International Licensing Agreements

International Licensing Agreements

IP, Technology Transfer and Competition Law

Michala Meiselles
Hugo Wharton

Wolters Kluwer

Published by:
Kluwer Law International B.V.
PO Box 316
2400 AH Alphen aan den Rijn
The Netherlands
E-mail: international-sales@wolterskluwer.com
Website: lrus.wolterskluwer.com

Sold and distributed in North, Central and South America by:
Wolters Kluwer Legal & Regulatory U.S.
7201 McKinney Circle
Frederick, MD 21704
United States of America
Email: customer.service@wolterskluwer.com

Sold and distributed in all other countries by:
Air Business Subscriptions
Rockwood House
Haywards Heath
West Sussex
RH16 3DH
United Kingdom
Email: international-customerservice@wolterskluwer.com

ISBN 978-94-035-0332-5

e-Book: ISBN 978-94-035-0213-7
web-PDF: ISBN 978-94-035-0223-6

This book is dedicated to Penelope Mansfield

Table of Contents

Preface

Contracts fulfil a number of functions spelling out the rights and obligations of the contracting parties, managing potential risks arising out of the contractual relationship, whilst at the same time supplying a contingency plan for each party in the event that an impasse is reached, or in the worst case scenario, the relationship itself breaks down.

Obviously no contract is perfect at addressing all eventualities; however, the parties contracting should aim as best as possible for such an optimal state of affairs.

This book aims to show readers how to achieve this outcome in the case of international licensing agreements.

What considerations need to be borne in mind during the planning, drafting, negotiation and post-negotiation review stages? What writing techniques will ensure that the international licensing agreement is suited to the precise business needs of the entity? What provisions should be included in such a contract to protect the parties' interests? How should the provisions be worded to maximise the protection afforded to the organisation and to pre-empt future legal concerns?

When planning, drafting and negotiating international licensing agreements, it is imperative to know exactly what essential issues need to be addressed. This book does this in an easy-to-use, clear and concise fashion.

Whilst the authors have set out to write as comprehensive a guide as possible, this book is not intended to replace the advice of a specialist lawyer.

At the time this book was finalised, there still remains uncertainty about the future of the EU and the UK post-Brexit, to use the layperson's term for the Withdrawal Talks.

List of Abbreviations

ADR	Alternative Dispute Resolution
EPC	European Patent Convention
EPO	European Patent Office
EUIPO	European Intellectual Property Office
GI	Geographic Indications
INTA	International Trade Mark Association
OHIM	Office for Harmonization in the Internal Market
NCA	National Competition Authority
TFEU	Treaty on the Functioning of the European Union
UKIPO	The UK Intellectual Property Organisation
VCL	Vienna Classification
WIPO	World Intellectual Property Organisation
WTO	World Trade Organisation

Acknowledgements

I would like to thank:

My sail ...

Mr Damien Béal

And my anchors ...

My father, Dr E. Meiselles
My mother, Mrs D. Meiselles
My brothers, Amit Meiselles and Dr Doron Meiselles
My sister, Danielle Shoval
My nieces and nephews
My dear friends, Angela Ginger, Sonia Le Monnier-Berri, and HsuehFang (Kay) Huang

Without your support, patience, encouragement and endless cups of tea, this project would have not been possible.

Also, I would like to thank Hugo Wharton, my co-author, for his enthusiasm, dedication, and energy.

Michala Meiselles

I would like to thank my dear late Mother, Penelope Mansfield, and my lovely sister, Angela Ginger, for all their encouragement, support and love over the years.

Also, Michala thank you so much for involving me in the writing of this book.

Hugo Wharton

We would both like to thank Christine Robben, our editor, for her professionalism, diligence and sterling guidance, and our reviewers for their insights, and recommendations.

Michala Meiselles and Hugo Wharton

CHAPTER 1
Introduction

§1.01 INTRODUCTION

In this chapter, a number of preliminary issues connected to international licensing agreements are considered by way of an introduction to the subject matter of this book.

The role of this genre of agreements will be examined in the first section of this chapter alongside the specific concerns of the contracting parties.

The second section of this chapter will explore the standard terms that should be considered by parties looking to conclude an international licensing agreement. This review will explore the function of each of these standard terms and will consider the possible wording of these terms.

§1.02 INTELLECTUAL PROPERTY DEFINED

The term 'intellectual property' has been variously defined. Frederick Gerhard furnished one such definition in 1868 in a book that he dedicated to the Members of the United States' Congress:

> A person's ideas or thoughts are his intellectual property only so long as they remain unuttered and unknown to others; but the moment he communicates them to the public, by speech, designs, writing, or any other mode, they cease to be his exclusive property and belong thenceforth to the community at large; for from that moment he has lost control of them, he can no longer alter or destroy them at will . . . We may therefore define the term 'intellectual property' as a man's thoughts and ideas, as long as they are not made public. The versification of the poet, the results of the philosopher's experiments, the ideas of the inventor, the patterns of the manufacturer, the fashions of the modiste, all are intellectual property until made the common property of everybody by verbal or written description, design, model, or any other mode. Once published and the poet cannot efface his poem

> from the memory of his readers, the philosopher hinder the utilization of his discovery, the inventor limit the benefits of his invention, the manufacturer withdraw his new pattern, or the modiste prevent the general adoption of the fashion introduced by her; all these thoughts and ideas cease to be the property of the individual and become the property of the many.[1]

§1.03 TAXONOMY OF PROPERTY

> Property is a word of different meanings. It may mean a thing owned (my watch or my house is 'my property'); it may mean ownership itself as when I speak of my 'property' in my watch which may pass to the person to whom I sell the watch before I actually hand the watch over or it may even mean an interest in a thing less than ownership but nevertheless conferring certain rights, as when we speak of the 'property' or 'special property' of a bailee in the thing bailed .... In English law, therefore, 'property' comprehends tangibles and intangibles, movables and immovables; it means a tangible thing (land or chattel) itself, or rights in respect of that thing, or rights, such as a debt, in relation to which no tangible thing exists.[2]

Personal property is made up of chattels real (comprising primarily of leasehold interests in land) and chattels personal (that are items of personal property that are not chattels real).[3]

Chattels personal encompass tangible movables (choses in possession), such as money and goods, and intangible movables (choses in action), which are made up of documentary intangibles and pure intangibles.[4]

Documentary intangibles are choses in action such as bills of lading, documentary letters of credit, negotiable instruments and insurance policies that are not only evidence of an underlying right to goods, money or securities but also an embodiment of the right itself.[5] As such the right the concerned document represents may be pledged or transferred by mere delivery of the physical document.[6] Occasionally endorsement may also be required to effect the transfer of title.[7] This is the case where a bill of lading is an order bill of lading rather than a bearer bill of lading. Where an

1. Frederick Gerhard, *Will the People of the United States Be Benefited by an International Copyright Law, or, Will Such a Law be an Injury to Them?* (1868, Harvard University) 6-8.
2. L S Sealy and RJA Hooley, *Commercial Law – Text, Cases, and Materials* (4th edn, Oxford University Press 2009) 57 (hereafter Sealy et al. 2009) citing James Crossley Vaines, Edward Lawson Griffin Tyler, and N. E. Palmer, *Crossley Vaines' on Personal Property* (5th edn, Butterworths 1973) 3.
3. Sealy et al. 2009: 56.
4. Sealy et al. 2009: 56.
5. Sealy et al. 2009: 56.
6. Sealy et al. 2009: 56.
7. Sealy et al. 2009: 56.

order bill of lading is involved it will need to be endorsed before it is delivered to effect transfer of title in the underlying cargo that the bill of lading represents. In contrast a bearer bill of lading requires mere delivery to transfer title to the underlying cargo that the bill represents.

Pure intangibles are choses in action that are not documentary intangibles such as debts, intellectual property rights and goodwill.[8]

§1.04 SCOPE OF THE TERM 'INTELLECTUAL PROPERTY' IN INTERNATIONAL LAW

'Intellectual property' as a term is defined in international law.

One such definition is provided in a Treaty concluded by the Members of the World Trade Organisation (WTO) entitled the Agreement on Trade-Related Aspects of Intellectual Property Rights (TRIPS).

This Treaty was developed under the aegis of the WTO through negotiations amongst its Members with the goal of reducing impediments to international trade whilst taking into account the need to promote effective and adequate protection of intellectual property rights.[9]

Intellectual property is deemed to encompass the following types of property:[10] copyright and related rights (addressed in Section 1 of Part 2, TRIPS), trademarks (Section 2), geographic indications (Section 3), industrial designs (Section 4), patents (Section 5), layout designs (topographies) of integrated circuits (Section 6) and undisclosed information (Section 7).

The rights derived from intellectual property are treated as being private rights[11] that nations have an incentive in protecting. The protection of intellectual property is a key public policy goal due to the developmental and technological objectives of countries.[12]

Another definition of intellectual property is given by the EU legislatures in the 2014 instrument setting out the block exemption for technology transfer agreements.[13] In this document, intellectual property is defined by reference to intellectual property rights as including industrial property rights in particular patents, trademarks, copyright and neighbouring rights.[14]

8. Sealy et al. 2009: 56.
9. Preamble to Agreement on Trade-Related Aspects of Intellectual Property Rights (signed in Marrakesh, Morocco on 15 April 1994) (hereafter TRIPS) Recital 1.
10. In sections 1 to 7 of Part 2 of TRIPS (Article 1(2), TRIPS).
11. Preamble to TRIPS Recital 4.
12. Preamble to TRIPS Recital 5.
13. Commission Regulation (EU) No 316/2014 of 21 March 2014 on the application of Article 101(3) of the Treaty on the Functioning of the European Union to categories of technology transfer agreements (hereafter TTBER 2014).
14. Article 1(h), TTBER 2014.

§1.05 COPYRIGHT AND RELATED RIGHTS

Copyright is the child of the printing press.[15] Creators of literary works had to wait until after the advent of printing to receive general recognition in law of their work.[16] The earliest rights were awarded by means of a special grant to publisher–printers.

The Statute of Anne enacted during the reign of Queen Anne in 1709 was the first fully fledged copyright act of its kind.[17] Intended for 'the encouragement of learning' the Statute of Anne vested 'the copies of printed books in the authors or purchasers of such copies'.[18] In order to encourage learned men to write, this act granted authors the rights in their works without first requiring them to obtain an individual grant from the sovereign.[19] This award of rights allowed authors to prevent others from delivering their works to the public without their permission.[20]

After the enactment of the Statute of Anne, similar acts were introduced in other jurisdictions, and in 1886 several countries concluded the first international treaty governing copyright.[21]

§1.06 LITERARY AND ARTISTIC WORKS IN THE CONTEXT OF COPYRIGHT

In the context of copyright, literary and artistic works are treated as including a production in the literary, scientific and artistic domain,[22] a translation, adaptation, arrangement of music and other alteration of a literary or artistic work,[23] a literary or artistic collection such as encyclopaedias and anthologies constituting intellectual creations by reason of the selection and arrangement of their contents.[24]

The expression 'literary and artistic works' encompasses 'every production in the literary, scientific and artistic domain, whatever may be the mode or form of its expression, such as books, pamphlets and other writings; lectures, addresses, sermons and other works of the same nature; dramatic or dramatico-musical works; choreographic works and entertainments in dumb show; musical compositions with or without words; cinematographic works to which are assimilated works expressed by a process analogous to cinematography; works of drawing, painting, architecture, sculpture, engraving and lithography; photographic works to which are assimilated

15. Richard C. De Wolf, An Outline of Copyright Law (John W. Luce 1925) (hereinafter De Wolf 1925).
16. De Wolf 1925: 1–2.
17. Copyright Act 1709 8 Ann. c.21 (hereinafter Statute of Anne). Full text of the Statute of Anne accessible at http://avalon.law.yale (last accessed 30 July 2016). edu/18th_century/anne_1710.asp (last accessed 28 January 2013).
18. Preamble, Statute of Anne.
19. Preamble, Statute of Anne.
20. §1 Statute of Anne.
21. Berne Convention for the Protection of Literary and Artistic Works (adopted in 1886) as amended on 28 September 1979 (hereafter Berne Convention as amended).
22. Article 2(1), Berne Convention 1971 as amended.
23. Article 2(3), Berne Convention 1971 as amended.
24. Article 2(5), Berne Convention 1971 as amended.

works expressed by a process analogous to photography; works of applied art; illustrations, maps, plans, sketches and three-dimensional works relative to geography, topography, architecture or science'.[25]

Copyright protection under the provisions of TRIPS extends to expressions rather than to ideas, procedures, methods of operation and mathematical concepts.[26]

§1.07 TRADEMARKS

A sign or combination of signs is capable of constituting a trademark if they have the ability to distinguish one entity's goods or services from those of other entities.[27] Personal names, figurative elements and an amalgamation of colours are all examples of signs that may be eligible for registration as trademarks.[28]

The character of goods or services to which trademarks may relate shall not form an obstacle to the registration of the trademark.[29]

Signs not 'inherently capable of distinguishing the relevant goods or services' may still be capable of registration depending upon distinctiveness acquired through use.[30]

Registration of a sign as a trademark may be made conditional upon visual perceptibility of signs.[31] Countries are permitted to make the ability to register a sign as a trademark dependent upon use.[32]

§1.08 GEOGRAPHIC INDICATIONS

Geographic indications (GIs) are indications identifying a good as originating in a territory, region or locality of a specific country 'where a given quality, reputation or other characteristic of the good is essentially attributable to its geographical origin'.[33]

Countries may introduce legal measures that allow interested parties to stop others from using 'any means in the designation or presentation of a good that indicates or suggests that the good in question originates in a geographical area other than the true place of origin in a manner which misleads the public as to the geographical origin of the good'.[34]

In the context of wines and spirits, national legislatures may introduce legal measures that allow interested parties to prevent the use of a GI identifying wines from wines, or spirits from spirits, not originating in the place indicated by the GI in

25. Article 2(1), Berne Convention 1971 as amended.
26. Article 9(2), TRIPS.
27. Article 15(1), TRIPS.
28. Article 15(1), TRIPS.
29. Article 15(4), TRIPS.
30. Article 15(1), TRIPS.
31. Article 15(1), TRIPS.
32. Article 15(3), TRIPS.
33. Article 22(1), TRIPS.
34. Article 22(2)a, TRIPS.

question.[35] This is true even in circumstances where the true origin of the goods is noted or in situations where the GI is used in translation or is accompanied by expressions (such as 'kind', 'type' and 'imitation'), which make it clear that the goods in question are not from the specific territory, region or locality alluded to.[36]

§1.09 INDUSTRIAL DESIGNS

The laws of most jurisdictions protect independently created industrial designs that are original or new.[37]

National legislatures have the discretion to provide that designs are not new or original when they are not significantly different from known designs or combinations of known design features.[38]

§1.10 PATENT

Patents are available in most jurisdictions in relation to inventions in all fields of technology, whether the inventions are products or processes, in circumstances where these inventions are new, involve an inventive step and are capable of industrial application.[39]

The term 'inventive step' may be used interchangeably with the term 'non-obvious', whilst the term 'capable of industrial application' can be used interchangeably with the term 'useful'.[40]

International law allows national legislatures to exclude certain inventions from patentability.

Countries are able to exclude from patentability inventions for public policy reasons in circumstances where the prevention of the commercial exploitation of the patentable invention is necessary in order to protect *inter alia* public morality, *ordre public* and to avoid serious prejudice to the environment.[41]

Nations are able to exclude from patentability diagnostic, therapeutic and surgical methods for the treatment of humans, animals and plants.[42]

Patents provide their owners with certain exclusive rights.[43]

The owner of a patent, the subject matter of which is a product, may exercise a right to prevent others (without his agreement) from carrying out certain acts such as producing, exploiting, offering for sale, selling or importing for these purposes the product that is the subject matter of the patent.[44]

35. Article 23(1), TRIPS.
36. Article 23(1), TRIPS.
37. Article 25(1), TRIPS.
38. Article 25(1), TRIPS.
39. Article 27(1), TRIPS.
40. Footnote 5 accompanying Article 27(1), TRIPS.
41. Article 27(2), TRIPS.
42. Article 27(3), TRIPS.
43. Article 28(1), TRIPS.
44. Article 28(1)a, TRIPS.

The owner of a patent, the subject matter of which is a process, may exercise a right to prevent others (without his permission) from carrying out certain acts including the act of using the process and the acts of exploiting, offering for sale, selling or importing for these purposes at least a product that is obtained directly by the process that is the subject matter of the patent.[45]

Other rights enjoyed by the owner of a patent include the right to grant a licence in relation to the patent and the right to assign the patent or transfer it by succession.[46]

§1.11 UNDISCLOSED INFORMATION

Information is undisclosed when it possesses commercial value and is lawfully within the control of a person (natural or legal) in circumstances where the person concerned has taken reasonable steps to keep the information secret.[47]

§1.12 COMMERCIAL VALUE AND SECRET NATURE OF THE INFORMATION

The information concerned will possess commercial value due to the fact that the information is secret.[48]

To be deemed a secret, the information will need to be information that it is not generally known amongst persons in the circles that would ordinarily deal with the kind of information involved or where the information is not readily accessible to this group of persons.[49]

Such information may either be consolidated (as a body of information) or take the form of a precise configuration and assembly of its components.[50]

A person is permitted to stop undisclosed information lawfully within their control from being disclosed to, acquired by or exploited by others, without their permission, in a manner that is inconsistent with honest commercial practices.[51]

An act will be inconsistent with honest commercial practices where it ensues from a breach of contract or a breach of confidence for example.[52]

Moreover a third party is capable of committing such an act in circumstances where the third party acquires this information either with the knowledge that it is acquiring such information or where it is grossly negligent in failing to know that it is doing so.[53]

45. Article 28(1)b, TRIPS.
46. Article 28(2), TRIPS.
47. Article 39(2), TRIPS.
48. Article 39(2), TRIPS.
49. Article 39(2), TRIPS.
50. Article 39(2), TRIPS.
51. Article 39(2), TRIPS.
52. Footnote 10 accompanying Article 39(2), TRIPS.
53. Footnote 10 accompanying Article 39(2), TRIPS.

The formula for the three products Coca-Cola, KFC and WD-40 are protected in this manner.[54]

Developed by a pharmacist, the formula for Coca-Cola has been closely protected by a select group of company employees for over a century.

Colonel Sanders' blend of herbs and spices for KFC and the formula for WD-40 are both closely guarded secrets.

Case study – WD-40[55]

WD-40 was developed in a laboratory in San Diego in 1953 by Rocket Chemical Company and its staff as part of a line of rust-prevention solvents.[56] After 40 tests, the team of researchers successfully developed the water displacing formula which is still in use today.[57] WD stands for Water Displacement and 40 stands for the 40 trials it took to develop the final product.[58]

First used in an industrial setting to protect the outer skin of the Atlas Missile from rust, it took several years before WD-40 was made available in aerosol cans as a result of experiments performed by Norm Larsen the founder of Rocket Chemical Company.[59]

In 1958, WD-40 made its first appearance on store shelves and in 1969, the company was renamed WD-40 Company Inc.[60]

WD-40 is the only product sold by WD-40 Company Inc.[61]

§1.13 ROLE OF INTELLECTUAL PROPERTY LAW

Just as law acknowledges ownership of tangible property, so it grants rights in intangible property as well.

Intellectual property law groups together the legal principles that govern such intangible, or intellectual, property. Such principles address *inter alia* ownership of intellectual property, the rights of the owners and the circumstances when the owner can stop others from using their property.

Regardless of its form, intellectual property is a creature of national law, although international law has and does put into place certain guidelines.

54. R. Mark Halligan and David A. Haas, 'The Secret of Trade Secret Success' *Forbes* (19 February 2010). Accessible at www.forbes.com/2010/02/19/protecting-trade-secrets-leadership-managing-halligan-haas.html (last accessed 27 February 2015).
55. Based on information found at wd40.com/cool-stuff/history (last accessed 27 February 2015).
56. Based on information found at wd40.com/cool-stuff/history (last accessed 27 February 2015).
57. Based on information found at wd40.com/cool-stuff/history (last accessed 27 February 2015).
58. Based on information found at wd40.com/cool-stuff/history (last accessed 27 February 2015).
59. Based on information found at wd40.com/cool-stuff/history (last accessed 27 February 2015).
60. Based on information found at wd40.com/cool-stuff/history (last accessed 27 February 2015).
61. Based on information found at wd40.com/cool-stuff/history (last accessed 27 February 2015).

Such international instruments aim to guarantee uniformity in terms of definitions, protection, assignment and licensing of rights, making it easier for rights owners to acquire other such rights in different countries.

The laws governing intellectual property confer exclusive rights on the owners of intellectual property, pursuant to which the owner is able to prevent the unauthorised use of its intellectual property and to exploit the same itself by, for example, issuing a licence to third parties or by assigning its rights in the intellectual property to others.[62]

§1.14 ROLE OF LICENSING

Licensing permits a person to capitalise on the investment that they have made. This investment entails an investment of time and money as well as operational risks associated with the undertaking.

Under the terms of a licensing agreement, the licensor will allow one or more entities to make use of the intellectual property rights associated with its invention, work of art, trademark, service mark, know-how and so forth.

By licensing, the party licensing should be able to secure a return on its investment. In addition to the financial remuneration, the licensing agreement may result in the development of an existing or new market for the product produced or services supplied under the terms of the licensing agreement. In certain circumstances, the licensing agreement may allow for the development of the intellectual property owned by the licensor. Pursuant to the terms of a technology licensing, the licensee may develop the existing technology.

§1.15 ROLE OF INTERNATIONAL LICENSING AGREEMENTS

A business looking to expand its domestic operations has at its disposal an array of strategies. One or more of these mechanisms may be used by the business contemporaneously.

First the business may decide to export its goods or services to one or more target markets. Such an operation may be undertaken by the business alone or with the assistance of another.[63]

An agent may be appointed by the business to source clients for it. In certain circumstances, the agent may also be delegated the authority to negotiate and conclude agreements with sourced clients on behalf of the appointing business (licensor).

The goods exported may be sold directly to the end customer, or the sale to the end customer may be performed via one or more intermediary parties. The business may decide, for example, to sell goods to one or more distributors in the designated territory for onwards sale.

62. 2014/C 89/03 Communication from the Commission — Guidelines on the application of Article 101 of the Treaty on the Functioning of the European Union to technology transfer agreements (hereafter TTBER 2014 Guidelines) para 6.
63. Michala Meiselles, *International Commercial Agreements: An Edinburgh Law Guide* (1st edn, Edinburgh University Press 2013) (hereafter Meiselles 2013), Chapter 1.

Under the agreements concluded with agents and distributors they may be given the right to make use of the rights associated with the intellectual property owned by the business. Agents and distributors may, for example, be given the right to market the goods or services using the trademark or service mark (respectively) owned by the business concerned.

A contract for the sale of goods may entail the supply of intellectual property, for example, the sale of a hardware system may entail the supply of a computer program or other intellectual property. As such an integral part of the transaction will be a licence granted by the owner of the intellectual property who may or may not be the seller of the goods.[64]

Where the seller is not the owner of the intellectual property, a separate agreement will exist between the owner of the intellectual property and the buyer in which the seller acts as an agent for the owner of the intellectual property.[65]

Second the business may enter into an agreement with an entity in the target market pursuant to which the latter is commissioned to manufacture or to assemble the goods designed and produced by the first party or to supply the services developed by the first party.

In the alternative, the entities may decide to collaborate for the purpose of developing and exploiting the technology developed by one or both of the parties.

These set-ups will typically entail licensing of intellectual property by one or more of the parties to the agreement.

A party producing or assembling goods in the target market may be licensed rights in relation to a variety of different types of intellectual property. Under the terms of such an agreement, the party producing or assembling the good may, for example, be granted a licence to make use of patents, trademarks, trade secrets and copyrighted materials owned by the first party.

A party providing a service in the target market may be licensed rights in relation to an array of different types of intellectual property. Under such an agreement, the party may be given the right to make use of patents, service marks, trademarks, trade secrets and copyrighted materials owned by the first party.

Third the business may decide to create a permanent presence in the target market.

Rather than engaging in exportation or in tandem with exportation, the business may decide to establish one or more operations in the target market. In such a context, the business may choose to establish an operation alone or in collaboration with one or more other entities.

The business may decide to establish an entity to run its operations in the target market. Such an entity may take the form of a branch, representative office or subsidiary.

In the alternative, the business concerned may opt to join forces with an entity established in the target market under the auspices of a joint venture or by means of a merger with the entity concerned.

64. Sealy et al. 2009: 292-3.
65. Sealy et al. 2009: 292-3.

Rather than joining forces, the business concerned may decide to acquire an entity already operating within the target market taking possession of the acquired party's assets, stock, contracts, networks and operations.

Such a strategy may be advantageous from the point of view of the acquiring entity with the requisite capital since the acquisition represents a turnkey solution for the acquiring entity.

Notwithstanding the advantages associated with an acquisition, there are certain considerations that should be borne in mind by the acquiring entity.

Beyond the cultural divide likely to exist between the acquiring and acquired entities that may adversely impact upon future operations, such an acquisition may be regulated entailing certain substantive and procedural prerequisites before the acquisition may proceed.

Licensing may require little or no capital investment on the part of the licensor, as the latter may be relying on the licensee to provide the investment. The licensor will also be relying on the licensee's knowledge of the target market and local regulation, its manufacturing, distribution and marketing capacities.

§1.16 CONCERNS OF THE CONTRACTING PARTIES

[A] The Concerns of the Licensor[66]

Beyond the financial incentive, due consideration should be given by the licensor to an assortment of other key considerations when negotiating a licence, *inter alia* quality control, the ability of the licensor to appoint others in the allocated territory or operate in the said territory in its own right, the promotional activities of the licensee and confidentiality.

[1] Promotional Activities[67]

The efficiency and effectiveness of the promotional activities undertaken by the licensee are going to be of vital importance to the licensor who may be concerned by brand recognition, revenue and market share.

With this in mind, the licensor may consider incorporating provisions into the licensing agreement that address the promotional and marketing activities of the licensee. Due consideration should be given by the licensor to the inclusion of certain key responsibilities on the part of the licensee such as an obligation to use its best efforts to develop a market for the products manufactured with the intellectual property licensed; to seek the authorisation of the licensor in relation to promotional materials; to expend a stipulated sum of money on such efforts and to report at regular intervals to the licensor on its promotional operations as well as on sales figures.

66. Further detail can be found in Meiselles 2013: 247-272.
67. Further detail can be found in Meiselles 2013: 247-8.

[2] Anti-competition Restrictions

The risk that the licensed intellectual property may come back into the home market of the licensor in the form of products that will compete with its own products is an issue that the licensor should consider addressing. This phenomenon known as the grey market or parallel imports may occur during or after the end of the term of the agreement.

There is no set view on parallel trade amongst the different jurisdictions. In certain countries, for example, the benefits of price competition are considered to be more important than the concerns of the licensor.

[3] Non-exclusivity and Retention of the Right to Grant a Licence to Other Parties[68]

The licensor may decide to reserve itself the right to grant further licences to parties other than the licensee. Moreover, the licensor may reserve itself the right to use the licensed property in the licensed territory effectively in competition with the licensee.

Such an arrangement may appeal to a licensor for a variety of reasons. First, it may appeal to a licensor where it is using a rolling royalty licensing agreement to generate a continuous return on its licensed property and is hoping to spread its risk amongst several different players in the assigned territory. Second, this arrangement may appeal to a licensor looking to enter into a new geographic market in circumstances where it wants to test the capability of the several prospective licensees in the territory involved before entering into a longer-term arrangement with the most competent licensee. Third, this arrangement may appeal to a licensor looking to secure itself the right to make use of the licensed property in the assigned territory.

[4] Confidentiality[69]

In a bid to safeguard proprietary information, the licensor should give due consideration to the inclusion of a confidentiality provision in the agreement concluded by the parties. In addition, in order to enhance management of the risk of leakage, the licensor should consider the inclusion of one or more of the following provisions in the licence:

- An obligation on the licensee to ensure that parties with access to the information agree to be bound by the terms of the agreement.
- An obligation on the licensee to ensure that persons with access to the information enter into confidentiality and non-exploitation agreements.
- A provision that the parties agree between them on the persons who should be allowed access to the information.

68. Meiselles 2013: 255-6.
69. Further detail can be found in Meiselles 2013: 263-4.

[5] *Unauthorised Use of Licensed Property*[70]

The licensor should give due consideration to the inclusion of provisions that curb the manner in which the licensee may exploit the licensed intellectual property, in a bid to safeguard the use made of the licensed intellectual property, which could have an adverse effect on the business of the licensor and to impede the creation of a potential competitor to the licensor.

In this context, the licensor should consider the inclusion of restrictions on the use that the licensee may make of the licensed intellectual property.

As such the licensor could, for example, insist that the licensee neither uses the licensed intellectual property in competition with the licensor (non-compete clause)[71] nor discloses the intellectual property licensed to another entity (confidentiality clause). The licensor may impose geographic limitations on the licensee's manufacturing or marketing activities by assigning a licensed territory. The licensor may insist on the inclusion of limitations on the licensee's field of use in the licensing agreement by restricting the applications for which the licensee may employ the intellectual property licensed, the output of the licensee and/or the customer base of the licensee.

[6] *Retention of Ownership in the Property Licensed*[72]

To ensure retention of ownership in the intellectual property licensed by the licensor to the licensee (the licensed property), due consideration should be given by the licensor for the inclusion of the following provisions in the licensing agreement. A provision:

- stating in clear terms that the licensee will not obtain any rights in relation to the licensed property;
- stating that all the rights and goodwill in the licensed property are and will remain vested in the licensor;
- obliging the licensee to inform the licensor if it becomes aware of an actual or threatened infringement of the licensed property;
- imposing an obligation on the licensee to assist the licensor in maintaining the validity and enforceability of the licensed property.

[7] *Quality Control*[73]

Poor quality control by the licensee is likely to have an adverse effect on the reputation and goodwill of the licensor. In order to ensure that a correct level of quality is maintained by the licensee, the licensor should give due consideration to the inclusion of certain material provisions in the licensing agreement concluded with the licensee *inter alia* a provision:

70. Further detail can be found in Meiselles 2013: 248.
71. Subject to competition law. More in a later chapter on competition law (Chapter 2).
72. Further detail can be found in Meiselles 2013: 258.
73. Further detail can be found in Meiselles 2013: 258.

- Allowing the licensor to inspect the facilities owned by or run by the licensee.
- Obliging the licensee to furnish the licensor with samples of the goods produced using the licensed property either at set intervals or in response to a request made by the licensor.
- Imposing certain training obligations on the licensee vis-à-vis its personnel and contractors.
- Impeding or restricting the licensee's ability to sublicense the licensed intellectual property.

[8] Right to Improvements and New Goods[74]

The licensor should give due consideration to preserving its rights in relation to improvements and new goods developed by it during the term of the agreement, as well as to securing itself rights in relation to new goods developed by the licensee using the licensed property and improvements made by the licensee using the licensed property.

With this in mind, the licensor may consider the inclusion of a provision allowing it to exploit the same (grant-back provision).[75]

[9] Regulation of the Licensing Agreement[76]

Competition law should be considered by the parties alongside taxation implications and any provisions that impact on the substantive terms of the licensing agreement.

Target market regulation of the terms of the licensing agreement will be a major concern for both the licensor and the licensee.[77] Regulation may exist in the target market in which the licensee is operating requiring, for example, the registration of the licensing agreement and imposing a requirement of prior approval. Such regulation is usually intended to guarantee that the licensing agreement and its provisions have no potential adverse effect on the local economy and its growth.[78] Such schemes will likely increase the cost and time associated with putting in place a licensing operation, whilst increasing the risk of leakage of confidential information.[79] In certain countries, for example, provisions that forbid or limit sublicensing will be prohibited due to the perceived centrality of sublicensing to the local economy and its growth. Other

74. Further detail can be found in Meiselles 2013: 258.
75. The use of grant-back provisions is regulated in certain countries. For a review of the subject of regulation *see* Ray August, Don Mayer, and Michael B. Bixby, *International Business Law: Text, Cases, and Readings* (5th edn, Pearson Education 2009), 510 (hereafter August et al. 2009).
76. Further detail can be found in Meiselles 2013: 250-1.
77. A review of licensing regulations is provided in August et al. 2009: 493–517.
78. August et al. 2009: 493–517.
79. Richard Schaffer, Filiberto Agusti, Lucien J. Dhooge, and Beverley Earle, *International Business Law And Its Environment*, International Edition (8th edn, South-Western Cengage Learning 2012) (hereafter Schaffer et al. 2012), 557.

provisions that may be scrutinised include grant-back requirements, export restrictions, price-fixing, non-competition clauses, exclusivity clauses and territorial restrictions.[80]

[B] The Concerns of the Licensee

Beyond the need to secure warranties and a grant from the licensor permitting it (the licensee) to make optimal use of the licensed intellectual property, the licensee will be motivated by the need to secure *inter alia* access to support services, exclusivity of use, the right to make use of improvements and new goods generated during the term of the licensing agreement and a minimal outlay on its part by reducing the payments due to the licensor.

[1] Support Services

The services offered by the licensor to the licensee under the terms of the licence add value to both parties.

From the point of view of the licensor, such services help improve sales whilst at the same ensuring the quality of production and service by the licensee, in turn safeguarding the reputation and goodwill of the licensor as well as the image of the intellectual property owned by the licensor. Moreover, such support may help the licensee develop improvements and new goods making use of the licensed intellectual property.

From the perspective of the licensee, these services offered by the licensor may not only assist it in improving sales but will also add value to the workforce of the licensee.

[2] Exclusivity[81]

An exclusive licence is the one that curtails the ability of the licensor to grant further licences in the assigned territory to other parties (such as agents, distributors and licensees). Moreover such a licence may also curtail the ability of the licensor itself to operate in the assigned territory.

Exclusivity will be beneficial from the perspective of the licensee as the latter will not be subject to direct competition in the assigned territory. For its part, a licensee is likely to require exclusivity in the assigned territory in order to safeguard its investment and prevent freeriding.

The licensee may be required to make a significant investment in terms of energy, time and money. This is especially true in situations where the licensor is a newcomer to the assigned territory; in which case, the licensee will be required to build up

80. August et al. 2009: 493–517.
81. Further detail can be found in Meiselles 2013:255-6.

demand for the licensed goods and to generate recognition of the licensed property. What is more, the licensee will typically be taking a risk when building up a new market, as such the licensee will be unwilling to permit others (the licensor included) to come along and benefit from the 'fruits of its labours' (freeriding).

[3] Right to Improvements and New Goods[82]

The right to use improvements and to exploit new goods developed using the licensed property is a right that will be important not only to the licensor but also to the licensee.

For its part, the licensee will probably endeavour to reserve itself rights in relation to improvements and goods developed by the licensor as well as the right to:

- sell any new goods developed by it (the licensee) in circumstances, for example, where the licensor is unwilling to agree on a mutually acceptable price for such goods; and
- grant a non-exclusive licence to the licensor in relation to improvements the licensee has made thereby allowing the licensee to grant a licence in relation to such improvements to parties besides the licensor.

[4] Royalty Payments

Royalty payments may be determined using the per-unit rate or some other measures such as quantity produced by reference, for example, to weight or length.[83]

The licensor is likely to attempt to secure itself a higher royalty rate whilst the licensee for its part is likely to aim for a lower royalty rate.

The licensor is likely to rely on certain arguments in support of a higher royalty rate, amongst them the suggestion that its energy, time and money were used to generate the licensed property, the subject matter of the licensing agreement, it assumed the risk associated with the legal protection.[84] The licensee for its part is likely to counter argue by suggesting that the sums of which the licensor is speaking are sunk costs that the licensor would have had to put in, that as licensee it assumes the largest part of the risk and investment as it is, for example, the party that is charged with production, promotion, distribution and sale of the products manufactured using the licensed intellectual property.[85]

§1.17 LEGAL STRUCTURES ASSOCIATED WITH LICENSING

Certain national and European level structures may function as useful business models in the context of licensing. Such structures may be used alongside a licensing

82. Further detail can be found in Meiselles 2013: 265-6.
83. Alexander I. Poltorak and Paul J. Lerner, *Essentials of Licensing Intellectual Property* (John Wiley & Sons 2004) (hereafter Poltorak et al. 2004), 101–2.
84. Further detail can be found in Meiselles 2013: 261.
85. Further detail can be found in Meiselles 2013: 261.

agreement or in lieu of such an agreement. European Economic Interest Groupings (EEIG), joint ventures and European Companies (SEs) are some of the structures that may be used in such a scenario.

One or more licensing agreements may, for example, be associated with a joint venture, European Company or an EEIG. In some situations, legal and natural entities may decide to develop intellectual property under the auspices of one of these structures. A European Company, joint venture or EEIG may, for example, be established for the purpose of pooling resources with the aim of developing technology.

The needs and strategic interests of the parties will usually influence their choice of structure, as will the type or types of intellectual property involved and occasionally the law applicable to the parties and the arrangement. Such arrangements are capable, for example, of being governed by EU competition law.

[A] European Economic Interest Grouping[86]

Formulated as a supranational corporate entity regulated by European law,[87] and comparable to 'an institutional form for joint venture partnerships between two or more companies, whether public or private',[88] the EEIG is intended to be used to facilitate cross-border activity amongst natural and legal persons.

Inspired by the French GIE (*groupement a l'intéret économique*) as an intermediate corporate form between a company and an association, the EEIG[89] is distinct from a company in a number of ways.[90] The EEIG is a vehicle for collaboration which neither replaces nor absorbs its constituent members[91] with each of the participating parties accordingly retaining its legal and economic independence throughout the lifecycle of the EEIG. At no point during its existence may this structure be utilised for absorption of its constituent members. In comparison with a company, whilst the EEIG is permitted to generate profits as a structure, it is not intended to be used as a profit-making entity in its own right.[92]

86. The history and features of the EEIG is considered in M. K. Meiselles, 'The European Economic Interest Grouping – A Chance for Multinationals?' (2015) 26 European Business Law Review, Issue 3 (hereafter Meiselles, 'The European Economic Interest Grouping – A Chance for Multinationals?').
87. Council Regulation (EEC) 2137/85 of 25 July 1985 on the European Economic Interest Grouping (EEIG), OJ 1985 L199/1 (1985) (EEIG Regulation).
88. Eric Engle, 'The EU Means Business: A Survey of Legal Challenges and Opportunities in the New Europe' (2006) 4 DePaul Bus. & Com. Issue 3, 377.
89. Erik Werlauff, *EU – Company Law* 119 (Copenhagen: DJØF, 2003) (hereafter Werlauff 2003), 116.
90. Werlauff 2003: 116.
91. Johan de Bruycker, 'EC Company Law – The European Company versus The European Economic Interest Grouping and the Harmonization of the National Company Laws' (1991) 21 Ga J Int'l & Comp L 19, 197-198.
92. Mark Abell and Robert Blin, 'EC Economic Interest Groupings come to life' (1989) 8 Int'l Fin L Rev 9, 9.

According to Professor Donald the 'closest American parallel to the EEIG would be a partnership form that allowed – or even required – the partners to reside in different states'.[93]

[1] Features Associated with an EEIG

Subject to certain minimum requirements governing the internal organisation of the EEIG, the manner in which the grouping is structured internally is largely at the discretion of the members of the grouping.[94] The organs prescribed by the regulation comprise a body of members acting collectively (collective body of members) which is permitted to make decisions implementing the objectives of the grouping, as well as an organ consisting of one or more managers (the management body).[95]

Notwithstanding the requirement that the grouping has a management body and a body of members acting collectively, the EEIG Regulation allows participating members to form further organs and delegate these organs management powers.[96]

[2] Advantages Associated with an EEIG

Amongst the benefits[97] associated with this structure are the absence of a minimum capital requirement,[98] uniformity of treatment (whilst each Member State can introduce its own version of the EEIG, each of the resulting national forms is strongly rooted in European law), European level endorsement and recognition (the legal existence of this legal form is rooted in European law), financial flexibility (the question of financing is at the discretion of the constituent members), operational versatility (European law provides the basic building blocks for the grouping leaving many substantive matters to the members themselves, as such the members have the discretion to determine how the grouping will be organised,[99] the composition of the grouping in terms of membership subject to the limits imposed by the EEIG Regulation,[100] the name, duration and objectives of the grouping.[101])

---

93. David Donald, 'Company Law in the European Community: Toward Supranational Incorporation' (1991) 9 Dick J Int'l L 1, 11.
94. Article 16, EEIG Regulation.
95. Article 16, EEIG Regulation.
96. Article 16(1), EEIG Regulation.
97. A detailed review of the benefits, and drawbacks associated with the EEIG can be found in Meiselles, 'The European Economic Interest Grouping – A Chance for Multinationals?'.
98. Professor Dine citing Mr Jean Pierson, Executive Director of Airbus Industries who praised the EEIG as a form lacking a minimum capital requirement (Janet Dine, 'The European Community's Company Law Directives – Changing the Balance of Power?' (1990-1991) 1 KCLJ 41, 44).
99. Article 16, EEIG Regulation.
100. As the grouping is only intended to be used to enhance cross-border cooperation between entities operating in different Member States, admissibility to the grouping, and the availability of such groupings to different entities is restricted. (Dominique Carreau and William L. Lee, 'Towards A European Company Law' (1988-1989), 9 Nw J Int'l L & Bus 501, 505 quoting from European Commission, Nineteenth General Report on the Activities of the European Communities 21, 112 (1986)).
101. Article 5, EEIG Regulation.

[3] Goals of Participating Parties

This multifunctional entity can be used for an array of ends by constituent members either on an ongoing basis or for a specific one-off project.

Such structures may be used, for example, for the submission of public tenders,[102] the supervision of projects,[103] the development, manufacturing, assembly and/or marketing of goods, the development of common technical knowledge,[104] the carrying out of common research, the development of common know-how, novel or improved processes and products, as well as the coordination of highly specialised services.[105] Groupings have, for example, been used in order to conduct research into high definition televisions and to provide common services to the legal profession.[106]

In the alternative, a grouping can be used by constituent members in order to gauge their ability to commit to each other on a long-term basis.[107] As such the grouping can, for example, be used by members as a precursor to a cross-border merger, the establishment of an SE or as a pilot study before the execution of an acquisition.

[B] Joint Venture

Two or more entities looking to collaborate may elect to do so using a joint venture as the vehicle for their collaboration. Once the parties have decided to establish a joint venture, they may decide to regulate their relationship using a contract or, in the alternative, through the creation of an equity structure, such as a joint venture corporation (JVC).[108]

[1] Features of the JVC

Unlike a contract-based joint venture, a JVC constitutes a distinct and new equity structure[109] with permanency.[110]

The founding entities of the JVC will typically become joint owners and managers of the ensuing entity.[111] The question of governance and the allocation of ownership

102. Werlauff 2003: 118.
103. Werlauff 2003: 118.
104. Werlauff 2003: 118.
105. Werlauff 2003: 118.
106. Examples given by Werlauff 2003: 118-9.
107. European Commission, Proposal for a regulation of the Council on the European cooperation grouping (ECG), COM (73) 2046 (1973) (hereafter Proposal 1973), 17.
108. Ayre 1982-1983: 1.
109. Michael Bergman, 'Corporate Joint Venture under the Antitrust Laws' (1962) 37 N.Y.U. L. Rev. 712 (hereafter Bergman 1962), 712 footnote 1.
110. Bergman 1962: 712 footnote 1 citing Forest Hodge O'Neal, *Close Corporations: Law and Practice, Volume 1* (Callaghan, 1958), 9.
111. Joint Venture Corporations: Drafting the Corporate Papers (Dec 1964) 78(2) Harvard Law Review 393, 395.

rights in the JVC are some of the matters that the co-investors will in many jurisdictions have the discretion to address privately.

Where each of the co-investors makes an equal contribution to the JVC, each will typically be allocated an equal share of the equity in the resulting entity alongside equal voting rights.[112] An unequal apportionment of ownership rights in the JVC may arise where, for example, the participating parties have made unequal contributions or host country regulation curtails the participation rights of foreign investors.[113] Notwithstanding the fact that the resulting ownership structure may be unequal, there is a possibility that the shares may be divided into classes that allow for the resolution of such inequality through weighted voting rights for example.

One of the simplest way of ensuring that co-investors are able to safeguard their respective interests is by allocating each of them with equal rights of representation on the board of directors of the JVC.[114]

The size, make-up and requirements for admission onto the board, the procedure for replacement of board members, the question of the right to veto, the classification of decisions by reference to whether they require a simple majority, qualified majority or unanimous decision, the procedure for addressing deadlocks (if applicable), the voting rights of co-investors, the sharing of profits and dividends, the transferability of shares and pre-emptive rights (compulsory buy-sell provisions) are some of the issues that are usually addressed in the agreement establishing the JVC.[115,116]

Typically the JVC will take the form of a limited liability company so that for all intents and purposes the liability of the co-investors will be limited to the value of their shares.[117]

[2] Advantages Associated with a Joint Venture

The decision to establish a JVC, argues Professor Brodley, is 'an implicit rejection of alternate forms of interfirm organization, such as merger or contractual arrangement'.[118,119] Notwithstanding the fact that the costs linked to the establishment of a JVC are comparatively high, it offers certain benefits that are not typically associated with a contract-based joint venture.

112. Simon Fisher and Damian Fisher, *Export Best Practice: Commercial and Legal Aspects* (The Federation Press 1998) (hereafter Fisher et al. 1998), 177.
113. Fisher et al. 1998: 177.
114. Joint Venture Corporations: Drafting the Corporate Papers (Dec 1964) 78(2) Harvard Law Review 393, 398.
115. Fisher et al. 1998: 184.
116. The procedures for addressing the replacement of directors and for resolving deadlocks is reviewed in detail in Joint Venture Corporations: Drafting the Corporate Papers (Dec 1964) 78(2) Harvard Law Review 393, 399-413.
117. Fisher et al. 1998: 177.
118. Joseph F. Brodley, 'Joint Ventures and Antitrust Policy', Harvard Law Review 95(7), 1521, 1527 (hereafter Brodley 1982).
119. Peter Schroth, 'United States Joint Ventures: Transideological and Otherwise' (1990) 38 Am. J. Comp. L. Supp. 213, 214 (hereafter Schroth 1990).

First, the creation of a JVC is comparatively more comprehensive than the formulation of a contractual arrangement. By establishing a JVC the participating entities are able to create a dedicated infrastructure with perenniality and permanence.[120]

Second, as contracts governing complex economic relationships often encounter a number of transactional difficulties, the JVC offers an effective mechanism for addressing these complications.[121]

Third, by using a joint venture as the vehicle for the collaboration some of the problems usually associated with a merger can be avoided.[122] Beyond the fact that the parties are able to avoid the risk of opportunism and informational asymmetry, they are also able to circumvent the need for a valuation of their respective contributions, as the joint venture permits the participant parties to await a market valuation.[123]

Fourth, the JVC offers a common identity internally vis-à-vis employees and investors and externally vis-à-vis outside parties transacting with the entity. Rather than each of the co-investors contracting in their own right, the JVC is able to deal on its own behalf generating transactional efficiency and expanding output whilst integrating the operations of the various co-investors.

[3] Goals of Participating Parties

The motives for the establishment of joint ventures, argues Professor Harrigan, may be divided into three main categories[124] - internal uses, competitive uses and strategic uses.[125]

[C] Internal Uses

Joint ventures may be formed in order to help participating entities build on existing internal strengths or indeed in a bid to create new ones.[126] Co-investors may form a joint venture in order, for example, to pool resources (assets, plant, technology and personnel), execute large industrial and financial projects[127] and formulate innovative management practices such as information systems and administrative techniques.[128]

---

120. Brodley 1982: 1527.
121. Brodley 1982: 1528.
122. Brodley 1982: 1528.
123. 'The problem of valuing the respective contributions of the participants is mitigated, because they can await an actual market judgement.' (Brodley 1982: 1528).
124. This categorisation is based on field studies discussed in Kathryn Rudie Harrigan, *Joint Ventures, Alliances, and Corporate Strategies* (Beard Books 1985) (hereafter Harrigan 1985), Chapters 7-12. The three key categories of motives posited by Professor Harrigan, she suggests can be subdivided into subcategories.
125. A review of these motives can be found in Harrigan 1985: Chapter 1.
126. Harrigan 1985: 29.
127. Bergman 1962: 714.
128. Harrigan 1985: 30. Such practices can also be updated through dialogue, the exchange of ideas, and brainstorming. (Harrigan 1985: 30).

[1] Competitive Uses

Joint ventures can function as a useful competitive weapon[129] with participating entities using such structures to generate 'first-mover' advantages by pre-empting competitors,[130] to influence the evolution of a given industry, to develop new industries and to reinforce their respective strategic positions.[131] By strengthening each of their negotiating positions, participating parties may also be able to 'tame potentially tough customers (such as the armed forces when purchasing armaments)'.[132]

[2] Strategic Uses

Entities may decide to use joint ventures to increase or decrease their respective domains.[133] Co-investors can use such structures to stabilise their existing domains and diversify into new but as yet unfamiliar areas of business operation.[134] Such a move could in the alternative allow a business to move away from an otherwise unattractive area of business to a novel or emerging area of operations.[135]

[D] European Company[136]

The European Company (SE) is the first European level public limited liability company. Governed by two pieces of European legislation, the Council Regulation on the Statute for a European Company (SE Regulation)[137] and the Council Directive supplementing this Regulation with regard to the involvement of employees (SE Directive),[138] this entity was formulated in order to facilitate cooperation between entities with headquarters in different Member States.[139,140]

---

129. Harrigan 1985: 31.
130. Harrigan 1985: 32.
131. Harrigan 1985: 28, 31.
132. Harrigan 1985: 31.
133. Harrigan 1985: 33. By way of illustration, Professor Harrigan gives the example of the joint venture involving Mitsui and AMAX.
134. Harrigan 1985: 33.
135. Harrigan 1985: 33.
136. The SE, its features, advantages and disadvantages are discussed in detail in Meiselles, M. and Graute, M. (2017) 'The Societas Europaea (SE) – Time to Start Over? Capturing the Zeitgeist of the 21st Century' European Business Law Review, Vol. 28 Issue 5, pp. 667–688.
137. Council Regulation (EC) No 2157/2001 of 8 October 2001 on the Statute for a European company (SE) OJ L294/1 Accessible at http://eur-lex.europa.eu/LexUriServ/LexUriServ.do?uri=OJ:L:2001:294:0001:0021:en:PDF (accessed 24 February 2014) (SE Regulation).
138. Council Directive 2001/86/EC of 8 October 2001 supplementing the Statute for a European Company with regard to the Involvement of Employees OJ L294/22 Accessible at http://eur-lex.europa.eu/smartapi/cgi/sga_doc?smartapi!celexapi!prod!CELEXnumdoc&lg=EN&numdoc=32001L0086&model=guichett (accessed 24 February 2014) (SE Directive).
139. The SE Regulation, and SE Directive both apply also throughout the European Economic Area (EEA); EEA comprises the EU Member States alongside the three EFTA countries that entered into the EEA Agreement, notably Norway, Iceland and Liechtenstein. All references in this thesis to the EU shall be construed to include Norway, Iceland and Liechtenstein.
140. Commission 'European Joint-Stock Company' Information Memo Note P29/70 dated June 1970 Accessible at http://aei.pitt.edu/31830/ (accessed 24 February 2014) (hereafter 1970 Information Note), part III.

Contrary to the intention of the drafters of the initial proposal of 1970 that created an autonomous legal form based purely European company law, the contemporary SE is a hybrid governed by European and national law. The result is a collection of 28 different national variants of the SE.[141]

The main characteristics of this hybrid corporate form[142] are determined by European level law (the SE Regulation and the SE Directive), whilst substantive issues *inter alia* governance, minority and creditor rights as well as the formation process are governed by national law.

[1] Features of the SE

Undertakings (public and private limited liability companies, firms and other legal bodies governed by public or private law) formed under the law of a Member State and having registered offices and head offices within the Union are permitted to establish SEs.[143,144,145] The registration of the SE should take place in a Member State of the EU[146] or a Member State of the European Economic Area.

As a public limited liability company, the SE will be able to offer its shares to the public. The co-founders of the SE may opt to list the entity or in the alternative keep it unlisted.[147]

A cross-border character is essential to the establishment of the SE with at least two of the companies involved in the formation of the SE being subject to the laws of different Member States or having had, for at least two years, a subsidiary governed by the law of another Member State or a branch located in another Member State.

[2] Advantages Associated with the SE

The European Company represents an entity recognised in national and European law with a unified management system and financial reporting rules. This entity also offers participating companies the option of maintaining offices in a number of Member

141. Bouloukos, 'Le Régime Juridique de la Société Européene (SE): Vers Une Société Européenne à la carte ? The Legal Status of the European Company (SE) Towards a European Company «à la carte »?' [2004] Int'l Bus. L.J. 489, 501 (hereafter Bouiloukas 2004), citing Michel Menjucq, *Droit international et européen des société (*Domat, 2001) 128.
142. Noëlle Lenoir 'The *Societas Europaea* (SE) in Europe – A Promising Start and an Option with Good Prospects' (2008) 4 Utrecht Law Review 13, 13 (hereafter Lenoir 2008).
143. Article 2, SE Regulation. Christoph Teichmann 'The European Company – A Challenge to Academics, Legislatures and Practitioners' (2003) 4 German Law Journal 309, 311 (hereafter Teichmann 2003).
144. Article 2(1)-(4), SE Regulation.
145. A Member State is permitted to allow a company whose head office is not in the Union to take part in the formation of an SE, if that company is formed under the law of a Member State, has its registered office in that Member State, and has a real and continuous link with a Member State's economy (Article 2(5), SE Regulation).
146. Article 7, SE Regulation.
147. For a more detailed description of the SE and its characteristics, *see* Dirk Van Gerven, 'Provisions of Community Law applicable to the Societas Europaea' in Dirk Van Gerven and Paul Storm (eds) *The European Company Volume I* (Cambridge University Press 2006), 29-30.

States whilst avoiding the need to establish a complex network of affiliated companies governed by the national laws of the different Member States.[148] The annual saving here has been estimated at over EUR 30 billion.[149]

In spite of the fact that the SE is a creature of national law and resembles a public limited liability company of the Member State in which it has its registered offices, the SE benefits from European legal personality and an 'unequalled freedom of movement'.[150] The registered office of an SE may be relocated throughout the EU[151] without the relocation resulting in the winding up of the SE or in the creation of a new legal person.[152] In contrast, national public companies are only generally allowed to transfer their registered office domestically, and national public companies incorporated in Member States supporting the real seat theory (such as Germany) cannot transfer their registered office to another Member State without winding up and creating a new legal person.

The co-founders of the SE may enjoy the freedom to formulate a management structure that suits their needs. In this context, they may choose between a monist management structure with a board of directors (referred to in the SE Regulation as the 'administrative organ') and a dualist structure with a supervisory organ and a management organ.[153] Whilst the SE has the discretion to choose between a one- or two-tier management structure, it is worthwhile noting that it is still obliged to have a general meeting of shareholders which must meet up at least once a year.[154]

In the case of two-tier structure, management of the company is entrusted, on the one hand, to the management organ, which is responsible for managing the company and, on the other hand, to the supervisory organ, entrusted with monitoring the activities of the management organ.[155] Whilst the supervisory organ may not itself exercise the power to manage the SE[156] it functions as a corporate custodian by assuming responsibility for amongst other matters the appointment and removal of members on the management organ,[157] the review of reports submitted to it by the management organ on the progress and foreseeable development of the SE's business and the launch of investigations.[158]

In the case of a one-tier system, the management of the company is only entrusted to an administrative organ.

148. Bouloukos 2004: 490.
149. Bouloukos 2004: 490.
150. Lenoir 2008: 15.
151. Article 8(1), SE Regulation reads 'The registered office of an SE may be transferred to another Member State in accordance with paragraphs 2 to 13. Such a transfer shall not result in the winding up of the SE or in the creation of a new legal person.'
152. 'Without dissolution and creation ab initio of a new legal person' (Bouloukos 2004: 491).
153. The two-tier system is governed by Articles 39-42, SE Regulation. The one-tier system is governed by Articles 43–5, SE Regulation. Articles 46–51 SE Regulation stipulate common rules.
154. Articles 38(a), and 52-60, SE Regulation.
155. Articles 39-42, SE Regulation.
156. Article 40, SE Regulation.
157. Article 39, SE Regulation.
158. Article 41, SE Regulation.

This option given to the companies - pursuant to Article 38(b) SE Regulation - depends in most cases on the terms of the company's statute and its business environment and not on a decision by the Member State. The type of management system to be chosen is, in most cases, predetermined by the respective country of incorporation. For example, German law only allows for public limited companies the two-tier system.[159]

[E] Assignment

Assignment is an alternative transactional arrangement to licensing. Whilst assignment entails a transfer, licensing is the extension of rights to the licensee to use the intellectual property of the licensor.

An assignment is a one-off transaction pursuant to which the intellectual property is purchased or sold for an agreed price.[160] Such an outright sale to another entity of the rights to the intellectual property will result in the permanent assignment of title to the intellectual property.

Assignment is likely to entail the sale of three categories of assets, namely the intellectual property itself, related know-how and associated materials.[161]

The formalities associated with assignments will vary from one jurisdiction to another, so that legal advice should be sought on the formalities in the jurisdiction concerned.

Under English law, an assignment of intellectual property typically needs to be made in writing, although it need not be executed in the form of a deed.[162] An assignment of a patent will also need to be registered with the UK IP Office.[163] This seems to be the case for registered designs as well.[164] Under English law, the issue of who must sign the document executing or recording the transaction will differ depending on the genre of intellectual property involved, although in the majority of situations, the assignor or transferor must sign the document in question.[165]

159. English law does not prescribe the one-tier system for public companies whereas German law prescribes the two-tier system for public companies. For more details regarding the British system see Jessica Schmidt *Deutsche vs. Britische Societas Europaea (SE)*, 478 (hereafter Sellier 2006).
160. Exchanging Value - Negotiating Technology Licensing Agreements (WIPO 2005), 17.
161. UNICO Practical Guides Commercialisation Agreements, Key issues in managing technology transfer agreements, 36-7 (hereafter UNICO guides key issues). Accessible at https://www.praxisunico.org.uk/sites/praxisunico.org.uk/files/unico_guides_keyissues_0.pdf (last accessed 30 July 2016).
162. Mark Anderson, Technology Transfer (Bloomsbury Professional 2010), 151 (hereafter Anderson 2010).
163. Anderson 2010: 89. The registration processes for patents, and registered designs are set out in regulations *inter alia* the Patents Rules 2007 (SI 2007/3291), and Registered Designs Rules 2006 (SI 2006/1975).
164. Anderson 2010: 155. Pursuant to the Registered Designs Act 1948, §19(1) as amended by the Copyright, Designs and Patents Act 1988 (UK) (hereafter CDPA 1988), §272. The registration processes for patents, and registered designs are set out in regulations *inter alia* the Patents Rules 2007 (SI 2007/3291), and Registered Designs Rules 2006 (SI 2006/1975) (UK).
165. For copyright assignments, §90(3), CDPA 1988, and for patent assignments, §30(5), Patents Act 1977 Chapter 37.

A sale of intellectual property may arise in a number of situations. Where the developer lacks the resources required in order to capitalise on the intellectual property or lacks the motivation to capitalise on the same.

Notwithstanding the fact that the former owner of the intellectual property may have relinquished its rights post-assignment in relation to the subject matter of the sale, this one-off transaction may occasionally entail certain sustained devoirs on the part of the former owner (the assignor) vis-à-vis the buyer (assignee). This may arise where payment is deferred.[166]

Frequently, the sale of the intellectual property rights is not a viable option. This may occur when the assignment of rights alone is insufficient, as the assignment is 'not attractive without human capital, a product, a developed market and/or an established business or revenue stream'.[167]

[1] Loss of Control and Ownership of Intellectual Property

In comparison with assignment, licensing may afford the licensor more flexibility and enhanced certainty.[168]

Under a licensing deal, the licensor will retain ownership and, if the terms of the agreement permit it, a certain level of control over the licensed intellectual property and the manner in which the licensed intellectual property is exploited by the licensee.[169]

Moreover, a licensor will typically secure itself a broad discretion to terminate the licence if certain circumstances arise (change of ownership, breach of a material obligation by the licensee, insolvency, administration or receivership of the licensee and so forth). Where the licensing agreement is terminated any licensed rights will revert to the licensor.[170]

Termination of an assignment and recovery of the assigned intellectual property may only be a possibility if the assignment agreement allows for the same. If such an option is afforded to the assignor it is likely to entail an application to the court for an order of reassignment.[171]

Assignment may also mean that the intellectual property assigned is developed in ways that the assignor had not wanted or in the alternative it may not be developed at all.[172]

Some assignment agreements will include provisions that stipulate the contingencies which will give rise to a reassignment. The assigned intellectual property may be reassigned, for example, in the event of insolvency or administration. Such reassignment may occur when there has been a failure to meet obligations defined in

166. Exchanging Value – Negotiating Technology Licensing Agreements (WIPO 2005), 17.
167. Exchanging Value – Negotiating Technology Licensing Agreements (WIPO 2005), 17.
168. UNICO guides key issues, 40.
169. UNICO guides key issues, 40.
170. UNICO guides key issues, 40.
171. UNICO guides key issues, 41.
172. UNICO guides key issues, 41.

the agreement. In circumstances where the assigned intellectual property is sold reassignment is unlikely to succeed.[173]

[2] Sub-assignment

Where intellectual property has been assigned, the assignee becomes the owner of the intellectual property sold to it and as such acquires the right to assign it in its own right. This process is known as sub-assignment. The party to whom the intellectual property is assigned (the sub-assignee) may not be necessarily bound by any of the contractual obligations that the original assignee agreed upon with the assignor.[174]

What is more, in the event that the assignee or the sub-assignee become insolvent or enter into an administration, the liquidator or administrator is likely to sell the property assigned which will in turn mean that the property in question will end up in the hands of a party that the assignor may not necessarily approve of. This is particularly important where the original assignor is a university and the sub-assignee is a party that the university would deem objectionable and exceptionable based on ethical considerations for example.[175]

§1.18 STANDARD PROVISIONS IN INTERNATIONAL LICENSING AGREEMENTS[176]

The following section of the chapter reviews certain standard terms commonly contained in international licensing agreements.

The precise terms that the contracting parties should consider including in their agreement will largely depend upon the subject matter of the agreement, the categories of intellectual property being licensed, the needs of the contracting parties and the law applicable to the agreement.

Notwithstanding this fact, certain concerns commonly arise when concluding such deals and certain standard provisions are incorporated into such agreements.

The provisions that are reviewed in the following section are representative of the types of provisions that the parties should consider incorporating into their cross-border licensing agreement.

The goal of this review is to provide an introductory overview of the key provisions and the matters that are habitually encountered in the context of these terms. This review is by no means intended to be exhaustive.

Due to the legal regulation governing such clauses in certain jurisdictions it is sensible for the parties to seek legal advice before incorporating these clauses into their licensing agreement.

173. UNICO guides key issues, 41.
174. UNICO guides key issues, 41.
175. UNICO guides key issues, 41.
176. Anderson 2010: Chapter 2. Exchanging value – Negotiating technology licensing agreements (WIPO 2005), 44-82; Fisher et al. 1998: 228-33; Cynthia Cannady, Technology Licensing and Development Agreements (OUP 2013) (available on Google books).

[A] Checklist of Provisions

The following checklist lists some of the key provisions that should be borne in mind by the parties reviewing, negotiating and drafting an international licensing agreement.

Not all of the provisions noted in the checklist are mandatory. However, when planning, negotiating and agreeing on the format of the terms of the contract it is sensible for each party contracting to consider each of these provisions in turn before deciding whether or not to use it.

Supplementary terms will be governed not only by the needs of the parties contracting but also by the intellectual property being licensed. These further terms will be reviewed in the various topic-specific chapters of this book.

Box 1 Checklist of provisions

Preface to the contract

✓ Cover sheet

✓ Table of contents (optional in longer contracts)

✓ Index of defined terms

Front of the contract (see section (§1.18[A][2]))

✓ Title

✓ Introductory clause (type of agreement, date of agreement, parties to agreement)

✓ Recitals

Body of the contract (see section (§1.18[A][3]) and the corresponding topic-specific chapter)

✓ Definitions clause

✓ Grant

✓ Term of the agreement

✓ Relationship of the parties

✓ Confidentiality

✓ Work obligations

✓ Obligations of the licensee

Payment terms

Non-compete provisions

Sublicencing

Quality control

Maintenance of licenced property

Restrictions on the fields of use

✓ Obligations of the licensor

Assistance and training to the licensee provided by the licensor

Warranties, liabilities and indemnities

✓ Termination (grounds and consequences)

Boilerplate clauses (see section (§1.36))

✓ Assignment clause

✓ Change of control and ownership clause

✓ Merger clause

✓ Modifications clause

✓ Severance clause

✓ Notice clause

✓ Representation clause

✓ Dispute resolution (informal discussions, renegotiation, adaption, ADR, choice of jurisdiction, choice of law)

✓ Language clause

Back of the contract (see section (§1.37))

✓ Concluding clause

✓ Signature blocks

✓ Attachment (exhibits and schedules)

[1] Preface to the Contract[177,178]

Box 2 Overall structure of contract

- Cover sheet
- Table of contents (in longer contracts; optional)

177. This topic is developed in Meiselles 2013: Chapter 2.
178. Two excellent guides on drafting of contracts are Kenneth Adams, *A Manual of Style of Contract Drafting* (2nd edn, American Bar Association 2007) (hereafter Adams 2007) in particular Chapters 2, 4 and 5, and Tina L. Stark, *Drafting Contracts: How and Why Lawyers Do What They Do* (Aspen 2007) (hereafter Stark 2007) in particular Chapters 5, 6 and 17.

- Index of defined terms (optional)
- Front of the contract
- Body of the contract
- Back of the contract

The body of the contract is prefaced by the front of the contract and followed by the back of the contract.

The central provisions that govern the relationship between the contracting parties are contained principally in the body of the contract. Occasionally certain key provisions will be contained in a separate agreement annexed, for example, to the contract.

- Cover sheet

A short version of the introductory clause will be set out on the cover sheet.

- Table of contents (optional)

In longer contracts, it is advisable to incorporate a table of contents. This typically comes after the cover sheet and lists the page numbers (for articles and sections) and attachments.

- Index of defined terms (optional)

Such an index alphabetically lists the defined terms indicating the page of the contract in which the definition of each defined term is given.

In the event that such an index is used, it is typically placed immediately after the table of contents.

[2] Front of the Contract[179,180]

Box 3 Overall structure of front of the contract

- Title
- Introductory clause
- Recitals

179. This topic is developed in Meiselles 2013: Chapter 2.
180. Adams 2007: Chapter 2; Stark 2007: Chapters 5–7.

The title, the introductory clause and the recitals constitute the front of the contract.

The following extract is taken from a technology licence.

> **Licence agreement**
>
> This licence agreement is dated (date the agreement becomes effective) and is between (name of Licensor) a (jurisdiction) (type of entity for example a company, a partnership and so on) ('LICENSOR') and (name of Licensee) a (jurisdiction) (type of entity) ('LICENSEE').
>
> The Licensor is the proprietor of (list intellectual property involved e.g. proprietor of certain patents and patent applications relating to).
>
> The Licensee desires to obtain a licence under the terms and conditions set out in this agreement.

The extract provided above encompasses:

1. A title

> Licence agreement

2. An introductory clause

> This licence agreement is dated (date the agreement becomes effective) and is between (name of Licensor) a (jurisdiction) (type of entity for example a company, a partnership and so on) ('LICENSOR') and (name of Licensee) a (jurisdiction) (type of entity) ('LICENSEE').

3. Recital

> The Licensor is the proprietor of (list intellectual property involved e.g. proprietor of certain patents and patent applications relating to).
>
> The Licensee desires to obtain a licence under the terms and conditions set out in this agreement.

[a] Title

Placed at the top centre of the first page, the title denotes the class of agreement involved.[181]

Such a title should be brief and should typically encompass within it the word 'agreement' or 'contract'.

[b] Introductory Clause[182,183]

The introductory clause appears after the title and sets out (in the following order):

(1) the type of agreement involved;
(2) the date of the agreement; and
(3) the parties to the agreement

[c] Type of Agreement[184,185]

The wording used in the title is incorporated into the introductory clause (in lower case) and preceded by the word 'This'. In the event that the agreement is defined in the definitions clause, initial capitals are used. Like any sentence the introductory clause will require a verb. 'Dated' is probably the simplest option and is clearer than 'made', 'concluded' or 'entered into'.

[d] Date of Agreement[186,187]

The date appearing in the introductory clause is the date on which the contract becomes effective unless the contract states otherwise. This date is crucial for a number of reasons. First it determines the dates on which the duties and rights of the contracting parties commence and second it defines the term of the agreement.

The contracting parties should take care to ensure that the date in the introductory clause corresponds with any other dates that appear in the contract.[188] In circumstances where the contracting parties are planning to postpone the signing of the agreement it is sensible for them to omit the date from the introductory clause and instead to date their signatures when signing the agreement. In such a situation, reference should be made within the terms of the agreement to the fact that the agreement will become effective only when the last party signs the agreement.

181. Adams 2007: 3.
182. Meiselles 2013: 49.
183. Adams 2007: 3–11.
184. Meiselles 2013: 49.
185. Adams 2007: 4-5.
186. Meiselles 2013: 49.
187. Adams 2007: 4–5.
188. The provision addressing the term of the agreement, and the initial period is reviewed in Meiselles 2013: Chapter 4.

[e] Parties to the Agreement[189]

An agreement binds the parties that sign it. For this reason, it is imperative that the identity of the parties contracting is clearly pinpointed and is ascertainable. To help the identity of the parties contracting stand out it is worthwhile using capital letters for these names.

Due consideration should be given to the question of whether a party representing an entity has the requisite authority to contract on behalf of the entity. This consideration is one that should be resolved before the negotiation process commences and well in advance of the contract being drawn up.[190]

The following information should be noted elsewhere in the contract:

- The addresses of the contracting parties. Such information should be referred to in the notice provision.
- Details of an authorised representative. These should be noted in the representation clause.

- Where the contracting party is a legal entity[191]

In the introductory clause, it is wise to not only identify the parties contracting but also to make a note of the following information:

(1) the category of entity involved (partnership, limited liability company, publicly listed company, JVC, European Company, European Economic Interest Grouping and so on);
(2) the designation of the form of entity ('LLP', 'Ltd', 'plc', 'Inc.', 'GmbH', 'AG', 'SE', 'EEIG' and so on);
(3) the organisation's governing jurisdiction (in this context as brevity is of the essence it is sensible for the parties to employ the phrase 'English company' rather than stating 'a company incorporated under English law');
(4) an indication of whether the entity is an affiliate of another entity; and
(5) where the entity is a company its company's registration number.

- Entity that is part of a group of companies

Where the contracting party is part of a group of companies, a concern that should be considered with care is the question of whether the parent company should be one of the contracting parties to the agreement (in order to furnish a parent company guarantee).[192] This genre of issue will be of importance in circumstances where the

189. Meiselles 2013: 50.
190. Meiselles 2013: Chapter 1.
191. Adams 2007: 5; Meiselles 2013: 50-1.
192. Anderson 2010: 53.

contracting party (that is a member of a group of companies) does not have the necessary assets to meet contractual liabilities and the parent company does.[193]

Where the contracting party is part of a large group of related companies, it is advisable for the registration number of the company contracting to be given, this is particularly important when a number of companies in the group possess similar names and where it is imperative to pinpoint the company in the group that is the party contracting.[194]

- Contracting with academics

Where an academic or indeed a group of academics are supplying consultancy services, due consideration should be given to the question of authority.[195]

In this context, before entering into negotiations, regard should be given to establishing whether the academics in question are permitted under the policy of the university to contract on behalf of the university.[196] Oftentimes, a consultancy agreement of this type will need to be handled by the central administration of the university or a company created by the university for this purpose.[197] If this is the case, then the university's central administration or the dedicated company should handle the negotiation and the conclusion processes.[198]

Certain categories of agreements will require the joining of certain personnel employed by the university or hospital.[199] In such instances the parties to the agreement will comprise the university or hospital and at a minimum the lead academic/researcher/doctor.[200]

This strategy may be employed in circumstances where the party joined is required to supply some express warranty in the agreement or is to be subjected to certain obligations.[201] For example, this may arise where there is a need to impose confidentiality obligations on the party in question.

- Contracting with large organisations[202]

Where a contract is contemplated with a large organisation (whether the organisation is corporate in character or is a university or hospital and so on), it may be sensible to refer in the contract to the appropriate department or section or unit by name (in the parties' clause).

193. Anderson 2010: 53.
194. Anderson 2010: 55.
195. Anderson 2010: 54.
196. Anderson 2010: 54.
197. Anderson 2010: 54.
198. Anderson 2010: 54.
199. Anderson 2010: 54.
200. Anderson 2010: 54.
201. Anderson 2010: 54.
202. Anderson 2010: 53-4.

[f] Recitals[203]

If used, these clauses will be situated after the title and before the body of the contract. Whilst such clauses are optional, the use of recitals can prove useful in a number of situations:[204] first, when certain terms in the contract are left vague and the arbiter needs to establish what the parties intended; and second, when certain terms are omitted completely from the contract and the arbiter is left to fill in the gap or gaps.

Headings such as 'RECITALS' and lead-ins such as 'WITNESSETH' can be dispensed with in recitals as the nature of the information and the location of these provisions mean that it is clear that these provisions are recitals.

[3] Body of the Contract

§1.19 GRANT

1. Subject to the terms set out in this agreement, the Licensor hereby grants to the Licensee the (revocable/irrevocable) (exclusive/non-exclusive) licence in the Licenced Territory to produce, have produced, sell, distribute and market the Licenced Goods [optional - together with the trademarks licenced by the Licensor defined in Schedule —— ('Licenced Trademarks')].

2. The Licensee shall negotiate separately with the Licensor any sales or exports of the Licenced Goods outside the Licenced Territory.

Optional provisions

3. (Where the licence is exclusive) The Licensee may exclusively produce, have produced, sell, distribute and market the Licenced Goods in the Licenced Territory [optional - together with the trademarks licenced by the Licensor defined in Schedule —— ('Licenced Trademarks')] to the exclusion of other parties (optional - including the Licensor).

4. The Licensee may exclusively use the technology licenced by the Licensor defined in Schedule —— ('Licenced Technology') in the Licenced Territory to the exclusion of other parties (optional - including the Licensor).

5. The Licensor grants the Licensee the (exclusive/non-exclusive) right to use the Licenced Trademarks in connection with the Licenced Goods in the Licenced Territory so long as the Licensee shall ensure that the Licenced Trademarks appear in a legible manner on all Licenced Good (optional - in the Licenced Territory).

203. Meiselles 2013: 50-1.
204. Stark 2007: 61.

6. Option A–

The Licensor grants the Licensee the (exclusive/non-exclusive) right to use the Licenced Trademarks in connection with the Licenced Goods in the Licenced Territory so long as the reference to and use of any the Licenced Trademarks by the Licensee is in a manner that is approved by the Licensor and that each reference to the Licenced Trademarks and use of any of the Licenced Trademarks by the Licensee is accompanied by an acknowledgement in a form approved by the Licensor that the same is a trademark of the Licensor.

Option B–

The Licensee shall have the sole discretion to determine the placement of the Licenced Trademarks. The Licensee may use the Licenced Trademarks alongside the trade names and trademarks of the Licensee.

The grant provision furnishes the licensee with a licence in relation to the intellectual property owned by the licensor. This provision is central to the parties for a number of reasons.

First, under the auspices of this provision the licensor extends the licensee certain rights in relation to the licensed intellectual property. Occasionally these rights granted pertain to one or more specific territory (licensed territory). In this provision the parties will typically indicate whether the licence granted is exclusive or non-exclusive.

Second, in this provision the licensor sets out the scope of the licence endowed upon the licensee. In circumstances where a non-exclusive licence is awarded, the licensor may insist on reserving itself the right to grant further licences to other parties aside from the licensee. It may also reserve itself the right to use the licensed property in the licensed territory effectively in competition with the licensee.

Once the parties have established the subject matter of their licence namely the component(s) that they wish to licence in or licence out, the licensee should give due consideration to that which it wishes to achieve using the licensed intellectual property and technology.[205] By identifying its business objectives, the licensee should be able to isolate the categories of rights that it will require under the licence.[206]

The rights granted under a licence will be governed not only by the needs of the contracting parties but also by the intellectual property law applicable to the agreement.[207]

205. Successful Technology Licensing (WIPO 2004), 21.
206. Successful Technology Licensing (WIPO 2004), 21.
207. Successful Technology Licensing (WIPO 2004), 21.

§1.20 TERRITORIAL EXCLUSIVITY

A licensor may grant the licensee a licence on either an exclusive basis or a non-exclusive basis in the territory assigned.[208]

[A] Non-exclusive Arrangements[209]

Under a non-exclusive licence, the ability of the licensor to award further licences in the assigned territory to other parties aside from the licensee is preserved.

Such a strategy is likely to be attractive to the licensor for a number of reasons. Beyond the fact that such a set-up will be of interest to a licensor keen on using the licensed property itself in the assigned territory, this arrangement is likely to be beneficial to a licensor looking to enter into a new geographic market in circumstances where it is attempting to gauge the commercial competence of a number of licensees on the designated market in the short term before concluding a long-term arrangement with the most competent licensee. Moreover, this set-up will offer the licensor the option of spreading its risk amongst several different actors in the assigned territory.

[B] Exclusive Arrangements[210]

Under an exclusive licence, the ability of the licensor to award further licences in the assigned territory to other parties aside from the licensee is curtailed.

A licensee is likely to insist on exclusivity in the context of technology licences for a variety of reasons.

Beyond the fact that the licensee is likely to be undertaking a major risk, it will probably be required to make a substantial investment in terms of energy, time and money. It may need to hire and train a corpus of specialised staff. It may be required to purchase or rent machinery and premises. There may be an expectation under the licensing agreement that the licensee invest resources in the development of the technology licensed to it.

By insisting on exclusivity, the licensee is able to ward against the risk of **freeriding** which occurs where a party other than the licensee (another licensee, a distributor, the licensor and so forth) is able to benefit from the work of the licensee on the given market.

From the vantage point of the licensor exclusivity may be problematic as it is effectively relying on one actor to generate revenue for it on the market designated. By placing all its resources in the hands of the exclusive licensee it is potentially running the risk of reducing its prospective revenue from the market in question if the licensee does not fare well.

---

208. The granting of an exclusive licence under English law will need to be in writing (§92, Copyright, Designs and Patents Act 1988).
209. For further details *see* the discussion in Meiselles 2013: 255.
210. For further details *see* the discussion in Meiselles 2013: 256.

In circumstances where exclusivity is extended to the licensee and the licensor is unable to generate an adequate return, the licensor will either have to wait until the agreement ends or if the terms of the licence permit it the licensor may have the right to terminate the agreement on the grounds of a breach by the licensee.

In order to mitigate or eliminate the risks borne in such circumstances by the licensor, certain protective measures should be considered in the licensing agreement. Such provisions could include:

(1) a provision stipulating a guaranteed annual minimum payment which guarantees a steady and fixed income to the licensor;
(2) where the licensee fails to meet a certain target set by reference to a base royalty payment or a minimum volume of sales (this target could be annual, biannual and so forth), the licensor could have the right to:
    (a) convert the exclusive licence into a non-exclusive licence; or
    (b) claw back exclusive territories reducing the areas in which the licensee enjoys exclusivity;
(3) where the licensee meets certain targets set by reference to income generated or volume of sales, the licensor could undertake to expand the territory of exclusivity;
(4) a provision limiting the period of exclusivity to an interval deemed sufficient for the licensee is able to recoup its initial sunk costs (**head start provision**);[211]
(5) a provision ring-fencing exclusivity to specific rights granted under the licensing agreement;[212]
(6) a provision ring-fencing exclusivity to certain technologies granted under the licensing agreement.[213]

§1.21 TERM OF THE AGREEMENT[214]

Option A – Without an initial period

1. This agreement shall enter into force on this —— day of —— in the year —— (or upon the date that this agreement is signed).

2. (Subject to earlier termination provided for within the terms of this agreement) This agreement will remain in force unless or until terminated by either Party giving the other not less than —— written notice.

Option B – With an initial period

1. This agreement shall enter into force on this —— day of —— in the year —— (or upon the date that this agreement is signed).

211. Successful Technology Licensing (WIPO 2004), 24.
212. Successful Technology Licensing (WIPO 2004), 25.
213. Successful Technology Licensing (WIPO 2004), 25.
214. For further details *see* the discussion in Meiselles 2013: 256-7.

2. (Subject to earlier termination provided for within the terms of this agreement) This will remain in force for a preliminary period of —— years ('Initial Period') and thereafter, unless and until terminated by either Party giving to the other not less than —— months' written notice.

3. (Optional) Neither Party shall give notice before the end of the Initial Period.

This clause indicates the date on which the agreement commences and in certain circumstances, the term of the agreement.

Care should be taken when concluding a fixed-term agreement or an agreement with an initial period to ensure the fixed term or the initial period is long enough to allow the licensee to develop a profitable business and to amortise its investment.

[A] Fixed-Term Agreement (Definite Term Agreement)

The clause fixing the term of the agreement will determine the time span of the contractual relationship between the parties as well as the time during which the licensee will be permitted by the licensor to exploit the licensed property in the assigned territory.

Where the parties agree to a fixed-term agreement, the contract will run its course unless there is some reason for its premature termination.

The parties that enter into a fixed-term agreement may agree to incorporate a **right of renewal**. In such circumstances they may agree that renewal be automatic or that certain steps be executed before the contract is renewed. In this context they may agree that renewal be achieved by means of a written agreement signed by the parties or that one party have the right to notify the other for renewal of the agreement to take place.

[B] An Agreement for an Indefinite Term

An agreement for an indefinite term will state that the agreement will continue unless and until one of the parties to the agreement provides the other with notice.

The prospective parties should give due consideration to the fact that in certain jurisdictions such arrangements result in the establishment of an agency relationship between the parties with all the responsibilities associated with the existence of such a relationship.[215]

215. This is the case in the European Union where under EU law the principal, and agent are subject to the provisions of Council Directive 86/653/EEC of 18 December 1986 on the coordination of the laws of the Member States relating to self-employed commercial agents. A detailed review of these obligations can be found in Meiselles 2013: Chapter 5.

[C] Initial Period or No Initial Period

The draft clause above provides for two alternatives. An agreement without an initial period (option A); an agreement with an initial period (option B).

A licensee is likely to insist upon the inclusion of an initial period for a variety of reasons. First to allow it to construct a market for the contract goods produced with the licensed intellectual property. Second to permit it to realise a return on its initial and continuing investment.[216] Third to enable it to amortise its investment.

The agreement may include an initial period along with a provision stating that the agreement cannot be terminated during that period (clause 3 in option B above).

Alternatively, the contracting parties may agree that the agreement can be terminated in specific situations (e.g., if one of the parties is declared insolvent or changes its business) or if specific obligations are not met by either party.

– Relationship of the parties

1. The Parties agree that the Licensor is separate and independent of the Licensee.

2. The Parties agree that the Licensee is not an agent or representative of the Licensor for any purpose, that the Licensee has not got authority to bind the Licensor in any way whatsoever and that the Licensee shall not contract in the name of the Licensor or on behalf of the Licensor.

3. Nothing in this agreement shall create or be treated as creating between the Parties a joint venture, a partnership, an employment relationship, a fiduciary relationship, an agency relationship or any other type of relationship.

4. Each Party shall be free to recruit or employ any staff or independent contractors and neither Party shall have the liberty to restrict or dismiss any staff or independent contractors recruited or employed by the other Party.

5. Each Party shall ensure that any staff and independent contractors recruited or employed sign an agreement not to use the Intellectual Property for any other purpose.

6. Neither Party shall be liable for the debts or liabilities of the other.

7. Save as expressly provided for in this agreement, neither Party shall enter into an agreement or have authority to enter into an agreement or provide any representation or warranty on behalf of the other Party or pledge the credit of the other Party or otherwise bind or oblige the other Party.

216. Richard Christou, *International agency, distribution, and licensing agreements* (Sweet & Maxwell 2004), 195.

This standard clause used in various commercial agreements clarifies the character of the relationship existing between the contracting parties.

This clause makes it clear that the licensee acts solely as a licensee. Establishing that the licensee is not acting as an agent, partner, employee and so on of the licensor.

This clause also establishes the distinctive character of the licensee and the licensor as separate and independent entities. This is beneficial to the parties as it prevents a situation where it may be argued that the agreement gives rise *inter alia* to a partnership, joint venture, agency or employment relationship. In other words, it will effectively ring-fence and curtail the power and authority of the parties to legally commit each other.

§1.22 CONFIDENTIALITY

1. The Parties agrees that any information disclosed regardless of source shall be kept confidential. This obligation shall extend to all information including but not restricted to technical data, information relating to the Licensed Goods, the Licensed Technology and the operations of each Party, its subsidiaries and its associated corporations.

2. The Parties agree to use the confidential information solely in connection with their respective activities under this agreement and for the purpose of executing their respective obligations set out in this agreement. The Parties agree not to use the confidential information for any other purposes.

3. The Parties may furnish information to (those officers, directors, employees and advisors that the Parties have agreed upon and who are listed in Schedule —— *(option A) or* those officers, directors, employees and advisors who need this information to carry out activities that the Parties have agreed upon under the terms of this agreement *(option B)*), on the proviso that such officers, directors, employees or advisors have confirmed their agreement to adhere to the terms of this agreement *(option C)* or that such officers, directors, employees or advisors have executed a confidentiality and non-exploitation agreement on terms that the Parties have confirmed by means of an agreement *(option D)*).

4. In order to impede unauthorised disclosure of information, the Parties shall safeguard any information disclosed using the same degree of care, no less than reasonable care, that each one of the Parties would use in order to safeguard its own information of a similar nature.

5. Unless expressly agreed upon within the terms of the agreement, the Parties shall not provide any information to a third person(s) including but not limited to an entity, an agent, a partner, an individual, a company belonging to the same group as the one the Party concerned belongs to and workers of the Party concerned who are not working at the branch, office or local establishment in the Territory.

6. Neither Party shall exploit the information at any time in order to compete in any manner with the other. Neither Party shall furnish this information to a third party so that it may compete with the other Party.

7. The obligations contained in this clause shall continue indefinitely after this agreement ends for whatever reason. (Optional – The obligations contained in this clause shall continue for a period ending () years from the date on which this agreement was terminated.)[217]

Optional provisions

8. Neither Party shall provide or sell or licence this confidential information to others without firstly obtaining the written authorisation of the other Party.

9. Any sublicence granted shall incorporate confidentiality requirements that are identical to the obligations applicable to the Licensee under this agreement.

10. Nothing contained within this agreement will adversely impact upon the right of either Party to exploit, disclose or otherwise deal with in its sole discretion any technology, know-how or other information either included or not in the Licensed Technology, which:

a. Was, is, or becomes, public knowledge otherwise than as a result of a breach of this agreement;[218]

b. Was rightly known to the Party (or to its affiliates) prior to such disclosure and the Party can provide written records demonstrating that this confidential information was previously known to it;[219]

c. Was developed by the Party independently of this agreement; or

d. Was or is lawfully acquired by the Party from sources that are independent of the other Party.[220]

In order to protect proprietary information in the possession of the contracting parties, to limit the risk of parallel imports and to remove the danger of freeriding, each of the contracting parties is likely to insist upon the inclusion of a confidentiality clause in the licence.

Due consideration should be given to the following optional provisions by the contracting parties when negotiating and drafting the confidentiality clause:

(1) A provision obliging the other party to ensure that those granted access to the information are bound by the terms of the agreement.

217. Exchanging Value – Negotiating Technology Licensing Agreements (WIPO), 46.
218. Exchanging Value – Negotiating Technology Licensing Agreements (WIPO), 46.
219. Exchanging Value – Negotiating Technology Licensing Agreements (WIPO), 46.
220. Exchanging Value – Negotiating Technology Licensing Agreements (WIPO), 46.

(2) A provision stipulating that those with access to the confidential information enter into a confidentiality and non-exploitation agreement.
(3) A provision setting out the details of those persons with authorised access to the confidential information.

Where the list of persons with access to the information is extensive or needs to be extended with time, the parties should consider using a schedule to list the details of the persons with access to the confidential information.

§1.23 WORK OBLIGATIONS

Where work is undertaken under a licensing agreement, a list of the tasks to be executed by the party or parties charged with these tasks should be comprehensively and accurately drafted either within the body of the agreement itself or in a schedule or attachment to the said agreement.[221]

§1.24 OBLIGATIONS OF THE LICENSEE[222]

The obligations imposed on the licensee under this genre of licence have as their goal the protection of the licensor and its interests *inter alia* the reputation, the goodwill and the revenue stream of the licensor.

From the vantage point of the licensor it will endeavour to incorporate into such a licensing agreement provisions that provide it with optimal and comprehensive protection. The licensee from its viewpoint will probably seek to limit the scope of these obligations as best it can.

The potential concerns of the licensor are numerous as are the corresponding obligations on the licensee.

The licensor should also consider the inclusion of a fail-safe in the event that something goes wrong or to prevent something going wrong. In such a situation the licensor should give thought to whether or not a breach of any of the provisions will give it the right to terminate the agreement.

First, the licensor will be concerned about protecting its financial return under the licensing agreement.

With this in mind, the licensor should consider the inclusion of comprehensive payment terms in the licence along with a provision ensuring a guaranteed minimum annual payment, which will safeguard the licensor's revenue stream in circumstances where the income generated by the licensee using the licensed property decreases.[223]

Second, beyond the financial component, the licensor will be concerned about limiting the licensee's ability to compete with it during the course of the agreement

221. Anderson 2010: 57.
222. For further details *see* the discussion in Meiselles 2013: 257-66.
223. More on minimum guaranteed annual royalties (also known as the minimum annual guarantee) later on in this chapter.

(**in-term non-compete clause**) and after the agreement comes to an end (**post-term non-compete clause**).

To protect its competitive position, the licensor will look to incorporate in-term and post-term non-compete clauses that are as widely drafted as possible bearing in mind the licensee's willingness to agree to such provisions and the position under national law which may restrict the use of such clauses and their scope.[224]

Third, in order to address the concerns associated with the loss of control by the licensor over the property that it has licensed to the licensee (the licensed property) and the potential loss of proprietary information belonging to it, the licensor will endeavour to secure certain protective measures within the agreement. Examples of such protective measures include:

(1) a provision *forbidding* the licensee to grant sublicences in relation to the licensed technology;
(2) a provision *restricting* the ability of the licensee to grant sublicences in relation to the licensed technology;
(3) the inclusion of a widely drafted confidentiality clause; and
(4) a provision restricting the fields of use of the licensed property.

Fourth to guarantee the licensor's retention of ownership in the licensed property it is sensible for the licensor to consider the inclusion of the following provisions in the licensing agreement:

(1) A provision clearly stating that the licensee will not acquire rights in relation to the licensed property.
(2) A provision stating that all rights and goodwill in the licensed property are and shall remain vested in the licensor.
(3) A provision compelling the licensee to advise the licensor of any actual or potential infringement of which it is aware or of which it becomes aware.
(4) A provision stipulating that the licensee must help the licensor safeguard the validity and enforceability of the licensed property (**maintenance of licensed property** clause).

Fifth to ensure that quality standards are adhered to by the licensee, due consideration should be given by the licensor to the inclusion of the following terms in the licensing agreement:

(1) An inspection provision

Such a provision would permit the licensor to inspect facilities used by the licensee for the production of goods using the licensed technology.

224. The regulation of non-compete clauses under EU law is addressed in Chapter 2 on competition law.

In this context, the licensor may insist on access to facilities *belonging to* the licensee and access to facilities *contracted to* the licensee, as well as access to facilities that the licensee is responsible for *running* or indeed *supervising*.

(2) A reporting requirement

By requiring the licensee to regularly report to the licensor, it will be able to ensure compliance and adherence to the terms of the agreement.

In this context to guarantee the provision of the information needed by the licensor in a full and accurate manner, the licensor should consider providing the licensee with a template report setting out the parameters that it would expect the licensee to report upon.

(3) A sampling provision

The licensor should consider the inclusion of a provision that requires the licensee to furnish it with samples of the goods manufactured using the licensed property either at regular interludes or on an ad hoc basis as and when required to do so by the licensor.

Finally, in a bid to preserve its rights in relation to new goods and improvements developed by the licensee using the licensed property, the licensor should give due regard to the inclusion of a **grant back clause** permitting it to exploit new goods and improvements developed by the licensee.[225]

§1.25 PAYMENT TERMS

- Payment terms (structure and time; currency; consequence of non-payment)

Paid-up licence

1. In consideration of the rights granted to the Licensee by the Licensor under this agreement in relation to (the Licenced Patents *or* Licenced Technology *or* Licenced Trademarks *or* any other property licenced by the Licensor to the Licensee) (and the technical assistance and support provided by the Licensor to the Licensee), the Licensee shall pay the Licensor an initial sum of ___ ('Initial Sum').

Option A

2. The Initial Sum shall be paid in full on ____ (insert due date).

Option B

2. The Licensee shall pay the Licensor the Initial Sum by means of instalments. The details of these instalments are as follows:a. The first instalment of ____ shall

225. The use of grant back clauses is regulated in certain jurisdictions. This topic is elaborating upon in August et al. 2009: 510.

be paid by the Licensee to the Licensor on ____;b. The second instalement of ____ shall be paid by the Licensee to the Licensor on ____;

c. [...]

Running royalty licence

1. In consideration of the rights granted to the Licensee by the Licensor under this agreement in relation to (the Licenced Patents *or* Licenced Technology *or* Licenced Trademarks *or* any other property licenced by the Licensor to the Licensee) (and the technical assistance and support provided by the Licensor to the Licensee), the Licensee agrees to pay the Licensor a royalty equal to ____ percent on (net receipts for example) ('Royalty').

2. The Licensee shall pay the Licensor the Royalty in (currency) within ____ days of the end of each [calendar month of each year, calendar quarter of each year, year and so forth]. (Optional) No account need be submitted nor payment made in respect of any (insert royalty period concerned) in which the sum due is less than (____) in which case the amount will be carried forward to the next accounting date.

3. The Licensee shall provide to the Licensor a written report (no later than ____ or with each Royalty payment) containing details of:

a. The total number of units sold;

b. The total sum invoiced by the Licensee;

c. The sales price for sales for the period covered by the Royalty;

d. (Optional) The permitted sublicenses granted by the Licensee; and

e. (Optional) All the transactions whatsoever in relation to the Licenced Patents *or* Licenced Technology *or* Licenced Trademarks *or* any other property licenced by the Licensor to the Licensee on which royalties are due,

during (e.g. the year to the immediately preceding ____).

4.

Option A – Right to interest

If the Licensee fails to make a payment to the Licensor when due, then provided the Licensor has given written notice of the overdue payment, the Licensor will be entitled to default interest at a rate equal to (____) per cent per annum above the published (____) base rate from time to time, from (____) business days after receipt of such notice until the date on which payment is received by the Licensor.

Option B – Automatic right to terminate

If the Licensee fails to make a payment to the Licensor when due, then the Licensor may end this agreement and terminate any rights granted to the Licensee under this agreement immediately without informing the Licensee.

Option C – Right to terminate on provision of notice

If the Licensee fails to make a payment to the Licensor when due, then provided the Licensor has given written notice of (____) business days of the overdue payment, the Licensor may end this agreement and terminate any rights granted to the Licensee under this agreement instantly without informing the Licensee.

5. The Licensee shall keep separate internal accounting records ('Accounting Records') pertaining to the:

a. Utilisation in the Licenced Territory of (the Licenced Patents *or* Licenced Technology *or* Licenced Trademarks *or* any other property licenced by the Licensor to the Licensee); and

b. Sales of Licenced Goods in the Licenced Territory.

6. For the purposes of verifying the sums paid by the Licensee to the Licensor, the Licensee shall allow an independent accountant/ accounting firm chosen by the Licensor and approved by the Licensee to review the Accounting Records kept by the Licensee. The Licensor shall pay the fees and expenses associated with this inspection.

Optional provisions

Minimum annual guarantee or minimum annual royalty payment

7. In the event that in any year ending on an anniversary date set out in the table displayed below:

a. The sales made by the Licensee fall below the corresponding minimum sums defined in the aforementioned table ('Minimum Sums') the Royalty will be calculated using the Minimum Sums;

b. The cumulative payments paid by the Licensee to the Licensor pursuant to the subsection above fall below the applicable royalty as calculated on the basis of the Minimum Sums then the Licensee shall pay the Licensor in (currency) within ____ days of the end of such year, the difference.

Table setting out the anniversary dates of this agreement and the corresponding Minimum Sums

Anniversary date of this agreement	Minimum Sum
()th	
()th	
()th	
()th …	

Deductions

8. The Licensee may deduct from the Royalty due the following items: Registration fees, Maintenance fees, payments required by any existing law or regulation of () and so forth.

9. The Licensee shall not be entitled to offset sums it claims are due to it without first obtaining the written permission of the Licensor.

The question of payment should be clearly and comprehensively addressed in a licensing agreement.[226]

The matters that should be addressed in the context of payment are the structure of payment, the currency and the timing of payments and the consequences of failing to pay or paying late.

[A] Structure of Payment

Where consideration for the licensing is monetary, the parties to the licensing agreement may agree to use the following methods of payment either alone or together, namely an initial sum and ongoing payments.[227]

[B] Paid-Up Licence Versus Running Royalty Licence[228]

A licence is said to be a **paid-up licence** in circumstances where the provisions of the licensing agreement entail the payment of an agreed sum by the licensee to the licensor. Such a sum may be paid in the form of a single lump sum payment or by means of instalments.

A **running royalty licence** is one under which periodic sums are paid by the licensee to the licensor.

From the perspectives of the licensor and the licensee, a paid-up licence is easier to formulate and to administer than a running royalty licence for a number of reasons.

[1] Running Royalty Licence

When negotiating a running royalty licence, the parties should bear in mind the fact that beyond the complications associated with agreeing on a royalty rate and on the

226. Anderson 2010: 57.
227. Pollzien, Götz and Bronfen, George (eds), *International Licensing Agreements* (Bobbs-Merrill 1965), 101–2 (hereafter Pollzien et al. 1965).
228. For a detailed discussion of paid-up licences *see* Meiselles 2013: 259-61.

frequency of payments, the administration of such a licence entails a myriad of difficulties. The reporting and auditing procedures that are typically incorporated into running royalty licences require the expenditure of time and money by both parties and have the potential of generating disputes that undermine commercial productivity and the sustainable development within the contractual matrix.[229,230]

A running royalty licence involving the payment of periodic payments is typically appropriate in scenarios where the parties to the agreement are uncertain about the forecasted sales or incapable of reaching an agreement on such sales.[231]

Alternately these set-ups may be suited to situations where the parties to the agreement are looking to share in the success of the venture[232] or where the licensee has limited cash flow and as such is unable to opt for a paid-up licence.[233]

[2] Paid-Up Licence

Paid-up licences are usually more appropriate where a short-term commitment is being considered by the contracting parties, which may occur where the licensee wishes to engage for the short term or where the term associated with the intellectual property licensed is coming to an end.[234]

From the vantage point of a licensor, a paid-up licence offers more certainty than a running royalty licence in circumstances where the commercial viability of the licensee is in question (this may be the case where the licensee is a start-up company) or where there are risks associated with the property licensed (where there is a potential for litigation).[235]

A paid-up licence is likely to be easier to negotiate when the future revenue of the licensee is relatively predictable as the parties contracting are less likely to dispute the figure to be paid over.[236]

Once the sum payable under the terms of the licence is defined by the contracting parties it will not fluctuate, whether the sales generated are high, low or non-existent.[237]

Notwithstanding this fact, the future sales anticipated by the contracting parties under the licensing agreement may be used as the basis for the computation of the sums due as royalties if the licence is a **part paid-up licence** (which combines a paid-up licence with a running royalty licence).

229. Pollzien et al. 1965: 15.
230. Poltorak et al. 2004: 101-2.
231. Poltorak et al. 2004: 101–2.
232. Poltorak et al. 2004: 101–2.
233. Pollzien et al. 1965: 101–2.
234. Poltorak et al. 2004: 101–2.
235. Poltorak et al. 2004: 101-2.
236. Poltorak et al. 2004: 99-100.
237. Pollzien et al. 1965: 15; Poltorak et al. 2004: Chapter 9.

[C] Initial Sum Payable[238]

Initial payments may be used not only in the context of paid-up licence but also in the context of a running royalty licence. Under the running royalty licence this sum will be paid to the licensor alongside royalties.

The agreed sum may be paid by the licensee to the licensor either as a one-off payment or in instalments.[239]

Where the sum is paid at once then the due date and figure involved should be addressed.

Where instalments are payable under the agreement then the due dates of the different instalments should be mentioned in the agreement alongside the sum of each instalment.[240]

[1] Drafting the Term Governing the Initial Sum

When drafting the term governing the initial sum, due consideration should be given by the parties to the following issues:

- whether the initial sum will represent an advance against royalties (in the case of running royalty licences);
- whether the initial sum is payable at once or in instalments;
- if the initial sum is payable at once:
  - what sum is due and when is it due;
  - what would be the consequences of non-payment of the sum due;
  - what would be the consequences of a late payment of the sum due.
- If the sum is payable in instalments:
  - what are the timings of these payments and what sums are due at each interval;
  - what would be the consequences of non-payment of one of the sums due;
  - what would be the consequences of a late payment of the said sums.

The consequences associated with the non-payment or late payment of the sums due could, for example, involve the imposition of interest.

If interest is due on the unpaid sums then reference should be made to the rate of interest, whether the rate is daily, monthly and so on, and whether the party to whom the monies are owing will have the right to terminate the agreement.[241]

238. For a detailed discussion of paid-up licences *see* Meiselles 2013: 259.
239. Pollzien et al. 1965: 101–2.
240. Pollzien et al. 1965: 101–2.
241. Anderson 2010: 57.

[D] Advance Against Future Royalties (Running Royalty Licence)

Where the licensee has agreed to pay the licensor an initial sum under a running royalty licence, the parties may agree that the initial sum paid will be an **advance against future royalties**. In which case, this advance is then offset against royalty payments that the licensee needs to pay to the licensor until such a time as the advance is reimbursed.[242]

Advances against future royalties may be brokered in circumstances where the licensee is in a stronger financial position than the licensor which may be the case, for example, where the licensor is a publicly funded entity or a start-up company that needs financing to continue with its research and development activities.[243]

[E] Ongoing Payments (Royalty Payments)

Ongoing payments in the context of a licence are intermittently referred to as **royalties**. Such sums may be due on top of the lump sum due under the agreement.

[1] Fixing Royalty Payments Versus Percentage-Based Royalties

In the context of a running royalty licence, the royalties payable may take the form of fixed sum royalties or percentage-based royalties.[244]

Fixed sum royalties typically involve the payment of a fixed sum on the sale of each item produced using the licensed IP.[245]

Percentage-based royalties fluctuate and depend upon the parameter(s) used as the basis for calculation. A number of variables may be used as the base for the calculation of royalty payments. Such payments may be calculated using the per unit rate or some other parameters such as quantity produced using, for example, weight or length.[246]

When royalties are computed using the per unit rate, the calculation reflects the number of units of licensed product sold.[247] Such payments may alternatively be linked to the volume of product sold where the product is manufactured using the licensed IP.[248]

242. Successful Technology Licensing (WIPO 2004), 31.
243. Successful Technology Licensing (WIPO 2004), 31.
244. The fixing of the royalty rate, and the considerations used in order to negotiate royalty rates are addressed in Meiselles 2013: 261-2.
245. Anderson 2010: 86.
246. Poltorak et al. 2004: 101–2.
247. Anderson 2010: 57.
248. Anderson 2010: 57.

Percentage-based royalties may be enumerated by reference to the royalties paid to the licensee by a sub-licensee or by reference to the revenue generated on the sales of goods produced using the licensed intellectual property (e.g., technology) or the services furnished using the said intellectual property.[249]

[F] Drafting the Royalty Provision

When drafting the royalty provision, due consideration should be given by the contracting parties to a variety of issues including:[250]

(1) the basis for the calculation of the royalty payment;
(2) the identity of those responsible for payment of the royalties;
(3) the timing of payments;
(4) the impact of non-payment or late payment of royalties;
(5) the use of a fixed rate or varying rates for the various categories of intellectual property;
(6) adjustable royalties;
(7) incorporation and its impact on the royalties due;
(8) minimum guaranteed annual royalty (also known as the minimum annual guarantee); and
(9) the inclusion of a cap on annual royalty payments.

[1] The Basis for the Calculation of the Royalty[251]

The basis for the calculation of the royalty should be dealt with within the terms of the agreement.

In this context reference should be made in the agreement to whether the royalty is fixed or percentage-based and the methodology that will be used in order to calculate the sums due under the running royalty licence.[252] Where appropriate, illustrations may be given as to how the methodology should be employed.[253]

In addition due consideration should be given by the parties to the right of the licensee to make deductions from royalty payments due for charges incurred by the licensee for registration charges, infringement litigation expenses and so forth.

The inclusion or not of value added taxes and other taxes should also be addressed within the royalty clause.[254]

249. Anderson 2010: 86.
250. Anderson 2010: 87.
251. Anderson 2010: 87.
252. Anderson 2010: 57.
253. Anderson 2010: 57.
254. Anderson 2010: 87.

[2] The Identity of Those Responsible for Payment of the Royalties

Within the agreement reference should be made to the identity of the party or parties responsible for payment of the royalties. In effect will royalties be due on the revenue generated by the licensee as well as the different sub-licensees.[255]

[3] The Timing of Payments

The parties contracting should take time to formulate a timetable for the payment of sums due under the agreement[256] and should indicate when the royalties fall due.

Royalties may be due, for example, at the time when the product is incorporated into a finished product, when the product is delivered, when it is invoiced or when payment is made in relation to the sums invoiced.[257]

[4] The Impact of Non-payment or Late Payment of Royalties

Within the terms of the agreement due consideration should be given to the consequences of non-payment or late payment.

The parties may negotiate a provision allowing for the imposition of interest on royalties owing (option A in the template clause abovementioned). If such a provision is included within the agreement, the parties should consider addressing the rate of interest payable on the overdue sums and the basis used for the calculation of interest. In other words, will interest accrue on a daily basis, on a monthly basis, on an annual basis and so on? And when will interest start accruing? And until when will interest accrue?

A further provision that the licensor may look to secure in the licensing agreement is the right to terminate the agreement on account of the failure to pay the royalties due (options B and C in the above-mentioned template clause).[258]

In the event that such a right is secured within the agreement, the parties should address the point in time when the right to terminate will arise (will this right be available 30 days from the due date, 60 days, 120 days etc.) and the procedure (if any) associated with the assumption of this right (will the licensor need to provide the licensee with written notice; if such notice is due, when should it be provided).

[5] Fixed Rate or Varying Rates for the Various Categories of Intellectual Property

Due consideration should be given by the contracting parties to whether one royalty rate will be applicable to the various categories of intellectual property or whether different rates will apply.[259]

---

255. Anderson 2010: 87.
256. Anderson 2010: 57.
257. Anderson 2010: 87.
258. Anderson 2010: 57.
259. Anderson 2010: 87.

[6] Adjustable Royalties

The parties may agree to use adjustable royalty rates. Such rates may be fixed by reference to different variables.[260]

Royalties could be linked to time. The parties may decide that the initial royalty rate will decrease by a set percentage each year over the term of the agreement.[261]

Another option would be to link royalties to the volume of licensed goods sold by the licensee. The more the licensee sells the lower the royalty rate.[262] By incorporating a sliding scale of this genre into the licensing agreement, the licensee has an incentive to sell more volume of product.

[7] Incorporation and Its Impact on the Royalties Due

In circumstances where a product manufactured using the licensed intellectual property such as technology is incorporated into another product, the question of incorporation should be addressed by the contracting parties within the terms of their agreement.

In this context the parties should address the following issues: Will royalties be determined by the price of the finished product or a proportion of this price, and if a proportion of the price is used to calculate the royalty due how will this proportion be computed.[263]

[8] Minimum Annual Royalty Payment

In order to ensure that the licensee is motivated to generate as many sales as possible each year, the licensor should give due consideration to the inclusion of a guaranteed annual minimum payment in the licence.

In order to protect its interests, the licensee is likely to challenge the inclusion of such a provision or, if it is willing to accept the inclusion of such a provision, the licensee will attempt to negotiate the minimum sums on which the minimum annual royalty payment is calculated.

When negotiating and drafting such clauses, the parties should take care to consider the following issues:

(1) The duration of such a clause

Where a technology licence is concerned, the duration of such a clause should reflect the period during which the technology remains commercially useable. The rate of technological development will have an impact upon the commercial useability of the

260. Successful Technology Licensing (WIPO 2004), 30.
261. Successful Technology Licensing (WIPO 2004), 31.
262. Successful Technology Licensing (WIPO 2004), 31.
263. Anderson 2010: 87.

technology licensed under the agreement. Where the rate of technological development is high, the commercial useability of the technology licensed under the agreement will be low.

As such, the licensee should pose the question whether the licensed technology will still be of commercial use in 2 years? 5 years? 9 years?

(2) The scope of such a clause

The parties should consider whether such a clause will encompass background technology or will extend to technology developed by the licensee using the background technology.

A further issue that should be borne in mind by the parties is whether this clause will encompass the technology developed by the licensor after the commencement of the agreement where this technology is licensed to the licensee.

[9] Cap on Annual Royalty Payment

In order to enhance certainty from the vantage point of the licensee, it may attempt to negotiate an upper limit on the annual royalty payments due to the licensor.[264]

If such a format is used, the licensee will pay royalties at the rate of x% per annum up to a maximum threshold.[265]

This ceiling may be renewed annually or may last for the duration of the agreement.[266]

[G] Fixing the Royalty Rate

Whilst the licensor will likely want to secure the highest royalty rate possible to enhance its return, the licensee will likely want to reduce the rate as much as possible.

When calculating the rate at which the royalty is set and negotiating the final royalty rate in the contract, the contracting parties should arguably give thought to the need to share the benefits produced by the agreement equally.

The extract below provides some illustrations of the strategies that may be utilised by the parties during negotiations to secure their respective interests.[267]

[1] Negotiation Strategies Associated with Royalty Rates

[a] Factors Supporting the Licensor's Claim for a Higher Royalty Rate

A licensor arguing for a higher royalty rate may rely on one or more of the following factors:[268]

264. Successful Technology Licensing (WIPO 2004), 30.
265. Successful Technology Licensing (WIPO 2004), 30.
266. Successful Technology Licensing (WIPO 2004), 30.
267. This table is inspired by a similar one used in Meiselles 2013: 261.
268. *See* factors listed in *Georgia Pacific Corporation v. United States Plywood* Corp. 318 F Supp 116 [SDNY 1970] (US).

(1) That it was due to the licensor's investment, the commitment of its personnel, its funding of research and development and its willingness to take a risk that the licensor was able to develop the licensed technology.
(2) That further research and development by the licensor will be made possible by the royalty payments and that any additional technology generated is likely to add value to the operations of the licensee (the case when the licensee is given access to future developments made by the licensor).
(3) That as licensor it assumed the risks related to the acquisition of the requisite legal protection. This will be the case where the licensor has carried out all the preparatory work leading up to the patent application or where the licensor has made an application for the patent or where such a patent has been granted.
(4) That the licensee is in a position to charge for the provision of after-sales service as a result of the grant of rights by the licensor to the licensee.
(5) That such an arrangement demonstrates the licensee's commitment to the product as well as to the licensor.
(6) That the licensee will not need to concern itself with actual or potential competition (where exclusivity is extended by the licensor).
(7) That the licensee is in a novel position due to the groundbreaking character of the technology licensed.
(8) That in order to qualify for a lower royalty rate, it is the responsibility of the licensee to show its commitment and ability to innovate (the case where a variable royalty rate is provided for in the licence).

[b] Factors Supporting the Licensee's Claim for a Lower Royalty Rate

A licensee arguing for a lower royalty rate or countering the licensor's arguments for a higher royalty rate may rely on one or more of the following factors:[269]

(1) That the sums invested by the licensor are sunk costs which the licensor would have been obliged to invest in order to generate the technology licensed.
(2) That the licensee's investment and infrastructure will permit it to commercialise the technology generated by the licensor. The infrastructure of the licensee will include its facilities, its personnel, the technology it owns, its know-how, its expertise in the given field of technology, its knowledge of the market, its networks on the given market and its global reach.
(3) That the investment required off the licensee to set-up an infrastructure is too high to warrant a high royalty rate.
(4) That any patent acquired by the licensor would be rendered valueless without the licensee's investment and infrastructure.

269. *See* factors listed in *Georgia Pacific Corporation v. United States Plywood* Corp. 318 F Supp 116 [SDNY 1970] (US).

(5) That the risk borne by the licensee warrants a lower royalty rate (the case where it is unclear whether the technology licensed can be commercialised).
(6) That the licensee will enhance the licensor's return on its investment.
(7) That finding new licensees is a time-consuming venture and that the licensor does not have time (the case where the licensor has developed technology in a field where there are other entities engaged in similar research and development or where there is term applicable to the intellectual property licensed).
(8) That the licensor should be considering the long-term profitability of the project.
(9) That once the commercial value of the licensed technology is clear, the licensee would be prepared to consider the royalty rate.
(10) That the licensee is willing to agree to a guaranteed minimum annual royalty payment only on the proviso that the royalty rate is slow.

[c] Factors Impacting on Royalty Rates[270]

Factors that have an impact on royalty rates include:

(1) The status of the technology (in a technology licence for example):
  (a) is the technology licensed a trade secret or the subject-matter of a patent;
  (b) the term of the patent/s or the remaining term of the patent/s (in cases where the technology licensed is the subject-matter of one or more patents);
  (c) the applications available in relation to the licensed technology (possible and proven);
  (d) the advantages that this new technology offers when compared with older technologies;
  (e) the proportion of profits that are associated with the licensed technology rather than the non-patent components (including the production process, the distribution network and the marketing operations of the licensee);
  (f) the profitability of the goods produced using the licensed technology (likely or proven);
  (g) the right to exploit further technology developed by the licensee or the licensor or both;
(2) the term of the licence and the availability of an option to renew the licence;
(3) the advantages associated with the licensed patent/s; and
(4) the provision of exclusivity (exclusivity will generally result in higher royalty rate).

270. These parameters are inspired by the factors listed by the court when assessing the royalty rate in default of an agreement by the parties in *Georgia Pacific Corporation* v. *United States Plywood Corp.* 318 F Supp 116 [SDNY 1970] (US).

§1.26 NON-COMPETE PROVISIONS

In consideration of the licences granted, during the term of this agreement (optional – and for a period of ____ after the end of this agreement), the Licensee shall not:

1. Enter into any agreements pursuant to which the Licensee obtains rights in the Licenced Territory to manufacture, have manufactured, use, sell, distribute or market any goods that directly compete with the Licenced Goods.

2. Without first obtaining the written consent of the Licensor, seek customers, establish any branch or any distribution depot for the Licenced Goods outside the Licenced Territory.

Optional provisions

3. For a period of ____ after this agreement comes to an end, the Licensee shall not enter into agreements pursuant to which it obtains rights in the Licenced Territory to manufacture, have manufactured, use, sell, distribute or market any goods that directly compete with the Licenced Goods.

4. The provisions in this clause will not apply to the goods listed in Schedule ____. By written agreement, the Parties may vary the list of goods in Schedule ____.

The licensor is likely to want to protect its competitive position by limiting the ability of the licensee to compete with it both during the term of the agreement and where possible after the agreement ends, through the inclusion of an in-term non-compete clause and a post-term non-compete clause (respectively).

Such clauses will address the rights of the licensee to engage in activities that could or would undermine the competitive position of the licensor, by addressing *inter alia* the risk of the licensee selling products that are in competition with the licensed goods in the assigned territory and addressing the risk of the licensee selling the licensed goods outside the assigned territory.

One of the key concerns that non-compete clauses aim to address is the risk of competing products entering into the home market of the licensor or other territories not assigned to the licensee. This phenomenon is known as the **grey market** or **parallel imports**.

The use of non-compete clauses is likely to be regulated, it is accordingly important that the parties consider the legal position of such clauses when drafting and negotiating their agreement.[271]

271. EU regulation of non-compete clauses in the context of technology transfer agreements is reviewed earlier on in this chapter.

In circumstances where the licensee is interested in possessing the right to sell competing goods, it should consider the inclusion of the following provisions in the agreement:

(1) A list of excluded competing goods that it is permitted to sell (optional provision listed above).
(2) The right to modify this list by prior agreement with the licensor (optional provision above).

A licensee may be interested in possessing the right to sell competing goods, if it has been responsible for manufacturing its own line(s) of products that compete in some way with the licensed goods.

§1.27 SUBLICENSING

1. The Licensee shall have no right to grant sublicence(s) under the licences granted without the prior written agreement of the Licensor.

Optional provisions

2. The Licensor shall assemble a list of criteria to be used by the Licensee when selecting potential sublicensees. The Licensee shall use this list of criteria when selecting potential sublicensees.

3. The Licensee shall inform the Licensor in writing once a potential sublicensee is sourced by it using the list of criteria. In such a situation, the Licensee shall provide the Licensor with all details and documents that support the Licensee's selection of the potential sublicensee.

5. The Licensor shall retain the right to veto any potential sublicensee.

6. The Licensor shall have sole responsibility for negotiating the sublicence with the approved sublicensee.

By securing itself the right to sublicence in the main licence, the licensee will have the right to grant rights in relation to the licensed intellectual property, belonging to the licensor, to one or more other entities.

In order to secure the right to sublicence, the licensee will need to acquire this right in terms of the licence.

Such an arrangement will typically enable the licensee to enhance its profitability and may allow for the (further) development of the licensed intellectual property benefiting the licensor and the licensee.

Sublicensing may be beneficial from the vantage point of the licensor. First the licensor is likely to be able to negotiate a share of the royalties generated by the sublicence. Second sublicensing may offer the potential for further research and development by the sublicensee/s. This is especially important when the sublicensee/s possess expertise, know-how, patents and technologies that neither the licensee nor the licensor have access to.

Sublicensing will be a key concern for the point of view of the licensor, as it is likely to be concerned by the potential loss of control and the potential loss of confidential information developed and owned by it (the licensor).

In order to address these risks, the licensor should consider the following options. First, it may include a provision in the licence prohibiting the grant of sublicenses. Second, it may decide to permit sublicensing on the proviso that it retains control over the selection of suitable sublicensees and over the substantive terms of the sublicences.

Where sublicensing is contemplated, due consideration should be given by the licensor to the inclusion of the following provisions:

(1) A provision obligating the licensee to approach the licensor for prior written authority before it looks into the possibility of sublicensing.
(2) A provision permitting the licensor to formulate the criteria for the selection of sublicensees with or without the input of the licensee.
(3) A provision permitting the licensor to veto sublicensees sourced by the licensee.
(4) A provision stipulating that the sublicensee enters into an agreement with the licensor as a precondition for the grant of the sublicence.

§1.28 QUALITY CONTROL

1. The Licensee shall ensure that any Licenced Goods produced by it or for it shall be constructed to the specifications stipulated by the Licensor as detailed in Schedule ____.

2. (Optional) The Licensee shall ensure that any Licenced Goods produced by it or for it shall be produced using comparable standards of performance to the standards of performance used at the relevant time by the Licensor and shall be of comparable quality to the goods produced at the relevant time by the Licensor.

3. The Licensor shall have the right to confirm the quality of the Licenced Goods produced by the Licensee or for the Licensee together with the quality of the use of Trademarks. Upon the provision of written prior notice of a reasonable period of time by the Licensor to the Licensee, the Licensee shall:

a. Permit one or more duly authorised representatives of the Licensor to inspect the facility or facilities at which the Licenced Goods are produced. (Optional) The Licensee shall not be bound to permit such visits if these have the potential of hindering its operations.

b. Provide the Licensor with free samples of the Licenced Goods manufactured by or for it.

(Optional) Notwithstanding this obligation, the Licensor confirms that its specifications for verification of quality shall be reasonable.

(Optional) Notwithstanding this obligation, the Licensor shall not raise objections to the quality of the Licenced Goods without having reasonable grounds for so doing.

4. The Licensee shall adhere to instructions relating to the quality of the Licenced Goods issued by the Licensor. Any instructions issued by the Licensor shall not be unreasonable in terms of practicality or financial cost.

Optional provisions:

5. The Licensor shall at its own discretion furnish the Licensee at no cost to the Licensee with promotional literature including but not limited to samples, catalogues, brochures, technical specifications and user manuals.

6. The Licensor shall endeavour to reply to technical queries regarding the Licenced Goods, the Licenced Technology, the Licenced Know-how and any information licenced by the Licensor to the Licensee.

7. The Licensee shall only use promotional literature that has been preapproved in writing by the Licensor when promoting the Licenced Goods.

Quality control will be a key concern from the vantage point of the licensor as such poor quality control by the licensee has the potential of adversely affecting the reputation and goodwill of the licensor as well as any intellectual property that it owns.

In a bid to reduce and if possible eliminate such a risk due regard should be given by the contracting parties to the inclusion of the following provisions in their agreement. A provision:

(1) granting the licensor a right to inspect facilities where the contract goods are produced;
(2) permitting the licensor to request samples of products produced by or for the licensee using the licensed technology or the licensed intellectual property of the licensor;
(3) requiring the licensee to furnish the licensor with samples (free or otherwise) of any goods that are manufactured by it or for it using the licensed intellectual property of the licensor;
(4) addressing the training of personnel employed by or on behalf of the licensee; and
(5) permitting the licensor to pre-approve marketing campaigns and promotional literature that concern the licensed intellectual property.

§1.29 MAINTENANCE OF LICENCED PROPERTY

During the course of this agreement:

1. The Licensee shall notify the Licensor in writing immediately of any actual infringement or suspected infringement of the Licenced Property (*or/and* Licenced Technology *or/and* Licenced Patents *and/or* Licenced Trademarks) of which the Licensee is aware or of which the Licensee becomes aware.

2. If within () days from the date of such notification, the Licensor has not taken action to arrange for the suspension of any such infringement, the Licensee may take action in its own right against the infringer or suspected infringer. In such a case, the Licensor shall provide the Licensor with all the necessary information, aid and authority required by the Licensee to take any such action. In circumstances where the Licensee is unable to pursue such action in its own right, the Licensor shall execute and deliver its agreement to be joined as a party to any such action. The costs and expenses associated with such action taken by the Licensee shall be borne by (the Licensee exclusively *or* the Licensor exclusively *or* the Parties in equal measure). The settlement of any action by the Licensee shall be conditional on the prior written consent of the Licensor which the Licensor shall not withhold without reason. The Licensor may take legal action against the infringer or suspected infringer in its own right and at its own expense on the proviso that the Licensor has first discussed this matter with the Licensee. (Optional – The Licensor may take legal action against the infringer or suspected infringer in its own right and at its own expense on condition that it has the prior written agreement of the Licensee). Where the Licensor or the Licensee take action and the other party does not join as a plaintiff, the plaintiff shall be permitted to keep all sums received pursuant to a judgement or settlement thereof.

3. The Licensee shall execute any necessary activities reasonably required of it by the Licensor in order to assist the Licensor in maintaining the validity and enforceability of the Licenced Property.

4. The Licensor shall indemnify the Licensee against all reasonable costs, damages and/or liabilities that ensue from or in connection with the execution of these activities.

5. The Licensor (*or* the Licensee) shall pay all maintenance fees or taxes.

6. The Licensor (*or* the Licensee) shall at its own expense undertake any activities that are needed in order to maintain in force the Licenced Patents (*or/and* Licenced Technology *or/and* Licenced Property *and/or* Licenced Trademarks) until the respective expiration date(s) thereof.

7. The Licensor (*or* the Licensee) shall at its own expense perform any tasks required in order to protect any New Goods or/and Improvements.

§1.30 RESTRICTIONS ON THE FIELDS OF USE[272,273]

1. The Licensee shall produce, have produced, use, distribute, market or sell the (Licenced Property *or/and* Licenced Technology *or/and* Licenced Patents *and/or* Licenced Trademarks) for the following purposes ().

2. The Licensee shall produce, have produced, use, distribute, market or sell the Licenced Goods (optional – together with the Licenced Trademarks relating to such Licenced Goods and to otherwise fully make use of the Licenced Technology *and/or* Licenced Patents) in the Licenced Territory.

3. The Licensee shall include a notice in all materials used on the Licenced Goods or in connection with Licenced Goods that denotes the fact that the Licensor is the sole proprietor of the Licenced Property and that the Licensee is an authorised licensee of the Licensor.

4. The Licensee shall ensure that every reference that is made to the Licenced Property *or/and* Licenced Technology *or/and* Licenced Patents *and/or* Licenced Trademarks by the Licensee or any parties connected to the Licensee will be accompanied by an acknowledgement in a form approved by the Licensor that the same is the Licenced Property *or/and* Licenced Technology *or/and* Licenced Patents *and/or* Licenced Trademarks of the Licensor.

5. The Licensee shall not do anything that may have an adverse impact on the goodwill of the Licensor.

6. The Licensee shall not reproduce or modify the Licenced Goods or any part thereof for use, sale or any other purpose.

7. The Licensee shall not make modifications to the packaging of the Licenced Goods.

8. The Licensee shall not modify, omit or adjust the Licenced Trademarks, numbers or other identifying features used on or in connection with the Licenced Goods.

9. The Licensee shall not use the Licenced Trademarks in any way that may prejudice their distinctiveness or validity or which may adversely impact upon the goodwill of the Licensor in the Licenced Trademarks.

10. The Licensee shall not use any trademark other than the Licenced Trademark(s), in relation to the Licenced Goods, without first obtaining the written consent of the Licensor.

272. For a detailed discussion, *see* Meiselles 2013: 248-9.
273. The provision governing the fields of use is linked to the grant clause discussed above. For this reason it is worthwhile considering the two together.

> 11. The Licensee shall not make use in the Licenced Territory of any trademark or trade name that is similar to the trademark(s) or trade name(s) of the Licensor and which may cause confusion or some form of deception.

It is commonplace for licensors to insist upon the inclusion of provisions in the licensing agreement defining the uses to which licensed technology may be put and the way in which the licensee may exploit and make use of the licensed intellectual property.

Non-compete clauses, confidentiality clauses, restrictions on territory and on customer groups are examples of such provisions.

From the vantage point of the licensor these provisions aim to ward against any potential loss of control over licensed intellectual property which may adversely affect the business interests of the licensor, to thwart the creation of a potential competitor and finally to guarantee adherence to national regulation. National regulation may impact upon uses and applications. This is the case, for example, where living materials are involved in certain jurisdictions such as the United Kingdom.

§1.31 ANTI-BRIBERY POLICY

> The Licensee shall
>
> 1. Adhere to applicable anti-bribery and anti-corruption laws and codes including but not limited to [] ('Relevant Regulation');
>
> 2. Adhere to the Licensor's policies relating to ethics, anti-bribery and anti-corruption [contained in Schedule () or of which the Licensee is advised by the Licensor] ('Relevant Policies');
>
> 3. Devise its own policies and procedures that ensure adherence with the Relevant Regulation and the Relevant Policies;
>
> 4. Ensure enforcement of such policies and procedures;
>
> 5. Inform the Licensor if and when it receives a request for undue financial or other advantage relating to the performance of the agreement;
>
> 6. Issue in writing a certificate on a (period e.g. annual, biannual) basis by (person e.g. CEO, CFO, Head Legal Counsel) of the Licensee confirming adherence with this clause by the Licensee;
>
> 7. Provide all evidence confirming such adherence to the Licensor as and when requested by the Licensor;
>
> 8. Ensure that it uses a written contract with all those persons with which it deals (in relation to its dealings connected to this agreement) containing terms that are equivalent to the terms imposed in this clause on the Licensee;

9. Ensure adherence with these terms by those persons; and

10. Be liable to the Licensor for any breach of these terms by such persons.

– Insurance

1. The Licensee shall acquire an all-risk insurance policy with a respectable insurance company. This policy cover shall be in compliance with the specifications denoted by the Licensor. The interest of the Licensor shall be specified in this policy.

2. The Licensee shall furnish the Licensor with a copy of the policy and evidence of the payment of premiums by the Licensee.

§1.32 OBLIGATIONS OF THE LICENSOR

The following review aims to highlight the key provisions that the licensee is likely to want to incorporate into the licensing agreement whilst reviewing certain material considerations pertaining to these terms.

Due to the legal regulation governing these clauses in certain jurisdictions, it is sensible for the parties to seek legal advice before incorporating the same into the licensing agreement.

§1.33 ASSISTANCE AND TRAINING TO THE LICENSEE PROVIDED BY THE LICENSOR

1. During the first year of this agreement (optional – during the term of this agreement) (optional – at no charge) the Licensor shall make available to the Licensee the services of a suitably experienced member of the Licensor's staff in order to:

a. Provide technical assistance relating to the use of the Licenced Patents *or/and* Licenced Technology *or/and* Licenced Property;

b. Assist the Licensee with marketing of the Licenced Goods;

c. Train the personnel of the Licensee to use the Licenced Patents *or/and* Licenced Technology *or/and* Licenced Property; and

d. Assist the Licensee to acquire the relevant authorisations and standards pertaining to the use of the Licenced Patents *or/and* Licenced Technology *or/and* Licenced Property.

2. During the first year of this agreement (optional – during the term of this agreement) (optional – at no charge) the Licensee may send to the premises of the Licensor suitably qualified employees of the Licensee for training by the

Licensor in connection with the use of the Licenced Patents *or/and* Licenced Technology *or/and* Licenced Property, the production of the Licenced Goods and the exploitation of the Licenced Know-how and any information licenced by the Licensor to the Licensee.

Optional provisions –

3. Any expenditure reasonably incurred by the employees of the Licensor in this context will be the exclusive responsibility of the Licensor *or* the Licensee *or* will be shared equally between the Parties.

4. Where the Licensee is solely or partially responsible for the expenditure of the Licensor in this context, the Licensee shall pay the Licensor no later than ____ days after the date on which the Licensor advises the Licensee of this expenditure.

5. The Licensee shall remain liable for the salaries and the employment expenses incurred by the employees of the Licensee.

6. When the employees of the Licensee attend the premises of the Licensor, the Licensee shall ensure that those employees in attendance adhere to regulations in place in the premises of the Licensor or applicable to the premises of the Licensor.

7. When the Licensor's employees attend the premises of the Licensee, the Licensor shall make sure that its employees in attendance adhere to regulations in place in the Licensee's premises or applicable to such premises.

The provision of training as well as technical support and assistance to the licensee by the licensor will be beneficial from the vantage point of both parties by enhancing profitability. These provisions also ensure quality of production and servicing by the licensee in turn safeguarding the reputation of the licensor and its goodwill as well as protecting the image of the intellectual property owned by the licensor.

§1.34 WARRANTIES, LIABILITIES AND INDEMNITIES

[A] Representations and Warranties

The Licensor represents and warrants:

1. That the Licenced Property *or/and* Licenced Technology *or/and* Licenced Patents comprise all the patents, patent applications, processes, formulations, specifications and rights required in order to produce, have produced and use the Licenced Goods. The Licensor shall execute all the activities required in order to maintain the Licenced Patents in full force and effect.

2. The Licenced Property *or/and* Licenced Technology *or/and* Licenced Patents is/are owned solely by the Licensor (or jointly with ____).

3. That no claims have been asserted nor to the best of the knowledge of the Licensor are any such claims threatened based on an alleged infringement by the Licensor of third party patents, trademarks or other industrial property rights in relation to the Licenced Property.

4. As of the date of this agreement, neither it nor any of its related companies and affiliates has provided or made available to a third party in the Licenced Territory all or any part of the Licenced Property *or/and* Licenced Technology *and/or* granted rights to a third party in the Licenced Territory in relation to the Licenced Patents.

5. During the term of this agreement, neither it nor any of its related companies and affiliates shall provide or make available to a third party in the Licenced Territory all or any part of the Licenced Property *or/and* Licenced Technology *and/or* grant rights to a third party in the Licenced Territory in relation to the Licenced Patents.

Optional provisions

6. The Licenced Trademark(s) is/are solely owned by the Licensor.

7. The Licensor has been granted exclusive licences (worldwide or in one or more territories) under the Licenced Trademark(s) utilised in connection with the Licenced Patents.

8. The Licenced Property *or/and* Licenced Technology *or/and* Licenced Patents is/are licenced exclusively to the Licensor (worldwide or in one or more territories) and the Licensor possesses full rights and powers to disclose and to licence the same to the Licensee.

9. The Licensor enjoys the right and has the authority to grant the Licensee the aforementioned licences.

10. During the term of this agreement, neither the Licensor nor any of its related companies and affiliates shall produce or have produced directly or indirectly the Licenced Goods in the Licenced Territory or use or permit the use of the Licenced Property *or/and* Licenced Technology *or/and* Licenced Patents in the Licenced Territory.

[B] Indemnities

1. The Licensor shall indemnify the Licensee for all expenditure, loss or damages sustained due to a claim pursued by a third party that is based on or results from the use made by the Licensee of the Licenced Property, if there has been

a. An infringement of the third party's intellectual property rights; or

b. A wrongful use of the third party's proprietary information.

Under English law, it is uncommon for warranties to be implied into a licensing agreement.[274] As such these agreements usually include warranties that are expressly stipulated by the contracting parties.[275]

Warranties explicitly set out by the contracting parties in terms of the agreement commonly address a number of matters.[276]

First warranties will address the position of the licensor.[277] Warranties contained within the terms of the licensing agreement will aim to clarify ownership of the subject matter of the licence. In this context, the contract should refer to whether the licensor is the sole owner of the intellectual property or not, whether the licensor is permitted to grant a licence to the intellectual property[278] and whether other technologies will be required in order to make use of the technology licensed.[279]

In the event that the licensor is the sole owner of the intellectual property, it is sensible for a representation to be included in the agreement noting that the licensed intellectual property is owned by the licensor thus preventing a situation from arising in which a third party attempts to argue that it is the rightful owner of the licensed intellectual property or technology and the licensor attempts to disclaim responsibility.[280]

In circumstances where the intellectual property is jointly owned a prospective licensee should ensure that all the joint owners of the said property agree to the grant of such a licence.[281]

Where the licensor and the licensee intend to collaborate in order to develop the technology (under the auspices of a research and development agreement or a joint venture for example), it is sensible for the parties to indicate in their licensing agreement who owns the intellectual property and the technologies generated by the parties jointly.[282]

The parties may agree on joint ownership or exclusive ownership by the licensor or the licensee of technology generated under the auspices of the collaborative project.[283]

Care should be taken in this context to establish the position under national law where joint ownership is the chosen model, since certain jurisdictions will require

274. Anderson 2010: 87.
275. Anderson 2010: 88.
276. Anderson 2010: 88.
277. Anderson 2010: 88.
278. Anderson 2010: 88.
279. Successful Technology Licensing (WIPO 2004), 18.
280. Successful Technology Licensing (WIPO 2004), 18.
281. Anderson 2010: 88.
282. Successful Technology Licensing (WIPO 2004), 18.
283. Successful Technology Licensing (WIPO 2004), 19.

parties to account to each other for profits made using the intellectual property generated which may not be an ideal set up when the parties no longer work together.[284]

Second the features of the intellectual property itself.[285] An indication will be given whether the intellectual property is capable of being licensed free from encumbrances and if it cannot be so licensed which encumbrances affect the property licensed.[286] Moreover in this context confirmation will be given as to whether licences or rights have been granted by the licensor to a third party that compromise the rights and licences granted to the current licensee.

The licensor may be unprepared to warrant the validity of the intellectual property due to the liability for damages it will then bear if it later transpires that the intellectual property is not valid.[287] As such the licensor is likely to agree to a more limited warranty in this context.[288] The licensor may be prepared to vouch that it has not done anything that is capable of invalidating the intellectual property and that it is unaware of anything that is capable of invalidating the intellectual property (without searches/investigations).[289]

Where the licensor is furnishing confidential information or trade secrets to the licensee, the licensor may be expected by the licensee to provide a number of warrants that the disclosure of the same to the licensee will not violate a duty that is owed to a third party, that the information has not entered into the public domain at the time the agreement is made and that the information has proven of use in the past in the production of products that are based on or make use of the licensed intellectual property.[290]

Third covenants granted by the licensor. A licensee in such circumstances is likely to seek the following covenants from the licensor. A promise by the licensor that it will not conduct itself in a manner that is at odds with the licensee's enjoyment of the licence.[291] An assurance that it will not assign the intellectual property which is crucial in circumstances where the licensee is dependent upon the assistance and support provided by the licensor as well as any new goods and improvements developed by the latter.[292] A guarantee by the licensor that it will inform the licensee of prospective assignments or encumbrances and acquire the written permission of the licensee before doing so.[293]

Technology transfer agreements will include warranties that differ in scope depending partially on the risk aversion of one or all of the contracting parties.[294] Other factors that will influence the scope of warranties include the sums of money involved

284. Successful Technology Licensing (WIPO 2004), 19.
285. Anderson 2010: 88.
286. Anderson 2010: 88.
287. Anderson 2010: 89.
288. Anderson 2010: 89.
289. Anderson 2010: 89.
290. Anderson 2010: 89.
291. Anderson 2010: 88.
292. Anderson 2010: 88.
293. Anderson 2010: 89.
294. Anderson 2010: 58.

in the transfer, the proximity of the technology licensed to the market as well as the practice in the country involved.[295]

Standard practices that have developed in this context include:[296]

(1) the warrantor granting warranties that are limited to the issues that are within the scope of his knowledge;
(2) the use of reservations to warranties where certain considerations have been made known by the warrantor (in a schedule or disclosure letter); and
(3) the imposition of limitations on liability and caps on the remedies implemented where a breach of the agreement occurs. Examples of these include caps on damages due, caps on duration and limitation of liability to financial damages.

§1.35 TERMINATION – GROUNDS AND RESULTS

[A] Grounds of Termination

1. Upon the occurrence of any of the following, this agreement may be terminated forthwith by either Party providing written notice of the termination to the other Party ():

a. Such other Party defaults in or breaches any of the materials terms of this agreement and the breach concerned is not rectified within () from the date the written notice detailing the breach and requiring rectification was received.

b. Such other Party becomes the subject of an administration order, becomes insolvent, enters into a voluntary arrangement or a receiver is appointed. In the alternative, such other Party is involved in something that resembles any of these procedures under the law of any jurisdiction.

c. The other Party either intends to or ceases to carry on business.

d. There has been a change in management, ownership or control of the other Party.

e. An event has occurred that prevents the other Party from executing its obligations under the agreement.

f. An assignment has taken place or is being attempted and the agreement of the Party intending to terminate this agreement has not been sought or obtained.

2. Rectification of a breach is deemed possible if the breaching Party is able to comply with the pertinent provision in all respects other than time of performance, on condition that time of performance is not of the essence.

295. Anderson 2010: 58-9.
296. Anderson 2010: 58.

3. In circumstances where a Party waives a breach under this agreement the waiver in question will not amount to a waiver of any subsequent breach of this agreement or any of its provisions.

4. A termination of this agreement will not prejudice any rights or remedies available to the Parties in relation to the breach in question or any other breach.

[B] Results of Termination

If this agreement is terminated for any reason, the Licensee shall:

a. Remain bound to perform its obligations under this agreement.

b. Liable to the Licensor for all sums due to its.

c. Pay the Licensor all sums due to it under the terms of this agreement.

d. Continue to properly assure at its own expense all maintenance and servicing of Licensed Goods sold by the Licensee in the Licensed Territory.

e. Return to the Licensor at no charge to the Licensor all materials furnished to the Licensee by the Licensor and all materials that the Licensee has used itself or that have been used on behalf of the Licensee.

When drafting licensing agreements, the contracting parties should give due consideration to the inclusion of the following provisions:[297]

(1) the expiration of fixed-term agreements and the possibility of their renewal;
(2) the circumstances that give rise to the right to terminate (breach of the provisions of the licence, insolvency, change of control or ownership and the occurrence of a force majeure event that subsists beyond a set time period);
(3) the right to terminate by the provision of notice; and
(4) the consequences of termination and in this context:
    (a) the matters to be addressed on termination (final reporting requirement, return of materials and data, rescission and termination of rights licensed under the agreement); and
    (b) the issues that will withstand the termination either temporarily (confidentiality, payment of sums due) and indefinitely (indemnities)

297. Anderson 2010: 59-60.

§1.36 BOILERPLATE CLAUSES

Boilerplate clauses are customary contractual provisions that are included in many agreements as a matter of course.

Box 4 Types of boilerplate clause

1. Assignment clause
2. Change of control and ownership clause
3. Merger clause
4. Modification clause
5. Severance clause
6. Language clause
7. Notice clause
8. Execution in counterparts
9. Jurisdiction clause
10. Choice of law clause
11. Alternative dispute resolution clause (including informal discussions, renegotiation and adaption)
12. Force majeure

[A] Assignment Clause[298]

> Neither Party, without the written agreement of the other, shall assign, transfer, mortgage, charge, dispose or delegate any of its rights, obligations or interests under this agreement. Neither Party shall unreasonably withhold such consent.

The contracting parties acquire rights under an agreement as well as undertaking certain responsibilities. An assignment will take place when there is a transfer of rights or obligations acquired under the agreement, from the contracting party, to a party who is not a contracting party (the assignee).[299] The contracting party transferring his rights or obligations under the agreement is the assignor.

298. Meiselles 2013: 55-7.
299. Stark 2007: 168.

Generally the assignee will acquire all the rights of the assignor under the agreement unless the contrary is stated.[300]

An assignment can take place in a variety of scenarios. First, when one of the contracting parties decides to sell off his business as a going concern and wishes to sell off his rights under the contract to the party to whom he is selling his business. As such the vendor of the business will need to assign rights that he has under the contract to the party acquiring his business. Second, one of the contracting parties may need to obtain financing (from a bank or financial institution) and in order to do so will need to assign the agreement as collateral. Third, an assignment can happen when the business of the contracting party is the subject matter of a merger or takeover.

When an assignment takes place, the contracting party or parties that remain party or parties to the agreement may wish to reassess their options, as they will be left with a new and unknown business partner (the assignee). As such the contracting parties have a number of options available to them in the agreement in order to address assignments. They may opt for an outright ban or limit the right to assign (by requiring prior written consent before assignment for example).

[B] Change of Control and Ownership Clause[301]

Change of control and ownership clauses and assignment clauses are of importance in the case of smaller technology businesses with outside investors.[302] Intellectual property and contracts occasionally represent the key possessions of such businesses.[303] The right to assign and the right to terminate an agreement in the event that there is a change in control or ownership significantly influence the value of the business to potential investors.[304]

[C] Merger Clause[305]

> This agreement expresses the full intent of the Parties to this agreement in relation to the subject matter of this agreement. This agreement sets out the entirety of the agreement made by the Parties and supersedes all prior agreements and understanding between the Parties.

Referred to intermittently as entire agreement clauses, zipper clauses or integration clauses,[306] such clauses indicate that the agreement consists of all the terms agreed

300. *Puget Sound National Bank v. Washington Department of Revenue* 868 P2d 127 (Wash 1994).
301. Anderson 2010: 62.
302. Anderson 2010: 62.
303. Anderson 2010: 62.
304. Anderson 2010: 62.
305. Meiselles 2013: 57.
306. Stark 2007: 176.

upon by the contracting parties and that the terms of the agreement cannot be contradicted or supplemented by any extrinsic evidence.[307]

Merger clauses are employed by the contracting parties in order to ensure legal certainty vis-à-vis the content of their agreement and *inter alia* their rights and obligations under the agreement. As such they are able to protect themselves against any later attempt by the other contracting party to argue that the parties in verbal transactions, by correspondence and so forth agreed upon different terms.

[D] Modification Clause[308]

> This agreement may only be varied by a written instrument signed by the Parties to this agreement or their duly authorised representatives.

To guarantee legal certainty in relation to the substance of the agreement, the parties contracting will typically agree that any modifications to the terms of the agreement will only be permissible if made using a written instrument signed by the parties themselves or their authorised representatives.

[E] Severance Clause[309]

> If any provision of this agreement is, becomes or is deemed to be invalid, illegal or unenforceable in any way or is abrogated or materially modified by the action of a competent authority, either the provision shall be deemed amended to comply with the applicable laws so as to be valid and enforceable; or if the provision cannot be amended as such, without substantially varying the intentions of the Parties, it shall be omitted and the remainder of the agreement shall remain in full force and effect.

Such a clause will allow for the removal or variation of a provision in the agreement when the said provision is rendered invalid, illegal or unenforceable for whatever reason.[310] The law governing the contract may be capable of removing certain clauses from the agreement. Under US law an unconscionable clause may be removed from the

307. Stark 2007: 178.
308. Meiselles 2013: 58.
309. Meiselles 2013: 58.
310. Stark 2007: 179.

body of an agreement or its effect limited so as to avoid any unconscionable result by a court.[311]

[F] Language Clause[312]

> The English text of this agreement is the only authentic text.

Where several language versions of the agreement exist it is sensible for the parties to indicate which language version of the agreement is the authentic text. This provision will effectively designate an official language by means of which the agreement will be construed in the event of a disagreement between the contracting parties. The UNIDROIT Principles address the matter of linguistic discrepancies. Article 4.7 of UNIDROIT states that where an agreement is made in two or more language versions of equal authority, then in the case of a discrepancy between the versions, preference is given for interpretative purposes to the version in which the agreement was first drawn up.

[G] Notice Clause[313]

> Where this agreement requires or permits the use of a notice, such notice shall be given in writing and shall be delivered or dispatched by prepaid first class airmail to the addresses supplied in this agreement or to any other addresses provided by the Parties in a notice hereunder. Such notices shall be treated as given either when delivered or () days after mailing by first class airmail, whichever is the earlier.

[H] Execution in Counterparts[314]

> This agreement may be executed in any number of counterparts, each of which when executed and delivered shall be equivalent to an original of this agreement, but all the counterparts shall together constitute the same agreement.

311. §2-302, Uniform Commercial Code (UCC). Formulated as model law by the National Conference of Commissioners on Uniform State Laws as well as by the American Law Institute, the UCC is effective in some form in nearly all the US jurisdictions.
312. Meiselles 2013: 58.
313. Meiselles 2013: 59.
314. Meiselles 2013: 59.

This provision permits the execution of the agreement in counterparts, where the parties contracting cannot be present in the same place or at the same time for the signing of the agreement.[315] The counterpart operates as a duplicate of the original agreement that the contracting parties can sign at different times.[316]

[I] Jurisdiction Clause

> The Parties to this agreement shall submit to the jurisdiction of _______ for the purposes of resolving any disputes and/or enforcing any claim arising under this agreement, or concerning this agreement.

Intermittently referred to as a forum clause or a choice-of-court clause, this provision allocates the forum with the power to handle the resolution of disputes under the agreement and the enforcement of claims under the same.

[J] Choice-of-Law Clause[317]

> This agreement shall be governed by and interpreted using the laws of _______.

Such a provision denotes the law that will govern the resolution of disputes under the agreement. In the absence of such a provision, the arbiter will apply conflict of law rules to ascertain the governing law.

[K] Alternative Dispute Resolution (ADR) Clause[318,319]

> The Parties shall resolve disputes under or connected to this agreement, any breach, termination or invalidity of this agreement, using [arbitration or mediation or some other form of alternative dispute resolution] in line with the rules of [include the name of the selected alternative dispute resolution body whose rules are to be used and indicate the version of these rules by reference to the year of publication].
>
> a. The authority shall be [name the organisation or person selected as the alternative dispute resolution body];

315. Stark 2007: 179.
316. Stark 2007: 179.
317. Stark 2007: 173; Meiselles 2013: 59-60.
318. Meiselles 2013: 60.
319. Alternative dispute resolution will be addressed in Chapter 7 on international dispute resolution.

b. The number of [arbitrators, mediators and so on] shall be [include the number agreed upon];

c. The locus of [arbitration, mediation and so on] shall be [insert the name of the town or country];

d. The language(s) that shall be employed in the [arbitration, mediation and so on] shall be [denote the language(s) of the proceedings];

e. The law that shall be used by the [body or person selected] shall be the law determined by the Parties in [cross-reference here to the choice-of-law clause].

[L] Multi-tiered Dispute Resolution Clauses[320]

(1) The Parties shall negotiate in good faith the resolution of disputes that arise out of or in connection with this agreement. (First Tier)

(2) If the Parties are unable to resolve the dispute using the procedure set out in §1 above, then either Party shall refer the dispute to an expert for consideration of the disputes. The expert to be chosen shall be a speciality in the following fields [] of [] years' standing. The expert to be chosen shall be chosen from amongst the members of the following institution [name the professional body, university etc from which the expert will be chosen]. The expert's examination shall be limited to the following fields [optional – note the fields to be determined by the expert]. (Optional – The expert's determination on the following matters shall be final and there will be no right of appeal). (Second Tier)

(3) If the Parties are unable to resolve the dispute using the procedures set out in §1 and §2, except as hereinafter provided, the Parties shall refer the matter to arbitration in accordance with the arbitration agreement annexed ('Arbitration Agreement'). (Third Tier).

These clauses, which are also known as escalation clauses, allow the contracting parties to adopt a phased approach to the resolution of disputes between them. Such clauses typically provide for two or more sequential tiers of ADR.

When the parties opt for this structure they are expected to reach a settlement of their disputes by progressing through 'the consecutive steps of different Private Dispute Resolution process'.[321] Commonly, this process commences with negotiations

320. Sample clause inspired by one provided in Klaus Peter Berger, *Private Dispute Resolution in International Business – Negotiation, Mediation, Arbitration Volume II: Handbook (*Kluwer Law International 2006), 48 (hereafter Berger 2006) citing ICC Award No 10256, printed in: Figueres, ICC International Court of Arbitration Bull., (2003) 82, 87.

321. Berger 2006: Preface.

proceeding through mediation or some other form of ADR ending with arbitration or litigation before national courts.

Such provisions aim to 'filter' out all or specific aspects of the disagreement narrowing down the scope of disagreement.

The question of whether each of the tiers 'is a condition precedent to proceeding to the next tier' is a matter of construction.[322]

[M] Force Majeure[323]

Option A

1. Neither Party shall be deemed to be in breach of this agreement, to the extent that performance of their obligations is delayed or prevented by circumstances that are beyond the reasonable control of that Party ('Force Majeure') and the Party in question could not reasonably be expected to have taken the impediment into account at the time this agreement was concluded, provided that each Party gives the other Party written notice promptly and uses its good faith efforts to cure the breach. Except in relation to the provisions governing (here reference can be made to those provisions in the contract that are not suspended by the Force Majeure clause).

2. In the event of Force Majeure, the time for performance will be extended for a period equal to the duration of the event of Force Majeure.

3. If the event of Force Majeure prevails for a continuous period in excess of —— months, the Parties shall be entitled to enter into good faith discussions with a view to alleviating its effects or to agreeing upon some other alternative arrangement or arrangements as may be fair and reasonable.

4. This clause shall not relieve either Party of the obligation to use all reasonable endeavours to mitigate the effect of such circumstances in relation to its obligations under this agreement.

Option B

1. Neither Party shall be deemed to be in breach of this agreement, to the extent that performance of their obligations is delayed or prevented by circumstances that are beyond the reasonable control of that Party ('Force Majeure') and the Party in question could not reasonably be expected to have taken the impediment into account at the time this agreement was concluded, provided that each Party gives the other Party written notice promptly and uses its good faith efforts to cure the breach. Except in relation to the provisions governing (here reference

322. Susan Blake, Julie Browne and Stuart Sime, A Practical Approach to Alternative Dispute *Resolution* (3rd edn, OUP), 426.

323. Meiselles 2013: 101-2. Template clause is based on clause in Meiselles 2013: 101.

can be made to those provisions in the contract that are not suspended by the Force Majeure clause).

2. In the event of Force Majeure, the time for performance will be extended for a period equal to the duration of the event of Force Majeure.

3. If the event of Force Majeure prevails for a continuous period in excess of —— months, the agreement will be automatically terminated (or terminated by written notice given by either Party to the other).

4. This clause shall not relieve either Party of the obligation to use all reasonable endeavours to mitigate the effect of such circumstances in relation to its obligations under this agreement.

Option C

This agreement is deemed cancelled and neither Party will be liable to the other for losses resulting from non-performance if performance of the Parties' obligations (except payment of sums due hereunder) is delayed or prevented by circumstances that are beyond the reasonable control of one or both of the Parties ('Force Majeure') provided that each Party gives the other Party written notice promptly and each Party uses good faith efforts to cure the breach.

Contracting parties should give due consideration to the various contingencies that could arise during the course of their dealings and the manner in which such contingencies will impact upon the execution of the contract. An unanticipated event either specified by the parties in this clause or encompassed within the scope of this clause will pursuant to this clause allow the contracting parties to be excused from performing their respective obligations under the contract (Force Majeure clause).

The contracting parties may include a force majeure clause that suspends and excuses performance until the event has passed (options A and B in the template clause). Such a provision will usually allow the parties to resume the performance of their obligations under the contract once the event has passed (options A and B in the template clause).

The parties may also include a provision in the contract addressing those scenarios when the event continues for a period that is longer than the one the parties envisaged within the contract (options A and B in the template clause). The length of the period will be determined largely by the concerns of the parties. Such a provision may allow at the end of the allowance period for renegotiation by the parties (option A in the template clause) or for termination of the agreement (automatically or by notice) (option B in the template clause).

§1.37 BACK OF THE CONTRACT[324]

This section of the contract that comes after the body of the contract is made up of the concluding clause, the signature blocks and where relevant the attachments.

Box 5 Structure of the back of the contract

- Concluding clause
- Signature blocks
- Attachments (exhibits and schedules)

[A] Concluding Clause[325]

The signature blocks (at the end of the agreement) are from time to time introduced by the concluding clause. Such a clause is optional. A concluding clause is often employed to prevent the otherwise abrupt transition from the body of the contract to the signature blocks.[326] Such a clause may state, for example, that 'each Party confirms that it has scrutinised and comprehends the terms of this agreement and duly signs below'.[327]

[B] Signature Blocks[328]

The signature blocks will either stand-alone or will be prefaced by the concluding clause. Each of the contracting parties will have its own separate signature block, containing its name and a signature line. Where the signing of the agreement needs to be witnessed, then a signature block will be included for the witness or witnesses.[329]

[C] Signing of the Agreement

In England and Wales, there exists no practice that necessitates the initialling of each page of the agreement by the parties contracting.[330] This mechanism used to address the risk of fraud ensures that the parties contracting are assenting to matching versions of the agreement.[331] Where manuscript amendments are made to the typed version of the agreement, such amendments should be initialled by the contracting parties to

324. Meiselles 2013: 60-3.
325. Meiselles 2013: 60.
326. Adams 2007: 63.
327. Adams 2007: 63.
328. Meiselles 2013: 60-1.
329. The processes of witnessing, and notarisation are addressed in Meiselles 2013: 62.
330. Anderson 2010: 62.
331. Anderson 2010: 63.

show their accord to the revisions made. Initialling usually takes place in the margin adjacent to the manuscript amendment.[332]

[D] Attachments[333]

Oftentimes documentation is annexed to the rear of the agreement. Such documentation is referred to intermittently as attachments, annexes or appendices. Two categories of attachments exist namely exhibits and schedules.

Within the agreement, references to exhibits and schedules are accentuated by ensuring that they are always underlined (Exhibit B or Schedule C). Exhibits are identified using sequential lettering or numbering. Schedules can be identified using sequential letters or numbers or in the alternative by reference to the sections in the agreement to which they relate (where a schedule is connected to section 5.1 then it would become Schedule 5.1).

An exhibit is a document that is dissociated from the agreement. It may be a document that either existed prior to the signing of the agreement or one that emerged at a time after the signing of the agreement. Exhibits to licences may comprise patent applications and template licence agreements for use in the context of sub-licensing. In the alternative, the agreement may incorporate as an exhibit some later agreement to be entered into by the contracting parties at some time after the pertinent agreement is concluded.

A schedule consists of items that are part of the agreement but have been displaced to the section after the signature blocks. Such displacement may be made for a plethora of reasons: first to conserve space; second to allow for an independent collation of materials; third to safeguard the confidentiality of proprietary information (as schedules are rarely annexed to the agreement when the agreement is filed externally).

332. Anderson 2010: 63.
333. Adams 2007: 68; Meiselles 2013: 62.

CHAPTER 2

Competition Law Considerations*

§2.01 INTRODUCTION

The purpose of this chapter is to address the competition law concerns that should be borne in mind when concluding a licensing agreement in an international context.

This chapter will look at European Union regulation of licensing agreements. In this context consideration will be given to the relevant provisions of the TFEU[1] and their impact on such arrangements and reference will be made to the various block exemptions relevant to licensing agreements.[2]

Worldwide there are now in excess of 120 systems of competition law.[3] India, China and Malaysia recently introduced competition laws, and several other countries are presently contemplating the introduction of such laws.[4] Beyond its geographic reach, competition law is now applied to an expanding array of economic activities.[5] A recent illustration of this is the series of negotiations between the IMF and Greece

* For further discussion, *see* Fairhurst, *Law of the European Union* (7th edn Pearson 2010), Chapters 19-22 (Fairhurst 2010); Jones and Sufrin, *EU Competition Law* (Oxford University Press 2011), Chapter 3 (hereinafter Jones and Sufrin 2011); Whish & Bailey, *Competition Law* (7th edn, Oxford University Press 2012), Chapters 16 and 19 (hereinafter Whish et al. 2012). For information about competition law and policy in the different jurisdictions, *see* the websites of the International Bar Association's Global Competition Forum (www.globalcompetitionforum.org), the International Competition Network (www.internationalcompetitionwork.org), the OECD (www.oecd.org), and UNCTAD (www.unctad.org).

1. Treaty of Lisbon amending the Treaty on European Union and the Treaty establishing the European Community (signed at Lisbon 13 December 2007) OJ C306 (hereinafter The Lisbon Treaty) retained, and revised the Treaty establishing the European Community OJ C325 (hereinafter TEC), and the Treaty on European Union OJ C326 (hereinafter TEU). The TEC was renamed the Treaty on the Functioning of the European Union (TFEU) whilst renumbering the articles in the TEU, and TFEU.
2. Where appropriate, the topic-specific chapters will elaborate on specific block exemptions.
3. Whish et al. 2012: 1.
4. Whish et al. 2012: 1.
5. Whish et al. 2012: 1.

regarding the latter's deficit in 2015, which included a proposal for the privatisation of certain state industries by the Greek government in a bid to reduce its spending.[6]

§2.02 BACKGROUND

Originating from the term *competere* which means 'to struggle for (something)' or 'campaign for (something)',[7] the word 'competition' is defined as 'the activity or condition of striving to gain or win something by defeating or establishing superiority over others'.[8]

The fundamental benefits associated with competition are lower prices, greater choice, better quality and enhanced efficiency.[9] A further side benefit of competition is 'the dynamic effect of stimulating innovation as competitors strive to produce new and better products for consumers ... as part of the continual battle of striving for consumers' business'.[10]

Though the terms **competition policy** and **competition law** are occasionally used interchangeably, a distinction should be made between these two distinct concepts.[11]

Broader in scope than competition law, **competition policy** describes the manner in which governments and, in the European Union, the Commission formulate and adopt measures intended to encourage competitive market structures and behaviour.[12]

Competition law by contrast refers to the body of rules, which aim to give effect to competition policy. Competition policy encompasses competition law.[13]

A common consideration underpinning competition policy in the various jurisdictions is the ability of one or more undertakings with market power to adversely affect consumer welfare.[14] Stifling technological development, fixing prices, limiting markets, curtailing the access of consumers to a variety of products and reducing output are all examples of the types of behaviour that competition policy typically addresses.[15]

§2.03 THE GOALS OF COMPETITION POLICY

Competition policy is dynamic in nature mirroring societal values and goals.[16] These ebbs and flows that shape and reshape competition policy and competition law are also

6. For further reading, *see* articles in August 2015 edition of the *New York Times*.
7. Oxford Dictionary (electronic) definition of the term 'compete'.
8. Oxford Dictionary (electronic) definition of the term 'competition'.
9. Whish et al. 2012: 4.
10. Whish et al. 2012: 4-5. An overview of the theory of competition can be found in Chapter 1, Whish.
11. Jones and Sufrin 2011: 4.
12. Jones and Sufrin 2011: 4.
13. Jones and Sufrin 2011: 4.
14. Whish et al. 2012: 1.
15. Whish et al. 2012: 1.
16. '... competition policy does not exist in a vacuum: it is an expression of current values and aims of society and is as susceptible to change as political thinking generally.' (Whish et al. 2012: 20).

a potential source of tension.[17] The considerations underlying competition law differ from jurisdiction to jurisdiction. This is apparent when one compares the development of competition law in the US and the EU for example.[18]

One goal associated with competition law is the protection of small entities against more powerful rivals. It has been argued that by promoting this goal competition law is effectively being used to protect the inefficient at the expense of the efficient party.[19]

This goal is linked to another goal of competition law namely the redistribution of wealth and the dispersal of economic power.[20] Pursuant to this view the concentration of resources 'in the hands of monopolists, multinational corporations or conglomerates could be considered a threat to the very notion of democracy, individual freedom of choice and economic opportunity'.[21] This is a view supported in a speech delivered by President Roosevelt in 1938 at a time when there was a prevailing mistrust of big business:

> The liberty of a democracy is not safe if the people tolerate the growth of a private power to a point where it becomes stronger than the democratic state itself.[22]

§2.04 THE GOALS OF COMPETITION POLICY IN THE EU

[A] Single Market Integration

One of the key objectives of competition policy in the EU is single market integration.[23] The establishment of a single market depends upon the removal of internal barriers to trade within the EU ensuring the free movement of goods, services, workers and capital and guaranteeing the ability of firms to expand beyond national borders so that they are able to operate 'on a more efficient, transnational, scale throughout the EU'.[24]

This approach is supported by the Commission[25] in its 2010 Guidelines on Vertical Restraints. In this document the Commission emphasises the importance of market integration in enhancing competition across the EU[26] and comments upon the need to address attempts by companies 'to recreate private barriers between Member States where States barriers have been successfully abolished'.[27] According to the

17. Whish et al. 2012: 20.
18. Whish et al. 2012: 20 citing Jebsen and Stevens, 'Assumptions, Goals and Dominant Undertakings; the Regulation of Competition under Article 86 of the European Union' (1996) 64 Antitrust Law Journal 443.
19. Whish et al. 2012: 21 citing the Chicago School of economists in the US that has been critical of this sentimentality.
20. Whish et al. 2012: 21.
21. Whish et al. 2012: 21.
22. Whish et al. 2012: 21 citing an extract from a speech President Roosevelt gave to Congress in 1938 (83 Cong Rec 5992 (1938)).
23. Fairhurst 2010: Chapter 20; Whish et al. 2012: 23.
24. Whish et al. 2012: 23.
25. Commission notice – Guidelines on Vertical Restraints (Text with EEA relevance) OJ C130, 19.05.2010, P. 0001-0046, para. 3. (hereinafter VRBER 2010 Guidelines).
26. Vertical Guidelines 2010): para. 7.
27. Vertical Guidelines 2010: para. 7.

Commission, EU competition law aims to prevent the negative effects on the market that may result from vertical restraints by addressing *inter alia* the 'creation of obstacles to market integration, including, above all, limitations on the possibilities for consumers to purchase goods or services in any Member State they may choose'.[28]

In the EU, the provisions governing competition compliment those governing the free movement of goods.[29] Whilst the latter target the measures adopted by governments that impede the free movement of goods within the EU, the former target restrictive and abusive practices of undertakings that do or may limit or even prevent the provision of goods and services in the Member States.[30]

[B] Protection of Consumer Interests

Another important goal associated with EU competition policy is the protection of consumer interests 'not by protecting the competitive process itself, but by taking action against offending undertakings, for example by requiring dominant firms to reduce their prices'.[31]

Whish and Bailey caution against the use of competition law for the promotion of a populist agenda referring to the attempt by the UK government in 1998 and 1999 to tackle the phenomenon referred to as 'rip-off Britain' when Ministers indicated that excessive prices were being charged by both monopolists and non-monopolists.[32] A key complication associated with using competition law to assume direct control over pricing, argue Whish and Bailey, is that competition authorities are 'ill-placed to determine what price a competitive market would set for particular goods or services, and indeed by fixing a price they may further distort the competitive fabric of the market'.[33]

[C] Consumer Welfare

Whish and Bailey argue that although a number of different policy goals have been pursued over the years in the context of competition law, consumer welfare is 'currently in the ascendancy'.[34] A fact which, they argue, is supported by a speech delivered in 2005, by the then Commissioner for competition policy, Neelie Kroes:

> Consumer welfare is now well established as the standard the Commission applies when assessing mergers and infringements of the Treaty rules on cartels and monopolies. Our aim is simple: to protect competition in the market as a means of enhancing consumer welfare and ensuring an efficient allocation of resources.[35]

28. Vertical Guidelines 2010: para. 100 in particular para. 100(iv).
29. Fairhurst 2010: 690.
30. Fairhurst 2010: 690.
31. Whish et al. 2012: 20.
32. Whish et al. 2012: 20.
33. Whish et al. 2012: 20.
34. Whish et al. 2012: 19.
35. Whish et al. 2012: 19 citing Speech/05/512 of 15 September 2005.

[D] Ancillary Goals

Ancillary objectives associated with competition policy in the EU include the levelling of the playing field and the enhancement of efficiency.[36]

Effective competition is the best stimulant of economic activity, making it easier for supply and demand structures to adjust to developments, whilst permitting enterprises to improve their efficiency.[37] Competition is crucial for the steady improvement of living standards throughout the EU and employment prospects within the respective Member States, in turn satisfying the individual and collective needs of society.[38]

§2.05 PROVISIONS OF EU LAW GOVERNING COMPETITION

EU competition law is specifically addressed in Articles 101 to 109 of the TFEU.

These substantive Treaty articles governing competition in the EU should be read alongside the objectives and principles set out in the TFEU and in the TEU. Beyond the establishment of an internal market,[39] which 'includes a system ensuring that competition is not distorted',[40] one of the key aims of the EU is a highly competitive social market economy.[41]

Article 101 TFEU prohibits 'all agreements between undertakings, decisions by associations of undertakings and concerted practices which may affect trade between Member States and which have as their object or effect the prevention, restriction or distortion of competition within the internal market'.

Article 102 TFEU prohibits the abuse by one or more undertakings of a dominant position within the internal market or in a substantial part of it in so far as it may affect trade between Member States.

Article 103 addresses the legislative procedure. Article 104 addresses the role of the authorities in the Member States. Article 105 addresses enforcement.

Article 106(1) addresses the responsibilities of Member States in relation to public undertakings and undertakings to which the Member States have granted special or exclusive rights.

Article 106(2) addresses the application of the rules in the Treaties and specifically the rules on competition to undertakings entrusted with the operation of services of general economic interest.

Articles 107–109 address aids granted by states. Article 107 generally prohibits aid granted by the State or through State resources 'which distorts or threatens to distort competition by favouring certain undertakings or the production of certain

36. Fairhurst 2010: Chapter 20.
37. Fairhurst 2010: Chapter 20.
38. Fairhurst 2010: Chapter 20.
39. Article 3(3), TEU.
40. Protocol (No 27) on the Internal Market and Competition annexed to the TEU, and the TFEU.
41. Article 3(3), TEU.

goods ... in so far as it affects trade between Member States'.[42] Certain categories of aid *are* deemed to be compatible with the internal market (Article 107(2) TFEU). Certain categories of aid *may be* deemed to be compatible with the internal market (Article 107(3) TFEU). Aid to remedy damage caused by a natural disaster is an example of aid that *is* compatible with the internal market.[43] Aid promoting cultural conservation and aid promoting economic development of areas where the standard of living is abnormally low or where this is serious unemployment are examples of aid that *may be* considered to be compatible with the internal market.[44]

A further instrument of EU competition law is the Merger Regulation.[45]

§2.06 ANTICOMPETITIVE ACTIVITY TARGETED BY EU COMPETITION POLICY

Competition policy within the EU targets three categories of anticompetitive activity.

First, horizontal and vertical agreements between otherwise independent undertakings which have as their object or effect the prevention, restriction or distortion of competition between the Member States. Such agreements are addressed principally in Article 101 TFEU (formerly Article 81 TEC).

Second, abusive practices of large undertakings, which dominate markets for goods, or services which affect trade between the Member States. Such behaviour is addressed primarily in Article 102 TFEU (formerly Article 82 TEC).

Third, mergers of undertakings resulting in positions of market dominance. Such mergers are addressed in the Merger Regulation.

Each one of these types of anticompetitive activities is subject to regulation and control by the Commission, the national competition authorities (NCAs) and the courts of the Member States.

There have been developments in the manner in which anticompetitive activity is dealt with within the EU. These changes have been implemented primarily through the use of secondary instruments. In addition, the Commission has been instrumental in issuing guidelines and notices which are intended to help industry.

§2.07 ROLE OF THE INSTITUTIONS AND THE MEMBER STATES

The Union and Member States are required to ensure the existence within the Union of the conditions needed for the competitiveness of industry.[46] This action is aimed at:[47]

- expediting the process of industrial adjustment to structural changes;

42. Article 107(1), TFEU.
43. Article 107(2)b, TFEU.
44. Article 107(3)a, and Article 107(3)d, TFEU.
45. Council Regulation 139/2004 on the control of concentrations between undertakings OJ [2004] L24/1 (hereinafter Merger Regulation 2004).
46. Article 173(1), TFEU.
47. Article 173(1), TFEU.

- promoting an environment that favours initiative, business development and cooperation between undertakings; and
- promoting improved utilisation of the 'industrial potential of policies of innovation, research and technological development'.

In this context, there is an expectation that Member States in collaboration with the Commission will consult with each other and coordinate their activities.[48]

The European Parliament is to be kept fully updated.[49] The Commission is encouraged to take steps to promote this cross-border coordination.[50]

For their part, both the European Parliament and the Council may adopt measures to support the action taken in the Member States in order to achieve these aims.[51] Such measures will be adopted by means of the ordinary legislative procedure, after consultation with the Economic and Social Committee.[52]

The Commission's Annual Reports on Competition Policy have, on several occasions, pointed out the linkage between competition policy, single market concerns and industrial policy.[53]

§2.08 POLICING COMPETITION POLICY

The introduction on 1 May 2004 of Regulation 1/2003[54] reformed the system of enforcement of EU competition policy. In order to meet 'the challenges of an integrated market and a future enlargement of the Community',[55] this Regulation set out to reform the system created by its predecessor, Council Regulation No. 17 of 6 February 1962 ('Regulation 17/62').

The centralised system (established by the Regulation 17/62) was deemed to be no longer able to balance the need for effective supervision on the one hand and the simplification of administration on the other hand[56] in turn hampering application of competition rules by the national courts and the national competition authorities, preventing the Commission from utilising its resources in an efficient manner to tackle the most grave infringements and imposing substantial costs on businesses.[57]

In order to tackle the difficulties associated with the former system (established by Regulation 17/62) the following changes were made.

First Regulation 1/2003 brought an end to the system of notification of individual exemption.[58]

48. Article 173 (2) TFEU.
49. Article 173(2), TFEU.
50. Article 173(2), TFEU.
51. Article 173(3), TFEU.
52. Article 173(3), TFEU.
53. Jones and Sufrin 2011: 32-4.
54. Council Regulation (EC) No 1/2003 of 16 December 2002 on the implementation of the rules on competition laid down in Articles 81 and 82 of the Treaty (hereinafter Regulation 1/2003).
55. Regulation 1/2003: Recital 1.
56. Regulation 1/2003: Recital 2.
57. Regulation 1/2003: Recital 3.
58. Whish et al. 2012: 116, 167.

Second the power to make decisions concerning the application of Article 101 TFEU is partitioned between the Commission, the NCAs and the national courts.[59] Prior to 1 May 2004, the Commission alone was responsible for applying Article 101(3) (formerly 81(3) TEC).[60]

The Commission, the NCAs and the national courts are jointly responsible for implementing EU competition policy by targeting:

(1) Restrictive trading agreements between otherwise independent business concerns which may affect trade between Member States and which have as their object or effect the prevention, restriction or distortion of competition in the internal market (Article 101 formerly Article 81 TEC).
(2) Abuse of a dominant position affecting trade between Member States (Article 102 formerly Article 83 TEC).
(3) Mergers of two or more undertakings that would significantly impede effective competition in the internal market (or a substantial part thereof) notably through the creation or strengthening of a dominant position (Article 2(3), Merger Regulation 2004).

§2.09 THE ROLE OF THE NATIONAL ENTITIES

Regulation 1/2003 provides an array of powers to designated national entities in the context of European competition law. The national entities endowed with these powers are the NCAs and the national courts.

First, in situations the NCAs or the national courts apply *national competition law* to agreements, decisions or concerted practices (within the meaning of Article 101 TFEU) that affect trade between the Member States (within the meaning of Article 101 TFEU), they will apply Article 101 TFEU to such agreements, decisions or concerted practices.[61] Similarly when the NCAs or the national courts apply *national competition law* to an abuse forbidden by Article 102 TFEU, they are also to apply Article 102 TFEU.[62]

However the rules of national competition law may not result in the prohibition of agreements etc. which may affect interstate trade *but which do not restrict competition within the meaning of Article 101(1) TFEU* or *which fulfil the conditions set out in Article 101(3) TFEU.*[63]

Second, NCAs enjoy the power to apply Articles 101 TFEU and 102 TFEU in individual cases.[64]

The national courts will also enjoy the power to apply Articles 101 and 102.[65] In proceedings 'for the application' of Article 101 TFEU or Article 102 TFEU, a national

59. Whish et al. 2012: 116. *See* Articles 5 and 6, Regulation 1/2003.
60. Whish et al. 2012: 116.
61. First sentence of Article 3(1), Regulation 1/2003.
62. Second sentence of Article 3(1), Regulation 1/2003.
63. Article 3(2), Regulation 1/2003. Italics added by authors.
64. Article 5, Regulation 1/2003.
65. Article 6, Regulation 1/2003.

court may approach the Commission for information it has or for its opinion on questions that involve the application of European competition rules.[66]

An NCA is permitted to submit written observations to the national courts of their Member State relating to the application of Article 101 TFEU or Article 102 TFEU[67] and with the permission of the court concerned, the NCA may make oral observations to the courts of their Member State.[68]

In the interests of the coherent application of these articles, the Commission is permitted to submit written observations to national courts and, with the permission of the court concerned, to make oral observations.[69]

Member States are expected to forward the Commission copies of judgments delivered by their respective courts in relation to Articles 101 and 102 TFEU.[70]

Third, acting in response to a complaint or at their own discretion, NCAs may adopt decisions requiring the cessation of an infringement, ordering interim measures, accepting commitments and imposing fines.[71]

Fourth, the Commission and the NCAs are expected to apply European competition law in close cooperation with each other.[72] The Commission and the NCAs will have the power to provide one another with any matter of fact or of law including confidential information[73] and to use in evidence any matter of fact or of law including confidential information.[74]

The Commission for its part is responsible for transmitting documentation that it has collated to the NCA and, at the request of the NCA, for providing copies of existing documentation needed for the assessment of a matter.[75]

The NCA for its part is responsible, when acting under Article 101 TFEU or Article 102 TFEU, for informing the Commission in writing before, or as rapidly as possible after, commencing the first formal investigative measure.[76] An NCA may also circulate this information to competition authorities based in other Member States.[77]

The NCA is responsible for notifying the Commission no later than 30 days before the adoption of a decision requiring the cessation of an infringement or the acceptance of commitments or withdrawing the benefit of a block exemption.[78] Such notice should include a case overview, a note of the envisaged decision or, in the absence thereof, any documentation denoting the course of action proposed.[79] At the request of the

66. Article 15(1), Regulation 1/2003.
67. First sentence of Article 15(3), Regulation 1/2003.
68. Second sentence of Article 15(3), Regulation 1/2003.
69. Third, and fourth sentences of Article 15(3), Regulation 1/2003.
70. Article 15(2), Regulation 1/2003.
71. Article 5, Regulation 1/2003.
72. Article 11(1), Regulation 1/2003.
73. Article 12(1), Regulation 1/2003.
74. Article 12(1), Regulation 1/2003.
75. First, and second sentences of Article 11(2) Regulation 1/2003.
76. First sentence of Article 11(3), Regulation 1:2003.
77. Second sentence of Article 11(3) Regulation 1:2003.
78. First sentence of Article 11(4), Regulation 1/2003.
79. Second sentence of Article 11(4), Regulation 1/2003.

Commission, the notifying NCA is responsible for furnishing the Commission with further documentation in its possession required for an assessment of the case.[80]

All information made available to the Commission may also be made available to counterparts in other Member States.[81]

Fifth, an NCA has the option of consulting with the Commission on any case involving the application of European competition law.[82]

Sixth, where the Commission commences proceedings for the adoption of a decision, the competition authorities of the Member States will be relieved of their competence to apply Article 101 TFEU or Article 102 TFEU.[83] In circumstances where an NCA is already acting, the Commission shall consult with the said NCA before initiating proceedings.[84]

Seventh, in circumstances where one or more other NCAs have received a complaint or are acting on their own initiative under Article 101 TFEU or Article 102 TFEU against the same agreement, decision or practice, the fact that one NCA is dealing with the case will be enough for the other NCAs to reject the complaint or to suspend the proceedings before them.[85] The Commission has the discretion to reject a complaint on the basis that an NCA is handling the case.[86]

§2.10 INDIVIDUAL REMEDIES

Articles 101 and 102 TFEU are both directly effective and so can be relied upon in proceedings brought before national courts.

As such a party hampered and harmed by concerted action between several undertakings may rely on Article 101 TFEU in domestic proceedings. Similarly, a party adversely affected by the abusive behaviour of a dominant player may rely on Article 102 TFEU in domestic proceedings.

§2.11 STANDARD OF PROOF

The party or the authority opposing the agreement, decision or concerted practice pursuant to Article 101 TFEU or the abuse pursuant to Article 102 TFEU is obliged to prove the infringement under the article concerned.[87]

The undertaking or the association of undertakings looking to claim the benefit of Article 101(3) TFEU is obliged to prove the conditions set out therein.[88]

80. Fourth sentence of Article 11(4), Regulation 1/2003.
81. Third, and fifth sentences of Article 11(4), Regulation 1/2003.
82. First sentence of Article 11(5), Regulation 1/2003.
83. First sentence of Article 11(6), Regulation 1/2003.
84. Second sentence of Article 11(6), Regulation 1/2003.
85. First sentence of Article 13(1), Regulation 1/2003.
86. Second sentence of Article 13(1), Regulation 1/2003.
87. First sentence of Article 2, Regulation 1/2003.
88. Second sentence of Article 2, Regulation 1/2003.

§2.12 'RELEVANT MARKET' DEFINED

Guidance on the definition of the term 'relevant market' is provided by the Commission in a notice published in the Official Journal in December 1997 (1997 Notice).[89]

The aim of the notice is the provision of guidance on the way in which the Commission applies the concept of relevant product and geographic market in its enforcement of European competition law[90] in order to enhance the transparency of the Commission's policy and decision-making in the field of EU competition[91] for the benefit of companies and their advisers.[92]

According to this guidance, the main aim of market definition is to 'identify in a systematic way the competitive constraints that the undertakings face. The objective of defining a market in both its product and geographic dimension is to identify those actual competitors of the undertakings involved that are capable of constraining those undertakings' behaviour and of preventing them from behaving independently of effective competitive pressure'.[93]

According to paragraph 9 of the 1997 Notice, the 'relevant market within which to assess a given competition issue is ... established by the combination of the product and geographic markets'.[94]

The 'relevant product market' includes 'all those products and/or services which are regarded as interchangeable or substitutable by the consumer, by reason of the products' characteristics, their prices and their intended use'.[95]

The 'relevant geographic market' consists of 'the area in which the undertakings concerned are involved in the supply and demand of products or services, in which the conditions of competition are sufficiently homogeneous and which can be distinguished from neighbouring areas because the conditions of competition are appreciably different in those area'.[96]

According to the Commission, the three key sources of competitive constraints that confront undertakings are demand substitutability, supply substitutability and potential competition.[97]

From an economic point of view when considering the definition of the relevant market, demand substitution represents 'the most immediate and effective disciplinary force on the suppliers of a given product, in particular in relation to their pricing decisions'.[98] When consumers are able 'to switch easily to available substitute products or to suppliers located elsewhere', the undertaking or group of undertakings

89. Commission Notice on the definition of relevant market for the purposes of Community competition law OJ [1997] C372/5, [1998] 4 CMLR 177 (hereinafter 1997 Notice).
90. 1997 Notice: para. 1.
91. 1997 Notice: para. 4.
92. 1997 Notice: para. 5.
93. 1997 Notice: para. 2.
94. 1997 Notice: para. 9.
95. 1997 Notice: para. 7.
96. 1997 Notice: para. 8.
97. 1997 Notice: para. 13.
98. 1997 Notice: para. 13.

are unable to exercise 'a significant impact on the prevailing conditions of sale, such as prices'.[99]

The exercise of market definition entails 'identifying the effective alternative sources of supply for the customers of the undertakings involved, in terms both of products/services and of geographic location of suppliers'.[100]

[A] Demand Substitution

Analysis of demand substitution involves 'a determination of the range products which are viewed as substitutes by the consumer'.[101] The question to be posited is 'whether the parties' customers would switch to readily available substitutes or to suppliers located elsewhere in response to a hypothetical small (in the range of 5% to 10%) but permanent relative price increase in the products and areas being considered'.[102] In circumstances 'substitution were enough to make the price increase unprofitable because of the resulting loss of sales, additional substitutes and areas are included in the relevant market. This would be done until the set of products and geographical areas is such that small, permanent increases in relative prices would be profitable'.[103]

[B] Supply Substitution

Supply substitution (or supply-side substitutability) is also relevant when defining markets in circumstances where its impact is equivalent to the effects of demand substitution in terms of effectiveness and immediacy.[104] This entails the ability of suppliers 'to switch production to the relevant products and market them in the short term without incurring significant additional costs or risks in response to small and permanent changes in relative prices'.[105]

Paper manufacturing can be used to illustrate the approach to supply substitution when defining product markets.[106] Paper plants suggest the Commission are able to adjust their production at a negligible cost and in a fairly short time-frame.[107] As such the Commission suggests that paper plants are able to compete for orders of the different grades of paper, when there are no particular difficulties involved with distribution, in particular when such orders are placed with sufficient lead time to permit an adjustment to the production line at the plants.[108]

99. 1997 Notice: para. 13.
100. 1997 Notice: para. 13.
101. 1997 Notice: para. 15.
102. 1997 Notice: para. 17.
103. 1997 Notice: para. 17.
104. 1997 Notice: para. 20.
105. 1997 Notice: para. 20.
106. 1997 Notice: para. 22.
107. 1997 Notice: para. 22.
108. 1997 Notice: para. 22.

For this reason, the Commission suggests that it 'would not define a separate market for each quality of paper and its respective use. The various qualities of paper are included in the relevant market, and their sales added up to estimate total market galue [sic. value] and volume'.[109]

§2.13 POTENTIAL COMPETITION

Potential competition is a third source of competition constraint which, the Commission suggests, should not be taken into account when defining markets since 'the conditions under which potential competition will actually represent an effective competitive constraint depend on the analysis of specific factors and circumstances related to the conditions of entry'.[110]

If necessary such an assessment is performed at a later stage 'once the position of the companies involved in the relevant market has already been ascertained, and when such position gives rise to concerns from a competition point of view'.[111]

§2.14 ARTICLE 101 TFEU: ANTICOMPETITIVE AGREEMENTS, DECISIONS AND CONCERTED PRACTICES[112]

Agreements, decisions and concerted practices caught by Article 101(1) TFEU, which fail to meet the conditions set out in Article 101(3) TFEU, are prohibited.[113] Any agreement or decision or concerted practice that is prohibited by Article 101(1) is automatically void.[114]

Agreements, decisions and concerted practices that are caught by Article 101(1) TFEU, which meet the conditions set out in Article 101(3) TFEU, are not prohibited.[115]

[A] Introduction to Article 101 TFEU

Article 101 TFEU prohibits 'all agreements between undertakings, decisions by associations of undertakings and concerted practices which may affect trade between Member States and which have as their object or effect the prevention, restriction or distortion of competition within the internal market'.

A general principle underlying Article 101(1) is the notion that 'each economic operator must determine independently the policy, which he intends to adopt on the

109. 1997 Notice: para. 22.
110. 1997 Notice: para. 24.
111. 1997 Notice: para. 24.
112. In the following discussion, the term 'agreement' includes concerted practices, and decisions of associations of undertakings.
113. Article 1(1), Regulation 1/2003.
114. Article 101(2), TFEU.
115. Article 1(2), Regulation 1/2003.

market'.[116] Examples of the types of restrictive agreements, decisions and concerted practices that infringe Article 101(1) are noted in the article itself.

The list contained in this article is illustrative and by no means exhaustive. In this context, the types of agreements, decisions and concerted practices covered by the article include those that:

(a) directly or indirectly fix purchase or selling prices or other trading conditions;
(b) limit or control production, markets, technical development or investment;
(c) share markets or sources of supply;
(d) apply dissimilar conditions to equivalent transactions with other trading parties, thereby placing them at a competitive disadvantage;
(e) make the conclusion of contracts subject to acceptance by the other parties of supplementary obligations, which, by their nature or according to commercial usage, have no connection with the subject of such contracts.

No distinction is drawn in Article 101 between agreements that distort competition in the internal market 'based on whether they are made between competitors operating at the same level in the economic process or between non-competing persons operating at different levels'.[117] As such this article applies to horizontal agreements (between parties operating at the same level of the economy, which are often actual or potential competitors) and vertical agreements (between parties operating at different levels, such as agreements between distributor and manufacturer or between licensor and licensee).[118]

Notwithstanding the wide scope of this article, the prohibition in Article 101(1) does not extend to specific categories of agreement, namely agreements concluded between undertakings that form part of a single economic entity[119] and genuine agency agreements.[120]

In a bid 'to protect competition on the market with a view to promoting consumer welfare and an efficient allocation of resources',[121] the prohibition contained in Article 101(1) extends to 'restrictions of competition between the parties to an agreement and to restrictions of competition between any of the parties and third parties'.[122]

116. Guidelines on the application of Article 101(3) TFEU, para. 14 (hereinafter Article 101(3) Guidelines) citing *inter alia* Case C-49/92 P, *Anic Partecipazioni* [1999] ECR I-4125, para. 116; and Joined Cases 40/73 to 48/73 and others, *Suiker Unie* [1975] ECR 1663 (hereinafter *Sugar Union* case), para. 173.
117. Case 56-64 and 58-64 *Consten & Grundig v. Commission* [1966] ECR 299, 339.
118. Jones and Sufrin 2011: 85; Whish et al. 2012: 117; Case 56-64 and 58-64 *Consten & Grundig v. Commission* [1966] ECR 299, [1966] CMLR 418.
119. This subject is reviewed later on in this chapter. The question of what constitutes a single economic entity is discussed at Jones and Sufrin 2011: 134-9.
120. This subject is reviewed later on in this chapter. *See also* Whish et al. 2012: 621-3.
121. Extract from Communication from the Commission – Guidelines on the application of Article 101 of the Treaty on the Functioning of the European Union to technology transfer agreements (2014/C 89/03), para. 5.
122. Extract from Communication from the Commission – Guidelines on the application of Article 101 of the Treaty on the Functioning of the European Union to technology transfer agreements (2014/C 89/03), para. 10.

Competition and market integration serve to enhance consumer welfare and ensure an efficient allocation of resources since 'the creation and preservation of an open single market promotes an efficient allocation of resources throughout the Community for the benefit of consumers'.[123]

[B] The Impact of Article 101(2) TFEU

Restrictive agreements are automatically void pursuant to Article 101(2). This article which states that agreements, decisions or concerted practices infringing Article 101(1) TFEU are automatically void (Article 101(2) TFEU) effectively renders an agreement, decision or concerted practice caught by Article 101(1) TFEU which does not satisfy the conditions set out in Article 101(3) TFEU automatically null without the need for a prior decision to this effect.[124]

Notwithstanding Article 101(2) TFEU, the Court of Justice of the EU (CJEU) has held that nullity will only affect those terms in an agreement prohibited by virtue of the provision, effectively, leaving the remainder of the agreement in situ.[125]

The entirety of the agreement will only be void where the prohibited terms within the agreement cannot be severed from the agreement.

[C] Substantive Requirements Contained in Article 101(1) TFEU

The applicability of Article 101(1) TFEU will be based on a number of factors:[126]

(1) the existence of an agreement between at least two undertakings or a similar arrangement such as a decision by an association of undertakings or a concerted practice between undertakings;
(2) that agreement or arrangement must be capable of affecting trade between Member States; and
(3) the agreement or arrangement must have as its object or effect the prevention, restriction or distortion of competition to an appreciable extent within the internal market.

In other words, this article will depend on the fulfilment of the following requirements:[127]

First, the existence of undertakings or an association of undertakings;

123. Article 101(3) Guidelines: para. 13.
124. Article 1(1), Regulation 1/2003.
125. Case 56/65 *Société Technique Minière (L.T.M.) v. Maschinenbau Ulm GmbH* (M.B.U.) [1966] ECR 235 [1966] CMLR 357. For further review, Jones and Sufrin 2011: Chapter 15.
126. Case T-41/96 *Bayer AG v. Commission of the European Communities* ECR II-3387, para. 4.
127. Jones and Sufrin 2011: 121.

Second, the existence of *collusion* by virtue of an agreement between these undertakings, a decision by an association of undertakings or a concerted practice;
Third, this collusion must have as its *object or effect* the prevention, restriction or distortion of competition;
Fourth, this collusion must have an *appreciable effect on competition*; and
Finally, an *appreciable effect on trade* between the Member States.

The following section of the chapter will examine the various components of Article 101 TFEU.

[1] Agreement, Decision or Concerted Practice Exists[128]

Article 101 TFEU applies to agreements and concerted practices between undertakings as well as to decisions by associations of undertakings.

The impact of the conduct of an undertaking on competition within the internal market can only be examined if it is *first established* that an agreement, a decision of an association of undertakings or a concerted practice within the meaning of Article 101(1) TFEU exists.[129]

The goal of Article 101(1) TFEU is not 'to "eliminate" obstacles to intra-Community trade altogether; it is more limited, since only obstacles to competition set up as a result of a concurrence of wills between at least two parties are prohibited'.[130]

This article effectively targets *cooperation* between undertakings which prevent, hinder or distort competition between Member States.[131]

The jurisprudence of the European Courts has defined the terms 'agreements', 'decisions' and 'concerted practices' as concepts, which allow for a distinction to be made between unilateral conduct of an undertaking (which is subject only to Article 102) and coordination of behaviour or collusion between undertakings.[132]

The kind of coordination of behaviour or collusion between undertakings that falls within the scope of Article 101(1) is that 'where at least one undertaking vis-à-vis another undertaking undertakes to adopt a certain conduct on the market or that as a result of contacts between them uncertainty as to their conduct on the market is eliminated or at least substantially reduced'.[133]

128. For a review of the meaning of an agreement, decision, and concerted practice, *see* Jones and Sufrin 2011: 141-170.
129. Case T-41/96 *Bayer AG v. Commission of the European Communities* ECR II-3387, para. 4.
130. Case T-41/96 *Bayer AG v. Commission of the European Communities* ECR II-3387, para. 4.
131. Whish et al. 2012: 99.
132. Article 101(3) Guidelines: para. 14.
133. Article 101(3) Guidelines: para. 15 citing *inter alia. See* Joined Cases T-25/95 and others, *Cimenteries CBR* [2000] ECR II-491, paras 1849 and 1852; and Joined Cases T-202/98 and others, *British Sugar* [2001] ECR II-2035, paras 58-60.

- The term 'agreement'

Agreement in Article 101(1) TFEU has been broadly defined encompassing binding and non-binding agreements, such as 'gentlemen's agreements' and circulars.[134] The scope of this article is not confined merely to binding legal agreements as this would effectively 'make the evasion of the law simple'.[135]

Agreements will fall under the scope of Article 101(1) TFEU irrespective of their enforceability under national law.[136] In other words, an agreement will fall within the scope of Article 101(1) TFEU without regard to whether or not the agreement concerned is an enforceable contract in accordance with national law.[137]

Agreements will also fall under the scope of Article 101(1) TFEU irrespective of their form.[138] Since this article makes no reference to formalities, it encapsulates agreements that are verbal as well as those that are written.[139]

It is also irrelevant in this context whether a sanction is imposed for failing to abide by the terms of the agreement.[140]

Whilst a decision taken by an undertaking which constitutes unilateral conduct on the part of the undertaking would escape the prohibition in Article 101(1) TFEU,[141] conduct adopted by the said undertaking in the context of its commercial relations with its partners could form the basis for an agreement between the undertakings when 'the acquiescence of those partners, express or implied, with the attitude adopted by the undertaking is established'.[142]

For an agreement to exist, it is enough for the undertakings involved to 'have expressed their joint intention to conduct themselves on the market in a specific way'.[143]

In the case of *Bayer AG v. Commission*, the General Court stated that the existence of an agreement depends on 'the direct or indirect finding of the existence of the subjective element that characterises the very concept of an agreement, that is to say a concurrence of wills between economic operators on the implementation of a policy, the pursuit of an objective, or the adoption of a given line of conduct on the market,

134. Joined cases 32/78, 36/78 to 82/78 *BMW Belgium SA and others v. Commission of the European Communities* ECLI:EU:C:1979:191.
135. Whish et al. 2012: 99.
136. Jones and Sufrin 2011: 109-10.
137. Case T-41/96 *Bayer AG v. Commission of the European Communities* ECR II-3387, para. 68, citing Sandoz, para. 13.
138. Jones and Sufrin 2011: 109-10.
139. Jones and Sufrin 2011: 109-10.
140. Jones and Sufrin 2011: 109-10.
141. Case T-41/96 *Bayer AG v. Commission of the European Communities* ECR II-3387 (summary of the judgement), para. 1.
142. Case T-41/96 *Bayer AG v. Commission of the European Communities* ECR II-3387 (summary of the judgement), para. 1.
143. Case T-41/96 *Bayer AG v. Commission of the European Communities* ECR II-3387, para. 67, citing Case 41/69 *ACF Chemiefarma v. Commission* [1970] ECR 661, para. 112; Joined Cases 209/78 to 215/78 and 218/78 *Van Landewyck and Others v. Commission* [1980] ECR 3125, para. 86; Case T-7/89 *Hercules Chemicals v. Commission* [1991] ECR II-1711, para. 256.

irrespective of the manner in which the parties' intention to behave on the market in accordance with the terms of that agreement is expressed'.[144]

By way of an illustration:

- Wholesalers that continue their commercial relationship with a producer when the producer adopts a new policy which it implements unilaterally will not be acquiescing in that policy when their de facto conduct is clearly at odds with the producer's policy.[145]
- A producer that adopts a supply policy, such as a partial or complete refusal of deliveries, intended to address an event that undermines its competitive position on the market is permitted to do so even if this conduct is intended to hinder parallel imports if the said producer complies with Articles 101 and 102 TFEU.[146] In other words, the producer in question has the right to adopt a solution on condition that the assertion of this right by the producer does not amount to abuse of its dominant position and there is no concurrence of wills between the producer and its wholesalers.[147]

  The existence of an agreement depends on 'the existence of a concurrence of wills between at least two parties'[148] the form of such an agreement is irrelevant on the proviso that 'it constitutes the faithful expression of the parties' intention'.[149]

  The types of arrangements deemed to be agreements include:

  - legal contracts;
  - gentlemen's agreements;[150]
  - simple understandings;[151]
  - protocols;[152]
  - an agreement which notwithstanding the fact that it has expired is still effective;[153]
  - constitution of a trade association;[154]
  - the formation agreement associated with the establishment of an EEIG or its byelaws;[155]
  - guidance issued by one party and followed by another;[156]

144. Case T-41/96 *Bayer AG v. Commission of the European Communities* ECR II-3387 (summary of the judgement), para. 3.
145. Case T-41/96 *Bayer AG v. Commission of the European Communities* ECR II-3387 (summary of the judgement), para. 3.
146. Case T-41/96 *Bayer AG v. Commission of the European Communities* ECR II-3387 (summary of the judgement), para. 4.
147. Case T-41/96 *Bayer AG v. Commission of the European Communities* ECR II-3387 (summary of the judgement), para. 4.
148. Case T-41/96 *Bayer AG v. Commission of the European Communities* ECR II-3387, para. 69.
149. Case T-41/96 *Bayer AG v. Commission of the European Communities* ECR II-3387, para. 69.
150. Whish et al. 2012: 100 footnote 161.
151. Whish et al. 2012: 100 footnote 162.
152. Whish et al. 2012: 100 footnote 164.
153. Whish et al. 2012: 100 footnote 168.
154. Whish et al. 2012: 100 footnote 169.
155. Whish et al. 2012: 100 footnote 171.
156. Whish et al. 2012: 101 footnote 173.

- correspondence exchanged between parties;[157]
- a partial agreement addressing certain but not all matters;[158]
- an agreement that is verbal.[159]

- Gentlemen's agreement

Where the parties to an agreement mutually declare themselves willing to abide by the gentlemen's agreement, this agreement is taken to amount to a faithful expression of the joint intention of the parties to the agreement with regard to their conduct on the common market.[160] Such a gentlemen's agreement will fall within the scope of Article 101 TFEU where it contains provisions that restrict competition in the internal market.[161]

- Decision by an association of undertakings[162]

Decisions made by associations of undertakings fall within the scope of Article 101 TFEU alongside agreements and concerted practices between undertakings.[163]

Although such associations often perform functions that are legitimate and intended to aid members, membership of such associations may tempt members to collude and coordinate their activities.[164] With this in mind Article 101(1) TFEU accordingly targets such illegitimate collusion.[165]

Even though the association itself may not have an economic activity it may fall within the scope of Article 101(1) TFEU and as such its decisions will be caught by this article.[166]

The following may be viewed as decisions within the meaning of Article 101(1) TFEU:

- the constitution of the trade association;[167]
- the regulations governing the activities of the association;[168]
- an agreement entered it by the association;[169] and
- a recommendation issued by the association (it is immaterial whether the recommendation is non-binding).[170]

157. Whish et al. 2012: 101 footnote 175.
158. Whish et al. 2012: 101 footnote 176.
159. Whish et al. 2012: 100 footnote 166.
160. Case 41/69 *ACF Chemiefarma NV v. Commission*, para. 111-2.
161. Case 41/69 *ACF Chemiefarma NV v. Commission*, para. 9.
162. For a fuller review *see* Jones and Sufrin 2011: 140-1.
163. *See* judgement of Roth J, *SEL-Imperial Ltd v. The British Standards Institution* [2010] EWHC 854 (Ch), paras 36, 41. Case 48/69 *Imperial Chemical Industries Ltd v. Commission of the European Communities* [1972] ECR 619 (hereinafter *Dyestuffs* case), para. 64.
164. Jones and Sufrin 2011: 118.
165. Jones and Sufrin 2011: 118.
166. Cases T-25/95 etc *Cimenteries CBR SA v. Commission* [2000] ECR II-491, [2000] 5 CMLR 204, para. 1320.
167. Whish et al. 2012: 111 footnote 279.
168. Whish et al. 2012: 111 footnote 280.
169. Whish et al. 2012: 111.
170. Whish et al. 2012: 111 footnote 281.

- Concerted practice between undertakings

By including the concept of concerted practice, Article 101 TFEU encompasses conduct that is neither attributable to an agreement nor a decision.[171] The difficulties in this context are associated with defining the form of coordination and the level of coordination that infringe Article 101 TFEU.[172] The existence of parallel price increases alone, for example, is not conclusive evidence of concerted practice.[173]

The purpose of this concept is to catch undertakings that do not enter into an agreement instead choosing to set their market policy in coordination with rival undertakings.[174]

Falling short of an agreement, concerted practice between undertakings *knowingly* substitutes practical cooperation between the undertakings for the risks of competition.[175]

As the following case illustrates, concerted practice could 'arise out of coordination which becomes apparent from the behaviour of the participants'.[176]

Imperial Chemical Industries Ltd v. Commission[177]

In this case, over the period spanning January 1964 to October 1967, three general and uniform increases in the prices of dyestuffs took place within the Community.[178]

In January 1964, there was 'a uniform increase of 15 per cent in the prices of most dyes based on aniline, with the exception of certain categories ... in Italy, the Netherlands, Belgium and Luxembourg and in certain third countries'.[179] An identical price increase took place in Germany on 1st January 1965.[180]

On 1st January 1965, 'almost all producers in all the countries of the Common Market except France introduced a uniform increase of 10 per cent on the prices of dyes and pigments excluded from the increase of 1964'.[181]

Around mid-October 1967, 'an increase for all dyes was introduced, except in Italy, by almost all producers, amounting to 8% in Germany, the Netherlands, Belgium and Luxembourg, and 12% in France'.[182]

171. Whish et al. 2012: 112.
172. Whish et al. 2012: 112.
173. Joined cases C-89, 104, 114, 116, 117 and 125-129/85, *Ahlstrom Osakeyhito v. Commission.*
174. Jones and Sufrin 2011: 113.
175. *Dyestuffs* case, para. 64 (italics added by authors).
176. *Dyestuffs* case, para. 65.
177. *Dyestuffs* case.
178. *Dyestuffs* case, para. 1.
179. *Dyestuffs* case, para. 2.
180. *Dyestuffs* case, para. 3.
181. *Dyestuffs* case, para. 4.
182. *Dyestuffs* case, para. 6.

The Commission commenced proceedings on its own initiative by its decision of May 1967, in relation to these increases for presumed infringement of Article 101(1) TFEU (at the time Article 85(1) EEC Treaty) against seventeen dyestuffs producers established inside and outside the Common Market and against various subsidiaries and representatives of those undertakings.[183]

In this case, the ECJ (now the CJEU) stated

64. Article 85 draws a distinction between the concept of "concerted practices" and that of "agreements between undertakings" or of "decisions by associations of undertakings"; the object is to bring within the prohibition of that article a form of coordination between undertakings which, without having reached the stage where an agreement properly so-called has been concluded, knowingly substitutes practical cooperation between them for the risks of competition.

65. By its very nature, then, a concerted practice does not have all the elements of a contract but may *inter alia* arise out of coordination which becomes apparent from the behaviour of the participants.

Parallel conduct alone is not concerted practice. Having said that parallel conduct may amount to strong evidence of a concerted practice if it leads to conditions of competition *that do not correspond to the normal conditions of the market*.[184] This may be the case if for example the parallel conduct is such that it allows competitors to attempt to stabilise prices at a level that is different from that to which competition would have led.[185]

The test set out in the *Dyestuffs* case was clarified in the 1975 decision of the Court in the *Sugar Cartel* case,[186] where it held that the existence of an *actual plan* is not essential, since the criteria of coordination and cooperation are defined by reference to the existence of autonomy:

> The criteria of coordination and cooperation ... which in no way require the working out of an actual plan, must be understood in the light of the concept inherent in the provisions of the Treaty relating to competition that each economic operator must determine independently the policy which he intends to adopt on the common market including the choice of the persons and undertakings to which he makes offers or sells.[187]

The need for independence will not prevent an undertaking from *intelligently adapting itself* to its competitors' existing and anticipated conduct, though it does prevent *strategic contact between operators*:

183. *Dyestuffs* case, para. 7.
184. *Dyestuffs* case: para. 66.
185. *Dyestuffs* case: para. 67.
186. *Sugar Union* case.
187. *Sugar Union* case: para. 173.

> Although it is correct to say that this requirement of independence does not deprive economic operators of the right to adapt themselves intelligently to the existing and anticipated conduct of their competitors. It does however strictly preclude any direct or indirect contact between such operators, the object or effect whereof is either to influence the conduct on the market of any actual or potential competitor or to disclose to such a competitor the course of conduct which they themselves have decided to adopt or contemplate adopting on the market.[188]

Both cases (the *Dyestuffs* case and the *Sugar Cartel* case) define the legal test to be used in order to assess concerted practice in the context of Article 101(1) TFEU.

Concerted practice, suggest, Whish and Bailey, depends on the existence of 'mental consensus whereby practical cooperation is *knowingly* substituted for competition; however the consensus need not be achieved verbally, and can come about by direct or indirect contact between the parties'.[189]

According to the Commission's 2011 Guidelines on Horizontal Agreements,[190] an exchange of strategic information between competitors may amount to a concerted practice 'if it reduces strategic uncertainty in the market thereby facilitating collusion'.[191]

A unilateral disclosure of strategic information, using mail, email, phone calls, meetings etc. by one undertaking to one or more of its competitors who accept(s) it may also constitute a concerted practice.[192]

A unilateral public announcement by one undertaking, in a newspaper, for example, that is followed by public announcements by competitors of a *strategic nature* could amount to 'a strategy for reaching a common understanding about the terms of coordination'.[193]

[2] An Agreement, Decision or Concerted Practice Between Two or More Undertakings

- The term 'undertaking' (in Articles 101 and 102 TFEU)

The term 'undertaking' is central to Articles 101 and 102 TFEU. Article 101 encompasses agreements and concerted practices between undertakings[194] whilst Article 102 covers abuse by dominant undertakings.[195]

In the context of EU competition law the issue is 'whether the distortion of competition is the responsibility of an undertaking: if it is, the behaviour in question may infringe Articles 101 and/or 102, subject to the availability of various defences

188. *Sugar Union* case: para. 174.
189. Whish et al. 2012: 113.
190. 2011 Communication from the Commission, Guidelines on the applicability of Article 101 of the Treaty on the Functioning of the European Union to horizontal cooperation agreements (2011/C 11/01) (hereinafter 2011 Guidelines on horizontal agreements).
191. 2011 Guidelines on horizontal agreements: para. 61.
192. 2011 Guidelines on horizontal agreements: para. 62.
193. 2011 Guidelines on horizontal agreements: para. 63.
194. Whish et al. 2012: 83.
195. Whish et al. 2012: 83.

such as state compulsion or Article 106(2)'.[196] Where the conduct distorting competition is not that of an undertaking, the conduct in question will not be subject to scrutiny under European competition law.[197]

As this term is not defined in the Treaty, it has fallen to the European courts to shed light on the meaning of this term.[198] The same meaning is given to the term 'undertaking' for the purposes of Articles 101 and 102 TFEU.[199]

A wide interpretation of this term has been adopted by the CJEU[200] embracing trade associations, agricultural cooperatives[201] and bodies set up by statute,[202] as well as natural persons.

– Presence of economic activity

The concept of an undertaking in the context of European competition law 'covers any entity that is engaged in an economic activity regardless of the legal status of the entity and the way in which it is financed'.[203]

The focus for the determination of whether an entity is an undertaking or not will depend on whether the entity engages in an economic activity,[204] which in this context is treated as encompassing 'any activity consisting of offering goods and services on a given market'.[205]

Even a public employment agency may be regarded as an undertaking as the fact that employment procurement activities are ordinarily entrusted to public agencies does not affect the economic nature of the activities it performs.[206]

Members of the Bar engaged in the provision of legal assistance for a fee who bear the financial risks associated with the performance of these activities are involved in the carrying on of an economic activity and are therefore undertakings for the purposes of Articles 101 and 102 TFEU.[207]

---

196. Whish et al. 2012: 84.
197. Whish et al. 2012: 84.
198. Whish et al. 2012: 83.
199. Cases T-68, 77 and 78/89 *Societa Vetro v. Commission* [1992] ECR II-1403, para. 358 ('The Court considers that there is no legal or economic reason to suppose that the term 'undertaking' in Article 86 has a different meaning from the one given to it in the context of Article 85.').
200. For a full review of the term undertaking, *see* Jones and Sufrin 2011: 124-140.
201. Case C-250/92 *Gøttrup-Klim e.a. Grovvareforeninger v. Dansk Landbrugs Grovvareselskab AmbA* ECLI:EU:C:1994:413.
202. Case 123/83 *Bureau national interprofessionnel du cognac v. Guy Clair* ECLI:EU:C:1985:33.
203. Case C-41/90 *Höfner and Elser v. Macrotron GmbH* [1991] ECR I-1979, [1993] 4 CMLR 306 (hereinafter *Macrotron* case) para. 21.
204. '... the concept of an undertaking covers any entity engaged in an economic activity, regardless of its legal status and the way in which it is financed.' (Case C-309/99 *Wouters, Savelbergh and Price Waterhouse Belastingadviseurs BV v. Algemene Raad van de Nederlandsche Orde van Advocaten* [2002] ECR I-I 1577, [2002] 4 CMLR 913 (hereinafter *Price Waterhouse* case), para. 46 citing *Macrotron* case: para. 21; Case C-244/94 *Fédération Française des sociétés d'assurances and Others* [1995] ECR I-4013, para. 14, and Case C-55/96 *Job Centre* [1997] ECR I-711, para. 21).
205. *Price Waterhouse* case: para. 47 citing Case 118/85 *Commission v. Italy* [1987] ECR 2599, para. 7; Case C-35/96 *Commission v. Italy* [1998] ECR I-3851, para. 36.
206. *Macrotron* case: para. 22.
207. *Price Waterhouse* case: para. 48-9.

Self-employed economic operators delivering services on a market (such as the market in specialist medical services) who are paid by their patients for these services whilst assuming the financial risks associated with the pursuit of their activities were held to be carrying on economic activity and were thus regarded as undertakings within the meaning of Articles 101 and 102 TFEU.[208]

In this context, it is irrelevant that the professional organisation is governed by public law statute, since Article 101 TFEU applies to agreements between undertakings and decisions by associations of undertakings regardless of the legal framework within which such decisions are taken and such agreements are made and the classification given in national law to the framework.[209]

Having said that, the CJEU has held that the rules on competition law do not apply to activity which, by its nature, its aim and the rules to which it is subject does not belong to the sphere of economic activity or which is connected with the exercise of the powers of a public authority.[210]

- Functional approach

It is possible for the same legal entity to be acting as an undertaking when it performs one activity but not when it performs another.[211] Accordingly, in order to determine the capacity in which the entity is operating a 'functional approach' should be adopted.[212,213]

As we saw earlier, the term 'undertaking' encompasses any entity that is involved in an economic activity.[214] In the *Höfner and Elser* case, the CJEU stated that the public employment agency may be regarded as an undertaking, as the fact that employment procurement activities are ordinarily entrusted to public agencies does not affect the economic nature of the activities it performs.[215] In *Pavlov*, the offering of services on

208. Case C-180/98 *Pavlov* [2000] ECR I-6451, [2001] 4 CMLR 30 (hereinafter *Pavlov* case), para. 75-6.
209. *Pavlov* case: para. 3; *Price Waterhouse* case: para. 66.
210. *Price Waterhouse* case: para. 57, citing Joined Cases C-159/91, C-160/91 *Poucet and Pistre* [1993] ECR I-637, paras 18 and 19 (concerning the management of the public social security system), Case C-364/92 *Sat Fluggesellschaft* [1994] ECR I-43, para. 30 (concerning the control and supervision of air space) and Case C-343/95 *Diego Cali oc Figli* [1997] ECR I-1547, paras 22 and 23 (concerning anti-pollution surveillance of the maritime environment).
211. Whish et al. 2012: 84.
212. Whish et al. 2012: 84.
213. By way of illustration *see* Commission Decision of 15 June 2001 relating to a proceeding under Article 81 of the EC Treaty and Article 53 of the EEA Agreement (COMP/34.950 – Eco-Emballages) OJ [2001] L233/37, [2001] 5 CMLR 1096, para. 70, and Case T-155/04 SELEX Sistemi Integrati SpA v. Commission of the European Communites ECLI:EU:T:2006:387, para. 54 ('since the Treaty provisions on competition are applicable to the activities of an entity which can be severed from those in which it engages as a public authority (Case 107/84 *Commission v. Germany* [1985] ECR 2655, paragraphs 14 and 15, and Case T-128/98 *Aéroports de Paris v. Commission* [2000] ECR II-3929, paragraph 108), the various activities of an entity must be considered individually and the treatment of some of them as powers of a public authority does not mean that it must be concluded that the other activities are not economic (*see*, to that effect, *Aéroports de Paris v. Commission*, paragraph 109).').
214. *Macrotron* case: para. 21; Case C-218/00 *Cisal di Battistello Venanzio & C. Sas v. Istituto nazionale per l'assicurazione contro gli infortuni sul lavoro* (INAIL), para. 22.
215. *Macrotron* case: para. 22.

the market in specialist medical services was viewed as the carrying on of an economic activity.[216]

The manner in which an entity is financed[217] and its legal status are immaterial when its status is determined; as such natural as well as legal persons are capable of being regarded as undertakings.[218] The rationale for this stance being that 'no advantage should be derived from the legal form in which an economic activity is exercised'.[219]

– Public powers

The rules on competition do not extend to activity 'which, by its nature, its aim and the rules to which it is subject does not belong to the sphere of economic activity[220]...or which is connected with the exercise of the powers of a public authority'.[221,222]

Where the State is involved, therefore, a distinction is made between cases involving the State acting in the exercise of official authority and cases involving the State carrying out economic activities.[223]

It is immaterial if the State is acting directly through a body forming part of the State administration or through a body on which the State has conferred special or exclusive rights, as the economic activities need not be executed by the public body itself.[224]

An entity is deemed to be acting in the exercise of its powers as a *public authority* when the activity 'is a task in the public interest which forms part of the essential functions of the State'.[225]

Anti-pollution surveillance in the port of Genoa entrusted to a private entity by port authorities[226] was held by the CJEU to be a task of public interest forming part of the essential functions of the States as regards the protection of the environment in

216. *Pavlov* case: paras 76-7.
217. Opinion of AG Jacobs delivered on 23 March 2000 in Cases C-180/98 to C-184/98, para. 107 citing *Macrotron* case: para. 21.
218. Opinion of AG Jacobs delivered on 23 March 2000 in Cases C-180/98 to C-184/98, para. 107 citing Case C-35/96 *Commission v. Italy*, paras 36-8.
219. Opinion of AG Jacobs delivered on 23 March 2000 in Cases C-180/98 to C-184/98, para. 107.
220. *Price Waterhouse* case: para. 57, citing C-159/91 and C-160/91 *Poucet and Pistre* [1993] ECR I-637, paras 18-9.
221. *Price Waterhouse* case: para. 57, citing C-364/92 *Sat Fluggesellschaft* [1994] ECRI-43, para. 30, and Case C-343/95 *Diego Cali & Figli* [1997] ECR I-1547 (Case C-343/95 Cali e Figli), para. 22-3.
222. Illustrations of this distinction can be found in the CJ decisions in Case 30/87 *Corrine Bodson v. Pompes Funèbres des Régions Libérées SA* [1988] ECR 2479, [1989] 4 CMLR 984, para. 18 and Case C-364/92 *SAT Fluggesellschaft v. Eurocontrol* [1994] ECR I-43, [1994] 5 CMLR 208, para. 30.
223. Case C-343/95 *Cali e Figli*, para. 16, citing Case 118/85 *Commission v. Italy* [1987] ECR 2599, para. 7.
224. Case C-343/95 *Cali e Figli*, para. 17, citing Case 118/85 *Commission v. Ital,* [1987] ECR 2599, para. 8.
225. Case C-343/95 *Cali e Figli*, para. 22.
226. At the material time, the port of Genoa was managed by the Consorzio Autonomo del Porto ('CAP'), a public body entrusted by legislation with administrative and economic functions relating to the management of the port (Case C-343/95 *Cali e Figli*, para. 3). By means of a Decree issued in August 1991, the President of CAP entrusted functions to SEPG (Case C-343/95 *Cali e Figli*, para. 7).

maritime areas. The Court in this case added that this type of surveillance 'is connected by its nature, its aim and the rules to which it is subject with the exercise of powers relating to the protection of the environment which are typically those of a public authority'.[227]

A professional body (such as the Bar of the Netherlands) created by the legislature (in this case the Netherlands legislature) as a body governed by public law and endowed with regulatory powers in order to perform a task in the public interest, which adopts a regulation 'is neither fulfilling a social function based on the principle of solidarity, unlike certain social security bodies,[228] nor exercising powers which are typically those of a public authority.[229] It acts as the regulatory body of a profession, the practice of which constitutes an economic activity'.[230] The fact that such a body is entrusted with the task of protecting the rights and interests of its members will not a priori exclude it from the scope of Article 101 TFEU even when it is performing its role as regulator.[231] Other elements that lend support to this conclusion include the fact that the governing bodies of the Bar of the Netherlands comprise 'exclusively of members of the Bar elected solely by members of the profession'[232] and the fact that when adopting measures, the Bar is not obliged to refer to specific public-interest criteria.[233]

The CJEU has highlighted the importance of context in making a determination on the nature of a given activity indicating that 'classification as an activity falling within the exercise of public powers or as an economic activity must be carried out separately for each activity exercised by a given entity'.[234]

An activity is an economic activity when it consists in offering goods or services on a given market; provided that this condition is fulfilled, the fact that the activity has a connection with a public function will not prevent the application of EU competition law.[235]

One entity is capable of performing both categories of activity (public and economic). In this context, an entity is capable of undertaking activities that fall within the exercise of public powers which are not of an economic nature justifying the application of European competition law (such as administrative decision-making)[236] as well as economic activities which fall within the scope of European competition law (such as the organisation of sporting events and the negotiation and conclusion of sponsorship, advertising and insurance contracts).[237]

227. Case C-343/95 *Cali e Figli* [1997] ECR I-1547, [1997] 5 CMLR 484, para. 23.
228. *Price Waterhouse* case: para. 58 citing C-159/91 and C-160/91 *Poucet and Pistre* [1993] ECR I-637, para. 18.
229. *Price Waterhouse* case: para. 58 citing *Sat Fluggesellshaft* [1994] ECRI-43, para. 30.
230. *Price Waterhouse* case: para. 58.
231. *Price Waterhouse* case: para. 59.
232. *Price Waterhouse* case: para. 61.
233. *Price Waterhouse* case: para. 62.
234. Case -49/07 *Motosykletistiki Omospondia Ellados NPID* (hereinafter *MOTOE* case) *v. Elliniko Dimosio* [2008] ECR I-4863, [2008] 5 CMLR 790, para. 25.
235. *MOTOE* case: para. 22 citing Case 36/74 *Walrave and Kock* [1974] ECR 1405, para. 4, and Case C-415/93 *Bosman* [1995] ECR I-4921, para. 73.
236. *MOTOE* case, para. 24.
237. *MOTOE* case, para. 19.

Elaborating on this point, Advocate General Juliane Kokott stated that 'aside from its considerable social importance, sport nowadays has a not insignificant economic dimension. Consequently, when it comes to the application of the competition rules, each individual activity that exhibits a connection with sport must on each occasion be examined to ascertain whether it is economic in nature or not'.[238] In this context it is immaterial whether the sportspersons taking part in the event 'practise the sport professionally or merely as amateurs, that is to say whether they are economically active or not'.[239] Where payments are made by those taking part in the event or those viewing the event, the organisation of such events is an economic activity.[240] Where agreements are concluded in relation to the marketing of the event there is also an economic activity.[241] It is immaterial in this context whether the entity is a non-profit-making association operating without seeking to make a profit, since this fact does preclude the assumption that its pursues an economic activity.[242]

An entity cannot be labelled an undertaking when it 'confines itself to an exclusively *social or public-interest activity* which is not pursued on the market in competition with other economic agents'.[243]

An entity that starts marketing its services will transition away from the sphere of exclusively social or public-interest activity; in such circumstances 'the mere fact that it continues at the same time to pursue an aim in the general interest … and does not seek to make a profit is no longer sufficient for it to be denied the status of undertaking within the meaning of competition law'.[244]

- Activities that are not economic in nature[245]

A distinction is drawn between the provision of social protection in a market context and the provision of such services on the basis of solidarity. Oftentimes the classification in this context is one of degree.[246] Solidarity is treated as meaning 'the inherently uncommercial act of involuntary subsidisation of one social group by another'.[247]

- Activities that are ancillary to a non-economic activity[248]

Procurement activity ancillary to a non-economic activity is also capable of being treated as a non-economic activity (as the following case illustrates) which will

238. AG Kokott's opinion in *MOTOE* case, para. 38.
239. AG Kokott's opinion in *MOTOE* case, para. 39.
240. AG Kokott's opinion in *MOTOE* case, para. 40.
241. AG Kokott's opinion in *MOTOE* case, para. 40.
242. AG Kokott's opinion in *MOTOE* case, para. 41.
243. AG Kokott's opinion in *MOTOE* case, para. 43 citing Case C-222/04 *Cassa di Risparmio di Firenze* [2006] ECR I-289, paras 120-1. Italics used by AG Kokott.
244. AG Kokott's opinion in *MOTOE* case, para. 44.
245. For further detail *see* Whish et al. 2012: 87.
246. Opinion of AG Jacob in Case C-264/01 etc *AOK Bundesverband* [2004] ECR I-2493, [2004] 4 CMLR 1261.
247. Opinion of AG Fennelly in *Sodemare v. Regione Lombardia* [1997] ECR I-3395, [1997] 3 CMLR 591, para. 29.
248. For further detail, *see* Whish et al. 2012: 89-90.

effectively mean that when an entity is engaged in the act of procuring it will not be deemed to be an undertaking under EU competition law.[249]

A complaint was submitted to the Commission by an association whose members are undertakings marketing goods and equipment used in Spanish hospitals, alleging that twenty-six bodies or organisations (including three ministries of the Spanish government) responsible for the administration of the Spanish national health service were guilty of an abuse of a dominant position under Article 102 TFEU, due to the comparatively long delays associated with payment of the invoices submitted by the members of the complainant association.[250] The accusation made was that the twenty-six entities concerned took an average of 300 days to pay debts to the members of the complainant when these same entities settled their debts to other suppliers within a far more reasonable period of time.[251]

This complaint was rejected by the Commission on two grounds.[252] First the Commission contended that the '26 ministries and other organisations in question [were] not acting as undertakings when they [participated] in the management of the public health service'.[253] Second the Commission indicated that 'the "demand" of the 26 ministries and other organisations [could not] be dissociated from the subsequent "supply" which they provide'.[254]

The General Court in this case stated that where the procurement of goods is associated with the provision of health care to the public, the ancillary act of procurement for a non-economic end (here the provision of health care) is not economic either:[255]

> 36. ...Thus, as the Commission has argued, it would be incorrect, when determining the nature of that subsequent activity, to dissociate the activity of purchasing goods from the subsequent use to which they are put. The nature of the purchasing activity must therefore be determined according to whether or not the subsequent use of the purchased goods amounts to an economic activity.
>
> 37. Consequently, an organisation which purchases goods — even in great quantity — not for the purpose of offering goods and services as part of an economic activity, but in order to use them in the context of a different activity, such as one of a purely social nature, does not act as an undertaking simply because it is a purchaser in a given market. Whilst an entity may wield very considerable economic power, even giving rise to a monopsony (sic monopoly), it nevertheless remains the case that, if the activity for which that entity purchases goods is not an economic activity, it is not acting as an undertaking for the

249. General Court judgement in Case T-319/99 *Federación Nacional de Empresas de Instrumentación Científica, Médica, Técnica y Dental (FENNIN) v. Commission* [2003] ECR II-357, [2003] 5 CMLR 34, paras 36 & 37 (hereinafter *FENNIN* case) upheld by the ECJ in Case C-205/03 P [2006] ECR I-6295, [2006] 5 CMLR 559, paras 25 & 26.
250. *FENNIN* case: para. 1.
251. *FENNIN* case: para. 1.
252. *FENNIN* case: para. 3.
253. *FENNIN* case: para. 3 (square brackets used in the judgement of the General Court).
254. *FENNIN* case: para. 3 (square brackets used in the judgement of the General Court).
255. *FENNIN* case: paras 36-7 upheld by the ECJ (now CJEU) in Case C-205/03 P [2006] ECR I-6295, [2006] 5 CMLR 559, paras 25 & 26.

purposes of Community competition law and is therefore not subject to the prohibitions laid down in Articles 81(1) EC and 82 EC.

- The status of individuals

Though a natural person may qualify as an undertaking, an individual who is acting as an employee or consumer would not qualify as an undertaking in view of the fact that the activities of the individual are unlikely to be deemed to be economic in character.[256]

- Individuals as consumers

Notwithstanding the classification of an individual as an undertaking, AG Francis Jacobs draws a distinction between an individual's activities related to the economic sphere and those activities related to their personal sphere.[257] Unlike legal persons 'who do not have a "private life," natural persons may act in their capacity as undertakings or in their capacity as final consumers'.[258]

Where a natural person acts as a final consumer he will be sheltered from EU competition law. A professional who arranges a holiday,[259] buys tickets to the opera[260] or sets up a supplementary pension scheme for himself[261] will accordingly fall outside the scope of EU competition law.

In contrast, when a professional engages in activities that closely relate to the practice of his profession, in other words to his professional activity, he will fall within the scope of EU competition law. A doctor buying medical equipment,[262] a lawyer renting premises[263] or a professional making contributions to a supplementary occupational pension scheme will qualify as an undertaking under EU competition law.[264]

The making of contributions to a supplementary occupational pension scheme by self-employed medical specialists, in circumstances where membership of the scheme stems from the practice of their profession, was considered to be an activity 'closely linked to the practice of their profession'.[265] In such circumstances the medical specialists were not deemed to be acting as end users and final consumers but instead as undertakings within the meaning of Articles 101 and 102 TFEU.[266]

256. Whish et al. 2012: 86 citing *Pavlov* case: paras 78-81.
257. Opinion of AG Jacobs delivered on 23 March 2000 in Cases C-180/98 to C-184/98, para. 115.
258. Opinion of AG Jacobs delivered on 23 March 2000 in Cases C-180/98 to C-184/98, para. 115.
259. Opinion of AG Jacobs delivered on 23 March 2000 in Cases C-180/98 to C-184/98, para. 115. Examples given by AG Jacobs.
260. Opinion of AG Jacobs delivered on 23 March 2000 in Cases C-180/98 to C-184/98, para. 115. Examples given by AG Jacobs.
261. *Pavlov* case: para. 78.
262. Opinion of AG Jacobs delivered on 23 March 2000 in Cases C-180/98 to C-184/98, para. 115. Examples given by AG Jacobs.
263. Opinion of AG Jacobs delivered on 23 March 2000 in Cases C-180/98 to C-184/98, para. 115. Examples given by AG Jacobs.
264. *Pavlov* case: para. 79.
265. *Pavlov* case: para. 79.
266. *Pavlov* case: para. 78-9, 81-2.

– Individuals as employees

Employees offering work for remuneration will in principle fall outside the scope of Article 101 TFEU. The category of employees excluded from the scope of Article 101 will not however include employed professionals, since 'their "pay" is directly linked to the profits and losses of their employer and they do not really work "under the direction" of that employer'.[267]

An employee acting in the course of his or her employment is regarded during the term of employment as being part of the undertaking that employs them.[268] Accordingly such an employee is not treated as constituting either individually or collectively an independent undertaking distinct from their employer for the purpose of EU competition law.[269]

Notwithstanding this fact, the position of the employee will change once the person is no longer employed; in circumstances where the employee concerned carries on an independent activity.[270]

– Regulation is immaterial

Regulation is irrelevant when assessing whether an entity is an undertaking.[271] The fact that the exercise of a profession is regulated will have no impact upon the classification of the profession for the purposes of EU competition law.[272273]

Customs agents for example were classified as undertakings.[274] Such agents were held to qualify as undertakings since their activity has 'an economic character, since they offered for remuneration services consisting in the carrying out of customs clearance formalities (including complementary services in monetary, commercial and fiscal matters), and since they assumed the financial risk involved in the exercise of their profession. The fact that the activity in issue was intellectual, required authorisation and could be pursued in the absence of a substantial organisational framework could not exclude it from the scope of Article 85 of the Treaty [now Article 101 TFEU]'.[275]

Entities entrusted by the State with an exclusively social role that are entirely non-profit-making are not generally regarded as undertakings in this context.[276]

267. Opinion of AG Jacobs delivered on 23 March 2000 in Cases C-180/98 to C-184/98, para. 112.
268. Whish et al. 2012: 90.
269. Whish et al. 2012: 90 citing Case C-22/98 *Jean Claude Becu* [1999] ECR I-5665, [2001] 4 CMLR 968, paras 26-7.
270. Whish et al. 2012: 90 citing *Reuter/BASF* OJ [1976] L254/40, [1979] 2 CMLR D44.
271. Opinion of AG Jacobs delivered on 23 March 2000 in Cases C-180/98 to C-184/98, para. 111.
272. Opinion of AG Jacobs delivered on 23 March 2000 in Cases C-180/98 to C-184/98, para. 111.
273. *Pavlov* case: para. 77.
274. Opinion of AG Jacobs delivered on 23 March 2000 in Cases C-180/98 to C-184/98, para. 108 citing Case C-35/96 *Commission v. Italy*.
275. Opinion of AG Jacobs delivered on 23 March 2000 in Cases C-180/98 to C-184/98, para. 108 citing Case C-35/96 *Commission v. Italy*.
276. C-159/91 & C-160/91 *Poucet & Pistre*, paras 18 & 19.

- Offer of goods or services[277]

According to the European Courts an economic activity is one that involves the offering of goods or services on a given market.[278]

The Commission argued that the Spanish Post Office was acting as an undertaking when it engaged in the provision of services on a given market.[279]

The same approach was adopted in the *Höfner and Elser* case,[280] in relation to the German Federal Employment Office and in the *Ambulanz Glöckner* case[281] in relation to medical aid organisations. In the latter case, it was held that since the medical aid organisations provide services in exchange for remuneration from users, the provision of such services in turn constitutes an economic activity and the medical aid organisations are regarded as undertakings.[282]

Though public service obligations may have the effect of rendering the services furnished by the medical aid organisation less competitive when compared with services rendered by other operators that are not subject to the same obligations, this fact alone will not prevent the activities concerned from being viewed as economic activities.[283]

- Lack of a profit motive or an economic purpose[284]

Lack of a profit motive or an economic purpose per se will not mean that an activity is not economic. This is the view adopted by the Commission[285] and the General Court.[286]

An economic activity will encompass 'any activity, whether or not profit-making, that involves economic trade'.[287]

Football clubs in national groupings for which the practice of football is an economic activity are regarded as undertakings and the national associations that group together these football clubs are regarded as associations of undertakings within the meaning of Article 101 TFEU.[288] It is immaterial in this context whether the national associations group together amateur and professional clubs.[289] The 'mere fact that a

277. *See* for further detail Whish et al. 2012: 85-6.
278. *Price Waterhouse* case: para. 47 citing Case 118/85 *Commission v. Italy* [1987] ECR 2599, para. 7; Case C-35/96 *Commission v. Italy* [1998] ECR I-3851, para. 36.
279. *Spanish Courier Services* OJ [1991] L 233/19, [1991] 4 CMLR 560.
280. *Macrotoron* case.
281. Case C-475/99 *Ambulanz Glöckner v. Landkreis Südwestpfalz (joined parties Arbeiter-Samariter-Bund Landesverband Rheinland-Pfalz eV, Deutsches Rotes Kreuz Landesverband Rheinland-Pfalz eV, and Vertreter des öffentlichen Interesses, Mainz)*.
282. Case C-475/99 *Ambulanz Glöckner v. Landkreis Südwestpfalz*, para. 20.
283. Case C-475/99 *Ambulanz Glöckner v. Landkreis Südwestpfalz*, para. 21.
284. *See* for further detail Whish et al. 2012: 86.
285. *Distribution of Package Tours During the 1990 World Cup* OJ [1992] L326/31, [1994] 5 CMLR 253, para. 43.
286. Case T-193/02 *Piau* [2005] ECR I-209, [2005] 5 CMLR 42, and Case C-519/04 *P Meca-Medina v. Commission* [2006] ECR I-6991 [2006] 5 CMLR 1023.
287. *Distribution of Package Tours During the 1990 World Cup* OJ [1992] L326/31, [1994] 5 CMLR 253, para. 43.
288. Case T-193/02 *Piau* [2005] ECR I-209, [2005] 5 CMLR 42, para. 69.
289. Case T-193/02 *Piau* [2005] ECR I-209, [2005] 5 CMLR 42, para. 70.

sports association or federation unilaterally classifies sportsmen or clubs as "amateur" does not in itself mean that they do not engage in economic activities'.[290]

- Single economic entity[291]

Where two or more legal persons form a single economic unit, collectively they are treated as being part of the same undertaking, as such any agreements reached between these parties are not treated as being agreements made between undertakings.[292]

This will be the case where the agreement is the one reached between a parent and its subsidiary or one concluded between entities in the same corporate group so long as these 'consist of a unitary organisation of personal, tangible and intangible elements, which pursue a specific economic aim on a long-term basis'.[293]

Though companies belonging to the same group and having the status of parent and subsidiary may have distinct legal personalities, if the undertakings form a single economic unit within which the subsidiary enjoys no real autonomy to decide on its course of action in the market and is instead expected to carry out instructions issued to it by the parent company that controls it, they will be treated for purpose of Article 101 TFEU as a single economic unit and as such there will be deemed to be no agreement between undertakings within the wording of Article 101(1) TFEU.[294]

This principle introduced in the 1971 decision in the case of *Béguelin Import v. GL Import Export*,[295] can be seen in *Viho v. Commission*. The approach adopted in *Viho v. Commission* was endorsed more recently in the Commission's 2011 Guidelines on the applicability of Article 101 TFEU to horizontal cooperation agreements (OJ [2011] C11/1).

In these Guidelines, the Commission stated that in the event that 'a company exercises decisive influence over another company they form a single economic entity and, hence, are part of the same undertaking' adding that this is the case for 'sister companies, that is to say, companies over which decisive influence is exercised by the same parent company'.[296]

In this context, determination centres on the influence exercised by one entity over the other. In other words, by whether the parties to the agreement are autonomous in their decision-making or whether one can or does exercise decisive influence over the other.[297] A variety of factors are borne in mind in this context including the shareholding held by the parent in the subsidiary, the composition of the board of

290. Case T-193/02 *Piau* [2005] ECR I-209, [2005] 5 CMLR 42, para. 70.
291. The question of what constitutes a single economic entity is discussed in detail in Jones and Sufrin 2011:134-9 and Whish et al. 2012: 92-9.
292. Whish et al. 2012: 92.
293. Case T-112/05 *Akzo Nobel NV v. Commission* [2007] ECR II-5049, [2008] 4 CMLR 321, paras 57 & 58.
294. Case C-73/95 *Viho Europe BV v. Commission*, para. 16.
295. Case 22/71 *Béguelin Import v. GL Import Export* [1971] ECR 949, [1972] CMLR 81.
296. Commission's 2011 Guidelines on the applicability of Article 101 TFEU to horizontal cooperation agreements (OJ [2011] C11/1), para. 11.
297. Whish et al. 2012: 94.

directors, the de facto influence that the parent exerts over the policies of the subsidiary and the directions issued by the former in relation to the latter.

This approach is exemplified in a number of decisions delivered by the European Courts (in the *AEG* case,[298] the *ICI* case[299] and then again in the case involving *Akzo Nobel NV*[300]).[301]

In these three cases, the substantive nature of the relationship between the parent and subsidiary companies was considered, albeit in the context of liability for infringements under Article 101 TFEU, in order to determine whether the entities were distinct legal entities or part of a single economic unit.

Where a parent company in exercise of its control over its subsidiaries[302] orders them to execute a decision to raise prices 'the conduct of the subsidiaries must be imputed to the parent company. For the purpose of applying the rules on competition, unity of conduct on the market as between a parent company and its subsidiaries overrides the formal separation between those companies resulting from their separate legal personality'.[303]

Viho v. Commission[304]

Viho challenged the Commission's refusal to accept that Parker and its subsidiaries form a single economic unit and that accordingly Article 85(1) TEC (now Article 101(1) TFEU) did not apply. The Court of First Instance ruled in favour of the Commission and Viho appealed.

The ECJ (now CJEU) held

15 It should be noted, first of all, that it is established that Parker holds 100% of the shares of its subsidiaries in Germany, Belgium, Spain, France and the Netherlands and that the sales and marketing activities of its subsidiaries are directed by an area team appointed by the parent company and which controls, in particular, sales targets, gross margins, sales costs, cash flow and stocks. The area team also lays down the range of products to be sold, monitors advertising and issues directives concerning prices and discounts.

16 Parker and its subsidiaries thus form a single economic unit within which the subsidiaries do not enjoy real autonomy in determining their course of

298. Case 107/82 *AEG-Telefunken v. Commission* [1983] ECR 3151, [1984] 3 CMLR 325, paras 47-53.
299. Dyestuffs case.
300. Case T-112/05 *Akzo Nobel NV v. Commission* [2007] ECR II-5049, [2008] 4 CMLR 321.
301. *See* recent decision in Case C-401/11 P *Elf v. Commission*.
302. In the *Dyestuffs* case the applicant held all if not a majority of the shares in the subsidiaries concerned and was in a position to 'exercise decisive influence over the policy of the subsidiaries as regards selling prices in the common market and in fact used this power upon the occasion of the three price increase (addressed in this case).' (*Dyestuffs* case, paras 136-7).
303. *Dyestuffs* case: para. 11.
304. Case C-73/95 *Viho Europe BV v. Commission P* [1996] ECR I-5457 [1997] 4 CMLR 419, para. 16.

> action in the market, but carry out the instructions issued to them by the parent company controlling them (Case 48/69 *ICI v Commission* [1972] ECR 619, paragraphs 133 and 134; Case 15/74 *Centrafarm v Sterling Drug* [1974] ECR 1147, paragraph 41; Case 16/74 *Centrafarm v Winthrop* [1974] ECR 1183, paragraph 32; Case 30/87 *Bodson v Pompes Funèbres* [1988] ECR 2479, paragraph 19; and Case 66/86 *Ahmed Saeed Flugreisen and Others v Zentrale zur Bekaempfung Unlauteren Wettbewerbs* [1989] ECR 803, paragraph 35).
>
> 17 In those circumstances, the fact that Parker's policy of referral, which consists essentially in dividing various national markets between its subsidiaries, might produce effects outside the ambit of the Parker group which are capable of affecting the competitive position of third parties cannot make Article 85(1) applicable, even when it is read in conjunction with Article 2 and Article 3(c) and (g) of the Treaty. On the other hand, such unilateral conduct could fall under Article 86 of the Treaty if the conditions for its application, as laid down in that article, were fulfilled.

In this context there is a presumption, which is rebuttable that 'the parent does in fact exercise such influence'.[305] Unless the parent can produce sufficient evidence to show that the subsidiary acts independently on the market, the two entities are treated as jointly and severally liable for fines imposed.[306]

In the following situations the single economic unit approach has been deemed inapplicable:

- A joint venture formed by four companies.[307]
- A joint subsidiary formed by two companies in which the participating companies enjoy equal voting rights and equal representation on the supervisory board.[308]
- An agreement between a parent and a subsidiary once it becomes autonomous.[309]

- Agency

The relationship that exists between a principal and an agent like the relationship between a subsidiary and its parent may be characterised by economic unity so that Article 101 TFEU does not catch agency agreements.[310]

305. Whish et al. 2012: 94.
306. Case C-97/08 P [2009] ECR I-8237, [2009] 5 CMLR 2633, paras 60-2.
307. *Ijsselcentrale* OJ [1991] L28/32, [1992] 5 CMLR 154, paras 22-4.
308. *Gosmé/Martell-DMP* OJ [1991]L185/23, [1992] 5 CMLR 586, para. 30.
309. Whish et al. 2012: 95; *see also Austin Rover/Unipart* OJ [1988] L45/34, [1988] 4 CMLR 513).
310. For a fuller review, *see* Chapter 9, Jones and Sufrin 2011.

[D] Effect on Trade Between Member States[311]

The prohibition in Article 101 TFEU is limited in its scope of application to those agreements, decisions or concerted practices capable of *affecting trade between Member States*. In the context of competition law, this requirement defines the boundary between the areas covered by European law and those falling within the purview of the law of the Member States.[312]

- Jurisdictional test

By denoting the 'boundary between the areas respectively covered by [EU] law and the law of the Member States'[313] this requirement effectively sets out the jurisdictional limit to the prohibition in Article 101.[314]

European competition law extends to any agreement, decision or concerted practice capable of constituting a threat to freedom of trade between the Member States, in particular through the partitioning of national markets.[315]

Conduct the effects of which are confined to the territory of a single Member State is governed in contrast by the national legal order.[316]

The entry into force of Regulation 1/2003 has enhanced the importance of this requirement, by partitioning the responsibility for enforcement. The role of the national courts and the NCAs in enforcing national competition law highlights the importance of determining whether an agreement, decision or concerted practice has an effect on interstate trade.

Due to the centrality of this issue, the Commission has issued guidance on this matter in the form of the Guidelines on the effect on trade concept contained in Articles [101 and 102 TFEU] OJ [2004] C101/81.

- Substantive test

An agreement, decision or concerted practice will be treated as having an effect on trade between Member States under Article 101 TFEU in circumstances where it either actually or potentially interferes with trade between Member States.[317]

It must be possible in this context to 'foresee with a sufficient degree of probability on the basis of a set of objective factors of law or of fact that the agreement

311. For a fuller review, *see* Jones and Sufrin 2011: 177-183.
312. Case 22/78 *Hugin Kassaregister AB and Hugin Cash Registers Ltd v. Commission of the European Communities*, para. 17.
313. Whish et al. 2012: 144 citing Case 22/78 *Hugin Kassaregister AB and Hugin Cash Registers Ltd v. Commission of the European Communities* [1979] ECR 1869, 1899, [1979] 3 CMLR 345, 373.
314. Jones and Sufrin 2011: 121.
315. Case 22/78 *Hugin Kassaregister AB and Hugin Cash Registers Ltd v. Commission of the European Communities*, para. 17.
316. Case 22/78 *Hugin Kassaregister AB and Hugin Cash Registers Ltd v. Commission of the European Communities*, para. 17.
317. Case 56/65 *Société Technique Minière (L.T.M.) v. Maschinenbau Ulm GmbH* (M.B.U.) [1966] ECR 235, 249.

in question may have an influence, direct or indirect, actual or potential, on the pattern of trade between Member States'.[318]

Article 101(1) TFEU will apply even though there is little trade between the Member States, as the possibility cannot be excluded that restrictions on the freedom of action may impede future trade between the Member States, since the situation may change from one year to another.[319]

An attempt to argue that an agreement did not produce an effect on trade between Member States, since the agreement increased trade volumes, was rejected by the CJEU in the case of *Consten & Grundig v. Commission*[320] on the basis that an agreement of this genre has the potential of affecting trade between Member States.[321]

The aim of the Treaty is not to increase trade between Member States but rather to create a system of undistorted competition in the EU.[322]

Consten & Grundig v. Commission[323]

Grundig (G), a German company, entered into a distribution agreement with a distributor in France, Consten (C) under which C was appointed as G's sole representative for France, Saar and Corsica.

C agreed to buy articles from G, and to market and service such items. C also undertook not to sell on its own account or upon that of another similar articles capable of competing with the goods which were the subject of the agreement, and not to deliver (directly or indirectly) for or to other countries from the contract territory. A similar prohibition was placed by G on all its sole distributors in other countries, and on its German wholesalers.

For its part, G undertook to grant C the retail sale rights, and not to make deliveries to other persons in the contract territory. For distribution purposes, C was permitted to use the name and emblem of G registered in Germany and other Member States. C registered in France under its own name the trademark GINT (Grundig International) which was placed on all appliances produced by G including those sold in Germany. C agreed to transfer to G as soon as it stopped being the sole distributor the registration of the trademark GINT with all the rights attached to it, or to cancel its registration.

318. Case 56/65 *Société Technique Minière (L.T.M.) v. Maschinenbau Ulm GmbH* (M.B.U.) [1966] ECR 235, 249, [1966] CMLR 357, 375.
319. Case 107/82 *AEG v. Commission*, para. 59 & 60.
320. Case 56-64 & 58-64 *Consten & Grundig v. Commission* [1966] ECR 299 [1966] CMLR 418.
321. Case 56-64 & 58-64 *Consten & Grundig v. Commission* [1966] ECR 299, 341 [1966] CMLR 418, 471-472.
322. Jones and Sufrin 2011: 122.
323. Case 56-64 & 58-64 *Consten & Grundig v. Commission* [1966] ECR 299 [1966] CMLR 418.

Another company (UNEF) bought G's appliances from German traders who delivered them in spite of the export prohibition imposed by G. UNEF resold these items in France at more favourable prices than C. C brought an action against UNEF for unfair competition and infringement of its trademark (GINT). C was successful at first instance and an appeal was brought by UNEF. At the same time, UNEF petitioned the Commission for a declaration that G and C had infringed Article 101 TFEU (at the time Article 85 of the EEC Treaty) through the provisions of the sole distributorship agreement and the ancillary agreement relating to the registration and use of the trademark GINT in France.

The court handling the appeal stayed the matter until a decision was taken by the Commission.

After an investigation, the Commission decided that the agreement between G and C breached Article 101 TFEU. G and C challenged this decision alleging *inter alia* that the Commission had relied on a mistaken interpretation of the concept of an agreement which may affect trade between Member States, and that the Commission had not shown that such trade would have been greater without the agreement between G and C.[324]

For its part, the Commission counter-argued that an infringement of Article 101(1) TFEU is fulfilled 'once trade between Member States develops, as a result of the agreement, differently from the way in which it would have done without the restriction resulting from the agreement, and once the influence of the agreement on market conditions reaches a certain degree'.[325]

The ECJ (now CJEU) dismissed the complaints raised in this respect stating that '[i]n this connexion, what is particularly important is whether the agreement is capable of constituting a threat, either direct or indirect, actual or potential, to freedom of trade between Member States in a manner which might harm the attainment of the objectives of a single market between States. Thus the fact that an agreement encourages an increase, even a large one, in the volume of trade between States is not sufficient to exclude the possibility that the agreement may "affect" such trade in the abovementioned manner. In the present case, the contract between Grundig and Consten, on the one hand by preventing undertakings other than Consten from importing Grundig products into France, and on the other hand by prohibiting Consten from re-exporting those products to other countries of the Common Market, indisputably affects trade between Member States. These limitations on the freedom of trade, as well as those which might

324. Case 56-64 & 58-64 *Consten & Grundig v. Commission* [1966] ECR 299, 341 [1966] CMLR 418, 471-2.
325. Case 56-64 & 58-64 *Consten & Grundig v. Commission* [1966] ECR 299, 341 [1966] CMLR 418, 471-2.

> ensue for third parties from the registration in France by Consten of the GINT trademark, which Grundig places on all its products, are enough to satisfy the requirement in question'.[326]

[E] Object or Effect the Prevention, Restriction or Distortion of Competition

An agreement etc. will not be prohibited under Article 101(1) TFEU unless the same prevents, restricts or distorts competition within the meaning of Article 101(1) TFEU; as such Article 101(1) TFEU only prohibits an agreement which has as its object or its effect the prevention, restriction or distortion of competition.[327]

The terms *object* and *effect* are read disjunctively; if it is clear from the terms of a given agreement in the economic context in which it is applied that the object of the agreement in question is the prevention, restriction or distortion of competition then there is in turn no need to look at the effects of the said agreement.[328] This prohibition effectively applies if one or the other requirement is proven.[329] In other words if the agreement either has as its object the prevention, restriction or distortion of competition or it has such an effect.[330]

- Agreements that have a restrictive object: *Agreements that have as their object the prevention, restriction or distortion of competition (restriction of competition by object)*

The differentiation between restrictions by object and restrictions by effect is paramount; as once 'it has been established that an agreement has as its object the restriction of competition, there is no need to take account of its concrete effects. In other words, for the purposes of applying Article [101(1)] no actual anticompetitive effects need to be demonstrated where the agreement has a restriction of competition as its object'.[331]

Restrictions of competition by object are those restrictions which by their very character have the potential of restricting competition; these are restrictions 'which in

326. Case 56-64 & 58-64 *Consten & Grundig v. Commission* [1966] ECR 299, 341-2 [1966] CMLR 418, 471-2.
327. Case 56/65 *Société La Technique Minière v. Maschinebau Ulm GmbH* [1966] ECR 234, 249; Case C-234/89 *Stergios Delimitis v. Henninger Bräu* [1991] ECR I-935 (hereinafter *Delimitis* case), para. 13 and Cases T-374, 375, 384 and 388/94 *European Night Services v. Commission* [1998] ECR II-3141, para. 136.
328. Jones and Sufrin 2011: 171; Whish et al. 2012: 118 citing Cases C-209/07, paras 15-6, C-8/08, paras 28, 30, C-501/06, para. 55.
329. Whish et al. 2012: 118.
330. Whish et al. 2012: 118 citing Case 56/65 *Société Technique Minière (L.T.M.) v. Maschinenbau Ulm GmbH (M.B.U.)* [1966] ECR 235, 249, [1966] CMLR 357, 375.
331. Article [101(3)] Guidelines, para. 20. Confirmed in Joined Cases 56/64 and 58/64 *Consten and Grundig* v. *Commission* [1966] ECR 299; Case C272/09 P *KME Germany and Others* v. *Commission* [2011] ECR I12789, paragraph 65; and Case C389/10 P *KME Germany and Others* v. *Commission* [2011] ECR I13125, paragraph 75 and Case C-226/11 *Expedia Inc v. Autorité de la Concurrence and Others* [2012] ECR I-795 (hereinafter *Expedia* case) paragraph 35.

light of the objectives pursued by the Community competition rules have such a high potential of negative effects on competition that it is unnecessary for the purposes of applying Article [101(1)] to demonstrate any actual effects on the market. This presumption is based on the serious nature of the restriction and on experience showing that restrictions of competition by object are likely to produce negative effects on the market and to jeopardise the objectives pursued by the Community competition rules'.[332]

The object of the agreement is viewed objectively with regard to 'the objective meaning and purpose of the agreement considered in the economic context in which it is to be applied'.[333] In such a context, an NCA will not be expected to show that an agreement produces 'adverse economic effects' in turn allowing it and the justice system to conserve resources.[334]

An organic approach is adopted in relation to the concept of object restriction (the restriction of competition by object); as such this notion cannot be limited to the examples articulated in Article 101(1).[335]

(1) Price fixing and the exchange of pricing information (Article 101(1)a)

The European courts take the view that the exchange of pricing information amongst competitors is 'tainted with an anticompetitive object if the exchange is capable of removing uncertainties concerning the intended conduct of the participating undertakings'.[336]

According to the Commission object restrictions include the sharing of information between competitors of 'individualised data regarding the intended future prices or quantities'[337] as well as pre-pricing communications involving the review of the factors used in the setting of prices amongst undertakings.[338]

(2) Market sharing (Article 101(1)c)[339]

(3) Control of output and export bans[340]

As the restriction on competition must be appreciable; where the object of the agreement is restrictive the agreement is capable of falling outside the scope of

332. Article 101(3) Guidelines: para. 21.
333. Whish et al. 2012: 119 citing Cases 29/83 and 30/83, paras 25-6; Case T-148/89, para. 79; Case C-551/03, paras 77-8.
334. Whish et al. 2012: 119 citing AG Kokott in Case C-8/08 *T-Mobile* [2009] ECR I-4529, [2009] 5 CMLR 1701, para. 43.
335. Whish et al. 2012: 122 citing AG Trstenjak, Case C-209/07 *Competition Authority v. Beef Industry Development Society Limited* [2008] ECR I-8637 [2009] 4 CMLR 310, para. 48.
336. Case C-8/08 *T-Mobile* [2009] ECR I-4529, [2009] 5 CMLR 1701, para. 43.
337. Whish et al. 2012: 122 citing Guidelines on Horizontal Co-operation Agreements.
338. Bananas Commission Decision of 15/10/08, paras 263-77.
339. For a detailed review, *see* Whish et al. 2012: 122-3.
340. Whish et al. 2012: 123 citing the decisions of General Court in *European Night Services*, and the decision of the CJ in Cases C501/06 P etc *GlaxoSmithKline v. Commission* [2009] ECR I-9291, [2010] 4 CMLR 50, paras 59-60, 62-4.

Article 101(1) TFEU if the 'likely impact on the market is minimal'.[341] Moreover the agreement will only infringe Article 101(1) TFEU where 'it has an *appreciable* effect on trade between Member States'.[342] Due to the need to demonstrate appreciability, it is necessary to define the relevant market.

- Agreements that have a restrictive effect: *Agreements that have as their effect the prevention, restriction or distortion of competition (restriction of competition by effect)*

The restrictive effect of the agreement will need to be demonstrated where its object is not the restriction of competition.[343]

Where an agreement does not possess a restrictive object, in order to ascertain if the agreement violates Article 101(1) TFEU it is essential to evaluate the effect of the agreement in the context of *the market* within which it is seen to operate and in light of 'the factual or legal circumstances causing it to prevent, restrict or distort competition'.[344]

In this context an assessment of whether an agreement violates Article 101(1) TFEU will require the adoption of a multi-phased approach.

Due consideration will firstly need to be given to the 'relevant product market' and the 'relevant geographic market'.[345] In the context of licensed public houses on the German market, for example, the 'relevant product market' and 'relevant geographic market' were deemed to consist of beer sales in licensed premises in Germany rather than beer sales in retail outlets.[346]

Once these relevant markets are assessed, two further questions will need to be considered.

The first question to be determined is *whether access to the market is hindered?* This question is assessed by looking at *whether the agreement hinders actual or potential competition that would have existed in the market without the agreement?*[347] In making such a determination, due regard should be given to the competition between the contracting parties as well as competition from third parties.[348] For example in this context consideration should be given to whether new competitors were able to access the market by purchasing existing breweries along with their respective networks of sales outlets or by opening new public houses.[349]

If this is the case and access is hindered, the next query is *whether the agreement concluded contributes to the foreclosure of the market?*[350] In other words 'does the

341. Whish et al. 2012: 120.
342. Whish et al. 2012: 120 (italics used by Whish).
343. Whish et al. 2012: 120 citing Cases T-374/94 etc *European Night Services v. Commission* [1998] ECR II-3141, [1998] 5 CMLR 718, para. 136.
344. Whish et al. 2012: 125-6, citing the decision of the CJEU in Case 23/67 *Brasserie de Haecht v. Wilkin* [1967] ECR 407, 415, [1968] CMLR 26, 40.
345. A review of the terms 'relevant market', 'relevant product market' and 'relevant geographic market' is provided in this chapter.
346. Whish et al. 2012: 125 citing *Delimitis* case: para. 16-8.
347. Article 101(3) Guidelines, para. 18(1).
348. Article 101(3) Guidelines, para. 18(1).
349. Whish et al. 2012: 126 citing *Delimitis* case: para. 19-23.
350. Whish et al. 2012: 126 citing *Delimitis* case: para. 24-7.

agreement restrict actual or potential competition that would have existed in the absence of the contractual restraint(s)?'[351]

Central to the assessment of whether an agreement has restrictive effect on competition is an assessment of the default position. Such an assessment can be achieved by considering 'what the position would have been in the absence of the agreement'.[352]

The Commission states that the determination 'of whether an agreement is restrictive of competitive must be made within the actual context in which competition would occur in the absence of the agreement with its alleged restrictions. In making this assessment it is necessary to take account of the likely impact of the agreement on inter-brand competition (i.e. competition between suppliers of competing brands) and on intra-brand competition (i.e. competition between distributors of the same brand)'.[353]

The impact of the agreement on potential competition on a given market is a relevant factor in the assessment of an agreement's restrictive effect though such an assessment should the General Court states be more than 'a hypothesis unsupported by any evidence or any analysis of the structure of the relevant market from which it might be concluded that it represented a real, concrete possibility'.[354]

Legitimate aims associated with an agreement that has a restrictive effect on competition may bring the agreement outside the scope of Article 101(1) TFEU.[355] In situations where it is demonstrated that the restrictions were essential to enable the contracting parties to accomplish a legitimate commercial aim the restrictions may be found to fall outside the scope of Article 101(1) TFEU due to the fact that they are 'ancillary to a legitimate commercial operation'.[356]

The grant of exclusivity in a licence to a licensee has been held to be necessary in order to enable the licensee to offset the risk assumed by it[357] and to protect its investment.[358] Certain restrictive provisions in licences may be warranted where their object is the protection of the intellectual property rights of the franchisor, the safeguarding of the common identity of the franchise system[359] and the preservation of the licensor's right to select and appoint licensees.[360]

351. Article 101(3) Guidelines, para. 18(2).
352. Whish et al. 2012: 127 citing Case T-328/03 [2006] ECR II-1231, [2006] 5 CMLR 258 258, para. 65-117.
353. Article 101(3) Guidelines, para. 17 citing *inter alia*. *See* Case 56/65 *Société Technique Minière (L.T.M.) v. Maschinenbau Ulm GmbH* (M.B.U.) [1966] ECR 235, 337, [1966] CMLR 357, 375, and Case C-7/95 P, *John Deere*, [1998] ECR I-3111, para. 76.
354. Whish et al. 2012: 127 citing Cases T-374/94 etc. *European Night Services v. Commission* [1988] ECR II-3141, [1998] 5 CMLR 718, paras 139-147.
355. Whish et al. 2012: 129.
356. Whish et al. 2012: 130.
357. Case 258/78 *LC Nungesser KG v. Commission* [1982] ECR 2015, [1983] 1 CMLR 278.
358. Case 262/81 *Coditel v. Ciné Vog Films SA* (No 2) [1982] ECR 3381, [1983] 1 CMLR 48.
359. Case 161/84 *Pronuptia de Paris v. Schilligalis* [1986] ECR 353, [1986] 1 CMLR 414.
360. Case 27/87 *Erauw-Jacquery Sprl v. La Hesbignonne Société Coopérative* [1988] ECR 1919, [1988] 4 CMLR 576; *Sicasov* OJ [1999] L4/27, [1999] 4 CMLR 192, para. 53-61.

- Regulatory and commercial ancillarity

The concept of regulatory ancillarity is distinct from the idea of commercial ancillarity but is equally capable of taking a restriction outside the scope of Article 101(1) TFEU.[361] Illustrations of the former can be found in the cases of *Price Waterhouse*[362] and *Meca-Medina*.[363]

The prohibition in Article 101(1) TFEU will not encompass every agreement between undertakings or decision made by an association of undertaking which restrict the freedom of action of one or more of the undertakings.[364] In order to assess the application of the prohibition in Article 101(1) TFEU to a certain case, account should be taken of a number of factors.[365]

Prime amongst these is the overall context within which the decision was taken or within which it produces its effects.[366] More specifically, consideration should be given to the objectives of the decision and to 'whether the consequential effects restrictive of competition are *inherent* in the pursuit of those objectives and are proportionate to them'.[367]

Applying this reasoning in the *Price Waterhouse* case, the CJEU takes the view that the decision of the Dutch Bar Council prohibiting Dutch lawyers from creating multi-disciplinary practices by partnering up with non-lawyers must be considered in light of the overall context within which the decision of this professional association was taken or the context within which the said decision produces its effect.[368] Bearing this context in mind, the CJEU notes that the Bar Council's decision was 'connected with the need to make rules relating to organisation, qualifications, professional ethics, supervision and liability, in order to ensure that the ultimate consumers of legal services and the sound administration of justice are provided with the necessary guarantees in relation to integrity and experience'.[369]

Assessing the compatibility of the anti-doping rules adopted by the IOC in *Meca-Medina*, the CJEU states that these rules were adopted in order to 'combat doping in order for competitive sport to be conducted fairly and that it included the need to safeguard equal chances for athletes, athletes' health, the integrity and objectivity of competitive sport and ethical values in sport'.[370] Speaking of the penalties imposed, the

361. Whish et al. 2012: 130.
362. *Price Waterhouse* case: para. 97.
363. Case C-519/04 P *Meca-Medina v. Commission* [2006] ECR I-6991 [2006] 5 CMLR 1023, paras 42-5.
364. *Price Waterhouse* case: para. 97.
365. *Price Waterhouse* case: para. 97.
366. Price Waterhouse case: para. 97.
367. Case C-519/04 P *Meca-Medina v. Commission* [2006] ECR I-6991 [2006] 5 CMLR 1023, para. 42 citing *Price Waterhouse* case: para. 97. (italics added by authors).
368. *Price Waterhouse* case: para. 97.
369. *Price Waterhouse* case: para. 97.
370. Case C-519/04 P *Meca-Medina v. Commission* [2006] ECR I-6991 [2006] 5 CMLR 1023, para. 43.

Court adds, that these penalties 'are necessary to ensure enforcement of the doping ban'[371] and thus 'their effect on athletes' freedom of action must be considered to be, in principle, inherent itself in the anti-doping rules'.[372]

As the decision in *Meca-Medina* demonstrates the judgment delivered in the *Price Waterhouse* case is not limited exclusively to professional ethics rules applicable to the legal profession or indeed to other professions,[373] as the decision in *Meca-Medina* concerns the rules of the International Swimming Federation.

Another route that could have been taken in the *Price Waterhouse* case would have been for the rules of the Dutch Bar Council to be held in violation of Article 101(1) TFEU (due to their impact on production and technical development pursuant to Article 101(1)(b) TFEU) and to then demonstrate that these rules satisfy Article 101(3) TFEU.[374] However at the relevant time, this strategy was unavailable as a decision under Article 101(3) TFEU could only have been made by the Commission in response to a notification under Article 4, Regulation 17 and no notification had been made.[375]

– The definition of appreciability & the impact of the *De Minimis* doctrine on the application of Article 101(1) (2014 Guidance)[376]

Put forth by the CJEU in *Völk v. Vervaecke*,[377] the *de minimis* doctrine is rooted in the idea that 'an agreement may fall outside the scope of Article 101(1) where it has an insignificant effect on the market, taking into account the weak position which the persons concerned have on the market of the product in question'.[378]

Guidance on the question of whether an agreement has a significant impact on competition has been produced by the Commission. The most recent version of this guidance (issued in 2014) replaces the guidance from 2001 (which replaced the 1997 guidance).[379]

371. Case C-519/04 P *Meca-Medina v. Commission* [2006] ECR I-6991 [2006] 5 CMLR 1023, para. 44.
372. Case C-519/04 P *Meca-Medina v. Commission* [2006] ECR I-6991 [2006] 5 CMLR 1023, para. 44.
373. Whish et al. 2012: 132.
374. Whish et al. 2012: 133.
375. Whish et al. 2012: 133.
376. Notice on agreements of minor importance which do not appreciably restrict competition under Article 101(1) of the Treaty on the Functioning of the European Union (*De Minimis* Notice) OJ 2014/C291/01 (2014 Guidance); Notice on agreements of minor importance which do not appreciably restrict competition under Article 81(1) of the Treaty establishing the European Community (*de minimis*) OJ 2001/C368/07 (2001 Guidance); Notice on agreements of minor importance published in OJ C372, 9.12.1997 (1997 Guidance).
377. Case 5/69 *Völk v. Vervaecke* [1969] ECR 295, [1969] CMLR 273.
378. Case 5/69 *Völk v. Vervaecke* [1969] ECR 295, [1969] CMLR 273.
379. Notice on agreements of minor importance which do not appreciably restrict competition under Article 101(1) of the Treaty on the Functioning of the European Union (*De Minimis* Notice) OJ 2014/C291/01 (2014 Guidance); Notice on agreements of minor importance which do not appreciably restrict competition under Article 81(1) of the Treaty establishing the European Community (*de minimis*) OJ 2001/C368/07 (2001 Guidance); Notice on agreements of minor importance published in OJ C372, 9.12.1997 (1997 Guidance).

The Guidance addresses *the ability of agreements to appreciably affect trade between Member States*[380] and aims to provide guidelines to undertakings, national courts and NCAs on the application of Article 101(1) TFEU.[381]

Though this Guidance is not binding on either national courts or NCAs,[382383] it does have the effect of limiting the exercise of discretion by the Commission.[384]

In the interests of transparency in the manner in which the Commission applies Article 101 TFEU, as the competition authority of the EU, by the *de minimis* notice the Commission effectively 'imposes a limit on the exercise of its discretion and must not depart from the content of that notice without being in breach of the general principles of law, in particular the principles of equal treatment and the protection of legitimate expectations.[385]'

Expedia[386]

Expedia (the online travel operator) created a joint subsidiary (Agence VSC) with SNCF (Société nationale des chemins de fer français) for the sale of travel services including train tickets.

The French competition authority found that the partnership between SNCF and Expedia creating Agence VSC constituted an agreement in violation of Article 101(1) TFEU, as the object and effect of this agreement is the promotion of the joint subsidiary 'in the market for travel agency services provided for leisure travel to the detriment of competitors'.[387] The French competition authority accordingly fined Expedia and SNCF.

The French competition authority determined *inter alia* that 'Expedia and SNCF were competitors in the market for on-line travel agency services, that their market shares were more than 10% and that, consequently, the "*de minimis*" rule, as set out in paragraph 7 of the "*de minimis*" notice and Article L. 464-2-1 of the Commercial Code, were not applicable.'[388]

Expedia challenged this decision arguing that the French Competition Authority had overestimated the market share held by Agence VSC.

On referral, the national court (Cour de cassation) asked the CJEU if the threshold in the *de minimis* notice is binding on the NCAs thereby precluding the NCAs from bring proceedings and imposing penalties 'in respect of a

380. Commission Notice – Guidelines on the effect on trade concept contained in Articles [101 and 102 TFEU] OJ C101, 27.4.2004, para. 4.
381. 2014 Guidance, para. 5 ex 2001 Guidance, para. 4.
382. 2014 Guidance, para. 5 ex 2001 Guidance, para. 4.
383. *Expedia* case: para. 27, 29 & 30.
384. *Expedia* case: para. 28.
385. *Expedia* case: para. 28 citing Joined Cases C-189/02 P, C-202/02 P, C-205/02 P to C-208/02 P and C-213/02 P *Dansk Rørindustri and Others* v. *Commission* [2005] ECR I5425, paragraph 211.
386. *Expedia* case.
387. *Expedia* case: para. 8.
388. *Expedia* case: para. 9.

practice under agreements, decisions of associations of undertakings or concerted action that may affect trade between Member States, but that does not reach the thresholds specified by the European Commission in its [*de minimis*] notice?'[389]

The Court ruled that the *de minimis* notice is non-binding on the NCAs and national courts, adding that an agreement which has an anti-competitive object 'constitutes, by its nature and independently of any concrete effect that it may have, an appreciable restriction on competition'.[390]

Replying to the question posed by the referring court, the Court said that Article 101(1) TFEU and Article 3(2) Regulation 1/2003 'must be interpreted as not precluding a national competition authority from applying Article 101(1) TFEU to an agreement between undertakings that may affect trade between Member States, but that does not reach the thresholds specified by the Commission in its de minimis notice, provided that the agreement constitutes an appreciable restriction of competition within the meaning of that provision'.[391]

The principles in the Guidance apply not only to agreements between undertakings, but also to decisions of associations of undertakings and to concerted practices.[392]

The 2014 Guidance is divided up into two parts.

– Part I of the 2014 Guidance

In Part I of the 2014 Guidance, reference is made to the jurisprudence of the CJEU which states that the prohibition in Article 101(1) TFEU 'is not applicable where the impact of the agreement on trade between Member States or on competition is not appreciable'.[393]

In the event that an agreement is covered by the Notice, the Commission will not initiate proceedings either in response to an application or on its own initiative.[394] Moreover, where an undertaking assumes or undertakings assume in good faith that an agreement comes within the scope of this Guidance, the Commission will not fine the undertaking or undertakings concerned.[395]

Paragraph 3 of the 2014 Guidance states that in the Guidance the Commission defines what is not an appreciable restriction of competition under Article 101(1) TFEU with reference to market share thresholds and based on whether the parties are actual

389. *Expedia* case in the section headed 'The dispute in the main proceedings and the questions referred for a preliminary ruling.'
390. *Expedia* case: para. 37.
391. *Expedia* case: para. 38.
392. 2014 Guidance, para. 6 ex 2001 Guidance, para. 5.
393. 2014 Guidance, para. 1 citing the decision in Expedia case, paras 16 & 17.
394. 2014 Guidance, para. 5 ex 2001 Guidance, para. 4.
395. 2014 Guidance, para. 5 ex 2001 Guidance, para. 4.

or potential competitors.[396] This paragraph adds that the negative definition of *appreciability* which defines what is not an appreciable restriction does not imply that agreements which exceed the market share thresholds appreciably restrict competition.[397]

Paragraph 4 of the 2014 Guidance confirms that agreements may not fall foul of Article 101(1) TFEU if *they are not capable of appreciably affecting interstate trade*.[398]

The issue of what constitutes *an appreciable effect on interstate trade* is not addressed in the Guidance; this issue being addressed elsewhere.[399]

– Part II of the 2014 Guidance

– Safe harbour provisions[400]

The pivotal provisions in the 2014 Guidance are the safe harbour provisions which define those agreements affecting interstate trade which all the same fall outside the scope of Article 101 TFEU. Two factors are used in this context, market share and the existence of competition between the contracting parties.

According to the safe harbour provisions, agreements between undertakings which affect interstate trade do not appreciably restrict competition within the meaning of Article 101(1) TFEU if:[401]

The *aggregate market share* held by the contracting parties does not exceed *10%* on any of the relevant markets affected by the agreement in circumstances where the undertakings that are party to the said agreement are *actual or potential competitors* on any of these markets (*10% market threshold*);[402] or

The *individual market share* held by each of the contracting parties does not exceed *15%* on any of the relevant markets affected by the agreement in circumstances where the agreement is concluded between undertakings that are *neither actual nor potential competitors* on any of those markets (*15% market threshold*).[403]

396. More on this below in the review of 2014 Guidance, para. 8 ex 2001 Guidance, para. 7.
397. 2014 Guidance, para. 3 ex 2001 Guidance, para. 2.
398. 2014 Guidance, para. 4 ex 2001 Guidance, para. 3.
399. This issue is addressed in the Commission Notice – Guidelines on the effect on trade concept contained in Articles [101 and 102 TFEU] OJ C101, 27.4.2004. Agreements between small- and medium-sized undertakings (SMEs) are rarely capable of appreciably affecting interstate trade as the Commission has stated that such agreements are not normally capable of affecting trade between Member States, as there is a presumption that the activities of such entities are normally local or at most regional in nature. (Commission Notice – Guidelines on the effect on trade concept contained in Articles [101 and 102 TFEU] OJ C101, 27.4.2004, para. 50) Notwithstanding this fact, 'SMEs may be subject to Community law jurisdiction in particular where they engage in cross-border economic activity.' (Commission Notice – Guidelines on the effect on trade concept contained in Articles [101 and 102 TFEU] OJ C101, 27.4.2004, para. 50). The definition of micro, small- and medium-sized enterprises is addressed in the Commission Recommendation OJ L 124 20.5.2003, 36.
400. 2014 Guidance, para. 8 ex 2001 Guidance, para. 7.
401. Though this provision makes reference to agreements, decisions and concerted practices are also encompassed within the purview of this Guidance (2014 Guidance, para. 6).
402. 2014 Guidance, para. 8(a) ex 2001 Guidance, para. 7.
403. 2014 Guidance, para. 8 ex 2001 Guidance, para. 7.

In circumstances where it is difficult to determine if the agreement is the one made between competitors or not, the 10% threshold should be used.[404]

Situations in which competition in a particular market is restricted by the cumulative foreclosure effect of agreements made are addressed within the Guidance.[405] Where in a relevant market, competition is restricted by the cumulative foreclosure effect of agreements, the market thresholds set out above are reduced to 5% (from 10%, 15% and 10% respectively) (*5% market threshold*).[406] This is the case irrespective of whether the agreement is the one concluded between competitors or not.[407] Where there is a cumulative foreclosure effect on a relevant market, individual suppliers or distributors with a market share not exceeding 5% are not generally regarded as contributing significantly to the cumulative foreclosure effect.[408]

Where less than 30% of the relevant market is covered by parallel agreements having similar effects, a cumulative foreclosure effect is unlikely to exist.[409]

In circumstances where the market share thresholds set out in paragraphs 8, 9 and 10 of the Guidance (discussed above) are surpassed by no more than 2 percentage points during two successive calendar years, the Commission takes the view that the agreements concerned are not restrictive of competition.[410]

Where an agreement outgrows the Guidance and the marginal relief provisions (for example paragraph 11 of the 2014 Guidance) it is unclear how it will be dealt with.[411] One option is that the agreement will be rendered void retrospectively.[412] Another possibility is that the agreement will be rendered unenforceable from the moment the Guidance is no longer applicable to the agreement.[413]

Market share is determined by reference to the term 'relevant market' and in turn by reference to the terms 'relevant product market' and the 'relevant geographic market'.[414] These terms are defined in guidance issued by the Commission.[415,416]

– Hardcore restrictions

As the aim of the Guidance relating to the *de minimis* doctrine is not to cover agreements which have as their object the prevention, restriction or distortion of competition within the internal market,[417] the safe harbour provisions (contained in the Guidance) will not encompass such agreements.[418]

404. 2014 Guidance, para. 9 ex 2001 Guidance, para. 7.
405. 2014 Guidance, para. 10 ex 2001 Guidance, para. 8.
406. 2014 Guidance, para. 10 ex 2001 Guidance, para. 8.
407. 2014 Guidance, para. 10 ex 2001 Guidance, para. 8.
408. 2014 Guidance, para. 10 ex 2001 Guidance, para. 8.
409. 2014 Guidance, para. 10 ex 2001 Guidance, para. 8.
410. 2014 Guidance, para. 11 ex 2001 Guidance, para. 9.
411. Whish et al. 2012: 142.
412. Whish et al. 2012: 142.
413. Whish et al. 2012: 142.
414. 2014 Guidance, para. 12 ex 2001 Guidance, para. 10.
415. Commission Notice on the definition of relevant market for the purposes of Community competition law OJ [1997] C372/5, [1998] 4 CMLR 177 (1997 Notice).
416. These terms are reviewed in this chapter.
417. 2014 Guidance, para. 13 citing 2014 Guidance, para. 2.
418. 2014 Guidance, para. 13.

With this in mind, the safe harbour provisions will not apply for example to agreements concluded between competitors which contain restrictions which either directly or indirectly have as their object:[419]

(a) the fixing of prices for sales of products to third parties;
(b) the limitation of output or sales; or
(c) the allocation of markets or customers.

Moreover, these safe harbour provisions will not extend to agreements containing any of the restrictions listed as hardcore restrictions in any current or future block exemption regarded by the Commission 'to generally constitute restrictions by object'.[420]

In contrast with the 2014 Guidance, the 2001 Guidance classifies hardcore restrictions by reference to the agreement within which they were contained.[421] In this earlier version of the Guidance, a distinction is drawn by the Commission between hardcore restrictions contained in agreements concluded between competitors and those contained within agreements concluded between non-competitors.[422]

In this context, the 2001 Guidance states that the safe harbour provisions are inapplicable to agreements made between competitors containing restrictions which, directly or indirectly, alone or in combination with other factors under the parties' control, have as their object a) the fixing of prices where there is a sale of products to third parties; b) the limitation of output or sales; c) the allocation of markets/customers.[423]

The 2001 Guidance also states that the safe harbour provisions are inapplicable to agreements made between non-competitors containing restrictions which, directly or indirectly, alone or in combination with other factors under the parties' control, have as their object *inter alia*[424] a) the restriction of the buyer's ability to decide the sale price

419. 2014 Guidance, para. 13.
420. 2014 Guidance, para. 13 citing the following provisions: (1) For supply and distribution agreements between non-competitors, Article 4 of Commission Regulation (EU) No 330/2010 of 20 April 2010 on the application of Article 101(3) of the Treaty on the Functioning of the European Union to categories of vertical agreements and concerted practices (OJ L 102, 23.4.2010, p. 1); (2) For licensing agreements between non-competitors, Article 4(2) of Commission Regulation (EU) No 316/2014 of 21 March 2014 on the application of Article 101(3) of the Treaty on the Functioning of the European Union to categories of technology transfer agreements (OJ L 93, 28.3.2014, p. 17); (3) For agreements between competitors: (a) Article 5 of Commission Regulation (EU) No 1217/2010 of 14 December 2010 on the application of Article 101(3) of the Treaty on the Functioning of the European Union to certain categories of research and development agreements (OJ L 335, 18.12.2010, p. 36) and (b) Article 4 of Commission Regulation (EU) No 1218/2010 of 14 December 2010 on the application of Article 101(3) of the Treaty on the Functioning of the European Union to certain categories of specialisation agreements (OJ L 335, 18.12.2010, p. 43) and (c) Article 4(1) of Commission Regulation (EU) No 316/2014 of 21 March 2014 on the application of Article 101(3) of the Treaty on the Functioning of the European Union to categories of technology transfer agreements (OJ L 93, 28.3.2014, p. 17).
421. 2001 Guidance, para. 11.
422. 2001 Guidance, para. 11.
423. 2001 Guidance, para. 11(1).
424. 2001 Guidance, para. 11(2).

(this is without prejudice to the supplier's ability to impose a maximum/recommended sale price on the proviso that they do not amount to a fixed or minimum sale price as a result of pressure from or incentives offered by any of the parties);[425] b) the curtailment of the territory into which the buyer may sell or supply the contract goods or services;[426] or c) the curtailment of the group of customers to whom the buyer may sell or supply the contract goods or services.[427]

The CJEU in its decisions in *Volk v. Vewaecke* and *Pedro IV Servicios SL v. Total Espana SA* seems to have adopted the view that Article 101(1) TFEU will only apply to a hardcore restriction where within the internal market competition is 'appreciably' restricted or 'perceptibly' restricted (respectively).[428] In *Volk*, the decision addresses the grant of absolute territorial protection to a distributor and in *Pedro IV* a resale price maintenance provision.[429]

As a matter of law, based on this case law, it appears likely 'that even hardcore restrictions might fall outside Article 101 because they have no appreciable impact'.[430]

– Agreements not covered by block exemptions and excluded restrictions

The safe harbour provisions are particularly relevant for those categories of agreements that are not covered by any block exemption[431] and for those agreements covered by a block exemption to the degree that those agreements contain restrictions that are not listed as hardcore restrictions but which are nevertheless not covered by the block exemption (also known as excluded restrictions).[432]

– Terms 'undertaking', 'party to the agreement', 'distributor', 'supplier' and 'connected undertaking'

The terms 'undertaking', 'party to the agreement', 'distributor' and 'supplier' include their respective connected undertakings in the context of the Guidance on *de minimis*.[433]

The term 'connected undertakings' include undertakings:[434]

(a) in which one of the parties to the agreement has, directly or indirectly:
   (i) the power to exercise a majority of the voting rights;
   (ii) the power to appoint more than half the members of the supervisory board, the management board or the bodies legally representing the undertaking; or

425. 2001 Guidance, para. 11(2)(a).
426. 2001 Guidance, para. 11(2)(b).
427. 2001 Guidance, para. 11(2)(b).
428. Whish et al. 2012: 142.
429. Whish et al. 2012: 142.
430. Whish et al. 2012: 142-3.
431. 2014 Guidance, para. 14.
432. 2014 Guidance, para. 14.
433. 2014 Guidance, para. 15; 2001 Guidance, para. 12(1). Paragraph 12(1) of the 2001 Guidance also includes the term 'buyer'.
434. 2014 Guidance, para. 16; 2001 Guidance, para. 12(2).

(iii) the right to manage the business of the undertaking.

(b) which directly or indirectly have the rights or powers listed in (a) over one of the contracting parties; or

(c) in which an undertaking referred to in (b) has, directly or indirectly, the rights or powers listed in (a).

§2.15 ARTICLE 101(3) TFEU[435]

Policy considerations have resulted in the exemption of certain agreements which are clearly harmful to the objectives of the EU but which have the net effect of promoting 'the very essence of the competitive process, namely to win customers by offering better products or better prices than those offered by rivals'.[436]

In circumstances where the pro-competitive effects of an agreement outweigh its anticompetitive effects, the agreement is 'on balance pro-competitive and compatible with the objectives of [EU] competition rules'.[437]

The objective of the competition rules in the EU is 'to protect competition on the market as a means of enhancing consumer welfare and of ensuring an efficient allocation of resources. Agreements that restrict competition may at the same time have pro-competitive effects by way of efficiency gains. Efficiencies may create additional value by lowering the cost of producing an output, improving the quality of the product or creating a new product'.

Article 101(3) TFEU sets out an exception rule, which provides a defence to undertakings against a finding of an infringement of Article 101(1) TFEU.[438]

The position under EU law is contrastable with the situation in the United States where under §1, Sherman Act 1890 certain agreements are characterised as per se infringements of the Act whilst others are addressed using the rule of reason analysis; there is no equivalent to Article 101(3) TFEU under US law.[439]

Agreements, decisions and concerted practices caught by the prohibition in Article 101(1) TFEU which satisfy the conditions set out in Article 101(3) TFEU are valid and enforceable without the need for a prior decision to this effect;[440] such agreements are effectively 'valid and enforceable from the moment that the conditions of Article [101(3)] are satisfied and for as long as that remains the case'.[441]

The converse is true as well; agreements caught by Article 101(1) TFEU that fail to meet the conditions set out in Article 101(3) TFEU are prohibited with 'no prior decision to that effect being required'.[442]

435. For a review of the relationship between Articles 101(1) and 101(3) TFEU. *See* Jones and Sufrin 2011: Chapter 4.
436. Communication from the Commission Notice – Guidance on the application of Article [101(3)] of the Treaty OJ [2004] C101/97 (Article 101(3) Guidelines), para. 33.
437. Article 101(3) Guidelines, para. 33.
438. Article 101(3) Guidelines, para. 1.
439. Whish et al. 2012: 121.
440. Article 101(3) Guidelines, paras 3 and 10 (para. 10 cites Article 1(2) Regulation 1/2003).
441. Article 101(3) Guidelines, para. 10 (para. 10 cites Article 1(2) Regulation 1/2003).
442. Article 101(3) Guidelines, para. 10 citing Article 1(1) Regulation 1/2003.

An agreement caught by Article 101(1) TFEU that fails to meet the conditions set out in Article 101(3) TFEU is null and void;[443] though such 'automatic nullity' is restricted to those parts of the agreement that are incompatible with Article 101 TFEU on the proviso that the parts concerned are capable of being severed from the remainder of the agreement.[444]

The Commission has issued guidance on the application of Article 101(3) TFEU in individual cases and in the context of the block exemption regulations.

The guidance on the application of Article 101(3) TFEU in individual cases is entitled the Guidance on the application of Article [101(3)] of the Treaty (Article 101(3) Guidelines).[445] This guidance is supplemented by the Commission's guidance on the application of Article 101(3) TFEU under the block exemption regulations[446] applicable to technology transfer agreements, vertical restraints and horizontal cooperation agreements.[447]

The Article 101(3) Guidelines set out the approach of the Commission to the interpretation of the conditions for exception contained in Article 101(3) TFEU;[448] effectively setting out the guidelines on how to apply Article 101(3) TFEU in individual cases.[449] The methodology used in the Article 101(3) Guidelines is rooted in an economic approach[450] and the standards set out in these Guidelines must be applied with reference to the facts of each specific case (a mechanical application is excluded in this context).[451]

In EU law, there are 'no agreements that are irredeemably, or *per se*, illegal'.[452] An illustration of this can be found in the Commission decision OJ [2004] L362/17.

With this in mind, as an exception to the prohibition in Article 101(1) TFEU, Article 101(3) TFEU provides that the prohibition in Article 101(1) TFEU may be declared inapplicable in the case of agreements, decisions and concerted practices that fall within the prohibition in Article 101(1) TFEU 'which contribute to improving production or distribution of goods or to promoting technical or economic progress, while allowing consumers a fair share of the resulting benefits, and which do not impose restrictions which are not indispensable to the attainment of these objectives,

---

443. Article 101(3) Guidelines, para. 41.
444. Article 101(3) Guidelines, para. 41 citing Case 56/65 *Société Technique Minière (L.T.M.) v. Maschinenbau Ulm GmbH* (M.B.U.) [1966] ECR 235, 249, [1966] CMLR 357, 375. According to the Commission the consequences of the activity of severing on the remainder of the agreement is governed by national law (Article 101(3) Guidelines, para. 41 citing Case 319/82 *Kerpen & Kerpen* [1983] ECR 4 173, paras 11 and 12.
445. Article 101(3) Guidelines, para. 4.
446. Article 101(3) Guidelines, para. 3.
447. Guidelines on the applicability of Article [101 TFEU] to horizontal cooperation agreements OJ [2011] C11/1.
448. Article 101(3) Guidelines, para. 3.
449. Article 101(3) Guidelines, para. 1.
450. Article 101(3) Guidelines, para. 5.
451. Article 101(3) Guidelines, para. 6.
452. Whish et al. 2012: 153 citing the decision of the General Court in Case T-17/93 *Matra Hachette v. Commission* [1994] ECR II-595, para. 85. *See also* Case T-168/01, para. 233 and Article [101(3)] Guidelines, para. 46.

and do not afford such undertakings the possibility of eliminating competition in respect of a substantial part of the products concerned'.[453,454]

An assessment under Article 101(3) TFEU is executed in two steps. Step one entails the assessment of whether the agreement is the one 'capable of affecting trade between Member States, has an anti-competitive object or actual or potential anti-competitive effects'.[455] Step two entails a determination of the pro-competitive benefits produced by the agreement that is found to be restrictive of competition and an assessment of whether these pro-competitive effects trump the anticompetitive effects.[456]

Since the goal of the EU rules on competition law is the protection of competition *on a given market* and these rules cannot be detached from this goal, the assessment under Article 101(3) TFEU is *market specific*; the benefits flowing from restrictive agreements are accordingly assessed 'within the confines of each relevant market to which the agreement relates'.[457]

With this in mind 'the condition that consumers must receive a fair share of the benefits implies in general that efficiencies generated by the restrictive agreement within a relevant market must be sufficient to outweigh the anti-competitive effects produced by the agreement within that same relevant market'.[458] Moreover, the adverse consequences for consumers in one geographic market or product market will not ordinarily be 'balanced against and compensated by positive effects for consumers in another unrelated geographic market or product market'.[459] In the event that the two markets are connected it may be possible to take into account efficiencies that have been achieved on these distinct markets on the proviso that 'the group of consumers affected by the restriction and benefiting from the efficiency gains are substantially the same'.[460]

Assessment of restrictive agreements within the context of Article 101(3) TFEU is made within the actual context within which it occurs and based on the facts existing at the given point in time.[461]

To qualify under Article 101(3) TFEU, the agreement, decision or concerted practice caught by Article 101(1) TFEU must satisfy the four cumulative conditions set out in Article 101(3) TFEU.[462] These four conditions consist of two sets of criteria (two that are positive and two that are negative).[463]

453. Article 101(3) Guidelines, para. 9.
454. Whish et al. 2012: 151.
455. Article 101(3) Guidelines, para. 11.
456. Article 101(3) Guidelines, para. 11.
457. Article 101(3) Guidelines, para. 43 citing Case T-131/99 *Shaw* [2002] ECR II-2023, para. 163 and Case C-360/92 P, *Publishers Association* [1995] ECR I-23, para. 29.
458. Article 101(3) Guidelines, para. 43.
459. Article 101(3) Guidelines, para. 43.
460. Article 101(3) Guidelines, para. 43.
461. Article 101(3) Guidelines, para. 44.
462. Article 101(3) Guidelines, para. 34.
463. Article 101(3) Guidelines, para. 34.

As the criteria articulated in Article 101(3) TFEU are cumulative; an agreement will only benefit from the exception in Article 101(3) TFEU if the affected agreement meets the ensemble of these criteria.[464] Given that these criteria are cumulative, in the event that the agreement fails to meet one of the delineated criteria it is then unnecessary to examine any of the remaining criteria.[465]

In circumstances where one of the four criteria is no longer met, Article 101(3) TFEU will cease applying to the agreement concerned.[466]

[A] The Two Positive Criteria in Article 101(3) TFEU

Article 101(1) TFEU may be declared inapplicable to agreements that, first, contribute in some way to improving the production of goods or their distribution or to promoting technical or economic progress (the issue of *pass-on to consumers*[467]); and second, permit consumers a fair share of the resulting benefit.

[B] The Negative Criteria in Article 101(3) TFEU

Article 101(1) TFEU may be declared inapplicable when agreements that meet the two positive criteria outlined above also fulfil the negative criteria contained in Article 101(3) TFEU. As such the prohibition in Article 101(1) TFEU may be declared inapplicable to agreements that improve production or distribution of goods or technical or economic progress and permit consumers a fair share of the resulting benefits on the proviso that these do not contain certain offending provisions.

Such agreements must not contain provisions that impose on the undertakings concerned restrictions which are *not indispensable to the attainment of the aforementioned objectives* (*indispensability*[468]) and that afford the undertakings concerned the possibility of eliminating competition in relation to a substantial part of the goods involved.

An agreement that fulfils all four conditions is deemed to enhance competition within the relevant market, 'because it leads the undertakings concerned to offer cheaper or better products to consumers, compensating the latter for the adverse effects of the restrictions of competition'.[469]

464. Whish et al. 2012: 153 citing Article 101(3) Guidelines, para. 42. *See* Cases 43/82 and 63/82 *VBVB and VVVB v. Commission* [1984] ECR 19, para. 61; Case C-238/05 *Asnef-Equifax v. Asociación de Usuarios de Servicios Bancarios (Ausbanc)* [2006] ECR I-11125, [2007] 4 CMLR 6, para. 65.
465. Article 101(3) Guidelines, para. 38 citing Case 161/84 *Pronuptia* [1986] ECR 353.
466. Whish et al. 2012: 153 citing Article [101(3)] Guidelines, para. 44.
467. Article 101(3) Guidelines, para. 39.
468. Article 101(3) Guidelines, para. 39.
469. Article 101(3) Guidelines, para. 34.

§2.16 INDIVIDUAL CASES AND THE BLOCK EXEMPTION REGULATIONS

Article 101(3) TFEU can be applied either to individual cases or to categories of agreements, decisions and concerted practices by virtue of the block exemption regulations.[470]

In circumstances where a restrictive agreement is covered by a block exemption regulation, the parties to the said agreement are 'relieved of their burden under Article 2 of Regulation 1/2003 of showing that their individual agreement satisfies each of the conditions of Article [101(3)]. They only have to prove that the restrictive agreement benefits from a block exemption'.[471]

The application of Article 101(3) TFEU to categories of agreements by means of a block exemption regulation 'is based on the presumption that restrictive agreements that fall within their scope fulfil each of the four conditions laid down in Article [101(3)]'.[472]

In circumstances where an agreement falls within the scope of Article 101(1) and the conditions set out in Article 101(3) are not fulfilled, the benefit of the block exemption may be withdrawn.[473] The Commission on its own initiative or in response to a complaint has the power to withdraw the benefit of a block exemption if it finds that in a specific case an agreement covered by a block exemption regulation has certain effects that are incompatible with Article 101(3) TFEU.[474]

An NCA also has the power to withdraw the benefit of a block exemption regulation where an agreement has effects which are incompatible with Article 101(3) TFEU in the territory of that Member State, or in part thereof, if the territory 'has all the characteristics of a distinct geographic market'.[475] In circumstances where a withdrawal is sought by the NCA it is for the NCA concerned to prove that that agreement infringes Article 101(1) TFEU and fails to meet the conditions of Article 101(3) TFEU.[476]

National courts have no power to withdraw the benefit of the block exemption regulations.[477]

[A] Procedure under Article 101(3) TFEU

Under Regulation 17/62 the Commission enjoyed the exclusive right to provide individual exemptions to agreements that were notified to it. With the entry into force of Regulation 1/2003 the system of notification and the individual grant of exemptions were removed and replaced with a new more streamlined system.

470. Article 101(3) Guidelines, paras 2 and 35.
471. Article 101(3) Guidelines, para. 35.
472. Article 101(3) Guidelines, para. 35.
473. Article 101(3) Guidelines, para. 36.
474. Article 101(3) Guidelines, para. 36 citing Regulation 1/2003, Article 29(1).
475. Article 101(3) Guidelines, para. 36 citing Regulation 1/2003, Article 29(2).
476. Article 101(3) Guidelines, para. 36.
477. Article 101(3) Guidelines, para. 37.

Pursuant to Regulation 17/62 an agreement that was in violation of Article 101(1) TFEU could only benefit from Article 101(3) TFEU if it was specifically exempted from the prohibition contained in Article 101(1) TFEU as a result of either an individual exemption (granted by the Commission following notification of the agreement) or a block exemption (extended by means of a Regulation to certain types of agreements).

From 1 May 2004 (pursuant to Regulation 1/2003) there is no longer a need to apply for an individual exemption and no prior decision is required on whether the agreement satisfies the conditions in A101(3) TFEU.[478]

The Commission, the NCAs and the national courts may now apply Article 101(3) TFEU individually to agreements, if there is a question about whether the agreement is compatible with this provision. As such the Commission, the NCAs or the national courts may exempt an agreement, decision or concerted practice which otherwise infringes Article 101(1) TFEU when it fulfils the criteria set out in Article 101(3) TFEU.

This new system is based on a sharing of competence in relation to the application of Article 101(3) TFEU; the application of this article is now shared by the Commission with the national courts and the NCAs.[479]

The new system has retained the system of block exemptions; as such Article 101(3) TFEU can be satisfied by ensuring that an agreement is formulated in such a manner so as to satisfy one of the block exemptions issued by the Council of the EU or the Commission.[480]

[B] Standard of Proof

Where an undertaking or an association of undertakings is looking to defend an agreement, decision or concerted practice by claiming the benefit of Article 101(3) TFEU it will bear the burden of proving that the requirements in this article are fulfilled.[481] In circumstances where the Commission reviews the evidence supporting the application of Article 101(3) TFEU and is unable to refute this evidence 'it may be that the undertakings will be taken to have discharged the burden of proof upon them'.[482]

In circumstances where the agreement is covered by a block exemption, the contracting parties will not be expected to show that the agreement meets each of the four conditions articulated in Article 101(3) TFEU; as 'there is a rebuttable presumption that agreements falling within the scope of a block exemption satisfy all four conditions'.[483]

478. Regulation 1/2003, Article 1(2).
479. Regulation 1/2003, Articles 5 and 6.
480. Whish et al. 2012: 152.
481. Regulation 1/2003, Article 2.
482. Whish et al. 2012: 152-3 citing Case 56-64 & 58-64 *Consten & Grundig v. Commission* [1966] ECR 299, 347 [1966] CMLR 418, 478.
483. Whish et al. 2012: 153 citing Article [101(3)] Guidelines, para. 35.

§2.17 VERTICAL RESTRAINTS BLOCK EXEMPTIONS (VRBER 2010)[484]

Upon the expiration of the VRBER 1999[485] in 2010 a revised legislative instrument was issued by the Commission. Dated 20 April 2010, this regulation came into force on 1 June 2010 and will expire 31 May 2022.[486] This regulation was issued alongside accompanying guidelines (Guidelines accompanying the VRBER 2010).[487]

Pursuant to this block exemption, where the market share of each of the parties to the vertical agreement on the specific market does not surpass 30% and the agreement does not contain within it certain categories of severe restrictive provisions then it is presumed that the agreement will general result in an improvement in production/distribution that permits the buying public a fair share of the resultant utility.[488]

[A] Structure of the VRBER 2010

Article 2	The block exemption (the operative provision in the VRBER)
Article 3	Market share threshold
Article 4	Hardcore restrictions
Article 5	Excluded restrictions
Article 6	Inapplicability of the block exemption
Article 7	Calculation and application of the market share threshold
Article 8	Calculation and application of turnover threshold
Article 9	Transitional period
Article 10	Validity period

[B] Scope of Application of the VRBER 2010

The VRBER 2010 governs the application of Article 101(3) TFEU to different types of vertical agreements and concerted practices.

484. Commission Regulation (EC) No 2790/1999 of 22 December 1999 on the application of Article 81(3) of the Treaty to categories of vertical agreements and concerted practices (Text with EEA relevance) OJ L 336, 29/12/1999 P. 0021 - 0025 (VRBER 1999) and its successor the Commission Regulation (EU) No 330/2010 of 20 April 2010 on the application of Article 101(3) of the Treaty on the Functioning of the European Union to categories of vertical agreements and concerted practices (Text with EEA relevance) OJ L 102, 23/4/2010 P.0001 - 0007 (VRBER 2010).
485. Commission Regulation (EC) No 2790/1999 of 22 December 1999 on the application of Article 81(3) of the Treaty to categories of vertical agreements and concerted practices OJ L 336, 29/12/1999 P. 0021 - 0025 (VRBER 1999).
486. Article 10 VRBER 2010.
487. Commission notice - Guidelines on Vertical Restraints (Text with EEA relevance) OJ C 130, 19.05.2010, P. 0001-0046, para. 3. (Guidelines on VRBER 2010).
488. VRBER 2010, Recital 8.

A vertical agreement is defined by Article 1 of the VRBER 2010 as 'an agreement or concerted practice entered into between two or more undertakings each of which operates, for the purposes of the agreement or the concerted practice, at a different level of the production or distribution chain, and relating to the conditions under which the parties may purchase, sell or resell certain goods or services'.[489] It is clear from the definition of the term 'vertical agreement' in Article 1 that the VRBER will apply also to concerted practices.[490]

The categories of agreement that are ordinarily deemed to meet the criteria set out in Article 101(3) TFEU encompass those that involve the purchase or sale of goods or services whether these are concluded between non-competing undertakings, made between certain competing undertakings (where the undertakings are actual or potential competitors)[491] or in the alternative by specific associations of retailers of goods.[492]

Also the categories of vertical agreement ordinarily deemed to meet the criteria set out in Article 101(3) TFEU encompass those containing auxiliary provisions governing the assignment or use of Intellectual property rights.[493]

Pursuant to Article 2 of the VRBER the block exemption applies to 'vertical agreements containing provisions which relate to the assignment to the buyer or use by the buyer of intellectual property rights, provided that those provisions do not constitute the *primary object of such agreements* and are *directly* related to the use, sale or resale of goods or services by the buyer or its customers. The exemption applies on condition that, in relation to the contract goods or services, those provisions *do not contain restrictions of competition having the same object as vertical restraints* which are not exempted under this Regulation'.[494]

Whilst franchising is not specifically addressed within the VRBER 2010 it is dealt with in the Guidelines accompanying the VRBER.[495]

This block exemption will not apply, however, to vertical agreements 'the subject matter of which falls within the scope of any other block exemption regulation, unless otherwise provided for in such a regulation'.[496]

489. Article 1(1)a, VRBER 2010.
490. The definition provided in Article 1(1)a, VRBER 2010 is reinforced by the wording of Recital 3 which defines the term 'vertical agreements' as including corresponding concerted practices.
491. A competing undertaking is defined as meaning 'an actual or potential competitor' (Article 1(1)c VRBER 2010) whilst an actual competitor is defined as an 'undertaking that is active on the same relevant market' (Article 1(1)c VRBER 2010) and a potential competitor is defined as an 'undertaking that, in the absence of the vertical agreement, would, on realistic grounds and not just as a mere theoretical possibility, in case of a small but permanent increase in relative prices be likely to undertake, within a short period of time, the necessary additional investments or other necessary switching costs to enter the relevant market'. (Article 1(1)c, VRBER 2010).
492. VRBER 2010, Recital 3.
493. VRBER 2010, Recital 3 and elaborated upon in Article 2(3), VRBER 2010.
494. Article 2(3), VRBER 2010 (italics added by authors).
495. Commission notice - Guidelines on Vertical Restraints (Text with EEA relevance) OJ C 130, 19.05.2010, P. 0001-0046, para. 3. (VRBER 2010 Guidelines).
496. Article 2(5), VRBER 2010.

Moreover this block exemption does not extend to vertical agreements entered into between competing undertakings unless these undertakings have entered into a non-reciprocal vertical agreement.[497]

[C] Main Change Introduced by the New Version of the Block Exemption

The main change introduced by the VRBER 2010 is the requirement that the respective market share of each party (the supplier and the buyer) should not exceed 30% (*30% market threshold*).[498] This revision was made 'to take into account the fact that some buyers may also have market power with potentially negative effects on competition'.[499]

[D] Market Share Threshold (Article 3 and Article 7, VRBER 2010)

Application of the block exemption (in Article 2) will depend upon the market share of the supplier and the buyer.[500]

The block exemption set out in Article 2, VRBER 2010 will apply on condition that:

- the market share held by the supplier does not surpass 30% 'of the relevant market on which it sells the contract goods or services'; and
- the market share held by the buyer does not surpass 30% 'of the relevant market on which it purchases the contract goods or services'.[501]

In other words, the supplier's market share and the buyer's market share must each be 30% or less.[502]

It is presumed that where the market share of each of the contracting undertakings does not exceed 30% and the agreement does not contain certain types of severe vertical restraints then generally the agreement will lead to an improvement in production or distribution allowing consumers a fair share of ensuing benefits.[503]

497. Article 2(4), VRBER 2010.
498. VRBER 2010, Recital 8, and Article 3(1), VRBER. In the former block exemption (VRBER 1999), Article 3(1) stated that the block exemption (in Article 2 of this instrument) would apply 'on condition that the market share held by the supplier does not exceed 30% of the relevant market on which it sells the contract goods or services.' (Article 3(1) VRBER 1999).
499. Press release IP/10/445 dated 20 April 2010.
500. Article 3(1), VRBER 2010.
501. VRBER 2010 Guidelines, para. 23.
502. Article 3(1), VRBER 2010.
503. VRBER 2010, Recital 8.

[E] Calculation of Market Share

In order to calculate the market share of the supplier, reference is made to the market sales value data for the preceding calendar year.[504]

In order to calculate the market share of the buyer, reference is made to the market purchase value data for the preceding calendar year.[505]

Where such data is unavailable, then estimates computed on the basis of other dependable market data can be used *inter alia* market sales and purchase volumes.[506]

[F] Multiparty Vertical Agreement

In a multiparty vertical agreement involving three parties who each operate at a different level of trade, the block exemption (in Article 2) will apply on the proviso that the market share of each respective party to the agreement is 30% or less.[507]

In the context of a multiparty arrangement, where one of undertaking acts as an intermediary (buying the contract goods or services from an undertaking that is party to the agreement and selling these on to another undertaking that is party to the agreement) the agreement will be covered by the VRBER 2010 on condition that the market share of the intermediary undertaking does not exceed the 30% market share threshold both as a buyer and a supplier.[508]

The example given by the VRBER 2010 Guidelines is that of an agreement concluded between a producer, wholesaler and retailer, which includes a non-compete clause. According to the Guidelines, for the block exemption to apply to this particular agreement the market shares of the producer and the wholesaler on their separate downstream markets must no surpass 30% and the market shares of the wholesaler and the retailer on their respective purchase markets must not surpass 30%.[509]

[G] Change in Market Share and the Phased Approach

Some flexibility is built into the VRBER 2010 to allow for changes in market share over time. Here a phased approach is adopted which uses the 35% market share threshold as a demarcation line.

In circumstances where the market share was initially no more than 30% and there is a subsequent increase in the market share over 30% *but not exceeding 35%*, the block exemption in Article 2 of the VRBER 2010 will remain in place for '*two consecutive calendar years* following the year in which the *30%* market share was first exceeded'.[510]

504. Article 7(a)-(b), VRBER 2010.
505. Article 7(a)-(b), VRBER 2010.
506. Article 7(a), VRBER 2010 as supplemented by VRBER 2010 Guidelines, para. 93.
507. VRBER 2010 Guidelines, para. 90.
508. Article 3(2), VRBER 2010 as supplemented by VRBER 2010 Guidelines, para. 90.
509. VRBER 2010 Guidelines, para. 90.
510. Article 7(d), VRBER 2010 (italics added by authors).

An increase in the market share *over 35%*, in circumstances where the initial market share did not surpass 30%, will mean that the block exemption in Article 2 of the VRBER 2010 will remain in place 'for *one calendar year* following the year in which the level of *35%* was first exceeded'.[511]

[H] Vertical Restraints (Hardcore and Excluded Restrictions)

[1] Hardcore Restrictions: Restrictions That Remove the Benefit of the Block Exemption (Article 4, VRBER 2010)

It is effectively presumed pursuant to the VRBER 2010 that 'where the market share held by each of the undertakings party to the agreement on the relevant market does not exceed 30%, vertical agreements which do not contain certain types of severe restrictions of competition generally lead to an improvement in production or distribution and allow consumers a fair share of the resulting benefits'.[512]

Vertical agreements containing certain categories of restrictions, known as hardcore restrictions, will not be capable of being exempted pursuant to the VRBER 2010.

The categories of restrictions classified as hardcore restrictions are those 'likely to restrict competition and harm consumers ... which are not indispensable to the attainment of the efficiency-enhancing effects'.[513]

The presence of one or more hardcore restrictions in a vertical agreement will effectively 'lead to the exclusion of the whole vertical agreement from the scope of application of the Block Exemption Regulation'.[514] As such hardcore restrictions are incapable of being severed from the vertical agreement within which they are contained.[515]

The inclusion of such a provision gives rise to the presumption that the agreement falls within the prohibition in Article 101(1) TFEU and is unlikely to satisfy the conditions set out in Article 101(3) TFEU.[516]

These severe anticompetitive provisions will effectively exclude the benefit of the block exemption without regard to the market share of the undertakings involved.[517]

Pursuant to Article 4 of the VRBER 2010, the block exemption will not apply to those vertical agreements that directly or indirectly, in isolation or in combination with other factors under the control of the parties set out to:

- Restrict the ability of the buyer to set its sale price.[518]

511. Article 7(e), VRBER 2010 (italics added by authors).
512. VRBER 2010, Recital 8.
513. VRBER 2010, Recital 10.
514. VRBER 2010 Guidelines, para. 47.
515. VRBER 2010 Guidelines, para. 70.
516. VRBER 2010 Guidelines, para. 47.
517. VRBER 2010, Recital 10.
518. Article 4(a), VRBER 2010; VRBER 2010 Guidelines, para. 48.

- Restrict the territory into which, or the customers to whom, a buyer party to the agreement may sell the contract goods or services, except:[519]
  - the restriction of active sales into the exclusive territory or to an exclusive customer group (reserved to the supplier or allocated by the supplier to another buyer) in circumstances where the restriction does not limit sales by the buyer's customers;[520]
  - the restriction of sales to end users by a buyer who is operating at the wholesale level of trade;[521]
  - the restriction of sales by members of a selective distribution system[522] to unauthorised distributors within the territory reserved by the supplier to operate that system;[523] and
  - the restriction of the ability of the buyer to sell parts (supplied for the purposes of incorporation) to customers who would use them in the production of the same type of goods as those supplied by the supplier[524]
- Restrict active or passive sales to end users by members of a selective distribution system operating at the retail level of trade (without prejudice to the possibility of forbidding a member of the system from operating out of a place of establishment that is unauthorised).[525]
- Restrict cross-supplies between distributors within a selective distribution system, including between distributors operating at different level of trade.[526]
- Restrict (in an agreement between a supplier of components and a buyer who incorporates those components) the ability of the supplier to sell components as spare parts to end users, repairers or other service providers who are not entrusted by the buyer with the repair or servicing of its goods.[527]

[2] When Is Fixing the Sale Price Not a Hardcore Restriction?[528]

In spite of the fact that a direct or indirect restriction on the ability of the buyer to set a sale price will result in an exclusion of the block exemption, a supplier will be able to set a maximum sale price or recommend a sale price without this resulting in the exclusion of the block exemption.[529]

519. Article 4(b), VRBER 2010; VRBER 2010 Guidelines, para. 50-5.
520. Article 4(b)(i), VRBER 2010.
521. Article 4(b)(ii), VRBER 2010.
522. A selective distribution system is defined by Article 1(1)e as 'a distribution system where the supplier undertakes to sell the contract goods or services, either directly or indirectly, only to distributors selected on the basis of specified criteria and where these distributors undertake not to sell such goods or services to unauthorised distributors within the territory reserved by the supplier to operate that system'.
523. Article 4(b)(iii), VRBER 2010.
524. Article 4(b)(iv), VRBER 2010.
525. Article 4(c), VRBER 2010; VRBER 2010 Guidelines, para. 56-7.
526. Article 4(d), VRBER 2010; VRBER 2010 Guidelines, para. 58.
527. Article 4(2), VRBER 2010; VRBER 2010 Guidelines, para. 59.
528. Article 4(a), VRBER 2010.
529. Article 4(a), VRBER 2010.

This will be the case provided that the imposition of a maximum sale price or the recommendation of a sale price do not amount to a fixed or minimum sale price as a result of pressure from, or incentives offered by, any of the parties.[530]

[3] Individual Applications in the Context of Hardcore Restrictions

Notwithstanding the existence of a hardcore restriction in the agreement, in individual cases, undertakings have the possibility to demonstrate pro-competitive effects under Article 101(3) TFEU,[531] in circumstances where an undertaking is capable of showing the likely efficiencies resulting from the inclusion of one or more hardcore restrictions and the fact that the requirements in Article 101(3) TFEU are met.

The Commission is then obliged 'to assess the likely negative impact on competition before making the ultimate assessment of whether the conditions of Article 101(1) are fulfilled'.[532]

The procedure for the individual assessment of such claims involves two sequential steps.[533]

First an assessment of the likely negative impact on competition associated with the inclusion of the hardcore restriction(s).[534]

Second an assessment of whether the conditions set out in Article 101(3) TFEU are met.[535]

Though the procedure is set out in a sequential manner, in practice the parties (the applicant undertaking and Commission) may engage in an iterative process involving a repetition of the process allowing an enhancement and improvement of the respective arguments of the parties and the Commission.[536]

[4] Excluded Restrictions: Restrictions Excluded from the Scope of the Block Exemption (Article 5, VRBER 2010)

Certain anticompetitive provisions known as excluded restrictions will not benefit from the block exemption.

The market share threshold of the parties contracting will have no bearing in this context. As such, such a restrictive provision will be excluded from the block exemption even if the market share threshold is not surpassed.[537]

Pursuant to the VRBER 2010, the following provisions are excluded restrictions:

530. Article 4(a), VRBER 2010.
531. VRBER 2010 Guidelines, para. 47.
532. VRBER 2010 Guidelines, para. 47.
533. VRBER 2010 Guidelines, para. 47.
534. VRBER 2010 Guidelines, para. 47.
535. VRBER 2010 Guidelines, para. 47.
536. VRBER 2010 Guidelines, para. 47, FT 26.
537. VRBER 2010 Guidelines, para. 65.

- Non-compete provisions of an indefinite nature or lasting for over 5 years[538] or tacitly renewable beyond a period of 5 years.[539]
- Obligations forcing the buyer not to produce, buy, sell or resell goods or services after the agreement comes to an end:[540]
    - Such an obligation is excluded from the coverage of the block exemption unless the obligation is:[541]
        - essential to the protection of substantial know-how[542] transferred by the supplier to the buyer;
        - relates to goods or services that compete with the contract goods or services;
        - confined to the premises and land from which the buyer operated during the term of the agreement (namely the point of sale); and
        - limited to a maximum term of one year after termination of the agreement.
- Obligations forcing members of a selective distribution system not to sell specific competing brands ('brands of particular competing suppliers').[543] Where a supplier stops his dealers from purchasing competing goods for resale this obligation cannot benefit from the coverage of the block exemption. Article 5 of the VRBER 2010 targets a strategy used in commence intended to allow a group of suppliers using the same distribution outlets from blocking access to these outlets to a specific competitor or a group of specific competitors.[544]

On condition that the excluded restriction may be severed successfully, leaving the remaining clauses operational, the block exemption will apply to the remainder of the vertical agreement.[545] The benefit of the block exemption is only lost in relation to the part of the agreement which fails to meet the conditions set out in the VRBER.[546]

538. Article 5(1)a, VRBER 2010 as supplemented by VRBER 2010 Guidelines, para. 65-7.
539. Article 5(1), VRBER 2010.
540. Article 5(1)b, VRBER 2010 as supplemented by VRBER 2010 Guidelines, para. 68.
541. Article 5(3), VRBER 2010 Guidelines, para. 68.
542. Know-how is defined by Article 1(g), VRBER 2010 as 'a package of non-patented practical information, resulting from experience and testing by the supplier, which is secret, substantial and identified'. Article 1(g), VRBER 2010 defines the key terms set out in the definition of 'know-how'. In this context, 'secret' is defined as meaning that 'the know-how is not generally known or easily accessible'; 'substantial' is defined as meaning that 'the know-how is significant and useful to the buyer for the use, sale or resale of the contract goods or services' and 'identified' is defined as meaning that 'the know-how is described in a sufficiently comprehensive manner so as to make it possible to verify that it fulfils the criteria of secrecy and substantiality'. (Article 1(g), VRBER 2010).
543. Article 5(1)c, VRBER 2010; VRBER 2010 Guidelines, para. 69.
544. VRBER 2010 Guidelines, para. 69.
545. VRBER 2010 Guidelines, para. 59.
546. VRBER 2010 Guidelines, para. 71.

[5] *Withdrawal of the Benefit of the Block Exemption*

In circumstances where the agreement to which the VRBER 2010 applies has consequences that are at odds with Article 101(3) TFEU, the Commission and indeed the NCAs may remove the benefit of the block exemption.[547]

The Commission is able to withdraw the benefit of the VRBER 2010 when it finds in a certain case that the 'qualifying agreement' (to which the exemption provided for in the VRBER 2010 applies) nevertheless has effects that are incompatible with Article 101(3) TFEU.[548]

The same is true for the NCA.[549] A competition authority at the Member State level is able to withdraw the benefit of the VRBER 2010 (in all or part of territory of that Member State) when the 'qualifying agreement' nevertheless has effects that are incompatible with Article 101(3) TFEU in the territory of that Member State, or in a part thereof, 'where such territory has all the characteristics of a distinct geographic market'.[550]

[6] *Licensing and the VRBER*

Vertical agreements containing IPR provisions are capable of benefiting from the block exemption if certain conditions are met by these agreements and in particular by the IPR provisions contained within these agreements.[551]

[I] Qualifying Agreements: When Will an Agreement Containing IPR Provisions Fall Within the Scope of the Block Exemption?

The point of departure in this context is Article 2(3) of the VRBER 2010 that brings within the scope of the block exemption vertical agreements containing IPR provisions. This article states that the block exemption (provided for in Article 2(1) VRBER 2010) applies 'to vertical agreements containing provisions which relate to the assignment to the buyer or use by the buyer of intellectual property rights, provided that those provisions do not constitute the primary object of such agreements and are directly related to the use, sale or resale of goods or services by the buyer or its customers. The exemption applies on condition that, in relation to the contract goods or services, those provisions do not contain restrictions of competition having the same object as vertical restraints which are not exempted under this Regulation'.[552]

The conditions set out in Article 2(3) of the VRBER 2010 are elaborated upon in the Guidelines accompanying the VRBER 2010. These conditions aim to ensure that the VRBER 2010 'applies to vertical agreements where the use, sale or resale of goods or

547. VRBER 2010, Recitals 13 & 14.
548. VRBER 2010, Recital 13.
549. VRBER 2010, Recital 14.
550. VRBER 2010, Recital 14.
551. The IPR provisions must meet the five conditions set out in VRBER 2010 Guidelines, para. 31.
552. Article 2(3), VRBER 2010.

services can be performed more effectively because the IPRs are assigned to or licensed for use by the buyer'.[553]

According to these Guidelines, Article 2(3) of the VRBER 2010 includes within its scope of application, vertical agreements containing provisions governing the:[554]

- assignment of IPRs to the buyer; or
- use of IPRs by the buyer

All other vertical agreements containing IPR provisions are excluded from the scope of the Block Exemption.[555]

According to the Guidelines, the block exemption in VRBER 2010 applies to vertical agreements containing IPR provisions if five cumulative conditions are met. The IPR provisions in these vertical agreements must:[556]

(1) be 'part of a vertical agreement';[557]
(2) be 'assigned to, or licensed for use by, the buyer';[558]
(3) not 'constitute the primary object of the agreement';[559]
(4) be 'directly related to the use, sale or resale of goods or services by the buyer or his customers';[560]
(5) not 'contain restrictions of competition having the same object as vertical restraints which are not exempted'[561] under the VRBER 2010.

- Condition one: IPR provisions 'must be part of a vertical agreement'

The agreement containing the IPR provisions will be a qualifying agreement (qualifying for the block exemption) if it is 'an agreement with conditions under which the parties may purchase, sell or resell certain goods or services'.[562]

This first condition makes it clear 'that the context within which the IPRs are provided is an agreement to purchase or distribute goods or an agreement to purchase or provide services and not an agreement concerning the assignment or licensing of IPRs for the manufacture of goods, nor a pure licensing agreement'.[563]

As such the VRBER 2010 will not apply to agreements under which one party provides to another a recipe, and licenses the other party the right to produce a

553. VRBER 2010 Guidelines, para. 32.
554. VRBER 2010 Guidelines, para. 31.
555. VRBER 2010 Guidelines, para. 31.
556. VRBER 2010 Guidelines, para. 31.
557. VRBER 2010 Guidelines, para. 31.
558. VRBER 2010 Guidelines, para. 31.
559. VRBER 2010 Guidelines, para. 31.
560. VRBER 2010 Guidelines, para. 31.
561. VRBER 2010 Guidelines, para. 31.
562. VRBER 2010 Guidelines, para. 31.
563. VRBER 2010 Guidelines, para. 33.

beverage using the recipe.[564] The block exemption neither will apply to copyright licensing[565] nor will it apply to a pure licence of a trademark.[566]

- Condition two – IPR provisions 'must be assigned to, or licensed for use by, the buyer'

The second condition makes it clear that the VRBER 2010 will not apply 'when the IPRs are provided by the buyer to the supplier, no matter whether the IPRs concern the manner of manufacture or of distribution'.[567]

- Condition three – IPR provisions 'must not constitute the primary object of the agreement'

The third condition makes it clear that in order to qualify for the block exemption in the VRBER 2010, the IPR provisions 'must serve the implementation of the vertical agreement'.[568] As such, the primary aim of the agreement 'must not be the assignment or licensing of IPRs',[569] but rather 'the purchase, sale or resale of goods or services'.[570]

- Condition four – IPR provisions 'must be directly related to'

This condition which requires that the IPR provisions be *directly related* to the use, sale or resale of goods or services by the buyer or his customers depends on the IPR provisions facilitating 'the use, sale or resale of goods or services by the buyer or his customers'.[571] These IPR provisions will usually involve the marketing of the goods or services.[572] In franchising, this is the case, as the franchisor sells goods for resale to the franchisee and licenses the franchisee to use its (franchisor's) trademark and know-how in order to market the goods.[573]

The contract goods or services are usually supplied by the licensor, though they may also be sourced by the licensee from a third supplier.[574]

- Condition five – IPR provisions must not contain non-exempted vertical restraints

The IPR provisions included in the agreements should not have the same object as any of the hardcore restrictions (noted in Article 4 of the VRBER 2010) or any of the excluded restrictions (noted in Article 5 of the VRBER 2010).[575]

564. VRBER 2010 Guidelines, para. 33.
565. VRBER 2010 Guidelines, para. 33.
566. VRBER 2010 Guidelines, para. 33.
567. VRBER 2010 Guidelines, para. 34.
568. VRBER 2010 Guidelines, para. 35.
569. VRBER 2010 Guidelines, para. 35.
570. VRBER 2010 Guidelines, para. 35.
571. VRBER 2010 Guidelines, para. 36.
572. VRBER 2010 Guidelines, para. 36.
573. VRBER 2010 Guidelines, para. 36.
574. VRBER 2010 Guidelines, para. 36.
575. VRBER 2010 Guidelines, para. 37.

CHAPTER 3

International Trademark Licensing

§3.01 BACKGROUND AND CONTEXT

Cross-border trademark licensing is one of the most complex forms of international licensing, and this is primarily due to the intricacies of trademark law which is a highly specialised area in its own right. However, as with software licences, trademark licences are also one of the more common forms of international licence that arise in commercial and corporate transactions.

In addition, being included within wider intellectual property licences, trademark licenses are often key components of wider commercial transactions such as franchising, manufacturing and distribution arrangements. This chapter will focus on a trademark licence in the context of a standalone license for goods, but the principles covered can be applied when reviewing or drafting other forms of agreement which incorporate a trademark license.

Before analysing the trademark licence structure and components in detail it is important that the reader has a working knowledge of trademarks and the laws and principles which govern them. The following summary is necessarily concise, due to the broad scope of the law on trademarks, but the intention is that it will provide an overview of the law in the UK and European context with illustrative references to other international jurisdictions to prompt further reading and research as needed. At the time of writing it is unclear how the exit of the UK from the EU will affect UK trademarks, so this is not considered further, although it is widely thought that the continuation of the existing arrangements, to the extent achievable, is desirable. The chapter's division into sections means that you can easily navigate the content based on your current knowledge and area of focus.

The nature of trademarks in a legal context is often misunderstood. The gaps are regularly demonstrated in the way intellectual property rights are described in the media, for example referring to the 'trademarking' of materials that are clearly the subject of copyright protection. Trademarks at their core can be thought of as signs used to differentiate the goods or services of one entity from those of another and can take the form of words, designs, letters, numerals and even the shape of goods or their packaging.[1] Note that trademarks can cover services as well as goods; however, to keep the content concise we will not be using the term 'service mark' separately in this chapter unless the context requires. References to trademarks should therefore be viewed as including service marks as well, unless stated otherwise. Trademarks are divided into classes of goods and services for registration, and this system is described in section §3.03[C] below.

The trademark owner must be a legal entity, but this can take several forms, so you will find individuals, businesses and other types of organisation that are trademark owners. For example, many charities and not-for-profit organisations have significant numbers of trademarks that are well known; the main World Wildlife Fund trademark has international recognition, and the association with the image of a panda will probably spring to mind when the name of that organisation is mentioned to you.

Trademarks are used at all levels of the commerce chain covering both 'Business to Business' suppliers and 'Business to Consumer' suppliers. Trademarks are used by a vast array of suppliers from heavy industrial equipment dealers through to confectioners and almost all types of supplier of goods and services in-between. The primary aim of a trademark is to enable the originator or maker of goods and services to be readily identified by the use of that sign. The all-pervasive use of trademarks in commerce today is easily demonstrated by looking around any supermarket, where it is hard to find any packaged products that do not utilise a trademark in one form or another.

Trademarks clearly play a pivotal role in the promotion of goods and services in the global marketplace as well. With increasing numbers of generic goods and services with relatively minor differentiators, in terms of functionality and specification, coming from a variety of sources, trademarks are a valuable method for businesses to instil identity and uniqueness in their products. Trademarks go beyond indicating that a supplier provided the product or service in that they also promote expectations of cost, quality and value in the target customers. The objective, of course, is to generate new customers and to create brand loyalty so that sales are repeated. An illustration of the value of trademarks and the importance of brands in the wider sense can be found in the Forbes annual list of the world's most powerful brands.[2]

Trademarks are not a recent creation and have been used in some form for centuries with their origins being traced back to craftsmen adding their fingerprints to the bottom of Egyptian, Greek and Roman pottery to indicate to the buyer who had made it.[3] The development of trademarks is also commonly associated with the markings on early weapons such as swords to indicate who had produced them. However, the modern trademark systems using formal registration originated in the 19th century in France and England with the first registered British trademark being a

1. Trade Mark Act 1994 (UK) s. 1.1.
2. Forbes Media LLC 'The World's Most Valuable Brands' (https://www.forbes.com/powerful-brands/list/#tab:rank) accessed 3 September 2017.
3. Helen E. Norman, *Intellectual Property Law* (2nd edn, Oxford University Press 2011).

Red Triangle logo for the brewer Bass, which was obtained under the Trade Mark Registration Act of 1875.[4]

A fundamental attribute of a trademark when compared to other intellectual property rights is that it can potentially be protected for an unlimited time, provided it is renewed and is not invalidated. In fact, the Bass Red Triangle logo referred to in the paragraph above is still registered to this day (albeit under different ownership). The ability to continually renew the protection of a trademark significantly increases its commercial value.

The impact of trademarks and their perceived value has increased exponentially in modern times. A factor at play here is the increased pace at which goods and services are replaced with new or enhanced ones. The product life cycle has shortened considerably because of faster innovation, cheaper manufacturing and lower retail prices, coupled with designed obsolescence. These changes have increased the importance of the consumer being able to identify the origin of new offerings with their supplier when the recognition could otherwise be compromised by the rapid pace of change. An illustrative example of this change is the transformation of the mobile phone and television markets to the point where replacement cycles now run 'year on year' with incremental changes within the cycle. The result of this is that products from only a few years ago can be significantly different to the latest offering and without trademarks they may not be readily identifiable as those of the manufacturer.

Brand valuation is not a definitive science, but a huge amount of money and expertise is used to estimate the market value of well-known marks and this corresponds with the status of trademarks as a core business asset. To illustrate this point, the brand consultancy Interbrand, in their 2015 survey,[5] lists the top 100 brands with individual values ranging from $4 billion for Tesla at 100 up to $178 billion for the number one brand, Apple.[6]

Brand value is also demonstrated by the amounts of money organisations are prepared to pay for the so-called rebrands – the Pepsi rebrand is reputed to have cost over a million dollars and the London Olympic 2012 logo several hundred thousand pounds. This money would not have been invested without a material return on investment being anticipated. However, the design of logos for trademarks does not have to involve large sums of money – the original Nike 'Swoosh' logo was bought from a graphic design student for a mere $15, and the original Google logo was developed by Sergei Brin, one of the company's co-founders.[7]

In common law jurisdictions such as the UK and the US you also have the concept of unregistered as well as registered trademarks, i.e., signs that have not been registered with the Governmental authorities but are still afforded protection under common law. This protection derived from principles of unfair competition such that a mark that has been used and established goodwill within a market over time should

4. David Bainbridge, *Intellectual Property* (Ninth edn, Pearson Education Limited 2012).
5. Interbrand Rankings http://interbrand.com/best-brands/best-global-brands/2016/ranking/ accessed 3 September 2017 (hereafter 'Interbrand Ranking').
6. Interbrand Ranking (n. 5).
7. StockLogos.com, www.stocklogos.com/topic/famous-logo-designs-and-how-much-did-they-cost accessed 19 July 2016.

not be taken advantage of by an unconnected third party even if they have not been officially registered.

In the UK the owner of an unregistered right can potentially bring an action for 'passing off' to prevent unfair use of their mark. However, making a successful claim for passing off is not straightforward as the owner of the unregistered mark will need to provide evidence to show that they have established a reputation and developed goodwill in the unregistered mark. In addition, the owner will need to demonstrate that the use of the conflicting mark constitutes a misrepresentation in the course of trade resulting in confusion between that mark and the unregistered mark resulting in a loss (e.g., sales under the unregistered mark have been lost as a result of the consumer buying the defendant's goods mistakenly thinking they were the goods of the claimant).[8] Another possible hindrance to making a successful passing off claim is that the mark's reputation may only cover a relatively small geographic area, such as the immediate locality of a restaurant outside of which it is substantially unknown. Protection can only apply where a reputation is established so that use of the same mark by another restaurant in another part of the country where no existing reputation can be demonstrated will not breach the rights in the unregistered trademark.

By contrast to the protection that can be sought using a passing off action in the UK, a registered trademark affords protection from conflicting use across England, Scotland, Wales, Northern Ireland and the Isle of Man. As you will appreciate, successfully proving a case of passing off will be time consuming and expensive whereas the process for enforcing a registered trademark is normally easier, faster and consequentially cheaper.

Assuming the criteria for registering a trademark can be met, the most prudent course of action will therefore be to seek registration and not rely on common law protection, where the burden of proof is high and the outcomes unpredictable. Consequently, the rest of this chapter will primarily focus on registered trademarks.

§3.02 WHAT CAN BE REGISTERED AS A TRADEMARK?

It is a common public misconception that trademarks are limited to names and logos, but in-fact less traditional signs can be the subject of a registered trademark including smells, colours, slogans, sounds, numbers and even gestures. For example, the number '911' is a trademark associated with Porsche, the Intel 'jingles' are a sound mark, Tiffany's blue pantone for jewellery (widely known as 'Tiffany Blue') is a colour mark and the 'pat on the back pocket' action used by Asda in the UK (part of Walmart) is a registered gesture mark. The common theme of these signs that enables them to be trademarks is that, notwithstanding their different forms, they are all capable of distinguishing the goods and services of one undertaking from those of another.

The wide adoption of the non-traditional forms of trademarks such as gestures and smells has been hindered to a certain extent by the difficulty in meeting certain

8. Three element test for Passing Off – *Reckitt & Colman Products Ltd v. Borden Inc. and others* [1990] 1 All ER 873.

registration requirements, but it is useful to understand their scope. One such requirement for registration is the need to be able to represent the potential mark graphically, which is obviously far more problematic for a sound or a smell. However, recent changes to increase trademark harmonisation in the EU introduced by the recasting of the Trade Mark Directive[9] means that from October 2017 graphical representation of a mark is no longer required provided that the subject matter of the trademark can be clearly identified in the application.[10] This may facilitate wider adoption of non-traditional marks in the future.

Even if the proposed mark fits into one of the categories identified above it may also be rejected for registration on other grounds which are covered in further depth in the next section.

§3.03 HOW ARE TRADEMARKS REGISTERED: AN INTERNATIONAL PERSPECTIVE

[A] Differences and Attempts to Harmonise

The process for registering a trademark varies considerably between jurisdictions and an in-depth overview here is not possible; however, many of the registration processes use a similar structure. Conscious attempts have been made to harmonise trademark registration processes through international agreements. The Trade Mark Law Treaty 1994[11] focusses on standardising the applications for and the administration of registered marks at both national and regional levels. At the date of writing there are 54 countries[12] which are signatories to the treaty, and this includes the UK and the US with Guatemala being the latest joiner in December 2016.[13]

In addition to specifying procedural requirements the Trade Mark Law Treaty 1994 standardised the trademark renewal timeline to a ten-year period and does not allow signatories to the Treaty (save in the case of surrender of a registration) to incorporate obligations of notarisation, certification or other legalisation. The overall objective of the Treaty is to make it easier for organisations to register trademarks in different jurisdictions by adopting broadly comparable registration processes which are familiar and easy to manage. The Treaty is administered by the World Intellectual Property Organisation[14] (WIPO) which is an agency of the United Nations. Established in 1967, this organisation, which currently has 188 members,[15] aims to create a balanced and effective IP system able to keep pace with the changing world whilst

9. Directive 2008/95/EC of The European Parliament and of the Council of 22 October 2008 to approximate the laws of the Member States relating to trademarks.
10. Article 3 (b) Directive (EU) 2015/2436 of the European Parliament (EP) and of the Council of 16 December 2015 to approximate the laws of the Member States relating to trademarks.
11. The Trade Mark Treaty 1994 text available at: www.wipo.int/treaties/en/ip/tlt/.
12. As of 3 September 2017.
13. List of Contracting Members: www.wipo.int/treaties/en/ShowResults.jsp?lang=en&treaty_id=5 (list of contracting members).
14. WIPO Website: www.wipo.int/portal/en/index.html.
15. List of members as at 1 May 2016: www.wipo.int/members/en/.

fostering a system that encourages innovation and creativity.[16] The WIPO website is a useful resource for IP information generally and can be referred to for, *inter alia*, a complete list of the countries that are currently signatories of the Trade Mark Law Treaty 1994.

[B] Pre-application Due Diligence and Grounds for Refusal of a Registration

Irrespective of harmonisation initiatives, each system of registration necessarily has differences and analysing these differences is beyond the scope of this chapter. However, there follows high-level description of the approach adopted in the UK for trademark registration as an illustrative example. This will hopefully provide some familiarisation with registration in the wider sense due to comparable themes adopted in other jurisdictions. The applicable legislation in the UK is the Trade Marks Act 1994.[17]

Potential grounds for the refusal of the registration of a mark should be assessed by the potential applicant, before an application is made to avoid wasted time and cost. The grounds for refusal of a trademark registration are normally divided into two categories, namely 'absolute' and 'relative' grounds.

Absolute grounds for refusal concern factors inherent in the mark itself. The following are some of the main types:

- Where the mark does not fit into one of the types of sign that can be registered as a trademark as referenced above. Further, certain types of marks will not be eligible for registration as a matter of public policy.[18] For example, signs that are considered offensive by being pornographic or by the inclusion of swear words. Applications that incorporate signs that benefit from special protection such as national flags, the Olympic symbols and hallmarks will also be rejected.
- If the mark is not inherently distinctive, i.e. where it is not capable of distinguishing the goods or services of one organisation from another.
- If the mark is descriptive of the goods or services which it is concerned with, for example, an application for 'Globe' as a trademark by a manufacturer of globes would fail for this reason but if it concerned a bike manufacturer it would not fail on this criterion. Note that the descriptive criteria extend not only the goods themselves but also to their characteristics so that if the mark is descriptive of the goods geographic origin, quality or purpose it will also not be accepted.

Relative grounds for refusal concern comparative criteria such as where the sign applied for has already been registered as a trademark by someone else in respect of

16. WIPO Policywww.wipo.int/policy/en/.
17. Trade Marks Act 1994: www.legislation.gov.uk/ukpga/1994/26/contents.
18. Trade Marks Act 1994, ss 3 and 4.

goods which are the same or similar to the ones in the application or where the proposed mark would be deceptively confusing or similar to another registered trademark. By way of example, an entity not related to Porsche A.G. trying to register 'Porsche' in relation to motor bikes would not have much success.

The process for assessing the suitability, or otherwise, of a proposed trademark is a complex process and applying the principles above can be very difficult particularly if the mark does not sit neatly 'inside the boxes' which is quite common. For this reason, and whilst not mandatory, the best route for establishing the likelihood of successful registration is to consult a trademark professional. They will be able to use their experience to assess whether the sign is suitable based on application of the absolute grounds and they can assess the likelihood of a challenge on relative grounds by searching databases of registered trademarks that could conflict.

[C] The Trademark Application and the Nice Classification System

In the UK, the fees of the Governmental registration body, the UK Trade Marks Registry, which is part of the UK Intellectual Property Office (an executive Division of the Department of Trade and Industry) (UKIPO) are non-refundable if an application fails.

The application for registration is made by completing standard forms which are then assessed by the body that deals with the registration process in the jurisdiction. In the UK, the application can be made either by traditional paper forms or online.

In addition to illustrating the mark being applied for, the applicant is required to identify the categories of goods and/or services which they want the trademark to be registered for.

The Nice Agreement,[19] which was concluded in 1957 and subsequently revised on several occasions since then,[20] provides a standard classification of goods and services for the purposes of registering trademarks.[21] The categorisation was established by a committee of expert representatives from signatory countries,[22] and the application of the categorisations is mandatory for the countries that have signed up to the agreement. The classification system (Nice Classification) has also been adopted by several International Intellectual Property Organisations (including the European Union Intellectual Property Office) and is also used by a number of countries even though they have not formally signed up to the agreement, so it is widely applicable on an international basis. The latest edition of the classification can be found on the WIPO website.

The Nice Classification system[23] has 45 classes, 34 of which relate to goods and the remaining 11 classes cover services. A huge range of different goods and services

19. Full title – Nice Agreement Concerning the International Classification of Goods and Services for the Purposes of the Registration of Marks (Nice Agreement).
20. On 14 July 1967, 13 May 1977 and 28 September 1979.
21. Text of Nice Agreement accessible at: www.wipo.int/treaties/en/text.jsp?file_id = 287532.
22. List of contracting parties accessible at: www.wipo.int/treaties/en/ShowResults.jsp?lang = en& treaty_id = 12.
23. The Nice Classification is accessible at: www.wipo.int/classifications/nice/en/.

are covered by the Nice Classification ranging from vehicles and wheelchairs in Class 12 through to things such as jellies, jams and compotes in Class 29. Notwithstanding the extensive range of goods and services covered, working out the correct classification for particular goods and services can be challenging and this is another area a trademark professional can assist with.

A filing can be made for one or more classes of goods and services, although fees are paid with reference to the number of classes applied for. This common classification system not only makes applications in other jurisdictions easier from the applicant's point of view but it also removes a significant administrative burden on the countries who are a party to the Nice Agreement who would otherwise need to develop and update their own classifications system.

In addition to the Nice Classification system, it is also worth mentioning the Vienna Classification (VCL) introduced by the Vienna Agreement[24] (concluded in 1973, amended in 1985). The VCL differs from the Nice Classification system in that it relates to the classification of figurative marks, i.e., marks that consist of pictures, graphics or images rather than words. It uses a three-level hierarchy starting with nineteen categories followed by divisions and numbered sections to accurately identify the mark at increasing levels of detail. The purpose of the VCL is to assist with exchange of information and documents concerning figurative marks at an international level. By using the same system, the speed at which trademark searches can be carried out is increased and the need for countries to develop their own classification is avoided.

[D] Examination of the Application by the Registry

Once an application has been received by the UKIPO a filing receipt will be issued. This is an important date as the trademark rights start from the date of filing rather than the date of registration if the application is successful. The filing date also has relevance in the international context and this is expanded later in this chapter. The application will then be examined to establish the suitability of the mark for registration using the criteria referred to at the start of this chapter, and an advisory search will be carried out for conflicting marks. This information is then summarised and sent back to the applicant in the form of an examination report (normally within about a month), highlighting any objections to registration on absolute grounds and referring to existing applications and registrations that the UKIPO consider could lead to a challenge from an existing trademark owner preventing the registration on relative grounds.

If the UKIPO has raised objections on absolute grounds, i.e., the mark is not suitable to be registered as a trademark, then these can be challenged by the applicant and if this is successful the objections can be waived, and the application can proceed. Even if there are citations warning of conflicting registrations raised in the report (i.e., potential challenges on relative grounds), this will not prevent the applicant from

24. Full title: Vienna Agreement Establishing an International Classification of the Figurative Elements of Marks (Vienna Agreement).

proceeding to the next stage involving advertisement of the application to see whether it is picked up and challenged by another trademark owner.

[E] The Advertisement Stage

The advertisement stage involves publishing the details of the application in the *Trade Marks Journal*[25] which is published weekly and contains details of accepted applications. If there have been no objections this stage will normally conclude within two months of the original application filing date. The purpose of the advertisement is to see whether there are any third party objections to the application when it is publicised. This provides the opportunity for oppositions to registration of the mark being raised by other trademark owners that may or may not have been picked up during the examination stage. For example, an opposition may be made if the proposed mark is considered by a third party to be identical or too similar to their own registration or existing application.

The advertisement stage can be extended for a further month at the request of a person raising an objection. In the event of a formal opposition being raised during the advertisement stage the timescales for registration can increase significantly whilst the issue is resolved (potentially years depending on the complexity). Due to the frequency and number of applications, trademark owners concerned about missing conflicting marks often commission a third party 'watching service' where all applications are systematically checked for conflicts with their own trademarks.

[F] Registration

If no objections are raised during the advertisement stage a certificate of registration will be issued by the UKIPO to the applicant, and the registration is published in the *Trade Marks Journal* to complete the process.

Overall, therefore, the registration process typically takes (assuming no objections are raised) anywhere from three to six months from the original filing of the application. The initial period of registration will be ten years, but the registration can be renewed indefinitely thereafter for successive periods of ten years, potentially giving a perpetual right.

Notwithstanding that a registration can continue to be renewed, this does not mean that the trademark rights cannot be lost. This can happen in several ways: first the registration can still be challenged as being invalid for absolute or relative grounds following registration. Anyone can bring an application for revocation and if successful, the trademark will be deemed to have not ever been in force. Non-use can also result in a registration being lost and removed from the register. In the UK non-use for a continuous period of five years (without a good reason such as a valid legal restriction) will expose the trademark to revocation. Note that the period of non-use allowed can vary in different jurisdictions. Finally, a trademark can be surrendered by

25. *Trade Marks Journal* available at: www.ipo.gov.uk/t-tmj.htm.

the rights holder. A reason for doing this might be where the holder has ceased to use or need the mark and therefore wishes to avoid incurring the on-going charges of maintaining the registration. Organisations with large numbers of trademarks often carry out audits to see whether it makes sense to remove particular marks from their portfolio.

§3.04 WHAT RIGHTS DOES A REGISTERED TRADEMARK GIVE TO THE RIGHTS HOLDER?

Trademarks are a form of intangible personal property and may therefore be licensed, assigned, bought, leased and passed by operation of law as is the case with other forms of property.

Subject to certain exceptions, a registered trademark is protected under the Trade Marks Act 1994 against unauthorised use in a number of permutations:[26]

- use in the course of trade of an identical mark for identical goods and services;
- use in the course of trade of an identical mark for similar goods and services where there is a likelihood of confusion on the part of the public;
- use in the course of trade of a similar mark for identical goods and services where there is a likelihood of confusion on the part of the public;
- use in the course of trade of a similar mark for similar goods and services where there is a likelihood of confusion on the part of the public;
- use in the course of trade of an identical or similar mark for non-similar goods and services where the registered trademark has a reputation in the UK and the use would be detrimental or harmful to the distinctiveness or repute of the registered trademark.

To explain use of identical mark for non-similar goods and services further, an example of this situation might be where one party has developed goods and services in the UK and created a reputation and the use on non-similar goods or services by a third party would dilute the distinctive of the registered mark such as if the registered name of a well-known perfume was used for a type of toilet cleaner by a third party.

Acts of infringement would include using a mark on packaging, offering the goods for sale using the mark, importing or exporting the goods under the mark and using the sign on business papers or advertising. As noted earlier, the protection of the mark runs from the filing date, but it is not possible to bring an action for infringement until the mark has been registered.

Not all use will constitute infringement, and the Trade Marks Act 1994 specifically excludes the following uses from infringement:[27]

- use by a person of their own name and address;

26. Trade Marks Act 1994, s. 10.
27. Trade Marks Act 1994, s. 11.

- use by persons other than the proprietor to provide indications of the characteristics of the goods such as kind, value, quality, geographic origin, intended purpose or quantity; or
- use of the mark where it is necessary to indicate the intended purposes of the goods or services – the most obvious example being where the use is to indicate the compatibility of spare parts and accessories.

Use of a mark for comparative advertising will not infringe a registered mark provided that the use is honest and fair in the circumstances. Any damages awarded for infringement will depend on the facts of each case and can range from an award for nominal damages to an account of any profits made in respect of the goods or services sold using the infringing marks.

After the trademark has been registered the registered trademark symbol ® can be used in connection with the mark. This symbol is used to give notice to third parties that you own the mark and that it has been registered with the applicable registry. The symbol is widely used internationally for the same purposes. There are no fixed rules regarding how the symbol is presented but it is often placed in superscript after the applicable trademark.

The registered trademark symbol may only be used with registered marks and it can be a criminal offence to use the symbol in relation to unregistered marks.[28] Where a mark is unregistered the symbols 'TM' and 'SM' can be used instead to put third parties on notice that the user of the mark believes they have rights in it, even though it has not been registered yet. The 'TM' and 'SM' symbols are often displayed where the user is in the process of making an application for the mark, but it does not mean that the user will necessarily be successful in registering the mark.

For further information on correct trademark usage, the International Trademark Association (INTA) provide a useful and straightforward guide on the subject which is available on their website (*A Guide to Proper Trade Mark Usage for Media, Internet and Publishing Professionals*).[29]

§3.05 HOW ARE TRADEMARKS PROTECTED ON A NATIONAL AND INTERNATIONAL LEVEL?

[A] Background

Trademarks are territorial rights, meaning that they can only give protection in the countries in which they are registered. Theoretically protection for a trademark in different jurisdictions would require separate applications to be made in all the countries where protection is sought. If the international protection for a trademark that is required is wide, then registration would constitute a very time-consuming and expensive process to be followed, not least because of the need to adhere to different application procedures, in different languages to obtain protection. Fortunately, to

28. Trade Marks Act 1994, s. 94.
29. INTA website accessible at www.inta.org.

address this situation, there are several international agreements and treaties that have been put in place to simplify the process for obtaining protection.

Evidently having protection in the correct jurisdictions forms the basis upon which international trademark licensing can operate. Before we look at the content of an international trademark licence in detail it is therefore important to understand the processes for registering trademarks in different jurisdictions.

[B] International Treaties Relating to Trademarks

[1] Overview

This section provides an overview of the most significant international treaties and agreements affecting trademarks. The extent to which arrangements will be beneficial will vary from case to case and if the field of use of the trademark is relatively narrow then making a few individual applications in the applicable countries, as and when needed, may be the most cost effective and efficient approach to take in the circumstances.

[2] The Paris Convention (1883) and the TRIPS Agreement (1995)

It is important to note that both the Paris Convention[30] and the Agreement on Trade-Related Aspects of Intellectual Property Rights (TRIPS Agreement)[31] have wider applicability than just trademarks in that their provisions deal with the protection of a number of different categories of intellectual property. For instance, the Paris Convention also implements common rules in relation to patents, industrial designs, trade names, indications of source and unfair competition. The following description restricts itself to the impact of agreements on trademarks. The Paris Convention and the TRIPS Agreement are considered together as they are complimentary in the way they operate.

The Paris Convention dates to 1883 and was one of the first treaties relating to the protection of intellectual property rights. It is still in force today having been revised and amended on a few occasions since its inception.[32] The Convention covers three main themes in relation to trademarks namely, national treatment, rights of priority and the common rules that contracting states are required to follow.

The Paris Convention is administered by WIPO and has extremely wide coverage with 177 Contracting Parties, with latest being Afghanistan in May 2017.[33] The Contracting Parties are collectively referred to as the Union. Membership is open to all

30. Paris Convention for the Protection of Industrial Property (Adopted 1883). Accessible at: www.wipo.int/treaties/en/text.jsp?file_id = 288514.
31. Accessible at www.wto.org/english/docs_e/legal_e/27-trips.pdf.
32. Entry into force on 20 March 1883. Revised on 14 December 1900, 2 June 1911, 6 November 1925, 2 June 1934, 31 October 1958, and 14 July 1967. Amended on 28 September 1979.
33. As of 1 September 2017. A list of Contracting Parties is accessible at: www.wipo.int/treaties/en/ShowResults.jsp?treaty_id = 2.

States. The Paris Convention is one of the most widely adopted international treaties in the world.

The provisions concerning the national treatment of trademarks ensure that persons (both natural and legal) who are nationals of, or domiciled within, a Contracting State receive equivalent protection under the laws of the other Contracting States. Consequently, even though the rules and protections will vary between the different Contracting States, a trademark applicant from one Contracting State will have their trademark application treated in the same way as if they were a national of, or domiciled in, the other Contracting State and will not be discriminated against. Further, if registration is ultimately granted in the other Contracting State the protections under law that would be afforded to a national holder of the rights will also be afforded to the foreign applicant on an equivalent basis.

The second key principle the Paris Convention introduced relates to so-called priority rights. This means that the date of first filing a trademark registration in one Contracting State will apply as the effective filing date for registrations in other Contracting States, provided that the trademark application is made in the other Contracting State within six months of the date of the first filing. As noted earlier, the filing date is important as protection of the mark, if successful, will be deemed to have started from the date of filing the application rather than the date the registration was in fact completed.

Each Contracting State is treated as being independent and allowed to adopt its own rules for registration and filing of trademarks. Consequently, Contracting States cannot refuse or invalidate an application or registration in their country, because the applicant or owner has not applied or registered the mark in their home country. Also, invalidation of a trademark in one Contracting State will not affect the registration in another Contracting State, i.e., they are viewed independently.

The Paris Convention also introduced limitations on the ability of Contracting States to revoke a trademark for non-use, requiring that this can only be done after a reasonable period of time and without there being a good reason for non-use. If a trademark has been registered in one Contracting State another Contracting State must accept that mark for application, but this is without prejudice to the other Member State's rights to subsequently refuse registration on other grounds such as conflicting marks, lack of distinctiveness, potential to create confusion/deceive, public policy. The Convention also provides for the prohibition from registration of categories of sign, without consent. For example, a prohibition on national emblems, hallmarks and official signs provided the same have been notified by the applicable Contracting State to WIPO.

The TRIPS Agreement is administered by the World Trade Organisation (WTO) and introduces many rules covering intellectual property that its member countries are required to follow. The total number of Contracting Parties to the TRIPS Agreement is 164.[34] As with the Paris Convention, the TRIPS Agreement has extensive international

34. As of 1 July 2016. The list of Contracting Parties is accessible at: www.wipo.int/wipolex/en/other_treaties/parties.jsp?treaty_id = 231&group_id = 22.

application. A list of TRIPS members can be found on the WTO website together with further information on how it affects other types of intellectual property rights.

The TRIPS Agreement is a relatively recent introduction, when compared to the Paris Convention, in that it only came into force on 1 January 1995 and is viewed as bolstering perceived inadequacies of the Paris Convention. Indeed, the TRIPS Agreement specifically requires compliance with the substantive provisions of the latest iteration of the Paris Convention.

The TRIPS Agreement specifies minimum standards of intellectual property rights protection that must be provided in the member countries and thereby goes a step beyond the requirements in the Paris Convention. Note that these are minimum standards and members are free to implement wider protection should they choose to do so if this does not conflict with the specified minimum rights. The members can determine how to implement their obligations under the TRIPS Agreement into their domestic legislation. The TRIPS Agreement also introduces procedures in respect of the enforcement of intellectual property rights together with remedies available in the member countries for the benefit of rights holders. A dispute resolution procedure for resolving disagreements between members concerning their obligations under the TRIPS Agreement was also implemented.

The TRIPS Agreement sets out the basic criteria upon which a sign can be eligible for trademark registration. To meet the criteria the sign must be capable of distinguishing the goods and services of one undertaking from those of another. Note the specific reference to services as well as goods, the TRIPS Agreement requires protection of service marks on an equivalent basis to those that are used to distinguish goods. A sign must be visibly perceptible, but members have the option to allow registration of marks such as sounds or smells which are not. Specific reference is made to the registrability of personal names, numbers, figurative elements and colours.

The protection that a trademark holder is afforded allows them to prevent use (without consent) of identical marks for identical goods and services and in such an instance a presumption of confusion is made. In other situations, such as where there are similar marks used with similar goods and services the rights holder can prevent use where it can show such use is likely to result in confusion. Special protection is also provided for 'well-known marks' of member countries and this can extend to use in relation to goods or services which are not similar if the use would lead to confusion as to whether those goods and services related to the rights holder in a detrimental way. This right can be exercised even in the absence of a registration of the 'well-known mark' in the other country.

The TRIPS Agreement requires a minimum initial protection period with subsequent renewal period of at least seven years, although as noted above, a ten-year protection period is usually the norm. Two other important points to note are:

(i) prior use of a sign before registration is precluded from being a reason for refusing an application; and
(ii) a minimum three-year period of uninterrupted non-use is required before a mark can be revoked for lack of use and the owner can defend the position if use was prevented by an independent cause. Use of the trademark by a

third party with consent (i.e., a valid license) is sufficient to constitute use by the holder when defending revocation for non-use.

[3] The EU Trademark

Legislative changes made in early 2016 are a logical place to begin with as they altered terminology that you may have read in older materials on the protection of trademarks in Europe. On 23 March 2016 the EU Trade Mark Regulation (EU 2015/2424)[35] came into force amending the existing Community Trade Mark Regulation. A new Trade Mark Directive (EU 2015/2436)[36] was also implemented that requires EU Member States to incorporate changes within their national legislation by January 2019.

The Directive and the Regulation are the most significant changes to trademark law in the EU since the introduction of the original Community Trademark. The primary purpose of the changes is to increase harmonisation between the old Community Trademark system and the registration of trademarks at the national level within EU Member States and to modernise the system generally. One of the most recognisable and immediate changes the Regulation has introduced is to change the name of the 'Community Trademark' to be known as the 'European Union Trademark'. The name of the body that deals with European trademark registrations has also changed from the 'Office for Harmonization in the Internal Market' (OHIM) to the more intuitive 'European Union Intellectual Property Office' (EUIPO). Whilst numerous changes have been introduced the following are the most material in this context:

- Changes to the fee structure with a view to reducing costs of applications.
- The removal of the requirement that a mark needs to be capable of being represented graphically to be registered (this will make the registration of non-traditional signs such as smells or sound easier).
- Previously trademark owners could register their goods and services against a whole class of the Nice System and that would cover all the goods and services listed under that class heading. In response to the successful challenge of this approach in the IP Translator Case in 2012,[37] this stance has been altered such that where only a class heading is listed it will only protect goods and services in the trademark application where their specification naturally falls within the literal meaning of the applicable class heading. The intention is that goods and

35. Full title – Regulation (EU) 2015/2424 of the European Parliament and of the Council of 16 December 2015 amending Council Regulation (EC) No. 207/2009 on the Community trademark and Commission Regulation (EC) No. 2868/95 implementing Council Regulation (EC) No. 40/94 on the Community trademark, and repealing Commission Regulation (EC) No. 2869/95 on the fees payable to the Office for Harmonization in the Internal Market (Trade Marks and Designs) (Text with EEA relevance).
36. Full title – Directive (EU) 2015/2436 of the European Parliament and of the Council of 16 December 2015 to approximate the laws of the Member States relating to trademarks (Text with EEA relevance).
37. Case C-307/10 *Chartered Institute of Patent Attorneys v. Registrar of Trade Marks (IP Translator case)*.

services are described with the necessary level of precision and clarity so that the extent of protection can be established.

- Changes have been made to the absolute grounds for refusal. Previously signs in the form of shapes that result from the nature of the goods themselves are for a technical effect or which give substantial value of the goods could not be registered. Now this ground is extended to apply to other characteristics of the goods and not just their shape.
- Changes have been made to the relative grounds of refusal so that protection of well-known marks with reputation now extends to similar goods and services as well and not just dissimilar ones. Designations of origin and geographic indications are now absolute and relative grounds for refusal.
- For greater harmonisation, the licensee of a mark can only bring proceedings for infringement of the mark with the owner's consent provided that exclusive licensees can now take proceedings if the owner has failed to act within an appropriate period from the licensee informing the owner of the infringement.
- Unless specifically agreed otherwise the trademarks of a business will transfer automatically with the transfer of the business itself.
- Other notable changes relate to defences to infringement and increased rights to combat counterfeiting.

Having described the recent changes, we can now elaborate on key features of the EU Trademark system which can be thought of as running alongside the registration systems in each of the Member States of the EU.

An EU Trademark registration provides protection for a trademark in all the Member States of the EU and was originally introduced in the form of the Community Trademark in 1996. An EU Trademark can be obtained through a single application, with a single fee (paid in Euros) to the EUIPO based in Alicante, Spain.[38] Renewals of protection can be made by the payment of one fee as well which makes on-going maintenance easier.

Applications can be done electronically on the EUIPO website or via paper application, although the Internet route has advantages because it is cheaper, and a filing receipt is issued immediately rather than having to wait for a few weeks as is the case for a paper application. This process is far easier from an administrative and cost standpoint than the pre-1996 position where individual applications at a national level in each EU Member State were required to obtain protection. Another advantage is that when the EU grows to include further Member States then the protection of the EU Trademark should apply automatically in those Member States as well.

The unitary nature of the EU Trademark offers many advantages in that it applies across the whole of the EU, and use within just one Member State (subject to certain caveats as to the types of goods or services) will be sufficient to protect the mark against a claim of invalidity for non-use. A downside to this unitary nature is that if the mark is successfully challenged by anyone in the EU who has prior rights to the mark in question the whole application will fail, and an EU Trademark will not be granted.

38. Website accessible at https://euipo.europa.eu/ohimportal/en/ (site of EUIPO).

All may not be lost in this situation; however, as it is still possible to convert the EU Trademark application to proceed based on a collection of individual national trademark applications, excluding of course the country or countries where a successful challenge was raised. The conversion will also be able to use the application date of the EU Trademark in terms of priority.

An important benefit for applicants (natural or legal) located outside the EU is that they can apply for an EU Trademark even if they are not a National of an EU Member State and even if they are not located in the EU. Note, however, that any infringement proceedings would need to be brought in an EU Member State, and there are rules setting out which Member States are applicable.

An application for an EU Trademark must be filed in one of the 23 official languages of the EU and then a second language must also be selected. Either the first or second language must be one of the five recognised by the EUIPO (English, French, Italian, German or Spanish). The second language is used for opposition and cancellation proceedings. Contrast this with the difficulty of having to make applications in multiple local languages if separate Member State registrations were used.

Following filing, the EUIPO will examine the application. It is important to note that the EUIPO only examines the application for refusal on absolute grounds and not relative grounds, so it will consider matters such as whether the mark is sufficiently distinctive, whether the class selections are appropriate and if the specification is sufficiently clear, but they will not verify whether there are grounds for refusal of the application because of the existence of conflicting marks. However, the EUIPO will carry out a search for conflicting marks where this option is selected in the application, but the results of the search are for information purposes only (a report used to be provided as a matter of course for Community Trademarks applications but this is no longer the case). In addition, some Member States produce reports of potentially conflicting marks which can be obtained for a fee. It is prudent for an applicant to carry out their own searches using a trademark professional prior to initiating an application. The new approach also puts the onus on existing trademark owners to monitor the publication of EU Trademarks to ensure that conflicting marks do not proceed to registration unnoticed.

Provided there are no objections, the application should be published within a month and then there will be a three-month period for oppositions or observations to be made by third parties to the EUIPO. Oppositions may be filed by holders of existing EU Trademarks or the holders of existing national rights in Member States, where a conflict with the application is identified. Oppositions can take quite a bit of time to resolve and whilst appeals are possible this can extend the timescale for resolution and registration considerably.

If there are no oppositions in the three-month period, the registration (as opposed to the application) will be published for the purposes of informing the public of the ownership of the mark and a certificate of registration will be issued. Following registration, the owner can take infringement actions and prevent registration of identical or similar signs in respect of similar or identical goods and non-similar goods where the EU Trademark has established a reputation in the EU. The initial period of protection is ten-years, and this may be renewed for successive ten-year periods thereafter, indefinitely.

EU Trademarks can be assigned or transferred but due to their unitary nature this must be an assignment or transfer of the whole registration. Licensing in part is a possible alternative to overcome this restriction.

Whilst the owner of a trademark in the EU has extensive rights to prevent third parties using it in the course of trade they are not limitless. In particular, there are restrictions based on the principle of 'exhaustion of rights' which are set out in the Trade Marks Directive (Article 15 Directive (EU 2015/2436)). In simple terms, exhaustion of rights in the EU context means that once the goods have been put in the market in the European Economic Area by the proprietor of the mark or with the consent of the proprietor they can no longer prevent any subsequent sale of those goods under the mark.

The purpose of the exhaustion of rights principle is to prevent the proprietor interfering with the free movement of goods within the EU and thereby the consequent benefits consumers can realise from parallel imports. For example, if goods were put on the market in France by the proprietor and those goods were more expensive in the UK, the proprietor will not be able to prevent a reseller taking the goods purchased in France and selling them in the UK at a price lower than they are currently sold in the UK whilst still making a profit.

The exhaustion of rights principle following a first sale does not apply if the goods were put on the market outside the EU as it only focusses on protection of free movement of goods within the EU. The proprietor can still act to prevent parallel imports from a non-EU country into the EU. In addition, the rights to undertake parallel imports in the EU after first being put on the market are not completely unfettered. The proprietor can still take action if the reseller changes the goods, de-brands, rebrands or repackages the goods for the subsequent sale.

[4] International Trademarks

The Madrid System is the basis for the international registration of trademarks. The system is based on two international treaties, the Madrid Agreement[39] concluded on 14 April 1891 (although subsequently revised and amended on a few occasions since then[40]) and the Madrid Protocol[41] adopted on 27 June 1989 (subsequently amended in

39. Full title – Madrid Agreement Concerning the International Registration of Marks. Text of Madrid Agreement accessible at www.wipo.int/wipolex/en/wipo_treaties/text.jsp?file_id = 283530. List of Contracting Members accessible at www.wipo.int/treaties/en/ShowResults.jsp?lang = en&treaty_id = 21.
40. Revised on 14 December 1900, 2 June 1911, 6 November 1925, 2 June 1934, 15 June 1957 and 14 July 1967. Amended on 28 September 1979.
41. Full title – Protocol Relating to the Madrid Agreement Concerning the International Registration of Marks. Full text accessible at www.wipo.int/wipolex/en/wipo_treaties/text.jsp?file_id = 283 484.

2006 and 2007).[42] The Madrid System provides a process for registering trademarks simultaneously in a number of countries and simplifies the on-going management of those registrations. Registrations are made in the International Register and the system is managed by WIPO, based in Geneva.

The Madrid Protocol was subsequently implemented to make the process introduced by the Madrid Agreement simpler. The Madrid System applies to countries that have signed up to either the Agreement or the Protocol and whilst it does not cover registrations in all countries of the world it does have extensive reach. As of September 2017, there were 99 members of the Madrid Union (Contracting Parties to the Madrid Protocol and the Madrid Agreement comprising of states and inter-governmental organisations), and this extends the protection of the International Trademarks to 113 countries, which has been estimated to cover approximately 80% of world trade. The EU is a party to the Madrid Protocol thus enabling an international registration to be used to obtain an EU Trademark. It provides protection in respect of a diverse range of major economies such as the US, China and Japan, although there are some notable exceptions in Canada, South Africa and Brazil.

All parties to the Paris Convention are eligible to become part of the Madrid Union by becoming a Contracting Party to the Madrid Agreement and/or the Madrid Protocol. Inter-governmental organisations are only eligible to become a party to the Madrid Protocol. Current details of the countries that have signed up to the Madrid Protocol can be found on the WIPO website which gives an indication of the extent of the protection that an International Trademark can provide.

Whilst the Madrid System has a similar objective to the EU Trademark in terms of simplifying registration and providing ongoing control of trademarks in multiple countries the approaches that they adopt have several significant differences.

Unlike an EU Trademark, International Trademark applications are restricted to people who are nationals of, or domiciled in, the country of a Contracting Party of the Madrid Protocol or, in the case of organisations, ones that have an industrial or commercial establishment in one of those countries. In contrast to the unitary system approach of the EU Trademark where the 'all or nothing' approach applies to registrations, an international registration will apply in respect of all the individual countries applied for and even if unsuccessful in certain countries, it will still be enforceable in respect of countries where the application is successful.

Even though an international registration is based on a single application form and fee as with the EU Trademark, the international application will be examined by the registries of all the countries where protection is sought. Effectively it is akin to making a bundle of national applications at the same time. This means that the success, or otherwise, of the international registration in any particular country is subject to that country's particular rules and processes for registration and their own grounds for refusal. Extension of the protection to other countries can be sought later following successful registration, if required.

42. List of Contracting Parties accessible at www.wipo.int/treaties/en/ShowResults.jsp?treaty_id = 8.

A prerequisite of an international application is that there must already be an existing application or registration in the 'home country' of the applicant. In addition, the classes of goods and services applied for cannot be any wider than the ones that were registered or applied for in the home country. In contrast to the EU Trademark, use of the mark in one country obtained by an international registration is not sufficient to defeat a claim of revocation for non-use in other countries. The use requirements (which may vary) must be complied with in accordance with the laws in each country where the international registration exists to avoid a local challenge. This is also reflected in the ability to use an injunction for stopping an infringement – action must be taken in the courts of each country where recourse is sought. Conversely, in the case of an EU Trademark it is possible to gain an injunction that covers the whole of the EU.

[5] Other International Arrangements That Concern Trademarks

The foregoing section has identified the most important treaties and agreements that relate to trademarks internationally; however, there are other regional arrangements which may need to be considered in the particular circumstances and the following are a few examples.

[a] The North American Free Trade Agreement

This agreement that came into effect in 1994 created a tri-lateral trade bloc between the US, Canada and Mexico. A key feature of the agreement is that it implements minimum standards for the protection of trademarks and other intellectual property in the member countries.

[b] African Intellectual Property Organization

African Intellectual Property Organization (OAPI) is an organisation of 17 West African countries tasked with protecting intellectual property rights within those countries. The underlying agreement is the Bangui Agreement which came into force in 1982. It joined the Madrid Protocol with effect from 2015.

[c] The Benelux Convention on Intellectual Property (Trademarks and Designs) 2005

The Benelux Convention was formed between Belgium, The Netherlands and Luxembourg (the term 'Benelux' is formed from the first two letters of the three countries) and is a political/economic union within the region. The Benelux Convention created a joint registration and administration system between these countries. The system is run by the Benelux Office for Intellectual Property, which also covers rights in designs.

§3.06 THE STRUCTURE OF AN INTERNATIONAL TRADEMARK LICENCE

[A] Initial Considerations

Having established the environment in which trademarks are controlled internationally and being given an insight into trademarks generally this part of the chapter will look in depth at the typical structure of an international trademark licence. In doing so the objective is to focus on practical points of drafting and negotiation. Consideration will also be given to some connected issues such as legal requirements to register licences, quality assurance and competition law. The underlying subject is a trademark licence under English law, but we will refer to differences of approach in some other jurisdictions where it is helpful to be aware of possible pitfalls.

As noted in the chapter on software, licensing trademarks, as opposed to assignment, is potentially a far more lucrative method of exploitation. Used internationally it can be a method of quickly leveraging brand value with a relatively little capital outlay. In addition, it can allow access to local expertise in another country that will allow for superior exploitation of the trademark and enable the rights holder to generate income from unexploited markets without the costs and complexities of setting up a local operation.

A trademark licence is, at its core, the granting of a permission by the rights holder (licensor) to another party (the licensee) to use a mark where use in the absence of such permission would infringe the trademark of the rights holder. Trademark law grants rights that automatically prohibit a third party from using the trademark without permission being obtained from the rights holder over and above the basic permission, the licence is the method by which control over the use of the trademark is exercised by the rights holder. In turn, the rights holder can control the permissions it provides to third parties to fit its commercial objectives. For example, the rights holder may license a third party to use the trademark on product x but not product y if the rights holder wants to market product y itself under the mark.

If the licence agreement does not govern the use of the trademark correctly this can not only have negative commercial consequences in terms of the extent of use permitted, it can potentially lead to the trademark being vulnerable to attack or even revocation if, for example, lack of quality control resulted in the trademark becoming generic and non-distinctive. Examples of some trademarks that have been affected by generic use include Hoover, Yo-Yo and Escalator which although originally created to identify them with particular companies have subsequently been adopted to generically refer to similar products to the originals.

Trademarks can be licensed on their own or, as is more often the case, in conjunction with a bundle of other intellectual property rights depending on the commercial situation. Consequently, the complexity of licence arrangements differs considerably.

Common commercial agreements where trademark licences are incorporated are franchise agreements where the franchisor is effectively giving the franchisee a right, for the term of the agreement, to replicate it business model. In this situation trademarks will pay a central role in identifying the brand under which the franchise operates. Other intellectual property rights such as patents, copyright and know how/trade secrets will also play a role in protecting the underlying method of doing business.

Merchandising agreements are another commercial agreement where trademark licenses are used extensively. In this context, the trademark owner licenses the use of their mark on other types of goods. Good examples of merchandising are the use of the trademarks of sports teams and film franchises on a multitude of consumer goods. At a more specialised level, trademark licenses can also be used to show the incorporation of a component product within another product – Teflon, Dolby, Intel and NutraSweet are well-known examples.

At the other end of the spectrum, and somewhat controversially, you may have intra-group licensing of trademarks and other intellectual property rights to achieve tax advantages. A group company based in a low tax jurisdiction can hold the intellectual property rights and then license them to other group companies for royalties thereby repatriating profits from group activities to a jurisdiction with a lower tax rate.

The licensing of a trademark to a third party may seem counter-intuitive to their primary purpose as an indication of origin, because the source of the goods under licence may not be the owner of the trademark but a potentially unknown third party that has been given the right to apply the mark to the goods. This issue is addressed by the licensor retaining control over the quality of the goods with which the third party uses the trademark such that the end user experience of the third-party goods is consistent with what is expected from the trademark indicator. Accordingly, the incorporation of detailed quality control provisions is a fundamental requirement of a good trademark licence and this concept is expanded on in the description of the licence structure in section §3.07. The quality of the third party products using the trademark needs to be consistent.

Licenses of trademarks should always be recorded in writing, not only for certainty as is the case with any contract, but also because in many jurisdictions such as the UK it is a legal requirement – the Trade Marks Act 1994 stipulates that licences need to be in writing and signed for and on behalf of the grantee to be valid.[43]

[B] Due Diligence Pre-licensing

Both the licensor and licensee will want to carry out certain checks before entering detailed licence negotiations.

From the licensee's perspective some points to consider will be:

- Does the licensor own the rights in the trademark that it is purporting to licence in the relevant jurisdictions? Searches can be done to establish the ownership position.

43. Section Trade Marks Act 1994, s. 28 (2).

- Are there existing licensees whose activities could negatively impact on the licensee's plans, e.g., the trademark may already have been licensed in respect of similar products that could reduce the potential market opportunities.
- Does the licensor have a standard form of licence or does one need to be prepared.
- Verification that the licensor is willing to licence the trademark for the purposes required, in terms of licence term, scope and royalty levels. If this is not done considerable time may be wasted in preparing the legal documentation when there is no chance of a deal being reached.
- Is the information provided sufficient to justify the business case and to therefore move to negotiation.
- What are the exit routes if things do not go as planned (*see* termination rights in section §3.07[M]). The licensee will not want to be tied into a non-productive arrangement.

From the licensor's position:

- ensure that the necessary trademarks that are to be the subject of the licence are already registered or an application has been submitted in the applicable jurisdiction(s) covered by the licence;
- carry out searches to establish the financial position of the licensee - can they be relied upon to meet the royalty payments? Obtain copies of credit reports, annual returns etc. to establish the exposure. Consider whether a parent company guarantee is necessary;
- will the scope of the proposed licensing conflict with any pre-existing licences of the trademark by the licensor, e.g., has exclusivity in that area been granted to another entity or even if other non-exclusive rights have been granted will it reduce payments from or compromise an existing relationship;
- is a license the best way to exploit the trademark in the short and longer term or might it be better to exploit the market yourself? Would a non-exclusive or an exclusive licence work better;
- take into consideration that if future licensees become aware of the terms that have been granted to one licensee they are going to try and achieve equivalent or better rights for their license, a long-term perspective is needed, and appropriate confidentiality obligations should be sought from the prospective licensee;
- what rules will you need to apply to the use of the trademark by the licensee to achieve sufficient quality control and appropriate use;
- even if the licensee is willing to meet your requirements are they capable of doing so? What is their track record? Have they licensed other trademarks before, do they have specialist expertise in the jurisdiction, is the image of the licensee in the market consistent with the trademark and what is their business plan;
- do you have a form of licensing agreement that you can put forward? As the licensor you will be in a better position if you take the lead in putting forward

the terms and you will want this in place before the licensee presents their own document which will naturally be skewed in their favour; and

- what are the exit routes for the licensor if things change (*see* termination rights at section §3.07[M] below)?

[C] Mandatory Local Law

As with any international contract, mandatory local laws can apply. Mandatory local laws can be considered as laws in a jurisdiction that will apply notwithstanding what the content of the contract provides and the choice of law governing it. Generally, these are laws which are made to apply as a matter of public policy. Key areas for trademark licences will be competition law, laws requiring contracting formalities (e.g., licence registration, notarisation and execution requirements), laws requiring payments to be made in the local currency and laws providing for compensation payments on termination, as is the case for many agency and some distribution arrangements. Local law advice should be sought to verify the effect any mandatory local laws may have on the proposed trademark licence.

[D] Registration of Trademark Licences

It is important to be aware that there is a possibility that a trademark licence will need to be registered with a governmental body in another jurisdiction where the mark is used. In the majority of countries registration of the licence agreement is no longer mandatory for the license to be enforceable (generally because this is viewed as an unnecessary administrative burden), but establishing the registration position is still important as it can impact on the protections afforded to the licensor and/or the licensee. For example, registration may be required for the licensee to act against an infringer or it may adversely impact the damages that can be sought from an infringer if the licence has not been registered.

The requirements and effect of registering a trademark licence vary from country to country and it should be therefore something that is considered at the outset of putting a licence in place, seeking local law advice where there is any doubt as to the position.

Another point to explore is whether registration of a licence in the jurisdiction means that it will become available as a public document. If this is the situation it may be worth separating out the license of the trademark from the rest of commercial agreement and simply recognise the grant of the trademark licence in a separate contract. By doing this, just the licence will become public and the other potentially commercially sensitive details of the deal can remain confidential.

§3.07 THE COMPONENT PARTS OF A TRADEMARK LICENCE AGREEMENT IN DETAIL

[A] Initial Considerations

The following is a generic example of how an international trademark licence may be structured. Each of the following headings will be commented on with explanation and some practical drafting suggestions.

- Parties
- Background/Recitals
- Definitions and Interpretation
- Grant of the Licence
- Confirmation of Title and Goodwill in the Trademark
- Maintenance of the Trademark and Warranties
- Quality Control
- Sales and Marketing relating to Licensed Products/Services
- Protection of the Trademark
- Royalties and Payment Mechanism
- Liability and Indemnities
- Term and Termination
- Dispute Resolution and Other boilerplate provisions of relevance (cross-refer to Chapter 7: International Dispute Resolution and Chapter 1: Introduction)

During negotiations, it is extremely important to mark all drafts as being 'Draft – Subject to Contract' to avoid any argument that a license has been granted before the formal agreement has been executed by both parties. Both parties will need to ensure that all aspects of the licence arrangements are reflected fully and accurately in the document as it is unlikely that additional provisions will be implied into the agreement itself by a court – this is especially the case in the UK.

Finally, it is worth noting that in some European countries (such as France) there can be an implied duty to negotiate contracts in good faith so if a licence was pursued but without any real intention of being concluded by one party (perhaps for an ulterior commercial reasons) then this could result in a damages claim from the other party. Local law advice should be obtained if this is a possible scenario.

[B] The Parties Clause

Trademark licences are often important strategic arrangements for the licensor which tend to put in place for a long time, so it is essential that the licensor is sure that the licensee is an appropriate entity to use the trademark. The parties' clause identifies the legal entities that are entering into the licence and your attention is directed to the issues to consider when populating the party's clause set out in the Software Chapter where the topic is dealt with in depth.

In the context of a trademark licence, the licensor will need to decide on the most appropriate entity to grant the licence – either directly from the ultimate rights holder or through an intermediary to which the right to grant sub-licences has been given. The licensor may wish to use an intermediary so that there is a level of separation in liability terms between the company that owns the trademark and the licensee. If a sub-licence structure is to be used, a formal intra-group arrangement setting out the exact scope of what can be sub-licensed by the intermediary should be put in place to create a chain of rights, particularly if there is the possibility that the group structure may change with group companies being divested.

The licensor will also need to think about whether the licensee needs a guarantor and whether the guarantor should be a party to the licence agreement. Alternatively, a standalone licence between the guarantor and the licensor could be put in place with an obligation placed on the licensee to get the standalone guarantee executed by the guarantor at the same time as the licence agreement. A typical situation where a guarantee would be needed is where the licensee is a local subsidiary of an international company, but the subsidiary has no material assets of its own. If the guarantee is to be signed after the main licence agreement (which may be the case for logistical reasons if the guarantor is located elsewhere), a contractually binding fixed timeline for the execution of the guarantee should be inserted which if not met constitutes a material breach allowing termination of the licence agreement. If use of the trademark will not follow immediately after the execution of the licence agreement the execution of the guarantee could be framed as a condition precedent such that if the guarantee is not executed, the licence agreement will be viewed as never having come into legal effect. Either of these approaches is a powerful leverage for ensuring that the licensee delivers on procuring the guarantee.

If a guarantee is required it should be brought to the table at the earliest opportunity, first to ensure that the licensee has an appropriate guarantor to put forward and to allow enough time for the form of guarantee to be negotiated and agreed so that it does not delay completion of the main licence agreement. The law of guarantees is complicated and varies by jurisdiction, so time will be needed, probably taking local law advice, to verify that the form of guarantee is enforceable against the guarantor in the jurisdiction it is located within, and that the procedures for enforcement are not so time consuming and expensive that the guarantee is of little practical benefit. It is quite possible that the guarantor will try and get the guarantee in a form they have prepared and subject to their local law and jurisdiction, but this should be resisted if possible.

[C] Background/Recitals

The 'background' or 'recitals' section, as noted in Chapter 4, International Software Licensing, is useful for putting the licence in context and can potentially act as an aid to interpretation in the event of a dispute. As trademark licences tend to be very specific to their circumstances and can be complicated, a headline summary of the arrangement, specifically referring to the main trademark rights being granted, is a helpful addition for subsequent interpretation.

[D] Definitions and Interpretation

Definitions are of course used to avoid the need to repeat explanations of terms that are used frequently in an agreement where the term in question has a precise and consistent meaning throughout.

In the context of an international trademark licence, the following terms are likely to be defined and will need to be drafted with care. As a point of good drafting, definitions should not be expressed as operative provisions as these should be in the main body of the licence agreement. If there is a particular right or obligation on either of the parties, then it should not be hidden within a definition.

Although English is generally regarded as the language of international business it is worth highlighting that certain countries may require contracts to be translated in the local language or it may be the case that the licensee's English language skills are too limited to fully understand the document. In these scenarios there may be a need to have a dual language licence agreement. This approach can create a risk for both parties as the translation of the two languages may result in different legal interpretations.

Where translation of the licence agreement cannot be avoided it is essential that the services of a professional translation firm are used to ensure that an accurate translation is produced. When selecting a translator, you should verify that they are used to dealing with legal translations due to the peculiarities of contractual language and the enhanced need for accuracy. Where the licence agreement is of significant importance the services of further translator are sometimes used to translate the original translation back into English so that a comparison can be done with the original to double check the accuracy. For ease of use, the English law version and the foreign law version can be set out in columns next to each other so that equivalent sections and clauses can be cross-referred straight away.

In any event, where a translation is undertaken, a contractual provision should be added stating which language will govern the licence agreement in the event of a dispute. Even if no translation is needed a well drafted international contract should aim to make the drafting as plain and clear as possible on the basis that the first language of one of the parties may not be English. The objective should always be to ensure that both sides fully understand their rights and obligations as even small misunderstandings can result in large disputes.

[1] Definition of 'Group'

If the license is to extend to group companies of the licensee it is important that the extent of usage beyond the primary licensee is fully understood. In the UK, statutory definitions are often used to cover the definition of what the 'Group' includes, e.g., by referring to the Company or Tax legislation to define 'Subsidiary' and 'Holding Company', and therefore provide certainty as to which entities form the group in question.

When dealing with a group located in another jurisdiction care needs to be taken to ensure that the terminology used still works for group structures created there as the form of companies and non-legal entities may vary. In this situation, it may be necessary to use a definition that provides a more generic description that can apply equally whether the group is in the UK or in another jurisdiction.

The licensor will need to check that the granting of a group license does not inadvertently extend the rights too far by obtaining details of the licensee's group structure to verify the scope. The definition of 'Royalties' will need to explicitly state that sales under the trademark by the other group companies will accrue Royalties as well.

Another approach to defining the 'Group' with sufficient certainty would be to specifically identify the licensed companies within the group by name, main/registered address and company/registration number (if used in the foreign jurisdiction). This has the advantage of being a fixed list whereas if the members of the Group altered at a later date and the clause did not restrict the licence to the members as at the date of the agreement unintended consequences could result.

[2] Definition of 'Net Sales Value/Receipts'

Royalty payments can be framed in many ways, but on-going royalties (as opposed to a one off payment) are often calculated with reference to a percentage of the Net Sales Value/Receipts of the goods sold by the licensee under the mark. This is reflective of the value of sales made by the licensee after taking out things like the costs of transport, tax, insurance, returns which would not be reasonable for the licensor to take a royalty on. The parties will be responsible for deciding what is and what is not included in this definition. The role of the lawyer is to accurately document the components. If the definition is incorrect or ambiguous for any reason it would not be surprising for a dispute to arise very early on in the relationship as minor discrepancies can lead to significant variations in return, so care needs to be taken. To avoid this situation, the definition should be questioned and tested by both parties to the point where they are comfortable that it covers all the bases and is being interpreted by both parties in the same way. Working out sample volume calculations and associated royalties is a good way to assess whether the provision operates as anticipated.

[3] Definition of 'Licensed Products/Services Field of Use'

This is another core definition as it is likely that use of the trademark will be restricted to specific goods and services. These goods and services will obviously need to be within the classes of the licensor's trademark registration, and they will normally be identified in a schedule if the detail cannot easily fit within the definition itself. Any ambiguity could lead to use of the trademark on a wider or narrower scale than anticipated which could adversely impact the licensor or the licensee. If it is anticipated that new or additional goods and services may be added or removed during the term of the licence then the definition can refer to the list of Licensed Products *'as may be varied by the written agreement of the parties, signed by their duly authorised representatives'*. This then gives a formal process for change within the existing agreement that removes the question as to whether an oral or non-formal change to the Licensed Products might be sufficient to alter the licence scope.

[4] Definition of the 'Licensed Trademarks'

Again, precision is important, and the exact details will generally be set out in a schedule rather than being included within the definition itself. The description should include the word 'mark' or an illustration of the registered figurative mark, the application or registered number, the classes in which it is registered, the location of registration and the filing date and the registered owner. These can usefully be put in the form of a table if there is more than one trademark to aid clarity.

[5] Definition of 'Territory'

This definition is used to define the geographic area of use within which the licensee can use the trademark in respect of the Licensed Products/Services. Superficially this may seem straightforward but the use of terms for geographic areas used in relation to some jurisdictions can have many different permutations (e.g., the UK, Great Britain, British Isles, United States of America, America, North America, South America etc.) coupled with the fact that over time political changes and conflicts can alter established borders. A brief look on the Internet for border changes in recent history will illustrate that this occurs more often than you might think. The exit of the UK from the EU is a good example of a material scope change.

As a result of this potential uncertainty the parties should check that the official definition of the terms used to define the territory are correct and in areas which are more prone to change perhaps indicate whether the territory relates to the geographic area of particular countries at the date of signature of the licence agreement or that area as it may change during the licence agreement. The EU is a good case in point - if you refer to Europe does it mean the members of the European Union as opposed to countries forming the European Continent, if it refers to the EU will the territory include new members of the EU over time or is the intention to limit it to the Member States as at the date of the agreement? When the EU is referred to, are both parties clear that this will not extend to the members of the European Economic Area as well? Alternatively, the parties can also simply refer to geographic areas as oppose to political boundaries if that is felt to be a better fit for the arrangements.

[E] The Grant of the Licence

The license grant sets out the fundamental basis upon which the license is being granted and not surprisingly is an area where both parties will need to focus on with their lawyers. A licence grant will typically address the following points:

- State clearly that the licensor is granting a license of the trademarks, as defined, as opposed to any form of assignment.
- The activities that are permitted in the context of that use, e.g., the sale, manufacture, marketing of goods or services.
- Confirm that the licence is restricted to use in respect of the defined Licensed Products.
- State that the licence is limited to use in the Territory, as defined.
- Provide that the licence is for a fixed term and will end at the same time as the licence agreement (whether that is due to simple expiry or earlier termination in accordance with the licence terms).
- Confirm whether the licence is exclusive, non-exclusive or a sole license (for commentary on the common meaning of these terms and the potential requirement to explicitly define them as between the parties, refer to the chapter on Software Licensing).

Based on the above, a clause might be structured as follows to tie all these together:

> *Subject to the other terms and conditions in this Licence Agreement, the licensor grants the licensee a non-exclusive license to use the Trade Marks on, or for the manufacture, distribution, marketing and sale, of the Licensed Products in the Territory for the duration of this Agreement.*

Sometimes the licence grant clause will refer to the licence being 'non-assignable' and 'without the right to grant sub-licences' within the clause itself, but in the interests of keeping the language clear these restrictions (and any others that are appropriate in the circumstances) are often carved out as separate clauses. Trying to bundle too much within the basic license grant can lead to a convoluted provision that covers the points but insufficiently describes nuances of how the rights are intended to work. The licensor should have selected the licensee carefully and will not want an assignment or sub-licence to result in use by an unspecified third party who may adversely affect the trademark. On this basis, a licensor's default starting position would normally be that sub-licensing and assignment by the licensee are prohibited or that they require the prior written consent of the licensor. The licensor may even stipulate that the licensor needs to grant any sub-licence directly to the third party if it is consented to rather than going through the licensee, so the licensor can ensure that they retain full control.

The grant also often includes a provision stating the rights that the licensor is retaining for itself, for example, if the licensor wanted to qualify the exclusivity it could add a statement that the licence is without prejudice to the licensor's right to sell Licensed Products within the Territory itself using the trademarks, but adding that it will not appoint any other third party licensees during the continuance of the licence agreement. If there have been prior license grants by the licensor that would contradict the exclusivity and the licensee accepts the position the grant can be expressed to be subject to those prior licenses.

Note that where the rights granted are exclusive in any respect thought will be needed as to whether the licence agreement may fall foul of competition law, whether this is EU competition law or other competition law applying in the area where the licence agreement has effect. This is a good example of mandatory law that has an impact irrespective of what the parties have agreed in the licence agreement and the choice of law governing it. The underlying justification for competition law restrictions in this context is that if the use of a mark is limited to one licensee then this may reduce competition in the market because other licensees of the trademark cannot enter the market with the result that consumers potentially get a worse deal.

Competition law is considered further in Chapter 2, but generally if one of the parties has a material market share or if the effect of the licence is to carve up the market in relation to the distribution of goods under the mark then that should raise a 'red flag' to consider the competition law position. Any implication of direct or indirect price fixing, such as if the licensor seeks to control the price of goods sold by the licensee is also something to watch out for. Analysis may require consultation with lawyers in other jurisdictions as, whilst the impact of EU Competition Law is well known, there are a multitude of similar competition laws applied throughout the world.

[F] Confirmation of Title and Goodwill in the Trademark

In addition to the licence grant the licensor will wish to add some other clauses to try and ensure that the licence and the actions of the licensee do not compromise the licensor's ownership of the registered trademark or affect its value in a negative way. The following protections will therefore be normally included within the licence agreement:

- A statement by the licensee acknowledging that that the licensor is the owner of the trademark and the only rights conferred on the licensee are those specifically set out in the licence document, i.e., wider rights should not be implied, although the value of this will of course be dependent on drafting of the license grant being clear and unambiguous.
- A so-called no challenge clause. These clauses are used to restrict the licensee's ability to challenge the validity as opposed to the ownership of the trademark. Care is needed when adding this sort of restriction as from an EU competition law perspective a clause which simply prevents the licensee challenging the validity of the mark will be an infringement of Article 101 of the Treaty on the Functioning of the European Union (TFEU). Notwithstanding this position, the licensor will want some form of protection where the licensee makes a challenge as to the validity of the licensed trademark, so the approach often adopted is to add a clause which allows the licensor to terminate the licence agreement if a challenge is made. Even if this less

restrictive approach is taken it should be noted that, depending on the fact scenario, the validity of the restriction could still be assessed as being an unreasonable restriction and therefore unenforceable but at least this stance would not invalidate the rest of the licence agreement.

- The licensor also needs to be mindful of the accrual of goodwill that the licensee may generate from using the trademark under the license. The licensee will endeavour to avoid this happening by stating that any goodwill generated from the licensee's use of the trademark will accrue to the licensor. This can in turn be bolstered by obligating the licensee to enter a formal assignment of any goodwill to the licensor upon request.
- The licensor will also normally require the licensee to include some form of notice on any materials or goods that incorporate the trademark stating that it is owned by the licensor and that it is therefore unambiguous that it is being used under licence and that the licensee does not own it. The prominence of this notice will ultimately depend on the circumstances and commercial negotiation and the licensor should therefore think about what it requires at the outset and detail what it requires in a schedule to the licence agreement or in the brand manual that specifies the way the trademark can be displayed.
- Other restrictions that a prudent licensor may want to include in the licence agreement are prohibitions on the licensee seeking to register confusingly similar trademarks, incorporating the trademark within the licensee's corporate name or indeed registering the same trademark for use in other fields of operation where the licensor has failed to protect its rights already in that jurisdiction. If the licensor has entered into an agreement before protecting its rights by way of an application or registration in the relevant jurisdiction, they could be left in a situation where the licensee registers the rights first for its own benefit. Failure to cover off these rights and obligations could result in time-consuming and expensive cross-border litigation.

[G] Maintenance of the Trademark and Warranties

Whilst the licensee can carry out searches to verify the licensor's ownership rights it will want a warranty from the licensor in the licence agreement confirming that it is the registered owner of the rights and that it is not aware of any challenge to those rights as at the date of the agreement. It would be unusual for a licensor to provide more extensive warranties in a trademark licence such that the trademark is valid and that it will not infringe the intellectual property rights of a third party. The reason for this is because of the wide range of grounds that a trademark can be challenged even after registration. The licensor cannot be sure that an existing conflicting mark, that was not identified previously, will not emerge or that there will not be a post-registration challenge to the trademark on relative grounds. If the licensee insists on more stringent warranties a compromise position might be to allow termination by the licensee if the warranty is breached but precluding other remedies such as damages, i.e., make termination of the licence agreement the sole and exclusive remedy.

An obligation should be placed on the licensor to maintain the renewals of the trademark during the term of the licence agreement, at the licensor's expense. This should not be an issue for the licensor as it will be in their own interests to ensure the trademark is retained on the register and to maintain control of the process. A possible exception to the expense of renewal obligation might occur if the license is exclusive; in this situation, the licensee will be the only entity allowed to utilise the trademark within the confines of the licence agreement, and the licensor may therefore expect some of the expense of renewal to fall to the licensee. The position reached will of course depend on commercial negotiations in the round.

An obligation to register the licence of the trademark may be placed on the licensee at its own cost but, again, this will depend on the circumstances.

[H] Quality Control

Quality control provisions should be treated as a fundamental component of the licence arrangement. As we have seen earlier, a key attribute of a trademark is to act as an indication to the market of a consistent source of goods and services of a particular quality notwithstanding that in the age of mass merchandising the identity of the actual source may not be known. From a purely commercial perspective, if the reputation of a trademark is lessened by its use on inferior or defective goods the purchaser may no longer trust the trademark as a sign indicating that they can rely on the goods bearing that mark to adhere to certain quality standards. This alienation could result in the customer selecting alternative products, particularly if the poor quality occurs on more than one occasion.

Irrespective of the direct damage to reputation and the devaluing of the trademark's value, failing to control the quality of the goods can ultimately lead to the loss of a trademark. There are provisions allowing for revocation in the UK under the Trade Marks Act 1994 or abandonment in the US under the Langham (Trademark) Act 1946 (the main federal statute concerning trademarks in the US). In the UK the argument would be that the lack of quality control has led to the failure of the mark to act as an indicator of goods or services of consistent quality. In the US the approach has been that where there has been 'bare licensing', i.e., licensing with no quality control the trademark can be contested as being 'abandoned' due to its inability to act as an indication of source.

Due to the inherent risks of failing to control quality, it is unusual to find a trademark licence (whether of goods or services) that does not include some provisions in this regard. The exact content of the quality control provisions will depend on the nature of the goods and services being licensed and accordingly legislation does not provide any detailed information on what is needed, but the following points provide some guidance on the factors that a licensor should consider when implementing quality control:

- the quality standards need to be sufficiently precise so that compliance or otherwise is measurable;

- where goods are manufactured under the trademark licence the quality standards may need to set out the formulations or standards or equipment that need to be used;
- regular samples of the goods may be stipulated together with inspections of production facilities although the licensee will be keen to ensure that the time and cost of compliance are not unduly onerous;
- restricting manufacture to pre-approved facilities;
- a contractual obligation on the licensee to inform the licensor of any customer complaints relating to the products or services so that problems can be addressed with the licensee at an early stage;
- an ability to halt distribution of the goods if the quality standards are failed, until the issues have been resolved.

Prescribing the quality standards and including them in the licence agreement is only one part of the process, and the licensor will also need to ensure that the procedures are followed and that the goods and services are checked. As a result, the obligations need to be realistic and workable for both parties. Notwithstanding the foregoing, the level of control exerted should not be so excessive or it might lead to an accusation that the arrangements go beyond a mere license. For example, you would not want the arrangement being construed as the licensing of a business model akin to a franchise agreement as that could put the licensor in conflict with legislation that controls franchising. Establishing what to include is not a matter of satisfying particular 'tick boxes', but rather the approach needs to be appropriate to the circumstances and commercially viable on a case-by-case basis.

[I] Sales and Marketing Relating to Licensed Products/Services

The licensor will want to exert control on the use of the trademark in relation to the sales and marketing of the goods not only to ensure correct use but also to maximise the commercial opportunities and therefore the royalties consequently achieved. A basic obligation to use 'best efforts'/'best endeavours' to promote the sale of the goods under the trademark is often used together with an obligation to comply with all applicable law when doing so. The parties may also choose to specify a marketing budget for advertising and promotion together with arrangements for who will pay these costs or how they will be apportioned. If the arrangement is long term, arrangements for the parties to meet and adjust the budget at regular intervals can be added.

Depending on the degree of quality control needed, the licensor may only require the licensee to use the trademark in accordance with the licensor's brand manual; however, licensors often require the right to pre-approve any advertising or marketing materials using the trademark. From the licensee's standpoint, a process and timescale for the approval process should be set out in the licence agreement so that undue delay by the licensor does not hinder the licensee's operations.

Non-compete provisions preventing the licensee carrying out competing activities during the term of the licence agreement are a standard protection. Care always needs to be taken with any post-termination restrictions due to potential competition law issues. In some jurisdictions an assessment of reasonableness of the post-termination restriction will be made to determine whether they are effective but in others they could be unenforceable per se and/or result in Governmental financial penalties for being anticompetitive.

[J] Protection of the Trademark and Infringement

Infringement has two perspectives in this context, either a third party suing the licensor and the licensee for infringement of a third party's mark or the infringement by a third party of the licensor's mark. In either case the situation will be of importance to both the licensee and licensor as it could affect the validity of the trademark and the licensee's ability to exploit it under the licence.

The licensor will normally place an obligation on the licensee to notify the licensor of any infringements it becomes aware of, as they will probably be the first to become aware of them because of their activities in the marketplace.

A decision will need to be made as to whether the licensor or the licensee acts against a third party for infringement. Quite often the licensor will wish to retain control of the action but will add a provision requiring the licensee to provide reasonable assistance as they may have important information that will be needed for the action to be successful. The licensee may also require the right to act itself if the licensor fails to do so within a certain time of becoming aware of the infringement to avoid being left in limbo with the infringers' action continuing to damage the licensee's legitimate use. In other situations, due to the geographic location and local knowledge of the licensee the licensor may let the licensee act against infringers with consent.

It will also be necessary to set out who is responsible for the costs of taking action, this will include not only legal costs but potentially the reimbursement of expenses that the licensee incurs in assisting. An agreement on the split of any damages recovered as between the parties may also be included on the assumption the infringement could negatively impact both the licensee and licensor (the licensee will lose sales and the licensor will in turn receive less royalties).

[K] Royalties and Payment Mechanism

Payment for trademark licenses are normally based on royalties payable by the licensee set by reference to a percentage of the net sale price of the goods or services sold by the licensee under the trademark (refer to the earlier comments in section §3.07[D] on the importance of defining the Net Sales Value or Price). The royalty structure and the percentage charged will vary considerably depending on the nature of the goods and the commercial situation. Upfront royalty payments and milestone payments that are then set off against future royalty earnings can also be used as well.

Commercial factors that will impact the level of the royalties payable include how well known the trademark is, the extent of the territory granted, whether the licence is exclusive and the potential market in the designated territory. A fixed rate royalty may be appropriate in some circumstances where the goods sold under the trademark are incorporated into another product – for example, bicycles and computers often incorporate branded components from third parties. Where a fixed amount is charged and the licence agreement lasts for some time then an ability to increase those prices for inflation will be important for the licensor.

The licensee will probably try to negotiate a tiered structure for the royalties such that the percentage paid decreases as the sales volumes increase. Notwithstanding that the royalties may be based on the net sales value the licensor will want to ensure that if the licensee makes non-arms' length sales at a reduced price or even for free (e.g., by the provision of samples or for use within its group companies) that there is provision for royalties not to be paid for these types of transaction, although a reduced rate may be an acceptable compromise. Obviously if sub-licensing is allowed, then sales by sub-licensees need to be specifically identified as transactions that attract a royalty payment.

A pure royalty payment structure exposes the licensor if the licensee underperforms, as all the sums received are wholly dependent on the amount of sales the licensee achieves. The risk is amplified if the licensor is granting a long term, exclusive licence covering a wide territory. This situation could leave the licensor caught in an unprofitable or under-utilised arrangement, so these issues need to be thought through at the negotiation phase. One way that the risk can be mitigated is by incorporating a minimum level of royalty payments that the licensee is required to meet. At one extreme a failure to meet this level would allow the licensor to terminate the licence agreement for failing to meet the minimum amount. However, if the licensee is well advised they will seek to remove the termination right or to lessen its impact by ensuring the licensee is given sufficient time to meet the minimum royalty taking into account the time required to penetrate the market. Another option would be to build in the right for the licensee to voluntarily pay a sum of money equivalent to any shortfall in royalties. The licensee may choose to do this where they believe the commercial returns from keeping the licence running outweighs paying the compensatory shortfall payment.

If the right of termination for failure to meet the minimum royalty payment is not acceptable to the licensee, the licensor may propose incorporating a right to convert an exclusive license to a non-exclusive one so that the licensor can make sales in the territory or appoint a third party to do so alongside the licensee. Whilst this is a better option than termination for the licensee it will not be lost on them that this may reduce their sales and take up unexploited opportunities, so the licensee may want the right to regain exclusivity if it subsequently increases sales to a level where the minimum royalty is met. If the licensor concedes to this approach it will need to check that it can bring its own or any third party activity within the territory to an end at the point exclusivity applies again, which may or may not be easily achievable. Transition periods are often used as the solution which provides sufficient time to terminate the third party arrangements or to wind down the licensor's own operations.

The regularity of royalty payments will need to be determined (normally monthly or quarterly payments are used) and an obligation placed on the licensee to record the basis of the calculations and provide information with the royalty payment of how the figure has been calculated so that the licensor can check at face value whether it has been paid the correct amount. On top of this audit rights will normally be included so that the licensor can gain access to the internal records of the licensee to verify that all the royalties due under the licence are being paid. An independent specialist third party would usually be used to carry out the audit. Most licensees will be concerned about this access in terms of confidentiality and disruption to their operations and their lawyers should therefore try to insert a maximum number of audits that can take place in any year, require the third party auditor to sign a confidentiality agreement and make the cost of the audit the responsibility of the licensor. These limitations should still enable the licensor to carry out adequate verification. The licensor will normally require the cost of an audit to be met by licensee if an adverse discrepancy in the royalty payments is identified and that exceeds a defined percentage (typically five percent), together with the obligation on the licensee to make good any identified shortfall of payments revealed by the audit. Of course, if the failure to pay royalties is material/has been deliberate then the licensor may wish to consider other remedies as well such as termination.

The trigger for royalties accruing should also be agreed and set out in the clause - the licensee will probably push for the trigger to be the date the payment is received from its end customer whereas the licensor will prefer the trigger to be the date the sale is concluded or the date of delivery of the product. The position ultimately reached will be a matter for negotiation, but the licensee may legitimately have concerns about their cash flow if it has to pay the royalties before it receives payment from its own customer, particularly if the royalty represents a significant proportion of their overall profit.

The following items will also need to be set out in the licence agreement in the context of the royalty payments:

- The currency in which the royalty payments will be made and consequently who will bear the exchange rate risk.
- The interest rate that will be applied to late payments.
- Tax - specialist advice should be sought on a case-by-case basis. Detailed analysis goes beyond the remit of this book, but issues will probably concern the application of VAT or other sales tax and whether the royalty payments could be subject to withholding tax. Whether any payments include or exclude VAT needs to be made clear. If withholding tax is applied the licensor will probably seek to ensure that the sums it is paid are gross as if no sums had been withheld.

[L] Liability and Indemnities

Whether either side obtains a limit on their liability will come down to negotiation. Due to the value of the trademark to the licensor and the damage that it would incur from use outside the scope permitted under the licence, the licensor is likely to resist a cap on the licensee's liability. Achieving a cap on the licensor's liability is probably more realistic but this may make the argument for no cap on the licensee's liability harder. If the licensor's liability is uncapped the best way for the licensor to protect its position will be to limit the scope of its obligations – if an obligation is not in the agreement it cannot be breached, and the licensee cannot incur a loss.

In addition to ensuring that the trademark is not used outside the scope of the licence agreement a major concern for the licensor (if the agreement concerns goods) will be product liability, particularly if the goods have the potential to cause damage to consumers. The fact that the goods are sold under the licensor's trademark means that the licensor (certainly in context of EU consumer protection law) could be held liable for defects in the licensee's goods. As a result, a licensor will normally expect an uncapped indemnity from the licensee in respect of third party claims made against the licensor in relation to the goods, backed up with an obligation on the licensee to take out an insurance policy that covers this potential liability.

In terms of indemnities from the licensor we have already explained that the licensor will resist any warranties that state that the trademark will not infringe any third party intellectual property rights and accordingly it is unlikely to provide any form of indemnification against it.

If the licensee uses the trademark outside the terms of the licence agreement, as well as claiming damages the licensor will want to stop the unauthorised use as soon as possible to limit damage to the trademark. Consequently, you will often see a provision whereby the licensee acknowledges that damages are not an adequate remedy and accordingly that the licensor is entitled to other remedies such as an injunction or specific performance. Whether these remedies are given is still at the court's discretion but a provision like this may persuade the court that the remedies are appropriate based on the circumstances.

[M] Term and Termination

Trademark licences normally last for a fixed period and can be relatively long term in nature (five or ten years or longer) when compared to the duration of other commercial agreements. The longer term is normally required to enable sufficient time for the licensee to get a return on their investment. The term can be stated to commence from the date the licence agreement is signed, on an effective date in the future (where time is required for commercial reasons for preparation by either party) or be deemed to have commenced from an earlier date. The latter option may be necessary if the parties have commenced performance of the licence agreement before the final form has been signed.

Commencing performance prior to signature of the licence agreement on the assumption of using a deemed commencement date is undesirable in that it leaves both parties exposed if the licence agreement is not ultimately executed. However, if the licence agreement is executed using a deeming earlier commencement date it will allow the terms of licence agreement to apply retrospectively to breaches or disagreements which subsequently come to light in relation to any performance during the pre-signature period. If this approach is taken there are two important points each party need to note. First, consider whether they have done anything during pre-signature performance that was inconsistent with the signed agreement as otherwise they could instantly find themselves in breach upon signature. Second the licence agreement itself must be dated as of the actual date it was signed and not the date the performance commenced, as failure to do so may be fraudulent. This is easily achieved by the insertion of a definition of 'Commencement Date' referring to the earlier date performance started whilst still putting the date of signature at the head of the agreement.

When it comes to termination of the licence agreement, the usual termination rights concerning material breach and insolvency events should be added but in relation to an international licence, there are a few additional considerations:

- The licensor will not usually want any uncertainty as to whether a non-payment of royalties constitutes a material breach. Depending on the amount of the non-payment in the context of the overall amounts due under the licence, the licensee may be able to argue that a non-payment was not sufficiently material to constitute a material breach and therefore termination. The risk to the licensor in this situation is that its purported termination of the arrangement is invalid. In the UK this could result in a claim of revocation of the licence agreement against the licensor. On this basis the licensor will ordinarily seek to build in a specific right for termination for any non-payment. The licensee's lawyer in turn will normally try and build in an obligation for notice from the licensor indicating that they intend to terminate if payment is not received within a defined period to avoid the licence being terminated for an administrative error such as an invoice going astray. This stance is not wholly unreasonable, but the licensor needs to ensure that an unduly long rectification period for non-payment is not inserted.
- Insolvency events encompass a wide variety of financial distress scenarios and the processes and terminology vary between jurisdictions so that using a detailed listing of the UK specific insolvency processes may not work if they do not correspond with the processes applying where the licensee is located. Working out the differences in the insolvency processes and reflecting them in the termination provisions is unlikely to be practical and accordingly it is sensible to add wording providing that termination is allowed if any events 'analogous' to the listed insolvency events occur in relation to the licensee in another jurisdiction. A termination event simply stating that termination is allowed if the licensee ceases to carry on business is an added protection that should be used as well as this is not contingent on defined insolvency events occurring, although this will not allow termination where the licensor is in financial difficulties but is still operating. From a licensee's view point it will want to check that the listed insolvency events do not allow termination for minor events such as a third party action over the failure to pay a small debt where the debt can be quickly resolved in the ordinary course of business. Events concerning solvent reconstruction or amalgamation of either party's business should also be excluded from allowing termination.
- As we noted in the earlier section on royalties, the licensor may want the right to terminate if a minimum level of royalties is not achieved to avoid being tied into a non-functioning relationship where alternatives could be sought.

- Change of control also has importance in a licence arrangement. Either party may have concerns if, for example, the other party is taken over by one of their direct competitors. If a change of control provision is included the party subject to it should ensure that it is reasonably balanced, i.e., by defining what is meant by a 'competitor' and prescribing a fixed timescale after a change of control within which the right of termination can be exercised.
- Where the breach of particular provisions of the licence agreement would severely expose the licensor (such as ones which would potentially expose the trademark to revocation) the licensee should consider whether breach of the provision should be specifically defined as constituting a 'material breach' allowing termination. Note that even when specific material breaches are identified they should be expressed as a non-exclusive list of such events as it is unlikely that all breaches that the licensor would consider material can be identified at the outset.
- Care must be taken to ensure that any termination notice follows the requirements of the licence agreement and that the notice states the basis for the termination, refers to the applicable provisions upon which it is being served and that the method of service of the notice complies with the formalities of the notices clause (including any stipulations concerning service in foreign jurisdictions).

Following termination, a few things will need to be covered in the agreement:

- Subject to any specified wind down processes (refer to the last point below), a clear statement that the license to use the trademark has ended (including any sub-licences, if applicable), and that the licensee (and any sub-licensees) will immediately cease all use of the trademark upon date of termination.
- An obligation to return any confidential materials to the licensor and to return or destroy any advertising materials that utilise the trademark.
- A provision setting out the clauses that will survive termination, typically including matters such as indemnification, liability caps, confidentiality and the clauses within the boilerplate that govern how the licence agreement operates that still have post-termination applicability such as definitions, severance, dispute resolution, governing law.
- A statement that termination will not affect any rights or obligations that have accrued up to the date of termination such as a claim for damages/outstanding payment.
- An obligation to immediately pay any outstanding royalties/ensure they are paid within the contractual period for making payment in the licence.
- A requirement to remove any registrations relating to the existence of the licence at the applicable registry.
- Where the license is in relation to goods there may be non-sold stock items or unfulfilled orders outstanding at the point of termination, particularly if the termination is not due to expiry in the ordinary course of events. From a practical viewpoint, the parties will need to agree a process for the stock to be

dealt with. The licensee will be concerned about having unsold stock which technically will be an infringement to dispose of once the licence ends or they may have contractual obligations to third parties to supply goods after the termination date. If the relationship has been good and comes to a natural end, then the licensor should be happy to allow 'wind down' provisions to deal with these issues whilst still being mindful that there must be an unequivocal end point for the licensee's use of the trademark. Possible options include allowing the licensee a defined period for the sale of current stock, the purchase of the stock by the licensor from the licensee at a defined price if the licensor can dispose of it directly, or the assumption of the fulfilment of outstanding orders under the licensee's third party contracts. If the termination is due to a breach of the licence agreement the licensor is likely to resist giving the licensee an orderly wind down option – and the issues will remain with the licensee.

[N] Dispute Resolution and Other Boilerplate Provisions of Relevance

For guidance on boilerplate provisions and dispute resolution, refer to Chapter 1 (Introduction) and Chapter 7 (International Dispute Resolution), respectively.

Selected Bibliography

Selected Readings

Wilkof, Neil J (2004), Trade Mark Licensing (Second Edition)
Bainbridge, David (2012) Intellectual Property (Ninth Edition)
Christou, Richard (2011) International Agency, Distribution and Licensing Agreements (Sixth Edition)
Christie, Andrew & Gare, Stephen (2014) Blackstone's Statutes on Intellectual Property (Twelfth Edition) – for reference to source Statutes

Useful Websites

World Intellectual Property Organisation Website: www.wipo.int
International Trade Mark Association Website: www.inta.org
World Trade Organisation Website: www.wto.org
GOV.UK Website: www.gov.uk/government/publications/protecting-your-uk-intellectual-property-abroad

CHAPTER 4

International Software Licensing

§4.01 INTRODUCTION

The licensing of software impacts on all aspects of modern life, with a global market value of enterprise software alone running to several hundred billion dollars.[1] The speed of technological progress has resulted in software being used for a vast array of business and personal applications. All sizes of organisation are heavily reliant on software from small businesses using basic accounts and word processing software through to international organisations using complex software to manage their multi-jurisdictional customer base and logistics. At the consumer level, the use of smart-phone applications to manage and organise peoples' day-to-day lives is becoming all pervasive.

Software has disrupted the way businesses operate with Internet start-up companies, utilising innovative software, achieving market capitalisation figures above that of established, 'blue chip' organisations within just a few years. There are hundreds of so-called Unicorn technical start-ups with a market capitalisation of over $1 billion operating in the retail, manufacturing and finance sectors. Uber Technologies Inc.'s development of a software platform enabling consumers to use a mobile application to contact drivers nearby to obtain a lift is a good example. The convenience to the consumer and the fact Uber drivers use their own cars to provide the cab service has resulted in a rapid expansion, disrupting the traditional taxi service model. Uber was only founded in 2009 and now it operates in over 400 cities in North and Central America, Asia, Africa, Australia and Europe. At the end of 2015, Uber had an estimated market value of $62.5 billion which would mean its value significantly exceeds the NASDAQ market capitalisation figures of both Ford and Twenty-First

1. Gartner Says Worldwide IT Spending is Forecast to Grow 2.4 Percent in 2017 – www.gartner.com/newsroom/id/3759763.

Century Fox.[2] Another high-profile example is Airbnb's online marketplace that connects consumers with accommodation worldwide. Airbnb began in 2008 and now covers 190 countries and has a market capitalisation of over $30 billion in 2017.[3] Notwithstanding the success of these companies, it should be noted that the massive effect on the markets they have entered has not been without controversy and it remains to be seen whether they can sustain their progression at the same rate. Issues of non-profitability, poor management and breaches of regulations have hampered Uber. Airbnb has also had regulatory issues and been criticised for its effect on accommodation prices for locals in tourist destinations.

Technology and software have changed the status quo, altering what people do and how they do it. The adoption of broadband technology in developed countries has opened up new channels for software distribution, allowing for the delivery of complex software across borders via Internet downloads and the wide spread use of 'Software as a Service' (software accessed over the Internet and run remotely from the users' hardware). Software is now the cornerstone of communication, risk reduction and innovation in business.

Consequently, it is not surprising that software licences are one of the most common forms of international licence agreement that legal advisors encounter. Even though software comes in a multitude of forms, there are a lot of similarities in terms of the main themes and issues to cover, irrespective of the type of software being licensed. The objective of this chapter is to explore these generic themes and issues in the context of the international licensing of software and in so doing assist the reader with the process of reviewing and drafting these types of agreement. Each subject area looks at issues from the perspective of the licensor and the licensor.

Much of this chapter assumes an alignment of UK and European law at the time of writing; however, with Brexit occurring at the end of March 2019 this may change. The current view is that there will be a significant period of transition where the status quo is maintained but the reader should consider the known position at the time of reading in relation to Brexit and any consequential differences between the UK and European law.

§4.02 WHY LICENSE SOFTWARE INTERNATIONALLY?

In most situations, licensing will be the most commercially effective way for a software developer to exploit the time and investment they have put into producing their software. The upfront cost of developing software can be considerable. Some of the latest video games have multi-million-dollar budgets exceeding those of Hollywood films, for example, the video game Grand Theft Auto IV by Rockstar games cost over $100 million to develop and it produced worldwide sales of $800 million within 24

2. www.uber.com and Matt Rosoff Uber is now more valuable than Ford, GM, and a bunch of huge public companies (Business Insider 4 December 2015) – www.techinsider.io/uber-valuation-vs-market-cap-of-publicly-traded-stocks-2015-12, accessed July 2016.
3. www.marketwatch.com/story/new-funding-round-pushes-airbnbs-value-to-31-billion-2017-03-09, accessed January 2018.

hours of going on sale.[4] Business targeted software is constantly enhanced to sell new versions offering new features and functionality. The incremental enhancement of the core Microsoft products is a good example of this strategy in action. Successes such as these are based on the developer retaining the underlying intellectual property rights in the software and licensing it widely on an international basis. In most cases, the one-time assignment/sale of the rights in software will not result in the necessary or maximum returns being achieved.

Licensing allows the owner to provide the same highly sophisticated product to multiple users at a much lower price point whilst achieving a higher overall return due to sales volume. New software versions and ongoing software maintenance also allow the software licensor to exploit new and additional revenue streams.

Most large software companies' success results from the successful implementation of licensing models rather than the one-off assignments. In fact, the foundation of Microsoft Inc.'s success was based on the decision to license. By licensing IBM, the Microsoft operating system for IBM personal computers, rather than selling the software for a one-off payment Microsoft could create its own market, offering the same software to third-party producers of 'IBM Compatible' PCs. Ironically the Microsoft operating system licensed to IBM was based on another company's operating system which Microsoft bought outright for just $50,000 and then adapted it for IBM.[5]

Expansion into international markets is a natural consequence of trying to achieve the maximum return on the licensing strategy. However, it is not without its difficulties due to the need to operate and contract in multiple jurisdictions with different legal systems.

This chapter will describe the alternative ways that software companies approach the issue of international licensing with their associated advantages and disadvantages. Of course, the risks are not limited to the licensor so the issues from the licensee's perspective will be covered as well.

§4.03 APPLICABILITY TO THE LEGAL ADVISOR

Legal practitioners, whether in-house or in private practice, can encounter international software licences in various situations. A common scenario is where a company or client has a requirement to license software from a company based in another jurisdiction. This is highly likely because of the increasing geographic spread of software developers worldwide. Moreover, this trend will continue as developing countries seek to move away from traditional manufacturing industries to high technology ones. Geographic location is no longer a hindrance to development resources either with the latest communication technology. Another situation where

4. Scott McCulloch, 'Revenues and Profits up for Grand Theft Auto Developer Rockstar North' (*The Daily Record*, 4 December 2014), www.dailyrecord.co.uk/business/company-results-forecasts/revenues-profits-up-grand-theft-4741016#dVDDMyDFQjreKx3v.97 accessed July 2016.
5. Sophie Curtis, 'Bill Gates a History at Microsoft', (*The Telegraph*, 4 February 2014), www.telegraph.co.uk/technology/bill-gates/10616991/Bill-Gates-a-history-at-Microsoft.html, accessed July 2016.

international licensing expertise may be needed is when a software company seeks legal advice on its own software licence to enable it to distribute its software to customers in other jurisdictions. International software licences are also frequently encountered when undertaking commercial due diligence in a corporate transaction.

As a general point it should always be borne in mind that irrespective of what is provided for in a licence agreement, mandatory rules of law in other countries can override licence terms irrespective of the choice of law and this is considered further later in this chapter.

The rest of this chapter will provide details on the underlying laws that have an impact on software licensing and will then analyse the skeleton structure and issues associated with an international software licence.

§4.04 THE UNDERLYING INTELLECTUAL PROPERTY RIGHTS APPLYING TO SOFTWARE

Before attempting to review a software licence it is important to have a general understanding of the intellectual property rights that underpin the software, so you can see how these may vary by jurisdiction, and the implications that this has for the licence agreement. Relatively limited prior knowledge of intellectual property and technology law has been assumed.

Several intellectual property rights can be found in, or are important to, software including copyright, patents, database rights and trademarks each of which is considered below with reference to the European and wider international position.

An in-depth analysis of these rights goes beyond the remit of this book, and accordingly the focus is placed on the implications for software protection and international licensing; however, the topics covered will direct the reader to the areas where further reading and research can be undertaken, if needed.

§4.05 COPYRIGHT: PROTECTION OF SOFTWARE

The most prevalent form of protection that software has on an international basis is copyright. This is because, in most jurisdictions, this form of protection arises automatically by operation of law (provided the fundamental requirements for copyright protection are met). That is to say, registration of the rights by the owner is not required. Note, however, that whilst registration is not normally required, in some jurisdictions such as the US voluntary registration of copyright confers additional benefits in terms of the ability to act against an infringer.

The emphasis in the summary below is on copyright from the UK/EU perspective, but references to other jurisdictions are made to provide examples of material differences that may apply in other jurisdictions. The main international treaties harmonising the application of copyright are described later in this chapter.

A key advantage of copyright when compared to most other intellectual property rights is the length of protection it can afford. Whilst the length of copyright protection can vary depending on the jurisdiction it mainly lasts for the life of the author, plus 50 or 70 years. Consequently, it is unlikely that copyright protection will expire before the end of the commercial usefulness of the software.

For copyright to exist the subject matter needs to be 'original' and fit into a categorisation of work, for example, literary, dramatic, musical or artistic works, sound recordings, films etc. The requirement of 'originality' is interpreted widely and provided the software has been produced by a developer using a moderate amount of labour and skill and it has not been copied the software is likely to meet the originality threshold, i.e., the software does not need to be unique as such. Copyright comes into existence as soon as the work is recorded in some tangible form.[6]

Software (or 'computer programs' as it is often referred to in legislation) is classified as a 'literary works' for the purposes of copyright on the basis it is written in computer code.[7] However, there may be other separate copyright works that exist in the components of the software, for example, images within the software can have copyright protection as 'artistic works' and music and songs output by the software can have copyright protection as a musical composition. Accordingly, multiple types of copyright can exist in just one piece of software. Depending on how the software components are developed these rights may be owned by different people. Software often utilises stock photographs and third-party music which have separate copyrights that are licensed to the developers for incorporation in the software by their owners.

The existence of copyright creates an intangible asset that may be licensed by the copyright owner. It gives the owner the right to allow or prevent a third party from using the copyright work in certain ways. In relation to the software owner the most important rights are the right to prevent copying, issuing copies to the public and making adaptations. A license is a contract enabling the software owner to permit a third party (the licensee) to use its software in pre-defined ways. In the absence of that licence right use will potentially put the licensee in breach of the copyright in the software. Most licences will limit the rights the licensee is granted to use the software so if the terms of the licence are not adhered to the licensee will potentially be liable for both breach of contract and infringement of copyright. The licence agreement therefore allows the licensor to control the software's use and to exploit it (commercially or otherwise).

Copyright protects the 'expression of an idea' rather than the idea itself. The EU Software Directive sets out this principle as it applies to 'computer programs' by providing that: *'Ideas and principles which underlie any element of a computer program, including those which underlie its interfaces, are not protected by copyright.'*[8] By way of illustration of this concept, copyright would protect the computer code of an anti-virus program and thereby prevent third parties producing their own version of the software by copying its code, but the underlying idea of an anti-virus protection software, i.e., to prevent malware infecting computers, would not be protected by copyright. Third parties can utilise that idea and develop their own anti-virus software provided that their software is original and not copied. Copyright does not create a

6. Copyright, Designs and Patents Act 1988, s. 3(2).
7. Copyright, Designs and Patents Act 1988, s. 3(1).
8. Directive 2009/24/EC on the Legal Protection of Computer Programs – Article 1(2).

monopoly right, and this is illustrated by the range of software available in any one market that essentially provides a very similar solution but by using proprietary methods of implementation.

One 'grey area' area of software copyright worth highlighting is the distinction made between so-called literal and non-literal copying. The former term concerns literal copying of underlying computer code or content and should be relatively easy to establish whilst the latter, more contentious area, concerns the extent to which the structure, layout and organisation of the software can be copied without using the computer code or content itself. Often cases of non-literal copying concern the 'look and feel' of the user interface, i.e., similarities between the look, layout and order of screen displays of the software as opposed to the non-viewable underlying computer code.

Proving infringement by non-literal copying is far harder than establishing literal copying and it has been the subject of several cases internationally with decisions veering both ways. The issue for the courts has been to balance providing legitimate protection for software whilst not extending its copyright protection beyond 'the expression of an idea' to create a monopoly right akin to patents. For example, if the layout of a computer screen is the only logical way to present a set of data efficiently, and that right is deemed to be protected by copyright it could act as a barrier to other market entrants producing competitive software as it would mean they cannot display the data to the user in a meaningful way without infringing copyright, even if their coding was original.

§4.06 AN OVERVIEW OF EUROPEAN AND INTERNATIONAL COPYRIGHT PROTECTION

Having established the basic premise that software is likely to benefit from copyright protection in some form and that this allows the owner to exploit the software using a licence arrangement we need to consider how copyright is treated in different jurisdictions.

If the copyright protection does not extend to the jurisdiction where the software is being licensed, then this will clearly be a problem. Even if a software owner only licensed the software in its domestic market and had copyright protection there, it could potentially leave the product exposed to piracy in other jurisdictions where there was no equivalent protection.

Copyright is extended to cover other jurisdictions through international treaties. Whilst there are a number of these treaties covering reciprocal copyright protection, the most important one is the Berne Convention for the Protection of Literary and Artistic Works ('the Berne Convention') which dates to 1886, albeit with several updates since that date.[9] The Berne Convention offers the most extensive protection for copyright

9. Text of the Berne Convention available at: www.wipo.int/treaties/en/text.jsp?file_id=283698.

internationally by having 171 Contracting Parties. The Berne Convention is administered by the World Intellectual Property Organisation (WIPO). For a complete understanding of this treaty's international reach, the list of the Contracting States which is available on the WIPO Website can be referred to.[10]

The Berne Convention operates by providing copyright protection to nationals of Contracting States with the same level of protection given to a national of another Contracting State. Membership also confers other rights under the Berne Convention such as a minimum term for which copyright protection must last in the Contracting States.

Another important treaty in the context of software is the WIPO Copyright Treaty of 1996. This treaty is a special agreement under the Berne Convention. It is adopted by WIPO Member States and was implemented to provide additional copyright protection to reflect technological advancements emanating from concerns that the existing copyright treaties did not address the issues adequately. The treaty expressly recognises computer programs' designation as 'literary works' for copyright protection, provides protection in relation to the organisation and selection of databases, provides rental and distribution rights that may not have been covered under the Berne Convention and prohibits the circumvention of technical methods used to protect works. Moreover, it recognises the right to authorise communication of works to the public through the Internet.

In the European context, there has been progressive harmonisation of the laws relating to copyright through the implementation of several directives. The Directive on the Harmonisation of Certain Aspects of Copyright in the Information Society (2001/29/EC) was used to reflect the WIPO Treaties in the National Law of the Member States of the EU. The first directive dealing with software specifically was the Directive on the Legal Protection of Computer Programs back in 1991. Due to changes since that date it was decided to implement the Directive on the Legal Protection of Computer Programs in 2009 (2009/24/EC) (commonly referred to as 'the Software Directive'). This directive did not alter the overall effect of the existing position but did require the implementation of the protection given to copyright in computer programs into the local law of EU Member States.

Subject to certain exceptions, which are covered in the sections below, the Software Directive provides the copyright owner with the exclusive rights to authorise copies (temporary or permanent) of the software; translate, adapt or alter the software, and allows the first distribution of the software to the public (including rental).[11] As the use of software will require copying to load or run the program on a computer, the control on the right to copy in turn provides control over who can use it. Note that there are exceptions to the rights in relation to software provided under the directive which cover a licensee's right to make back-up copies, test the software and carry out reverse decompilation. These exceptions are explained further in section §4.13[C][9] below[12]

10. List of Contracting Parties of the Berne Convention available at: www.wipo.int/treaties/en/ShowResults.jsp?lang=en&treaty_id=15.
11. Directive (2009/24/EC), Article 4 (1).
12. Directive (2009/24/EC), Articles 5 and 6.

as it is important that software licensors operating in the EU are aware of these licensee rights when operating in the EU.

In summary, therefore, assuming the software meets the basic requirements for copyright, the protection afforded will have wide international application.

§4.07 PATENTS: PROTECTION OF SOFTWARE

If a software patent can be obtained it is potentially a valuable right for the owner as a patent effectively gives a monopoly right in relation to the product (unlike copyright). The period of patent protection in most jurisdictions is 20 years. The relevant statute in the UK is the Patents Act 1977. Whilst at first glance patents may appear to be anticompetitive by excluding others from the same market, the trade-off is that the patent owner is required to publish their invention. Accordingly, in the longer term, it is a method of sharing information and encouraging future innovation in the market. If an organisation knows that it will get sufficient time to get a significant return on its innovation without direct competition because of a patent they are more likely to invest in new developments.

As with copyright, patents are a form of intangible property right that can be licensed, but the protection a patent provides goes far wider, despite the period of protection being far shorter. Because patents are a monopoly right they protect the underlying ideas of the software and not just the expression of those ideas.

The pharmaceutical industry illustrates the benefits of patents particularly well. At one end of the industry you have the major pharmaceutical companies expending millions on drug trials (most of which will fail to reach commercialisation) on the premise that if they patent just one drug from all the trials the returns they will make through the patent protection period without competitors will be more than enough to compensate for all the wasted trial costs and to secure a profit. After a patent expires, so-called generic pharmaceutical companies can replicate the drug from the information published in the patent and manufacture and sell it at a much lower cost (as they do not have any research and development overheads) and still make a profit. The originating company, the generic company and the end user all benefit in some way. You may have observed that the share price of large pharmaceutical companies varies significantly if they abandon trials of a promising drug that could be patentable or where one of its major drug's patent protection is about to expire, and this reflects the huge sums at stake.

The potential value of a patent is reflected in the process for obtaining one in that it involves a complex application process that will normally require extensive examination by a government body against the designated criteria for patentability. The general requirements for something to be patentable in the UK are that it must be new, involve an inventive step and be capable of industrial application.[13] Patent applications can be costly and time-consuming and will normally require professional assistance from patent agents.

13. Patents Act 1977, s. 1 (1).

In the context of international protection, it should be noted that patents are territorial rights with the protection and the laws governing the patent being on a 'country-by-country' basis. Accordingly, if you have a patent in one country, the patent protection applies to that jurisdiction only and not wider. This means that a separate patent will, prima facie, need to be obtained in each jurisdiction where protection is required. Moreover, the Patent Cooperation Treaty of 1970 (PCT) allows a single patent application to be made to obtain patent protection in other countries that are party to the Treaty. Note that even though it is one application it does not result in a single patent with a wide area of protection – the output is a collection of separate national patent registrations being granted.

In addition to the PCT, the European Patent Office (EPO) created by European Patent Convention 1973 (EPC) provides for EU patent applications in all the countries designated by the applicant, but these still need to be enforced before the applicable national courts and will be subject to their legislation.

The EPC is not a European Union derived body, and it covers patents in 38 EPC Member States, i.e., its reach extends beyond the current 28 EU Member States. There has been considerable debate about introducing a unitary patent system in Europe for a long time. A unitary system would allow a single patent to apply across the EU but to date the attempts to implement this have failed, most notably in 2005 when a proposed directive by the EPO was roundly rejected. Patents can of course also be obtained in any required country individually by applying through the relevant national patent office as well.

In summary, irrespective of the route taken to get the patent in the different jurisdictions the laws applying to the patent will vary depending on the laws applied in the relevant country.

In addition to the general complexities of obtaining a patent there is also the issue of the extent to which software is patentable under the laws of any particular jurisdictions. The US has a more relaxed approach than Europe in this context with software patents being relatively common whereas in Europe the patentability of software is often contentious and complicated.

Under Article 52 (2) c of the EPC a computer program 'as such' is not patentable. This ambiguous wording is not elaborated on in the EPC, and this has caused much disagreement and debate as to the circumstances in which software may be granted a patent and in turn to differing approaches of interpretation being adopted by the countries within Europe. The wording has been interpreted to mean that the software must have a technical character/effect to be patentable so, for example, control software that is used in relation to an industrial manufacturing process might meet this requirement. Nevertheless a significant number of software patents have been granted in Europe by the EPO which has taken a robust approach in approving software patents over the years but the stance at a national level varies, with the courts in the UK, for example, veering towards refusing the grant of patents for software. Because of these differences, coupled with copyright protection arising automatically, encountering a software with patent protection is far less likely than coming across software which is only protected by copyright. If there is patent protection it should be readily easy to determine by looking at the Licence Agreement which will refer to the patent.

§4.08 TRADEMARKS AND DATABASE RIGHTS

Whilst of less significance than copyright and patents there are other intellectual property rights that are relevant to software protection and these are summarised below.

Trademarks can be used to distinguish the software products of one provider from those of another. Trademarks do not protect the software itself but the use of a distinguishing mark in relation to a software product can be a useful way of protecting a company's business. Trademarks are also an excellent method of associating a product with implied characteristics of quality and value to the customer. Microsoft and Apple are good examples of companies that have leveraged trademarks and branding to great effect. Windows, Outlook, Excel and PowerPoint are just a few of the well-known registered trademarks of Microsoft Inc. The Apple logo, iTunes, iPhone and iPad registered trademarks are recognised internationally. For details of the extent to which these companies use trademark protection you can go to their websites which contain a list of their registrations.[14] For further information on how trademarks can be obtained internationally refer to the Trademark Licensing chapter.

If a licensor has a strong trademark in relation to its software product in one jurisdiction it makes sense to ensure that the trademark is protected in any new market before launching the product there under the mark to avoid losing the rights to a third party. This may require the assistance of trademark agents and branding experts. These specialists will be able to verify that the mark does not conflict with an existing trademark and that the brand does not need localising to avoid an inadvertent and undesirable interpretation in another jurisdiction. An amusing but expensive mistake Mercedes-Benz made when first entering the Chinese market was using the brand name 'Bensi,' without knowing that the Chinese translation meant 'rush to die', a fantastic message to potential car buyers that was quickly addressed![15]

Databases within software can benefit from copyright protection as literary works if they meet the required criteria. The database will need to meet the requirement of originality and this may not be achieved if the database merely comprises a simple collation of information categories. Even so, copyright is the most common form of protection for databases internationally and a database with copyright will have the benefit of the wider protection afforded by Berne Convention and the WIPO Copyright Treaty, as explained in section §4.06. In Europe there is also another level of protection for databases aside from copyright. If the database required substantive effort to produce but could not qualify for copyright protection due to a lack of originality it may still have Database Right.

The requirement for additional protection of databases in the EU arose because of the harmonisation of the 'originality' test for software in the EU, which was required

14. Microsoft Inc. trademarks: www.microsoft.com/en-us/legal/intellectualproperty/trademarks/en-us.aspx and Apple Inc. trademarks: www.apple.com/legal/intellectual-property/trademark/appletmlist.html.
15. Geoffrey James, '20 Epic Fails in Global Branding' (*Inc.com*, 29 October 2014) www.inc.com/geoffrey-james/the-20-worst-brand-translations-of-all-time.html accessed July 2016.

because EU Member States used different tests to determine what could be protected. This gap was addressed by the EU Database Directive (96/9/EC)[16] which is implemented into local law of EU Member States. Database right is an independent or 'sui generis' right that offers protection for up to 15 years from the end of the year the database is completed. Database Right specifically excludes software that operates or creates databases which should in any event have copyright protection, but it can cover databases which software refers to or accesses when operating.

§4.09 COMPETITION LAW ISSUES

As with other licences of intellectual property, licensors should be aware that software licences have the potential to create competition law issues. For further consideration of this topic, refer to Chapter 2 (Competition Law Considerations).

§4.10 THE IMPORTANCE OF A FORMAL WRITTEN LICENCE AND THE TYPES OF SOFTWARE LICENCE ENCOUNTERED IN AN INTERNATIONAL CONTEXT

It is vital that licensors utilise a comprehensively written licence when exploiting their software, on a national or international basis. The software licence, as with any contract, is intended to create certainty between the parties. It determines what the licensee can, and cannot do with the software and for how long and protects the licensor's rights and exposure to liability.

A badly drafted licence agreement puts both the licensee and licensor at risk. From the licensee's viewpoint they may not be permitted to use the software in the intended way and from the licensor's side, failure to put in appropriate licensee restrictions may mean that they lose valuable rights to exploit their product in the future. In an extreme situation, a licensor could inadvertently assign the rights in their software rather than license them or open themselves up to claims from the licensee for loss of profits if the software does not operate correctly.

Time and attention spent on ensuring a licence agreement is correct in the first instance will have a significant effect on the software product's success and can mitigate against the risk of litigating in an unfamiliar foreign jurisdiction.

Software licences take several forms, primarily depending on the use to which the software will be put rather than the jurisdiction in which the software will be used. At one end of the spectrum there will be bespoke, individually negotiated licences such as in arrangements between computer companies where one company wants to incorporate the other company's software product into their own software or where one company wants to procure a bespoke piece of software for their own use. At the other extreme will be straightforward 'click through' licences that are presented and accepted on screen before access to the product is allowed or for older software licences contained with software on physical media so-called shrink wrap licences. In between

16. Council Directive 96/9/EC on the Legal Protection of Databases.

these types of licence will be standard form corporate licences completed by online acceptance or by signature of a physical licence agreement. The length and complexity of the licence agreement will also be influenced by the value of the software and whether the software is targeted at 'business to consumer' or 'business to business' transactions. Note that in the latter scenario there may be sectoral or regulatory requirements that affect the contents of a software license. This is often the case in the financial services sector, and so this aspect should be investigated when dealing with regulated industries.

For most standard 'off the shelf software' click through licenses are the norm. The licensor will not allow the software to be accessed or used without the licensee actively confirming agreement to the terms, usually by clicking an electronic acceptance button. The acceptance process may occur online or be on the media on which the software is provided. The licensor needs to take care when designing the click through process to ensure that the terms and conditions are incorporated into the contract correctly. Accordingly, it is important that the licensee can access and review the licence terms before they accept the terms as if they are only available after clicking 'accept' then they will not form part of the contract. This situation can be avoided by having a link clearly providing access to the terms and conditions above the acceptance button or better still requiring the licensee to scroll through the license terms before being presented with the acceptance button. It is also essential that the software cannot be accessed without pressing the acceptance button; otherwise, there will be an evidential gap, if it is disputed whether the terms have been accepted. The licensor needs to be able to show that without acceptance the user could not have physically used the program.

For high value software there is often a hard-copy licence based on the licensor's standard document that is then negotiated in relation to commercial and legal points. Whether the document is negotiable and to what extent will depend on the relative bargaining power of the licensor and licensee, but in any event it is vital that the licensee reviews the licence terms to see whether they permit the intended use.

When reviewing a standard form licence from a large software vendor for a commoditised software product the licence terms can be extremely hard to follow, with numerous online provisions. These types of licence can be a challenge even for experienced technology lawyers. The difficulties arise not only because of their length (which can be considerable) but also because different provisions apply dependant on which product is being purchased, the region you are in and the options being selected. Moreover, the agreements often use hyperlinks to cross-refer to ancillary terms for software components that apply as well but how the two sets of terms interrelate in detail is often unclear. Further, where the terms and conditions are accessed online they may be updated over time and identifying the terms that were originally entered into can be a problem particularly if they were not printed out in full at the time the contract was entered into. Even though this less than user-friendly approach has caused controversy, it is still prevalent. Often IT departments print out contract summaries omitting the underlying contract terms which can cause problems in identification of contract terms later. The issue often materialises when the company is being sold, and due diligence identifies the absence of license terms applicable to the software used on the company's systems.

When presented with a maze of applicable licence terms it is important that the licensee identifies the various strands and obtains a working knowledge of how they interact, seeking clarification from the licensor/software reseller if necessary.

Failing to understand and follow licence terms creates not only the financial risk of an action for breach of contract but also a reputational risk. The situation can be particularly embarrassing if the licensee derives its revenue stream from the licensing of its intellectual property. Being shown to not respect the intellectual property rights of a third party, when you expect your customers to respect your own, is not a message that any company wants to convey.

Effective licence management is important for all organisations, and the final form licence agreements should be kept and indexed electronically or in hard copy so that they are readily accessible as a record of the terms and scope of use that were agreed. If this is not done at the time of entering into a licence agreement verifying the basis on which the software was licensed down the line can be hard to establish. Anyone who carries out due diligence will be aware of how often draft, unsigned or undated copies of licence agreements are included for review and the uncertainty that this creates.

The need to obtain copies of agreements tends to arise at the point where there is a software dispute or where it is not known whether the desired scope of use is permitted. The last thing that you will want to do as a licensee is not to be able to find the licence terms. From a practical viewpoint, it does not matter whether the contract management is done by the business at a commercial level or within the legal department, but someone needs to take on this responsibility.

Another licensing model for software distribution is the value-added re-seller agreements, commonly known as VAR agreements. In this model the licensor deals with a commercial intermediary who distributes the software to the end user. They may offer additional services or products that are sold with the licensor's software, hence the reference to 'value add'. The advantage to the licensor is that they can sell their software in larger numbers to the VAR whilst in turn the VAR should get a material discount on the unit price enabling them to sell on and still make a profit. In terms of the licence of the software, the end user will be required by the VAR to enter the licence terms directly with the licensor, or alternatively the licensor may allow the VAR to sub-license the software to the end user ensuring that the sub-license does not give wider rights than those granted to the VAR. The VAR route to market may be desirable if there are VARs in the target jurisdiction with well-established local market knowledge and presence. A key downside however is losing direct control of the distribution process.

The use of agents in the local jurisdiction is another option whereby the agent introduces or introduces and negotiates licenses of the software on behalf of the licensor. It should be noted however that there are often laws that protect an agent's interests that could expose the licensor. For example, in Europe the Directive on the

Coordination of the Laws of the Member States[17] relating to self-employed commercial agents, implemented in the UK as the Commercial Agent Regulations 1993,[18] amongst other things, controls the principal's ability to terminate the agent and can lead to compensatory payments to the agent on termination for loss of the agency. This legislation only applies to the sale of goods so whether software is determined to be goods or services is important and there has been significant debate on the topic. The wider implications of this distinction are considered in section §4.13[C][14] below, but a recent case in the UK[19] concluded that electronic distribution of software was not goods for the purpose of the regulations and so they did not apply; however, if software is distributed via a tangible medium such as a CD then they may well be viewed as goods. This is an area which would benefit from legislative clarification. The overall message therefore is before appointing an agent it should be verified whether there is any agency law that could cause a problem.

More complex standard form corporate licences are most likely to be encountered by the legal practitioner in an international context as these will tend to be viewed by the business as requiring legal review. The rest of this chapter will therefore focus on these types of licence agreement, but many of the principles explained can be applied more generally to other forms of licence. Most licenses cover similar issues but vary in the extent to which they are covered depending on the nature and value of the software and the context in which they will be used.

§4.11 WHAT ARE THE INITIAL POINTS TO CONSIDER WHEN DRAFTING OR REVIEWING ANY FORM OF SOFTWARE LICENCE?

Having set the background to international licensing in respect of the law relating to the protection of intellectual property rights, this section covers the initial questions that need to be asked, whether you are acting for the licensee or the licensor of the software.

[A] Software Delivery and Software as a Service

A good place to start with a licence agreement is to consider the method by which the software will be delivered to the licensee; for example, will the software be provided on a physical medium such as on a CD-Rom or downloaded to the user's computer from the Internet or will it be accessed and used remotely through an Internet.

Where the software is accessed and used through the Internet it is often referred to as 'Software as a Service', 'SaaS' or cloud computing and this is one of the primary methods for software delivery. Technically speaking the customer is not granted a licence with a standard SaaS arrangement as they merely access the software remotely and as they do not need to use the software locally and they do not host the software no copying is carried out. However, notwithstanding this distinction' the basis of a

17. Council Directive (86/653/EEC) on the coordination of the laws of the Member States Relating to Self-Employed Commercial Agents.
18. The Commercial Agents (Council Directive) Regulations 1993.
19. Computer Associates UK Limited v. Software Incubator [2018] EWCA Civ 518.

SaaS agreement and a software licence are very similar in structure, and many of the same issues arise.

The improvements in Internet speeds using broadband and fibre technology mean that it is now practicable to run software on a licensor's servers in a location that is remote from the user's computer. The core processing is carried out by the licensor's servers remotely with the results passed back over the Internet to be displayed on the licensee's equipment. This method of delivery is used for a range of standard commercial software – Microsoft 365 (which provides a suite of their productivity software) is a good example of a service of this type. Whilst the contract to deliver software remotely will quite often be framed as the provision of a service in real terms this is still just another method of licensing, and most of the licensing issues considered below will apply equally notwithstanding some changes in terminology.

Remote provision via Software as a Service has increased the ease with which licensors can make their software available internationally as the end user will only need access to the Internet to make use of the software in different locations. Benefits to the licensor are that it should provide greater protection for the software's underlying code because there is no need to provide the customer with a copy of the software to run on their computer. It also allows the licensor to make changes and introduce updates and new versions centrally for wide access by the licensee population.

Notwithstanding the comments above, Software as a Service is not without disadvantages for the user. For example, the move to this method of delivery by vendors means that there are fewer providers of bespoke solutions and this gives customers less opportunity to develop their own software which might offer them a competitive advantage in the marketplace. Whilst it is helpful to have the software updated and new versions implemented for you by the vendor, in terms of knowing you are up to date, the corresponding downside is that the customer has less control over the version that they use. This might be a problem if the new version is less stable, as is often the case with newly released software or if it requires corresponding changes and costs to other software used by the customer to maintain interoperability. The customer may therefore wish to agree on a policy in relation to the obligation to update to new versions to mitigate this risk. As the software is hosted remotely so is the customer's data, accordingly this represents a risk to the customer if they do not have their own copies. They need to ensure there is a mechanism to get their data back on termination of the agreement and what happens to data access if the Internet is down or the vendor becomes insolvent?

[B] Source Code and Object Code: Escrow

Software can be provided in source code or object code form. Object code is the executable form of the code that the computer can directly process to run the software but is not in a form that the licensee can amend. Source code is the underlying code originally written by the programmer in the chosen computer language to create the software. An experienced programmer with access to the source code and associated notes would be able to establish how the software works and therefore to adapt and alter it by using the source code. The source code is compiled (converted) into object code which is the form of code that allows the computer to process and run the software. As a licensee will not normally need the source code to operate the software, the licensor will not usually provide it as this increases the risk that a licensee might seek to use and exploit it unfairly. It is possible, but not easy, to convert object code to source code in certain situations, and therefore there are normally prohibitions in licence agreements prohibiting reverse engineering.

Most software licences will not allow the licensee to access the source code of the software. Access will mainly be needed where the software is being purchased outright by the licensee such that they will want the ability to amend it independently or where the licensee needs access to support the software to correct errors in the software, where the licensor has failed to do so.

Where the software being licensed is fundamental to the business operations of the licensee and the availability of alternative software products in a timely fashion is limited, the licensee may want the reassurance of knowing that they can have access to the source code for support purposes if, for example, the software provider went out of business. By way of illustration, if an online retailer's website platform is unavailable even for a relatively short period of downtime due to problems with the software which are not promptly remedied the losses suffered might be considerable. The risks in this area are increased if the software being licensed has been amended specifically for the licensee or if the licensor is a relatively small operation because the options for assistance are restricted. Where the type of software is widely used in the marketplace this is less of a concern as there are likely to be plenty of support specialists available with experience that can be drawn upon.

Source code escrow is one option available to the licensee to reduce the risks of not having source code access. Source code escrow is a compromise between the licensor's understandable desire to keep their source code confidential and the licensee's need to know that they can access the source code for support of the software if the licensor goes out of business or fails to meet its support obligations. It involves a trusted third party being provided with a copy of the source code of the software by the licensor with the right to release that source code to the licensee if defined circumstances occur – so-called release events. The primary release event would be where the licensor becomes insolvent and is therefore unable to support the software. Other release events might include the licensor's refusal to support the software in breach of the licence terms or where the intellectual property rights in the software are sold by the licensor, and the new owner is not prepared to provide support to the licensee. It is worth noting that bespoke release events can be negotiated but obviously these will need to be agreed by all the parties and the escrow agent will charge fees for making changes to their standard offering. The escrow agent may also refuse the amendments if they believe the changes are not workable or expose them to greater risk.

If a valid release event occurs, the licensee will be given access to the source code; however, the use of the source code by the licensee following release will not be without restriction because it will still be subject to extended licence conditions. Typically, this licence will allow the licensee to use the source code to the extent needed to support and maintain the software itself or via a third party so that licensee can continue to use the software in the way intended under the original licence but not wider. This provides an additional layer of protection for the licensor in that the licensee will only get access to the source code in exceptional circumstances and even if it is released the licensor knows that the licensee is only permitted to use it in a restricted way consistent with the original license scope.

Escrow arrangements are normally put in place using the standard form agreements of third-party escrow agents. The arrangement is tripartite being entered into by the escrow agent, the licensor and the licensee. The escrow agreement will set out the terms and conditions for lodging the software and the circumstances in which it may be released. The escrow agent is paid recurring fees for holding the software in escrow and a separate charge for releasing the software if a release event occurs.

Licensors who have more significant customer bases and know that their licensees will probably require source code escrow often put in place group escrow arrangements with a recognised agent. Under a group arrangement, the licensee signs up to become one of the licensee members who is allowed access if a release event occurs. The advantage for the licensor is that they only need to put in place one underlying arrangement with the escrow agent that can then be used for multiple licensees as required. The fact that the licensor has a standard agreement in place means that they can argue the escrow terms are non-negotiable because the escrow arrangements need to be consistent across the client base. In addition, it can be put in place quickly and cheaply. The time taken to individually negotiate a bespoke escrow arrangement should not be underestimated as it can delay the completion of a licence arrangement if the licensee insists it is put in place contemporaneously or within a short time of completion of the main licence agreement.

When reviewing a group escrow arrangement, the licensee would be prudent to see whether the form of agreement varies from the escrow agent's standard and moreover whether all the standard release events have been covered and if its obligation to pay the escrow fees have been allocated/changed from the escrow agent's default position to its detriment.

The licensee also needs to view the extent of protection afforded by escrow from a practical viewpoint. Whilst having such an arrangement in place may be needed to satisfy corporate governance requirements for mitigating risk, the time and complexity taking over support of the software may take too long to be of practical use.

Another consideration with any escrow of software is the completeness and quality of the lodged code. If the lodged source code is incomplete or badly prepared, it may make taking over support impossible. Escrow agents often provide a basic verification of the source code that the licensor lodges these days, but a full verification where the materials are tested for their fitness for purpose can be very expensive. In the light of this the licensee may need to consider what other options are available if the key piece of software cannot be supported; for example, can a paper-based system be used until an alternative system was implemented? One of the leading escrow agents is

NCC International Limited and its website is a good source of additional information on the escrow process providing sample forms of agreement.[20]

Finally, looking at escrow from the licensor's standpoint, whether they agree to their source code being put in escrow can be a difficult decision if the software in question represents the primary revenue stream of the licensor and it has a significant user base. The risk of their source code being disclosed may be viewed as being too great. The reality is that licensors are far more likely to agree to escrow when they have created a bespoke piece of software just for the licensee. On the plus side for the licensor, the deposit of the software can be used evidentially as proof of ownership of the intellectual property rights in the software.

[C] Third-Party Materials and Open Source Software Used Within the Software

The next question to consider is what is included within the software package being licensed, as it may require third-party components to work. Often software utilities need third-party products to operate and so the consistency across the different licence terms needs to be checked. For example, one licence may allow use by group companies and the other may not, software use may be restricted to a different number of users or maybe no support is provided for the third-party product. Many licensors merely append licence terms for third-party products that need to be complied with in a schedule to the licence agreement and require compliance with the terms by the user in the front end. A responsible licensor will have ensured that the terms are internally consistent, but this should not be assumed by the licensee. If there are material differences the licensor should ordinarily put the onus on the licensor to resolve them because it is outside the licensee's control.

Another issue in this context is 'open source' software which is widely included in software products these days. In an international context this is relevant as many forms of open source licences emanate from the US and are stated to be subject to its laws. Open source software is computer code that is made available free of charge by various entities for general use. However, whilst open source is free to use that does not mean that use is unfettered, a licence will be granted which restricts what the licensee can do with it. There are a huge variety of open source licences, but the obligations can range from including an acknowledgement that the software includes the open source code to a requirement that the code in which it is incorporated is made available as open source as well. There are limited examples of cases in respect of the enforcement of open source licenses at present but again, licensors and licensees need to be sure that the inclusion of any open source software is consistent with the main licence terms.

20. NCC Website available at: www.nccgroup.trust/uk.

[D] 'Business to Business' or 'Business to Consumer'

In terms of a licensor seeking to license their software in different jurisdictions whether the licensee is a business user, or a consumer is a fundamental point as in many jurisdictions there will be enhanced statutory legal protection for consumers over businesses and this means that what a licensor can put in a contract for a consumer and for a business may be very different if the contract is to be enforceable under the local law.

Sometimes software may have both consumer and business customers due to its wide applicability. Email and word processing are obvious examples of software of this type and accordingly different versions of the software licence may be needed, one for businesses and one for consumers. It is possible for a single licence document to accommodate both scenarios by stating that certain sections of the licence will not apply if the licensee is contracting as a consumer. Whilst this may seem to be the easiest and most cost-effective solution, drafting a license in this way to cover off the issues whilst keeping the terms concise and retaining sufficient levels of clarity can be difficult. Often producing separate licence versions for businesses and consumers with a similar format and structure produces a better result that is faster and therefore cheaper to put in place. A licensor putting in place licenses in foreign jurisdictions for use by consumers will certainly need to verify the position under local law to be comfortable that their licence will be enforceable.

[E] Who Will Be Using the Software?

Licensees will at the outset need to think about who will be accessing and using the software they are licensing to make sure that they are sufficiently licensed. Not surprisingly, licensors will try to ensure that their licence terms restrain usage so far as possible to protect their rights in the product.

At the business level an assumption may be made that the licence will cover use by the wider group companies, but each group member may well be a different legal entity and require a separate license. This issue often arises where the software can be utilised by the whole group such as in the case of payroll processing software. If the licence is stated to be for the 'internal use' of the licensee, it is debatable whether this would permit one part of the group to carry out the payroll processing for its wider group companies if they are separate legal entities.

The possibility of third-party use by outsourced service providers is another key consideration that must also be raised at the outset. Does the licensee have an outsourced service provider that will be using the software on behalf of the licensee or is this a possibility in the future? Many industries have a tradition of outsourcing non-core (but potentially critical) services such as software support so they can focus on the principal activities that make them money. If so this needs to be specifically recognised in the license grant or by allowing the assignment of the software licence to the outsource provider as is sometimes the case. The licensee will be in a far better place to negotiate this right into the license pre-contract rather than gaining consent later when the licensor may seek additional fees to extend the use.

[F] Restrictions to Specific Locations and Specifications

Where the licence places restrictions on the location where the software can be used the ability to alter this should be anticipated. Whilst the licensor is unlikely to allow un-restricted relocations, if the licensee is simply moving its business operations locally the licensee will not want relocation of the software to be unreasonably restricted or subject to consent. Building in the ability to change the location within reasonable parameters, coupled with an obligation to notify the licensor of the change in writing may be a reasonable compromise for both parties. A specific carve out for temporary use of the software in a disaster recovery location by a third party is a scenario where the licensee may want to be able to relocate the software without consent.

Often software licences provide minimum specifications for the hardware and operating system that the software needs to run on. This is understandable on the basis the software may have been designed for or optimised to run in this environment, and the licensor may have concerns that it cannot meet its obligations in terms of warranties, support or upgrades if this is not followed. The licensee will need to verify with their IT team that their current software environment meets the requirements and that any pending upgrades to internal systems will not cause a problem.

The licence agreement may also require the licensee to keep the version of the software they use to be no more than a certain number of versions behind the then current version of the software offered by the licensor. This requirement is on the basis that the licensor will not want to keep supporting older versions of the software for different customers indefinitely. Whilst the licensor's approach to this issue is understandable the licensee will need to highlight this to the relevant technical contacts. Also, if the licensee is required to keep the software current what is the licensor's process for adding new versions – how often will this occur and is the cost of upgrade included in the licence fee or will additional fees be payable.

§4.12 THE DIFFERENT APPROACHES LICENSORS TAKEN WITH INTERNATIONAL SOFTWARE LICENCES

The approach to putting in place international licences varies; some licensors take the view that they will simply choose to rely on an unamended licence agreement under their own local law when expanding their markets in other jurisdictions. This approach is more likely to be the case where the two countries share a common language as few licensees will sign up to a licence which is in another language and will not want to go to the trouble and expense of having a licence translated. The licensor may take the view that on a cost-benefit analysis it is not worth having specific amendments made to their standard licence agreement particularly where the number of international sales is limited or if the software is low value and low risk and therefore unlikely to be legally reviewed by the licensee.

By not amending the license for use in another jurisdiction the licensor is effectively taking a risk (calculated or otherwise) that issues will not arise. The downside is that the licensor may not be able to take effective action against the licensee in the case of a breach of the licence agreement. For example, the standard licence may provide for the exclusive law and jurisdiction of the home courts, but there might not be a reciprocal enforcement arrangement with the country of licensee leading to complications. In addition, the licensor might not be aware of mandatory laws that apply in the jurisdiction of the licensee. Mandatory rules of law can be thought of as laws that apply in a country notwithstanding that a contract may be subject to a different law and provides otherwise. These tend to be laws that are applied as a matter of public policy and would typically relate to things such as competition, consumer protection and employment matters, but there are other areas such as the rights afforded to the licensee under the Copyright Designs and Patents Act 1988 referred to below. The net effect is that the unamended licence may be subject to laws which change the intended effect or scope of the licence to the detriment of the licensor. Consequently, local law advice may be needed to cover off concerns in this area.

Another potential downside of not changing the standard form of licence for another jurisdiction is that the prospective licensee may simply not be prepared to accept the licence agreement in that form. This may be because it does not understand the terms of the agreement sufficiently or that the net effect of the terms puts them at a significant disadvantage. Customers are unlikely to invest significant sums in a business-critical software solution if their only method of legal redress requires them to act in the home courts of the licensor, on the other side of the world using the local law of the licensor.

Even if the licensee does not make significant changes to the licence presented by the licensor but simply asks for a change in law and jurisdiction this can still leave material risks for the licensor. A case in point would be limitations of liability where the provision could be unenforceable under the amended choice of law without drafting changes.

Another risk is that in the absence of the licensor providing a license in the local law of the licensee the licensee may put forward a licence agreement on their own terms which the licensor will then have to spend time and money reviewing if it wants to win the business. The terms of the licence will inevitably start from a position which favours the licensee as well.

The failure to produce a localised licence agreement may result in the licensor spending more time and money in the long run and accepting a greater level of risk than if the effort had been put in up-front to produce one.

Another common approach is to have a standard licence with country-specific changes in the same document depending on where the licensee is located. Key changes might be to the governing law, the contracting entity for the licensor and the liability provisions. For example, If the licensor is in the US and the licensee is based in the UK, the licensor could contract with the licensee through the UK subsidiary of the licensor's US parent company, under English Law, replacing the US-based limitation of liability with one drafted for English Law set out in a Schedule. The advantage for the licensor is that they have one document for all their licensees in different jurisdictions, and they will have the comfort of knowing that it takes effect in a way that accommodates the local law of each licensee. From a usability context this can create quite a convoluted document to follow from a licensee's perspective, and careful drafting is needed to achieve the necessary clarity so that the licensee can identify the variables that apply to their scenario quickly and easily.

Another option would be to produce separate, bespoke licences adapted for every country where the software is licensed. For legal clarity and risk management this might be the 'gold standard' but the legal costs and management time of implementing this in multiple countries may be prohibitive. A practical solution to reduce costs, whilst still achieving sufficient risk limitation might be to use English Law for all EU countries (in the knowledge that there will be a common underpinning of EU law) and then produce alternative versions for non-EU Countries as and when material volumes of business are predicted.

For sophisticated licensing solutions, the licensor may need external local legal support to produce licence agreements for other jurisdictions due to the expertise required in different laws. When selecting an external law firm for support choosing a firm that specialises in technology and either has regional offices or affiliations in the countries where the licences will be used is probably the easiest route. This approach will be more efficient because the licensor can deal with a single point of contact at the firm in their home jurisdiction who can then coordinate the adaptation of the licence for other jurisdictions using that firm's established contacts. As the coordinating firm will have pre-vetted their foreign affiliates this is less risky than independently trying to select an appropriate firm in the jurisdiction. Whilst this is not the cheapest option it may be prudent for software with significant revenue streams or the potential to achieve them.

As we have seen the structure of the licence for dealing with multiple jurisdictions can be developed in several ways each with different risk and cost profiles. Which is the correct one in any situation will depend on the nature of the software, the potential returns and perceived risk. This is something that can be worked through with the client using a cost-benefit analysis to enable them to make an informed decision.

Whilst it may seem appealing for a licensor to put extremely one-sided terms into their standard licence agreement this can end up being a false economy. It is naïve to assume that a document that provides all the things that the licensor would want will have an easy path to signature. Experienced business people as well as legal advisors will quickly be able to identify the absence of intellectual property warranties/indemnities, low liability caps and extensive exclusions of liability. If the licence agreement is reasonably balanced, greater consistency between the licence agreements can be achieved across the user base because fewer changes will need to be negotiated. This consistency means that licensor can achieve a better overall view of the risk position. The similarity of licence terms also allows the commercial team to readily answer the core questions that potential licensees tend to raise. If a one-sided document is presented it is far more likely to be challenged by licensees and require negotiation and change before it is accepted, which takes time and costs money. The benefits of a balanced agreement will be increased if the licence is under the laws of another country where local legal advisors would need to be consulted on changes requested by the prospective licensees. Getting the balance right is vital and requires analysis but listing the 'must have' positions of both the licensee and licensor is a good place to start when preparing a standard form of licence agreement.

If a licensor has several group companies, there are options as to which company to use as the contracting entity for the licence. A straightforward option is of course to license the software through the main entity, in the home jurisdiction. However, from a liability and tax position this may not be the best choice. Tax advisors should be asked about the relative benefits of doing this as opposed to setting up a local subsidiary to contract through. Framework agreements can provide flexibility and tax efficiency when carrying out multi-jurisdictional licensing. A carefully thought out tax strategy can significantly reduce the amount of tax paid by a licensor by minimising exposure to double taxation and maximising available reliefs, so getting specialist advice makes sense.

From a liability aspect, the licensor may not want the licensee to have a direct route of action against the part of the company holding the key asset of the intellectual property rights in the software. If a new subsidiary company is established in the country where the licensees will be located, the chain of liability could stop at that point if things go wrong. However, if the cost of the software is high or performs a business-critical function a reasonably sophisticated licensee will probably consider the background of the local subsidiary to verify it has the financial standing to meet a claim under the licence agreement. If the financial position is not sufficient the licensee may request a parent company guarantee. If this scenario is likely a standard form of guarantee, drafted on terms that are acceptable to the licensor's parent company, would be a useful document to have available so that is used as the starting position before the licensee sends over their own guarantee document which will probably be skewed heavily in their favour.

At a practical level, the process of supporting the software in other jurisdictions will need to be worked out. Do the support manuals need translating? If there is a support help desk will different time zones mean that support cannot be provided during the normal office hours of the licensee? Can this be dealt with by having help desk staff work a couple of extra hours or will a local support team be needed? If the language is different, do the support staff have sufficient proficiency in the local language to enable them to provide technical advice?

The way a licence agreement is presented to a licensee can increase or decrease the likelihood of it being negotiated. If the licence agreement is structured with the variables such as licence numbers, support levels, party details as a front sheet contract summary with the actual terms and conditions governing them attached then this will give the impression that there is little room for negotiation on the part of the licensee, particularly if the agreement is well thought through, reasonable and supplied in a non-amendable format such as PDF. This approach may not be appropriate for highly complex or bespoke software, but it is an approach worth considering. From the licensee's perspective, even if they are not able to negotiate the licence (or only to a limited extent) care needs to be taken to ensure that the standard form does allow use as required and that there is a viable remedy against the licensor if things go wrong.

Developing approved negotiation positions for the most contentious licence provisions may make sense for larger licensors as this will enable the standard licence agreement to be negotiated commercially to a certain degree before needing to consult with legal advisors. The legal advisors can produce various alternative clauses that can be proposed based on the common concerns that licensees may raise. This tactic will allow a legally approved response to the licensee's concern to be delivered quickly, and this will hopefully close a point without the need for additional legal input. This strategy requires an up-front investment of time from the licensor's legal advisors because they need to prepare the alternative clauses, ensure the personnel dealing with negotiation understand the implications of the alternatives and what they can and cannot change. The payoff for this investment is that the negotiation process is streamlined and potentially easier to manage in multiple jurisdictions.

Another approach licensors sometimes take when entering a new jurisdiction is to identify a 'trophy customer' to trial the software solution. The negotiation and implementation of the software for the first customer will enable the licensor to get a feel for the issues of licensing in this jurisdiction, not only in terms of the approach to licensing but also the practical issues with supporting the solution. Based on this live experience the licensor can then develop their offering before offering it to the wider market. The 'trophy customer' selected may need to be incentivised to be the trial licensee through favourable pricing, but this can be a good method of understanding the potential for a software product in a new market, whilst limiting the licensor's initial investment and risk. If the software is innovative enough, the chance of being first in the market with the potential for competitive advantage may be sufficient for the licensor not to seek preferential pricing. Ideally the customer chosen will be high profile so that it can act as a reference site for the software product. A licensee with a similar demographic to the target customer group will add to the value of undertaking this step.

If the software solution incorporates any third-party software, then the basis on which it is licensed will need to be checked to ensure that those terms do not have a limitation on cross-border licensing. Again, this is something that should be verified at the start so that any problems can be identified and addressed by consultation with the third party before a substantial amount of money is invested.

If a licensor has used third parties to develop their software product care needs to be taken to ensure that copyright in the third party developed software is owned by the licensor before it is licensed. Unless otherwise agreed, the 'author' is the first owner of the copyright in a work, so even if a contractor or other third party has been specifically engaged in developing a software product for someone else, the third party will, in the first instance, own the copyright in what they produce despite being paid for the work. To avoid this issue, any such third parties should be contracted on terms that automatically assign all copyright in the software which they develop to the licensor at the time of its creation. In addition, it is also prudent to obtain a waiver of moral rights that might arise. Moral rights which derive from the Berne Convention are not ownership or economic rights but protect the author of a copyright work such that they have a right to be identified as the author and to object derogatory treatment of their work. These rights do not apply to computer programs or computer-generated works under the Copyright, Designs and Patents Act 1988 but might be applicable to documentation, specifications or databases relating to the software and the approach to moral rights may vary in different jurisdictions, hence the importance of including a waiver.

One final consideration, that will probably only apply to limited number of software developers, is whether the nature of the software is subject to export control pursuant to US or EU law or otherwise. Examples of where restrictions may apply are software which has a military use or where the destination country is subject to embargos. Note that these controls can cover electronic distribution via the Internet as well as by physical transfer. In some situations, a specific export licence can be obtained. Guidance on this issue can often be found on government websites which have information to assist exporting businesses.

§4.13 KEY PROVISIONS AND ISSUES IN A SOFTWARE LICENCE

[A] Parties Clause

The Parties clause whilst seemingly innocuous needs greater attention from a drafting and risk perspective in an international licence agreement. As for any contract it is vital that the correct parties are identified in the licence. Corporate legal entities are referred to and created by different methods in other jurisdictions so rather than referring to a 'limited' company the correct designation of the entity maybe 'Inc.' in the US (Incorporated), 'GBMH' (Gesellschaft mit Beschränkter Haftung) in Germany, S.r.l. (Società a responsabilità limitata) in Italy etc. Also, in some countries you may not have the concepts of company numbers or registered offices, so the Parties clause may need to be adapted to refer to a principal place of business instead. Other formalities may need to be followed in this context, for example, when referring to a corporate entity in the US the State where the company was incorporated is normally identified.

The wide use of company identification numbers in Europe is helpful because even if the name of a company or its registered office changes the company number will stay the same, so tracking down that entity will involve a search against the company number.

Taking the time to verify the proposed parties to the licence unambiguously will hopefully prevent future pitfalls. A good starting point for this due diligence is to identify the website of the body responsible for registering corporate entities in the country of the licensee. For example, Companies House in the UK provides free searches to check whether a company name exists, its registered office and its company number. You can also find out when it was incorporated and any previous corporate names. Further company details can be obtained as required for a small fee. The corporate information section of a licensee's website is another way that information can be cross-checked, although this is not as reliable as Government sources for obvious reasons.

From the licensee's viewpoint, it is not unusual to find that whilst the software owner is a foreign entity the company licensing the software is a local subsidiary of the main entity, e.g., instead of 'Sparkle Software, Inc.' the licensor is stated to be 'Sparkle Software Limited'. Whilst it may seem positive that the licensor has invested in a local subsidiary the primary driver for the foreign entity may be to avoid any direct legal liability to the licensee if a claim arises. Licensee's that are concerned about this should obtain further information on the subsidiary's background. If the subsidiary has just been set up and has no material resources, the licensee may not have a remedy if it has a claim. If this is the situation a parent company guarantee for the subsidiary can be requested.

Early discussion with the licensor and the parent company is recommended if a parent company guarantee is needed so that the guarantee can be drafted in parallel with the licence to avoid delays.

[B] Background or Recitals

The Background or Recital section is another area of a licence that is often not considered sufficiently on the assumption that it does not form part of the legally binding contract in many jurisdictions. However, this ignores the fact that it may be used to assist with the interpretation of the contract where there is ambiguity. Including, a precise statement of the basis of the licence in this section can help to highlight any discrepancies between the parties understanding and therefore be of use if a dispute arises. Licensors need to be careful that the inclusion of statements in the recitals are not construed as warranties, as whilst the recitals may not form part of the contract, this does not preclude other forms of legal liability arising from these statements such as a tortious liability for misrepresentation. If a statement is added by the licensee, consider whether it is objectively true and whether you are comfortable adding it in as this is sometimes used as a method of surreptitiously adding additional assurances into an agreement.

[C] Licence Grant and Associated Definitions

The license grant goes to the root of the licence agreement and needs to be reviewed carefully from the perspective of both parties. The licensor needs to ensure that the clause wording cannot be interpreted as giving wider rights than anticipated and the licensee needs to check that any restrictions do not prevent the intended and legitimate use of the software. The grant of use will normally include the basic license followed by more specific descriptions of restrictions elsewhere in the contract to keep the clause at a reasonable length. This is often achieved by making the licence grant 'subject to' certain other provisions of the licence agreement and accordingly the scope of use can only be fully determined by looking at all the relevant provisions in the round.

A statement asserting the ownership by the licensor of the intellectual property rights in the software is also usual because it can be used to contradict any assertion by a licensee that the rights granted go beyond a simple license to use.

Common variables affecting the scope of the licence grant are set out below with a corresponding analysis:

[1] Sole, Exclusive and Non-exclusive

Licences can be expressed to be exclusive, sole and non-exclusive. As these terms can sometimes be open to alternative interpretations, it is generally considered advisable in the context of exclusive and sole licenses to elaborate on the parties understanding of these terms by either defining the term or by adding further explanatory provisions. For example, a lay client may not appreciate that an exclusive license would ordinarily be interpreted as preventing their own internal use of the software as well as third parties. If those rights need to be retained it should be expressed as a sole licence. The implications of not getting this correct could be considerable, so it is prudent to make the rights as unambiguous and explicit as possible in the licence.

[2] Royalty Free and Non-transferable

Quite often the license grant includes reference to the license being 'royalty free' this indicates that the license does not involve recurring payments to use the software and so would be consistent with a one-time license fee to use the software with no further payments for ongoing use are applicable.

Stating that the license is 'non-transferable' in the license grant means that the license is personal as between the parties and cannot be transferred by the licensee to a third party. It should be checked whether this is consistent with the assignment clause as if the licensee is permitted to assign the Agreement to other Group companies it would presumably expect the right to use the software to transfer with the Agreement. This can be clarified by making the statement of non-transferability subject to the provisions in the assignment provisions.

It is worth noting that there has been a lot of discussion in the EU as to whether licensees have the right to sell on second-hand software based on the exhaustion of rights principle notwithstanding what the licence provides concerning transferability. This is a complex and much-debated area and accordingly it is not appropriate to elaborate on this further here but to find out more it is worth referring to the decision in the Court of Justice of the European Union case of UsedSoft GmbH v. Oracle International Corp [2012] C-128/11.

[3] Identifying the Software That Is the Subject of the License and the Purpose of Use

A simple reference to the name of the software is unlikely to be sufficient to clarify the scope of what is being licensed. Software can have multiple versions and optional modules comprised within the whole. To avoid confusion, it is always prudent to make sure that the licence identifies exactly what is included and excluded by perhaps appending a specification of the software as a schedule, separately identifying optional modules that are included and referring to the version number of the software.

In relation to the purpose of use, a reference to 'the internal business purposes' of the licensee is terminology that is often used. It has the benefit of not unduly restricting the licensee's legitimate use within its business by being overly prescriptive but does not allow commercial exploitation (the contract will usually expressly prohibit this as well). Where there is an intended use that does not sit squarely within internal business purposes a clarificatory statement can be added. For example, stating that internal use includes the licensee running the payroll software for the benefit of other group companies as well.

[4] Territorial Restrictions

Licenses are often restricted by territory as well. Precision and accuracy are important, and the way geographic areas are described can have distinct meanings. For example, the UK includes Northern Ireland as well as England, Scotland and Wales, whereas Great Britain does not include Northern Ireland. Despite being islands located close to the UK the Channel Islands and the Isle of Man are in fact self-governing Crown Dependencies and are not part of the UK. Tasmania is an Island State of Australia and so forms part of Australia as such. Reference to Europe could be interpreted to include 47 countries within the European continent or just the current EU Member States.

The licensee should look at their requirements holistically. For example, it might be easy to overlook that a company's outsourced disaster recovery site is in Eastern Europe and their call centres are in India and therefore the software needs to be licensed for use in these locations as well.

These examples illustrate the issues that can arise with geographic designations where there is a lack of familiarity and emphasises the need to explicitly clarify the parties' understanding of these terms in the licence agreement.

[5] Time Limited, Perpetual and Irrevocable Licenses

Whether a licence is stated to be 'perpetual' is often driven by the licence fee model chosen. Self-sufficient software where no ongoing maintenance is needed is more likely to allow ongoing use following the payment of a one-time licence fee but if the software is high value with active ongoing involvement of the licensor a time limited license with regular licence/support fees is more likely.

The reference to 'perpetual' is slightly misleading because the licensor will want to make it clear that the licence is still subject to termination rights if the licensee is in breach of the terms of the licence agreement or becomes insolvent and accordingly you would expect the licence grant to be made subject to the termination provisions.

The use of the term 'revocable' or 'irrevocable' can cause similar confusion. If a license is stated to be revocable it could mean that the license could be ended at any point the licensor wanted irrespective of the license ending on termination. Conversely does irrevocable override the license ending on termination? Accordingly, it is important to understand the parties' intentions and draft the licence on terms that removes these potential ambiguities.

Where the licence agreement has a relatively short term, but the licensee anticipates long-term use, it would be prudent to try and negotiate assurances that onerous price increases will not be imposed come the time a new licence is needed. This situation can occur where the licensee wants to evaluate a piece of software through use before committing to integrating it in the long term. One method of allowing price increases whilst giving reassurance to the licensee is to use indexation, against an appropriate price index which will allow independent and objective changes to pricing to be made over time.

[6] Sub-licensing

In most situations, the licensor will insert a specific prohibition on the licensee sub-licensing the software, i.e., granting a third party the rights to use the software within the scope of the license that has been granted to them. However, it may be appropriate in some circumstances such as for software distribution or value-added reseller arrangements where the licensee will be involved in an onward transaction with an end user of the software. In these situations, the licensor will seek to protect their rights in the 'downstream' licence by requiring that it is done on pre-defined terms leaving only the commercial arrangements to be negotiated by the licensee with their end user or by mandating that particular terms are inserted in the sub-licence that the licensee puts in place. These additions are intended to protect the underlying ownership of the intellectual property rights by the licensor but should not of course extend to fixing the prices at which the licensee sub-licenses the software for competition law reasons.

[7] User Number Restrictions

Another common way that software use is restricted is by prescribing the number of users within the licensee organisation that can make use of the software. The amount the licensee pays is adjusted based on the extent to which the software is made use of. From the licensee stance this will require them to know from the outset the numbers of employees who will need to be able to use the software. Failure to anticipate future use may also create a cost exposure so if the number of users in the organisation might increase it would make sense to agree within the licensor the costs of adding further users later. The licensee's negotiating position will be stronger pre-contract. The pricing for such additions may be on a per user basis, groups of users or within bands of users. Where there is a lot of uncertainty and the licensee is concerned about its ability to monitor and control user numbers an alternative that is sometimes available is an 'Enterprise Licence' where the number of users is not constrained provided that the new or different users are employed within the organisation.

It is also worth pointing out that you can get different classes of user with some having greater rights of use or the ability to carry out administrative activities within the software. Where this is the case the licence needs to set out the class as well as number of users and the licensee needs to have a clear understanding of its present and future requirements for different user rights within the organisation.

[8] Concurrent Users

User numbers can also be controlled by reference to 'named users' or 'concurrent users'. Named users may simply mean each of the user licences must be assigned to a named employee or contractor but depending on how this is structured it can expose the licensee. For example, if the licensee has a high turnover of staff and a license ends when a named user leaves and cannot be transferred this can prove to be a costly licensing model. A licensee in this situation will therefore want the right to substitute another named user if someone leaves – the number of users will not have changed just their identity, so this should be acceptable to the licensor.

Another permutation is the licensing of 'Concurrent Users'. This normally means that there is no need to identify the different users by name but at any point in time the number of people using the software at the same time is limited to the agreed number. The licensee will need to assess their anticipated usage and perhaps put internal rules in place to secure the most economic number of concurrent users to purchase licenses for.

[9] Under-licensing

You may question how the licensor will know whether the user numbers have been exceeded. For commercial software, the licensor normally addresses this by building in rights to audit the use of the software. As well as physical audits the rights often include a right to remotely log into the licensee's system to verify usage at random points in time. The licence agreement will often provide that if the agreed user numbers are exceeded then the licensor is entitled to charge for them. This effectively defines the remedy for under-licensing upfront thereby avoiding the need to pursue contractual damages. The licensee may feel relatively relaxed with this approach, if the licence fees will regulate themselves with further fees just applying if the business use increases. However, this may not be the case as the licensor will often add a provision stating that the then applicable published costs of a user (without negotiated discounts) will be charged for the additional unlicensed users.

Many large licensors substantially discount their published list prices using price reductions as a marketing tool to attract the licensee's business with no expectation by the licensee that full rates will be charged in the ordinary course of business. The net effect therefore is that the calculation of the fees due for the non-authorised additional users will not only be adjusted for future higher prices but will also be calculated on the notional full list prices. To illustrate, if the standard licence fee discount is sixty percent, paying the full list price for additional users can escalate to a significant amount. The lesson for the licensee is therefore to correctly estimate, anticipate and monitor correct usage or negotiate an alternative pricing model that does not have the potential to result in large unexpected fees being imposed.

It is also worth highlighting that anti-piracy organisations seek changes in the law to protect rights owners and sometimes take legal action on behalf of their members against infringers. A good example of such an organisation in the UK is FAST or the Federation Against Software Theft whose primary focus is preventing copyright infringement of software.

[10] Exceptions to Copyright Protection for Software in the EU

As stated previously, the EU Software Directive identifies the exclusive rights that the owner of the copyright in the software enjoys and this will form the basis upon which the licensor grants rights to the licensee under the licence agreement.[21] Notwithstanding this point, in the EU there are certain exceptions to these rights which need to be reflected in a well-drafted software license.[22]

The exceptions to the restricted rights that the licensee benefits from include the right to make a back-up copy of the software where this is required for legitimate use and the right to observe, study and test the functioning of the software to determine its underlying principles and ideas. Moreover, any restriction on reverse engineering the software cannot prevent the licensee from de-compiling the software for the specific purpose of ensuring that the software can operate with other software or devices. Any such decompilation is restricted to the part of the software necessary to achieve interoperability, and the right will not apply if the information needed to achieve interoperability has been made readily available to the licensee.

The provisions are implemented into English Law under Sections 50 A (Back-up Copies) and Section 50 B (De-compilation) of the Copyright Designs and Patents Act 1988. Any term or condition in a licence agreement which prohibits or restricts these rights must be made subject to these statutory rights or the provision will be void under Section 296A.

[11] Supporting Documentation

The supporting documentation such as operating manuals, whether provided in hard copy or electronically, will have separate copyright protection from the software as a literary work. The licensor will normally place restrictions on the number of hard copies that can be made by the licensee without additional payment and the licensee should confirm that it will be entitled to sufficient copies for their intended use.

The licensor will need to consider whether any supporting documentation will need to be translated for a foreign licensee and if any other changes are required to

21. Directive 2009/24/EC – Article 4.
22. Directive 2009/24/EC – Articles 5 and 6.

reflect use in another jurisdiction such as alterations to support hours, and contact details.

[12] Delivery of the Software

The licence agreement will have to identify how and when the software will be made available to the licensee. This may be as simple as gaining access to a license key (an activation code) for software delivered electronically or it may require physical delivery and professional installation on the licensee's system by a fixed date.

The licensee should verify when the license commences, when payment commences and when it will have access for use. If the license and payment commence on signature, but there is a gap before delivery of the software, the licensee could be paying for a period when the software is not available for use where the licence term is fixed.

If the software is being developed specifically for the licensee, liquidated damages and ultimately termination may be appropriate protections for late delivery. To be enforceable however the liquidated damages cannot be penal. Under English law the assessment of whether they are a penalty focuses on whether the liquidated damages are proportionate to protecting the innocent party's legitimate interest in enforcing the other party's obligations.[23]

[13] Licence Fees

As noted above, licence fees can be a one-time payment, recurring, based on user numbers or number of licenses. In an international context the parties will need to decide what currency payment will be made in and in turn who will bear the exchange rate risk. The tax position will also need review – do the sums in the Agreement include or exclude VAT or other sales taxes? Note that in the UK if a contract does not state whether VAT is included or excluded the contract will be interpreted as if the sums already include VAT, so it is important to address the point explicitly.

As well as seeking advice on the tax position generally the licensor needs to establish whether payments under the licence could be subject to withholding tax in the licensee's jurisdiction and agree how this will be dealt with. Often the licensor requires that payments are 'grossed up' notwithstanding that tax will be withheld so that they receive the full anticipated amount straight away.

Remedies for late payment such as suspension of support and maintenance and late payment interest can be effective remedies for inducing payment by the licensee before recourse to termination or litigation.

23. Cavendish Square Holding BV v. Talel El Makdessi and ParkingEye Limited v. Beavis [2015] UKSC 67.

[14] Confidentiality

The confidentiality provisions will normally explicitly identify the software and its associated documentation as being confidential in addition to more general commercially sensitive information. The potential losses for the licensor arising from disclosure of the software materials could be significant, and the licensor will normally require that any breach of confidentiality claim is not subject to any liability cap. In turn, the licensee will need to check that the confidentiality provisions are not so stringent that they cut across their legitimate licensed use of the software. For example, if disclosure of the software and documentation is limited to employees of the licensee in the confidentiality clause but the license grant allows use by the licensee's contractors the licence agreement will be internally inconsistent and there will be uncertainty.

Standard exclusions from the obligations of confidentiality should be included in the clause. These exclusions include matters such as disclosure to legal authorities under a court order, independent development by the licensee, receipt of the information from a third party who was not under any duty of confidentiality and where the confidential information is already in the public domain through no fault of the licensee.

[15] Support and Maintenance

Support and maintenance can be provided at varying levels. It may range from basic telephone support for queries to remote diagnostics and full on-site support. The support can form part of the general license agreement or may be set out in a separate agreement with separate fees. Sometimes licensors also include limited warranties, without additional payment particularly where the software is a bespoke development. These are normally for a defined period where the licensor will resolve issues and bugs that the licensee has identified after the software has been put into live use. It is worth considering whether the support period should start after the warranty period if the assistance under the warranty and the support service are the same otherwise the licensee is paying for something that is being provided for free. However, it is likely that the warranty will be limited to resolving issues caused by the licensor's own default and accordingly licensee initiated problems, updates and user help may well not be included within the warranty protection, so the exact wording should be checked.

The licensee needs to analyse the level of support it requires. For example, does the support cover user queries on how to operate the software as well as technical issues? Will training on the use of the software be needed and if so how will this work if the licensor and licensee are in different countries? Computer based training may be an option or it may be necessary to set up local workshops. A 'train the trainer' approach may be a cost-effective solution in that a limited number of licensee staff can be trained to a high level by the licensor, so they have the necessary skill set to roll out the training to the wider licensee user base.

As noted above time zones need to be factored in when setting support hours and if on-site support is offered, the logistics for doing this in another jurisdiction need to be put in place. Sometimes this is resolved by the licensor setting up an arrangement with a third party in the jurisdiction who can support the local licensees on a call off basis. This approach can be a cheaper alternative than the licensor setting up its own operations.

Some licensors offer different levels of support such as 'gold', 'silver' or 'bronze' at different prices with different levels of coverage and responsiveness that the licensee can select depending on the business need. Service levels and associated credits may be something the licensee insists on so that it has a benchmark for the support provided and has a remedy, short of litigation or termination, it can rely on if the licensor fails to meet the support standards.

Sometimes the licensor pre-empts the request for service levels and service credits by inserting a standard offering into the licence agreement. In these situations, the licensee will need to analyse the way the regime works as they may be drafted for presentation rather than to act as a robust system for obtaining the correct levels of service. For example, the service levels may be expressed as 'targets' rather than absolute response or correction times with no service credits applying. Where service credits are offered the calculations can intentionally be made convoluted by the licensor to disguise the limited levels of recourse. To check the position the licensee should work through real-world examples of potential service failures. It may become clear that the licensor must fail a service level catastrophically before a service credit accrues and the monetary value of the service credit might be low. Service credits may be framed as being 'in full and final settlement' for the service failure. The licensee should challenge this position as it will prevent other remedies such as damages or termination applying, and these may be appropriate if the failure is material. Accumulation of a certain amount of service credits should ultimately provide a right of termination as well. If the value and type of the licence does not justify a service credit regime, escalation for resolution by the licensor should be initiated where service levels are not met.

The licensee should also check the basis upon which the support charges may increase – it could be based on an index, capped at a certain percentage or at the discretion of the licensor. If it is at the licensor's discretion when are there any restrictions about when and how often an increase can be applied? If it does not apply at the point of support renewal can the licensee terminate if the increase is unacceptable or will they be locked in at the new higher charge until the point of renewal? These are all important points for the licensee to check when reviewing the terms of support.

[16] Warranties and Indemnities

Normally a software warranty will be framed by reference to the product's compliance with a software specification or a software manual. The licensee will need to ensure that they been provided with these materials and that they adequately describe all the functionality and performance required, if they do not cover the points sufficiently the warranty may be of little practical use. The warranty may be limited to compliance 'in all material respects' with the specification or the manual, and the licensee will ideally want this qualification removed, particularly if the specification and manual have been produced independently by the licensor.

Occasionally a software warranty is limited to the physical media upon which the software is delivered which in real terms means that if the CD Rom containing the software is defective (e.g., scratched or broken) then it will be replaced as opposed to any reassurance being provided in relation to the software itself. This may be acceptable for low value software which has an established market reputation and a wide user base but not otherwise. Software warranty periods vary in length, but a 90-day period is often used for 'off the shelf software', following which the standard support terms take over. Licensors will not generally warrant that their software will operate completely 'uninterrupted or error free' due to the inherent unpredictability of software and it is normal to see an explicit caveat to this effect in a licence agreement.

The licensee should consider whether any additional warranties are needed as well. An example, for financial software, might be that the software can process other currencies such as Euros or that it complies with applicable financial services legislation in the way that it processes information.

An intellectual property rights warranty and indemnity should be sought by the licensee. Be aware, however, that the way that an indemnity is drafted can materially affect the protection it provides. An assessment of the following points should be made by a licensee as a matter of course:

- Is the indemnity subject to the limit of liability? IPR infringement claims can be large and accordingly it is market practice to expect this risk (which is in the licensor's control) to be uncapped or at the very least only limited to a large amount that can reasonably be expected to cover any claim.
- Is the IPR indemnity limited by reference to the heads of loss that can be claimed and if so what might that affect in terms of recoverability?
- Does the indemnity cover the manuals and any third-party elements included within the package?
- Does it refer to all intellectual property rights or just those in the licensor's home jurisdiction? What if the rights that are infringed are registered elsewhere?
- Does it cover all potential losses or just damages awarded by a court of final appeal? This may result in some losses not being recovered dependant on the extent of the court award. What if the claim is settled by the licensor and the third party before court – the indemnity should make the licensor liable.

Often the indemnity cover is subject to a course of conduct procedures which requires the licensee to notify the licensor of any claim promptly, give the licensor control over the litigation, and an obligation on the licensee to help with the defence and not admit liability. Whilst not inherently unreasonable the licensee needs to ensure that it is aware of these provisions and can comply with them.

From the licensor's perspective it is prudent to ensure that the indemnity is not unduly wide, i.e., the cover should not apply to the extent the infringement is caused by the licensee's use of the software outside the licence terms, such as claims caused by unauthorised modification by the licensee or a third party. As added protection if a claim arises the licensor can reserve the right to modify or replace the software, so the period of potential infringement is minimised. The licensor can change the software so that it becomes non-infringing and the licensee can continue to use it thereby reducing potential claims from the licensee if the action would require use to stop. The licensee should in turn ensure that any such changes to the software will not adversely affect its functionality or performance. If the licensor cannot alter the software to make it non-infringing, which may be the case if the infringing element is fundamental, then the licensor will also want the right to terminate the licence and perhaps return a proportion of the license fee to the licensee as compensation. If the licensee agrees to this provision, they should state that the reimbursement of the proportion of the license fee is without prejudice to the intellectual property rights indemnity and the licensee's other rights and remedies where the costs of discontinuing use of the software could be significant.

There has been a lot of debate as to whether software constitutes goods or services. This debate is relevant as the remedies available at law can vary based on this categorisation. In the UK certain implied terms can apply depending on whether the subject of the agreement is the supply of goods or services. The statutory protections given for the supply of goods are more extensive than those provided for the supply of services, so it is an important issue. A detailed analysis of this position goes beyond the remit of this book, but some of the implications of this distinction are set out below:

- Whilst the situation is not fully resolved the prevailing view seems to be that services will generally be viewed as services unless the software is provided on some physical medium such as a disk or CD-ROM in which case it may be viewed as the supply of goods with the implications that follow;
- Certain implied terms cannot be excluded when the transaction is 'business to consumer' and where it is a 'business to business' transaction some (but not all) can be excluded but whether that is effective will be subject to a test of 'reasonableness' in the circumstances;
- In 'business to business' licence agreements, the licensor will attempt to exclude as many statutory implied terms as possible. This is usually drafted as full exclusion save in the event of terms which cannot legally be removed;
- When dealing with a 'business to consumer' licence much wider implied terms apply which cannot be excluded and the drafting needs to ensure that the licence could not be interpreted as an attempt to exclude these rights. Wide consumer protection provisions are likely to apply in other jurisdictions so local law advice is advisable;
- Where the supply of the software is likely to be viewed as a supply of goods, then this can have further implications and in particular the application of the United Nations Convention on Contracts for the International Sale of Goods (Vienna 1980). This Convention applies where the law of a contracting state of the Convention applies to the contract or the parties who are a party to the agreement are in different Contracting States. It covers business to business contracts but not those relating to consumers and currently has extensive

international coverage with over 80 Contracting States.[24] The Convention provides certain rules, rights, obligations and remedies that apply to qualifying international sale of goods agreements that can alter the effect of a software licence agreement and consequently its effect is generally excluded by contract from applying. Note that whilst the UK is not a Contracting State it is common to see an explicit exclusion of the Convention and care needs to be taken if the law of a Contracting State applies or the licence agreement is made between two different Contracting States;

- Changes to the consumer protection regime in Europe introduced by the Consumer Rights Directive (2011/83/EC) provide protections for consumers in respect of the downloading of 'Digital Content' which could include software, so these will need to be considered when dealing with consumers in a European context. The Directive was introduced into UK Law by the Consumer Protection Act 2015 and came into force on the 1 October 2015.

[17] Limitation of Liability

The licensor's limitation of liability is typically set by reference to the fees paid or a multiple of it. The default position tends to be a multiple of the license fees 'paid or payable' in simpler arrangements where there is a one-time payment. If the fees are recurring by nature, then the limit may be by reference to sums paid or payable in a period of twelve months as the value of the accumulated licence fees over many years of use may be considerable. The twelve-month period can be consecutive periods from the date of the licence agreement, often these are defined as 'Contract Years'. Sometimes the twelve months' period is linked to the period prior to the date of a claim. The latter needs to be reviewed carefully in conjunction with the payment cycle as if substantive payments are not made up front at the start the cap on liability in the early stages of the contract term may be unreasonably low, as only small payments will have been made at that point. Clarification on what is meant by the 'date of claim' will be needed – does that mean the date of the breach or the date proceedings were issued and so on. Also, what might be the position if the breach straddles two Contract Years, what will be the liability limit in that situation?

Whilst the licensee may also want a cap on their liability this will normally be rejected by the licensor as the obligations on the licensee will primarily relate to payment of the fees and not breaching the licensor's intellectual property rights by using or disclosing the software outside the licence terms and in these circumstances the licensor will not consider it appropriate to insert a notional limit.

The liability clause should not attempt to limit or exclude things that are prohibited under the applicable law, for example under English Law, e.g., death or personal injury caused by the negligence of a party cannot be excluded and neither can

24. http://www.uncitral.org/uncitral/en/uncitral_texts/sale_goods/1980CISG_status.html.

certain provisions as to title. The whole limitation clause may become unenforceable if the limitation of liability could be construed as excluding these types of loss.

The licensor is likely to exclude heads of loss such as loss of profits, loss of anticipated savings, and loss of goodwill. These heads are often classified by the courts as direct losses so identifying them as or implying that they are types of indirect or consequential forms of loss could mean that the licensor is inadvertently fully exposed to these types of claims. Drafting these heads of loss as severable sub-clauses separate from any reference to indirect and consequential loss and explicitly stating that the exclusions apply whether these losses are direct or indirect is a sensible approach to reduce these risks.

It should be appreciated by the licensee that the licence fee will not in many cases justify the licensor accepting unlimited liability for the heads of loss referred to above. By way of illustration, if a trading website cannot operate and this was due to the failure of the software the licensor could have unlimited exposure for the profits on lost sales. The potential claim could be out of all proportion to the licence fee received. Also, if this risk was assumed for several customers it might not take much for the licensor to be put out of business. However, what it is reasonable to allow the licensor to exclude will depend on the circumstances in each case, so if the limit of liability was low and loss of profits was the only damage that could realistically be claimed by the licensor it may be reasonable for the licensor to accept it.

As noted previously where the consequences of the breach are considerable it is often appropriate to bring such liability outside the cap on liability or potentially agree a much higher liability cap for that type of liability. This is often the case for liability in the cases of IP infringement, data protection and confidentiality.

Another point the licensee needs to be wary of is that the licensor is not using the liability clause to try and exclude items for which it should be liable. For example, if the licensor was responsible for backing up data and the licensee could not back up the data itself an exclusion of liability by the licensor for loss of data would not be a fair allocation of risk.

[18] Dispute Resolution and Other Boilerplate Provisions of Relevance

Refer to Chapter 1 (Introduction) for guidance on boilerplate provisions and Chapter 7 (International Dispute Resolution) for dispute resolution.

Selected Bibliography

Selected Readings

Reed, Chris, *Computer Law*, 2011 (Seventh Edition)
Morgan, Richard and Burden, Kit, *Computer Contracts*, 2013 (Ninth Edition)
Klinger, Paul and Burnett, Rachel, *Drafting and Negotiating IT Contracts*, 2013 (Third Edition)

Christou, Richard, *International Agency, Distribution and Licensing Agreements*, 2011 (Sixth Edition)

Other Resources for Technology Law

The Society for Computers and Law (www.scl.org) – this is the leading UK organisation for Lawyers working in Technology. Annual Membership is required but it provides excellent resources, and training. There is also a useful society magazine published every two months. Academic and Professional memberships are available.

CHAPTER 5
Franchising*

§5.01 INTRODUCTION

This chapter starts with a review of the term 'franchise' followed by an examination of the central characteristics that underlie a franchise arrangement.

Due consideration will be given to a variety of regulatory structures developed in order to either govern or guide the parties engaged in this commercial arrangement. Such systems address the manner in which both the franchisor and the franchisee conduct themselves.

* Franchising is reviewed in the following textbooks: Abell, Mark (2013), *The Law and Regulation of Franchising in the EU*, 1st ed., Edward Elgar Publishing Ltd; Felstead, Alan (1993), *The Corporate Paradox: Power and Control in Business Franchise*, 1st ed., Routledge; Mendelsohn, Martin (1979), *The Guide to Franchising*, 2nd ed., Pergamon Press; Mendelsohn, Martin (ed.) (1984), *International Franchising: An Overview*, Elsevier; Mendelsohn (1992); Konigsberg, Alex S. (1996), *International Franchising*, Juris; Mendelsohn, Martin (2004), *The Guide to Franchising*, 7th ed., Thomson Learning. In Mendelsohn (1979), Chapter 2 discusses the features offered by the franchisor to the franchisee, Chapter 3 addresses the advantages and disadvantages of franchising, Chapter 4 the subject-matter of a franchise arrangement, Chapter 5 the setting up of a franchise, Chapter 6 the sources of income for the franchisor, Chapters 7 and 8 the initial and ongoing support structures (respectively) offered by the franchisor and Chapter 9 the provisions in a franchise agreement. In Mendelsohn (1984), Chapter 1 (written by Lewis G. Rudnick) examines the history of franchising in the US, Chapter 2 (Iain Baillie) examines franchising of trademarks, Chapter 3 (Nicholas Fyfe) examines franchising of images, and Chapters 4–11 look at franchising in the US, Canada, Latin America, the Asia/Pacific region, the UK, Europe, France and Germany respectively. In Mendelsohn (1992), Chapter 2 (written by Martin Mendelsohn) looks at the European treatment of franchise arrangements, Chapter 3 (Martin Mendelsohn) looks at the international exploitation of franchising arrangements, Chapter 4 (Manzoor G. K. Ishani) looks at the tax concerns associated with franchising arrangements, and Chapters 5–16 address the treatment of such arrangements in the then member states of the European Union. Konigsberg (1996) looks at the law governing franchising arrangements (Chapters 3 and 4), the concerns associated with international franchising operations (Chapter 5) and the formats available for international expansion of a franchising operation (Chapters 6–12).

The authors would like to thank Dr Mark Abell, Partner at Bird & Bird for his valuable insights and recommendations during the writing of this chapter.

A franchise agreement will need to contain certain material terms in order to ensure the workability of the relationship and guarantee the protection of the distinct interests of the contracting parties. A selection of these provisions is explored in the second part of this chapter. The final part of this chapter will provide an illustration of the way in which franchises operate in practice.

§5.02 FRANCHISING DEFINED

The difficulty in formulating a definition for the term 'franchise' stems from the fact that the term is used to designate a wide array of marketing systems[1] and business models.

Notwithstanding the wide variety of arrangements that may be classified as franchises, many of these structures possess a number of common intrinsic features.

Franchising is by no means a new concept in law or indeed marketing. As a technique it 'did not derive from one moment of inventiveness by an imaginative individual. It evolved from the solutions developed by businessmen in response to the problems with which they were confronted in their business operations'.[2]

The term 'franchise' derived from the French word 'franc' denoting freedom, was used to denote 'the acknowledgement of a privilege'.[3] As such settlements extended privileges ordinarily reserved for lords were named *ville-franches*.

The historical DNA of franchising can be traced back to the 1215 Magna Carta, which 'enfranchised' Barons to collect taxes.[4]

From the 1600s onwards in Japan, the *Norenkai* system of restaurant chains[5] used a system akin to that of a contemporary franchise; in the context which an employer would permit an employee to create a restaurant in a different location using both the same name and same menu as their employer.[6]

In the 1700s, the 'Tied House' system developed in the UK to secure the distribution of beers by brewers used an early form of franchising.[7]

It is generally believed that franchising emerged as a business model in the US after the end of the Civil War.[8]

The McCormick Harvesting Machine Company (McCormick) and the Singer Sewing Machine Company (Singer) are two of the earliest examples of franchising in

1. Barbe, Erwin (1975), 'Fraud in Connection with Franchise or Distributorship Relationship', *American Law Reports 3d* 64, 11; Martin Mendelsohn 2004, Chapter 1.
2. Mendelsohn 1992: 1.
3. Emerson, Robert W. (2009), Franchise Contracts and Territoriality: A French Comparison, Entrepreneurial Business Law Journal Vol 3, 315-353, Footnote 2.
4. Abell 2013: 12. The Crown 'offered feudal lords the right to maintain civil order, determine and collect tax revenues' and barons paid the Crown a set sum of money from the tax revenues collected. In 1562, this system of patronage was ended by the Council of Trent. (Abell 2013: 13, footnote 1).
5. Abell 2013: 12. Under the Japanese-based *Norenkai* system, an employer would permit an employee to create a restaurant in a different location using the same name and same menu as their employer. (Abell 2013: 14, footnote 2).
6. Abell 2013: 14, footnote 2.
7. Abell 2013: 12.
8. Mendelsohn 2004: 16.

the US.[9] Around 1850, McCormick commissioned local agents to sell and service its machines,[10] and during the same period, Singer used agents, working on a commission basis, to demonstrate, sell, and repair their sewing machines.[11]

At the start of the 20th century, this business model began to be used in the US in the beverage and the motor industries 'followed by a trickle of developments until the 1930s, when Howard Johnson[12] started his famous chain in the USA, and the 1940s and 1950s, which saw the birth of so many of the modern giants of the franchising community'.[13]

In the 1950s, the classic franchise structures were developed in the US, with the likes of McDonalds (1955),[14] KFC (1955),[15] and IHOP (1959),[16] and in the UK, with the likes of Wimpy (1955),[17] and Service Master (1958).[18]

The significant increase in the use of franchising as a business model in the mid-1950s is attributable to a number of factors.[19] First, the development of television meant 'more efficient nationwide information technology, reducing the cost of establishing national brand names'.[20] Second, an increase in travel meant that consumers were shopping more frequently in unknown geographic areas in which national brands often served as indicators of quality.[21] Finally, the increase in real income of consumers.[22]

A first wave of growth was experienced in the 1960s,[23] and then a second in 1970s.[24]

9. Abell 2013: 14 (footnote 3), citing Mendelsohn 1999.
10. Abell 2013: 14 (footnote 3), citing Mendelsohn 1999.
11. Mendelsohn 2004: 16.
12. Howard Johnson bought a small shop in Massachusetts in 1925, where he started producing his own ice creams. In 1929, he opened his first restaurant. In 1935, the first of his franchises were opened in Cape Cod. By the end of 1935, Howard Johnson had franchised restaurants and ice cream stands in Massachusetts. In 1940 he opened a road restaurant on the Pennsylvania Turnpike. In 1954, he franchised his first motor lodge in Savannah, Georgia. At the time of his retirement from the position of president in 1959, the nationwide company that he established had '675 restaurants, 175 motor lodges and annual sales of $127 million'. (Sanmarco, Anthony M., (2013), A History of Howard Johnson's: How a Massachusetts Soda Fountain Became an American Icon, Introduction).
13. Mendelsohn 2004: 16.
14. Abell 2013: 14 (footnote 6) citing Love, J.F., McDonalds: Behind the Arches (2008), 45.
15. Abell 2013: 14 (footnote 7) citing Felstead 1993: 42.
16. Abell 2013: 14 (footnote 7) citing Felstead 1993: 42.
17. Abell 2013: 14 (footnote 9), citing Stanworth, J. and Smith B. (1991), *Barclays Guide to Franchising for Small Businesses*, Blackwell.
18. Abell 2013: 14 (footnote 10). ServiceMaster, a cleaning franchise launched in the United States in 1958, and based in Chicago, arrived in the United Kingdom in 1958 when Raymond Crouch acquired a master licence for Europe. Abell 2013: 14 (footnote 10).
19. Mathewson G. F. and Winter R. A. (1985) The Economics of Franchise Contracts, Journal of Law and Economics, Vol. 28 No. 3, 503-526, 504.
20. Mathewson et al 1985: 504.
21. Mathewson et al 1985: 504.
22. Mathewson et al 1985: 504.
23. Abell 2013: 13.
24. Abell 2013: 13.

In the 1960s, several large franchises opened in the UK (in 1965, Golden Egg Restaurants, and in 1966, Dyno Rod),[25] and Germany (Ihr Platz, Nordsee and OBI).[26]

The second wave saw the introduction of the first Franchise Regulation (adopted in California in 1971),[27] the adoption of franchise relationship laws in fourteen States (USA), the establishment of the European Franchise Federation (1972), French and German Franchise Associations (1973), and British Franchise Association (1978).

Nowadays, franchising involves all levels in the chain from manufacturing to consumer, and is found in the relationship existing between manufacturers and retailers, manufacturers and wholesalers, wholesalers and retailers and retailers and retailers.[28]

Franchising contributes significantly to the GDP of the UK (£15.1 billion),[29] Germany (€48 billion),[30] and France (€47.6 billion).[31]

According to the British Franchise Association, the contribution of franchising to the economy of the UK has increased by 46 % over a ten year period.[32] Franchising in the UK employs 621,000 people.[33] The number of UK-based franchisee-owned businesses is 44,200, with approximately 29% of franchisees running multiple units.[34]

The following review considers some of the definitions developed to explain the structure referred to as a franchise. This two-part review examines the legislative and non-legislative definitions of this concept. Whilst the first part of this review will consider legislative definitions, the second part of the review will assess definitions of this concept derived from non-legislative sources.

[A] Franchise as Defined by Legislation

Articulated by legislatures, these definitions reflect policy considerations.

Guided by competition policy considerations, the European Commission (Commission) has developed a definition of the term 'franchise' within the context of the block exemptions it has issued.

25. Abell 2013: 13.
26. Abell 2013: 13.
27. Abell 2013: 13. The California Franchise Investment Law (California Corporations Code, Division 5, Parts 1-6, Sections 31000-31516) was adopted in 1970, and came into effect in January 1971. (Abell 2013: 15, footnote 13).
28. Mendelsohn 1992: 1–2.
29. British Franchise Association statistics for 2015 (published in January 2016) available at https://www.thebfa.org/external-relations-pr/franchise-industry-research/ (last accessed 19/4/2018).
30. Abell 2013: 1, citing Deutsche Bank, Report on Franchising (January 2008).
31. Abell 2013: 1, citing French Franchise Federation Report 2010.
32. British Franchise Association statistics for 2015 (published in January 2016), available at https://www.thebfa.org/external-relations-pr/franchise-industry-research/ (last accessed 19/4/2018).
33. British Franchise Association statistics for 2015 (published in January 2016), available at https://www.thebfa.org/external-relations-pr/franchise-industry-research/ (last accessed 19/4/2018).
34. British Franchise Association statistics for 2015 (published in January 2016), available at https://www.thebfa.org/external-relations-pr/franchise-industry-research/ (last accessed 19/4/2018).

One such definition was issued in 1988 under the auspices of the block exemption governing franchises. Another was promulgated in 2000 under the aegis of the guidelines issued alongside the block exemption governing vertical restraints.[35]

A definition of the term 'franchise' that may be contrasted with the one provided by the Commission is the one furnished by the US-based federal agency, the Federal Trade Commission (FTC).

Guided not only by the need to protect consumers and promote competition but also by the need to protect prospective franchisees, the FTC has developed a set of rules, which is primarily intended to protect the interests of the franchisee during the initial stages of the contracting process (FTC Rule).[36]

[1] European Union Definition of the Term 'Franchise'

[a] Earlier Definition of the Term (Block Exemption on Franchise Agreements)[37]

Empowered by EU law (Regulation No 19/65/EEC) to apply Article 85(3) of the EEC Treaty (TEEC) to different categories of bilateral exclusive agreements falling within the remit of this article of the Treaty, the Commission after consultation with the Advisory Committee on Restrictive Practices and Dominant Positions issued the Block Exemption on Franchise Agreements.[38]

Based on the experience of the Commission, the Block Exemption on Franchise Agreements defines those franchise agreements which prima facie fall within the scope of the prohibition in Article 85(1) TEEC, but which normally are viewed as meeting the criteria laid out in the exemption in Article 85(3) TEEC.[39]

Franchise agreements are deemed to be able to impact upon intra-Community trade, when 'they are concluded between undertakings from different Member States or where they form the basis of a network which extends beyond the boundaries of a single Member State'.[40]

The Franchise Block Exemption highlights the fact that franchise agreements are capable of enhancing interstate competition, by targeting those arrangements which in the normal course of events 'improve the distribution of goods and/or the provision of services as they give franchisors the possibility of establishing a uniform network with limited investments, which may assist the entry of new competitors on the market, particularly in the case of small and medium-sized undertakings, thus increasing

35. Commission notice – Guidelines on Vertical Restraints (Text with EEA relevance) OJ C291, 13/10/2000 p. 0001-0044 (Guidelines on VRBER 1999).
36. The FTC Rule is discussed in more detail later on in this chapter.
37. Full title – Commission Regulation (EEC) No 4087/88 of 30 November 1988 on the application of Article 85(3) of the Treaty to categories of franchise agreements OJ L 359/46 – 359/52 (Block Exemption on Franchise Agreements).
38. Full title – Commission Regulation (EEC) No 4087/88 of 30 November 1988 on the application of Article 85(3) of the Treaty to categories of franchise agreements OJ L 359/46 – 359/52 (Block Exemption on Franchise Agreements).
39. Paragraph 4 of the preamble to the Block Exemption on Franchise Agreements.
40. Paragraph 6 of the preamble to the Block Exemption on Franchise Agreements.

interbrand competition. They also allow independent traders to set up outlets more rapidly and with higher chance of success than if they had to do so without the franchisor's experience and assistance. They have therefore the possibility of competing more efficiently with large distribution undertakings ... (and those arrangements) also allow consumers and other end users a fair share of the resulting benefit, as they combine the advantage of a uniform network with the existence of traders personally interested in the efficient operation of their business. The homogeneity of the network and the constant cooperation between the franchisor and the franchisee ensures a constant quality of the products and services. The favourable effect of franchising on interbrand competition and the fact that consumers are free to deal with any franchisee in the network guarantees that a reasonable part of the resulting benefits will be passed on to the consumers'.[41]

A distinction is made by the Franchise Block Exemption between a franchise on the one hand and a franchise agreement on the other.[42]

A franchise is defined by the Franchise Block Exemption as 'a package of industrial or intellectual property rights relating to trademarks, trade names, shop signs, utility models, designs, copyrights, know-how or patents, to be exploited for the resale of goods or the provision of services to end users'.[43]

In contrast with the definition of a franchise as a bundle of rights for use in the resale of goods and the provision of services to end users, the Franchise Block Exemption defines the contractual arrangement that is the franchise agreement.

According to this definition, the franchise agreement is 'an agreement whereby one undertaking, the franchisor, grants the other, the franchisee, in exchange for direct or indirect financial consideration, the right to exploit a franchise for the purposes of marketing specified types of goods and/or services; it includes at least obligations relating to:

- the use of a common name or shop sign and a uniform presentation of contract premises and/or means of transport,
- the communication by the franchisor to the franchisee of know-how,
- the continuing provision by the franchisor to the franchisee of commercial or technical assistance during the life of the agreement'.[44]

Such agreements states the preamble to the Franchise Block Exemption are in essence 'licenses of industrial or intellectual property rights relating to trade marks or signs and know-how, which can be combined with restrictions relating to supply or purchase of goods'.[45]

41. Paragraphs 7 and 8 of the preamble to the Block Exemption on Franchise Agreements.
42. This document entered into force on 1 February 1989 and remained in force until 31 December 1999 (Article 9, Block Exemption on Franchise Agreements). It has since been superseded by the Vertical Restraints Block Exemption.
43. Article 1(3)a, Block Exemption on Franchise Agreements.
44. Article 1(3)b, Block Exemption on Franchise Agreements.
45. Paragraph 2 of the preamble to the Block Exemption on Franchise Agreements.

Two structures are delineated in the provisions of the Franchise Block Exemption.[46]

In the first category are those agreements concluded between two undertakings (the franchisor and the franchisee) involving the sale of products and/or the provision of services.

In the second category are those agreements concluded with the help of an intermediary. This third entity acting as an intermediary is granted by the franchisor 'in exchange of direct or indirect financial consideration, the right to exploit a franchise for the purposes of concluding franchise agreements with third parties, the franchisees'.[47] The go-between is known as the master franchisee. Effectively this structure entails a relationship that is made between a franchisee and a franchisor through the master franchisee.

The different categories of franchise, suggest the Franchise Block Exemption, are distinguished in accordance with its underlying goal.[48] An industrial franchise relates to the production of goods.[49] A distribution franchise involves product retail.[50] A service franchise involves the provision of services.[51]

[b] Later Definitions of the Term (Vertical Restraints Block Exemptions)[52]

Guidelines[53] were issued in October 2000 by the Commission alongside the block exemption governing vertical restraints in order 'to help companies to make their own assessment of vertical agreements under the EC competition rules'.[54]

These Guidelines[55] which address the exemption of qualifying franchise agreements defines these as agreements that 'contain licences of intellectual property rights relating in particular to trademarks or signs and know-how for the use and distribution of goods or services. In addition to the licence of IPRs, the franchisor usually provides the franchisee during the life of the agreement with commercial or technical assistance.

46. Paragraph 5 of the preamble to the Block Exemption on Franchise Agreements.
47. Article 1(3)c, Block Exemption on Franchise Agreements.
48. Paragraph 3 of the preamble to the Block Exemption on Franchise Agreements.
49. Paragraph 3 of the preamble to the Block Exemption on Franchise Agreements.
50. Paragraph 3 of the preamble to the Block Exemption on Franchise Agreements.
51. Paragraph 3 of the preamble to the Block Exemption on Franchise Agreements.
52. Commission Regulation (EC) No 2790/1999 of 22 December 1999 on the application of Article 81(3) of the Treaty to categories of vertical agreements and concerted practices (Text with EEA relevance) OJ L 336, 29/12/1999 P. 0021 – 0025 (VRBER 1999) and its successor the Commission Regulation (EU) No 330/2010 of 20 April 2010 on the application of Article 101(3) of the Treaty on the Functioning of the European Union to categories of vertical agreements and concerted practices (Text with EEA relevance) OJ L 102, 23/4/2010 P.0001 – 0007 (VRBER 2010).
53. Commission notice – Guidelines on Vertical Restraints (Text with EEA relevance) OJ C291, 13/10/2000 p. 0001-0044 (Guidelines on VRBER 1999).
54. Guidelines on VRBER 1999, para. 3.
55. Commission notice – Guidelines on Vertical Restraints (Text with EEA relevance) OJ C291, 13/10/2000 p. 0001-0044 (Guidelines on VRBER 1999).

The licence and the assistance are integral components of the business method being franchised. The franchisor is in general paid a franchise fee by the franchisee for the use of the particular business method. Franchising may enable the franchisor to establish, with limited investments, a uniform network for the distribution of his products. In addition to the provision of the business method, franchise agreements usually contain a combination of different vertical restraints concerning the products being distributed, in particular selective distribution and/or non-compete and/or exclusive distribution or weaker forms thereof'.[56]

Upon the expiration of the VRBER 1999 in 2010, a revised legislative instrument was issued by the Commission. Dated 20 April 2010, this regulation came into force on 1 June 2010[57] and like its predecessor it does not specifically address franchise agreements which are once again addressed within the accompanying guidelines. The guidelines accompanying the VRBER 2010 which aim to fulfil the same goal as the earlier guidelines[58] use the same definition as the one used in the earlier guidelines.[59]

[c] *Conclusion*

By way of a synopsis, according to the guidelines issued by the Commission a franchise agreement will possess certain key characteristics.

First such an agreement will entail the grant of a licence of intellectual property rights. Second beyond the licence the franchisor will provide the franchisee with assistance which is both commercial in character and technical in nature. Third this arrangement will effectively amount to a business method. Fourth a franchise fee will be paid by the franchisee for the use of this business method. Fifth the franchisor will be in a position to develop a uniform distribution network for his products. Finally the arrangement will entail a collection of vertical restraints that will relate to the distribution of these products.

There are minor differences between the definition of a franchise agreement in these guidelines and the earlier definition of such an agreement put forth by the Franchise Block Exemption.[60]

A franchise agreement in the Franchise Block Exemption is defined as possessing the following attributes. First it is an agreement which grants the franchisee the right to exploit a package of intellectual property rights (referred to in the Franchise Block Exemption as the franchise) in the marketing of specific goods and services. Second the franchisor is expected not only to provide the franchisee with continuing assistance

56. Guidelines on VRBER 1999, para. 199.
57. Article 10, VRBER 2010. This regulation will expire on 31 May 2022.
58. Commission notice – Guidelines on Vertical Restraints (Text with EEA relevance) OJ C 130, 19.05.2010, P. 0001-0046, para. 3. (Guidelines on VRBER 2010).
59. Guidelines on VRBER 2010, paras. 43 and 189.
60. Article 1(3)b, Block Exemption on Franchise Agreements.

throughout the term of the agreement but to also communicate know-how to the franchisee. Third in exchange for the grant of intellectual property rights, the franchisee will provide direct or indirect financial consideration.

[2] Definition in English Law

Franchise arrangements are defined in UK legislation. One such definition is that given in the Financial Services Act 1986 which describes franchise arrangements as 'arrangements under which a person earns profits or income by exploiting a right conferred by the arrangements to use a trade name or design or other intellectual property or the good-will attached to it'.[61]

[3] US Definition

Franchising is defined in US case law as 'the license from the owner of a trademark or trade name permitting another to sell his product or service under that name'.[62]

The FTC promulgated the original Franchise Rule on 21 December 1978. This Rule was revised in 2007 and became effective on 1 July 2007 (FTC Rule).

Primarily a set of rules governing disclosure before sale, both sets of Rules were introduced in a bid to address and 'prevent deceptive and unfair practices in the sale of franchises ... and to correct consumers' misimpressions about franchise ... offerings'.[63]

The FTC Rule defines a franchise as:[64]

> 'any continuing commercial relationship or arrangement, whatever it may be called, in which the terms of the offer or contract specify ... orally or in writing that:
>
> > The franchisee will obtain the right to operate a business that is identified or associated with the franchisor's trademark, or to offer, sell, or distribute goods, services, or commodities that are identified or associated with the franchisor's trademark;
> > The franchisor will exert or has authority to exert a significant degree of control over the franchisee's method of operation, or provide significant assistance in the franchisee's method of operation; and
> > As a condition of obtaining or commencing operation of the franchise, the franchisee makes a required payment or commits to make a required payment to the franchisor or its affiliate'.[65]

61. (§75(6)f, Financial Services Act 1986). The 1986 Act has been repealed (by the Financial Services and Markets Act 2000), but the definition is still of relevance. The 2000 Act was amended by the Financial Services Act 2010.
62. *Aaron E. Levine & Co.* v. *Calkraft Paper Co.*, 429 F. Supp. 1039 (E.D. Mich. 1976), 1050, citing *Rubinger* v. *Int'l Tel. & Tel. Corp.*, 310 F. 2d. 552 (2nd Cir. 1962) cert. denied, 375 US 820 (1962) (US).
63. Federal Register, Vol 72 No 61, Friday March 30 2007, Rules and Regulations, p.15445.
64. Federal Register, Vol 72 No 61, Friday March 30 2007, Rules and Regulations (2007 Rule).
65. 16 CFR 436.1(h).

In this context, a franchisee is defined as 'any person who is granted a franchise'.[66] Whilst a franchisor is defined as 'any person who grants a franchise and participates in the franchise relationship'.[67]

According to the FTC, a commercial arrangement will be deemed to be a franchise when it fulfils 'the three elements of a franchise' irrespective of the terminology used and in circumstances where the 'franchisor represents that the relationship being offered has the characteristics of a franchise, regardless of any failure on the franchisor's part to perform as promised'.[68]

[4] French Definition

In the 1930s, the French company La Lainière de Roubaix devised a system of distribution under the trade name Pingouin.[69]

In the 1960s, and 1970s, the franchise business model gained in popularity with the number of franchisors increasing from 34 to 203 over an eight-year period spanning 1971-1979.[70] Over the same period, there was an increase in the number of franchisees from 2,000 (1971) to 10,700 (1979).[71]

By 2007, the number of franchise networks in France reached circa 141.[72]

Defined by French law, as a contract pursuant to which a person (franchisor) grants another (franchisee) 'its own distinctive signs and an original commercial "savoir-faire", i.e., know-how, in consideration for a royalty'.[73] In franchise arrangements, beyond the grant of distinctive signs, and the sharing of savoir-faire, the franchisor usually provides the franchisee with ongoing assistance,[74] whilst controlling the use of the savoir-faire[75] by the franchisee.[76]

Franchise arrangements are a genre of intuitu personae agreements, entered into 'in consideration of the person',[77] so that 'the personal characteristics of the other party to the agreement determine the implementation and conclusion of that contract'.[78] As such under French law, a franchise is viewed as a personal arrangement with the

66. 16 CFR 436.1(i).
67. 16 CFR 436.1(k). In the 2007 Rule, the term 'franchisor' encompasses the term 'subfranchisor'. [16 CFR 436.1(k)] A subfranchisor is defined as a person 'who functions as a franchisor by engaging in both pre-sale activities and post-sale performance.' [16 CFR 436.1(k)].
68. Federal Register, Vol 72 No 61, Friday March 30 2007, Rules and Regulations, p.15459.
69. Emerson 2009: 320, citing from Louisa Igoudjil, Le regime des contrats d'entreprise 57 n.268 (2006).
70. Emerson 2009: 316.
71. Emerson 2009: 317, citing Dominique Baschet (2005), La Franchise: Guide Juridique - Conseils Pratiques, 31.
72. Emerson 2009: 317, citing figures issued by the French Franchise Federation, Les chiffres de la franchise en 2007.
73. Emerson 2009: 319-320.
74. Emerson 2009: 320, Footnote 11, citing Baschet 2005: 21.
75. 'Know-to-do' would be a literal translation of the phrase *savoir-faire (savoir* means 'to know'; *faire* 'to do') (translated by M Meiselles).
76. Emerson 2009: 320.
77. This Latin phrase is defined in French as '*en fonction de la personne*' (Emerson 2009: 316).
78. Emerson 2009: 320.

franchisor providing the right to exploit its distinctive features and savoir-faire, and the franchisee providing the capital, experience, and ability.[79]

This concept which is by no means unique to French law can be found in Belgian and Italian franchise law as well.[80] Since the professional attribute and financial capacity of the franchisee are crucial to such an arrangement, most franchise agreements will include an 'intuitus personae' clause which is exclusively and unilaterally linked to the franchisee in person.[81]

[B] Non-legislative Definitions

Whilst the first part of the review of the term 'franchise' considered several definitions derived from legislative sources (international and national), the second part of this review looks at some definitions of the term deriving from non-legislative sources.

Here a number of definitions are explored. The first is a definition developed by the World Franchise Council (the Council). The second is the definition that has been developed by the European Franchise Federation (EFF). The third definition is the definition contained within the Draft Common Frame of Reference (DCFR) developed by the EU. The fourth definition is the definition contained in the Model Franchise Disclosure Law (September 2002) developed by UNIDROIT for use by state legislatures.

[1] World Franchise Council

Established in 1994[82] this independent international representative body of national franchise associations[83] has been entrusted by its members with a number of key objectives. Not only is it a forum for dialogue and cooperation between its member associations, it is also responsible for providing its members with information, for representing the views of its members to national and international legislatures and policy-makers, as well as non-governmental organisations.[84]

Since its establishment, the Council has successfully promoted the idea that each member country should have a single franchise association (the 'Recognition of One

79. Emerson 2009: 320-321.
80. Emerson 2009: 321.
81. Emerson 2009: 321, citing Baschet 2005: 430 – *'Le plupart des contrats prévoit une clause d'intuitus personae unilatérale en la seule personne du franchisé: le franchiseur signe un contrat de franchise en fonction des aptitudes professionnelles et des capacités financières du franchisé.'* (translated by M Meiselles).
82. At the 1994 Annual Convention of the IFA, a team of executives from various national franchise associations led by the IFA and the European Franchise Federation decided as one to establish the Council – Information available on home page of World Franchise Council at http://www.worldfranchisecouncil.net (accessed on 2/8/2014).
83. Member associations come from countries including Canada, China, Europe, India, Japan, Russia and Switzerland. A full listing can be found at http://www.worldfranchisecouncil.net/members.html (last accessed 14/5/2018).
84. Information available on home page of World Franchise Council at http://www.worldfranchisecouncil.net (last accessed 14/5/2018).

Association per Country' campaign)[85] whilst its work with UNIDROIT has led to the adoption of a common stance with regards to the formulation of the model law on franchising.[86]

The Council's constitution was initially worked on by a team of representatives from a number of countries including Mexico, Canada, Europe and the US.[87] The final draft of this document was produced by a working group led by the British Franchise Association with representatives from several national associations.[88] In June 1995, the final draft of the constitution was adopted.[89] The current constitution is the result of several consecutive revisions.[90,91]

A franchise agreement is defined by the Council as 'a commercial development strategy based on an interdependent partnership between independent commercial entities, the franchisor and the franchisees; The franchisor and the franchisee commit themselves reciprocally in view of their common and mutual success; To attain this objective, the commitments of both parties, throughout their relationship, are based on fundamental ethical principles; The principles apply to the relationship between the franchisor and franchisee, as well as to the relationship between master-franchisee and sub-franchisee'.[92]

[2] European Franchise Federation

Constituted in 1972 this not-for-profit organisation based in Brussels represents national franchise associations established throughout Europe both in countries that are EU Member States and in those that are not.[93]

85. This campaign has brought about the merger of the former Philippines-based associations and the creation of a single association in Korea (Information accessed on home page of World Franchise Council at http://www.worldfranchisecouncil.net on 2/8/2014).
86. Information available on home page of World Franchise Council at http://www.worldfranchisecouncil.net (last accessed 2/8/2014).
87. Information available on home page of World Franchise Council at http://www.worldfranchisecouncil.net (last accessed 2/8/2014).
88. Information available on home page of World Franchise Council at http://www.worldfranchisecouncil.net (last accessed 2/8/2014).
89. Information available on home page of World Franchise Council at http://www.worldfranchisecouncil.net (last accessed 2/8/2014).
90. The Constitution was amended 2 April 2007 and then 13 April 2011 and 19 September 2013 (information available on home page of World Franchise Council at https://www.worldfranchisecouncil.net/wfc-constitution.html (last accessed 14/5/2018).
91. The updated version of the Constitution is accessible at https://www.worldfranchisecouncil.net/wfc-constitution.html (last accessed 14/5/2018).
92. The World Franchise Council's Principles of Ethics dated 12 November 2001 are accessible at https://s3-ap-southeast-2.amazonaws.com/wh1.thewebconsole.com/wh/3181/images/Code-of-Ethics.pdf (last accessed 14/5/2018).
93. Accessed on the home page of the EFF at http://www.eff-franchise.com (last accessed 1/8/2014).

A 'single Voice for Franchising with regards to the institutions of the European Union'[94] the EFF aims to campaign for this business model by formulating uniform policies, and best practice, whilst promoting self-regulation of this business model.[95]

Each of the founding members of the EFF assisted in the compilation of the Code of Ethics (the Code)[96] (last amended 6 December 2016)[97] with all EFF National Franchise Association Members, and their respective memberships committed to following the provisions of the Code.[98] All EFF Member Franchise Associations have endorsed the Code, and are committed to its promotion, and implementation in their respective countries.[99]

This Code represents 'a practical ensemble of essential provisions for the governance of the relations between a franchisor and each of its franchisees, operating together in the framework of the franchise network'.[100]

The definition of franchising encapsulated within the Code was developed by the EFF in consultation with the Commission to ensure that it accords with the definition set out in the Franchise Block Exemption.[101]

According to this definition, franchising 'is a system of marketing goods and/or services and/or technology, which is based upon a close and ongoing collaboration between legally and financially separate and independent undertakings, the Franchisor and its individual Franchisees, whereby the Franchisor grants its individual Franchisee the right, and imposes the obligation, to conduct a business in accordance with the Franchisor's concept. The right entitles and compels the individual Franchisee, in exchange for a direct or indirect financial consideration, to use the Franchisor's trade name, and/or trade mark and /or service mark, know-how, business and technical methods, procedural system, and other industrial and /or intellectual property rights, supported by continuing provision of commercial and technical assistance, within the framework and for the term of a written franchise agreement, concluded between parties for this purpose'.[102]

94. Accessed on the home page of the EFF at http://www.eff-franchise.com (last accessed 1/8/2014).
95. Missions of the EFF accessible at http://www.eff-franchise.com/80/membership.html (last accessed 14/5/2018).
96. The Code of Ethics can be accessed at http://www.eff-franchise.com/77/regulation.html (last accessed 14/5/2018).
97. Part II, European Franchise Federation Code of Ethics accessible at http://www.eff-franchise.com (last accessed 1/8/2014).
98. Paragraph 2, Preamble to the European Franchise Federation Code of Ethics accessible at http://www.eff-franchise.com/Data/Code%20of%20Ethics2.pdf (last accessed 14/5/2018).
99. Paragraph 2, Preamble to the European Franchise Federation Code of Ethics accessible at http://www.eff-franchise.com/Data/Code%20of%20Ethics2.pdf (last accessed 14/5/2018).
100. Paragraph 2, Preamble to the European Franchise Federation Code of Ethics accessible at http://www.eff-franchise.com/Data/Code%20of%20Ethics2.pdf (last accessed 14/5/2018).
101. UNIDROIT in a document entitled 'The European Union and Franchising' accessible at http://www.unidroit.org/english/guides/2007franchising/country/eu.pdf (last accessed 31/1/2014), footnote 7, page 2.
102. Article 1, EFF Code of Ethics accessible at http://www.eff-franchise.com/Data/Code%20of%20Ethics2.pdf (last accessed 14/5/2018).

Due to its centrality, the term 'know-how' is defined in the Code alongside its component elements (secret, substantial and identified).[103]

'Know-how' is defined by the Code, as 'a package of non-patented practical information, resulting from experience and testing by the Franchisor, which is secret, substantial and identified'.[104]

The term 'secret' in this context means 'that the know-how is not generally known or easily accessible; it is not limited in the narrow sense that each individual component of the know-how should be totally unknown or unobtainable outside the Franchisor's business'.[105] 'Substantial' means 'the know-how is significant and useful to the buyer for the use, sale or resale of the contract goods or services'.[106,107] 'Identified' refers to the fact that 'the know-how must be described in a sufficiently comprehensive manner so as to make it possible to verify that it fulfils the criteria of secrecy and substantiality'.[108109]

[3] Draft Common Frame of Reference

A franchise is defined in the DCFR as a 'legal relationship arising from a contract under which one party, the franchisor, grants the other party, the franchisee, in exchange for remuneration, the right to conduct a business (franchise business) within the franchisor's network for the purposes of supplying certain products on the franchisee's behalf and in the franchisee's name, and whereby the franchisee has the right and the

103. Article 1, EFF Code of Ethics accessible at http://www.eff-franchise.com/Data/Code%20of%20Ethics2.pdf (last accessed14/5/2018).
104. Article 1, EFF Code of Ethics accessible at http://www.eff-franchise.com/Data/Code%20of%20Ethics2.pdf (last accessed14/5/2018).
105. Article 1, EFF Code of Ethics accessible at http://www.eff-franchise.com/Data/Code%20of%20Ethics2.pdf (last accessed14/5/2018).
106. Article 1, EFF Code of Ethics accessible at http://www.eff-franchise.com/Data/Code%20of%20Ethics2.pdf (last accessed14/5/2018).
107. Previously the term 'substantial' in the context of know-how was defined as meaning 'that the know-how includes information which is indispensable to the franchisee for the use, sale or resale of the contract goods or services, in particular for the presentation of goods for sale, the processing of goods in connection with the provision of services, methods of dealing with customers, and administration and financial management; the know-how must be useful for the Franchisee by being capable, at the date of conclusion of the agreement, of improving the competitive position of the Franchisee, in particular by improving the Franchisee's performance or helping it to enter a new market.' (Part II, EFF Code of Ethics accessed at http://www.eff-franchise.com on accessed 1/8/2014).
108. Article 1, EFF Code of Ethics accessible at http://www.eff-franchise.com/Data/Code%20of%20Ethics2.pdf (last accessed 14/5/2018).
109. Previously the term 'identified' in the context of know-how was more widely defined as 'the know-how must be described in a sufficiently comprehensive manner so as to make it possible to verify that it fulfils the criteria of secrecy and substantiality; the description of the know-how can either be set out in the franchise agreement or in a separate document or recorded in any other appropriate form.' (Part II, EFF EFF Code of Ethics accessed at http://www.eff-franchise.com on accessed 1/8/2014).

obligation to use the franchisor's trade name or trademark or other intellectual property rights, know-how and business method'.[110]

[4] UNIDROIT Model Franchise Disclosure Law

In the Model Franchise Disclosure Law 2002[111] (Model Law) developed by the International Institute for the Unification of Private Law (UNIDROIT) and discussed below, a franchise is defined as meaning:

> 'the rights granted by a party (the franchisor) authorising and requiring another party (the franchisee), in exchange for direct or indirect financial compensation, to engage in the business of selling goods or services on its own behalf under a system designated by the franchisor which includes know-how and assistance, prescribes in substantial part the manner in which the franchised business is to be operated, includes significant and continuing operational control by the franchisor, and is substantially associated with a trademark, service mark, trade name or logotype designated by the franchisor. It includes:
>
> (A) the rights granted by a franchisor to a sub-franchisor under a master franchise agreement;
> (B) the rights granted by a sub-franchisor to a sub-franchisee under a sub-franchise agreement;
> (C) the rights granted by a franchisor to a party under a development agreement.
>
> For the purposes of this definition "direct or indirect financial compensation" shall not include the payment of a bona fide wholesale price for goods intended for resale'.[112]

Keywords in the definition of the term 'franchise' are further developed in the definitions provision in Article 2, Model Law. According to this article:

> A franchise agreement 'means the agreement under which a franchise is granted'.[113]

A franchised business 'means the business conducted by the franchisee under a franchise agreement'.[114]

110. Annex entitled Definitions accompanying the Draft Common Frame of Reference (IV.E.-4:101) reproduced in Principles, Definitions and Model Rules of European Private Law, Prepared by the Study Group on a European Civil Code and the Research Group on EC Private Law (Acquis Group), Edited by Christiian von Bar, Eric Clive, and Hans Schulte-Nölke, Hugh Beale, Johnny Herre, Jerome Huet, Matthias Storme, Stephen Swann, Paul Varul, Anna Veneziano and Fryderyk Zoll (published by Sellier, 2009), 554.
111. Model Franchise Disclosure Law (2002) accessible at https://www.unidroit.org/instruments/franchising/model-law (last accessed 14/5/2018).
112. Article 2, Model Franchise Disclosure Law (2002) accessible at https://www.unidroit.org/instruments/franchising/model-law (last accessed 14/5/2018).
113. Article 2, Model Franchise Disclosure Law (2002) accessible at https://www.unidroit.org/instruments/franchising/model-law (last accessed 14/5/2018).
114. Article 2, Model Franchise Disclosure Law (2002) accessible at https://www.unidroit.org/instruments/franchising/model-law (last accessed 14/5/2018).

A franchisee 'includes a sub-franchisee in its relationship with the sub-franchisor and the sub-franchisor in its relationship with the franchisor'.[115]

A franchisor 'includes the sub-franchisor in its relationship with its sub-franchisees'.

A master franchise 'means the right granted by a franchisor to another party (the sub-franchisor) to grant franchises to third parties (the sub-franchisees)'.[116]

A sub-franchise agreement 'means a franchise agreement concluded by a sub-franchisor and a sub-franchisee pursuant to a master franchise'.[117]

The intention of the drafters of the Model Law and the Explanatory Report was to limit the definition of the franchise under the Model Law to the arrangement known as a 'business format franchise'[118] thereby exclude from its scope certain other arrangements *inter alia* the arrangement known as an 'industrial franchise' (which is defined by the drafters of the Model Law and the Explanatory Report as a franchise that concerns the manufacture of goods and which consists 'in manufacturing licences based on patents and/or technical know-how combined with trademark licences'),[119] as well as the arrangements known respectively as a 'distribution franchise' (which concerns the sale of goods) and a 'service franchise' (which concerns the supply of services).[120]

By referring to the fact that in the definition of a franchise the phase direct or indirect financial compensation excludes 'payment of a bona fide wholesale price for goods intended for resale',[121] the drafters intended to exclude transactions involving a simple sale of goods as opposed to the granting of a franchise system[122] from the scope of this definition.

By mentioning the fact that the franchisee is engaging in the sale of goods and services 'on its own behalf', the intention is 'to make it clear that the franchisee is independent from the franchisor, that the franchisee is an entrepreneur in its own right who invests and risks its own funds and that the franchisor and the franchisee are not liable for each other's acts or omissions'.[123]

By referring in the definition to 'a system designated by the franchisor', the drafters of these instruments have devised the definition 'franchise' to encompass

115. Article 2, Model Franchise Disclosure Law (2002) accessible at https://www.unidroit.org/instruments/franchising/model-law (last accessed 14/5/2018).
116. Article 2, Model Franchise Disclosure Law (2002) accessible at https://www.unidroit.org/instruments/franchising/model-law (last accessed 14/5/2018).
117. Article 2, Model Franchise Disclosure Law (2002) accessible at https://www.unidroit.org/instruments/franchising/model-law (last accessed 14/5/2018).
118. Explanatory Report, para. 46 accessible at https://www.unidroit.org/instruments/franchising/model-law (last accessed 14/5/2018).
119. Explanatory Report, para. 46 accessible at https://www.unidroit.org/instruments/franchising/model-law (last accessed 14/5/2018).
120. Explanatory Report, para. 46 accessible at https://www.unidroit.org/instruments/franchising/model-law (last accessed 14/5/2018).
121. Explanatory Report, para. 47, accessible at https://www.unidroit.org/instruments/franchising/model-law (last accessed 14/5/2018).
122. Explanatory Report, para. 47, accessible at https://www.unidroit.org/instruments/franchising/model-law (last accessed 14/5/2018).
123. Explanatory Report, para. 49, accessible at https://www.unidroit.org/instruments/franchising/model-law (last accessed 14/5/2018).

those situations in which the franchisor is not the owner of trademarks or distinctive signs involved, which could arise when the franchisor has designed a system in which goods are sold with particular trademarks even if the franchisor has nothing to do with their production and does not own the trademark.[124] This notion is reinforced further on in the definition where it is stated that the system designated by the franchisor 'is substantially associated with a trademark, service mark, trade name or logotype designated by the franchisor'.[125]

The related requirements in the definition provided in the Model Law, that the franchise entail a 'system designated by the franchisor ... (that) prescribes in substantial part the manner in which the franchised business is to be operated', and 'includes significant and continuing operational control by the franchisor', were included by the drafters to ensure that there exists not merely control over the use of the trademarks (that would in any event be exercised in a trademark licence) but also control over the 'very nature of the business'[126] exercised by the franchisor, enabling the franchisor to prescribe *inter alia* to the operating hours of the outlet.[127]

The nature of the control in the definition exercised by the franchisor is intended to be 'significant and continuing operational control'.[128] This requirement is intended to exclude share-holding control and to ensure 'control over certain functions'[129] thereby assuring that the definition encompasses arrangements where 'the franchisee operates the franchise following the franchise system developed by the franchisor and that the quality of the performance is the same irrespective of outlet'.[130]

§5.03 CHARACTERISTICS OF FRANCHISING[131]

A franchise agreement is a mechanism permitting the franchisor to distribute goods or services through a network of independent entities (franchisees).

It is a model that has developed over the years out of a series of business transactions and practices sharing a number of key characteristics namely:[132]

- ownership by one party of a name, idea, process or piece of equipment with the accompanying goodwill;

124. Explanatory Report, para. 51, accessible at https://www.unidroit.org/instruments/franchising/model-law (last accessed 14/5/2018).
125. Explanatory Report, para. 51, accessible at https://www.unidroit.org/instruments/franchising/model-law (last accessed 14/5/2018).
126. Explanatory Report, para. 55, accessible at https://www.unidroit.org/instruments/franchising/model-law (last accessed 14/5/2018).
127. Explanatory Report, para. 55.
128. Explanatory Report, para. 50, accessible at https://www.unidroit.org/instruments/franchising/model-law (last accessed 14/5/2018).
129. Explanatory Report, para. 50, accessible at https://www.unidroit.org/instruments/franchising/model-law (last accessed 14/5/2018).
130. Explanatory Report, para. 50, accessible at https://www.unidroit.org/instruments/franchising/model-law (last accessed 14/5/2018).
131. Mendelsohn 2004, Chapter 1.
132. Mendelsohn 1979, Chapter 1.

- the grant of a licence for exploitation of the same by the owner to another party (the licensee);
- the inclusion of directions within the licensing agreement governing the operation of the business in the conduct of which the licensee exploits his rights under the licensing agreement; and
- the payment by the licensee of a royalty or other consideration for the rights extended under the licensing agreement.

These same features characterise every single franchise transaction. In addition to the four elements described above, with a franchise a fifth element is present, which is the presence of a continuing relationship between the franchisor and the franchisee consisting of the franchisee receiving the full and ongoing support of a comprehensive range of expert know-how in the running of the operation.[133]

Under a franchise agreement, the franchisee is:

- allowed to offer goods or services to the public using a business model developed by the franchisor under the trade name, trademark, service mark or other form of branding developed and owned by the franchisor; and
- provided with a range of services furnished by the franchisor which are intended to ensure as best as possible that the franchisee enjoys the same level of success as the franchisor, such services including selection of trading sites, training in the operation of the business model, the provision of know-how and other trade secrets, and provided with ongoing support from the franchisor (which usually includes operational support, marketing support, research and development).[134]

From the point of view of the franchisee, the franchisor:

- supplies specialised knowledge and experience;
- provides initial training and support and ongoing assistance and back-up;
- furnishes 'the benefit of a name and reputation (a brand image) and goodwill which are already well established in the mind and eye of the consumer';[135] and
- promotes the trademark, service mark or trade name.[136]

From the point of view of the franchisor, the franchisee:

- supplies the capital investment and the manpower;
- takes on the vast majority of the capital risk;
- takes charge of the day-to-day running of the business;
- provides entrepreneurial commitment; and

133. Mendelsohn 1979: 4.
134. Mendelsohn 1992: 3.
135. Mendelsohn 2004: 48.
136. Mendelsohn 2004: 48–51.

- furnishes on-site management and local knowledge.[137]

The term 'franchising' is used to describe *inter alia* the dealer appointed by the car manufacturer and the petrol station owner appointed by the oil company. As an operational tool, franchising is used in many industries amongst them fast-food retailing, hotels, video rental stores and cinema chains.

The difference between a franchisee and any other party establishing a business is the presence of pre-opening training and an external entity which assumes responsibility for the provision of ongoing training, support and guidance.

From the point of view of the franchisor, a franchise is distinct from a branch. A branch invariably involves dealing with a branch manager with all the problems associated with operating a branch in terms of motivation, control and responsibility. A franchise involves dealing with a business owner (franchisee).[138] The motivation, control and responsibility of the franchisee are rarely going to be an issue from the point of view of the franchisor.

Many of the difficulties associated with creating and running a business (lack of capital, a bad business concept, a poor trading position, lack of specialised know-how, failure to pinpoint risks and so on) should not typically be present in a franchising operation. The knowledge of the franchisor should ensure that these difficulties are pre-empted and addressed[139] through the pre-opening training and ongoing support structure.

§5.04 ADVANTAGES ASSOCIATED WITH FRANCHISING

[A] Advantages Associated with Franchising from the Stance of the Franchisee

In contrast with an employment relationship, franchising allows for profit-sharing between the contracting parties, coupled with considerable autonomy on the part of the franchisee who enjoys the freedom to make decisions about the running of the franchise.[140]

[1] Turnkey Solution[141]

The franchisee does not need to expend time, money and effort developing a presence in a market nor does it need to assume risk.[142] In fact the franchisee is entering into a

137. Mendelsohn 2004: 40–2.
138. Mendelsohn 1979: 12.
139. Mendelsohn 1979: 13.
140. Mathewson et al 1985: 503.
141. UNIDROIT Guide 2007, 252.
142. UNIDROIT Guide 2007, 252.

business with an established trademark or trade name. In other words, the franchisee will already have a potential clientele.[143]

[2] Failure Risk[144]

The failure risk will be lower when compared to that associated with a traditional business[145] though the maturity of the franchise system is vital in this context. Maturity is the result of the experience acquired by the franchisor in testing the system and operating the network.[146]

[3] Training[147]

Of particular note is the provision of training at the beginning of the relationship in order to enhance the efficiency of the franchisee's operations and thereafter in order to keep the franchisee informed of new developments as well as to help the franchisee solve problems that it encounters in the running of the business.[148] Certain larger franchisors will offer a 24-hour support and assistance service to their network of franchisees.[149]

[4] Marketing, Advertising and Public Relations

Marketing, advertising and public relations are typically coordinated by the franchisor to ensure that a common image of the network is promoted.[150] National campaigns are usually the responsibility of the franchisor on behalf of the whole franchise network with the cost being borne by all the members of the network.[151] Local advertising is typically the responsibility of the local franchisee or franchisees.[152]

[5] Preferential Rates for Bulk Buying[153]

Preferential rates for bulk buying are oftentimes offered to franchisees.[154]

143. UNIDROIT Guide 2007, 252.
144. UNIDROIT Guide 2007, 253.
145. UNIDROIT Guide 2007, 253.
146. UNIDROIT Guide 2007, 253.
147. UNIDROIT Guide 2007, 253.
148. UNIDROIT Guide 2007, 253.
149. UNIDROIT Guide 2007, 253.
150. UNIDROIT Guide 2007, 253.
151. UNIDROIT Guide 2007, 253.
152. UNIDROIT Guide 2007, 253.
153. UNIDROIT Guide 2007, 253.
154. UNIDROIT Guide 2007, 253.

[B] Advantages Associated with Franchising from the Stance of the Franchisor

Franchising emerges as an efficient organisational form in some settings as it helps minimise agency costs (including monitoring) whilst permitting franchisees to capitalise on their knowledge of the local markets 'to produce local services efficiently to the mutual benefit of the franchisor and franchisee'.[155]

[1] Reduction of Risk[156]

The prospect of expanding its business over a relatively short period of time without the franchisor needing to invest capital as the funds are provided by the franchisee.[157]

[2] Financial Incentive[158]

The franchisor will usually receive remuneration from the franchisee.[159]

[3] Access to Smaller and More Complex Markets[160]

By relying on the franchisees' knowledge of the market and local regulation, the franchisor is able to gain access to smaller and more complex markets.[161]

[4] No Liability[162]

No liability will typically be borne by the franchisor for the acts or omissions of the franchisee since these are deemed to be distinct entities.[163]

[5] Motivation and Business Acumen[164]

The franchisor will be relying on the motivation and business acumen of the franchisees who as business owners will be motivated to generate a profit and to use their business acumen in doing so.[165]

155. Mathewson et al 1985: 505.
156. UNIDROIT Guide 2007, 254.
157. UNIDROIT Guide 2007, 254.
158. UNIDROIT Guide 2007, 254.
159. UNIDROIT Guide 2007, 254.
160. UNIDROIT Guide 2007, 254.
161. UNIDROIT Guide 2007, 254.
162. UNIDROIT Guide 2007, 254.
163. UNIDROIT Guide 2007, 254.
164. UNIDROIT Guide 2007, 254.
165. UNIDROIT Guide 2007, 254.

Businesses, other than sole traders, entail a relationship between a principal, and the individuals hired by the principal (agents) who provide a service or produce or distribute goods on behalf of their principal.[166] Since the interests of the principal and agents will not always coincide, a costly management structure typically needs to be introduced to address the risk of underperformance by agents.[167]

Franchising helps mitigate the need for such a system of management by replacing the need for oversight with powerful financial incentives, namely the benefit of profits gained, and the risk of loss of capital invested in the venture.[168] Franchising creates a synergy between the franchisee and franchisor in turn reducing the need for monitoring and increasing the probability for optimal performance by the franchisee.[169]

[6] Motivation of Staff[170]

As staffing and supervision of personnel are the responsibility of the franchisee they will possess the tools needed to select staff with care, to train and supervise personnel and to motivate members of the workforce which will in turn result in increased productivity.[171]

§5.05 DISADVANTAGES ASSOCIATED WITH FRANCHISING[172]

[A] Disadvantages Associated with Franchising from the Stance of the Franchisee

[1] Lack of Autonomy[173]

The franchisee is not entirely independent and is not accordingly in a position to make decisions regarding the policy, the strategy and the operations for its business.[174] Key decisions are either exclusively made by the franchisor or jointly with the network of franchisees.[175] As such the professionalism and responsiveness of the franchisor are critical from the point of view of the franchisee.[176]

166. Abell 2013: 27.
167. Abell 2013: 27.
168. Abell 2013: 27.
169. Abell 2013: 27.
170. UNIDROIT Guide 2007, 254.
171. UNIDROIT Guide 2007, 254.
172. UNIDROIT Guide 2007, 253.
173. UNIDROIT Guide 2007, 253.
174. UNIDROIT Guide 2007, 253.
175. UNIDROIT Guide 2007, 253.
176. UNIDROIT Guide 2007, 253.

[2] Lack of Control[177]

Excessive control may be exercised by the franchisor which will probably become an issue once the franchisee is starting to understand the business and to form its own views on the running of the business.[178]

[3] Lack of Guarantees

The franchise is granted for a fixed period which is usually renewable. Notwithstanding this fact there is no absolute guarantee of renewal.[179] As such the franchisee may spend time, money and effort building up a business whilst at the same time undertaking the risk associated with establishing a business only to see it being taken over by the franchisor at the end of the fixed term.[180]

As it is difficult to estimate the financial return on the business, the franchisee is bearing a substantial risk at least initially.[181] This is compounded by the fact that if the business fails the franchisee will lose the entirety of its investment.[182]

[4] Problems with the Franchisor

During the term of the franchise, the franchisee may become dissatisfied with the level of service,[183] with the quality of support[184] and with the marketing and promotional activities furnished by the franchisor.[185] Moreover communication between the franchisee and the franchisor's staff may be poor,[186] and the behaviour of the franchisor may be viewed by the franchisee as autocratic.[187]

In circumstances where the franchise is not sufficiently developed, the franchisee may come to believe that the franchisor has failed to execute comprehensive pilot tests of the operations.[188]

All in all the franchisee may consider that the level of success of the business falls short of the level of success the franchisee had expected.[189]

177. UNIDROIT Guide 2007, 254.
178. UNIDROIT Guide 2007, 254.
179. UNIDROIT Guide 2007, 254.
180. UNIDROIT Guide 2007, 254.
181. UNIDROIT Guide 2007, 254.
182. UNIDROIT Guide 2007, 254.
183. Mendelsohn 2004, 154.
184. Mendelsohn 2004, 154.
185. Mendelsohn 2004, 155.
186. Mendelsohn 2004, 155.
187. Mendelsohn 2004, 155.
188. Mendelsohn 2004, 154.
189. Mendelsohn 2004, 155.

[B] Disadvantages Associated with Franchising from the Stance of the Franchisor[190]

[1] Domino Effect[191]

If the franchisee causes damage due to its acts or omissions the damage suffered by the franchisor and the whole of the franchise network will be substantial impacting on profitability, image and goodwill.[192]

[2] Relative Limited Control[193]

The control that a franchisor will have over the units will be substantially lower than the control it would have if these units were owned by it.[194]

In such a context, the franchisor may have limited control over the franchisee and may encounter difficulties ensuring the franchisee adheres to requisite operational standards.[195] The franchisee may be unwilling to pay fees due and may fail to file its reports.[196] Moreover the franchisee may be unwilling to improve its premises and may be reticent about making changes to its systems and its operations when required to do so by the franchisor.[197]

All in all the business of the franchisee may not meet the expectations of the franchisor.[198]

[3] Potential for a Mutiny[199]

There is a risk of the franchisees acting in concert against the franchisor.[200] There is also a risk of the franchisees breaking away and establishing a competing business venture or ventures.[201]

[4] Erosion[202]

Reticence on the part of a franchisee to modernise its premises and equipment may erode the reputation and goodwill associated with the franchise.[203]

190. UNIDROIT Guide 2007, 255.
191. UNIDROIT Guide 2007, 255.
192. UNIDROIT Guide 2007, 255.
193. UNIDROIT Guide 2007, 255.
194. UNIDROIT Guide 2007, 255.
195. Mendelsohn 2004, 154.
196. Mendelsohn 2004, 155.
197. Mendelsohn 2004, 155.
198. Mendelsohn 2004, 155.
199. UNIDROIT Guide 2007, 255.
200. UNIDROIT Guide 2007, 255.
201. UNIDROIT Guide 2007, 255.
202. UNIDROIT Guide 2007, 255.
203. UNIDROIT Guide 2007, 255.

[5] A Lower Return[204]

The return is lower when compared with that of an integrated unit.[205] The potential returns made using a branch or subsidiary are likely to be higher than those associated with a franchise.[206]

§5.06 CATEGORIES OF FRANCHISE AGREEMENTS

[A] Overview

According to Martin Mendelsohn, franchising 'is not an industry; it is a method of marketing goods and services which knows almost no boundaries in terms of business categories'.[207] Though many transactions are described as franchises, each has a different application.[208]

[1] Types of Franchise Arrangements

Franchises may be classified in a variety of ways, as the following classifications demonstrate.

Franchises are often classified into three categories:[209]

(1) Industrial franchises that concern the production of goods and consist of manufacture under licence agreements containing trademarks, patents and technology grants.
(2) Distribution franchises that concern the sale of goods.
(3) Service franchises that concern the supply of services.

On occasion, a different categorisation is used which classifies franchise agreements into:[210]

- Product distribution franchises that involve the franchisee selling goods produced or supplied by the franchisor using the franchisor's trademark in exchange for payment of fees and often an assurance from the franchisee that it will only sell the products produced or supplied by the franchisor.
- Total business franchises (also known as the business format franchises) that involve the right to use a specific business format.

204. UNIDROIT Guide 2007, 255.
205. UNIDROIT Guide 2007, 255.
206. UNIDROIT Guide 2007, 255.
207. Mendelsohn 2004: 1.
208. Mendelsohn 2004: 3.
209. UNIDROIT Guide to International Master Franchise Arrangements (2nd Edition) Published by International Institute for the Unification of Private Law (UNIDROIT) ISBN 88-86449-16-X (UNIDROIT Guide 2007), 1.
210. UNIDROIT Guide 2007, 1.

[2] *Different Levels of Service*

In addition to the different classifications of franchises, a franchisor may offer different levels of service under the auspices of the franchise. A number of these structures will be considered in the section that follows.

[B] Types of Franchise Arrangements: Total Business Franchise[211]

The main type of franchise is the total business franchise.[212]

This form of franchise which 'is increasingly coming to symbolise franchising as a whole'[213] involves not only 'the exploitation of goods identified by a trademark or services identified by a service mark, but the preparation of a 'blueprint' for the successful way of carrying on a business in all its aspects'.[214]

In a total business franchise a party develops a complete method for founding and operating a business and grants licences to others to trade using the same particular business method.[215]

The total business franchise concept entails the exploitation of the goods or services identifiable by a trademark, trade name, service mark or other brand name developed and owned by the franchisor, and the sale of the blueprint of how to successfully operate the business.[216]

In this context, the franchisor will have paved the way so to speak for the franchisee by preparing and by smoothing the way for the franchisee through the formulation of a blueprint.[217][218]

This blueprint developed by the franchisor aims to reduce the risks typically associated with the creation of a new business[219] by addressing all aspects of the business including the parameters used for the selection of sites for the positioning of the business, the training of parties buying the business in the business methods used to distinguish it from other similar businesses as well as the training of parties in the methods of marketing.[220]

211. Reviewed in Mendelsohn (2004: 3–5).
212. Mendelsohn 2004: 3.
213. UNIDROIT Guide 2007, 1.
214. Mendelsohn 2004: 3.
215. Mendelsohn 1979: 3.
216. Mendelsohn 2004: 4–5.
217. Mendelsohn 2004: 4.
218. 'The seller of the blueprint (the franchisor) will have prepared and smoothed the way for a person (the franchisee), who invariably has never previously owned or operated a business of his own, not only with a predetermined and established format, but with the backing of an organization which would not otherwise be available to him at a cost which makes economic sense.' (Mendelsohn 2004: 4).
219. Mendelsohn 2004: 4.
220. Mendelsohn 2004: 3–4.

The party acquiring this franchise will obtain the blueprint developed by the franchisor coupled with the continuing support of the franchisor and in return the franchisee will pay the franchisor a fee or other consideration.[221]

The franchisor will typically supply the franchisee with the requisite know-how and training to enable the franchisee to make use of the said know-how.[222] Moreover in many cases the franchisor will provide the franchisee with a detailed manual containing all the instructions required for the running of the business.[223]

Formulation of the blueprint is executed with care by the prospective franchisor in a bid to mitigate the risks associated with the launch of a new business.[224] In this context, the criteria for the selection of sites for the positioning of the business are tested (these criteria are formulated 'by reference to the availability of potential customers within a given marketing area'[225]) as are the facilities for the training of franchisees.[226]

In a total business franchise, five key features are present.[227] First, ownership of a trademark, trade name and business system by the franchisor. Second, the grant of a licence by the franchisor to the franchisee in order to permit the latter to exploit the trademark, trade name and business system owned by the franchisor. Third, the inclusion of provisions controlling and regulating the manner in which the franchisee exploits the rights granted in the context of the operation of the business. Fourth, the payment of a fee or other consideration in exchange for the grant of rights and the provision of services by the franchisor to the franchisee. Finally, the provision of ongoing support in order to ensure that the franchisee has access to continuing expert advice and support in the operation of his business (this takes the form of 'the "head office organization" of the franchisor[228]').

Whilst the obligations and rights of the parties in the context of the total business franchise may differ depending on the needs of the parties, the law governing the parties and the agreement as well as the subject-matter of the agreement, such arrangements have certain common underlying features:[229]

- The franchisor has perfected a business system and decides to grant one or more entities the right to exploit this business system.
- The franchisor and franchisee are distinct entities (natural or legal) that are legally and financially separate.
- The franchisee invests capital and assumes the totality of the risk associated with the grant under the franchise.

221. Mendelsohn 2004: 4–5.
222. UNIDROIT Guide 2007, 1-2.
223. UNIDROIT Guide 2007, 1-2.
224. Mendelsohn 2004: 3.
225. Mendelsohn 2004: 3.
226. Mendelsohn 2004: 4.
227. Mendelsohn 2004: 4-5.
228. Mendelsohn 2004: 5.
229. UNIDROIT Guide to International Master Franchise Arrangements (2nd Edition) Published by International Institute for the Unification of Private Law (UNIDROIT) ISBN 88-86449-16-X (UNIDROIT Guide 2007), 249.

- The franchisee is granted the right to use and to exploit the property of the franchisor, its know-how, trade secrets, trademarks, patents and other intellectual property.
- The franchisee commits itself to adhering to the business method developed by the franchisor.
- The franchisee promises to compensate the franchisor for the grant. Such compensation takes the form of an entrance fee and/or continuing fees which are typically a percentage of the turnover.
- The franchisor has a right of supervision over the operations of the franchisee in order to observe the manner in which the franchisee gives effect to the franchise system.
- The franchisor typically commits itself to providing the franchisee with continuing training and support.

Additional commitments will be included within the franchise agreements or in agreements that supplement the franchise agreement:[230]

- The grant of territorial exclusivity in other words an undertaking by the franchisor not to grant other franchises or not to engage in the franchised business itself within the assigned territory. In the alternative, the franchisor may reserve itself the right to sell or distribute goods which are the subject-matter of the franchise and to thus compete directly or indirectly with the franchisee.[231]
- The grant of product exclusivity in other words an undertaking by the franchisee to sell the franchisor's products exclusively.[232]
- A commitment from the franchisee to buy products sold or utilised in the franchise exclusively from the franchisor or its approved suppliers or its recommended suppliers.[233]
- The provision of an indicative price list to the franchisee pertaining to the goods sold or services provided by the franchisee. Such a list may give rise to competition law concerns as a type of price fixing thus care should be taken when using such a list.[234]
- The provision of equipment by the franchisor to the franchisee for use in the operations of the franchisee under the franchise agreement.[235]
- The provision of premises owned or leased by the franchisor to the franchisee for use by the franchisee. As such, the franchisor will be leasing or subleasing these premises to the franchisee.[236]

230. UNIDROIT Guide 2007, 249-250.
231. UNIDROIT Guide 2007, 250-251.
232. UNIDROIT Guide 2007, 250.
233. UNIDROIT Guide 2007, 250.
234. UNIDROIT Guide 2007, 250.
235. UNIDROIT Guide 2007, 250.
236. UNIDROIT Guide 2007, 250.

- In order to ensure that the premises of the franchisee conform with the other units in the network, the franchisor may provide the franchisee with decorating tips, instruction or assistance regarding the interior decoration of the unit or units run by the franchisee.[237]
- A franchisor may aid the franchisee in sourcing of finance.[238]
- The franchisor may centralise certain administrative functions such as accounting for the entire franchise network.[239]
- A franchisor may provide the franchisee with market studies about the community in which the prospective unit is to be located with an estimate of the prospects of success and of the likely revenue (earning claim).[240]
- An undertaking by the franchisee to adhere to standards and/or procedures stipulated by the franchisor.[241]
- An undertaking by the franchisee not to engage in competing activities during and after the duration of the franchise.[242]
- An undertaking by the franchisee not to disclose confidential information to unauthorised third parties such as operational information, trade secrets and know-how.[243]
- A right to control an adherence by the franchisee to standards set under the franchise.[244]
- A right to terminate the franchise for a failure on the part of the franchisee to adhere to the standards set.[245]

In order to ensure that members of the franchise network have the benefit of a common image vis-à-vis consumers, the franchisor will preserve itself certain protective measures that permit it to oversee the quality of the goods or services offered by the franchisee. As such the franchisor may insist on inspection and auditing provisions enabling the franchisor to inspect the franchise outlet and sample any goods sold at the outlet (respectively).

[C] Structuring International Franchises

Cross-border franchising may be done using a variety of mechanisms.[246]

237. UNIDROIT Guide 2007, 250.
238. UNIDROIT Guide 2007, 250.
239. UNIDROIT Guide 2007, 250.
240. UNIDROIT Guide 2007, 251.
241. UNIDROIT Guide 2007, 251.
242. UNIDROIT Guide 2007, 251.
243. UNIDROIT Guide 2007, 251.
244. UNIDROIT Guide 2007, 251.
245. UNIDROIT Guide 2007, 251.
246. UNIDROIT Guide 2007, 11.

[1] Company-Owned Operations

When looking to enter a foreign market a business may decide to establish and to maintain company-owned operations.[247]

Such a strategy requires manpower and outlay and as such may not necessarily be a viable option for certain businesses.[248] Moreover such a strategy may prove to be a major drain on the resources of the business.[249]

However should the resources be available to pursue such a strategy, the business will be able to use this mechanism as the basis for the establishment of a franchise network in the target market[250] and may be able to use the experience that it gains to select potential franchisees.[251]

[2] Direct Franchises

Direct franchises involve the franchisor contracting directly with each franchisee in the target market.[252]

Several problems may arise in such a context. First the distance between the franchisor and the franchisee may mean that the provision of services is difficult.[253] Second the franchisor's lack of familiarity with the target market may mean that the franchisor fails to identify the differences between its home market and the target market.[254]

[3] Area Development Agreements

An area development agreement is a type of direct franchise, which entails an agreement between the franchisor and a developer in the target market.[255] Pursuant to this agreement, the developer may be charged with establishing an agreed number of units within a set period of time in the assigned territory.[256] Franchisors may appoint one or more developers in the assigned territory.[257]

In this context, the franchisor benefits from having to deal with fewer franchisees and from the existence of a direct relationship with the appointed franchisees.[258] The shortfalls in this context include the fact that the franchisor will be reliant on one developer or a small number of developers, which may be a risky strategy for the franchisor if the businesses of the developers fail or do not do as successful as the

247. Mendelsohn 2004, 260.
248. Mendelsohn 2004, 260.
249. Further discussion can be found in the Starbucks' case study at the end of this chapter.
250. Mendelsohn 2004, 260.
251. Mendelsohn 2004, 260.
252. Mendelsohn 2004, 261.
253. Mendelsohn 2004, 261.
254. Mendelsohn 2004, 261.
255. Mendelsohn 2004, 262.
256. Mendelsohn 2004, 262.
257. Mendelsohn 2004, 262.
258. Mendelsohn 2004, 262.

franchisor had expected.[259] Also if there exists a problem in the relationship between the franchisor and the developer the fallout may be significant.[260] There is also a risk that the dissatisfied developers may more easily group together to challenge the franchisor.[261] In circumstances where the developer is established this could lead to clashes in the working cultures of the franchisor and the developer.[262]

[4] Master Franchise[263]

According to data collated, master franchise agreements are the most common franchise agreement used in cross-border transactions.[264]

A master franchise is an arrangement entailing the grant of a right by the franchisor to another (the sub-franchisor or the master franchisee).[265] Such arrangements may be domestic or international.[266] Under the terms of such an agreement, the sub-franchisor will be entrusted with opening its own units or with sub-franchising.[267] A sub-franchisor may be entrusted with pilot-testing its own outlet or outlets.[268]

Such a grant is 'in most cases exclusive, to grant franchises to sub-franchisees within a certain territory (such as a country) and/or to open franchise outlets itself'.[269] In this set-up the sub-franchisor effectively acts as franchisor in the target territory.[270] In consideration the sub-franchisor pays the franchisor for this right.[271] Such compensation usually takes the form of an initial fee and/or ongoing royalties that usually take the form of a percentage of the income generated by the sub-franchisor from the sub-franchised outlets.[272] The structure of the compensation package 'will vary from country to country and from franchise to franchise.[273]'

Master franchise arrangements entail two agreements, one between the franchisor and the sub-franchisor (the master franchise agreement) and the other between the sub-franchisor and each of the sub-franchisees (the sub-franchise agreement).[274]

In the main there will be no direct contractual relationship between the franchisor and sub-franchisees.[275] It is effectively, the sub-franchisor who owes duties to

259. Mendelsohn 2004, 262.
260. Mendelsohn 2004, 262.
261. Mendelsohn 2004, 263.
262. Mendelsohn 2004, 263.
263. UNIDROIT Guide to International Master Franchise Arrangements (2nd Edition) Published by International Institute for the Unification of Private Law (UNIDROIT) ISBN 88-86449-16-X (UNIDROIT Guide 2007).
264. UNIDROIT Guide 2007, 2.
265. UNIDROIT Guide 2007, 2.
266. UNIDROIT Guide 2007, 3.
267. Mendelsohn 2004, 263.
268. Mendelsohn 2004, 263.
269. UNIDROIT Guide 2007, 2.
270. UNIDROIT Guide 2007, 2.
271. UNIDROIT Guide 2007, 2.
272. UNIDROIT Guide 2007, 2-3.
273. UNIDROIT Guide 2007, 3.
274. UNIDROIT Guide 2007, 3.
275. UNIDROIT Guide 2007, 3.

sub-franchisees, as franchisor in the territory, and who takes charge of enforcement under the sub-franchise, as well as assuming responsibility for the general development and management of the network in the assigned territory.[276]

In circumstances where the sub-franchisee fails to meet its obligations, it is the duty of the sub-franchisor to intervene.[277] As such the franchisor will not usually have the right to take direct action to secure compliance by sub-franchisees though the franchisor may be able to sue the sub-franchisor for non-performance if the sub-franchisor has not fulfilled its obligation to enforce the sub-franchise agreements.[278]

In exceptional circumstances, a direct contractual relationship may be established between the franchisor and the sub-franchisee/s.

[a] *Benefits Associated with Master Franchise Agreements*

[i] Benefits Associated with Master Franchise Agreements from the Point of View of the Franchisor

Beyond the fact that the master franchise allows the franchisor to delegate responsibility for daily supervision of sub-franchisees to the sub-franchisor,[279] the master franchise provides a set-up that allows the franchisor to develop a network without incurring the costs associated with foreign direct investment and[280] to rely on the expertise of the sub-franchisor and indirectly the sub-franchisees (their knowledge of the market and national regulation, their distribution network, their capacity to market and occasionally their ability to engage in the provision of after-sales services).[281] Moreover, the franchisor will also have a direct relationship with the sub-franchisor.[282]

This arrangement is especially important bearing in mind the geographic distances involved.[283] The proximity of the sub-franchisor to the designated territory will also enable it to oversee and control performance by the sub-franchisees.[284]

[ii] Benefits Associated with Master Franchise Agreements from the Points of View of the Sub-franchisors and the Sub-franchisees

Sub-franchisors and sub-franchisees will benefit from the franchisor's investment in the development of its unique business model[285] ('a well-known and tested business

276. UNIDROIT Guide 2007, 3.
277. UNIDROIT Guide 2007, 3.
278. UNIDROIT Guide 2007, 3.
279. Mendelsohn 2004, 263.
280. UNIDROIT Guide 2007, 4.
281. UNIDROIT Guide 2007, 4.
282. Mendelsohn 2004, 263.
283. UNIDROIT Guide 2007, 4.
284. UNIDROIT Guide 2007, 4.
285. UNIDROIT Guide 2007, 4.

concept[286]') and on occasion the investment made in the development of technical know-how that accompanies the franchise.[287]

[b] *Concerns Associated with Master Franchise Agreements*

Certain concerns are associated with master franchise agreements from the stance of the different parties.

[i] Concerns Associated with Master Franchise Agreements from the Franchisor's Point of View

- Limited control over the franchise network

The franchisor is heavily reliant on the sub-franchisor due to the distance between the country of the franchisor and the territory within which the network is established, the fact that the establishment, supervision and control of the franchise network and the trademarks is entrusted to the sub-franchisor and the fact that there is no direct contractual relationship between the franchisor and the sub-franchisees.[288]

These concerns may accordingly impede the ability of the franchisor to oversee and control performance of the operations of the various units.[289] This effectively means that the franchisor is 'obliged to rely on the sub-franchisor to enforce the sub-franchise agreements and to ensure that its rights, such as intellectual property rights, are not infringed upon'.[290]

Though the sub-franchisor is likely to be as interested in enforcing the obligations as the franchisor due to a desire to guarantee the proper functioning of the network and the protection of licensed IP, there is no guarantee that the sub-franchisor will execute its obligations in an effective manner.

In this context the franchisor should verify that the sub-franchisor is competent[291] and should check and monitor the quality of:[292]

- the sub-franchisor's procedures for selection of sub-franchisees and sites;
- the training provided to sub-franchisees; and
- the support provided to sub-franchisees.

Moreover, the franchisor should establish and maintain channels of communication between it and the sub-franchisees.[293] With this in mind, the franchisor should endeavour to:

286. UNIDROIT Guide 2007, 4.
287. UNIDROIT Guide 2007, 5.
288. UNIDROIT Guide 2007, 5.
289. UNIDROIT Guide 2007, 5.
290. UNIDROIT Guide 2007, 5.
291. Mendelsohn 2004, 263.
292. Mendelsohn 2004, 263.
293. Mendelsohn 2004, 263.

- attend meetings organised by the sub-franchisor;
- convene annual meetings for sub-franchisees; and
- visit the sub-franchisees' premises.

Although caution should be exercised in this context by the franchisor to ensure that it does not undermine the position of the sub-franchisor.

- Difficulties ending the master franchise

The difficulties associated with terminating the master franchise arise from the impact such an action would have on the sub-franchisees that derive their rights from the master franchise agreement.[294]

- Financial return

The financial return of the franchisor under the master franchise agreement will be considerably lower than in the context of a direct franchise.

One of the key features associated with a master franchise is 'the sharing of the income'.[295] The initial franchise fees will be shared between the franchisor and the sub-franchisor as will royalty fees.[296] Occasionally, the franchisor's initial and ongoing investments (especially the continued provision of support to the sub-franchisor to ensure the viability of the franchise network) are not adequately compensated for.[297]

[ii] Concerns Associated with Master Franchise Agreements from the Stance of the Sub-franchisor

The uncertainty borne by the sub-franchisor who will not know with certainty whether the master franchise agreement will be renewed once it comes to the end of the term.[298]

The share of the revenue generated may not necessarily be sufficient to compensate the sub-franchisor for its investment in the development of the franchise network and its ongoing expenditure associated with administering the network.[299]

[D] Different Levels of Service

A franchisor may offer different levels of service under the auspices of the franchise. In this context the franchise may take a number of forms:

- The turnkey franchise
- Equipment package
- Equipment purchasing

294. UNIDROIT Guide 2007, 6.
295. UNIDROIT Guide 2007, 7.
296. UNIDROIT Guide 2007, 7.
297. UNIDROIT Guide 2007, 8.
298. UNIDROIT Guide 2007, 7.
299. UNIDROIT Guide 2007, 7.

- Equipment leasing
- Future obligation to buy.

[1] Turnkey Franchise

Franchisors may buy the premises as well as shopfitting and equipping these premises ready for commencement of business.[300] Franchisees will typically contract to pay in stages if the works of the franchisor are still ongoing.[301]

[2] Equipment Package

A franchisor may offer to sell the franchisee all the items of equipment required by the franchisee for installation in the premises.[302]

[3] Equipment Purchasing

A franchisor may furnish the franchisee with details of the specifications and the plans so that the franchisee can arrange for the shopfitting itself.[303] In such situations the franchisor may supply a list of branded equipment or a list of approved equipment for use by the franchisee.[304]

[4] Equipment Leasing

In order to reduce the cost of the initial package the franchisor may offer to lease equipment to the franchisee in which case the franchisor may receive a commission from the leasing company.[305]

In situations where the equipment is patented, the franchisor will lease it to the franchisee, as the franchisor will be reluctant to sell such equipment to the franchisee.[306]

§5.07 DISTINGUISHING FRANCHISES FROM OTHER COMMERCIAL ARRANGEMENTS[307]

The elements associated with franchise agreements may cause them to be identified with other categories of agreement especially in countries where no dedicated legislation is available to specifically address franchises.[308]

300. Mendelsohn 2004, 136.
301. Mendelsohn 2004, 136.
302. Mendelsohn 2004, 137.
303. Mendelsohn 2004, 136.
304. Mendelsohn 2004, 137.
305. Mendelsohn 2004, 137.
306. Mendelsohn 2004, 138.
307. UNIDROIT Guide 2007, 8 onwards.
308. UNIDROIT Guide 2007, 8.

In certain jurisdictions, the courts have applied legislation adopted for commercial agents and other arrangements by way of analogy to franchise agreements.[309]

[A] Distinguishing Franchising and Agency[310]

A franchisee deriving his rights from the grant in the franchise agreement is an entity that is distinct from the franchisor. Each of the two entities invests in their own right assuming risk in their own name.[311]

In contrast, an agent is granted authority by a principal and though the agent and principal are distinct, the agent acts on behalf of the principal.[312] For example, the agent may solicit clients, orders and occasionally engage in negotiations on behalf of the principal.[313]

Due to the fact that the agent represents the principal and has authority to act in the place of the principal, the agent may render the principal liable.[314]

In principle this is not the case where a franchise arrangement exists, as the franchisee does not represent the franchisor, has no authority to act for the franchisor and is generally incapable of rendering the franchisor liable.[315] Though caution should be exercised in this context by ensuring the inclusion of suitable provision in the franchise agreement stating clearly that the relationship between the parties is not intended to be that of agent and principal.

[B] Distinguishing Franchise from Distribution[316]

Whilst distribution and franchising arrangements may share certain common features, these arrangements are distinct.[317]

Whilst a vendor and purchaser relationship may be present in a franchise relationship, the franchise agreement will also include a licensing component (licensing of a trademark, a service mark, know-how and so forth) coupled with an agreement to furnish services in the form of training, support and assistance.[318]

Having said this on occasion depending on the definition of franchising used there is scope for overlap between a franchising arrangement and distribution arrangement. In a distribution set-up, a distributor may have limited use of the intellectual property of the manufacturer for the duration of the agreement (e.g., use of a trademark in the marketing and sale of goods produced under the distribution agreement) coupled

309. UNIDROIT Guide 2007, 8.
310. The agency relationship is reviewed in detail in Chapter 5, Meiselles, Michala (2013) *International Commercial Agreements – An Edinburgh Law Guide*, 1st ed., Edinburgh University Press.
311. UNIDROIT Guide 2007, 9.
312. UNIDROIT Guide 2007, 9.
313. UNIDROIT Guide 2007, 9.
314. UNIDROIT Guide 2007, 9.
315. UNIDROIT Guide 2007, 9.
316. The agency relationship is reviewed in detail in Chapter 4, Meiselles, Michala (2013) *International Commercial Agreements – An Edinburgh Law Guide*, 1st ed., Edinburgh University Press.
317. UNIDROIT Guide 2007, 10.
318. UNIDROIT Guide 2007, 10.

with some ongoing support. The distinction here between a franchise and distribution relationship is the presence and exercise of control that the franchisor will have over the manner in which the licensed intellectual property is exploited by the recipient of the grant.

[C] Distinguishing Franchising from Licensing

A franchise arrangement will involve supplementary features not necessarily present in a licensing arrangement.[319]

Whilst under a licence and a franchise, the licensor and the franchisor respectively will control the manner in which the licensed intellectual property is exploited by the recipient of the grant, the licensor will have 'no control over the business format or the manner in which the licensee carries on business'.[320]

The franchisor in contrast will have a wider array of powers at its disposal than a licensor, since the franchisor may exercise direct control over the business and operational aspects of the unit/s operated by the franchisee.[321]

[D] Distinguishing Franchise from Area Representative Agreements

Area representative agreements may be used in the context of franchising however such agreements are more akin to agency set-ups.[322]

Where area representation agreements are used in the context of franchising the area representative may be entrusted with the right to solicit prospective franchisees (seek, interview and makes recommendations for their suitability to the franchisor) and to exercise certain supervisory responsibilities on behalf of the franchisor (training and monitoring).[323]

The area representative is distinct from a franchisee or sub-franchisor as the area representative does not invest capital in the construction of the network and does not develop goodwill in the same way that a franchisee or sub-franchisor would, as such a franchisor cannot expect the area representative to possess the same qualities as a franchisee or a sub-franchisor.[324]

§5.08 REGULATION OF FRANCHISE ARRANGEMENTS

This section considers the practice rules developed by the EFF and enshrined within its Code, the model franchise disclosure law (produced by UNIDROIT) and the provisions governing franchise arrangements as articulated in the DCFR.

319. UNIDROIT Guide 2007, 10.
320. UNIDROIT Guide 2007, 11.
321. UNIDROIT Guide 2007, 11.
322. UNIDROIT Guide 2007, 14.
323. UNIDROIT Guide 2007, 14.
324. UNIDROIT Guide 2007, 14.

[A] EFF's Code

The founding associations of the EFF formulated a body of rules[325] contained in the EFF's Code [326] (last amended 6 December 2016). Originally written in 1972, this Code was reviewed in 1992 to reflect developments in the franchising sector, and the EU's regulatory framework.

The entire text of the Code is binding on all EFF National Franchise Association Members, and their respective memberships.[327] All EFF Member Franchise Associations have endorsed the Code, and are committed to its promotion, and implementation in their respective countries.[328]

[1] Obligations of the Franchisor

A franchisor is defined as 'the initiator and long-term guardian' of the franchise network made up of itself and its individual franchisees.[329] The franchisor is subject to certain specific obligations set out in the Code. These range from duties that are more general in scope, to those that are more specific in their remit.

[a] General Obligations Imposed on the Franchisor

Beyond its status as a 'long-term guardian' of the franchise network,[330] certain general obligations are owed by the franchisor.

In its dealings with the individual franchisees the franchisor is required to exercise both fairness and good faith.[331] This dual obligation is defined as one of an ongoing nature.[332]

Though there is no indication of whether this duty arises prior to contracting there is nothing to displace this assumption. Which would arguably mean that this twofold obligation not only applies during the term of the franchise agreement but before the agreement itself is concluded.

In particular in this context, the franchisor has a duty to advise its individual franchisees of breaches under the terms of the agreement, and where relevant to extend

325. Paragraph 9, Preamble to the European Franchise Federation Code of Ethics accessible at http://www.eff-franchise.com/Data/Code%20of%20Ethics2.pdf (last accessed 14/5/2018).
326. The Code of Ethics can be accessed at http://www.eff-franchise.com/77/regulation.html (last accessed 14/5/2018).
327. Paragraph 2, Preamble to the European Franchise Federation Code of Ethics accessible at http://www.eff-franchise.com/Data/Code%20of%20Ethics2.pdf (last accessed 14/5/2018).
328. Paragraph 2, Preamble to the European Franchise Federation Code of Ethics accessible at http://www.eff-franchise.com/Data/Code%20of%20Ethics2.pdf (last accessed 14/5/2018).
329. Article 2.1, European Franchise Federation Code of Ethics accessible at http://www.eff-franchise.com/Data/Code%20of%20Ethics2.pdf (last accessed 14/5/2018).
330. Article 2.1, European Franchise Federation Code of Ethics accessible at http://www.eff-franchise.com/Data/Code%20of%20Ethics2.pdf (last accessed 14/5/2018).
331. Article 2.4 (ii), European Franchise Federation Code of Ethics accessible at http://www.eff-franchise.com/Data/Code%20of%20Ethics2.pdf (last accessed 14/5/2018).
332. Article 2.4, European Franchise Federation Code of Ethics accessible at http://www.eff-franchise.com/Data/Code%20of%20Ethics2.pdf (last accessed 14/5/2018).

such franchisees the opportunity of rectifying their faults.[333] Moreover the franchisor must attempt 'to resolve complaints, grievances and disputes with good faith and goodwill through fair and reasonable direct communication and negotiation'.[334]

In addition to the exercise of fairness in its dealings with franchisees, the franchisor has an obligation to test-run the operation before establishing a franchise network by first operating the 'business concept with success in the relevant market, for *at least one year* and in at least one pilot unit'.[335] This last provision has been redrafted in order to refine the test-run period; an earlier version of this provision read – 'The Franchisor ... shall have operated a business concept with success in the relevant market, for a reasonable time and in at least one pilot unit'.[336]

Furthermore, the franchisor must either be the owner of the pertinent distinguishing identification associated with the business concept that it developed and operated (trade name, trademark and so forth), or be in possession of legal rights thereto.[337]

[b] Specific Obligations Owed by the Franchisor

Beyond the generic obligations owed by a franchisor, it owes certain supplementary duties to prospective individual franchisees in the pre-contract phase, and to selected individual franchisees during the term of the agreement.

[i] During the Pre-contract Phase

During the course of pre-contractual negotiations, certain duties are imposed on the franchisor by the rules set out in the Code.

Transparency and honesty are crucial in this context. Franchisors are accordingly required to use clear materials to promote their franchises, 'free of ambiguity and misleading statements',[338] and where these contain references to prospective revenue such information should be of an objective nature, and should not be misleading in character.[339]

333. Article 2.4, European Franchise Federation Code of Ethics accessible at http://www.eff-franchise.com/Data/Code%20of%20Ethics2.pdf (last accessed 14/5/2018).
334. Article 2.4, European Franchise Federation Code of Ethics accessible at http://www.eff-franchise.com/Data/Code%20of%20Ethics2.pdf (last accessed 14/5/2018).
335. Article 2.2, European Franchise Federation Code of Ethics accessible at http://www.eff-franchise.com/Data/Code%20of%20Ethics2.pdf (last accessed 14/5/2018) (italics added by authors).
336. Article 2.2, European Franchise Federation Code of Ethics at http://www.eff-franchise.com (accessed at 1/8/2014) (italics added by authors).
337. Article 2.2, European Franchise Federation Code of Ethics accessible at http://www.eff-franchise.com/Data/Code%20of%20Ethics2.pdf (last accessed 14/5/2018).
338. Article 3.1, European Franchise Federation Code of Ethics accessible at http://www.eff-franchise.com/Data/Code%20of%20Ethics2.pdf (last accessed 14/5/2018).
339. Article 3.2, European Franchise Federation Code of Ethics accessible at http://www.eff-franchise.com/Data/Code%20of%20Ethics2.pdf (last accessed 14/5/2018).

In order to allow for an objective assessment of the merits, and the viability of such arrangements, potential franchisees should be provided with 'full and accurate written disclosure of all information material to the franchise relationship, within a reasonable time prior to the execution of these binding documents'.[340]

Also, the prospective franchisee should be furnished with a copy of the Code, along with a 'full and accurate written disclosure of all information material to the franchise relationship, within a reasonable time prior to the execution of these binding documents'.[341]

In circumstances where a pre-contract is used by the franchisor, the latter should provide the prospective individual franchisee, that is a candidate for the franchise, with the following information in writing 'prior to the signing of any pre-contract':[342]

1. Its purpose.
2. Any consideration due to the franchisor in relation to the latter's actual expenditure incurred during, and in relation to the pre-contract phase.
3. The duration of the pre-contract.
4. Any termination rights that may arise in the context of the pre-contract.

In circumstances where the agreement is executed, and a pre-contract fee has been paid to the franchisor, the said fee should either be refunded or offset against any entry fee due from the franchisee in question.[343]

A franchisor will retain the right to impose a non-compete and/or confidentiality obligation on the prospective individual franchisee in order 'to protect its know-how and identity'.[344]

Beyond the obligation to ensure limpidity, fairness is of the essence during the pre-contractual phase. As such the franchisor should ensure that the selection and acceptance of individual franchisees are limited to 'those who, upon reasonable investigation, appear to possess the basic skills, education, personal qualities and financial resources sufficient to carry on the franchised business'.[345]

[ii] During the Term of the Agreement

Throughout the duration of the contractual relationship, a franchisor is obligated to provide individual franchisees in the franchise network not only with initial training

340. Article 3.3, European Franchise Federation Code of Ethics accessible at http://www.eff-franchise.com/Data/Code%20of%20Ethics2.pdf (last accessed 14/5/2018).
341. Article 3.3, European Franchise Federation Code of Ethics accessible at http://www.eff-franchise.com/Data/Code%20of%20Ethics2.pdf (last accessed 14/5/2018).
342. Article 3.6(i)-(ii), European Franchise Federation Code of Ethics accessible at http://www.eff-franchise.com/Data/Code%20of%20Ethics2.pdf (last accessed 14/5/2018).
343. Article 3.6(i), European Franchise Federation Code of Ethics accessible at http://www.eff-franchise.com/Data/Code%20of%20Ethics2.pdf (last accessed 14/5/2018).
344. Article 3.6(iii), European Franchise Federation Code of Ethics accessible at http://www.eff-franchise.com/Data/Code%20of%20Ethics2.pdf (last accessed 14/5/2018).
345. Article 4, European Franchise Federation Code of Ethics accessible at http://www.eff-franchise.com/Data/Code%20of%20Ethics2.pdf (last accessed 14/5/2018).

but also with ongoing support of a commercial and/or technical nature.[346] In addition the franchisor is duty-bound to grant the franchisee 'the right to use the know-how transferred and/or made available' to the franchisee,[347] and invest means (financial and human) in promotion of its brand, and in research and innovation thereby ensuring 'the long-term development and continuity' of its concept.[348]

Beyond these framework obligations, the Code also addresses the substantive terms governing the relationship between the parties. According to the Code, a franchise agreement should include *inter alia* the rights, and duties of the franchisor, and individual franchisees, the rights of the franchisor in relation to the intellectual property rights relating to the brands, signs and so forth, the payment terms applicable to the individual franchisees, the basis for renewal, the right of the individual franchisee to sell or transfer the franchised business along with the franchisor's pre-emption rights in this context, as well as the provisions governing termination and the consequences arising out of such termination.[349]

[2] Obligations of the Individual Franchisees

During the term of the agreement, the franchisee is obliged to 'devote its best endeavours to the growth of the franchise business and to the maintenance of the common identity and reputation of the franchise network',[350] to furnish the franchisor with verifiable operational information to allow for determination of performance, and any financial records needed 'for effective management guidance'.[351]

Beyond these obligations that arise during the term of the franchise agreement, the individual franchisee also owes an ongoing duty to keep confidential any information material to the franchise concept.[352] Such information is likely to include know-how granted to it by the franchisor under the terms of the franchise.

[3] Obligations Common to the Parties

Certain obligations set out in the Code are applicable to the franchisor and the franchise.

346. Article 2.2(iv), European Franchise Federation Code of Ethics accessible at http://www.eff-franchise.com/Data/Code%20of%20Ethics2.pdf (last accessed 14/5/2018).
347. Article 2.2(iv), European Franchise Federation Code of Ethics accessible at http://www.eff-franchise.com/Data/Code%20of%20Ethics2.pdf (last accessed 14/5/2018).
348. Article 2.2(ix), European Franchise Federation Code of Ethics accessible at http://www.eff-franchise.com/Data/Code%20of%20Ethics2.pdf (last accessed 14/5/2018).
349. Article 5.5, European Franchise Federation Code of Ethics accessible at http://www.eff-franchise.com/Data/Code%20of%20Ethics2.pdf (last accessed 14/5/2018).
350. Article 2.3(ii), European Franchise Federation Code of Ethics accessible at http://www.eff-franchise.com/Data/Code%20of%20Ethics2.pdf (last accessed 14/5/2018).
351. Article 2.3(v), European Franchise Federation Code of Ethics accessible at http://www.eff-franchise.com/Data/Code%20of%20Ethics2.pdf (last accessed 14/5/2018).
352. Article 2.4(iii), European Franchise Federation Code of Ethics accessible at http://www.eff-franchise.com/Data/Code%20of%20Ethics2.pdf (last accessed 14/5/2018).

Both parties are required to exercise both fairness and good faith in their dealings with each other, notify the other if there has been a breach of contract, provide each other with an opportunity to cure the breach, and 'respect the confidentiality of information material to the franchise concept provided by the one to the other'.[353]

These obligations are set out under the heading 'the ongoing obligations of both parties'.[354] Though there is no indication as to whether these duties arise prior to contracting, and after the end of term there is nothing to displace this assumption, which would arguably mean that these obligations not only apply during the term of the franchise agreement but both before the agreement is concluded, and after the agreement comes to an end.

In addition each party is required to attempt 'to resolve complaints, grievances and disputes with good faith and goodwill through fair and reasonable direct communication and negotiation'.[355]

[B] World Franchise Council

Certain analogies can be made between the rules promoted by the Council and those advocated by the EFF. Both impose obligations upon franchisors before the contract is concluded and during the course of the contractual term, and on individual franchisees during the term of the agreement.

[1] Obligations of the Franchisor

[a] During the Pre-contract Phase

During the acquisition phase the franchisor is expected to adhere to certain obligations, which are comparable to those defined by the Code.

The prospective franchisee should be provided with all the information it needs in order to determine whether it wishes to conclude a franchise agreement. Such information should be 'objective, verifiable and devoid of delusion or deceit', and should be provided within a reasonable period of time before the date set for the signing of the agreement so long as the period in question is no shorter than 7 days.[356]

Where a pre-sale contract is concluded by the franchisor and prospective franchisee (contract of reservation) then the franchisor should indicate if and when the sums paid by the prospective franchisee(s) (guarantee payment) will be reimbursed.[357]

353. Article 2.4(ii)-(iii), European Franchise Federation Code of Ethics accessible at http://www.eff-franchise.com/Data/Code%20of%20Ethics2.pdf (last accessed 14/5/2018).
354. Article 2.4, European Franchise Federation Code of Ethics accessible at http://www.eff-franchise.com/Data/Code%20of%20Ethics2.pdf (last accessed 14/5/2018).
355. Article 2.4 (iv), European Franchise Federation Code of Ethics accessible at http://www.eff-franchise.com/Data/Code%20of%20Ethics2.pdf (last accessed 14/5/2018).
356. Part 3, The World Franchise Council's Principles of Ethics dated 12 November 2001 accessible at http://www.worldfranchisecouncil.net/code-of-ethics.html (last accessed 14/5/2018).
357. Part 3, The World Franchise Council's Principles of Ethics dated 12 November 2001 accessible at http://www.worldfranchisecouncil.net/code-of-ethics.html (last accessed 14/5/2018).

The Council elaborates here on the selection, and the contracting processes by stating that any determination by the franchisor should be informed by the objective of 'achieving their common and mutual success', and should not be discriminatory in nature,[358] and indicating that the franchisor should prompt the prospective franchisee to confer with other franchisees in the network (that the prospective franchisee is seeking to join), and to seek professional advice before signing the agreement.[359]

[b] During the Term of the Agreement

The collective needs of the individual franchisees in the franchise network require franchisors to generate and preserve 'the commercial and technical know-how that supports the franchise network', and promote ongoing 'structured dialogue with the franchisees to aid the protection and development of the franchisor's know-how'.[360]

In this context, the franchisor is duty-bound to guarantee that each of the franchisees in the network adheres to its duties for the general good of the network.[361]

Akin to the Code, the rules developed by the Council aim to promote the longevity of the working relationship by stating that a franchisor should permit a franchisee to rectify breaches once notice is given to the defaulting party.[362]

[2] Obligations of the Franchisee

Whilst the Code of the EFF imposes more detailed obligations upon franchisees, the body of rules developed on behalf of the Council impose obligations upon the parties that are articulated using broader terms.

Akin to the Code of the EFF, during the term of the agreement under the Council's rules a franchisee is obliged to participate in the 'life of the network' whilst protecting the interests of the franchise network.[363] In this context, the Code of the EFF stipulates that a franchisee 'devote its best endeavours to the growth of the franchise business and to the maintenance of the common identity and reputation of the franchise network'.[364]

Whilst a franchisee must provide a franchisor with 'verifiable operating data to facilitate the determination of performance and the financial records necessary for

358. Part 3, The World Franchise Council's Principles of Ethics dated 12 November 2001 accessible at http://www.worldfranchisecouncil.net/code-of-ethics.html (last accessed 14/5/2018).
359. Part 3, The World Franchise Council's Principles of Ethics dated 12 November 2001 accessible at http://www.worldfranchisecouncil.net/code-of-ethics.html (last accessed 14/5/2018).
360. Part 4, The World Franchise Council's Principles of Ethics dated 12 November 2001 accessible at http://www.worldfranchisecouncil.net/code-of-ethics.html (last accessed 14/5/2018).
361. Part 4, The World Franchise Council's Principles of Ethics dated 12 November 2001 accessible at http://www.worldfranchisecouncil.net/code-of-ethics.html (last accessed 14/5/2018).
362. Part 4, The World Franchise Council's Principles of Ethics dated 12 November 2001 accessible at http://www.worldfranchisecouncil.net/code-of-ethics.html (last accessed 14/5/2018).
363. Part 4, The World Franchise Council's Principles of Ethics dated 12 November 2001 accessible at http://www.worldfranchisecouncil.net/code-of-ethics.html (last accessed 14/5/2018).
364. Article 2.3(ii), European Franchise Federation Code of Ethics accessible at http://www.eff-franchise.com/Data/Code%20of%20Ethics2.pdf (last accessed 14/5/2018).

effective management guidance'[365] along similar lines the rules of the Council impose a more general obligation on the franchisee to supply the franchisor 'with the operational information concerning his franchise business'.[366]

Beyond these obligations that arise during the course of the contractual engagement, the individual franchisee owes a duty of confidentiality to the franchisor that subsists during as well as after the term of the agreement.[367]

[3] Obligations Common to the Parties

Certain obligations that are common to the franchisor and franchisee are articulated in the rules of the Council.

Beyond the obligation imposed on the parties to resolve disagreements using mediation (where the dispute is litigated), and the duty to protect the interests of the consumer (in the execution of their responsibilities), the franchisor and the franchisee are required to 'co-operate in all loyalty and in respect of their mutual obligations and commitments'.[368]

Nowhere in these rules is the term 'loyalty' defined; however, arguably this term may be interpreted with the help of the principles elaborated upon within the definition of a franchise arrangement found in the introduction to these rules.

A dual commitment is elaborated upon within these principles. First, the parties share a commitment to the success of the franchise project ('The franchisor and the franchisee commit themselves reciprocally in view of their common and mutual success'[369]). Second, the parties are jointly committed to adhere to certain ethical standards ('To attain this objective, the commitments of both parties, throughout their relationship, are based on fundamental ethical principles'.[370])

[C] UNIDROIT Model Franchise Disclosure Law

[1] Introduction

Drafted by the UNIDROIT (International Institute for the Unification of Private Law) Study Group on Franchising and finalised by a Committee of Governmental Experts, convened by the organisation to examine the draft prepared by the former, the Model

365. Article 2.3 (v), European Franchise Federation Code of Ethics accessible at http://www.eff-franchise.com/Data/Code%20of%20Ethics2.pdf (last accessed 14/5/2018).
366. Part 4, The World Franchise Council's Principles of Ethics dated 12 November 2001 accessible at http://www.worldfranchisecouncil.net/code-of-ethics.html (last accessed 14/5/2018).
367. Part 4, The World Franchise Council's Principles of Ethics dated 12 November 2001 accessible at http://www.worldfranchisecouncil.net/code-of-ethics.html (last accessed 14/5/2018).
368. Part 4, The World Franchise Council's Principles of Ethics dated 12 November 2001 accessible at http://www.worldfranchisecouncil.net/code-of-ethics.html (last accessed 14/5/2018).
369. Part 2, The World Franchise Council's Principles of Ethics dated 12 November 2001 accessible at http://www.worldfranchisecouncil.net/code-of-ethics.html (last accessed 14/5/2018).
370. Part 2, The World Franchise Council's Principles of Ethics dated 12 November 2001 accessible at http://www.worldfranchisecouncil.net/code-of-ethics.html (last accessed 14/5/2018).

Franchise Disclosure Law (Model Law) was adopted on 25 September 2002 by the Governing Council of UNIDROIT.

[2] Background to the Model Law[371,372]

On 25 September 2002 the Governing Council of UNIDROIT adopted the Model Law finalised by a Committee of Governmental Experts that was convened by the organisation to examine a draft prepared by the UNIDROIT Study Group on Franchising.

[3] UNIDROIT Goals in Relation to the Model Law and Explanatory Report Thereto

This instrument was developed by UNIDROIT with several goals in mind.

Beyond the fact that the Model Law and the Explanatory Report thereto were developed as 'as an example that is not compulsory',[373] these documents were developed 'for States[374] legislators ... as an instrument intended to be a recommendation for States that have decided to adopt franchise specific legislation'.[375] As such the intention is to allow States to institute the changes that they consider to be necessary in order to address their specific requirements.[376]

This instrument is intended to serve as a source of inspiration, as an instrument that may be consulted and used as a model or blueprint by 'national legislators who have decided that legislation specifically aimed at franchising should be introduced into their legal system...'[377]

In recognition of the fact that 'franchising is playing an ever greater role in a wide range of national economies',[378] UNIDROIT suggest that 'State legislators may wish to consider a number of different elements including:

371. According to UNIDROIT, in January 1999, work on the Model Franchise Disclosure Law started with the preparation of a first draft by the Drafting Committee. In December 1999 and then in December 2000, this draft was submitted to the Study Group in Plenary. The draft text of the Model Franchise Disclosure Law with the accompanying Explanatory Report to the Model Law were submitted to the Committee of Governmental Experts in line with the instructions of the Governing Council of UNIDROIT. In April 2002, the Committee of Governmental Experts completed its work. In September 2002, the draft Model Law and the draft Explanatory Report to the Model Law were transmitted to the Governing Council of UNIDROIT. On 25 September 2002, the Governing Council of UNIDROIT adopted the Model Franchise Disclosure Law. (Source http://www.unidroit.org/overview-franchising-model-law (last accessed 1/8/2014)).
372. A more detailed background can be found in the Explanatory Report, notably in paragraphs 8-26 (inclusive).
373. Preamble, Model Law.
374. According to Article 2, Model Law the term State is deemed to include 'the territorial units making up a State which has two or more territorial units, whether or not possessing different systems of law applicable in relation to the matters dealt with in this law'.
375. Preamble, Model Law.
376. Explanatory Report, para 6.
377. Explanatory Report, para. 1.
378. Preamble, Model Law.

- whether it is clear that there is a problem, what its nature is, and what action, if any, is necessary;
- whether prospective investors are more likely to protect themselves against fraud if they have access to truthful, important information in advance of their assent to any franchise agreement;
- whether the nation's economic and social interests are best served by legally requiring a balance of information between the parties to a franchise agreement;
- whether there is a pattern of abusive conduct, or whether this conduct is isolated or limited to particular industries;
- the nature of the evidence of abuse;
- whether existing laws address the concerns and whether they are adequately applied;
- whether an effective system of self-regulation exists;
- the financial burden the new legislation will place upon franchisors and investors as compared to the benefits of legally-required disclosure;
- whether the proposed legislation inhibits or facilitates entry to franchisors, and its effect on job creation and investment; and
- the views of interested organisations including national franchise associations'.[379]

One further objective behind the Model Law is 'to encourage the development of franchising as a vehicle for conducting business'.[380]

This body of soft law is viewed as 'a means to create a secure legal environment between all the parties in a franchise arrangement. To that end, the Model Law ensures that the prospective franchisees intending to invest in franchising receive material information about franchise offerings thus permitting them to make an informed investment decision. In addition, the Model Law brings security to franchisors in their relationships with franchisees, administrative authorities and courts'.[381]

The emphasis in the Model Law is on the imposition of obligations on the franchisors, the reasoning being that 'the experience and economic size of franchisors, which permit them to have access to legal counsel, do not make it necessary to provide franchisors with the same degree of protection as franchisees. Furthermore, as is the case with other entrepreneurs, it is normal business practice for franchisors to ask prospective franchisees for information. Franchisors will naturally want to be able to assess the capabilities and reliability, as well as the financial conditions, of prospective franchisees before entrusting them with the development of a business that carries their trade name'.[382]

379. Preamble, Model Law.
380. Explanatory Report, para. 2.
381. Explanatory Report, para. 3.
382. Explanatory Report, para. 33.

[4] *Scope of the Model Law*

[a] *Substantive Scope*

The Model Law is 'limited to pre-contractual disclosure'.[383] It deals neither with the contractual relationship between the parties nor the consequences of termination.[384]

It addresses neither the issue of the validity of the franchise agreement[385] nor its provisions, unless this is expressly provided for in the law of the State adopting this law.[386]

[b] *Topical and Territorial Scope*

This body of law is intended to apply to domestic and international franchise agreements[387] and is applicable both when the franchise is granted and when it is renewed 'for the operation of one or more franchised businesses within the [State adopting this law]'.[388]

This instrument is intended for use in relation to franchise agreements and not other types of agreement.[389] It will apply to existing categories of franchise agreements (including master franchise agreements,[390] development agreements[391] and traditional unit agreements)[392] and any future types of franchise agreements that may develop with time.[393]

The Model Law applies 'in the State adopting the Model Law'[394] which effectively means that it 'applies to franchises that are operated in the national territory of the State adopting this law irrespective of whether the franchise originates as a domestic franchise or as a foreign franchise'.[395] In contrast, the Model Law is not intended 'to apply to franchises that are exported from a country that has adopted the Model Law

383. Explanatory Report, para. 30.
384. Explanatory Report, para. 30.
385. Explanatory Report, para. 40.
386. Article 1(2), Model Law.
387. Explanatory Report, para. 32.
388. Article 1(1), Model Law.
389. Explanatory Report, para. 36(1).
390. A master franchise is defined as 'the right granted by a franchisor to another party (the sub-franchisor) to grant franchises to third parties (the sub-franchisees).' (Article 2, Model Law) this definition is elaborated upon in the Explanatory Report, para. 44 where it is explained that a master franchise is one in which 'the franchisor grants the sub-franchisor (also called the "master franchisee") the right not only to operate franchise outlets itself, but also to grant sub-franchises to sub-franchisees in the territory the franchisor has granted it the right to develop.' (Explanatory Report, para. 44).
391. A development agreement is defined as 'an agreement under which a franchisor in exchange for direct or indirect financial compensation grants to another party the right to acquire more than one franchise of the same franchise system. (Article 2, Model Law) This definition is elaborated upon in the Explanatory Report, para. 44 where it is explained that a development agreement is used to develop large territories often as an alternative to master franchising.
392. Explanatory Report, para. 32.
393. Explanatory Report, para. 32.
394. Explanatory Report, para. 36(2).
395. Explanatory Report, para. 36(3).

into a country that has not, nor is it intended to apply to a franchise which is not operated in the country even if the agreement has been signed there'.[396]

The State legislature possesses the discretion to determine whether the national law inspired by the Model Law should apply only to situations where the franchise agreement is concluded at the end of the negotiation process, or whether it should also apply to those cases where the franchise agreement is not concluded at the end of the negotiation process.[397]

Affiliates of both the franchisee and franchisor are addressed within the Model Law. Whilst the Model Law uses the term 'affiliate' to cover those parties who are referred to as associates in legislative instruments, in the context of franchising the intention is to extend State legislatures the discretion to determine the type of control that needs to be exercised by a natural or legal person for them to qualify as an affiliate.[398]

Reference to an affiliate of the franchisee is intended to encompass 'the different legal entities into which a franchisee might be organised'.[399]

Reference to an affiliate of the franchisor is intended to encompass the parent company, the daughter companies and 'companies on the same organisational level as the franchisor'.[400]

[5] Disclosure Requirements in the Model Law

[a] Timing of Disclosure

According to the disclosure requirements in the Model Law, a franchisor is generally obligated to provide each prospective franchisee with a disclosure document subject to specific exceptions,[401] to which the franchise agreement proposed must be annexed, at least fourteen days before the earlier of:

396. Explanatory Report, para. 36(3).
397. Explanatory Report, para. 36(3).
398. Explanatory Report, para. 41.
399. Explanatory Report, para. 42.
400. Explanatory Report, para. 43.
401. The exceptions are listed in Article 5, Model Law.

According to Article 5, no disclosure document is required in the following situations. Firstly where the grant of the franchise is made to a 'person who has been an officer or director of the franchisor or of an affiliate of the franchisor for at least one year immediately before the signing of the franchise agreement.' (Article 5(A), Model Law) Secondly, where there is an assignment or other transfer of the rights and the duties of the franchisee under the existing franchise agreement 'where the assignee or transferee is bound by substantially the same terms as the assignor or transferor, and the franchisor has not had a significant role in the transaction other than approval of the transfer.' (Article 5(B), Model Law) Thirdly, where a franchise is granted to a person (natural or legal) who has been for the previous two years been engaged in the same or a similar business, 'if the sales of the franchise, as reasonably anticipated by the parties at the time the franchise agreement is entered into, will not during the first year of the relationship exceed 20% of the total aggregate sales of the combined business of the franchisee and its affiliates.' (Article 5(C), Model Law) Fourthly, if the franchise that is granted is one to 'which the prospective franchisee commits to a total financial requirement under the franchise agreement in excess of [X].' (Article 5(D), Model Law) Fifthly, if 'the grant of a franchise to a

(1) the signing of any agreement relating to the franchise by the prospective franchisee, excluding confidentiality agreements relating to information delivered or to be delivered by the franchisor; or
(2) the payment of any non-refundable fees or fees the refund 'of which is subject to such conditions as to render them not refundable'[402] to the franchisor or its affiliate by the prospective franchisee pertaining to the purchase of the franchise.[403]

The disclosure document must be updated within a set number of days of the end of the fiscal year of the franchisor.[404]

[b] Timing of Disclosure of a Material Change

Where there has been a material change to the information to be disclosed (pursuant to Article 6, Model Law), a written notice of the change should be delivered to the prospective franchisee 'as soon as practicable' before either:[405]

1) the signing of any agreement relating to the franchise by the prospective franchisee, excluding confidentiality agreements relating to information delivered or to be delivered by the franchisor; or
2) the payment of any non-refundable fees or fees the refund 'of which is subject to such conditions as to render them not refundable'[406] to the franchisor or its affiliate by the prospective franchisee pertaining to the purchase of the franchise.[407]

A material change in the information required to be disclosed (in Article 6, Model Law) is 'a change which can reasonably be expected to have a significant effect on the prospective franchisee's decision to acquire the franchise'.[408]

[c] Formalities Associated with the Disclosure Document

The law set out in thc Model Law will apply whenever a franchise agreement is concluded or renewed after the law enters into force.[409] The rights granted by the law

prospective franchisee who together with its affiliates has a net worth in excess of [Y] or turnover in excess of [Z].' (Article 5(E), Model Law) Sixthly, where an existing franchise agreement is either being renewed or extended on the same terms.(Article 5(F), Model Law).

402. Article 3(1)B, Model Law.
403. A security (bond or deposit) paid on the conclusion of a confidentiality agreement is excluded from the scope of this provision.
404. Article 3(2), Model Law.
405. Article 3(2), Model Law.
406. Article 3(1)B, Model Law.
407. A security (bond or deposit) paid on the conclusion of a confidentiality agreement is excluded from the scope of this provision.
408. Article 2, Model Law.
409. Article 9, Model Law.

are non-derogable as such any waiver of a right given by this law to the franchisee is void.[410]

The requisite disclosure document should be in writing[411] and should set out the information stipulated in the Model Law.[412]

The format of the disclosure document is at the discretion of the franchisor on condition that 'the information contained therein is presented as a single document at one time and meets the requirements imposed by this law'.[413]

If so requested by the franchisor, the prospective franchisee is required to provide written acknowledgement to the franchisor of the receipt of the disclosure document.[414]

[d] Remedies Available to the Franchisee

Certain remedies are available to the franchisee if the disclosure document or the notice of material change has not been delivered within the time stipulated (in Article 3, Model Law), contains a misrepresentation[415] of a material fact[416] or makes an omission[417] of a material fact.[418]

Such rights do not derogate from any right or rights that the franchisee may be entitled to under the applicable law[419] governing all other matters relating to termination and damages that are not expressed addressed within this provision of the Model Law.[420]

In such circumstances, the franchisee may upon giving the franchisor thirty days prior written notice terminate the franchise agreement and/or claim for damages against the franchisor for the conduct described,[421] unless the franchisee has the information required to be disclosed through some other means, did not rely on the misrepresentation, or the termination is disproportionate given the circumstances.[422]

410. Article 10, Model Law.
411. Article 4(1), Model Law.
412. Article 2, Model Law elaborated upon by Article 6, Model Law.
413. Article 4(2), Model Law.
414. Article 7, Model Law.
415. A misrepresentation is defined as 'a statement of fact that the person making the statement knew or ought to have known to be untrue at the time the statement was made.' (Article 2, Model Law).
416. A material fact is defined as 'any information that can reasonably be expected to have a significant effect on the prospective franchisee's decision to acquire the franchise.' (Article 2, Model Law).
417. An omission is defined as 'the failure to state a fact of which the person making the statement was aware at the time the statement ought to have been made.' (Article 2, Model Law).
418. Article 8(1)(A)-(C), Model Law.
419. Article 8(3), Model Law.
420. Article 8(4), Model Law.
421. Article 8(1), Model Law.
422. Article 8(1), Model Law.

[e] Substantive Content of the Disclosure Document

Certain information must be provided by the franchisor to the prospective franchisee in the disclosure document.[423] This information addresses the franchisor, the subject-matter of the franchise agreement and other franchisees.

Information relating to the franchisor includes the following:

- its legal name,[424] its legal form,[425] its legal address,[426] the address of its principal place of business[427] and the address of its principal place of business in the State where the prospective franchisee is located;[428]
- information regarding the business experience[429] of the franchisor and its affiliates[430] including the period each has operated 'a business of the type to be operated by the prospective franchisee'[431] and the period 'each has granted franchises for the same type of business as that to be operated by the prospective franchisee';[432]
- background information of any person with senior management responsibilities in the business operations of the franchisor relating to the franchise including their names, business addresses, positions held and business background;[433]
- details of criminal convictions or findings of liability in civil actions or arbitrations of the franchisor or of any of its affiliates[434] involving franchises or other businesses relating to fraud, misrepresentation or similar acts or practices;[435]
- details of whether any criminal action or civil action or civil arbitration is pending against the franchisor or its subsidiary;[436]
- details of any bankruptcy, insolvency or comparable proceedings relating to the franchisor and its affiliate(s) over the period of the previous five years;[437] and

423. Article 6, Model Law.
424. Article 6(1)(A), Model Law.
425. Article 6(1)(A), Model Law.
426. Article 6(1)(A), Model Law.
427. Article 6(1)(A), Model Law.
428. Article 6(1)(C), Model Law.
429. Article 6(1)(E), Model Law.
430. Where these affiliates are responsible for 'granting franchises under substantially the same trade name…' (Article 6(E), Model Law).
431. Article 6(1)(E)(i), Model Law.
432. Article 6(1)(E)(ii), Model Law.
433. Article 6(1)(F), Model Law.
434. Where the affiliate has been 'engaged in franchising for the previous five years…' (Article 6(1)(G)(ii), Model Law).
435. Article 6(1)(G), Model Law.
436. Article 6(1)(G), Model Law.
437. Article 6(1)(H), Model Law.

- the financial statements of the franchisor[438] including balance sheets and statements of profit and loss for the previous three years.[439]

Information relating to the subject-matter of the franchise includes details of the:

- trademark, trade name, business name or similar name under which the franchisor trades or intends to trade in the State in which the prospective franchisee plans to operate the franchise business;[440]
- information concerning the franchise to be operated by the prospective franchisee;[441]
- information concerning[442] the intellectual property of the franchisor to be licensed to the prospective franchisee (including registration, application for registration, the name of the owner of the intellectual property right/s (IPR), the name of the applicant for registration, the date on which registration of the IPR expires and any litigation or legal proceedings which could have a material effect on the legal right of the franchisee to make use of the intellectual property under the franchise agreement);[443]
- categories of goods and/or of services that the franchisee will be required to buy or lease (including the details of the supplier of such goods and/or services and any discretion the franchisee will enjoy to recommend other providers to the franchisor for approval).[444] Any entitlement to revenue or other benefits that may be received by the franchisor or its affiliates from any supplier of goods and/or services to the franchisee, will be passed on to the prospective franchisee;[445]
- the estimated total initial investment to be made by the prospective franchisee;[446]
- any financing offered or arranged by the franchisor;[447]
- historical or projected financial performance of outlets owned by the franchisor, the franchisor's affiliates or franchisees.[448] This information must 'have a reasonable basis at the time it is made'[449] and indicate 'the material assumptions underlying its preparation and presentation',[450] 'whether it is

438. Article 6(1)(N)(i)(c), Model Law.
439. Where these financial statements do not go back three years, the franchisor is still obliged to disclose the same documents that have been prepared since they began their activity. (Article 6(1)(N)(i)(c), Model Law).
440. Article 6(1)(B), Model Law.
441. Article 6(1)(D), Model Law.
442. Where such affiliates grant 'franchises under substantially the same trade name'(Article 6(1)(I), Model Law).
443. Article 6(1)(L), Model Law.
444. Article 6(1)(M), Model Law.
445. Article 6(1)(M), Model Law.
446. Article 6(1)(N)(i)(a), Model Law.
447. Article 6(1)(N)(i)(b), Model Law.
448. Article 6(1)(N)(ii)(a), Model Law.
449. Article 6(1)(N)(ii)(aa), Model Law.
450. Article 6(1)(N)(ii)(bb), Model Law.

based on actual results of existing outlets',[451] 'whether it is based on franchisor-owned and/or franchisee-owned outlets'[452] and 'the percentage of those outlets that meet or exceed each range or result';[453]
- state of the general market of the products or services forming the subject matter of the franchise;[454]
- state of the local market of the products or services forming the subject matter of the franchise;[455] and
- development prospects of the market.[456]

Information relating to other franchisees including:

- information concerning the total number of franchisees[457] and the total number of company-owned outlets of the franchisor and of its affiliates 'granting franchises under substantially the same trade name';[458]
- details (names, business addresses and business phone numbers)[459] of the franchisees and of the franchisees of any of the franchisor's affiliates 'granting franchises under substantially the same trade name'[460] where their outlets are 'located nearest to the proposed outlet of the prospective franchisee ... in the State of the franchisee and/or contiguous States, or, if there are no contiguous States, the State of the franchisor';[461]
- information about franchisees of the franchisor and franchisees of any of the franchisor's affiliates that 'grant franchises under substantially the same trade name'[462] that have ceased to be franchisees during the three fiscal years prior to the one during which the franchise agreement is concluded with a note of the reasons why the franchisees concerned stopped to be franchisees of the franchisor.[463]

Certain further information should be provided by the franchisor in either the franchise agreement (in which case the franchisor can make reference in the disclosure document to the relevant section(s) of the franchise agreement) or the disclosure document (where the items are not included in the franchise agreement, the fact should be noted in the disclosure document). This information encompasses:[464]

451. Article 6(1)(N)(ii)(cc), Model Law.
452. Article 6(1)(N)(ii)(dd), Model Law.
453. Article 6(1)(N)(ii)(ee), Model Law.
454. Article 6(1)(O)(i), Model Law.
455. Article 6(1)(O)(ii), Model Law.
456. Article 6(1)(O)(iii), Model Law.
457. Article 6(1)(I), Model Law.
458. Article 6(1)(I), Model Law.
459. Article 6(1)(J), Model Law.
460. Article 6(1)(J), Model Law.
461. Article 6(1)(J), Model Law.
462. Article 6(1)(K), Model Law.
463. Article 6(1)(K), Model Law.
464. Article 6(2), Model Law.

- the terms and conditions of renewal of the franchise (if any);[465]
- a description of the initial training programmes;[466]
- a description of the on-going training programmes;[467]
- the extent of the exclusive right to be granted to use trademarks covered by the franchise agreement, or to licence the use of trademarks covered by the franchise agreement or to sell or distribute goods and/or services authorised for sale by the prospective franchisee (if any) including exclusive rights to territory and exclusive rights to customers;[468]
- information about reservations made by the franchisor relative to any exclusive rights granted to the prospective franchisee;[469]
- the grounds for termination of the franchise agreement by the franchisor and the consequences of such termination;[470]
- the grounds for termination of the franchise agreement by the prospective franchisee and the consequences of such termination;[471]
- a description of limitations imposed upon the prospective franchisee (if any) relative to the territory and/or to customers;[472]
- a description of restrictions or conditions imposed on the prospective franchisee relative to the goods and/or service that it may sell;[473]
- non-compete covenants (in-term and post-term);[474]
- the initial franchise fee[475] and any other fees and payments;[476]
- an indication of whether any portion of the initial fee is refundable and the conditions under which a refund will be made;[477]
- the conditions for assignment or other transfer of the franchise;[478]
- any forum selection provision;[479]
- any choice of law provision;[480] and
- an indication of the dispute resolution mechanism selected.[481]

465. Article 6(2)(A), Model Law.
466. Article 6(2)(B), Model Law.
467. Article 6(2)(B), Model Law.
468. Article 6(2)(C), Model Law.
469. Article 6(2)(C), Model Law.
470. Article 6(2)(D), Model Law.
471. Article 6(2)(E), Model Law.
472. Article 6(2)(F), Model Law.
473. Article 6(2)(J), Model Law.
474. Article 6(2)(G), Model Law.
475. Article 6(2)(H), Model Law.
476. Article 6(2)(I), Model Law.
477. Article 6(2)(H), Model Law.
478. Article 6(2)(K), Model Law.
479. Article 6(2)(L), Model Law.
480. Article 6(2)(L), Model Law.
481. Article 6(2)(L), Model Law.

[D] Draft Common Frame of Reference[482]

Presented to the Commission by the Study Group on the European Civil Code and the Research Group on Existing EC Private Law in December 2008, the DCFR was published in 2009.

The DCFR is intended to be used as a stand-alone tool[483] and to act as a source of inspiration for the resolution of private law questions.[484]

[1] Composition and Scope of DCFR

The DCFR consists of ten books, most of which are subdivided into chapters, sections, subsections and articles.

Various commercial agreements are addressed in Book IV. This book is subdivided into eight parts with each part addressing a different class of contract. Part E (in Book IV) addresses the formulation and regulation of commercial agency, franchise and distributorship agreements.

[2] Regulation of Commercial Franchise Agreements by the DCFR

The general provisions contained in IV.E.-1 of the DCFR and the rules contained in IV.E.-2 govern all the agreements addressed in Part E of Book IV namely commercial agency, franchise and distribution agreements.

Each of these agreements is also addressed separately by a set of dedicated and supplementary rules (IV.E.-3 covers commercial agency agreements, IV.E.-4 covers franchise agreements and IV.E.-5 covers distribution agreements).

[3] General Provisions and General Rules Governing Commercial Franchise Agreements[485]

Part E of Book IV addresses contracts for the creation and regulation of a commercial agency, franchise or distributorship agreement.[486] Pursuant to the DCFR, the parties contracting are obliged to comply with certain obligations at the pre-contractual stage and during the term of the agreement.

482. The DCFR is reviewed in Meiselles, Michala (2013) International Commercial Agreements - An Edinburgh Law Guide, 1st ed., Edinburgh University Press, Chapter 7.
483. Paragraph Intr. 7 DCFR (Introduction, paragraph 7).
484. Paragraph Intr. 8 DCFR.
485. Contained in Chapters 1 and 2 of Part E of Book IV (respectively).
486. Paragraph IV.E.-1:101(1) DCFR (Book IV, Part E, Chapter 1, Section 1, sub-section 1, paragraph 1).

[4] *Pre-contractual Obligations*

At the pre-contractual stage the contracting parties are obliged to provide each other with the information needed in order to permit the other party to ascertain on a reasonably informed basis whether or not it wishes to conclude a contract.[487] Such information must be furnished within a reasonable period of time before the contract is concluded.[488]

A franchisor is also obliged pre-contract to provide the putative franchisee with information concerning its business and its experience; the scope and structure of the network involved; the relevant intellectual property rights; the franchise method and operation; the proposed terms of the franchise agreement; and the fees, royalties or other periodical payments.[489]

[5] *Miscellaneous Obligations*

Beyond the obligation to provide information, each of the parties contracting must cooperate with the other,[490] provide in due time all the information in its possession which the other party needs in order to achieve the objectives of the contract[491] and ensure the confidentiality of all information received from the other party both throughout the duration of the contractual relationship and upon termination of the relationship.[492] Whilst a party is permitted to use confidential information to achieve the goals of the agreement,[493] it may not use this confidential information for any other purpose.[494]

[6] *Contracts for a Fixed Term*

Each of the parties to the contract may decide not to renew their fixed term contract.[495] In the event that one of the parties would like to renew the contract it is free to do so by informing the other party of their intention to renew.[496] In such a case, the contract will be renewed for an indefinite period unless the recipient of the notice of renewal provides notice of non-renewal not later than a reasonable time before the expiry of the contract period.[497]

487. Subsection IV.E.–2:101 DCFR.
488. Subsection IV.E.–2:101 DCFR.
489. Subsection IV.E.–4:102 DCFR.
490. Subsection IV.E.–2:201 DCFR.
491. Subsection IV.E.–2:202 DCFR.
492. Paragraph IV.E.–2:203(1) DCFR.
493. Paragraph IV.E.–2:203(2) DCFR.
494. Paragraph IV.E.–2:203(2) DCFR.
495. Subsection IV.E.–2:301 DCFR.
496. Subsection IV.E.–2:301 DCFR.
497. Subsection IV.E.–2:301 DCFR.

[7] Contracts for an Indefinite Term

Each of the parties to an indefinite term contract will have a right to terminate the contractual relationship by providing the other party with notice.[498]

When the notice provides for termination after a reasonable period of time no damages will be payable.[499] In contrast when the notice provides for immediate termination or termination after a period of time which is not reasonable in length then damages will be payable.[500,501]

[8] Entitlement to a Lien over Property Held[502]

When one of the contracting parties fails to perform its obligation to pay (remuneration, compensation, damages and/or indemnity), the other party to the contract may have the right to retain movables belonging to this party until such a time as this party performs its obligation.

[9] Statement of Terms[503]

Each one of the contracting parties may request that the other party provides it with a signed statement of the terms of the contract in textual form on a durable medium. The parties are not permitted to exclude this duty or to derogate from or vary its effects.

[10] Rules Specific to Franchise Agreements

Franchise agreements are governed by general provisions (set out in IV.E.-1), general rules (set out in IV.E.-2) and specific provisions (set out in IV.E.-4).

The specific provisions governing franchise agreements (in IV.E.-4) are intended to cover contracts pursuant to which one party (franchisor) grants another party (franchisee) the right to conduct business within the network of the franchisor using the trade name or trademark of the franchisor along with any other intellectual property belonging to the franchisor as well as the franchisor's know-how and business method.[504]

The franchisor is obliged *inter alia* to:[505]

498. Paragraph IV.E.-2:302(1) DCFR.
499. Paragraph IV.E.-2:302(2) DCFR. The calculation of the length of a reasonable period is addressed in subsection IV.E.-2:302.
500. Paragraph IV.E.-2:302(2) DCFR. The calculation of the length of a reasonable period is addressed in subsection IV.E.-2:302.
501. Subsection IV.E.-2:303 addresses the determination of damages for termination with inadequate notice.
502. Subsection IV.E.-2:401 DCFR.
503. Subsection IV.E.-2:402 DCFR.
504. Subsection IV.E.-4:101 DCFR.
505. The duties of the franchisor are reviewed in Section IV.E.-4:2.

- furnish the franchisee with the right to use the IPRs to the degree necessary in order to operate the franchise business;[506]
- furnish the franchisee with support including training, guidance and advice without additional charge;[507]
- update the franchisee regarding market conditions, relevant communication between the franchisor and customers in the territory and marketing campaigns;[508] and
- ensure the supply of products ordered by the franchisee within a reasonable time.[509]

The franchisee is obliged *inter alia* to:[510]

- pay the franchisor the agreed fees, royalties or other periodical payments;[511]
- inform the franchisor about claims brought or threatened by third parties in relation to the IPRs of the franchisor;[512]
- update the franchisor regarding infringements of its IPRs by third parties;[513]
- adhere to the business method of the franchisor;[514] and
- allow the franchisor to inspect its premises and accounting books.[515]

[E] US Franchise Disclosure Rules[516]

In the US, franchise arrangements are addressed by a dual level of legislation (federal and state) defining the relationship itself, as well as certain substantive obligations owed by the parties.[517]

The specific characteristics associated with franchise arrangements are defined separately by federal law on the one hand, and state law on the other hand,[518] with the law varying from one state to another.[519] Whereas the statute of one state may define a relationship as a franchise, another state's laws may classify the same relationship as

506. Subsection IV.E.-4:201 DCFR.
507. Subsection IV.E.-4:203 DCFR.
508. Subsection IV.E-4:205 DCFR.
509. Paragraph IV.E.-4:204(1) DCFR.
510. The duties of the franchisee are reviewed in Section IV.E.-4:3.
511. Subsection IV.E.-4:301 DCFR.
512. Subsection IV.E.-4:302 DCFR.
513. Subsection IV.E.-4:302 DCFR.
514. Subsection IV.E.-4:303 DCFR
515. Subsection IV.E.-4:304 DCFR.
516. Selected bibliography includes: (1) Compliance Guide dated May 2008 issued by the FTC (Federal Trade Commission); (2) 16 CFR Part 436 (FTC Rule replaced its predecessor which came into effect 21 Oct 1979); (3) Staff opinions found on FTC website (www.ftc.gov/bcp/franchise/netadopin.shtm).
517. Emerson 2009: 329.
518. Emerson 2009: 322.
519. Emerson 2009: 322.

merely a distribution or licensing relationship.[520] The classification given by the parties themselves is accordingly merely of secondary importance.[521]

The FTC at the federal level delineates three key elements as being material in a franchise arrangement, namely an offer to use a trademark, exercise of significant control and assistance, and payment.[522]

At the state level, in the US, two sets of laws are applicable. The first set of laws - Regulation laws (also known as Sales laws) - cover the initial offer and the sale of the franchise.[523] The second set of laws - Relationship laws - govern the post-sale relationship between the parties.[524]

[1] FTC Rule: Overview and Comparison Between the New Rule and Old Rule

The FTC Rule obliges franchisors to provide prospective franchisees with key information.

The FTC Rule differs from its predecessor in several key respects.[525] First it addresses new technologies such as the Internet. Second, it requires more extensive disclosure about the substance of the franchise relationship. Third, it exempts certain entities originally caught by its forerunner. Fourth, it prohibits certain practices not previously addressed in the former body of law.

A further revision made to the earlier body of law removes the requirement that the prospective franchisees always have at least five business days within which to review the completed franchise agreement.[526]

[2] Applicability[527]

The FTC Rule will apply to the offer of the franchise as well as the sale of the franchise.[528] The applicability of the FTC Rule will be determined by reference to whether or not the underlying relationship meets the definition of a franchise set out in the FTC Rule and whether or not an exemption or exclusion applies.[529]

A relationship is capable of qualifying as a franchise regardless of the label used by the parties themselves to describe the relationship on the proviso that the three prerequisites reviewed below are met.[530]

520. Emerson 2009: 322.
521. Emerson 2009: 322.
522. Emerson 2009: 322 citing 16 CFR 436.1 (h)(1)-(3)(2008).
523. Emerson 2009: 322.
524. Emerson 2009: 323.
525. Compliance Guide dated May 2008 issued by the FTC, pp. (i) and (ii).
526. Compliance Guide dated May 2008, p. 22.
527. Compliance Guide dated May 2008, pp. 1-16; 16 CFR §436(1).
528. Compliance Guide dated May 2008, p. 1.
529. Compliance Guide dated May 2008, p. 1.
530. Compliance Guide dated May 2008 p. 1. 16 CFR 436(1)h.

Conversely, an arrangement referred to by the contracting parties as a franchise will not be such a relationship unless the three conditions denoted below are met.[531]

A franchise is defined by the FTC Rule as a 'continuing commercial relationship or arrangement'[532] fulfilling three key elements. First the franchisee 'will obtain the right to operate a business that is identified or associated with the franchisor's trademark, or to offer, sell, or distribute goods, services, or commodities that are identified or associated with the franchisor's trademark'.[533] Second the franchisor 'will exert or has authority to exert a significant degree of control over the franchisee's method of operation, or provide significant assistance in the franchisee's method of operation'.[534] Third as a prerequisite for 'obtaining or commencing operation of the franchise, the franchisee makes a required payment or commits to make a required payment to the franchisor or its affiliate'.[535]

Such a relationship may exist regardless of whether the relationship is represented orally or in writing as having the necessary characteristics associated with such a relationship and regardless of whether the representations are true or capable of being fulfilled.[536] So if for example the prospective franchisor represents that it will licence a trademark, in circumstances where it promises to provide assistance and will charge a minimum payment, the arrangement will be qualify as a franchise under the FTC Rule and will accordingly be covered by this Rule, even if it later transpires that the prospective franchisor does not in fact have a trademark or if it has a trademark it is unable to provide the assistance promised.[537]

[a] Requirement One: Provide a Trademark or Other Commercial Symbol[538]

A franchise will involve 'the right to operate a business that is 'identified or associated with the franchisor's trademark, or to offer, sell, or distribute goods, services, or commodities that are identified or associated with the franchisor's trademark'.[539]

The term 'trademark' has broad application covering not only trademarks, but also service marks, names, logos as well as other commercial symbols.[540] In this context, it is not necessary for the franchisor to be the owner of the mark itself so long as it has 'the right to licence the use of the mark to others'.[541]

531. Compliance Guide dated May 2008 p. 1. 16 CFR 436(1)h.
532. 16 CFR 436(1)h.
533. 16 CFR 436(1)h (definition of a franchise).
534. 16 CFR 436(1)h (definition of a franchise).
535. 16 CFR 436(1)h (definition of a franchise).
536. Compliance Guide dated May 2008 p. 1 citing 16 CFR 436(1)h.
537. Compliance Guide dated May 2008 p. 1.
538. Compliance Guide dated May 2008 p. 2.
539. Compliance Guide dated May 2008 p. 2 citing 16 CFR 436(1)h.
540. 16 CFR 436(1)v (definition of trademark).
541. Compliance Guide dated May 2008 p. 2.

[b] Requirement Two: Promise to Exercise Significant Control or Provide Significant Assistance in the Operation of the Business

'Significance' in the context of this second requirement is correlated to the level of reliance displayed by the prospective franchisee. In other words, the more the franchisees reasonably rely on the control or assistance of the franchisor the more likely the control or assistance will be deemed to be significant.[542]

The reliance of a franchisee may be greater where the franchisee lacks experience in the business being offered for sale or when they take on a large commercial risk or where 'the control or assistance is unique to that specific franchisor, as opposed to a typical practice employed by all businesses in the same industry'.[543]

To be viewed as significant, the control or assistance must concern the 'franchisee's overall method of operation - not a small part of the franchisee's business'.[544]

Significant types of control will encompass the exercise of control over *inter alia* the approval of sites, the design and appearance of sites; the operational timetable, the human resource policies, the accounting systems, the promotional activities and the production mechanisms.[545]

Significant assistance in the operation of the business includes assistance with training, the creation of accounting systems, the selection of locations and the provision of advice on management, marketing or personnel as well as the provision of a comprehensive operations manual.[546]

[c] Requirement Three: Minimum Payment

The final requirement for applicability is the requirement that the franchisor or an affiliate be paid a minimum sum as a condition for obtaining a franchise or starting operations[547] at any time before the commencement of operations of the franchised business or within the first six months of the commencement of operations of the franchised business.[548]

The required payment may entail other forms of payment that the franchisee is expected to pay the franchisor or an affiliate under the terms of the contract.[549] Required payment will encompass *inter alia* the initial franchise fee, the rent, the security deposit, the non-refundable charges and the continuing royalties.[550]

542. Compliance Guide dated May 2008, p. 3.
543. Compliance Guide dated May 2008, p. 3.
544. Compliance Guide dated May 2008, p. 3.
545. Compliance Guide dated May 2008, p. 3.
546. Compliance Guide dated May 2008, p. 3.
547. Compliance Guide dated May 2008, p. 4.
548. Compliance Guide dated May 2008, p. 5.
549. Compliance Guide dated May 2008, p. 5.
550. Compliance Guide dated May 2008, p. 5.

[3] Relationships Excluded from the FTC Rule

The FTC Rule exempts minimum requirement payment,[551] fractional franchise[552] and leased departments[553] whilst adding several new exemptions (sales governed by the Petroleum Marketing Practices Act and sales involving sophisticated investors).[554]

A fractional franchise is defined by the FTC Rule as 'a franchise relationship that satisfies the following criteria when the relationship is created:

(1) the franchisee, any of the franchisee's current directors or officers, or any current directors or officers of a parent or affiliate, has more than two years of experience in the same type of business; and
(2) the parties have a reasonable basis to anticipate that the sales arising from the relationship will not exceed 20% of the franchisee's total dollar volume in sales during the first year of operation'.[555]

A leased department is defined by the FTC Rule as 'an arrangement whereby a retailer licences or otherwise permits a seller to conduct business from the retailer's location where the seller purchases no goods, services, or commodities directly or indirectly from the retailer, a person the retailer requires the seller to do business with, or a retailer-affiliate if the retailer advises the seller to do business with the affiliate'.[556]

[4] Disclosure Requirements

The FTC Rule addresses the following issues: (1) who must prepare the disclosures, (2) who must furnish the disclosure to the prospective franchisees, (3) how the prospective franchisees receive the disclosures and (4) the period of review available to prospective franchisees.

[5] Responsibility for Preparation of the Disclosure Documents

The onus of preparing disclosure documents is borne by the franchisor and any sub-franchisors.

Under the FTC Rule the term 'franchisor' is treated as including 'any person who grants a franchise and participates in the franchise relationship. Unless otherwise stated, it includes subfranchisors. For purposes of this definition, a "subfranchisor"

551. 16 CFR 436.8 Exemptions '(a) The provisions of 16 CFR 436 shall not apply if the franchisor can establish any of the following: (1)The total of the required payments, or commitments to make a required payment, to the franchisor or an affiliate that are made any time from before to within six months after commencing operation of the franchisee's business is less than $570.'
552. 16 CFR 436.8(a).
553. 16 CFR 436.8(a).
554. Compliance Guide dated May 2008, pp. 7-16 citing 16 CFR 436.8(a).
555. 16 CFR 436.1(g).
556. 16 CFR 436.1(l).

means a person who functions as a franchisor by engaging in both pre-sale activities and post-sale performance'.[557]

In order to qualify as a franchisor, the person in question must not only grant the franchise but also participate in the relationship. As such persons that take part in the pre-sale activities alone will not qualify as franchisors.[558]

Pursuant to the FTC Rule, the franchisor and sub-franchisor are responsible for each other's compliance with the provisions of the FTC Rule and are accordingly collectively and individually liable for violations by the other party.[559]

Certain fields of information may need to be provided exclusively by one or the other party (franchisor and sub-franchisor). In other situations, both the franchisor and sub-franchisor will need to supply the information to ensure that the requisite disclosure is accurate.[560]

Disclosure items 1–4 and 21 will require the provision of information by the franchisor and sub-franchisor/s, whilst disclosure item 20 requires information from the sub-franchisor and in certain circumstances the franchisor.[561]

[6] Responsibility for Providing the Disclosure Documents

Responsibility for providing the disclosure documents to each prospective franchisee is borne by the prospective franchisor including any prospective sub-franchisor/s.

A prospective franchisee is defined as 'any person (including any agent, representative, or employee) who approaches or is approached by a franchise seller to discuss the possible establishment of a franchise relationship'.[562]

There is no obligation to provide disclosure documentation to persons who do not approach or are not approached by a franchise seller.[563]

[7] Methods of Disclosure

Under the FTC Rule, disclosure documents must be furnished in writing.

Though in this context the terms written and in writing are widely defined, to include 'any document or information in printed form or in any form capable of being preserved in tangible form and read. It includes: type-set, word processed, or handwritten document; information on computer disk or CD-ROM; information sent via email; or information posted on the Internet. It does not include mere oral statements'.[564]

557. 16 CFR 436.1(k).
558. Compliance Guide dated May 2008, p. 17.
559. Compliance Guide dated May 2008, p. 17.
560. Compliance Guide dated May 2008, p. 17.
561. Compliance Guide dated May 2008, p. 18.
562. 16 CFR 436.1(r).
563. Compliance Guide dated May 2008, p. 18.
564. 16 CFR 436.1(w).

[8] The Point in Time When the Disclosure Documents Must Be Provided

Unless a transaction is exempted under the FTC Rule, where an offer or sale of a franchise (situated in the US or its territories) is made, then the franchisor must furnish the prospective franchisee/s with a current disclosure document 'at least 14 calendar-days before the prospective franchisee signs a binding agreement with, or makes any payment to, the franchisor or an affiliate in connection with the proposed franchise sale'.[565] In this context, an affiliate is defined as 'an entity controlled by, controlling, or under common control with, another entity'.[566]

The period of fourteen calendar days commences the day after the delivery of the disclosure document. In other words, the signing of the agreement or the receipt of payment can take place on the fifteenth calendar day following delivery.[567]

The prospective franchisor may be required to provide the disclosure documents more than fourteen calendar days before the franchisee signs or pays if a reasonable request is made to this effect.[568] A failure to comply with a reasonable request for early delivery will be an independent violation of the FTC Rule.[569]

[9] Further Review Period

Any franchisor wishing 'to alter unilaterally and materially the terms and conditions of the basic franchise agreement or any related agreements attached to the disclosure document'[570] is obliged to provide the prospective franchisee 'with a copy of each revised agreement at least seven calendar-days before the prospective franchisee signs the revised agreement'.[571]

Where the modifications to the agreement are the result of negotiations initiated by the prospective franchisee then the seven calendar day period will not be triggered.[572]

[10] Methods of Furnishing Disclosure Documents

Disclosure documents may be furnished in a variety of ways.[573] The franchisor will have provided such documentation by the requisite date if:[574]

- copies of the documents are hand-delivered, faxed, emailed, or otherwise delivered by the requisite date to the prospective franchisee;

565. 16 CFR 436.2(a).
566. 16 CFR 436.1(b).
567. Compliance Guide dated May 2008, p. 20.
568. Compliance Guide dated May 2008, p. 21.
569. Compliance Guide dated May 2008, p. 21.
570. 16 CFR 436.2(b).
571. 16 CFR 436.2(b).
572. 16 CFR 436.2(b).
573. Compliance Guide dated May 2008, p. 21.
574. 16 CFR 436.2(c)(1)-(3).

- instructions are provided to the prospective franchisee by the required date indicating how the documentation may be accessed on the Internet; or
- a paper or tangible electronic copy (computer disk, CD-ROM and so forth) is dispatched to the address provided by the prospective franchisee by first-class US mail at least three calendar days before the requisite date.

[11] Disclosure Document – Substance

[a] Cover Page[575]

The disclosure document must commence with a cover page adhering to the order and form set out in the FTC Rule.

After the title in bold capitals reading franchise disclosure document, the cover page should *inter alia* note the franchisor's details (the name of the franchisor, the type of business organisation, the principal business address and the franchisor's contact information), include a sample of the primary trademark and review the franchised business.[576]

[i] Issuance date

The issuance date means any date on which the prospective franchisor finalises the version of the disclosure document for future use. States in the US that require the registration of disclosure documents by franchisors may use the term effective date to refer to the date on which the State in question formally approved the registration of the disclosure document.[577]

[b] Table of Contents[578]

After the cover page, a table of contents will need to appear listing all twenty-three disclosure items and the page on which each disclosure item commences. This table should also list all exhibits by letter.

[c] Item 1: The Franchisor, Any Parents, Predecessors and Affiliates[579]

Item 1 of the FTC Rule requires disclosure of background information pertaining to the franchisor and any parents, predecessors and affiliates.

575. 16 CFR 436.3. Review of the cover page can be found in Compliance Guide dated May 2008, pp. 24-27. A template of the cover page is provided in the Compliance Guide dated May 2008, p. 27.
576. 16 CFR 436.3.
577. Compliance Guide dated May 2008, p. 26.
578. 16 CFR 436(4). Reviewed in the Compliance Guide dated May 2008, pp. 27-28. A template can be found in the Compliance Guide dated May 2008, p. 28.
579. 16 CFR 436(5)a. Reviewed in Compliance Guide dated May 2008, pp. 29-32. A template can be found in the Compliance Guide dated May 2008, p. 32.

The information in this item should include the names and principal business addresses of the franchisor, any parents, predecessors (in the ten year period leading up to the close of the franchisor's most recent fiscal year)[580] and affiliates (offering franchises in any line of business or providing products or services to the franchisor's franchisees),[581] the 'name that the franchisor uses and any names it intends to use to conduct business',[582] the type of business entity employed by the franchisor and the state in which the said entity is organised,[583] information about the business of the franchisor and the franchises offered[584] and information about the previous business experience of the franchisor.[585]

[d] Item 2: Business Experience of Key Personnel[586]

Substantially identical to its predecessor the FTC Rule requires disclosure of the business experience of certain key individuals for the last five years.

This item should note the name and position of the franchisor's directors, trustees, general partners, principal officers and other individuals with management responsibility, as well as their principal positions and employers over the period of five years.

Under the FTC Rule the franchisor's obligation to disclose extends to the business experience of all individuals with management responsibilities, irrespective of their formal title and regardless of whether they are employed by the franchisor, an affiliate or parent.

[e] Item 3: Litigation[587]

There is an obligation to disclose to the prospective franchisee certain lawsuits involving the franchisor and other entities associated with the franchisor.

Under the FTC Rule, this obligation extends to the disclosure of lawsuits commenced against franchisees.[588]

The disclosure requirement extends to pending lawsuits, lawsuits involving the franchise relationship, previous lawsuits and current governmental injunctive or restrictive actions.[589]

---

580. 16 CFR 436(5)a(2).
581. 16 CFR 436(5)a(1).
582. 16 CFR 436(5)a(3).
583. 16 CFR 436(5)a(5).
584. 16 CFR 436(5)a(6).
585. 16 CFR 436(5)a(7).
586. 16 CFR 436(5)b. Reviewed in the Compliance Guide dated May 2008, p. 33. A template can be found at Compliance Guide dated May 2008, p. 34.
587. 16 CFR 436(5)c. Reviewed in the Compliance Guide dated May 2008, pp. 34-41. A template is included in the Compliance Guide dated May 2008, p. 41.
588. Compliance Guide dated May 2008, p. 34.
589. 16 CFR 436(5)c(1)-(2).

[f] Item 4: Bankruptcy[590]

Pursuant to the FTC Rule, the franchisor is obliged to disclose the bankruptcy history of the franchisor itself, all its affiliates and parents, as well as its predecessors.

In addition, this obligation extends to officers, general partners and any individuals who have a management responsibility in relation to the sale or operation of the franchises offered by the disclosure document.

[g] Item 5: Initial Fees and the Conditions for the Refund of Such Fees[591]

Initial fees are defined as 'all fees and payments, or commitments to pay, for services or goods received from the franchisor or any affiliate before the franchisee's business opens, whether payable in lump sum or installments'.[592]

The franchisor is obliged to disclose initial fees and the conditions under which if any such fees are refundable.[593]

In circumstances where the initial fees are not uniform, the franchisor must disclose the range or formula used in order to compute the initial fees paid in the fiscal year prior to the issuance date and the factors used to determine the sum.[594]

[h] Item 6: Other Fees[595]

The FTC Rules require disclosure by the franchisor of recurring or occasional fees associated with the operation of the franchise including but not limited to[596] royalties, advertising fees and training fees, whether or not these payments are made directly to the franchisor or an affiliate or collected by the franchisor or affiliate for another.

This information should be set out in a tabular form and should include the type of fee, the amount of the fee and the due date of the fee.[597]

[i] Item 7: Estimated Initial Investment[598]

The FTC Rule provides an illustrative list of expenses that are typical; however, this list is not exhaustive.

590. 16 CFR 436(5)d. Reviewed in the Compliance Guide dated May 2008, pp. 42-43. A template can be found in the Compliance Guide dated May 2008, p. 43.
591. 16 CFR 436(5)e. Reviewed in the Compliance Guide dated May 2008, pp. 43-45. A template can be found in the Compliance Guide dated May 2008, p. 45.
592. 16 CFR 436(5)e.
593. 16 CFR 436(5)e.
594. 16 CFR 436(5)e.
595. 16 CFR 436(5)f. Reviewed in the Compliance Guide dated May 2008, pp. 45-47. A template is included in the Compliance Guide dated May 2008, p. 47.
596. 16 CFR 436(5)f.
597. 16 CFR 436(5)f.
598. 16 CFR 436(5)g. Reviewed in the Compliance Guide dated May 2008, pp. 48-51. A template is included in the Compliance Guide dated May 2008, pp. 50-51.

The rationale for this requirement is to give 'prospective franchisees a much more detailed picture of their likely investment than Item 5 (initial fees) and Item 6 (other fees paid to the franchisor or affiliates)'.[599]

This information should be set out in tabular form and should include a note of the type of expenditure, the amount of expenditure, the method of payment, the due date and to whom the payment is to be made.[600]

[j] Item 8: List of Obligatory Purchases, Restrictions on Sources of Products and Services[601]

This item will list the franchisee's obligations to buy or lease *inter alia* goods and services related to the establishment or operation of the franchised business from the franchisor, its designee or approved suppliers.

[k] Item 9: Franchisee's Obligations[602]

The disclosure document should list the key obligations of the franchisee in tabular form. Each obligation listed in the table should also be cross-referenced with the applicable section of the franchise or other agreement and with the relevant disclosure document provision.[603]

[l] Item Ten: Financing[604]

The FTC Rule requires disclosure of all material terms and conditions of any financing arrangement that the franchisor, its agent or affiliates offer to the franchisee including:

- the cover of the finance;
- the identity of each lender providing finance and their relationship to the franchisor;
- the amount of financing offered;
- the rate of interest and finance charges (expressed on an annual basis);
- the number of payments due or the period of repayment;
- the nature of any security interest exerted by the lender; and
- details of any penalties due in relation to defaults.

599. Compliance Guide dated May 2008, p. 48.
600. 16 CFR 436(5)g.
601. 16 CFR 436(5)h. Reviewed in the Compliance Guide dated May 2008, pp. 51-57. A template is provided in the Compliance Guide dated May 2008, pp. 56-57.
602. 16 CFR 436(5)i. Reviewed in the Compliance Guide dated May 2008, pp. 57-59. A template is provided in the Compliance Guide dated May 2008, pp. 57-59.
603. 16 CFR 436(5)i.
604. 16 CFR 436(5)j. Reviewed in the Compliance Guide dated May 2008, pp. 59-63. A template can be found in the Compliance Guide dated May 2008, pp. 61-63.

[m] Item 11: Assistance, Support and Training Provided to the Franchisee[605]

The franchisor is obliged to disclose information about assistance etc. provided pre-opening and during the operation of the franchise. In addition the franchisor should also describe the advertising programme for the franchise.

[n] Item 12: Territory[606]

The obligation to disclose will encompass the following information:

- whether the franchise is for one or more specific locations to be approved by the franchisor;
- details of any minimum territory granted to the franchisee (noting for example the specific radius);
- the conditions if any under which the franchisor will approve the relocation of the business of the franchisee;
- the options available to the franchisee (such as rights of first refusal);
- whether an exclusive territory will be granted by the franchisor;
- the conditions if any under which the franchisor will permit the franchisee to establish further outlets; and
- any plans that the franchisor has to operate a competing franchise offering similar goods or services.

[o] Item 13: Associated Trademarks[607]

The obligation to disclose will encompass the following information:

- details of each principal trademark that the franchisee will be licensed (a principal trademark is defined in this context as 'the primary trademarks, service marks, names, logos, and commercial symbols the franchisee will use to identify the franchised business. It may not include every trademark the franchisor owns'[608]);
- details of whether the trademarks are registered with the US Patent and Trademark Office;
- details if any of litigation pending, settlements and restrictions that impact on the franchisee's use of the trademark/s.

605. 16 CFR 436(5)k. Reviewed in the Compliance Guide dated May 2008, pp. 63-72. A template can be found in the Compliance Guide dated May 2008, pp. 69-72.
606. 16 CFR 436(5)l. Reviewed in the Compliance Guide dated May 2008, pp. 72-74. A template can be found in the Compliance Guide dated May 2008, p. 74.
607. 16 CFR 436(5)m. Reviewed in the Compliance Guide dated May 2008, pp.74-76. A template can be found in the Compliance Guide dated May 2008, pp. 75-76.
608. 16 CFR 436(5)m.

[p] Item 14: Other Associated Intellectual Property[609]

The obligation to disclose will encompass disclosure of information relating to any intellectual property related to the franchise. In this context the franchisor must disclose the following information:

- the types of intellectual property associated with the franchise;
- the duration of the same;
- the ownership rights or licences enjoyed by the franchisor in relation to each type of intellectual property;
- the duration of the rights of the franchisor;
- details of any legal proceedings, settlements and restrictions that may affect the ability of the franchisor to use such property.

[q] Item 15: Participation Duties[610]

The franchisor will be obliged to disclose to the franchisee any obligation to participate personally in the actual operation of the franchise business. In this item the franchisor should also indicate whether it recommends participation.

[r] Item 16: Restrictions on What the Franchisee May Sell[611]

The franchisor is obliged to disclose any restrictions concerning the goods or services that a franchisee may sell or supply.

[s] Item 17: Renewal, Termination, Transfer and Dispute Resolution[612]

The franchisor should disclose in tabular form, cross-referencing each enumerated franchise related item with a provision in the franchise or related agreement, *inter alia* the length of the franchise, renewal or extension of the term and the requirements for such a renewal or extension, termination by the franchisee, termination by the franchisor (with or without cause), the obligations of the franchisee on termination or non-renewal, assignment by the franchisor and transfer by the franchisee (the pre-approval process, the conditions, the franchisor's right of first refusal).

609. 16 CFR 436(5)n. Reviewed in the Compliance Guide dated May 2008, pp. 76-77. A template can be found in the Compliance Guide dated May 2008, p. 77.
610. 16 CFR 436(5)o. Reviewed in the Compliance Guide dated May 2008, pp. 78-79. A template can be found in the Compliance Guide dated May 2008, pp. 78-79.
611. 16 CFR 436(5)p. Reviewed in the Compliance Guide dated May 2008, pp. 79-80. A template can be found in the Compliance Guide dated May 2008, pp. 79-80.
612. 16 CFR 436(5)q. Reviewed in the Compliance Guide dated May 2008, pp. 80-83. A template can be found in the Compliance Guide dated May 2008, pp. 81-83.

[t] Item 18: Public Figure's Involvement[613]

The franchisor disclosure in this context should include reference to:

- any compensation or other benefit given to a public figure for their endorsement or the use of the public figure in the franchise name or symbol;
- the degree of involvement that a public figure has in the management or control of the franchisor; and
- the total investment of the public figure in the franchisor.

[u] Item 19: Financial Performance Representations[614]

Where the franchisor makes representations on financial performance to the prospective franchisees, the franchisor 'must have a reasonable basis and written substantiation for the representation at the time the representation is made and must state the representation in the Item 19 disclosure'.[615]

In this context, the franchisor must provide further specific information pertaining to these representations.

[v] Item 20: List of Outlets and Franchisee Information[616]

In this item, the disclosure by the franchisor must include a note of 'the total number of franchised and company-owned outlets for each of the franchisor's last three fiscal years'.[617] In this context, an outlet will include 'outlets of a type substantially similar to that offered to the prospective franchisee'.[618]

[w] Item 21: Audited Financial Statements[619]

The franchisor is required to provide audited financial statements prepared in line with the generally accepted accounting principles ('GAAP') for the most recent fiscal years to show the financial condition of the franchisor.

613. 16 CFR 436(5)r. Reviewed in the Compliance Guide dated May 2008, pp. 83-84. A template can be found in the Compliance Guide dated May 2008, p. 84.
614. 16 CFR 436(5)s. Reviewed in the Compliance Guide dated May 2008, pp. 85-95. A template can be found in the Compliance Guide dated May 2008, pp. 93-95.
615. 16 CFR 436(5)s(3).
616. 16 CFR 436(5)t. Reviewed in the Compliance Guide dated May 2008, pp. 95-112. A template can be found in the Compliance Guide dated May 2008, pp. 98-112.
617. 16 CFR 436(5)t.
618. 16 CFR 436(5)t.
619. 16 CFR 436(5)u. Reviewed in the Compliance Guide dated May 2008, pp. 112-116. A template can be found in the Compliance Guide dated May 2008, p. 116.

[x] Item 22: Contracts[620]

Franchisors are required to attach a copy of all proposed agreements relating to the franchise offered pursuant to item 22. This requirement encompasses the franchise agreement, leases, options, financial and purchase agreements.

[y] Item 23: Receipts[621]

The FTC Rule requires franchisors to obtain a signed receipt for the disclosure document furnished to each prospective franchisee. The prospective franchisee is permitted to 'sign' the document receipt electronically.

[F] Regulation of Franchise Arrangements in France

The first attempt in France to regulate the franchise relationship was taken in 1972 by the French Franchise Federation (FFF) with the formulation of a Code of Ethics (the Code).[622] Ultimately this Code had little bearing upon the moral conduct of the parties since its enforcement was not mandatory.[623] Notwithstanding this fact, the Code is still referred to by the courts as a testament to custom and usage; since the fact that a franchisor joins the FFF implies that the Code becomes part of any franchise agreement the franchisor in question then concludes.[624]

[1] Legislation

The French legislature intervened in this context with the introduction of the Law of Doubin (*Loi Doubin*).[625] Named after the Minister François Doubin who introduced the law, this Law adopted on 31 December 1989 (Law No. 89-1008) set-out to redress the disparity of power between contracting parties.[626]

620. 16 CFR 436(5)v. Reviewed in the Compliance Guide dated May 2008, pp. 116-117. A template can be found in the Compliance Guide dated May 2008, pp.116-117.
621. 16 CFR 436(5)w. Reviewed in the Compliance Guide dated May 2008, pp. 119-120. A template can be found in the Compliance Guide dated May 2008, pp.119-120.
622. Emerson 2009: 323.
623. Emerson 2009: 323.
624. Emerson 2009: 324.
625. Loi n° 89-1008 du 31 décembre 1989 relative au développement des entreprises commerciales et artisanales et à l'amélioration de leur environnement économique, juridique et social, in Journal Officiel, 2 January 1990. Law No. 89-1008 of 31 December 1989 related to the development of commercial and artisanal businesses and the improvement of their economic, legal and social environment.
626. Emerson 2009: 324.

Though Law No. 89-1008 is not specific to franchises, it nevertheless encompasses such relationships, with Article 1 of Law No. 89-1008 addressing franchises (now set out in Article L330-3 of the Commercial Code[627]).[628]

The details of Article of Law No. 89-1008 were subsequently laid out in Decree No. 91-337 of 4 April 1991.[629] Published in the Official Journal (JO) dated 4 April 1991, the goal of Decree No. 91-337 was to apply Article 1, Law No. 89-1008.[630]

Article L330-3 of the Commercial Code (L330-3)[631] applies to any person who grants another the right to exploit a commercial name, trademark or sign, whilst obliging the latter to be exclusive or quasi-exclusive in the exercise of their activity.[632] Pursuant to Article L330-3, the first party must provide the second party with information of a sincere nature.

In this context, a franchisor is mandated by Article L330-3, as the party granting the other the right to exploit a commercial name and so forth, to furnish a Disclosure Document to potential franchisees containing full and honest information (*'des informations sincères'*)[633] sufficient to allow potential franchisees to determine whether to proceed with the transaction (*'qui lui permettre de s'engager en connaissance de cause'*).[634]

This Disclosure Document must contain the information mandated by the Decree addressing more precisely the following particulars:[635]

- date of establishment (*l'ancienneté*) and experience of the franchisor's business;
- state and developmental prospects of the market concerned;

627. *Code de commerce.*
628. Article L330-3 is found in the Commercial Code (*Code de commerce*) Found in Book III entitled 'Certain forms of sale and exclusivity clauses' (*Livre III - De certaines formes de ventes et des clauses d'exclusivité*) in Title III entitled 'Exclusivity Clauses' (*Title III - Des clauses de'exclusivité*).
629. Décret n° 91-337 du 4 avril 1991 *portant application de l'article 1er de la loi n° 89-1008 du 31 décembre 1989 relative au développement des entreprises commerciales et artisanales et à l'amélioration de leur environnement économique, juridique et social.* Translated by M. Meiselles – Decree No.91-337 of 4 April 1991 addressing the application of Article 1 of Law No. 89-1008 of 31 December 1989 related to the development of commercial and artisanal businesses and the improvement of their economic, legal and social environment.

    Decree No. 91-337 can be found in the Journal Officiel (JO) dated 6 April 1991 (a correction to the Decree was published in the Journal Officiel (JO) dated 4 May 1991).
630. Emerson 2009: 324 Footnotes 33 and 34.
631. L330-3.
632. *'Toute personne qui met à la disposition d'une autre personne un nom commercial, une marque ou une enseigne, en exigeant d'elle un engagement d'exclusivité ou de quasi-exclusivité pour l'exercice de son activité, est tenue, préalablement à la signature de tout contrat conclu dans l'intérêt commun des deux parties, de fournir à l'autre partie un document donnant des informations sincères, qui lui permette de s'engager en connaissance de cause.'* (translated by M. Meiselles).
633. L330-3.
634. L330-3.
635. L330-3 reads *'Ce document, dont le contenu est fixé par décret, précise notamment, l'ancienneté et l'expérience de l'entreprise, l'état et les perspectives de développement du marché concerné, l'importance du réseau d'exploitants, la durée, les conditions de renouvellement, de résiliation et de cession du contrat ainsi que le champ des exclusivités.'* (Translated by M. Meiselles).

- size of the network;
- duration of the contract;
- conditions for renewal, termination, and transfer of the contract; and
- scope of exclusivity.

Other information which must be provided by the franchisor to the prospective franchisee includes the:[636,637]

- address of the seat of the franchisor;
- legal status of the entity that is the franchisor; and
- franchisor's activity, capital, banking information and history.

At least 20 days before the date assigned for signing the contract or the date on which a signature fee is due, the Disclosure Document along with a draft of the contract must be disclosed.[638]

In the event that payment of a fee is required prior to the signing of the contract intended to secure a territory for the potential franchisee, then written confirmation must be provided as well, addressing the benefits secured in exchange for this sum (*'prestations assurées en contrepartie de cette somme'*), and the reciprocal obligations of the parties in the event of cancellation (*'en cas de dédit'*).[639]

Where a party either fails to provide this mandated information or tender all the information promptly, it may sustain civil and criminal sanctions.[640] In this context, the franchisee may also seek civil damages for any harm resulting from either the failure of the franchisor to provide the documents or furnish accurate information.[641]

Where there has been a premature or abusive termination of the relationship, the franchisee may seek civil damages for any harm resulting from such termination.[642]

636. R330-1 *reads 'Le document prévu au premier alinéa de l'article L. 330-3 contient les informations suivantes:*

1° L'adresse du siège de l'entreprise et la nature de ses activités avec l'indication de sa forme juridique et de l'identité du chef d'entreprise s'il s'agit d'une personne physique ou des dirigeants s'il s'agit d'une personne morale; le cas échéant, le montant du capital'. According to R330-1, the Disclosure Document mentioned in Article L330-3 should include – '1) The address of the seat of the enterprise, the nature of its activities, with an indication of its legal form, the identity of the head of the enterprise if this involves a physical person, or the dirigents if this involves a moral person, and the capital reserve.' (Translated by M. Meiselles).

637. Emerson 2009: 333-334.

638. L330-3 reads *'Le document prévu au premier alinéa ainsi que le projet de contrat sont communiqués vingt jours minimum avant la signature du contrat, ou, le cas échéant, avant le versement de la somme mentionnée à l'alinéa précédent.'* (Translated by M.Meiselles).

639. L330-3 reads *'Lorsque le versement d'une somme est exigé préalablement à la signature du contrat mentionné ci-dessus, notamment pour obtenir la réservation d'une zone, les prestations assurées en contrepartie de cette somme sont précisées par écrit, ainsi que les obligations réciproques des parties en cas de dédit.'* (Translated by M. Meiselles).

640. Emerson 2009: 334.

641. Emerson 2009: 334.

642. Emerson 2009: 334.

In the event of a mistake or misrepresentation, the franchisee has the option of voiding the contract.[643] The right to void the franchise contract was upheld by the *Cour de Cessation* in cases where consent was obtained improperly through mistake, misrepresentation or by means of duress.[644] The *Cour d'Appel de Lyon (*Court of Appeal of Lyon) also ruled in 2008 that a franchise agreement is void if the franchisor fails to provide the franchisee with information in the pre-contractual documents regarding the condition of the franchise.[645]

The legislative framework introduced by the French legislature is supplemented by EU law notably EU Competition Law, and to a limited degree, by the opt-in Ethics Code of the FFF.

[2] Ethics Code of the FFF

The FFF adopted an Extension to the EFF Code. This Extension, which was last revised in June 2011, sets out the individual responsibilities of the parties alongside their shared obligations.[646]

[a] Franchisee's Responsibilities

The franchisee for his part is responsible for the human and financial means, and any acts taken vis-à-vis third parties in the context of exploitation of the franchise.[647]

Second, the franchisee must remain loyal to other franchisees in the network,[648] as well as the network itself, and be involved in the life of the network contributing to its general interest.[649] He must collaborate in a loyal manner to ensure the success of the network he belongs to.[650]

Third, when the term of the franchise agreement is nearing its end, the franchisee must inform the franchisor if he does not wish to renew the agreement.[651]

[b] Franchisor's Responsibilities

The franchisor for its part is responsible for guaranteeing the franchisee the right to use the savoir-faire it maintains and develops and must transmit it to the franchisee.[652] The validity of the franchisor's rights to the brands conferred to the franchisee must also be guaranteed by the franchisor.[653]

643. Emerson 2009: 334, citing Article 1109, French Civil Code which *reads 'Il n'y a point de consentement valable si le consentement n'a été donné que par erreur ou s'il a été extorqué par violence ou surpris par dol.'*
644. Emerson 2009: 334, citing Cass.com, 5/12/2000 pourvoi no. 97-21.631.
645. Emerson 2009: 334 Footnote 74 citing *Cour d'Appel de Lyon* 24/1/2008 pourvoi no. 06/07033.
646. Extension found in Part 4, EFF Code of Ethics (last visited 7/5/2018).
647. Article 1, Extension to EFF Code of Ethics (last visited 7/5/2018).
648. Article 8, Extension to EFF Code of Ethics (last visited 7/5/2018).
649. Article 4, Extension to EFF Code of Ethics (last visited 7/5/2018).
650. Article 1, Extension to EFF Code of Ethics (last visited 7/5/2018).
651. Article 14, Extension to EFF Code of Ethics (last visited 7/5/2018).
652. Article 4, Extension to EFF Code of Ethics (last visited 7/5/2018).
653. Article 7, Extension to EFF Code of Ethics (last visited 7/5/2018).

Moreover, the franchisor is responsible for promotion of the brand, research and innovation, as well as investment in the development and sustainability of its concept.[654] Full rights to exploit the brands, signs and so forth must be guaranteed by the franchisor to the franchisee.[655]

The franchisor must draw up a written agreement setting out, in a complete and precise manner, the rights, obligations, and responsibilities of the parties.[656]

During the term of the agreement, the franchisor must strive first to define quality norms, and see to it that these are respected by the franchisee in the context of the latter's relations with the end customer,[657] second to ensure that the franchisee is aware of his responsibilities vis-à-vis the end customer,[658] and third to draw to the franchisee's attention the necessity of guaranteeing down-payments made by the customer, in circumstances where the customer must make full or partial advance payment.[659] These last three duties relate to the franchisor's responsibility for the identity, and reputation of the network.[660]

In the event the franchisor does not wish to renew the contract, as the term of the agreement nears its end, the franchisor must provide advance notice to the franchisee of a sufficient length.[661]

Bearing in mind the obligation of loyalty owed, the franchisor will not look to develop sales using the Internet, when such a move is prejudicial to the franchisees.[662]

A franchisor is not permitted to adopt unwarranted restrictions intended to deprive the franchisee of his right to leave the network when the franchise agreement is coming to an end.[663]

§5.09 EU COMPETITION LAW AND ITS IMPACT ON FRANCHISE AGREEMENTS[664]

[A] Franchising and the VRBER 2010[665]

[1] Definition of Franchising under the Guidelines

The Guidelines accompanying the VRBER 2010 define a franchise as an agreement containing 'licences of intellectual property rights relating in particular to trademarks or signs and know-how for the use and distribution of goods or services. In addition to the licence of IPRs, the franchisor usually provides the franchisee during the life of the

654. Article 5, Extension to EFF Code of Ethics (last visited 7/5/2018).
655. Article 7, Extension to EFF Code of Ethics (last visited 7/5/2018).
656. Article 12, Extension to EFF Code of Ethics (last visited 7/5/2018).
657. Article 13(1), Extension to EFF Code of Ethics (last visited 7/5/2018).
658. Article 13(2), Extension to EFF Code of Ethics (last visited 7/5/2018).
659. Article 13(3), Extension to EFF Code of Ethics (last visited 7/5/2018).
660. Chapeau to A13, Extension to EFF Code of Ethics (last visited 7/5/2018).
661. Article 14, Extension to EFF Code of Ethics (last visited 7/5/2018).
662. Article 16, Extension to EFF Code of Ethics (last visited 7/5/2018).
663. Article 17, Extension to EFF Code of Ethics (last visited 7/5/2018).
664. Discussed in detail in Jones and Sufrin (2011: 656).
665. A detailed review of the VRBER 2010 can be found in the chapter on competition law.

agreement with commercial or technical assistance. The licence and the assistance are integral components of the business method being franchised. The franchisor is in general paid a franchise fee by the franchisee for the use of the particular business method. Franchising may enable the franchisor to establish, with limited investments, a uniform network for the distribution of his products. In addition to the provision of the business method, franchise agreements usually contain a combination of different vertical restraints concerning the products being distributed, in particular selective distribution and/or non-compete and/or exclusive distribution or weaker forms thereof'.[666]

[2] Qualifying Franchise Agreements

Licensing addressed within the terms of a franchise agreement will be covered by the VRBER 2010 in circumstances where five prerequisites are met.[667] These five conditions are discussed in detail in Chapter 2 on Competition Law.

[a] Qualifying Agreements: When Will an Agreement Containing IPR Provisions Fall Within the Scope of the Block Exemption?

The point of departure in this context is Article 2(3) of the VRBER 2010 that brings within the scope of the block exemption vertical agreements containing IPR provisions. This article states that the block exemption (provided for in Article 2(1) VRBER 2010) applies 'to vertical agreements containing provisions which relate to the assignment to the buyer or use by the buyer of intellectual property rights, provided that those provisions do not constitute the primary object of such agreements and are directly related to the use, sale or resale of goods or services by the buyer or its customers. The exemption applies on condition that, in relation to the contract goods or services, those provisions do not contain restrictions of competition having the same object as vertical restraints which are not exempted under this Regulation'.[668]

The conditions set out in Article 2(3) of the VRBER 2010 are elaborated upon in the Guidelines accompanying the VRBER 2010. According to these Guidelines, the block exemption in VRBER 2010 applies to vertical agreements containing IPR provisions if five cumulative conditions are met. The IPR provisions in these vertical agreements must:[669]

- be 'part of a vertical agreement';[670]
- be 'assigned to, or licensed for use by, the buyer';[671]

666. VRBER 2010, para 189.
667. The IPR provisions must meet the five conditions set out in VRBER 2010 Guidelines, para 31.
668. Article 2(3) VRBER 2010.
669. VRBER 2010 Guidelines, para 31.
670. VRBER 2010 Guidelines, para 31.
671. VRBER 2010 Guidelines, para 31.

- not 'constitute the primary object of the agreement';[672]
- be 'directly related to the use, sale or resale of goods or services by the buyer or his customers';[673] and
- not 'contain restrictions of competition having the same object as vertical restraints which are not exempted'[674] under the VRBER 2010.

In the context of franchising, it is commonly the case that these five prerequisites are fulfilled, since under most franchise agreements the franchisor furnishes goods and/or services (notably commercial or technical assistance services) to the franchisee[675] and the IPR provisions help the franchisee to resell the goods (supplied by the franchisor or by the supplier designated by the franchisor) or to use those goods and sell the resulting goods or services.[676] Where the franchise agreement 'only or primarily concerns licensing of IPRs', this agreement is unlikely to be covered by the Block Exemption Regulation,[677] though the Commission will generally apply to this agreement the principles denoted in the VRBER 2010 and the Guidelines accompanying the VRBER 2010.[678]

IPR-related restrictions that are generally viewed as necessary to safeguard the IPRs of the franchisor which fall within the scope of Article 101(1) TFEU (hereinafter Article 101(1)) and in turn within the scope of the VRBER 2010 include the following obligations:[679]

- the obligation imposed on the franchisee 'not to engage, directly or indirectly, in any similar business';[680]
- the obligation imposed on the franchisee not to buy a financial interest in the capital of a competing undertaking which would provide the franchisee with 'the power to influence the economic conduct of such undertaking';[681]
- the obligation imposed on the franchisee not to make known to a third party the know-how furnished by the franchisor 'as long as this know-how is not in the public domain';[682]
- the obligation imposed on the franchisee to pass onto the franchisor 'any experience gained in exploiting the franchise and to grant it, and other franchisees, a non-exclusive licence for the know-how resulting from that experience';[683]

672. VRBER 2010 Guidelines, para 31.
673. VRBER 2010 Guidelines, para 31.
674. VRBER 2010 Guidelines, para 31.
675. VRBER 2010 Guidelines, para 44.
676. VRBER 2010 Guidelines, para 44.
677. VRBER 2010 Guidelines, para 44.
678. VRBER 2010 Guidelines, para 44.
679. VRBER 2010 Guidelines, para 45.
680. VRBER 2010 Guidelines, para 45.
681. VRBER 2010 Guidelines, para 45.
682. VRBER 2010 Guidelines, para 45.
683. VRBER 2010 Guidelines, para 45.

- the obligation imposed on the franchisee to inform the franchisor of any infringements of the licensed IPRs, to pursue such infringements and to aid the franchisor with the pursuit of such infringements;[684]
- the obligation imposed on the franchisee not to make use of the licensed know-how for any purpose other than the exploitation of the franchise;[685]
- the obligation imposed on the franchisee not to assign to another without the agreement of the franchisor any of the rights provided or duties imposed under the franchise agreement.[686]

[3] Market Share Threshold in Franchise Agreements and the Block Exemption

The block exemption in the VRBER 2010 applies up to the 30% market share threshold.[687]

In the case of a vertical agreement containing IPR provisions that aid the buyer to market the contract goods (such as the use of the supplier's trademark), then the market share of the supplier on the market where he sells the contract goods is relevant to the application of the Block Exemption.[688]

Where the franchisor is not supplying goods for resale but rather is providing 'a bundle of services and goods combined with IPR provision which together form the business method being franchised, the franchisor needs to take account of his market share as a provider of a business method. For that purpose, the franchisor needs to calculate his market share on the market where the business method is exploited, which is the market where the franchisees exploit the business method to provide goods or services to end users. The franchisor must base his market share on the value of the goods or services supplied by his franchisees on this market. On such a market the competitors may be providers of other franchised business methods but also suppliers of substitutable goods or services not applying franchising'.[689]

In the context of a franchise arrangement [690] 'the more important the transfer of know-how, the more likely it is that the restraints create efficiencies and/or are indispensable to protect the know-how and that the vertical restraints fulfil the conditions of Article 101(3)'.[691]

A franchise agreement containing a non-compete obligation on the goods or services acquired by the franchisee will fall outside the scope of Article 101(1) if 'the obligation is necessary to maintain the common identity and reputation of the franchised network. In such cases, the duration of the non-compete obligation is also

684. VRBER 2010 Guidelines, para 45.
685. VRBER 2010 Guidelines, para 45.
686. VRBER 2010 Guidelines, para 45.
687. VRBER 2010 Guidelines, para 190.
688. VRBER 2010 Guidelines, para 92.
689. VRBER 2010 Guidelines, para 92.
690. VRBER 2010 Guidelines, para 190.
691. VRBER 2010 Guidelines, para 190.

irrelevant under Article 101(1), as long as it does not exceed the duration of the franchise agreement itself'.[692]

§5.10 GOVERNING LAW

[A] Conflict of Law Rules[693]

If the parties have failed to select the body or indeed the bodies of law governing their contract and their contractual relationship then the law applicable to the contract will be determined by the final arbiter using conflict of laws rules.

[B] Conflict of Laws Rules Governing Franchise Agreements under European Union Law

In circumstances where one or more of the contracting parties is based and/or is operating in a Member State of the European Union, the arbiter will refer to the provisions of Rome I[694] in order to determine the law applicable to the contract.

Rome I governs all contracts concluded after 17 December 2009. Contracts concluded either before or on 17 December 2009 are governed by the Rome Convention[695] the predecessor to Rome I.

Rome I and the Rome Convention both apply to contractual obligations in situations where there is a choice between the laws of different countries. Both instruments contain rules that define the law applicable to a contract, and those rules are mandatory in application.

Where Member States have several territorial units each of which has its own rules of law in relation to contractual obligations then each territorial unit will be treated as a country for the purposes of identifying the law applicable under Rome I.[696]

---

692. VRBER 2010 Guidelines, para 190.
693. For English and European law *see* McClean, David and Beevers, Kisch (2005), *Morris: The Conflict of Laws*, 6th ed., Sweet & Maxwell, Chapters 1, 13; for US law *see* Scoles, Eugene F., Hay, Peter, Borchers, Patrick J. and Symeonides, Symeon C. (2004), *Conflict of Laws*, 4th ed., Thomson West. *See also* Ferrari, Franco and Leible, Stefan (eds) (2009), *Rome I Regulation: The Law Applicable to Contractual Obligations in Europe*, Sellier European Law Publishers; Murray et al. (2007), Chapter 21.
694. The full title of Rome I is Regulation (EC) No 593/2008 of the European Parliament and the Council of 17 June 2008 on the Law Applicable to Contractual Obligations. It is available at http://eur-lex.europa.eu/ LexUriServ/LexUriServ.do?uri=OJ:L:2008:177:0006:0006:en:PDF (last accessed 21 January 2013).
695. 80/934/EEC: Convention on the Law Applicable to Contractual Obligations Opened for Signature in Rome on 19 June 1980, available at http://eur-lex.europa.eu/LexUriServ/ LexUriServ. do?uri=CELEX:41980A0934:EN:HTML (last accessed 21 January 2013).
696. Article 22.1 Rome I.

[1] Freedom to Choose the Governing Law

Article 3.1 of Rome I permits the parties contracting to choose the law governing their contract. The parties may choose the law applicable to the whole of their contract or alternatively to just part of it.[697] Furthermore, Article 3.2 of Rome I permits the parties contracting to modify by agreement the law governing the contract. Any such selection must be made expressly or clearly demonstrated by the terms of the contract or the circumstances of the case.[698]

Wherever possible, it is advisable for the contracting parties to expressly identify the law that they have chosen to govern the contract concluded between them. This will ensure certainty and clarity in their relationship and will ward against any potential litigation that could later ensue on this very question.

[2] In the Absence of a Choice by the Parties

Whilst the contracting parties are free to choose the law applicable to the contract between them,[699] if they do not do so Rome I will intercede to make the selection for them in accordance with the rules set out in Article 4.

Article 4.1 of Rome I sets out specific choice of law rules for particular categories of cases. Where Article 4.1 does not supply a conclusive choice of law then the general rule articulated in Article 4.2 applies. Further general displacement rules – included in Articles 4.3 and 4.4 – are intended to introduce flexibility in those situations where the application of one of the specific choice of law rules does not produce the appropriate result.

Pursuant to Article 4.1, in circumstances where the law applicable to the contract has not been selected by the contracting parties (in line with Article 3), a franchise contract will be governed by the law of the country where the franchisee has his habitual residence.[700]

[3] Habitual Residence

The phrase habitual residence, used in this context, is defined by Article 19 Rome I which states that for:

- companies and other bodies (corporate or unincorporated) habitual residence shall be the place of central administration;
- a natural person acting in the course of a business activity habitual residence will be his principal place of business;

697. Article 3(1) Rome I.
698. Article 3(1) Rome I.
699. Article 3 Rome I.
700. Article 4.1(d) Rome I.

- a contract concluded in the course of the operations of a branch, agency or any other establishment the place where the branch, agency or any other establishment is located will be deemed to be the place of habitual residence;
- contracts for which performance is the responsibility of a branch, agency or establishment, the place where the branch, agency or any other establishment is located will be deemed to be the place of habitual residence.

When ascertaining the habitual residence, the relevant point in time is the time when the contract is concluded.

§5.11 CATEGORIES OF AGREEMENTS ASSOCIATED WITH FRANCHISING

The process of franchising will typically entail a number of distinct phases. These phases are listed in chronological order below:[701]

- the creation and the development of the franchise system;
- the promotion of the franchise system;
- the period between the recruitment of the franchisee and the launch of the franchisee's operation;
- the ongoing relationship between the franchisor and the franchisee;
- termination of the relationship;
- post-termination.

The recruitment of the franchisee, the launch of the relationship and the ongoing relationship between franchisor and franchisee will be dealt with to a large extent contractually.[702] Typically these matters will be addressed in one or occasionally two agreements.[703]

The agreement used to address the period between the recruitment of the franchisee and the launch of the franchisee's operation is usually referred to as a purchase agreement. The agreement used to address the ongoing relationship between the parties is known as the franchise agreement, franchise or licence agreement.[704]

[A] Purchase Agreement

The purchase agreement will address the following items:

- franchise package;
- price; and
- initial support services provided by the franchisor to the franchisee.

701. Based on a classification provided by Mendelsohn 2004: 187-8.
702. Mendelsohn 2004: 188.
703. Mendelsohn 2004: 188.
704. Mendelsohn 2004: 188.

Each of these three items addressed in the purchase agreement is briefly reviewed below.

[1] Franchise Package

The scope, substance and subject matter of the franchise package being acquired from the franchisor is set out in a list referred to as the inventory (schedule of equipment or equipment list).

Such an inventory may be confidential in nature; in which case, the contract will impose an obligation on the franchisee to this effect. Moreover the contract will typically indicate that if the transaction does not proceed the list will need to be returned.

[a] Location of Premises

The contracting parties will not necessarily need to agree upon the premises from which the franchisee will operate before the contracts are concluded on the proviso that the area within which the premises are to be situated is ascertainable.[705]

An agreement may be concluded which is conditional upon a mutually agreeable location being found.[706] In circumstances where there are several prospective franchisees at a time where premises are not readily available, a waiting list may be used; in which case a prospective franchisee will be added to the list.[707] In certain situations, it may be possible for the prospective franchisee to obtain an option for an area.[708]

[b] Layout of Premises

The manner in which the premises or mobile units is dealt with may be addressed in the franchise package.[709] To this end, the franchisor may provide the franchisee with:[710]

- standard plans and specifications for the premises (responsibility for adapting the premises may be assumed by either the franchisor or franchisee with the latter using its own personnel and contractors subject to the prior authorisation of the franchisor);
- a manual containing property specifications (which the personnel and contractors of the franchisee may use to draft precise plans);

705. Mendelsohn 2004: 188.
706. Mendelsohn 2004: 188.
707. Mendelsohn 2004: 188.
708. Mendelsohn 2004: 188.
709. Mendelsohn 2004: 189.
710. Mendelsohn 2004: 189.

- the entire package of services needed to prepare the outlet (this package will encompass the preparation of plans and specifications and the execution of all the necessary works needed to prepare the outlet).

Alternately the franchisee may take charge of selecting a shop-fitter without consulting the franchisor or using the franchisor's list of approved contractors.[711] Such a shop-fitter will then use the plans and specifications of the franchisor in order to execute the conversion of premises.[712]

When the franchisee assumes responsibility for the fitting of the premises, it will assume responsibility for the day-to-day supervision of the project whilst the franchisor will monitor works for compliance with its standards.[713]

[2] Price

Pricing should be addressed clearly in the terms of the purchase agreement with due regard being given by the contracting parties to the method and timing of payment.

Various options are available with regard to timing.[714] Full payment may be due upon the signing of the agreement (rare), though more often than not only part of the payment will be due on signing with the remainder of the price falling due at some later stage (on delivery of the equipment, upon commencement of training and so forth).[715]

A payment provision may factor in the need to generate financing for the franchise.[716] In which case, the contract may be made conditional upon the arrangement of satisfactory finance; though in this context due care should be taken by the parties to define with care the phrase 'satisfactory finance'.[717]

The parties contracting should give consideration to whether or not the deposit will be refunded if the transaction does not proceed.[718] Such a provision should address the circumstances in which the deposit is refundable and whether the deposit will be refunded in full or in part.[719] Where partial refund is due, a method for the computation of the part due should be included.[720]

In circumstances where a franchisor wishes to withdraw from a transaction if for example it transpires that the franchisee is not suitable, the parties may provide that the entire deposit may be refunded to the franchisee subject to the reimbursement of expenditure incurred by the franchisor in relation to training and so on.[721]

711. Mendelsohn 2004: 189.
712. Mendelsohn 2004: 189.
713. Mendelsohn 2004: 189.
714. Mendelsohn 2004: 189.
715. Mendelsohn 2004: 189.
716. Mendelsohn 2004: 189.
717. Mendelsohn 2004: 189.
718. Mendelsohn 2004: 190.
719. Mendelsohn 2004: 190.
720. Mendelsohn 2004: 190.
721. Mendelsohn 2004: 189.

[3] *Initial Support Services Provided by the Franchisor to the Franchisee*

The franchisor will provide to the franchisee an array of services initially and throughout the term of the agreement including assistance with the selection and the identification of trading locations, guidance on the application for occupation rights relating to the trading location, preparation of layout plans, assistance with the fitting of the outlet, general assistance with the calculation of the correct level and mix of inventory, training of staff and franchisees in the operation of the business format, relevant manufacturing or preparation procedures, accounting, business controls, marketing, promotion and merchandising.[722] Furthermore, the franchisor will supply its franchisee with the operations manual.[723]

§5.12 MATERIAL TERMS IN A FRANCHISE AGREEMENT[724]

The following section of the chapter reviews the key terms typically contained in franchise agreements.

Whilst the terms that should be contained in such licensing agreements depend largely on the nature of the technology being licensed, certain common matters frequently arise in such deals.

The provisions that are reviewed are representative of the types of provisions that the parties should consider incorporating into their licensing agreement. The goal of this review is to provide an introductory overview of the key provisions and the matters that are frequently encountered in the context of these terms. This review is by no means intended to be exhaustive.

Due to the legal regulation governing such clauses in certain jurisdictions it is sensible for the parties to seek legal advice before incorporating these clauses into their licensing agreement.

[A] Overview

According to the rules contained in this Code developed by the EFF, a franchise agreement should set out in clear and unambiguous terms, the duties of the contracting parties whilst also defining the following basic terms:[725]

- the products and/or services furnished by the franchisor to the individual franchisee;
- the rights granted to the individual franchisee;

722. Mendelsohn 2004: Chapter 4.
723. Mendelsohn 2004: Chapter 4.
724. Selected bibliography includes Mendelsohn, The Guide to Franchising (7th Edition, Thomson), European Franchise Federation Code of Ethics and World Franchise Council Code of Ethics.
725. Article 5.5, European Franchise Federation Code of Ethics accessible at http://www.eff-franchise.com/Data/Code%20of%20Ethics2.pdf (last accessed 14/5/2018).

- the rights granted to the franchisor including any right that the franchisor enjoys to update the franchise system to align the system with 'new or changed methods';[726]
- the payment terms;
- the duration of the arrangement which should be sufficiently long in order to enable the individual franchisee 'to amortize their initial and subsequent investments specific to the franchise';[727]
- the option of renewing the agreement (renewal terms); and
- the termination provisions.

[B] Checklist of Provisions

In the preface to this section, a checklist of the key provisions reviewed is included. This checklist aims to help the reader plan their agreement before the drafting and negotiation of the said accord.

The following checklist lists some of the key provisions that should be borne in mind by the parties contracting or the party drafting the agreement.

This agreement is intended for use in cross-jurisdictional transactions between commercial parties. Not all of the provisions noted in the checklist are mandatory. However, when planning, negotiating and agreeing on the format of the terms of the contract it is sensible for each party contracting to consider each of these provisions in turn before deciding whether or not to use it.

Box 12.1 Checklist of provisions

Preface to the contract

✓ Cover sheet

✓ Table of contents (optional in longer contracts)

✓ Index of defined terms

Front of the contract

✓ Title

✓ Introductory clause (type of agreement, date of agreement, parties to agreement)

✓ Recitals

726. Article 5.5 (xii), European Franchise Federation Code of Ethics accessible at http://www.eff-franchise.com/Data/Code%20of%20Ethics2.pdf (last accessed 14/5/2018).
727. Article 5.5 (viii), European Franchise Federation Code of Ethics accessible at http://www.eff-franchise.com/Data/Code%20of%20Ethics2.pdf (last accessed 14/5/2018).

Body of the contract

✓ Definitions clause

✓ Grant

✓ Term of the agreement

✓ Shared obligations

Relationship of the parties

Confidentiality

Work obligations

✓ Obligations of the franchisee

Fees and accounts

Non-compete provisions

Sublicencing[728]

Protection of proprietary information and goodwill of the franchisor

Retention of ownership in the property licenced

Quality control

Future obligation to buy equipment

Anti-bribery policy of the franchisee

Insurance

Maintenance of licenced property[729]

Restrictions on the fields of use[730]

✓ Obligations of the franchisor

Franchisor's initial obligations

Franchisor's ongoing obligations

Assistance and training

Promotion

Warranties, liabilities and indemnities

✓ Termination (grounds and consequences)

728. *See* the corresponding section in the introduction chapter for detail and template clause.
729. *See* the corresponding section in the introduction chapter for detail and template clause.
730. *See* the corresponding section in the introduction chapter for detail and template clause.

✓ Death

Boilerplate clauses

✓ Assignment clause

✓ Change of control and ownership clause

✓ Merger clause

✓ Modifications clause

✓ Severance clause

✓ Notice clause

✓ Representation clause

✓ Dispute resolution (informal discussions, renegotiation, adaption, ADR, choice of jurisdiction, choice of law)

✓ Language clause

Back of the contract

✓ Concluding clause

✓ Signature blocks

✓ Attachment (exhibits and schedules)

[C] Preface of the Contract[731]

[D] Front of the Contract[732]

Franchise agreement

This franchise agreement is made [on this __ day of __ in the year __ *or* upon the date of the signature hereof] and is between:

1. __ of __ ('Franchisor')

2. __ of __ ('Franchisee')

The Franchisor and Franchisee will be referred to in this agreement individually as a Party or collectively as the Parties.

731. The preface of the contract is addressed in Chapter 1 of this book.
732. The front of the contract is addressed in Chapter 1 of this book.

The following information will appear in the front of the contract:

[1] Title

'Franchise agreement' in the extract above.

[2] Introductory Clause

This clause sets out the nature of the agreement, the details of the parties concluding the contract (in this case the franchisor and the franchisee) and occasionally the date of the agreement.

In the extract above the introductory clause is as follows:

> This franchise agreement is made [on this __ day of __ in the year __ *or* upon the date of the signature hereof] and is between:
>
> 3. __ of __ ('Franchisor')
>
> 4. __ of __ ('Franchisee')
>
> The Franchisor and Franchisee will be referred to in this agreement individually as a Party or collectively as the Parties.

[3] Recital(s)[733]

Whilst the recital is optional and may be dispensed with, when a recital is included in a contract it is likely to vary from one contract to another in length and detail according to the role it fulfils within the contract.

A recital may be there to set out the context, to denote the intentions of the parties contracting and to refer to other agreements entered into either prior to the agreement concerned or alongside this agreement.

Whilst no recital is included in the extract above, a recital of the type sampled below may be used when a franchise agreement is concluded.

> The Franchisor has carried out considerable research and has developed know-how, practical business experience and expertise in the Business and desires to develop this Business further. The Business uses bespoke goods ('Licenced Goods') and bespoke services ('Licenced Services') developed and perfected by the Franchisor.

733. A detailed review of recitals and their role is provided in the introduction chapter.

The Business, developed by the Franchisor, is carried out under marks ('Licenced Marks'). The Licenced Marks are owned exclusively by the Franchisor.

The Franchisor is prepared to grant certain defined rights described in this agreement to the Franchisee to enable the Franchisee to sell and market the Licenced Goods and to provide and promote the Licenced Services using the Licenced Marks.

The Franchisee desires to acquire the right and franchise to operate the Business pursuant to this agreement.

The Franchisee desires the right during the term of this agreement to sell the Licenced Goods and to provide the Licenced Services from the premises defined in this agreement ('Premises') using the Licenced Marks in accordance with the operations manual furnished by the Franchisor to the Franchisee as updated from time to time ('Manual').

[E] Body of the Contract

[1] Definitions Clause[734]

The definitions clause denotes the key terms used throughout the agreement and determines the scope of these terms. Due to the importance of these definitions to the ensuing relationship between the parties, it is sensible to verify the precision of these terms.

In franchise agreements the definitions clause will encompass terms such as Business, Licenced Territory, Franchisee's Business, Licenced Marks, Licenced Intellectual Property, Licenced Technology, Licenced Goods, Licenced Services, Premises, Manual, Equipment, Financial Package, Initial Fee, Start-up Package and Term.

[2] Grant[735]

1. In consideration of the payments agreed upon in this agreement, the Franchisor shall grant the Franchisee a licence during the Term (optional: limited to the Licenced Territory) and in line with the provisions of this agreement to:

a) Operate the Franchisee's Business;

734. *See* corresponding section in the introduction chapter.
735. *See* the corresponding section in the introduction chapter for detail and template clause.

b) Make use of the Licenced Marks and of the Licenced Intellectual Property in relation to the Franchisee's Business;

c) Make use of the Licenced Technology; and

d) Employ the Franchisor's knowledge and experience in relation to *inter alia* accounting, marketing, distribution, sales and management

From the Premises in accordance with the System.

2. Any sales of the Licenced Goods or exports of the Licenced Goods outside the Licenced Territory will be negotiated separately by the Franchisee with the Franchisor.

Option A: non-exclusive licence

3. This agreement is non-exclusive.

Option B: exclusive licence

3. The Franchisor grants the Franchisee a licence on an exclusive basis. As such the Franchisee may, to the exclusion of others [optional – including the Franchisor], exclusively:

1. Produce, have produced or use the Licenced Goods in the Licenced Territory;

2. Sell the Licenced Goods in the Licenced Territory; and

3. Use Licenced Technology.

The array of rights granted by the franchisor to the franchisee will largely be dictated by the subject matter of the franchise agreement and relevant surrounding circumstances. Such a provision will typically list the various rights that the franchisor is granting to the franchisee including, but not limited to, the right to use the:[736]

- blueprint of the franchisor and its methods of operation;
- trademarks, service marks and trade names belonging to the franchisor and any goodwill associated with these;
- trade secrets and confidential know-how of the franchisor;
- copyright materials of the franchisor (operations manual for example);
- recipes, formulas, designs, processes and manufacturing processes created and refined by the franchisor; as well as
- the brand image developed by the franchisor.

736. Mendelsohn 2004: 174, 191.

[a] Territorial Restrictions

Under the terms of the franchise agreement, the franchisee will be obligated to conduct the franchised business from one or more premises approved by the franchisor.[737]

[b] Exclusivity and Territory

Exclusivity is often associated with the grant of rights. The precise scope and the exact substance of the exclusive rights awarded to the franchisee will be governed to a large degree by the nature of the franchised business and whether the franchised business is fixed (an outlet for example) or mobile (a vehicle for example).[738]

Where a fixed unit is used for the franchised business, exclusivity if granted will usually be associated with a defined territory encompassing the area within a specific radius from the franchisee's unit.[739] No franchises will be granted by the franchisor within this specific territory.[740]

Where a mobile unit is used under the terms of the franchise, an area will typically be assigned to the franchisee within which it may operate on an exclusive or non-exclusive basis.[741] Under the terms of such an agreement, the franchisee will be prohibited from soliciting for business outside the assigned territory.[742]

A franchisor interested in retaining the right to sell into the territory allocated under the franchise agreement (using for example the Internet and mail order), should address this right within the terms of the franchise (optional clause in the Option B above).[743]

[3] Term of the Agreement[744]

Option A: Indefinite term agreement with no initial period

> 1. This agreement shall come into force [on this ___ day of ___ in the year ___ *or* upon the date of the signature of this agreement] and remain in force unless terminated by one Party providing the other Party prior written notice of no less than ___ [subject to the right to early termination provided by the terms of this agreement].

737. Mendelsohn 2004: 191.
738. Mendelsohn 2004: 191.
739. Mendelsohn 2004: 191-2.
740. Mendelsohn 2004: 192.
741. Mendelsohn 2004: 192.
742. Mendelsohn 2004: 192.
743. Mendelsohn 2004: 192.
744. For further detail *see* corresponding section in the introduction chapter.

Option B: Indefinite term agreement with an initial period

> 1. This agreement shall come into force [on this ___ day of ___ in the year ___ *or* upon the date of the signature of this agreement] and remain in force for an initial term of ___ years from the date of this agreement ('Initial Term').
>
> [Optional: No right to terminate during the Initial Term. Neither Party shall provide notice to the other Party before the end of the Initial Term.]
>
> [Optional: The Initial Term is subject to early termination pursuant to clause ()].
>
> 2. The agreement shall remain in force after the Initial Term unless terminated by one Party providing the other Party with prior written notice of no less than ____. [Optional: Subject to the right to early termination provided by clause ()].
>
> 3. In the event the Franchisee continues to perform the Franchisee's Business after the Initial Term ends, then the Franchisee will be deemed to do so in accordance with the terms and conditions of this agreement.

Option C: Requirement for renewal after the end of the initial period

> 1. This agreement shall come into force [on this ___ day of ___ in the year ___ *or* upon the date of the signature of this agreement] and remain in force for an initial term of ___ years from the date of this agreement ('Initial Term'). [Optional: No right to terminate during the Initial Term. Neither Party shall provide notice to the other Party before the end of the Initial Term.][Optional: Subject to early termination pursuant to clause ().]
>
> 2. No less than [] and no more than [] before the end of the Initial Term, the Franchisee at its discretion may provide the Franchisor with written notice of its desire to renew the term of this agreement for a period of [] after the end of the Initial Term ('Renewal Term').
>
> 3. The Franchisor shall accept this request for renewal by providing the Franchisee with written notice no less than [] before the end of the Initial Term, on the proviso that:
>
> a) The Franchisee has paid the Renewal Fee within [] before the end of the Initial Period and has executed all its obligations under this agreement to the reasonable satisfaction of the Franchisor;
>
> b) The Franchisee's Business satisfies the requirements imposed by the Franchisor as defined in the Manual and the franchise agreement applicable at the time in question;

c) There are no material breaches outstanding on the part of the Franchisee at the end of the Initial Term; and

d) There are no grounds for termination by the Franchisor pursuant to clause [].

4. Renewal pursuant to this clause will be executed by the Parties' written and signed confirmation of the renewal or, if so stipulated by the Franchisor, by the Parties concluding a new franchise agreement that uses the Franchisor's then current form of the franchise agreement, on the proviso that on renewal, the Franchisee has:

a) Paid the Initial Fee; and

b) Fulfilled its obligations in clauses [].

5. The provisions in clauses [] or any equivalent provision/s in the new agreement shall [or shall not] apply during the Renewal Term.

6. Any renewal under this clause shall not prejudice the rights or the obligations of [the Parties or the Franchisor] outstanding at the end of the Initial Term.

7. Optional: This agreement shall terminate at the end of Renewal Term unless this agreement shall be terminated earlier in accordance with clause [].

Option D: Fixed term agreement

1. This agreement shall come into force [on this ___ day of ___ in the year ___ *or* upon the date of the signature of this agreement] and remain in force for a period of ___ years from this date.

2. (Optional: Automatic renewal) This agreement is renewable automatically for successive periods of ___ years, unless it is terminated by one Party providing the other Party with prior written notice of no less than ____. The provisions in clauses [] shall [or shall not] apply. Any renewal under this clause shall not prejudice the rights or the obligations of [the Parties or the Franchisor] outstanding at the end of the earlier term.

2. (Optional: Active renewal) Either Party is able to renew this agreement for successive periods of ____ years, by providing the other Party with prior written notice of no less than ____. The Party who receives the request for renewal shall object to the renewal of this agreement by providing a written reply within _____ to the Party requesting a renewal. If no written reply is provided within _____ to the Party requesting a renewal, the agreement will be renewed automatically.

The provisions in clauses [] shall [or shall not] apply. Any renewal under this clause shall not prejudice the rights or the obligations of [the Parties or the Franchisor] outstanding at the end of the earlier term.

This provision may stipulate the date on which the agreement will commence and if appropriate the term of the agreement.

[a] Initial Period and Definite Term

Where the parties contracting agree on a definite term or an initial period, they should take care to ensure that the definite term or the initial period is sufficiently long to allow the franchisee to amortise its initial investment[745] and to generate a return on its investment.[746]

When setting the duration of their contractual relationship, due consideration should be given by the contracting parties not only to the sums invested but also to the concerns of the franchisee's lenders who will be concerned about ensuring that the franchisee will have sufficient time to repay its loans.[747]

[b] Renewal

When negotiating the terms of the franchise, the parties should address the issue of renewal and the format of any such renewal.[748] In this context, the Code of the EFF and the Council suggest the inclusion of a provision in the agreement setting out the basis for renewal of the agreement.[749]

In template clauses C and D above renewal is provided as an option. The first option (in template clause D) allows for automatic renewal, whilst the second option allows for active renewal.

[c] Revamp Provision

Renewal may be used by certain franchisors as an occasion to impose further obligations upon the franchisee using a revamp provision or relocation provision.[750]

745. Mendelsohn 2004: 175; *see also* EFF Code of Ethics: 5.4.
746. WFC Code of Ethics: IV.
747. Mendelsohn 2004: 175.
748. Mendelsohn 2004: 175.
749. Article 5.5 (ix), European Franchise Federation Code of Ethics accessible at http://www.eff-franchise.com/Data/Code%20of%20Ethics2.pdf (last accessed 14/5/2018). A similar requirement is set out in WFC Code of Ethics: IV.
750. Mendelsohn 2004: 175.

A revamp provision will typically oblige the franchisee to completely refit its premises and bear the full cost of such an endeavour which may be equal if not greater than those originally incurred by the franchisee.[751]

Such a revamp will usually be required by the franchisor in order to ensure that its business remains competitive and contemporary.[752] Per se the use of such clauses is not unfair but the way in which they are enforced may be.

Before contemplating such a provision, the franchisor should consider trial running the revamp using a sufficient number of representative operational units to ascertain the worth of such a venture.[753] In the event that a revamp is required, the franchisor should consider assisting the franchisee with the arrangement of funding for the project.[754]

Moreover, when making a decision in this regard, the franchisor should take into account the franchisee's need to reap the financial rewards from any such expenditure.[755] Thereby ensuring that the franchisee is able within a reasonable period of time to recover their investment and to increase their profitability.[756]

[d] Relocation Provision

The renewal of the franchise may be made conditional on relocation obliging the franchisee to close down its present premises and to relocate to new ones which the franchisor considers offer a better trading opportunity or larger location in which to exhibit the franchisor's new ideas.[757]

From the perspective of the franchisee, such a provision will effectively oblige it to set up a completely new operation with all the inherent risks, expenditure (including the cost of the existing premises until such a time as these are disposed of) and potential losses (e.g., losses associated with the disposal of the existing premises) associated with such a venture.[758]

Before contemplating such a provision, due consideration should be given by the franchisor to its necessity and the alternatives available[759] as such the franchisor should consider whether it would be possible for the new concept to be installed in the existing premises.[760]

If the franchisor decides to insist on an obligation to relocate, it should be able to demonstrate the cost effectiveness of any relocation from the point of view of the franchisee based on existing and sufficient testing and to justify this provision by

751. Mendelsohn 2004: 176.
752. Mendelsohn 2004: 176.
753. Mendelsohn 2004: 176.
754. Mendelsohn 2004: 176.
755. Mendelsohn 2004: 176.
756. Mendelsohn 2004: 176.
757. Mendelsohn 2004: 176-7.
758. Mendelsohn 2004: 177.
759. Mendelsohn 2004: 177.
760. Mendelsohn 2004: 177.

reference to future competitiveness.[761] Moreover it should assist the franchisee to source financing for the relocation.[762]

A franchisor should act with utmost good faith in such circumstances and should not use such an obligation as a mechanism for ridding itself of a franchisee.[763]

[4] Shared Obligations

The agreement may include certain shared obligations borne by both parties throughout the term of their relationship.

Beyond an agreement on the nature of the relationship[764] that exists between them, the parties should consider agreeing on a duty of confidentiality[765] and their working obligations.[766]

In this context, the parties may agree that they are obligated to exercise good faith and fairness in their dealings with each other,[767] to settle their differences 'with good faith and goodwill through fair and reasonable direct communication and negotiation',[768] and where appropriate in the case of litigation to resort to mediation in order to resolve conflicts between them.[769]

Moreover the franchisee and franchisor may agree to 'cooperate in all loyalty and in respect of their mutual obligations and commitments'.[770]

The Council's Code of Ethics[771] and the EFF Code of Ethics[772] both suggest that the provisions of the agreement set out the respective rights and duties of the franchisor and franchisee. Such terms, the Council suggests, should be 'equitable for both of the parties'.[773]

[5] Obligations of the Franchisee[774]

The following obligations imposed on the franchisee under the terms of the franchise agreement are intended to protect the interests of the franchisor, its reputation, its goodwill, its property and earnings.

761. Mendelsohn 2004: 177.
762. Mendelsohn 2004: 177.
763. Mendelsohn 2004: 177.
764. *See* the corresponding section in the introduction chapter for detail and template clause.
765. *See* the corresponding section in the introduction chapter for detail and template clause.
766. *See* the corresponding section in the introduction chapter for detail and template clause.
767. Article 2.4 (ii), European Franchise Federation Code of Ethics accessible at http://www.eff-franchise.com/Data/Code%20of%20Ethics2.pdf (last accessed 14/5/2018).
768. Article 2.4 (iv), European Franchise Federation Code of Ethics accessible at http://www.eff-franchise.com/Data/Code%20of%20Ethics2.pdf (last accessed 14/5/2018).
769. WFC Code of Ethics: IV.
770. WFC Code of Ethics: IV.
771. WFC Code of Ethics: IV.
772. Article 5.5, European Franchise Federation Code of Ethics accessible at http://www.eff-franchise.com/Data/Code%20of%20Ethics2.pdf (last accessed 14/5/2018).
773. WFC Code of Ethics: IV.
774. Reviewed in detail in Meiselles 2013: 257-8.

The franchisor for its part will probably endeavour to ensure the incorporation into the agreement of provisions protecting its interests effectively and comprehensively. From its perspective, the franchisee will probably attempt to contain such obligations as best as it can.

The provisions discussed below are representative of the type of provisions that a franchisor should consider including in a franchise agreement and of the kind of interests that such a franchisor will look to protect by so doing.

[a] Fees and Verification of Accounts

1. The Franchisee shall pay the Franchisor the sum of [] in [currency] ('Initial Fee'). The Initial Fee will be payable on []. The Initial Fee will encompass all the obligations furnished by the Franchisor pursuant to clause(s) [] in this agreement.

2. The Franchisee shall pay the Franchisor [x% of for example the Gross Monthly Receipts] in [currency] on [] each [week or month or year] ['Management Fee'].

3. The Franchisee shall pay the Franchisor [x% of for example the Gross Monthly Receipts] in [currency] on [] each [week or month or year] ['Advertising Fee'].

4. All payments by the Franchisee will be made [by cheque or by wire transfer using the following information], unless the Franchisor stipulates otherwise by written notice given to the Franchisee.

5. All sums due from the Franchisee are exclusive of all sales taxes. The Franchisee shall pay all sales taxes [on the due date for payment or on receipt of the Franchisor's invoice].

6. The Franchisee shall be responsible for paying all invoices due to third party suppliers.

7. The Franchisee shall:

a. Maintain records of all sales;

b. Report to the Franchisor on its sales on the [] day of each [] using the template report [provided in the Manual or approved by the Franchisor];

c. Keep at its Premises updated and comprehensive accounts and records pertaining to the Franchisee's Business. Such accounts and records should conform to the template [provided in the Manual or approved by the Franchisor];

d. Provide an audited copy of the accounts of the Franchisee on a [period] basis on [date] and all information and documentation reasonably requested by the Franchisor;

e. Retain its accounting and financial records for at least [] years after the end of the accounting year to which such records relate;

f. Permit an independent auditor appointed [by the Franchisor or by the Parties] to inspect such records. The cost of this audit shall be borne [by the Franchisor or the Franchisee or by the Parties].

[i] Introduction

In a franchise arrangement, the franchisee's revenue will be the revenue generated from the operation of the individual unit.[775]

The revenue of the franchisor will come from a number of possible sources.[776] First from the income generated from the sale of the franchise packages (initial fees).[777] Second from the continuing franchise fees (management services fees).[778] Third from the mark-up on the sale of goods.[779]

From the point of view of the franchisee, it is imperative that the franchise business generates enough revenue to allow it to make a return on its investment, to earn remuneration for its work and to be able to pay the sums that are due to the franchisor.[780]

[ii] Initial Fee

In the majority of cases the franchisor will charge the franchisee an initial fee.

Standard franchise

In its simplest form the initial fee will reflect the range of services that the franchisor will furnish the franchisee with in order to aid the franchisee with the establishment of its operational unit.[781] This fee will encompass the services and the training furnished by the franchisor.[782]

775. Mendelsohn 2004: 132.
776. Mendelsohn 2004: 132.
777. Mendelsohn 2004: 132.
778. Mendelsohn 2004: 132.
779. Mendelsohn 2004: 132.
780. Mendelsohn 2004: 132.
781. Mendelsohn 2004: 134.
782. Mendelsohn 2004: 134.

In addition the initial fee will include the price charged for permitting the franchisee to join the franchised network.[783] The price charged for allowing the franchisee to join the network will be commensurate with 'the strength of the name and the goodwill associated with it'.[784]

Turnkey franchise

In certain franchises, the franchisor may also buy the premises and then equip these premises.[785]

In which case, the franchisee will be charged an initial fee, which represents a mark-up on the cost of the various components that make-up the package furnished by the franchisor.[786] This fee will also probably include a charge for joining the franchise network.[787]

Equipment package

Another category of franchises consists of an arrangement in which the franchisor sells the franchisee an equipment package consisting of all the items of equipment required by the franchisee in order to commence trading.[788] In such a franchise, the franchisor will also supply the core services referred to above.[789]

In this category of franchise, the sale price will encompass the initial franchise fee 'by way of a mark-up on the cost of the equipment to include the [aforementioned] elements'.[790]

[iii] Ongoing Fees (Management Services Fee)

The franchisor will charge its franchisees an ongoing fee to pay for the continuing services supplied by the franchisor to the franchisee.[791]

This fee often referred to as the management services fee will in the majority of franchises be a percentage-based fee, calculated using the gross revenues generated by the franchisee.[792]

In some cases, this fee is fixed.[793] In other cases the franchisor may insist on the payment of a minimum fee.[794]

783. Mendelsohn 2004: 134.
784. Mendelsohn 2004: 134.
785. Mendelsohn 2004: 134.
786. Mendelsohn 2004: 134.
787. Mendelsohn 2004: 134.
788. Mendelsohn 2004: 134.
789. Mendelsohn 2004: 134.
790. Mendelsohn 2004: 134.
791. Mendelsohn 2004: 139.
792. Mendelsohn 2004: 139.
793. Mendelsohn 2004: 139.
794. Mendelsohn 2004: 134.

Fixed management services fee v. Percentage-based management services fee

A fixed management services fee may be more beneficial to the franchisee if the level of the fee is reasonable.[795] Where a fixed fee is used, due consideration should be given by the franchisee to the fact that the fee may be subject to regular adjustments. Where adjustments are made, the franchisor should endeavour to ensure that the franchisee is not prejudiced in order to guarantee a sustainable contractual relationship.[796]

In a percentage-based fee franchise, the franchisee will benefit from a certain amount of certainty, as it will be aware of the method used for calculating the fee due and will be conscious of the fact that the franchisor will not be charging any further fees.[797]

From the point of view of the franchisor, a percentage-based fee structure offers certain benefits.[798] First, the franchisor will benefit from the growth generated by the franchisee, which is achieved to some degree with the help of the franchisor (its ongoing support and its work and investment in developing and in maintaining the franchise system).[799] Second the franchisor will benefit from the inflationary increase in gross revenues.[800] Third it will benefit from the ease of administering this fee structure and the competitive nature of this arrangement.[801]

It has been argued that the management services fee has a negative impact on the franchisee since the franchisee will be reluctant to pay the franchisor especially initially when the franchisee is investing time and effort in constructing its business.[802] With time, when the franchisee's business is more successful, the franchisee will be reticent about paying the franchisor if it starts enjoying 'a degree of independence from the franchisor'.[803]

In situations where the franchisor is supplying a product, the management services fee will often consist of a fixed fee component representing the mark-up on the product and a percentage-based fee.[804]

A distinction should be made between the management services fee on the one hand and a royalty payment on the other. Whilst a royalty payment is a type of income that is passive in nature relating to the use of the intellectual property of the franchisor, the management services fee is largely a payment made to remunerate the franchisor for the ongoing services it furnishes to the franchisee.[805]

795. Mendelsohn 2004: 140.
796. Mendelsohn 2004: 140.
797. Mendelsohn 2004: 140.
798. Mendelsohn 2004: 140.
799. Mendelsohn 2004: 140.
800. Mendelsohn 2004: 140.
801. Mendelsohn 2004: 141.
802. Mendelsohn 2004: 141.
803. Mendelsohn 2004: 141.
804. Mendelsohn 2004: 141.
805. Mendelsohn 2004: 141.

[iv] Sums Received on the Sale of Assets

In some franchises the franchisee will contract to buy products from the franchisor or its assigned supplier.[806] Where the franchisor sells these products to the franchisee the franchisor will receive a return in the form of a mark-up on the goods.[807] Where the franchisor's approved supplier sells the goods, the franchisor's return may take the form of a rebate paid by the supplier.[808]

[v] Advertising Levy

In many franchise schemes, a provision will be made for advertising and promotion expenditure incurred by the franchisor or the franchisee or both.[809]

In situations where the franchisor is responsible for paying for such activities it may choose to deal with the issue of costs in one of three ways.[810]

First it may charge the franchisee a percentage-based fee calculated on the basis of the franchisee's gross income.[811] In such a situation, the franchisor may agree to spend the entire fee on advertising and promotional activities.

Second it may charge a fee for such activities which will be included in the management services fee. In such cases the franchisor may agree to spend a part of these fees on advertising and promotional activities.[812]

Third it may agree to perform such activities without making a charge.[813] The franchisor may be willing to bear these costs if it is 'a substantial advertiser on its own account'.[814]

If regional or local advertising and promotion are required, the franchisor may delegate all or some of the responsibility for these activities to the franchisee.[815] In which case the franchisor may ask the franchisee for an annual minimum financial commitment in relation to these activities.[816] The minimum annual expenditure figure may be fixed or may fluctuate (it may be a percentage of the gross income generated by the franchisee).[817]

806. Mendelsohn 2004: 141.
807. Mendelsohn 2004: 141.
808. Mendelsohn 2004: 141.
809. Mendelsohn 2004: 143.
810. Mendelsohn 2004: 143.
811. Mendelsohn 2004: 143.
812. Mendelsohn 2004: 143.
813. Mendelsohn 2004: 143.
814. Mendelsohn 2004: 143.
815. Mendelsohn 2004: 143.
816. Mendelsohn 2004: 143.
817. Mendelsohn 2004: 143.

[vi] Verification of Accounts

The fees paid to the franchisor by the franchisees largely or wholly represent the franchisor's gross revenue.[818] As such the franchisor should ensure not only the timely payment of fees but also its ability to verify the accuracy of fees paid to it by the franchisees.

By requiring the franchisee to furnish audited accounts or by auditing the accounts of the franchisee, the franchisor is able to verify the accuracy of the fees paid to it by the franchisee.

Another way of checking the accuracy of fees paid is for the franchisor to access the supply sources of the franchisee. If the franchisor knows what the franchisee is buying it will have a clearer picture of what the gross sales figures of the franchisee should be.[819] By checking the franchisee's supplies, the franchisor is also able to verify whether the franchisee is buying goods from non-approved sources in turn allowing the franchisee to falsify its figures.[820]

In this context, the franchisor is likely to insist the franchise agreement includes provisions requiring:

- timely payment of fees due;
- the franchisee to follow accounting and reporting standards stipulated by the franchisor;
- the franchisee to allow the franchisor or its agent/s (e.g., an accountant appointed by the franchisor or one agreed upon by the parties) access to accounting and financial records including VAT returns and assessments.[821] By checking this data, the franchisor will be able not only to verify the accuracy of fees but also to monitor the performance of the franchisee and notably its attainment of projected gross and net profit margins and its managerial operations.[822] Such checks may be scheduled or unscheduled by means of spot checks carried out by the franchisor or its agents;[823]
- the franchisee to allow the franchisor or its agent/s to carry out spot checks of the franchisee's supplies thus permitting the franchisor to determine whether the franchisee is buying goods from non-approved sources; and
- the franchisee to obtain and maintain insurance cover for the business in order to protect the business and livelihood of the franchisee.[824] In certain circumstances, the franchisor may be able to negotiate cover for the network.[825]

818. Mendelsohn 2004: 178.
819. Mendelsohn 2004: 179.
820. Mendelsohn 2004: 179.
821. By checking VAT returns and assessments, the franchisor will be able to obtain an accurate picture of the franchisee's performance and to compare the figures declared by the franchisee against the figures submitted to the relevant tax authority. (Mendelsohn 2004: 179).
822. Mendelsohn 2004: 179, 194.
823. Mendelsohn 2004: 179, 194.
824. Mendelsohn 2004: 194.
825. Mendelsohn 2004: 194.

[b] Non-compete Provisions[826]

Beyond the financial obligation borne by the franchisee, the franchisor is likely to want to ensure that the franchisee cannot compete with it either during the term of the licensing agreement or after the end of this term. To this end the franchisor is likely to insist on the inclusion of a widely drafted non-compete clause in the agreement.

The incorporation of such a clause will largely depend not only upon the willingness of the franchisee to agree to such a clause, but also on the position under national law. As we have seen competition law may restrict the scope of such a clause or even forbid its use altogether.

[c] Protection of Proprietary Information and Goodwill of the Franchisor

Due to the potential loss of proprietary information belonging to it, the franchisor is likely to insist upon the inclusion of the following provisions:

- a prohibition or limitation on sublicensing;[827]
- a broadly drafted confidentiality clause forbidding the franchisee from disclosing to third parties any of the know-how provided to it by the franchisor at any point during the term of the agreement and at any time after the agreement comes to an end;
- a stipulation that the franchisee does nothing that is likely to prejudice or damage the goodwill in the licensed marks;
- a stipulation that the franchisee does nothing that is likely to adversely affect the reputation of the franchisor; and
- a provision that limits the manner in which the licensed property is used by the franchisee.[828,829] The franchisor may for example stipulate that the franchisee is entitled to use licensed marks solely for the purpose of promoting the business and only in accordance with directions provided by the franchisor.

[d] Retention of Ownership in the Property Licensed[830,831]

In order to ensure the retention of ownership in the licensed property, the franchisor should give due consideration to the inclusion of the following in the franchise agreement. A provision stating that:

826. A detailed review of non-compete can be found in the introduction chapter. A template clause can also be found in the introductory chapter. A review of competition law in the EU can be found in the chapter on competition law.
827. A detailed review of sublicensing can be found in the introduction chapter. A template clause can also be found in the introduction chapter.
828. A detailed review of restrictions on the fields of use can be found in the introduction chapter. A template clause can also be found in the introduction chapter.
829. For a detailed discussion, *see* Meiselles 2013: 248-249.
830. A detailed review of this topic can be found in the introduction chapter. A template clause can also be found in the introduction chapter.
831. Further detail can be found in Meiselles 2013: 258.

- the franchisee shall acquire no rights to the licensed property;
- the franchisee only use the licensed marks in connection with the franchise operation;
- the franchisee only use and present the licensed marks in line with instructions issued to it from time to time by the franchisor;
- all the rights and the goodwill in and associated with the licensed property are vested in the franchisor and remain vested in the franchisor;
- the franchisee immediately inform the franchisor of any infringement of the licensed property and/or licensed marks of which the franchisee becomes aware; and
- the franchisee assist the franchisor in maintaining the validity and enforceability of the licensed property.

[e] Quality Control

1. The Franchisee shall start trading on the Start Date.

2. During the term of this agreement, the Franchisee shall:

a. Ensure the Franchisee's Business is conducted in line with the Manual;

b. Use its best endeavours to promote, protect and develop the Business and the goodwill in the Business;

c. Utilise only stationery provided by the Franchisor [or the Franchisor's approved supplier];

d. Utilise only the signage approved by the Franchisor in connection with the Business;

e. Utilise only the packaging approved by the Franchisor in connection with the Business;

f. Provide the Franchisor with samples of the goods produced [at specific intervals or as required by the Franchisor];

g. Provide the Franchisor with documentation relating to the running of the Premises including but not limited to cleaning of the Premises, feedback forms completed by customers, complaints filed by customers and so forth;

h. Ensure the Premises are open during specified hours;

i. Ensure the Premises are kept clean and maintained to the standards stipulated [by the Manual or by the Franchisor];

j. Ensure the Premises are maintained to the highest standard;

k. Ensure the Premises are refurbished, redecorated or improved as stipulated by the Franchisor;

l. Ensure that all changes to the Premises are approved in writing by the Franchisor;

m. Provide access to the Premises to the Franchisor, at a reasonable time on the provision of reasonable written notice to the Franchisee, so that the Franchisor may inspect inter alia the Premises, the equipment, the inventory and the accounts of the Franchisee's Business;

n. Supply goods and services solely in accordance with the conditions of sale stipulated in the Manual;

o. Ensure that all staff employed by it are at all times clean, presentable and tidily dressed [in the designated attire or where no uniform is required professionally attired];

p. Ensure adherence with the procedures for [auditing, invoicing, ordering etc] stipulated by [the Franchisor or the Manual];

q. Keep adequate stocks to meet the demands of customers of the Franchisee's Business;

r. Not licence another to administer the Business the Licenced Name;

s. Inform the Franchisor of any development or change made to the Business or the System;

t. Advise the Franchisor of any business opportunities of which the Franchisee becomes aware;

u. Implement improvements or changes required by the Franchisor relating to the Franchisee's Business;

v. Use the Website in compliance with [the Manual or the Franchisor's instructions];

w. Acquire, maintain and comply with all licences and consents;

x. Comply with legislation and regulations applicable to the Premises and the use of the Premises;

y. Comply with the Intellectual Property and the Franchisee's Business; and

z. Do nothing that may bring the Business into disrepute or that may damage the goodwill of the Business.

In order to ensure that the franchisee maintains uniform and high quality standards and protects the integrity of the licensed marks, the reputation and the goodwill of the franchisor and the franchise network, due consideration should be given by the franchisor to the inclusion of provisions in the franchise agreement:

- requiring the franchisee to carry on the business franchised from the agreed premises in line with the methods and standards developed by the franchisor and the operations manual of the franchisor (this manual may be updated intermittently by the franchisor so that it reflects organisational improvements and changes in marketplace);[832]
- permitting the franchisor to inspect the agreed premises operated by the franchisee periodically to verify compliance with the standards imposed on the franchisee by the franchisor;
- requiring the franchisee to purchase goods from the franchisor or its nominated suppliers;[833]
- compelling the franchisee to use its best endeavours and the highest standards in all matters related to the licensed business and to carry on the said business in a meticulous way and in a way that is in all material respects to the reasonable satisfaction of the franchisor;
- requiring the franchisee to ensure that all its members of staff before they commence work are trained either by the franchisor or in the methods of the franchisor;
- obligating the franchisee to ensure that its business premises are clean and updated as required.[834] In this context modernisation is seen as a way of guaranteeing 'the freshness of the image appeal to the consumer and competitiveness in the market place'.[835] Franchisees may be expected periodically to install new technology (such as point-of-sale systems). Where such an obligation is incorporated into the franchise agreement, the franchisor may look to ensure that the franchisee invest any sums needed in order to ensure the correct installation and running of the new system regardless of the benefits, whilst the franchisee will be concerned about capping its expenditure. One of way of balancing the often-opposing interests of the parties is to include a clause in the contract obliging the franchisor to detail the extent of the planned requirements, the initial and running costs thereby permitting the franchisee to reach an informed decision before undertaking the improvements;[836]
- compelling the franchisee to ensure that all staff employed by it in the licensed business are at all times clean, presentable and either tidily dressed in the designated attire or (where no uniform is required) professionally attired;[837]
- obliging the franchisee to provide the franchisor with samples of the goods produced either at specific intervals or as required by the franchisor;
- obliging the franchisee to provide the franchisor with documentation relating to the running of the premise(s) including but not limited to cleaning of the premises, feedback forms completed by customers, complaints filed by customers and so forth;

832. Mendelsohn 2004: 193.
833. Mendelsohn 2004: 194.
834. Mendelsohn 2004: 194.
835. Mendelsohn 2004: 177.
836. Mendelsohn 2004: 178.
837. Mendelsohn 2004: 194.

- permitting the franchisor to speak to customers of the franchisee and staff members working for the franchisee without prior notice being given (spot checks);
- requiring the franchisee to carry on the business covered by the franchise agreement using the licensed marks and no other names or marks;
- requiring the franchisee to carry on its business from the premises agreed upon with the franchisor;
- obliging the franchisee to provide the agreed services from the premises between agreed hours and on agreed days. Such a provision aims to maximise profitability by ensuring that the business is operated in an optimal manner without the incurrence of disproportionate overheads;[838]
- obligating the franchisee to use and display point-of-sale advertising materials as dictated by the franchisor (such materials may be provided to the franchisee at no charge);[839]
- stipulating that the franchisee promote and improve the business (such an obligation may or may not be linked to minimum performance requirements)[840] and actively partake in the life of the network;[841]
- forbidding the franchisee from registering domain names on the Internet (altogether or without the prior agreement of the franchisor)[842] and using promotional materials without the prior agreement of the franchisor (though the franchisor is likely to assume responsibility for promotion and advertising at the national level, the parties may agree that the franchisee engage in local advertising and promotion);[843] and
- forbidding the franchisee from assigning the contract altogether or without the prior authorisation of the franchisor (more on this below).

Pursuant to the EFF Code, a franchisee is further obligated to devote its best endeavours to the growth of the franchise business and to the maintenance of the common identity and reputation of the franchise network.[844]

[f] Future Obligation to Buy Equipment

In certain franchises there may be a continuing obligation on the franchisee to buy new or essential equipment from the franchisor.[845] If this is the case, due consideration should be given by the franchisee to its obligation to buy such equipment especially when the existing equipment acquired by the franchisee is in perfect working order; the

838. Mendelsohn 2004: 193.
839. Mendelsohn 2004: 194.
840. Mendelsohn 2004: 195.
841. WFC Code of Ethics: 1V.
842. Mendelsohn 2004: 195.
843. Mendelsohn 2004: 194.
844. Article 2.4 (iii), European Franchise Federation Code of Ethics accessible at http://www.eff-franchise.com/Data/Code%20of%20Ethics2.pdf (last accessed 14/5/2018).
845. Mendelsohn 2004, 138.

mark-up (of the franchisor) in order to ensure it is not over-charged by the franchisor[846] and whether such an obligation will be 'justified in terms of increased efficiency and output, resulting in a cost-effective alternative'.[847]

[g] Anti-bribery Policy of the Franchisee[848]

[h] Insurance[849]

[6] Obligations of the Franchisor

[a] Franchisor's Initial Obligations

The Franchisor shall provide the Franchisee within [] days of the date of the agreement with:

1. The selection criteria for the Premises;

2. Advice on the selection of Premises;

3. Advice on inter alia equipment, furniture, display equipment and signage listed [in the Manual or in the Start-up Package];

4. Advice on the establishment of the Franchisee's Business;

5. Assistance to inaugurate the Business;

6. A public relations launch [as detailed in the Manual or the Start-up Package];

7. A training programme providing training on [details of the programme]. This initial training will be provided to new staff members recruited by the Franchisee. Such training shall be furnished by the Franchisor or by one of its Affiliates at [location] in [city, country] [or at a location which the Franchisor shall select]. The expense for this training is itemised in Schedule []. The Franchisor shall not bear any obligation for any salaries, benefits, travel or living expenses incurred by the Franchisee's staff members during the course of such training. [Optional – This training shall be provided free of charge];

8. An opening crew or Manager of Operations Standards to assist with the opening of the Premises for a maximum period of [];

846. Mendelsohn 2004, 138.
847. Mendelsohn 2004, 138.
848. *See* the introduction chapter for further detail and a template clause.
849. *See* the introduction chapter for further detail and a template clause.

9. The Manual [provided on loan]; and

10. The Financial Package in accordance with the terms set out in [the Manual or in Schedule ()].

[b] Franchisor's Ongoing Obligations

1. During the term of this agreement, the Franchisor shall provide the Franchisee with:

a. Know-how, advice and guidance relating to the Business;

b. Ongoing training in the Services and relating to the correct operation of the Business. This training shall be provided by the Franchisor or by one of its Affiliates at [location] in [city, country] [or at a location which the Franchisor shall select]. Such training shall be provided to the Franchisee, to new staff members working for the Franchisee and to existing staff members working for the Franchisee. The expense for this training is itemised in Schedule []. The Franchisor shall not bear any obligation for any salaries, benefits, travel or living expenses incurred by the Franchisee's staff members during the course of such training. [Optional – This training shall be provided free of charge];

c. Reasonable levels of ongoing support and assistance. Such support and assistance shall be provided by head office personnel with knowledge of the Business. [Optional: Such support and assistance will be provided at the Franchisor's discretion as the Franchisor considers requisite in order to guarantee the efficient running of the Business and to promote and enhance the operation of the Business];

d. Assistance with the running of the Business from the Premises; and

e. Stationery subject to availability.

2. During the term of the agreement, the Franchisor shall ensure that:

a. The Manual is updated to reflect developments in the Business and connected to the Business;

b. The System is updated;

c. A conference take place for all franchisees of the Business at a time and a place that is convenient for the majority of the franchisees of the Business ['Conference']. This Conference shall take place on a [] basis;

d. A website promoting the Business ['Website'] be maintained and updated on a [] basis;

e. There is an ongoing and structured dialogue between franchisees in the network; and

f. Individual franchisees in the network respect their obligations and commitments.

3. The Franchisor shall allow the Franchisee to conduct the Franchisee's Business online.

[i] Assistance and Training

Responsibilities borne by the franchisor may include an obligation to:[850]

- train new staff;
- train existing staff where appropriate in relation to new techniques developed by the franchisor or other franchisees, new technology generated by the franchisor or other franchisees and so forth;
- provide ongoing support and continuous assistance required in order to guarantee the efficient running of the franchise operation;
- provide the operations manual and ensure it is updated to take account of improvements connected to the franchise operation;
- maintain a permanent and structured dialogue with franchisees in a bid to protect and develop the know-how of the franchisor; and
- beyond its initial obligations, the franchisor may assume responsibility for ongoing support and training as well as for continuous development and maintenance of 'the commercial and technical know-how that supports the franchise network'.[851]

Any ongoing commitments owed by the franchisor should be clearly defined in the franchise agreement and in any amendments made to this agreement.

Pursuant to the EFF Code a franchisor is obliged to have operated a business concept with success for at least one year, and in at least one pilot unit[852] and to be the owner, or be in possession of legal rights to the use, of its network's trade name, trademark or other distinguishing identification.[853]

Moreover in the general interest of the network, the franchisor may also be duty-bound to ensure that individual franchisees respect their obligations and commitments.[854]

850. WFC Code of Ethics: IV.
851. WFC Code of Ethics: IV.
852. Article 2.2 (i), European Franchise Federation Code of Ethics accessible at http://www.eff-franchise.com/Data/Code%20of%20Ethics2.pdf (last accessed 14/5/2018).
853. Article 2.2 (ii), European Franchise Federation Code of Ethics accessible at http://www.eff-franchise.com/Data/Code%20of%20Ethics2.pdf (last accessed 14/5/2018).
854. WFC Code of Ethics: IV.

Even where the commitments of the franchisor are set out in a dedicated clause, attention should also be given to the scope and wording of the grant clause in order to ensure that comprehensive rights are awarded to the franchisee by the franchisor.

[ii] Promotion

1. The Franchisor shall:

a. Promote the Licenced Marks and Business [in the Territory] as it thinks fit;

b. Furnish the Franchisee with promotional literature as it thinks fit;

c. Pay the Advertising Fee into a separate account to be kept on trust for the franchisees. The Franchisor may use this Advertising Fee to satisfy its obligations under this clause; and

d. Furnish the Franchisee on [] with an audited account of the income and the expenditure relating to this account. The audited account shall be paid for using the monies in this account.

2. (Optional: Where promotion is partial the responsibility of the Franchisee) The Franchisee shall:

a. Promote the Franchisee's Business in the Territory in compliance with [the Manual or the Franchisor's instructions] [making use of materials furnished to the Franchisee by the Franchisor];

b. Cooperate with the Franchisor in relation to specific promotional campaigns where the Franchisor deems this necessary; and

c. Spend no less than an amount equal to [per cent of () or (set amount)] per year on promotion of the Franchisee's Business in the Territory.

Where promotional activities are partially the responsibility of the franchisee the franchisor should consider using limitations on these activities by referring the franchisee to its instructions or to specifications in the operations manual. In some circumstances the franchisee may be required to expend a minimum sum over a set period on such promotional activities.

[c] Warranties, Liabilities and Indemnities

See the introduction chapter for further detail and a template clause.

[7] Termination (Grounds and Consequences)[855]

[a] Grounds of Termination

The contracting parties should give due consideration to when either party will have the right to terminate the agreement, the consequences of termination and the possibility of rectifying certain breaches in order to salvage the working relationship between the parties (right to cure).

The EFF Code places an obligation on a franchisor to provide written notice to it individual franchisees of any breaches of contract and where appropriate to provide the defaulting party with a reasonable time to rectify the default.[856]

An agreement may be for a fixed term without any provision being made for renewal; in such circumstances if no offer of a new agreement is forthcoming the relationship between the parties will effectively come to an end.[857]

A provision may be made for the termination in the event that certain contingencies arise either automatically upon the occurrence of the contingency or upon the provision of notice.[858]

In many circumstances, the agreement will include a provision allowing the breaching party to rectify certain breaches within a set period of time, effectively displacing the right of the innocent party to terminate the agreement.[859] Where the franchisee fails to respect the terms of the agreement, the franchisor may be obligated to provide the franchisee with a reasonable delay to conform to its obligations after due notice is given to the franchisee by the franchisor.[860]

A failure to rectify the breach within the time stipulated will typically permit the innocent party to employ its right to terminate.[861] Breaches that are fundamental in nature may be excluded from the scope of the cure provision; such breaches include those that go to the heart of the relationship between the parties undermining the relationship of trust presumed to exist between the parties. Examples of such breaches may include the provision of false or misleading information or the disclosure of confidential information.[862] Even in circumstances where a franchisee has defaulted, consideration should be given to the possibility of finding a solution which will not result in the termination of the agreement between the parties.[863] For example, attempts may be made to persuade the franchisee to resume performance of its obligations under the contract and supplementary support and assistance may be offered in circumstances where the franchisee unable to adhere to its obligations.[864]

855. *See* the introduction chapter for further detail and a template clause.
856. Article 2.4 (ii), European Franchise Federation Code of Ethics accessible at http://www.eff-franchise.com/Data/Code%20of%20Ethics2.pdf (last accessed 14/5/2018).
857. Mendelsohn 2004: 201.
858. Mendelsohn 2004: 201.
859. Mendelsohn 2004: 201.
860. WFC Code of Ethics: IV.
861. Mendelsohn 2004: 201.
862. Mendelsohn 2004: 201.
863. Mendelsohn 2004: 202.
864. Mendelsohn 2004: 202.

[b] Consequences of Termination

Upon termination of the franchise agreement, the franchisor will be concerned about ensuring that it recovers complete control of its intellectual property rights, its system and its goodwill.

Accordingly provision may be made in the agreement that in the event of termination the franchisee stop:[865]

- using the brand name, trademarks, service marks and so forth alongside the goodwill associated therewith;
- using the system and know-how of the franchisor;
- using any outward signs that may create confusion in the mind of the consuming public whilst permitting the franchisee to take advantage of the goodwill of the franchisor; and
- soliciting custom from existing customers who make up part of the goodwill of the franchisor.

In addition, the franchisee may be forbidden from competing with the franchisor and the network in the event of termination.[866]

In circumstances where the franchisee occupies premises leased or subleased to it by the franchisor, it may be asked to vacate such premises in the event of termination. In which case, during the negotiation of the agreement, the franchisee should consider whether the agreement provides it with safeguards for the cash investment that it has made.[867]

[8] ***Death***

To address the possible death of the franchisee or the principal shareholder of the franchisee (where the franchisee is a company) due consideration should be given by the parties to the rights of the beneficiaries of the franchisee.

In this context, regard should be given by the parties to the question of whether or not the beneficiaries of the franchisee should be allowed to assume the responsibilities of the franchisee and to run the business of franchisee as a going concern until one of them is capable of qualifying as a franchisee in turn taking an assignment of the franchisee's business.

In the alternative, the parties should consider the question of whether in such circumstances the business of the franchisee is sold at the earliest opportunity available or at a suitable later date. In such circumstances, the franchisor may agree for a fee to provide management services for a period of several weeks following death.[868]

---

865. Mendelsohn 2004: 203.
866. Mendelsohn 2004: 203.
867. Mendelsohn 2004: 202.
868. Mendelsohn 2004: 180, 196-7.

[9] General Clauses, Boilerplate Clauses and the Back of the Contract[869]

[a] Assignment[870]

The franchisor should give due consideration to reserving its right to assign the agreement without restrictions, so that it can for example sell its business on as a going concern or use the business or even the Licencsd Property as collateral for a loan.

As the franchisor is reliant on the work of the franchisee to generate revenue, to safeguard its licensed property and to enhance and preserve its reputation and brand image, the franchisor should give due consideration to whether or not it wishes to allow individual franchisees to assign the franchise.

In circumstances where assignment by the franchisee is permitted, the franchisor should give due consideration to the inclusion of preemption rights,[871] and the right it has to scrutinize a prospective assignee before allowing the assignment to proceed.

Assignment by the franchisee may occur for example where the franchisee is looking to sell its business and where the franchisee or a principal shareholder of the franchisee (if the franchisee is a company) dies.

In practice it is seldom hard to organise the transfer of the franchised business on the proviso that the prospective purchaser of the franchisee's business fulfils the selection criteria set out by the franchisor and successfully completes all the necessary training requirements specified by the franchisor.[872]

Most franchise agreements will include a fee to cover the expenditure incurred by the franchisor in processing the application of the prospective franchisee and in training the prospective franchisee; this fee will either be fixed or linked to the sale price (percentage of the sale price).[873] Occasionally the franchisor may be able to introduce a prospective franchisee from its waiting list (in exchange for an introductory fee).[874]

In the event of a sale by the franchisee of its business, certain contracts may provide the franchisor with an option to buy. Any such option must guarantee the franchisee as good a deal as it would receive on the open market in a bona fide arms' length deal.[875]

869. General clauses, boilerplate clauses and the back of the contract are addressed in Chapter 1 of this book.
870. For full review, *see* Meiselles 2013: 272. *See* the introduction chapter for a template clause.
871. Article 5.5 (x), European Franchise Federation Code of Ethics accessible at http://www.eff-franchise.com/Data/Code%20of%20Ethics2.pdf (last accessed 14/5/2018).
872. Mendelsohn 2004: 195.
873. Mendelsohn 2004: 195.
874. Mendelsohn 2004: 195.
875. Mendelsohn 2004: 195.

[b] Alternative Dispute Resolution[876]

Common complaints made by franchisees include assertions that certain pre-contractual representations made by the franchisor are incorrect or inaccurate (principal amongst these profit predictions), that the franchisor has failed to perform its contractual obligations or has failed to properly perform such obligations, that the franchisor has failed to innovate, that the franchise network is becoming out of date and that the franchisor has introduced changes that prove to be ineffective or that advertising or promotional campaigns of the franchisor are ineffective.[877]

Common complaints by franchisors include assertions that the franchisee has failed to operate the system properly, has failed to comply with its reporting obligation, has failed to pay fees due or has done so in a tardy fashion, has failed to adhere to quality assurance standards, has failed to market the business in a proper manner, has failed to devote enough time to the business and has failed to redecorate the premises or update the equipment or has engaged in a competing business.[878]

Whilst certain complaints are capable of being resolved using ADR, others are so fundamental in nature that they arguably go to the root of the relationship. If such breaches are not rectified within the time specified in a notice, arguably these may lead to the termination.[879]

§5.13 CASE STUDY

In sports, the Giants and Red Sox are examples of baseball franchises.[880] Franchises are also used in football.[881] In media, Disney Pixar has employed franchises in relation to its brands such as the Toy Story brand.[882] The warriors' line of video games developed by the Japanese video game developer Koei is the subject matter of a franchise.[883]

US restaurant chains such as Burger King, McDonald's Corp, Wendy's Co and Dine Equity Inc's Applebee have for decades used franchising as a preferred model for overseas' expansion due to the fact that they offer a steady and predictable revenue stream in the form of royalties.[884] As investors prefer to focus on markets that generate

876. *See* the introduction chapter for a template clause.
877. Mendelsohn 2004: 199-200.
878. Mendelsohn 2004: 199-200.
879. Mendelsohn 2004: 200.
880. Jake Appleman (2014), Brooklyn Bounce: The Highs and Lows of Nets Basketball's Historic First (Scribner), page 104; Glenn Stout, Richard A. Johnson (2004) Red Sox Century: The Definitive History of Baseball's Most Storied Franchise, page 5.
881. Kevin Carroll (2007), Dr Eddie Anderson: Hall of Fame College Football Coach - A Biography (McFarland & Co Inc, Publishers), page 91.
882. Carmen Liliana Medina & Karen E. Wohlwend (2014), Literacy, Play and Globalization: Converging Imaginaries in Children's Critical and Cultural Preferences (Taylor & Francis), page 97.
883. Edited by Gretchen Papazian and Joseph Michael Sommers (2013), Game On, Hollywood! Essays on the Intersection of Video Games and Cinema (McFarland & Company Inc Publishers), page 136.
884. Julie Jargon, Wall Street Journal, Starbucks Tries Franchising to Perk Up Europe Business, updated 29 November 2013.

higher returns, franchising has proven to be particularly attractive in Europe due to its struggling economy.[885]

Starbucks in contrast with other leading brands in the food industry has generally resisted using franchising in an effort to control its brand.[886] Franchised cafes have historically made up a small proportion of the European, Middle Eastern and African (EMEA) Starbucks' stores.[887] Joint ventures have been concluded in China and India.[888] Licensing agreements have been used worldwide. Starbucks have granted licences to retailers and travel companies operating stores in airports and shops.[889]

In 2013 this US chain decided to change its strategy in an effort to enter markets that it had not previously considered.[890] Over a three-year period (2010-2013) the number of company operated stores in the UK fell whilst the corresponding number of franchised and licensed stores increased.[891] At the end of 2013, the number of franchised and licensed stores in the UK was approximately 200, representing an increase of over 150 stores over a three-year period spanning early 2010 to late 2013.[892] According to more recent figures, Starbucks owns 397 UK stores, 209 of its other UK stores are operated under franchises and 226 of its further stores are operated under a licence (these are located in train stations and airports).[893]

Operating profit in the EMEA region increased dramatically between 2012 fiscal year and 2013 fiscal year (in 2013 fiscal year operating profits were recorded at $64.2 million), as did restaurant traffic (a growth of 3%).[894] In 2014 UK sales dropped from £408.7 million to £405.6 million after Starbucks shut 17 loss-making stores and granted franchises to 74 of its cafes.[895]

885. Julie Jargon, Wall Street Journal, Starbucks Tries Franchising to Perk Up Europe Business, updated 29 November 2013 citing Sharon Zackfia, analyst with William Blair & Co.
886. Julie Jargon, Wall Street Journal, Starbucks Tries Franchising to Perk Up Europe Business, updated 29 November 2013.
887. As at November 2013. Julie Jargon, Wall Street Journal, Starbucks Tries Franchising to Perk Up Europe Business, updated 29 November 2013.
888. Julie Jargon, Wall Street Journal, Starbucks Tries Franchising to Perk Up Europe Business, updated 29 November 2013.
889. Julie Jargon, Wall Street Journal, Starbucks Tries Franchising to Perk Up Europe Business, updated 29 November 2013.
890. Julie Jargon, Wall Street Journal, Starbucks Tries Franchising to Perk Up Europe Business, updated 29 November 2013 citing Kris Engskov head of Starbucks in EMEA.
891. Julie Jargon, Wall Street Journal, Starbucks Tries Franchising to Perk Up Europe Business, updated 29 November 2013.
892. Julie Jargon, Wall Street Journal, Starbucks Tries Franchising to Perk Up Europe Business, updated 29 November 2013.
893. Ashley Armstrong, Telegraph, Starbucks UK brews up record profits - but pays less tax, 15 December 2015.
894. Julie Jargon, Wall Street Journal, Starbucks Tries Franchising to Perk Up Europe Business, updated 29 November 2013.
895. Ashley Armstrong, Telegraph, Starbucks UK brews up record profits - but pays less tax, 15 December 2015.

Due to the centrality of its culture, its standards and the importance of its brand, Starbucks exercises caution when selecting its partners.[896] In order to perfect selection, Starbucks spends time getting to know potential franchisees and their families.[897]

Starbucks has indicated its intention recently to limit the number of franchise partners. Franchisees are expected to open 10 or more stores, to agree to a ten-year term, to possess pre-existing experience in real-estate development or with operating branded retailers and to have £500,000 in liquid assets.[898]

Anil Patil, the first UK based Starbucks franchisee raised £10 million to create 16 stores (the first store was opened in 2013) and plans to open 100 more stores over a five-year period.[899] Mr Patil owned and sold an eighteen-site Domino's Pizza franchise.[900]

Franchising permits Starbucks to access local knowledge to guarantee the success of its new stores, whilst allowing it to "capitalise on latent demand in under-served areas of the country."[901]

Starbucks' French partners include the Casino Group.[902] The Monoprix Group that owns a chain of stores recently opened two Starbucks' stores in Lyon in the context of a deal concluded between Casino Group and Starbucks.[903]

§5.14 FUTURE LANDSCAPE IN THE EU

On 12 September 2017, the Members of the European Parliament passed a Resolution calling on the Commission to open up a public consultation to illicit information on the 'real situation in franchising', before drawing up 'non-legislative guidelines' on how to improve the state of the franchising sector in the EU.[904] At the time of writing, these guidelines have yet to be released.

This resolution aims to find ways to improve the take-up of franchising as a business model in the EU retail sector, due to poor performance across the various Member States, when compared with the US and Australia.[905] Franchising represents 5.95 percent of GDP in the US, 10.83 percent of GDP in Australia, and only 1.89 percent

896. Julie Jargon, Wall Street Journal, Starbucks Tries Franchising to Perk Up Europe Business, updated 29 November 2013 citing Kris Engskov head of Starbucks in EMEA.
897. Julie Jargon, Wall Street Journal, Starbucks Tries Franchising to Perk Up Europe Business, updated 29 November 2013 citing Kris Engskov head of Starbucks in EMEA.
898. Julie Jargon, Wall Street Journal, Starbucks Tries Franchising to Perk Up Europe Business, updated 29 November 2013.
899. Rebecca Burn-Callander, Telegraph, Starbucks' first UK franchise raises warchest for mass expansion, 28 September 2015.
900. Rebecca Burn-Callander, Telegraph, Starbucks' first UK.franchise raises warchest for mass expansion, 28 September 2015.
901. Rebecca Burn-Callander, Telegraph, Starbucks' first UK franchise raises warchest for mass expansion, 28 September 2015 citing Anil Patil, founder of 23.5 Degrees.
902. Le Figaro, La recette de Starbucks pour doubler de taille en France d'ici à 2020, 11 January 2016 (author unnamed).
903. Les Echos, Monoprix accélère ses ouvertures et innove (undated and author unnamed).
904. Motion for a European Parliament Resolution on the functioning of franchising in the retail sector 2016/2244 (INI), para. 26.
905. Motion for a European Parliament Resolution on the functioning of franchising in the retail sector 2016/2244 (INI), para. c.

of the GDP in the EU.[906] Moreover, this resolution acknowledges that 83.5 percent of franchising turnover is concentrated in only seven Member States in the EU.[907]

Franchising is viewed as a business model with significant cross-border dimensions[908] able to help in completing the Single Market in the retail sector. Also it is regarded as a convenient mechanism 'to establish business through shared investment by the franchisor and franchisee'[909] leading to job creation, SME and entrepreneurship development, and the acquisition of new skills.[910]

Inconsistent laws between the different Member States and a lack of uniformity amongst the national measures introduced to target unfair practices in the field of franchising[911] have culminated in the creation of technical barriers capable of hindering the establishment of cross-border activities by both franchisors and franchisees.[912] This lack of harmonisation is harmful not only to the economic activities of the parties themselves but also to the consuming public due to the adverse impact this state of affairs has on consumer choice.[913]

To encourage a broader dissemination of the franchise business model across the EU, the European Parliament adopts a multi-faceted strategy highlighting a number of key priorities.[914]

Transparency is key in this sector, where information is either unwritten or kept confidential, by creating a platform on which potential and actual franchisors and franchisees can access information regarding their rights and obligations.[915]

Harmonisation of protection afforded to the parties, notably the franchisee, will enable the EU to address the lack of legislative/regulatory convergence at the national level.[916] Such protection will be achieved not only through the formulation of guidelines, but also by the enhancement of enforcement at the national level. The formulation of guidelines of a non-legislative standing will help address any unfair trade

906. Motion for a European Parliament Resolution on the functioning of franchising in the retail sector 2016/2244 (INI), para. c.
907. Motion for a European Parliament Resolution on the functioning of franchising in the retail sector 2016/2244 (INI), para. c.
908. Motion for a European Parliament Resolution on the functioning of franchising in the retail sector 2016/2244 (INI), para. D.
909. Motion for a European Parliament Resolution on the functioning of franchising in the retail sector 2016/2244 (INI), para. C.
910. Motion for a European Parliament Resolution on the functioning of franchising in the retail sector 2016/2244 (INI), para. D.
911. Motion for a European Parliament Resolution on the functioning of franchising in the retail sector 2016/2244 (INI), para. 2.
912. Motion for a European Parliament Resolution on the functioning of franchising in the retail sector 2016/2244 (INI), para. E.
913. Motion for a European Parliament Resolution on the functioning of franchising in the retail sector 2016/2244 (INI), para. E.
914. Motion for a European Parliament Resolution on the functioning of franchising in the retail sector 2016/2244 (INI), para. c.
915. Motion for a European Parliament Resolution on the functioning of franchising in the retail sector 2016/2244 (INI), para. G.
916. Motion for a European Parliament Resolution on the functioning of franchising in the retail sector 2016/2244 (INI), para. 4.

practices that exist[917] ensuring adherence to 'labour standards and a decent and high-quality service'.[918] Lack of effective enforcement mechanisms at the Member State level, the European Parliament acknowledges, has a dampening effect on the franchise sector, due to the high risk assumed by persons looking to become franchisees and existing franchisees. Enforcement measures, the European Parliament hopes, will help secure the continuity of the franchise relationship.[919]

In a sector dominated by established associations representing the interests of franchisors, the establishment of associations representing the interests of franchisee will help promote the interests of franchisees ensuring that the views of franchisees are heard when legislation and policies are being formulated.[920] This is especially true when one considers the fact that the franchisee is typically the party that is in a far weaker bargaining position.[921] A situation compounded by limited access to information regarding the rights and obligations of the parties to the franchise arrangement.[922]

Collection of strategic information at the national and European levels will allow the European Parliament and the EU institutions to formulate a comprehensive view of the sector[923] enabling both levels to determine progress in the sector, whilst pinpointing gaps, and deficits. Information will be collated first by national contact points, which will then share this gathered information with the Commission.[924] The Commission is also asked to gather information about unfair trade practices, and unfair contract terms,[925] and to instruct Eurostats to focus on this model when assembling statistical data about the sector.[926]

To ensure the existence of a balanced set of rights and obligations, the European Parliament recognises the need for specific principles, covering pre-contractual disclosure and confidentiality of information.[927] Pre-contractual information needs to be comprehensive, clear and accurate allowing the prospective franchisee to make an

917. Motion for a European Parliament Resolution on the functioning of franchising in the retail sector 2016/2244 (INI), para. 4.
918. Motion for a European Parliament Resolution on the functioning of franchising in the retail sector 2016/2244 (INI), para. 3.
919. Motion for a European Parliament Resolution on the functioning of franchising in the retail sector 2016/2244 (INI), para. 5.
920. Motion for a European Parliament Resolution on the functioning of franchising in the retail sector 2016/2244 (INI), para. 10.
921. Motion for a European Parliament Resolution on the functioning of franchising in the retail sector 2016/2244 (INI), para. 6.
922. Motion for a European Parliament Resolution on the functioning of franchising in the retail sector 2016/2244 (INI), para. 6.
923. Motion for a European Parliament Resolution on the functioning of franchising in the retail sector 2016/2244 (INI), para. 11.
924. Motion for a European Parliament Resolution on the functioning of franchising in the retail sector 2016/2244 (INI), para. 11.
925. Motion for a European Parliament Resolution on the functioning of franchising in the retail sector 2016/2244 (INI), para. 12.
926. Motion for a European Parliament Resolution on the functioning of franchising in the retail sector 2016/2244 (INI), para. 12.
927. Motion for a European Parliament Resolution on the functioning of franchising in the retail sector 2016/2244 (INI), para. 20.

informed decision about whether to enter into the franchise arrangement proposed.[928] Such information should be provided in writing, with sufficient notice before the signing of the franchise agreement.[929]

928. Motion for a European Parliament Resolution on the functioning of franchising in the retail sector 2016/2244 (INI), para. 20.
929. Motion for a European Parliament Resolution on the functioning of franchising in the retail sector 2016/2244 (INI), para. 20.

CHAPTER 6

Technology Transfer Agreements*

§6.01 TECHNOLOGY AND ITS IMPORTANCE IN THE BUSINESS CONTEXT[1]

[A] Definition of the Term 'Technology'

'Technology' as a term has a variety of definitions.

Technology is defined, by WIPO, as the '*end products* of scientific research and development in the form of inventions and know-how which are *used as tools or processes for creating new or improved products and services* that better serve the needs of the market'.[2]

In contrast, according to the United Nations Conference on Trade and Development, technology is '*systematic knowledge* for the manufacture of a product, for the application of a process or for the rendering of a service'.[3] This definition, which excludes goods that are either sold or hired, defines technology as encompassing '*the knowledge that goes into the creation and provision of the product or services* that constitutes "technology," not the finished product or service as such'.[4] According to this definition, the knowledge that goes into the production of goods and the supply of

* Books - Anderson M, Technology Transfer (3rd Edition, Bloomsbury Professional Ltd); Jones A and Sufrin B, EU Competition Law (4th Edition, OUP).

1. Exchanging value - Negotiating technology licensing agreements (WIPO); Kanwar, Intellectual Property Protection and Technology Licensing: The Case of Developing Countries, Journal of Law and Economics, Vol 55, No 3 (August 2012), 539, 540; Larson and Anderson, Technology Transfer, Licensing Contracts, and Incentives for Further Innovation, American Journal of Agricultural Economics, Vol 76, No 3 (Aug 1994), 547, 547-549.
2. Exchanging Value - Negotiating Technology Licensing Agreements (WIPO), 15. Emphasis added by writers.
3. UNCTAD Report entitled 'Transfer of Technology' (UNCTAD 2001) Reference UNCTAD/ITE/IIT/29, 5-6, citing the Draft International Code on the Transfer of Technology 1985 (Draft TOT Code 1985), Chapter 1 paragraph 1.2.) Emphasis added by writers.
4. UNCTAD 2001, 6. Emphasis added by writers.

services encompasses not only the '*technical knowledge* on which the end product is based' but also 'the *organizational capacity to convert the relevant productive inputs into the finished item or service*, as the case may be'.[5] The emphasis is placed in this context not only on the 'knowledge or methods that are necessary to carry on or to improve the existing production and distribution of goods and services' or indeed to develop entirely new products or processes but also on 'entrepreneurial expertise and professional know-how'.[6]

Technology suggests the European Commission (Commission) 'is an input, which is integrated either into a product or a production process'.[7]

[B] Sources of Technology

The product of research and development, technology may be produced by one entity alone or in collaboration with others. In the alternative technology that has been previously developed by another entity may be purchased or licensed ('licensing-in').[8]

Oftentimes it is far more efficient to purchase or to licence technology developed by others due to the savings generated by such a move or due to the lack of the human resources needed in order to develop the said technology.[9] It is however worthwhile noting that certain countries impose restrictions on the sale and/or licensing of certain technologies deemed sensitive to national security.[10]

The innovation strategy that a business adopts will depend to a large extent on the objectives, scope and time horizons of the product portfolio of the business concerned, the competitive environment within which the business operates and the positioning of the business in the value chain.[11]

[C] Internal Versus External Transfer of Technology

[1] Features of Internal and External Transfers

Corporations – national or multinational – are amongst the main generators of new technology. Such entities may transfer their technology using one of two mechanisms.[12] Such a transfer may be internal or external.

An internal transfer may for instance be made to entities that are affiliated with the transferor. Such affiliates are usually ones under the ownership and control of the

5. UNCTAD 2001, 6. Emphasis added by writers.
6. UNCTAD 2001, 6, citing Santikarn, Miagsam (1981), Technology Transfer (Singapore: Singapore University Press), 4.
7. Communication from the Commission – Guidelines on the application of Article 101 of the Treaty on the Functioning of the European Union to technology transfer agreements. (2014/C 89/03), C89/9, para. 20.
8. Exchanging Value – Negotiating Technology Licensing Agreements, WIPO, 15.
9. Exchanging Value – Negotiating Technology Licensing Agreements (WIPO), 15.
10. Exchanging Value – Negotiating Technology Licensing Agreements (WIPO), 15.
11. Pathways to Innovation Excellence, Arthur D Little 2010, 10.
12. UNCTAD 2001, 12 citing UNCTAD 1999a, 203.

transferor.[13] The investment may take the form of a Greenfield Investment (where the entity establishes a new entity in the host country) or a Brownfield Investment (when it acquires an existing firm in the target market).[14]

Development resulting from internal transfers offers a number of substantial advantages.[15] Financing is likely to be provided alongside the transferred technology. Access may be given to technology available to the transferor that would not necessarily be made available through an external transfer coupled with access to a system of support and assistance provided by the transferor. Such a transfer is likely to be achieved more rapidly than a transfer out of technology.

Internal transfers do however entail a number of potential disadvantages. Such transfers may necessitate the acquisition of an entire package of the transferor which may encompass brand names and infrastructure. Whilst the retention of certain key skills and know-how by the transferor may impede the efficiency and effectiveness of the transfer of technology.[16]

In contrast with internal transfers, an entity may choose to transfer out the technology developed by it. Such external transfers of technology may assume a number of forms, including joint ventures, franchises, licenses, subcontracting or production deals.[17]

The advantages associated with external transfers of technology will be determined principally by the form such transfers assume. In the main such transfers offer a turnkey solution allowing the parties to capitalise on the assets of each other. Moreover such transfers may afford a transferor an ongoing revenue stream and financial package (in the form of an advance) enabling it for example to fund further research and development.

[2] Choosing Between an Internal and External Transfer

Certain criteria are used by entities to determine the manner of the technology transfer. Such criteria include the character of the technology involved, the strategy of the party looking to transfer its technology, the competences of the recipient and any applicable national regulation affecting the transfer of technology.[18]

Internal transfers are common when the technology transferred is intricate or alternatively if it is part of a fast-moving area of technology.[19]

By using an internal transfer, the transferor is able to protect and enhance its competitive position, as it remains not only the proprietor of the technology but also the party responsible for the development of the technology.[20]

13. UNCTAD 2001, 12 citing UNCTAD 1999a, 203.
14. UNCTAD 2001, 13, citing UNCTAD 2000a, 174-176.
15. UNCTAD 2001, 14-5.
16. UNCTAD 2001, 15.
17. UNCTAD 2001, 14 citing UNCTAD 1999a, 203.
18. UNCTAD 2001, 13.
19. UNCTAD 2001, 13.
20. UNCTAD 2001, 13.

The owner of the technology may decide to create an entity that it controls and owns which it then entrusts with 'an exclusive global mandate' to assume production of a specific product line.[21]

The competences of the transferee will determine whether the transfer by the transferor is internal or external. The absence of a competent licensee is likely to result in an internal transfer of the technology by the transferor.[22]

Host country may mandate strategy as the policy of the host country may necessitate the transfer of technology to a local partner.[23,24]

[D] Scope of Technology

One or more types of intellectual property may be associated with technology. Technology may give rise to a variety of different types of intellectual property.

The technology may entail patents, copyrights, trademarks and trade secrets amongst other types of intellectual property.

Patents may be associated with novel or improved products or processes. Copyright may be associated with the works of authorship which may encompass

---

21. UNCTAD 2001, 13.
22. UNCTAD 2001, 13.
23. UNCTAD 2001, 13.
24. Other host country restrictions are reviewed in UNCTAD 2001, 23-4. A host country may adopt measures that restrict the employment of foreign nationals and require the employment and training of local personnel; require the transfer of certain technologies deemed strategically important by the host country; control the royalty rates charged by the foreign entity in relation to the transferred technology; and demand the establishment of certain R&D activities in the host country to ensure the development of technology in line with the demands of the host country. Such restrictions are now the subject of certain international treaties which in turn affect the ability of the host country to utilise these measures. Chapter 3 of the Draft International Code of Conduct on the Transfer of Technology (1985 version) emphasises the discretion of nations to adopt measures affecting the transfer of technology but also stresses the responsibilities of the host country. Subject to the prerogative enjoyed by States to decide on the national measures they wish to adopt in the context of technology transfer, such measures should (according to §3.1 of this document) '(i) Recognize that a close relationship exists between technology flows [and] the conditions under which such flows are admitted and treated; (ii) Promote a favourable and beneficial climate for the international transfer of technology; (iii) Take into consideration in an equitable manner the legitimate interests of all parties; (iv) Encourage and facilitate transfers of technology to take place under mutually agreed, fair and reasonable terms and conditions having regard to the principles and objectives of the Code; (v) Take into account the differing factors characterising the transactions such as local conditions, the nature of the technology and the scope of the undertaking; (vi) Be consistent with their international obligations.' Measures adopted by States – states §3.2 of this document – should be fairly and equitably applied and should be applied on the same basis to all parties. In the adoption of legislation, States are encouraged to give due consideration to local economic and social development needs. (§3.3) Factors that States may take into account when adopting measures regulating the flows and effects of technology transfer (§3.4) include financial factors (such as tax treatment, transferability of payments and currency regulations governing exchange of currency), renegotiation, technical considerations (such as use of components produced locally and imported) and organisational factors (including regulation of collaborative agreements involving foreign entities, the scope of such agreements in terms of duration, terms and the fields of activity). (UNCTAD Report 2001, 55-8, citing UNCTAD 1996a vol I, 184-8).

technical manuals, specifications, schematics and formulae. Trademarks may be associated with distinctive features associated with the products and technologies such as logos and names.[25]

Due to the value associated with technology, once developed the intellectual property rights associated with the technology may either be sold outright to another or alternatively such intellectual property rights may become the subject-matter of a licence.

§6.02 TECHNOLOGY TRANSFER: DEFINITION OF THE CONCEPT AND THE TYPES OF TRANSACTIONS

[A] Definition of the Concept of 'Technology Transfer'

The promulgation of commercial technology is a process referred to as technology transfer.[26]

This transmission of knowledge by the transferor to the recipient may or may not be dealt with by means of contract involving the transferor and recipient or recipients as the case may be.[27]

Consideration for the transfer may be in the form of cash consideration or non-cash consideration. Certain transfers of technology may for example be made in exchange for technologies developed and owned by the licensee, for options in relation to technology generated by the transfer and for shares.

Such a transfer may originate from the private or public sector and may be to the public or private sector. Technology transfers may involve transfers by government or public bodies to entities which are either private or public in nature. The national laboratories affiliated with the Department of Energy (DOE) in the US, for example, are involved in the regular and recurrent transmission of 'knowledge, intellectual property or capabilities developed at DOE national laboratories'.[28] Such transferences are typically made to entities including but not limited to the private sector, universities, research centres and the government (state and federal).[29]

25. Successful Technology Licensing (WIPO 2004), 4.
26. UNCTAD 2001, 6 citing Blakeney 1989, 136.
27. UNCTAD 2001, 6 citing Blakeney 1989, 136.
28. Report of GAO to Congressional Committees entitled 'Technology Transfer – Clearer Priorities and Greater Use of Innovative Approaches Could Increase the Effectiveness of Technology Transfer at Department of Energy Laboratories' (June 2009) reference GAO 09 548 DOE, 14 citing Secretarial Policy Statement on Technology Transfer at Department of Energy Facilities (January 31, 2008).
29. Report of GAO to Congressional Committees entitled 'Technology Transfer – Clearer Priorities and Greater Use of Innovative Approaches Could Increase the Effectiveness of Technology Transfer at Department of Energy Laboratories' (June 2009) reference GAO 09 548 DOE, 8. (GAO Report 2009).

[B] Types of Transactions Involving Technology Transfer

A variety of commercial transactions may be used to deal with technology. Such transactions share one common denominator namely their subject matter – technology.[30]

The review that follows looks at the use of the term (technology transfer) by the UNCTAD (the United Nations Conference on Trade and Development) and compares this usage with that made by European Union law and by the US government.

Technology transfer agreements may be commercial and non-commercial in nature.[31] Non-commercial technology transfer agreements may take the form of cooperation agreements such as those concluded between different countries. Developed and developing countries may enter into technology transfer agreements of a non-commercial nature that govern *inter alia* infrastructure and agricultural development, research, education, employment and transport.[32]

The discussion that follows does not address non-commercial agreements nor does it address the diffusion of technology. In the context of the discussion that follows technology diffusion is treated as an activity that is distinct from the transfer of technology.[33]

[1] UNCTAD

According to the report of the UNCTAD from 2001, technology transfer agreements encompass an array of agreements differentiate by their subject matter. Such contracts cover amongst other items industrial property, know-how and technology expertise.

In the first category are the transactions that assign, sell and licence the different categories of industrial property excluding trademarks, service marks and trade names when these are not encompassed in the subject matter transferred.[34]

In the second category are those transactions concerning the supply of know-how and technical expertise. Such know-how and technical expertise could encompass studies, operational strategies, designs, specifications, services and training.[35]

In the third category are the transactions that involve the provision of the technological expertise needed in order to set in place and operate hardware and instruments.[36]

In the fourth category are the transactions that involve the provision of technological expertise needed in order to procure, to install and to utilise hardware, instruments, intermediate products and/or raw materials that have been procured.[37]

30. UNCTAD 2001, 6-7, citing the Draft TOT Code 1996a volume I, 183.
31. UNCTAD 2001, 7 citing Blakeney 1989, 3.
32. UNCTAD 2001, 7 citing Blakeney 1989, 3.
33. UNCTAD 2001, 7 citing Blakeney 1989, 3.
34. UNCTAD 2001, 7 citing Blakeney 1989, 3.
35. UNCTAD 2001, 7 citing Blakeney 1989, 3.
36. UNCTAD 2001, 7 citing Blakeney 1989, 3.
37. UNCTAD 2001, 7 citing Blakeney 1989, 3.

In the fifth category are those transactions that involve the supply of the technological elements of cooperation arrangements of an industrial and a technical character.[38]

[2] European Union

European Union law adopts a comparatively narrow definition when compared with the one put forth by the UNCTAD. Pursuant to European Union law[39] a technology transfer agreement refers to licensing agreements and assignments.[40]

[a] Licensing Arrangements

In this context a licensing agreement is defined as an agreement pursuant to which the licensor permits one or more parties to use its technology rights in the production of contract products, by the licensee and/or its sub-contractor(s).[41][42]

The term encompasses licensing agreements concluded between two undertakings or more. It also extends to agreements made between entities that are in competition with one another (horizontal agreements) and those which are not competing (vertical agreements).[43]

In the case of horizontal agreements, the contracting parties are typically active on the same level of the production or supply chain. In the case of vertical agreements, these parties are actors participating in different levels of the production or supply chain.[44]

[b] Assignments

An assignment of technology rights in this context is defined as an agreement between two undertakings for the purpose of producing contract products 'where part of the risk associated with the exploitation of the technology remains with the assignor'.[45]

38. UNCTAD 2001, 7 citing Blakeney 1989, 3.
39. Pursuant to the Technology Transfer Block Exemption Regulation (TTBER) as supplemented by the Guidance Accompanying the TTBER.
40. TTBER 2014, Art. 1(c).
41. European Commission Memo entitled 'Antitrust: Commission consults on proposal for revised competition regime for technology transfer agreements – frequently asked questions Memo/13/120 (Brussels, 20 February 2013), 1.
42. TTBER 2014, Art. 1(c) read alongside Art. 1(f) and Art. 1(g). A contract product refers to a product (a good or a service) manufactured directly or indirectly using the technology rights that have been licenced.
43. European Commission Memo entitled 'Antitrust: Commission consults on proposal for revised competition regime for technology transfer agreements – frequently asked questions Memo/13/120 (Brussels, 20 February 2013), 1.
44. European Commission Memo entitled 'Antitrust: Commission consults on proposal for revised competition regime for technology transfer agreements – frequently asked questions Memo/13/120 (Brussels, 20 February 2013), 1.
45. TTBER 2014, Art. 1(c) read alongside Art. 1(f) and Art. 1(g). A contract product refers to a product (a good or a service) manufactured directly or indirectly using the technology rights that have been licensed.

[3] US Government

Technology transfer agreements as a term can be used to refer to a plethora of arrangements.

According to an official report written by the US Government Accountability Office (GAO) transfers of technology involving the US Department of Energy (DOE) laboratories only encompass 'some of the laboratories' technology – and knowledge-sharing activities'.[46]

Based on field-based interviews the report of the GAO indicates that the following arrangements and activities at the laboratories of the DOE are said to constitute technology transfer agreements.[47]

[a] Cooperative Research and Development Agreements[48]

Cooperative research and development agreements commonly referred to as CRADA entail public-private collaborations[49] which include alliances between governmental departments (such as the DOE) and non-federal partners.[50]

These collaborations may be formulated for a number of reasons including the enhancement of the technology developed by the government department, the commercialisation of such technology and the furtherance of the respective research and development objectives of the collaborating partners.

Such efforts may result *inter alia* in studies, analyses, improvements and new products in the form of goods and services, which are directly beneficial to the research goals of the government department and its private sector partner.[51]

Under the auspices of such an arrangement, the laboratories of the government department contribute resources such as personnel, equipment and other in-kind resources, whilst at the CRADA partner contributes funding and/or in-kind resources.[52]

Ownership of any intellectual property generated by the collaboration will be an issue determined by negotiation between the parties.[53]

Case study – CRADA

One illustration of a CRADA is the joint field test in which the National Renewable Energy Laboratory (Laboratory) in Colorado collaborated with Sacramento's utility district,. This project saw the design, development and

46. GAO Report 2009, 8.
47. GAO Report 2009, 8.
48. GAO Report 2009, Appendix 2 displays and analyses the data provided by the DOE.
49. GAO Report 2009, 8.
50. GAO Report 2009, 8.
51. GAO Report 2009, 8.
52. GAO Report 2009, 8.
53. GAO Report 2009, 8.

construction of housing incorporating the energy efficiency technology developed by the Laboratory.

This collaboration allowed the Laboratory to test its research whilst the construction company was given the opportunity to develop design specifications for energy efficient housing.[54]

[b] Non-federal Work-for-Others Agreements[55]

These privately funded research projects typically involve the governmental laboratory carrying out research for a non-federal sponsor.[56] This research is not directly intended for the benefit of the laboratory or the government department to which the laboratory is affiliated.[57]

Under the auspices of such a scheme, the sponsor bears the entire cost of the project concerned and typically opts to receive ownership of any intellectual property generated as a result of the research carried out by the governmental laboratory.[58]

In such circumstances, the private sector sponsor will be obligated to award government a licence to make use of any technology and intellectual property generated by means of the research carried out by the public sector body.[59]

Case study – Non-federal work-for-other agreements

An example of such an arrangement is the work performed by a government laboratory based in Los Alamos (the Los Alamos National Laboratory – Laboratory) alongside the University of California which set out to develop a detection and response early alert system for avian influenza.

Under the auspices of this project, the objective of the Laboratory was the development of software and hardware systems alongside analysis tools and protocols.

[c] Licensing Agreements[60]

Once a governmental body (such as a laboratory) has developed technologies it has the option of licensing the same to another entity in exchange for a fee or using a royalty

54. GAO Report 2009, 9.
55. GAO Report 2009, Appendix 2 displays and analyses the data provided by the DOE.
56. GAO Report 2009, 9.
57. GAO Report 2009, 9.
58. GAO Report 2009, 9.
59. GAO Report 2009, 9.
60. GAO Report 2009, Appendix 2 displays and analyses the data provided by the DOE.

based scheme.[61] Using this strategy, the government body is able to raise a profit from the licensing of patented inventions or discoveries, copyrighted software programmes and so forth.[62]

> **Case study – Licencing**
>
> The Ames Laboratory licenced a lead-free solder developed by it alongside Sandia National Laboratories to industry.[63] The licencing of this technology yielded roughly five million USD in the fiscal year 2007.[64]

In the fiscal years 2006-2008 sixteen out of the seventeen national laboratories affiliated to the DOE licenced technologies netting approximately forty four million USD in fees and royalties.[65]

[d] *User-Facility Agreements*[66,67]

Under user-facility agreements, the facilities of the governmental body (the DOE for example) are made available for use by external entities for their own research ends.[68] On occasion the research is performed in collaboration with public sector personnel (such as the personnel working at the laboratory).[69]

Facilities may be offered on a gratuitous basis or for a negotiated fee on the proviso that the research resulting from the use of these resources is made available to the public.[70]

Where the results are not made available to the public, the parties using the facilities are usually obligated to reimburse the costs associated with the use of the amenities provided.[71]

> **Case study – User-facility agreement**[72]
>
> Under the aegis of the user-facility agreement, the private party entrusted with the management and operations of one of the DOE's national laboratory (the Washington state-based Pacific Northwest National Laboratory) was given

61. GAO Report 2009, 10.
62. GAO Report 2009, 10.
63. GAO Report 2009, 10.
64. GAO Report 2009, 10.
65. GAO Report 2009, 10.
66. GAO Report 2009, 10-11.
67. GAO Report 2009, Appendix 2 displays and analyses the data provided by the DOE.
68. GAO Report 2009, 10.
69. GAO Report 2009, 10.
70. GAO Report 2009, 11.
71. GAO Report 2009, 11.
72. GAO Report 2009, 44.

access to resources owned by the DOE and to personnel working at the laboratory in question in order to further its own private research goals.[73]

This arrangement, which lasted for almost five decades (from 1964 to 2012) and generated ten percent of all the work performed annually at the laboratory (equating to approximately 70 million USD per annum), was pioneered in order to 'stimulate economic diversity and private investment in the local community by encouraging the contractor (Battelle Memorial Institute) to pursue private research and development work and to invest in facilities and equipment at the laboratory beyond what the federal government would invest, in part to support this private research work'.[74]

Several hundred distinct agreements were concluded every year with federal and non-federal bodies, under the auspices of the user-facility agreement, by the contractor (Battelle Memorial Institute).[75] In the three-year period spanning fiscal years 2006 to 2009, the contractor concluded approximately 700 to 800 such agreements.[76] This in turn meant that the laboratory did not have to enter into as many CRADAs or nonfederal work-for-others agreements as other DOE national laboratories did.[77]

[e] Conclusion

Based on a review and analysis of figures provided to the GAO by the DOE, in the fiscal years 2006 to 2008, the vast majority of agreements concluded by the DOE were user-facility agreements, with non-federal work-for-others agreements coming in in second place, patent licenses in third place and CRADAs in the final place.[78]

Quite apart from the four categories of agreements reviewed above which are classified by the GAO and the DOE as technology transfer agreements, the laboratories of the DOE are also involved in collaborative agreements with federal bodies. In the fiscal years spanning 2006 to 2008, sixteen out of the seventeen national DOE laboratories were involved in such federal work-for-others agreements. Out of 4900 such agreements in the fiscal year 2008, approximately 600 were funded by the Department of Homeland Security.[79]

Though officials at ten out of the seventeen such laboratories classify federal work-for-others agreements as technology transfer agreements, officials at other laboratories argue that these accords are not technology transfer agreements on

73. GAO Report 2009, 44.
74. GAO Report 2009, 44.
75. GAO Report 2009, 44.
76. GAO Report 2009, 44.
77. GAO Report 2009, 44.
78. GAO Report 2009, 13 (figure 2).
79. GAO Report 2009, 13-4.

account of the fact that these arrangements entail a federal agency partner rather than a private sector partner.[80]

§6.03 CHALLENGES ASSOCIATED WITH TECHNOLOGY TRANSFER AGREEMENTS

In an official public report published in June 2009 by the GAO on the operations of seventeen national laboratories owned by the DOE, the GAO highlights a number of challenges associated with technology transfer agreements. The data collected from these laboratories and the field-based interviews are summarised in this report which was submitted to the Congressional Committees.

Three key challenges are highlighted by the technology transfer officials working for the various laboratories, states the GAO. These in turn limit the volume of technologies transferred out of the laboratories and restrain the ability of these laboratories to share their capabilities.[81]

Competing internal priorities is the first of the three challenges. The second is the lack of resources needed in order to commercialise the technology generated. The third and final challenge is bureaucracy. These different challenges are reviewed below.

[A] Competing Internal Priorities

The ability to transfer technologies generated is often hindered by the fact that interests diverge across the organisations. This coupled with a general lack of interest in the transfer of such technologies has meant that the scope for technology transference is limited.

Within organisations, public and private, the interests of management do not necessarily coincide and converge with those of the personnel responsible for the research and development operations of the organisation.

In its report, the GAO highlights its findings, which are based on submissions made to it by officials working in the different laboratories of the DOE. According to certain officials at these laboratories, there exists a general lack of interest in the transfer of technology and the processes associated with the same.[82] Other officials attest to the fact that the priorities for their researchers are the research they are conducting and the publication of any data and information generated by the same, rather than collaborations with the private sector.[83]

Notwithstanding the fact that federal law in the US makes the transfer of technology a responsibility for all federal laboratory scientists and engineers,[84] the divergent concerns of management and the researchers coupled with a lack of interest

80. GAO Report 2009, 14.
81. GAO Report 2009, 22.
82. GAO Report 2009, 22-3.
83. GAO Report 2009, 22-3.
84. Federal Technology Transfer Act of 1986 Pub. L. No. 99-502, § 4, 100 Stat. 1785, 1790 (1986).

in the processes involved in transferring technologies are capable of producing a dampening effect on the transfer of technologies.[85]

[B] Lack of Resources

This second challenge is instrumental in exacerbating the first of the three challenges.

Lack of specialised personnel with the business acumen needed to commercialise the technology generated is a major concern for many of the laboratories reviewed in the GAO's report.[86]

For them, the challenge is the recruitment of staff with an entrepreneurial background and the expertise needed to identify and promote technologies possessing commercial potential.[87]

Whilst the DOE acknowledges that its staff excels at research, innovation and invention it admits that not all staff notably scientists 'look beyond their research to possible applications in the marketplace'.[88]

In the context of this second challenge, one cannot overlook the shortage or lack of the financial resources needed in order to develop and demonstrate the technologies generated. Technology transfer officials from fourteen (out of the seventeen) national laboratories belonging to the DOE attest to this fact.[89]

For an organisation to find itself in a position to promote its technology to outside investors it requires not only specialised personnel but also the requisite capital needed in order to show the commercial applications of its technology.[90] Many investors will require such evidence before providing the means needed to commercialise the know-how.[91]

Once the research effort has come to an end and technologies have been developed, outside investors are needed by the organisation in order to help them commercialise these technologies.[92] Further development or analysis is often required before the laboratories can attract industry and commercialise the technologies available.[93]

This state of affairs (oftentimes termed the **valley of death**) may arise out of 'a failure to transfer promising technologies because, on the one hand, DOE has limited funding to continue research beyond its initial mission scope and, on the other, potential industry partners are often reluctant to assume the risks of investing in

85. GAO Report 2009, 23.
86. GAO Report 2009, 22.
87. GAO Report 2009, 22.
88. GAO Report 2009, 22.
89. GAO Report 2009, 23. At page 24 several examples are given of 'promising technologies currently languishing in the "valley of death."'
90. GAO Report 2009, 23.
91. GAO Report 2009, 23.
92. GAO Report 2009, 23.
93. GAO Report 2009, 23.

technologies whose potential has not been demonstrated with a prototype, performance data, or similar evidence'.[94]

[C] Bureaucratic Constraints

The final challenge, highlighted by the DOE's technology transfer officials, is the obligation to make use of standard contracts or clauses during negotiations for the transfer of technology.[95]

By undermining the ductility of being able to negotiate the substance of the contracts governing the transfer of technology, this duty placed on DOE officials has the effect of hindering such negotiations and on occasion deterring potential partners.[96]

In the context of the DOE's work, whilst laboratory contracting officials are generally responsible for negotiation of contracts with potential collaborators, such agreements must be approved by the DOE and their terms need to be those set out by federal law or DOE policy.[97]

An illustration of one such constraint is the obligation imposed on the party negotiating with the federal laboratory to pay in advance (for 90 days' work for example) before a work-for-others agreement can be concluded.[98] This obligation, it is contended, not only fails to reflect commercial practices but has also proven to be an obstacle in negotiations with certain small enterprises that do not have the requisite capital to advance the funds demanded.[99]

Another term that acts as a barrier to negotiations is the requirement on partners (under CRADAs) and licensees (under licensing agreements) to 'substantially manufacture' in the US commercial goods incorporating the technologies developed by the DOE laboratories[100] or, in the case of CRADA partners, a binding obligation to furnish an 'alternate net benefit to the US economy'.[101] Whilst these obligations based on federal and DOE policies aim to support industry in the US they may act as deterrents to businesses that generally manufacture overseas.[102]

[D] Solutions for Valley of Death Technologies

In order to enhance the identification and utilisation of technologies developed by scientists at its national laboratories, the DOE have formulated certain strategies. Whilst these mechanisms were developed in order to tackle difficulties confronted by the DOE, these mechanisms are transferable having application beyond the DOE laboratories.

94. GAO Report 2009, 23.
95. GAO Report 2009, 25.
96. GAO Report 2009, 25.
97. GAO Report 2009, 25.
98. GAO Report 2009, 25.
99. GAO Report 2009, 25.
100. GAO Report 2009, 25.
101. GAO Report 2009, 25 footnote 25.
102. GAO Report 2009, 25.

First technology transfer officials are appointed internally at each laboratories and charged with identifying technologies developed at the laboratories that have commercial applications and may be used in the production of commercial goods.[103]

Such officials typically possess a business background enabling them to appreciate the commercial utilisation of such technologies.[104] In order to carry out their role these officials have been willing to use an assortment of techniques including regular evaluation of pending publications by researchers at the laboratory, promotion of technologies selected as having commercial potential alongside the public relations officers at the laboratories and collaboration with the officers at the laboratories charged with applying for patent protection and management of intellectual property.[105]

Second, certain laboratories use the services of entrepreneurs-in-residence who represent venture capitalists and who take charge of identifying and commercialising technologies developed by the scientists and researchers at the laboratories.[106]

Such entrepreneurs funded by the DOE are given one year in which to identify a minimum of one energy-efficiency/renewable-energy technology and to prepare a strategy for the commercialisation of the said technology.[107] One of the entrepreneurs posted in one of the DOE's laboratories estimated that 80% of the technologies developed by the laboratory in question were commercially promising and could be commercialised within approximately one year after a period of further development or testing.[108]

Third, funding through the provision of grants may allow laboratories to fund further research and development efforts. One illustration of a public-private initiative involving the National Renewable Energy Laboratory entailed a 250,000 USD grant, which was matched by a private entity. As a result of this joint investment the laboratory was able to develop a prototype for industry based on its advanced cooling fan technology (a technology resulting from its research into geothermal energy).[109]

A fourth strategy employed by select laboratories owned by the DOE is the policy of rolling-back funds into the operations of the laboratory. These laboratories are effectively a sustainable model whereby they use monies generated by licensing of their technology to develop other technologies in need of further R&D in order to render these technologies more attractive to external investors.[110]

A fifth strategy is adopted by certain laboratories that have developed mechanisms to streamline the negotiation process. In an effort to enhance the efficiency of the negotiation process, certain DOE laboratories have worked in collaboration with officials of the DOE in order to formulate technology transfer agreements with

103. GAO Report 2009, 26.
104. GAO Report 2009, 26.
105. GAO Report 2009, 26.
106. GAO Report 2009, 26.
107. GAO Report 2009, 26.
108. GAO Report 2009, 26.
109. GAO Report 2009, 27.
110. GAO Report 2009, 26.

pre-approved terms and conditions.[111] As a result of these efforts, these laboratories are no longer required to seek the prior approval of the DOE for technology transfer agreements negotiated with prospective partners.[112]

Certain laboratories have introduced umbrella CRADAs with major industrial partners such as Goodyear or Chevron. As such these laboratories, which regularly contract with these partners, now make use of these umbrella agreements as the basis for their contractual relations with these specific partners.[113] These agreements may contain certain pre-agreed terms and conditions, such as the right of review which permits the contracting parties to review each other's publications before their submission for publication, as well as a right of joint ownership in any intellectual property generated by the collaboration between the parties.[114]

A further strategy is the development of permanent alliance with private partners. Certain laboratories owned by the DOE have developed permanent partnerships with the private sector. One such laboratory has a contract with a non-profit research organisation.[115] Under the terms of the agreement concluded between the laboratory and the private sector organisation (which is referred to as a 'use-permit') the latter operates the laboratory and in exchange is permitted to make use of the facilities owned by the laboratory and the personnel working at the laboratory for its own research and technology-sharing operations.[116]

Another mechanism used to help assist with the commercialisation of technologies are government-sponsored training and networking events.[117] Representatives from the private sector searching for partnerships with federally run laboratories are invited to partake in these events.[118] Besides these sessions, searchable web-based tools have been launched.

§6.04 THE BUSINESS MODELS AVAILABLE IN THE CONTEXT OF TECHNOLOGY

[A] Introduction[119,120]

Technology transfer is commonly associated with a number of associated agreements.

Licenses, assignments, materials transfer agreements (MTAs), option agreements, the right of first opportunity, the right of first refusal, research and development agreements, sponsored clinical trials agreements, heads of agreement (alternately heads of terms, term sheet, letter of intent and memorandum of understanding),

111. GAO Report 2009, 28.
112. GAO Report 2009, 28.
113. GAO Report 2009, 28.
114. GAO Report 2009, 28.
115. GAO Report 2009, 28.
116. GAO Report 2009, 28.
117. GAO Report 2009, 29.
118. GAO Report 2009, 29.
119. A review of these various agreements can be found in Chapter 2, Anderson 2010.
120. Exchanging value – Negotiating technology licensing agreements (WIPO); UNICO guides key issues, Chapter 6.

confidentiality agreements (CDAs) or non-disclosure agreements (NDAs), employment agreements, consultancy agreements, agreements with students and spin-out company agreements are all examples of agreements associated with technology transfer.

This section compares two business models that may be used in the context of technology namely assignments of technology and technology licensing agreements.

[1] Assignment

Once developed, technology may be sold by the entity that developed the technology to one or more other entities.

A sale of technology may arise in situations where the party responsible for developing the technology does not possess the means, the experience or the motivation required to capitalise on the technology. As such the developer may decide instead to source a buyer for the technology.[121]

Assignment is a one-off transaction pursuant to which the technology is purchased by the assignee and sold by the assignor for an agreed price.[122] This one-off transaction may on occasion entail certain sustained devoirs on the part of the parties to the transaction namely the party selling (assignor) and the party buying (assignee).[123] This may arise where payment is deferred.[124]

Frequently, the sale of the intellectual property rights (associated with the technology) without more is not a viable option.[125] This may occur when the assignment of rights alone is insufficient as the assignment is 'not attractive without human capital, a product, a developed market and/or an established business or revenue stream'.[126]

A sale of technology entails the sale of rights relating to three categories of assets namely the intellectual property itself, the know-how and materials.[127]

The know-how assigned will encompass technical data as well as non-technical (commercial) data relating to the intellectual property.[128] This know-how is intended to assist the party purchasing the technology to make use of the intellectual property sold.[129]

Materials available to the party selling the technology may be required by the purchaser in order to exploit the intellectual property sold. In certain situations such materials are provided under a distinct agreement known as a Materials Transfer Agreement (MTA).[130]

121. Exchanging Value - Negotiating Technology Licensing Agreements (WIPO), 17.
122. Exchanging Value - Negotiating Technology Licensing Agreements (WIPO), 17.
123. Exchanging Value - Negotiating Technology Licensing Agreements (WIPO), 17.
124. Exchanging Value - Negotiating Technology Licensing Agreements (WIPO), 17.
125. Exchanging Value - Negotiating Technology Licensing Agreements (WIPO), 17.
126. Exchanging Value - Negotiating Technology Licensing Agreements (WIPO), 17.
127. UNICO guides key issues 36-37.
128. UNICO guides key issues, 37.
129. UNICO guides key issues, 37.
130. UNICO guides key issues, 37.

[2] Comparing Licensing with Assignments

In contrast with a licence, an outright sale to another entity of the rights to the intellectual property associated with the given technology results in the permanent assignment of title to the pertinent technology and in turn to the rights to the intellectual property connected with the relevant technology.

Assignment may mean that the intellectual property assigned is developed in ways that the assignor had not wanted or in the alternative it may not be developed at all.[131]

Some assignment agreements will include provisions that stipulate the contingencies which will give rise to a re-assignment.[132] The assigned intellectual property may be re-assigned for example in the event of insolvency or administration.[133] Such reassignment may occur when there has been a failure to meet obligations defined in the sale agreement.[134]

In comparison with assignment, licensing will typically enable the licensor to retain ownership of the intellectual property licensed whilst maintaining a degree of control over the exploitation of the licensed intellectual property through the retention of authority over the manner in which the intellectual property is used, developed, marketed and distributed, affording the licensor far more operational certainty and flexibility.[135]

Pursuant to the terms of the licensing agreement, the licensor will oftentimes retain the right to bring the licensing agreement to an end.[136] This right to terminate may for example be associated with a breach of diligence obligations on the part of the licensee.[137] Termination may arise in the event of the insolvency of the licensee or in circumstances where the licensee enters into a voluntary arrangement.[138] Other contingencies that may give rise to a right to terminate include a change in ownership or management of the licensee and an actual or threatened cessation of operations by the licensee.[139]

Typically where the agreement is terminated, the licensed rights will instantaneously revert back to the licensor.[140]

Termination of an assignment and recovery of the assigned intellectual property may only be a possibility if the assignment agreement allows for the same. If such an option is afforded to the assignor it is likely to entail an application to the court for an order for re-assignment.[141]

131. UNICO guides key issues, 41.
132. UNICO guides key issues, 41.
133. UNICO guides key issues, 41.
134. UNICO guides key issues, 41.
135. UNICO guides key issues, 40.
136. UNICO guides key issues, 40.
137. UNICO guides key issues, 40.
138. UNICO guides key issues, 40.
139. UNICO guides key issues, 40.
140. UNICO guides key issues, 40.
141. UNICO guides key issues, 41.

Where technology has been assigned, the assignee becomes the owner of the technology and may in turn assign the assigned technology to a third party. The party to which the technology is assigned (sub-assignee) may not be necessarily bound by any of the contractual obligations that the original assignee agreed upon with the assignor.[142]

What is more, in the event that the assignee or the sub-assignee become insolvent or enter into an administration, the liquidator or administrator is likely to sell the property assigned which will in turn means that the property in question may end-up in the hands of a party that the assignor may not necessarily approve of.[143] This is particularly important where the original assignor is a university and the sub-assignee is a party that the university would deem objectionable and exceptionable based on ethical considerations for example.[144]

[3] Technology Licensing Agreements

The next part of this chapter focuses in on technology licensing agreements. This section of the chapter starts with an exploration of the subject matter of such agreements. Here the distinction between foreground intellectual property, background intellectual property and side-ground intellectual property is discussed alongside the distinction between exclusive, sole and non-exclusive agreements. Thereafter the different advantages associated with the licensing technology are deliberated on and a review of the disadvantages associated with such agreements is provided.

[a] Introduction

Licensing of technology will occur where one party owns one or more forms of intellectual property associated with the technology in question. Ownership in this context of the intellectual property associated with the technology will mean that the owner of the technology has the right in law to prevent another party from making use of the intellectual property in question.

The grant of a licence will permit the owner of the technology to allow one or more other parties to make use of the intellectual property in question. The grant of such a licence will be tightly controlled by the terms of the agreement drawn up in order to govern the relationship between the parties to the contract.[145]

Under a licensing set-up, the intellectual property rights connected to the technology are licensed by the owner of the technology (licensor) conjointly or severally to one or more other entities (licensees). This arrangement involving the licensing of technology to another is referred to as licensing-out.

Such a grant may either be for a specified period (definite term) or indefinitely (indefinite term). Under an indefinite term licence, the grant may remain in place

142. UNICO guides key issues, 41.
143. UNICO guides key issues, 41.
144. UNICO guides key issues, 41.
145. Successful Technology Licensing (WIPO 2004), 4.

indefinitely or at least until the expiration of the term applicable to the intellectual property type or types licensed (applicable where a patent or copyright is involved for example).

Licensing may involve the grant of rights to the intellectual property in a certain limited geographic area (territory).

Diverse rights are associated with intellectual property. Consequently, under a licensing agreement, the rights that may be conferred by the licensor on the licensee are wide-ranging. Such rights may encompass the right to produce, to have produced, to make use of, to reproduce, to display and to distribute, as well as the right to make use of a trademark in the distribution of and the sale of goods produced using the licensor's intellectual property.[146]

[b] *Categories of Technology Licensing Agreements*

Licensing agreements associated with technology typically fall into three categories.[147]

The first category comprises licensing agreements under which a licence is granted that is *limited to certain rights relating to the intellectual property*.[148] Under such a licensing agreement, the licensee may be granted for example the right to copy and distribute certain materials protected by copyright that relate to the technology developed by the licensor.[149] The licensee may accordingly have the right to copy and distribute formulae and schematics linked to the technology.[150]

The second category encompasses licensing agreements under which a licence is granted in relation to *all rights associated with the intellectual property or intellectual properties connected with the technology*.[151] As such the licensee will have all the rights to the relevant intellectual property or intellectual properties.[152] This licence will allow the licensee to produce, have produced, distribute, market, sell and use the products made using the pertinent technology.[153]

A third type of licence may be one that *grants all intellectual property rights which are essential to the production and marketing of a product* that meet a certain technical standard or specification.[154] By way of illustration, a group of entities formulate a technical specification to ensure the interoperability of devices and based on the agreed technical specification the participating entities pool their intellectual property rights and licence each other all the rights needed in order to produce and sell the product.[155]

146. Exchanging Value – Negotiating Technology Licensing Agreements (WIPO), 17.
147. Successful Technology Licensing (WIPO 2004), 4-5.
148. Successful Technology Licensing (WIPO 2004), 4-5.
149. Successful Technology Licensing (WIPO 2004), 4-5.
150. Successful Technology Licensing (WIPO 2004), 4-5.
151. Successful Technology Licensing (WIPO 2004), 4-5.
152. Successful Technology Licensing (WIPO 2004), 4-5.
153. Successful Technology Licensing (WIPO 2004), 4-5.
154. Successful Technology Licensing (WIPO 2004), 4-5.
155. Successful Technology Licensing (WIPO 2004), 5.

§6.05 SUBJECT MATTER OF A LICENSING AGREEMENT

Licensing-out usually involves the granting of rights in relation to three categories of assets namely the intellectual property itself, the know-how and materials.[156]

The know-how licensed comprises technical and non-technical (commercial) data related to the intellectual property licensed.[157] This know-how is intended to assist the licensee in making use of the intellectual property licensed.[158]

Materials available to the licensor may be required by the licensee in order to exploit the intellectual property licensed.[159] For example in scenarios where a university licenses technology the licensee may require access to certain materials that only the university possesses including biological or chemical compounds of human tissue.[160] In certain situations such materials are provided under a distinct agreement known as a Materials Transfer Agreement (MTA).[161]

[A] Background Intellectual Property and Foreground Intellectual Property[162]

A licensing agreement involving a university will occasionally entail the licensing-out of technology developed not only prior to the conclusion of the agreement, but also after the date the agreement was made.

In this context, a distinction is drawn between background intellectual property (formerly referred to as pre-existing know-how or knowledge) and foreground intellectual property.[163]

These terms refer respectively to the intellectual property or know-how developed before the date the licensing agreement was concluded or the work started and the intellectual property or know-how developed during the term of the agreement in the performance of the activities under the agreement.[164]

Intellectual property developed during the term of the agreement, which does not result from the execution of activities under the agreement concluded by the parties, is oftentimes included in the definition of the term 'background intellectual property' or 'background know-how.[165]

Where intellectual property or know-how is introduced into the project whilst the project is in progress, in circumstances where the intellectual property or know-how in question was not anticipated at the conception of the project, that intellectual property

156. UNICO guides key issues, 36-7.
157. UNICO guides key issues, 37.
158. UNICO guides key issues, 37.
159. UNICO guides key issues, 37.
160. UNICO guides key issues, 37.
161. UNICO guides key issues, 37.
162. UNICO guides key issues, 37.
163. UNICO guides key issues, 37.
164. UNICO guides key issues, 37.
165. UNICO guides key issues, 37.

or know-how is known as side-ground intellectual property.[166] Occasionally such intellectual property or know-how is treated as being encompassed within the definition of background intellectual property.[167]

The terms of a licensing agreement will address the ownership of the particular foreground and background intellectual property or know-how, as well as dealing with the identity of the party or parties that may have the right to make use of such intellectual property or know-how and the types of use that may be made of the same.[168] Moreover, the agreement may include provisions addressing remuneration for the said usage.[169]

[B] Exclusive – Sole – Non-exclusive

Reference may also be made in the agreement as to whether the licence to use the foreground or background intellectual property or know-how is on an exclusive, sole or non-exclusive basis.[170]

Though in the context of UK IP legislation, some statutory definitions are given for the term 'exclusive', such definitions only relate to the use made of the term (exclusive) in the pertinent legislative instruments.[171] The common understanding of these terms is noted below.

Exclusive means that once rights are granted under a licence exclusively to a specific entity in relation for example to certain intellectual property in a certain field and territory, then the licensor is not permitted to grant another licence relating to the same rights to another party nor to make use of those licensed rights itself.[172]

Sole means that once rights are granted under a licence to particular rights solely to one entity, the licensor is not permitted to grant another licence of the same rights to another entity.[173] In this context and in contrast with an exclusive licence, the licensor is permitted to make use of those licensed rights itself.[174]

Non-exclusivity means that the licensor can if it wishes grant one or more licenses of the same rights to other entities, whilst retaining the right to make use of the licensed rights itself.[175]

166. UNICO guides key issues, 38.
167. UNICO guides key issues, 38.
168. UNICO guides key issues, 38.
169. UNICO guides key issues, 38.
170. UNICO guides key issues, 39.
171. UNICO guides key issues, 39.
172. UNICO guides key issues, 39.
173. UNICO guides key issues, 39.
174. UNICO guides key issues, 39.
175. UNICO guides key issues, 39.

§6.06 THE BENEFITS AND CONCERNS ASSOCIATED WITH TECHNOLOGY LICENSING[176]

The advantages and disadvantages of licensing technology is a major concern for entities whether these are prospective or actual licensors or licensees. Such matters should be borne in mind in the pre-pre-contractual stage when the party looking to exploit the technology that it owns is faced with several courses of action.

[A] Benefits Associated with Technology Licensing

Licensing of technology may occur where a licensor wishing to focus on one geographic zone or in the alternative on one or more unique fields of use is willing to allow another entity in possession of a greater proficiency or involvement in other territories or fields of use, the use of the pertinent technology.[177]

In so doing, the licensor may receive remuneration in the form of a capital payment (an advance or an initial payment) and a regular stream of revenue (in the form of royalties), whilst contemporaneously benefiting from the distinct knowledge of the licensee (knowledge of the target market or markets in terms of demand and regulation) as well as the specific resources available to the licensee (such as the production, distribution and marketing capacities of the licensee) in turn permitting the licensor to expand its market share more effectively.

In addition, the licensing agreement may permit the delegation of research and development functions to the licensee. Under such an agreement, the licensee may be delegated the freedom to develop the technology licensed further. In turn permitting both the licensee and licensor to benefit from any resultant developments.

Licensing, from the point of view of the licensee, provides the licensee with access to readily available technologies thereby allowing the licensee to benefit from the investment and efforts of the licensor in developing the technology.

Licensing-in allows the licensee to pair the licensed-in technology with the licensee's existing technology portfolio which in turn allows the licensee to offer new products and services and to create new market opportunities.

[B] Concerns Associated with Technology Licensing

The licensing of technology entails a number of concerns. In order to preempt and address these it is sensible for each of the parties looking to negotiate such an arrangement to bear in mind these concerns prior to the commencement of negotiations.

Certain concerns should be borne in mind well before the period leading up to the negotiation (in the pre-pre-negotiation planning stage). From the vantage point of the

176. Exchanging Value – Negotiating Technology Licensing Agreements (WIPO), 17-20; Fisher & Fisher, Export Best Practice – Commercial and Legal Aspects, 220.
177. Exchanging Value – Negotiating Technology Licensing Agreements (WIPO) 17-9.

prospective licensor for example such matters should shape the selection of prospective licensees and in turn the formulation of the criteria used to make the initial selection.[178]

[1] Concerns of the Licensor

Licensing may result in the creation of competition. By licensing technology to the licensee, the latter may evolve into a potential competitor to the licensor. This is especially the case when the licensee is more effective or efficient than the licensor.

Where the licensor is expected to invest further time and expense in the development of the technology under the terms of the licensing agreement, this may prove to be a burdensome undertaking on the part of the licensor.

The licensing arrangement may create a dependency with the licensor depending on the expertise, experience and infrastructure of the licensee. During the term of the licence, the licensor may have no incentive or may not be permitted (by the terms of the agreement) to develop a market share within the allocated territory or territories. In addition, the licensor may in time become reliant on the stream of revenue generated by the licensee.

Licensing of technology may increase the overheads associated with the final product produced. This may mean that the final cost of the product may be prohibitive and unsustainable.

From the viewpoint of the licensor, licensing may also mean that the licensor does not enjoy the same freedom it would otherwise enjoy, as it may not be able to change its licensees with the same ease as for example its distributors.[179]

[2] Concerns of the Licensee

Whilst licensing may be advantageous for the licensor, the licensee may not have the necessary level of certainty that it requires in order to build a sustainable operation.[180]

From the perspective of the licensee, there is a risk that the licensor may elect to use its right to terminate the agreement bringing an end to the licensing arrangement. Such a step is likely to result in heavy losses and liabilities from the point of view of the licensee. The licensee will probably not only have invested time and money in entering into the licensing agreement (expenses associated with due diligence, legal expenses, the acquisition of relevant authorities needed in order to administer the operation and so forth), but also in relation to the establishment of the infrastructure needed in order to exploit the licensed technology (leasing or purchase of premises, machinery and equipment and the hiring of personnel and consultants).

178. Discussed further within this chapter.
179. Fisher & Fisher, Export Best Practice (The Federation Press 1998), 216.
180. UNICO guides key issues, 41.

Licensing may create dependency from the viewpoint of the licensee. This dependency could manifest itself in the licensee becoming reliant on the technology of the licensor. This may act as a barrier to the future expansion of the licensee and to their ability to create products for different markets.

Where the licensor is expected to invest further time and expense in the development of the technology under the terms of the licensing agreement, from the point of view of the licensee this could mean that a commitment is made to a technology that is only partially ready for commercial exploitation.

§6.07 CONSIDERATIONS FROM THE POINT OF VIEW OF THE TECHNOLOGY OWNER/DEVELOPER[181]

Before entering into a technology licensing agreement, certain strategic concerns should be borne in mind by the owner of the technology.[182] The prospective licensor is encouraged to analyse the terrain in which it operates, to assess the viability of licensing versus the other transfer of technology options and to then formulate its own bespoke procedure for the selection of prospective licensees.[183]

As a majority of the steps reviewed in this section of the chapter take place before negotiations are even contemplated by the licensor, these steps are referred to by the authors as the pre-pre-contractual considerations.

[A] Pre-pre-contractual Considerations

By using a stepped approach, the owner of technology is arguably in a better position to decide on the strategy it wishes to employ with regards to the technology that it owns.

This phased analysis that is carried out in distinct stages will allow the owner of the technology to assess first its business and the objectives of the said business, second the context within which the business concerned operates and, where the context warrants the licensing of technology, the process the business intends to use in order to proceed with the selection of its licensee(s) in the target market.[184]

The process of analysis will vary depending on the entity involved. Each entity will have its own particular and unique considerations which will in turn shape its review.[185]

181. Fisher & Fisher, Export Best Practice (1998, The Federation Press), 215.
182. Fisher & Fisher, Export Best Practice (1998, The Federation Press), 215.
183. Fisher & Fisher, Export Best Practice (1998, The Federation Press), 215.
184. Fisher & Fisher, Export Best Practice (1998, The Federation Press), 215-216. Whilst Fisher & Fisher use a two-step approach, the authors have modified this test by incorporating a third step (the analysis and assessment of the business and its objectives).
185. Fisher & Fisher, Export Best Practice (1998, The Federation Press), 216.

[1] Step One: Analysis and Assessment of the Business and Its Objectives

Arguably before a business is able to determine the merits of licensing its technology it should first analyse its actual approach on innovation and its long-term strategy on innovation.[186]

Once a business has identified its approach to innovation, in a bid to enhance its level of innovation it should assess its position on innovation through a process of benchmarking, before deciding upon its long-term strategy with regards to innovation.[187]

[a] Approaches to Innovation (Innovation Engines)

Businesses will typically adopt one of three approaches to innovation. These approaches (referred to as innovation engines) - in a 2010 report prepared by the consulting firm Arthur D Little[188] - are the analysis-driven, idea-driven and research-driven innovation engines.

Approximately 400 companies participated in a global survey performed in 2009 by Arthur D Little[189] with the highest level of responses coming from the following sectors: Engineering, machinery and high-tech; telecommunications, IT, software and media; automotives; and pharmaceuticals.[190] The results of this survey and ensuing study are summarised and analysed in a 2010 report prepared by the firm.[191]

This study looked at the upstream activities of the business (the planning and decision-making that the business makes) as well as its downstream activities (the implementation of these choices made by the business).[192]

[i] Analysis-Driven Approach to Innovation[193]

Adopted by the majority of those companies that took part in the survey (42% of the respondents), this top-down approach is rooted in the notion that a thorough analysis of the market, competing businesses and internal competences should come before the making of decisions regarding the selection of products for the marketplace.[194]

186. This three-step approach has been developed based on the information set out in Pathways to Innovation Excellence, Arthur D Little 2010 (with particular reference to pages 8-10).
187. This three-step approach has been developed based on the information set out in Pathways to Innovation Excellence, Arthur D Little 2010 (with particular reference to pages 8-10).
188. Pathways to Innovation Excellence, Arthur D Little 2010, 8.
189. Pathways to Innovation Excellence, Arthur D Little 2010, 3.
190. Pathways to Innovation Excellence, Arthur D Little 2010, 3.
191. Pathways to Innovation Excellence, Arthur D Little 2010, 3.
192. Pathways to Innovation Excellence, Arthur D Little 2010, 3.
193. Pathways to Innovation Excellence, Arthur D Little 2010, 8-10.
194. Pathways to Innovation Excellence, Arthur D Little 2010, 10.

Suited to industry sectors such as automotive, telecommunications equipment and software, this approach typically involves a one to five-year time horizon before the execution phase.[195]

The analysis-driven stance to innovation is prominent in the manufacturing of goods sector with 60 % of respondents using this approach.[196]

[ii] Idea-Driven Approach to Innovation[197]

The idea-driven approach to innovation is centered on the generation of a large number of ideas before the implementation of the best ones.[198] With each idea corresponding with one product or service, this approach usually takes one to five years to implement.[199] This approach is the second most prominent approach to innovation according to the survey conducted by Arthur D Little with 39 % of the respondents using it.[200]

The idea-driven approach is the most popular of the three approaches in the fast-moving consumer goods and retail industry[201] with 68 % of the respondents using this innovation engine.

[iii] Research-Driven Approach to Innovation[202]

In contrast with the analysis-led and the idea-driven innovation engines, the least popular approach to innovation is the research-driven one.[203]

With 19 % of the respondents to the 2009 survey conducted by Arthur D Little endorsing it, this research-intensive stance fosters the generation of ideas.[204] Once generated, the best concepts are selected whilst the remaining ones are discarded.[205]

This approach is suited to sectors of industry that are mainly research-driven such as pharmaceuticals as well as oil and gas exploitation.

With a time horizon of up to ten years, even projects in the downstream developmental stages may be halted before their launch.[206]

195. Pathways to Innovation Excellence, Arthur D Little 2010, 8.
196. Pathways to Innovation Excellence, Arthur D Little 2010, Figure 7 at page 10.
197. Pathways to Innovation Excellence, Arthur D Little 2010, 8-10.
198. Pathways to Innovation Excellence, Arthur D Little 2010, 8.
199. Pathways to Innovation Excellence, Arthur D Little 2010, 8.
200. Pathways to Innovation Excellence, Arthur D Little 2010, 8.
201. Pathways to Innovation Excellence, Arthur D Little 2010, Figure 7 at page 10.
202. Pathways to Innovation Excellence, Arthur D Little 2010, 8-10.
203. Pathways to Innovation Excellence, Arthur D Little 2010, 8.
204. Pathways to Innovation Excellence, Arthur D Little 2010, 8.
205. Pathways to Innovation Excellence, Arthur D Little 2010, 8.
206. Pathways to Innovation Excellence, Arthur D Little 2010, 8, 10.

[iv] Overview

The 2010 study of Arthur D Little found evidence of each one of the three approaches in almost every one of the sectors of industry examined.[207]

The only sector within which only two of the approaches were found was manufacturing of goods with no evidence in the replies of the research-driven approach to innovation.[208]

In the chemical and pharmaceutical sector for example 39 % of companies use the analysis-driven approach, 32 % the idea-driven approach, with 29 % using the research-based approach to innovation.[209]

In the automotive industry, whilst most manufacturers and suppliers use the analysis-driven approach (47 %), the other two approaches are present as well (with 31 % using the idea-driven approach and 22 % the research-driven approach).[210]

[b] Benchmarking

By benchmarking itself a business is arguably in a far better position to determine its long-term strategy to innovation.[211]

In order to enhance innovation, businesses are encouraged to use one of two strategies depending on their level of innovation.[212]

Whilst a low or medium innovator is encouraged to benchmark itself against businesses in the same sector of industry that are leaders in innovation,[213] a business that is a top innovator in a sector of industry is encouraged to look to the most successful businesses that use the same innovation engine irrespective of the industry within which they operate.[214]

[c] Planning an Innovation Strategy

The innovation strategy that a business adopts will be determined to a large extent by the aims, scope and time horizons of the product portfolio of the business concerned, the competitive nature of the environment within which the business operates and the positioning of the business in the value chain.[215]

Once a business has identified its point of departure it should be in a better position to first make use of its resources and skill base, second comprehend the value

207. Pathways to Innovation Excellence, Arthur D Little 2010, 10.
208. Pathways to Innovation Excellence, Arthur D Little 2010, Figure 7 at page 10.
209. Pathways to Innovation Excellence, Arthur D Little 2010, 10.
210. Pathways to Innovation Excellence, Arthur D Little 2010, 10.
211. Pathways to Innovation Excellence, Arthur D Little 2010, 8.
212. Pathways to Innovation Excellence, Arthur D Little 2010, 8.
213. Pathways to Innovation Excellence, Arthur D Little 2010, 8.
214. Pathways to Innovation Excellence, Arthur D Little 2010, 8.
215. Pathways to Innovation Excellence, Arthur D Little 2010, 10.

of its technology base and finally determine what to buy, sell, review, retain and enhance.[216]

[i] Enhancing Innovation Performance

A structured approach may be adopted in order to achieve high innovation performance.

By looking at the upstream and downstream components of the business' innovation system, the Innovation Excellence Model – introduced in 1995 by Arthur D Little (and gradually refined since) – sets out a range of best practices that businesses are able to use in order to improve their innovative performance.[217]

The key factors associated with innovation success are the ability to comprehend the contribution that each technology makes to the goals of the business,[218] the ability to take advantage of business intelligence acquired from diverse external sources (including lead users, suppliers, external experts and crowdsourcing) thus pre-empting potential problems before they emerge,[219] the capacity to react to change[220] and the capacity to mobilise the entire organisation to generate new concepts.[221]

By reacting to changes in targeted sectors through a regular review of the product/service portfolio under development, the business is able to optimise its allocation of resources and to eliminate 'waste'.[222]

By assessing the portfolio throughout its lifecycle (in the product planning and product development modes as well as the maintenance mode), the business is able to strategically manage its product/service portfolio.[223]

By isolating '*where, when* and *against whom* the company chooses to compete'[224] the business is able to formulate a structured approach to its reviews. With this in mind, it is then able to translate the 'decision on *how* to compete ... into a product and services portfolio that needs to be managed over the lifecycle, populated and made responsive to business changes, new innovations, new ideas and revised strategic directions'.[225]

216. Pathways to Innovation Excellence, Arthur D Little 2010, 9.
217. Getting a Better Return on Your Innovation Investment, Arthur D Little 2013, 5.
218. Reviewed in detail at Getting a Better Return on Your Innovation Investment, Arthur D Little 2013, 12.
219. Reviewed in detail at Getting a Better Return on Your Innovation Investment, Arthur D Little 2013, 12-13.
220. Reviewed in detail at Getting a Better Return on Your Innovation Investment, Arthur D Little 2013, 13-14.
221. Getting a Better Return on Your Innovation Investment, Arthur D Little 2013, 12.
222. Reviewed in detail at Getting a Better Return on Your Innovation Investment, Arthur D Little 2013, 13-14.
223. Reviewed in detail at Getting a Better Return on Your Innovation Investment, Arthur D Little 2013, 13.
224. Getting a Better Return on Your Innovation Investment, Arthur D Little 2013, 14 (italics in the original text).
225. Getting a Better Return on Your Innovation Investment, Arthur D Little 2013, 14 (italics in the original text).

The ability to mobilise a workforce to generate new ideas will rely on either a push-logic ('within which idea generation is stimulated for pre-defined opportunity areas supported by a structured enrichment process and reward systems'[226]) or a pull-logic (based on no/little guidance).[227]

By mobilising its workforce in this fashion, the business should be better able to achieve a myriad of objectives.[228]

First, this approach will allocate employees a proactive role in the development of the business itself[229] in turn transforming employees into active and involved stakeholders in the business. Second, as employees are called upon to generate new ideas they will become visible contributors to the development of the business. Third by making all the ideas visible to the workforce, the business it is better able to stimulate an urge for discovery.[230] Finally, by enhancing participation by employees in the running of the business, it can demonstrate its commitment to new ideas.[231]

Certain businesses encourage an inclusive approach by organising regular company-wide creative sessions in which persons or teams with complementary profiles take part in brainstorming sessions.[232] Other companies adopt more innovative strategies which make use of social media platforms, idea jam sessions and idea boot camp sessions.[233]

[2] Second Step: Analysis of Context[234]

Once the owner of the technology has assessed its business and the objectives of its business, it should give due consideration to the context within which the business concerned operates, before assessing the process that the business should use in order to select licensee(s) in the target market.[235]

In order to determine whether licensing is the best strategy for the business, the owner of the technology should arguably give due consideration to a number of contextual factors. These factors, which are specific to the owner of the technology, will encompass:[236]

- import barriers (tariff and non-tariff barriers) – Which import barriers affect the products of the entity? Do these import barriers render the products of the entity uncompetitive on the target market?

226. Getting a Better Return on Your Innovation Investment, Arthur D Little 2013, 15.
227. Getting a Better Return on Your Innovation Investment, Arthur D Little 2013, 15.
228. Getting a Better Return on Your Innovation Investment, Arthur D Little 2013, 15.
229. Getting a Better Return on Your Innovation Investment, Arthur D Little 2013, 15.
230. Getting a Better Return on Your Innovation Investment, Arthur D Little 2013, 15.
231. Getting a Better Return on Your Innovation Investment, Arthur D Little 2013, 15.
232. Getting a Better Return on Your Innovation Investment, Arthur D Little 2013, 15.
233. Getting a Better Return on Your Innovation Investment, Arthur D Little 2013, 15-16.
234. Fisher & Fisher, Export Best Practice (The Federation Press 1998), 215.
235. Fisher & Fisher, Export Best Practice (1998, The Federation Press), 215-216. Whilst Fisher & Fisher use a two-step approach, the author of this chapter has revised this test to incorporate a third step (the analysis and assessment of the business and its objectives).
236. The criteria are based on those found in Fisher & Fisher, Export Best Practice (The Federation Press 1998), 215.

- transport costs, time and risk – Do transport costs and time render the products of the entity too expensive on the target market?
- production costs – Are the costs of production comparatively high when compared with the production costs of the entity's actual and potential competitors globally and in the target market?
- profitability of the business – Will the entity be able to create a business in the target market that is profitable? Does it possess the needed competences to emerge as a successful player in the target market? Will licensing generate more revenue than export?

[3] Third Step: Identification and Assessment of Potential Licensee[237]

Once the owner of the technology has assessed the business and its objectives, the context within which the business concerned operates and the suitability of licensing to the technology developed, due consideration should be given by it to the process that the business intends to utilise in order to proceed with the selection of its licensee(s) in the target market.[238]

From the point of view of the licensor it is worthwhile taking all the necessary steps it is practicable able to take in order to safeguard its competitive advantage which is typically though not exclusively its intellectual property rights.[239]

Since licensing may mean that the licensor may not be able to change its licensees with relative ease,[240] once the prospective licensor has assessed the market potential of its technology, it should put together a list of criteria for the selection of potential licensees. Using this list, the prospective licensor should isolate, categorise and then assemble a list of prospective licensees from which its final selection will be made.[241]

Owners of technology will occasionally settle for a suboptimal return. This may occur for a number of reasons. Perspective licensors will often rely on potential licensees to assess the market potential and the market value of its technology.[242] Oftentimes a licensor will not endeavour to select the licensee for its technology but will instead enter into a licensing agreement with a licensee that proactively approached it and made an offer that appears to cut the entry costs of the licensor whilst earning it a return on its technology as rapidly as possible.[243]

In order to carry out an identification and assessment of potential licensees, the prospective licensor should assemble a list of selection criteria before assessing the

237. Fisher & Fisher, Export Best Practice (The Federation Press 1998), 215.
238. Fisher & Fisher, Export Best Practice (1998, The Federation Press), 215-216. Whilst Fisher & Fisher use a two-step approach, the author of this chapter has revised this test to incorporate a third step (the analysis and assessment of the business and its objectives).
239. Fisher & Fisher, Export Best Practice (The Federation Press 1998), 216.
240. Fisher & Fisher, Export Best Practice (The Federation Press 1998), 216.
241. Fisher & Fisher, Export Best Practice (The Federation Press 1998), 216.
242. Fisher & Fisher, Export Best Practice (The Federation Press 1998), 216.
243. Fisher & Fisher, Export Best Practice (The Federation Press 1998), 216.

distinct qualifications and aptitude of the potential licensees.[244] In all situations, it is worthwhile addressing the following matters:[245]

- identity of the prospective licensee - Have the business name and address of the prospective licensee been verified?
- confidentiality agreement - Has a confidentiality agreement been entered into with the prospective licensee?
- regulation in the target market - Is there regulation in place in the target market affecting the ability to enter into the agreement (product liability legislation and competition law) and the substantive terms of the agreement?
- protection in the target market - Does the law in the target market protect the technology? If so, how effective is the intellectual property right protection available and what enforcement procedures are available to restrain infringements?
- improvements and new products - What procedural steps should be undertaken in order to notify the other party in relation to improvements and new products? What rights does the prospective licensor enjoy in relation to improvement and new products during the term of the agreement? What rights will it enjoy after the agreement comes to an end?
- territorial scope and exclusivity - Which territory is assigned? Will the prospective licensee be exclusive, sole or non-exclusive? Will the prospective licensee have the right to sub-licence?
- duration - What is the term of the proposed licensing agreement?
- due diligence - Does the prospective licensee possess the necessary expertise and resources to effectively exploit the licensed technology in the target market(s)? In this context, due consideration should be given to:
  - the manufacturing, distribution and marketing capability of the prospective licensee (in order to assess the manufacturing capability of the prospective licensee, consideration should be given to the possibility of visiting the manufacturing plants and operations of the potential licensee);
  - the prospective licensee's access to financing;
  - its past experience (has it been a licensee for similar technology in the past? If so, for whom and for how long?) and the profitability of these past relationships (were these past contractual relationships profitable for the licensor?);
  - its know-how, patents and technologies;
  - the calibre and knowledge base of its personnel and the potential licensee's ability to develop the licensed technology;
  - the financial position of the prospective licensee? In order to assess the financial position of the entity a review of financial records and references

244. The criteria are based on those found in Fisher & Fisher, Export Best Practice (The Federation Press 1998), 216.
245. The criteria are based on those found in Fisher & Fisher, Export Best Practice (The Federation Press 1998), 216.

from creditors may be necessary. If there are concerns about the financial status of the prospective licensee, consideration should be given to whether or not it will be necessary to ask the prospective licensee to post a performance bond with monies in an escrow account;
- the need for governmental approvals before the production of the appointed products.

[a] Confidentiality Agreements

Oftentimes before the start of negotiations, consideration is given to the conclusion of confidentiality agreements.[246]

Such agreements impose legally binding obligations pertaining to the usage that may be made of confidential information made known during the negotiation phase or the disclosure of such information to others.[247] Such information may be technological information (such as prototypes, designs, specifications and formulae) or business information (such as operational data, strategic information, price lists and customer lists).[248]

By using such an agreement, the licensee is able to examine the technology that they are considering licensing off the owner of the technology and in turn to consider the worth and functionality of the same.[249]

Care should be taken where standstill agreements are being proposed during the pre-contractual phase as these agreements limit the ability of the party to consider competitive alternatives during the negotiation phase.[250] As such the party's negotiation leverage and flexibility are limited which is especially important when negotiations are long-term in nature.[251]

The material issues that should be borne in mind by the parties in the context of confidentiality agreements are first whether the recipient of the confidential information will be estopped from using the same, second whether they will be forbidden from disclosing the confidential information to others, and third the jurisdiction and the law that will be used if a dispute arises between the parties.[252]

§6.08 PRE-CONTRACTUAL CONSIDERATIONS FOR THE LICENSEE[253]

Certain issues should be borne in mind by the prospective licensee before committing to a licensing agreement.

246. Successful Technology Licensing (WIPO 2004), 19.
247. Successful Technology Licensing (WIPO 2004), 19.
248. Successful Technology Licensing (WIPO 2004), 19.
249. Successful Technology Licensing (WIPO 2004), 19.
250. Successful Technology Licensing (WIPO 2004), 19.
251. Successful Technology Licensing (WIPO 2004), 19.
252. Successful Technology Licensing (WIPO 2004), 19.
253. Fisher & Fisher, Export Best Practice (1998, The Federation Press), 218.

From the perspective of the potential licensee it should consider the following matters before deciding whether to enter into a licensing agreement in relation to the pertinent technology:[254]

- the costs of developing the technology versus the time to market;
- the price per unit versus the sale potential;
- the size of the market versus the minimum market share; and
- the profit margin versus the implementation costs.

§6.09 EUROPEAN UNION REGULATION OF TECHNOLOGY TRANSFER AGREEMENTS

Technology is viewed by the Commission as 'an input, which is integrated either into a product or a production process'.[255] As such, the licensing of a technology right is capable of impacting upon upstream competition (in input markets) and downstream competition (in output markets).[256]

Competition in innovation is capable of being impacted upon by technology licensing agreements as such agreements may adversely impact upon the development and indeed the issuing of enhanced products or novel products that will eventually substitute existing products.[257] Due to this potential impact that innovation has on competition, it is borne in mind when determining the impact of the technology licensing agreements on the product markets and the technology markets.[258]

A review of European Union regulation of technology transfer agreements follows. The first part of this section reviews block exemptions generally in the context of Article 101 of the Treaty on the Functioning of the European Union (TFEU).[259] The latter part of this section looks in more detail at the block exemptions available in the context of technology transfer agreements.

As this book focuses on licensing agreements, Article 102 TFEU will only be mentioned briefly.[260] Article 102 TFEU compliments Article 101 TFEU.[261] Whilst

254. Fisher & Fisher, Export Best Practice (1998, The Federation Press), 218, citing information from the webpage of Arthur D Little (http://www.adlenterprises.com/select2.html).
255. Communication from the Commission – Guidelines on the application of Article 101 of the Treaty on the Functioning of the European Union to technology transfer agreements. (2014/C 89/03), C89/9, para. 20.
256. Communication from the Commission – Guidelines on the application of Article 101 of the Treaty on the Functioning of the European Union to technology transfer agreements. (2014/C 89/03), C89/9, para. 20.
257. Communication from the Commission – Guidelines on the application of Article 101 of the Treaty on the Functioning of the European Union to technology transfer agreements. (2014/C 89/03), C89/9, para. 26.
258. Communication from the Commission – Guidelines on the application of Article 101 of the Treaty on the Functioning of the European Union to technology transfer agreements. (2014/C 89/03), C89/9, para. 26.
259. A more detailed review of competition law and Article 101 TFEU can be found in Chapter two on competition law.
260. For further reading on Article 102 readers are referred to Richard Whish and David Bailey, Competition Law (Oxford University Press, 2012), ch 5.
261. Whish et al 2012: 173.

Article 101 TFEU targets agreements, decisions and concerted practices that are anti-competitive, Article 102 TFEU[262] (formerly Article 82 TEC) targets abuse of dominance on the internal market. This Article prohibits, not dominance per se, but rather the abuse of dominance.

Behaviour will fall foul of Article 102 TFEU if three components are present. First, the presence of dominance 'within the internal market or in a substantial part of it'.[263] Second, the existence of an abuse of such dominance.[264] Third, the abuse of the dominant position must impact upon trade between Member States.[265]

Article 102 TFEU will only apply if one undertaking has a 'dominant position' or if two or more undertakings are 'collectively dominant'.[266]

Examples of conduct that may infringe Article 102 TFEU include[267] the imposition of 'unfair purchase or selling prices or other unfair trading conditions',[268] the placement of limitations on 'production, markets or technical development to the prejudice of consumers',[269] the application of 'dissimilar conditions to equivalent transactions with other trading parties,[270] thereby placing them at a competitive disadvantage' and the imposition of supplementary obligations as a prerequisite for contracting where such obligations 'by their nature or according to commercial usage, have no connection with the subject of such contracts'.[271]

[A] Block Exemptions Generally

Anticompetitive agreements and practices are prohibited pursuant to the law of the European Union and more specifically in accordance with Article 101 TFEU.

The responsibility for assessing whether an agreement concluded or a practice undertaken is anticompetitive is borne by the entities themselves. To assist with this analysis and assessment, the Commission describes certain categories of agreements that are unproblematic from a competition standpoint.[272] This approach adopted by the Commission, which intends to 'meet the two requirements of ensuring effective protection of competition and providing adequate legal security for undertakings' takes into account 'the need to simplify administrative supervision and the legislative framework to as great an extent as possible'.[273]

262. Article 102 TFEU reads 'Any abuse by one or more undertakings of a dominant position within the internal market or in a substantial part of it shall be prohibited as incompatible with the internal market in so far as it may affect trade between Member States.'
263. Article 102 TFEU.
264. Article 102 TFEU.
265. Article 102 TFEU.
266. Whish et al 2012: 179. Further reading on the issue of dominance can be found in Whish et al 2012: ch 14.
267. Examples of conduct that may infringe Article 102 TFEU are listed in the provision itself.
268. Article 102 TFEU.
269. Article 102 TFEU.
270. Article 102 TFEU.
271. Article 102 TFEU.
272. European Commission Memo entitled 'Antitrust: Commission consults on proposal for revised competition regime for technology transfer agreements – frequently asked questions Memo/13/120 (Brussels, 20 February 2013), 1.
273. TTBER 2014, recital para. 3.

In circumstances where the agreement concerned respects all the criteria set out by the Commission, then the agreement in question is exempted from the prohibition contained in Article 101 TFEU.[274]

[B] Block Exemptions in the Context of Technology Transfer Agreements

In the context of technology transfer agreements, the Commission is empowered by the Enabling Regulation (in this context, pursuant to Regulation No 19/65/EEC) to apply Article 101(3) TFEU to specific types of technology transfer agreements and corresponding concerted practices to which two undertakings are party that fall foul of the prohibition in Article 101(1) TFEU.[275] The Enabling Regulation defines the types of technology transfer agreements, which the Commission regard 'as normally satisfying the conditions' found in Article 101(3) TFEU.[276]

This the Commission has done by means of regulations. The latest such regulation was adopted in 2014 (the 2014 Technology Transfer Block Exemption Regulation). This regulation replaced the former block exemption from 2004 (the 2004 Technology Transfer Block Exemption Regulation).

The review that follows compares the block exemption from 2004 (the 2004 Technology Transfer Block Exemption Regulation) with its predecessor (the 1996 Technology Transfer Agreements Regulation) and with its successor (the 2014 Technology Transfer Block Exemption Regulation).

[1] TTBER 2004: The New Wave[277]

[a] Background to the TTBER 2004

In 2004, the Commission adopted a revised block exemption[278] replacing the 1996 Technology Transfer Agreements Regulation, which ceased to apply from 31 March 2006.[279]

274. European Commission Memo entitled 'Antitrust: Commission consults on proposal for revised competition regime for technology transfer agreements – frequently asked questions Memo/13/120 (Brussels, 20 February 2013), 1.
275. TTBER 2014, recital para. 1.
276. TTBER 2014, recital para. 2.
277. Commission Regulation (EC) No 772/2004 of 27 April 2004 on the application of Article 81(3) of the Treaty to categories of technology transfer agreements (OJ L 123/11 dated 27 April 2004) (TTBER 2004). Commission Regulation (EU) No 316/2014 of 21 March 2014 on the application of Article 101(3) of the Treaty on the Functioning of the European Union to categories of technology transfer agreements (OJ L93/17 dated 28 March 2014) (TTBER 2014).
278. Commission Regulation (EC) No 772/2004 of 7 April 2004 on the application of Article 81(3) of the Treaty to categories of technology transfer agreements (OJ L 123, 27.4.2004, p. 11) (TTBER 2004).
279. Commission Regulation (EC) No 240/96 of 31 January 1996 on the application of Article 85 (3) of the Treaty to certain categories of technology transfer agreements (OJ L031 dated 9 February 1996, 2.

The 1996 Technology Transfer Agreements Regulation was criticised for being complicated and far too limited in its breadth of application.[280] Moreover, it was lambasted for not encompassing licensing agreements that did not pose a risk to competition and for failing to make use of the updated model employed in the context of the reforms made to horizontal and vertical agreements.[281] It was also argued that the 1996 Technology Transfer Agreements Regulation imposed unnecessary burdens on businesses forcing industry into 'a legal straight-jacket' whilst skewing 'enforcement toward over deterrence'.[282]

The process of reviewing the 1996 Technology Transfer Agreements Regulation process started in December 2001.[283] Based on a fact-finding performed by the Commission it concluded that industry favoured a review arguing for a simplification and clarification of the 1996 Technology Transfer Agreements Regulation.[284] Its review of the Regulation highlighted the following findings.[285] First that the criteria used in the 1996 Technology Transfer Agreements Regulation were focused on the *form of the agreement* rather than its *actual impact upon the market*.[286] Second that this instrument was 'too prescriptive and seems to work as a straitjacket, which may discourage efficient transactions and hamper dissemination of new technologies'.[287] Third that the Regulation's scope of application was too narrow (the Regulation covered certain patent and know-how licensing agreements) thereby rendering it 'increasingly inadequate to deal with the complexity of modern licensing arrangements (e.g., pooling arrangements, software licenses involving copyright)'.[288] Fourth that certain restraints were deemed illegal or excluded from the 1996 Technology Transfer Agreements Regulation without a proper economic justification, in spite of the potential of certain restraints to enhance efficiency, accordingly the Commission stated that the restraints should be judged by reference to the nature of the competitive relationship existing between the parties, the market structure and the market power of the contracting parties.[289]

280. Anderson 2010: 664, citing Evaluation Report on the Transfer Technology Block Exemption Regulation 240/96.
281. Anderson 2010: 664, citing Evaluation Report on the Transfer Technology Block Exemption Regulation 240/96.
282. Anderson 2010: 664, citing Evaluation Report on the Transfer Technology Block Exemption Regulation 240/96, para. 175.
283. Speech by Mario Monti, the European Commissioner for Competition Policy delivered in Paris 16 January 2004 (available at http://europa.eu/rapid/press-release_SPEECH-04-19_en.htm?locale=en last accessed 11 April 2014), 2.
284. Commission Press Release entitled 'Competition Policy: Commission opens debate on block exemption for licensing agreements' (IP/02/14) dated 7 Jan 2002, 1.
285. Commission Press Release entitled 'Competition Policy: Commission opens debate on block exemption for licensing agreements' (IP/02/14) dated 7 Jan 2002, 1.
286. Commission Press Release entitled 'Competition Policy: Commission opens debate on block exemption for licensing agreements' (IP/02/14) dated 7 Jan 2002, 1.
287. Commission Press Release entitled 'Competition Policy: Commission opens debate on block exemption for licensing agreements' (IP/02/14) dated 7 Jan 2002, 1.
288. Commission Press Release entitled 'Competition Policy: Commission opens debate on block exemption for licensing agreements' (IP/02/14) dated 7 Jan 2002, 1.
289. Commission Press Release entitled 'Competition Policy: Commission opens debate on block exemption for licensing agreements' (IP/02/14) dated 7 Jan 2002, 1.

Bearing in mind its findings from the review, the Commission invited comments on a wide array of issues including:

- whether the scope of the block exemption should be widened to encompass further forms of intellectual property (copyright, design rights and trademarks), which are essential to certain industries such as software engineering (which rely on chains of copyright licenses for manufacture and distribution);[290]
- whether the new block exemption should embrace multilateral licensing agreements (such as licensing pools) due to their commercial importance bearing in mind the growing complexity of new technologies and their ability to enhance efficiency (notably in situations where the pooling of patents is essential to the exploitation of new technologies);[291]
- whether a more flexible approach should be adopted vis-à-vis licensing agreements between non-competing entities (i.e., vertical agreements) bearing in mind the efficiency enhancing nature and pro-competitive character of exclusive licenses concluded between such parties. For example where the proprietor of the intellectual property has not got the means needed to manufacture and distribute the licensed products, it may be more efficient for it to grant a licence to a party in possession of the requisite capital. Such a licence may be granted on an exclusive basis in order to prevent the licensee from free-riding and to motivate both parties to invest in further R&D;[292] and
- whether a more prudent approach should be embraced where agreements between competing parties (horizontal agreements) are concerned. A licence between competing parties is capable of resulting in competition concerns where the licence has the effect of restricting or indeed blocking potential competition between the parties, due for, e.g., to the inclusion of territorial and customer restrictions and production quotas.[293]

This review aimed to modify the 1996 Technology Transfer Agreements Regulation so that it was more consistent with, what Mario Monti the European Commissioner for Competition Policy at the time called, 'the new generation of Commission block exemption regulations'.[294] Moreover it was motivated by 'the changing forms and importance of licensing', the over formalistic and legalistic character of the 1996 Technology Transfer Agreements Regulation and the fact that the 1996 Technology

290. Commission Press Release entitled 'Competition Policy: Commission opens debate on block exemption for licensing agreements' (IP/02/14) dated 7 Jan 2002, 1-2.
291. Commission Press Release entitled 'Competition Policy: Commission opens debate on block exemption for licensing agreements' (IP/02/14) dated 7 Jan 2002, 2.
292. Commission Press Release entitled 'Competition Policy: Commission opens debate on block exemption for licensing agreements' (IP/02/14) dated 7 Jan 2002, 2.
293. Commission Press Release entitled 'Competition Policy: Commission opens debate on block exemption for licensing agreements' (IP/02/14) dated 7 Jan 2002, 2.
294. Speech by Mario Monti, the European Commissioner for Competition Policy delivered in Paris 16 January 2004 (available at http://europa.eu/rapid/press-release_SPEECH-04-19_en.htm?locale=en last accessed 11 April 2014), 3.

Transfer Agreements Regulation did not adhere to the 'more economic approach adopted under the rules on distribution and horizontal co-operation agreements'.[295]

In 2002, the Commission consulted with stakeholders before working out the details of the draft block exemption and guidelines.[296] This consultation launched in 2002 by the Commission to explore and evaluate the operation of the 1996 Regulation was rooted in the centrality of innovation in economic development, the importance of competition in the evolution of innovation and the need 'to find the right balance between protecting competition and protecting intellectual property rights'.[297]

The overarching rationale of this evaluation was grounded in the fact that 'the economic development of the Community and its ability to draw abreast of its competitors in the rest of the world depends on the capacity of industry to devise new technologies and to disseminate them at a large scale'.[298]

In September 2003, these draft texts were discussed with the various Member States (the Member States endorsed the approach adopted by the Commission) and the proposals were published in October 2003 for public consultation.[299] Over 70 responses were received. These came from a variety of sources including industry, trade associations, law societies, law firms, national authorities, companies and universities.[300]

The approach of the Commission when it started work on the TTBER 2004 was regarded by industry as being well-grounded and cogent.[301] By this time, the Commission possessed a far more extensive working knowledge of technology licenses along with an understanding that in most cases such agreements do not pose major competition concerns, on the proviso that they do not contain hardcore provisions.[302] On the basis of these experiences, the Commission decided in the TTBER 2004 to change its stance on block exemptions.

Rather than listing clauses that were acceptable and unacceptable (as it did in the 1996 Technology Transfer Agreements Regulation), the Commission employed – in the TTBER 2004 – a framework structure 'within which technology transfer agreements are viewed as acceptable from a competition standpoint'.[303]

295. Speech by Mario Monti, the European Commissioner for Competition Policy delivered in Paris 16 January 2004 (available at http://europa.eu/rapid/press-release_SPEECH-04-19_en.htm?locale=en last accessed 11 April 2014), 2.
296. Speech by Mario Monti, the European Commissioner for Competition Policy delivered in Paris 16 January 2004 (available at http://europa.eu/rapid/press-release_SPEECH-04-19_en.htm?locale=en last accessed 11 April 2014), 3.
297. Commission Press Release entitled 'Competition Policy: Commission opens debate on block exemption for licensing agreements' (IP/02/14) dated 7 Jan 2002, 1.
298. Commission Press Release entitled 'Competition Policy: Commission opens debate on block exemption for licensing agreements' (IP/02/14) dated 7 Jan 2002, 1.
299. Speech by Mario Monti, the European Commissioner for Competition Policy delivered in Paris 16 January 2004 (available at http://europa.eu/rapid/press-release_SPEECH-04-19_en.htm?locale=en last accessed 11 April 2014), 3.
300. Speech by Mario Monti, the European Commissioner for Competition Policy delivered in Paris 16 January 2004 (available at http://europa.eu/rapid/press-release_SPEECH-04-19_en.htm?locale=en last accessed 11 April 2014), 3.
301. Anderson 2010: 662.
302. Anderson 2010: 662.
303. Anderson 2010: 662.

Far less appealing from the perspective of industry was the attitude of the Commission to certain types of technology transfer agreements perceived as being more worrisome from a competition point of view, namely agreements involving competing undertakings and those involving undertakings with substantial market shares.[304]

[2] The Differences Between the TTBER 2004 and Its Predecessor the 1996 Technology Transfer Agreements Regulation

The TTBER 2004 differed from its predecessor the 1996 Technology Transfer Agreements Regulation in a number of key respects:[305]

First, under the TTBER 2004 the scope of the regulation was broadened to encompass a far more diverse range of agreements. Not only patent and know-how licenses qualified for the exemption but also software computer licenses and design rights licenses.[306]

The responses to the draft TTBER 2004 did not, according to Mario Monti, display a 'consensus on further broadening the scope to also include copyrights in general and trademarks'.[307] In this context, Mario Monti added that 'the licensing of copyrights in general can not be covered by regulation because of limits of the enabling Council Regulation 19/65, which only allows the Commission to block exempt the licensing of industrial property rights'.[308] Accordingly, the TTBER 2004 did not encompass database licensing as the materials contained on such databases are oftentimes addressed by copyright.[309] The licensing of trademarks was not addressed in the TTBER 2004 either as 'it is not related to technology transfer of an innovation but the use of a symbol that helps to differentiate and identify products. The licencing of these other types of intellectual property rights will therefore only be covered when ancillary to the technology transfer'.[310]

Second, under the TTBER 2004 the exemption only applied when a market share threshold was not surpassed. The threshold differed depending on whether the undertakings were competitors or not.

304. Anderson 2010: 662.
305. Anderson 2010: 663.
306. Speech by Mario Monti, the European Commissioner for Competition Policy delivered in Paris 16 January 2004 (available at http://europa.eu/rapid/press-release_SPEECH-04-19_en.htm?locale=en last accessed 11 April 2014), 3.
307. Speech by Mario Monti, the European Commissioner for Competition Policy delivered in Paris 16 January 2004 (available at http://europa.eu/rapid/press-release_SPEECH-04-19_en.htm?locale=en last accessed 11 April 2014), 3.
308. Speech by Mario Monti, the European Commissioner for Competition Policy delivered in Paris 16 January 2004 (available at http://europa.eu/rapid/press-release_SPEECH-04-19_en.htm?locale=en last accessed 11 April 2014), 3.
309. Speech by Mario Monti, the European Commissioner for Competition Policy delivered in Paris 16 January 2004 (available at http://europa.eu/rapid/press-release_SPEECH-04-19_en.htm?locale=en last accessed 11 April 2014), 3.
310. Speech by Mario Monti, the European Commissioner for Competition Policy delivered in Paris 16 January 2004 (available at http://europa.eu/rapid/press-release_SPEECH-04-19_en.htm?locale=en last accessed 11 April 2014), 4.

The proposed use of market share thresholds in the draft TTBER 2004 was the main point of criticism in the responses received by the Commission.[311] Three types of categories of responses were received in this regard.[312] The first category of responses objected to the use of such thresholds all together.[313] The second category of responses endorsed the use of such thresholds but argued that these thresholds should be increased.[314] The third category of responses called for a longer transitional period under the TTBER 2004 (specifically Article 8, TTBER 2004).[315]

The use of thresholds was objected to largely because it is argued that 'market shares are of no relevance in high tech sectors, that the assessment of market shares throughout the life of the agreement decreases legal certainty and is costly and furthermore that relevant product and geographic markets are often difficult to define'.[316]

Notwithstanding these different forms of criticism, market share thresholds are used in the TTBER 2004.

Mario Monti replied to this reprobation by stating that the TTBER 'applies to all sectors not just high tech ones. It is fair to state that most sectors are mature and that even sectors that are in such a state of flux are so usually only for a limited period. Therefore in most sectors, and that also means in most sectors where licencing takes place, market shares do matter. In addition, usually licencing concerns products that either will continue to compete with existing products or that will replace existing products. There are not many products which cater to a human need for which nothing existed before. Therefore market definition in case of licencing will not be markedly more difficult than market definition for most other agreements ... . Market share thresholds do not divide good agreements from bad agreements. They only create a safe harbour for those types of restrictions and situations where the Commission can safely assume that either Article 81(1) does not apply or that the conditions of

311. Speech by Mario Monti, the European Commissioner for Competition Policy delivered in Paris 16 January 2004 (available at http://europa.eu/rapid/press-release_SPEECH-04-19_en.htm?locale=en last accessed 11 April 2014), 6.
312. Speech by Mario Monti, the European Commissioner for Competition Policy delivered in Paris 16 January 2004 (available at http://europa.eu/rapid/press-release_SPEECH-04-19_en.htm?locale=en last accessed 11 April 2014), 6.
313. Speech by Mario Monti, the European Commissioner for Competition Policy delivered in Paris 16 January 2004 (available at http://europa.eu/rapid/press-release_SPEECH-04-19_en.htm?locale=en last accessed 11 April 2014), 6.
314. Speech by Mario Monti, the European Commissioner for Competition Policy delivered in Paris 16 January 2004 (available at http://europa.eu/rapid/press-release_SPEECH-04-19_en.htm?locale=en last accessed 11 April 2014), 6.
315. Speech by Mario Monti, the European Commissioner for Competition Policy delivered in Paris 16 January 2004 (available at http://europa.eu/rapid/press-release_SPEECH-04-19_en.htm?locale=en last accessed 11 April 2014), 6.
316. Speech by Mario Monti, the European Commissioner for Competition Policy delivered in Paris 16 January 2004 (available at http://europa.eu/rapid/press-release_SPEECH-04-19_en.htm?locale=en last accessed 11 April 2014), 6.

Article 81(3) are fulfilled. Above the market share thresholds there is no presumption of illegality'.[317]

Third, under the TTBER 2004 the treatment of competing undertakings differed from the treatment of non-competing undertakings. The rationale for this distinction was the notion that potential competition concerns are distinct based on the nature of the competitive relationship that exists between the contracting parties.[318]

The existence of a competitive relationship may arise before the contract is concluded or after it is made.[319] The latter may occur when the licensee develops technology of its own and licenses this technology or uses it to produce.[320] To ensure legal certainty, in circumstances where the undertakings become competitors after the agreement is concluded the hardcore list that will be applicable throughout the duration of the agreement will be the list applicable to non-competitors.

Finally, under the TTBER 2004 a list of hardcore provisions was used that had the effect of taking the agreement outside the scope of the exemption furnished by the TTBER 2004.

Competition risks are generally regarded as being higher where there is licensing between competing undertakings and where there is reciprocal licensing rather than non-reciprocal licensing. The hardcore provisions, argued Mario Monti, should reflect this.[321]

[3] TTBER 2014: The Second Wave

Bearing in mind 'the overall positive experience with the application of (the TTBER 2004)[322] ... and taking into account further experience acquired since its adoption', in 2014 the Commission adopted a revised and updated Technology Transfer Block Exemption Regulation.[323]

317. Speech by Mario Monti, the European Commissioner for Competition Policy delivered in Paris 16 January 2004 (available at http://europa.eu/rapid/press-release_SPEECH-04-19_en.htm?locale=en last accessed 11 April 2014), 6-7.
318. Speech by Mario Monti, the European Commissioner for Competition Policy delivered in Paris 16 January 2004 (available at http://europa.eu/rapid/press-release_SPEECH-04-19_en.htm?locale=en last accessed 11 April 2014), 4.
319. Speech by Mario Monti, the European Commissioner for Competition Policy delivered in Paris 16 January 2004 (available at http://europa.eu/rapid/press-release_SPEECH-04-19_en.htm?locale=en last accessed 11 April 2014), 4.
320. Speech by Mario Monti, the European Commissioner for Competition Policy delivered in Paris 16 January 2004 (available at http://europa.eu/rapid/press-release_SPEECH-04-19_en.htm?locale=en last accessed 11 April 2014), 4.
321. Speech by Mario Monti, the European Commissioner for Competition Policy delivered in Paris 16 January 2004 (available at http://europa.eu/rapid/press-release_SPEECH-04-19_en.htm?locale=en last accessed 11 April 2014), 4.
322. Wording in brackets added by authors.
323. TTBER 2014, recital para. 2.

The TTBER 2014 was issued following a consultation that was commenced on 6 December 2011.[324] This public consultation initiated by the Commission concerned the technology transfer regime in place since 2004.

This consultation, which came to an end on 3 February 2012, resulted in the redrafting of both the TTBER 2004 and the Guidance Accompanying the TTBER 2004.[325]

The revised TTBER (TTBER 2014) and the Guidance Accompanying this TTBER were issued on 28 March 2014 in time for the expiration of the former TTBER (the TTBER 2004 expired on 30 April 2014).

§6.10 TECHNOLOGY TRANSFER BLOCK EXEMPTION REGULATION (TTBER 2014)

Presently the specific rules governing technology transfer agreements are set out in two instruments, the Technology Transfer Block Exemption Regulation (TTBER) and the guidance accompanying the TTBER.[326]

[A] The Aims of the TTBER

Technology transfer agreements entailing the licensing of rights in technology are viewed as pro-competitive agreements under EU law as they typically improve economic efficiency.

A number of reasons are given in support of providing a block exemption to technology transfer agreements.[327]

First, these agreements bring about a reduction in the replication of research and development.[328] Second, such agreements enhance the stimulus for the initial research and development.[329] Third, these agreements 'spur incremental innovation'.[330] Fourth, these agreements promote diffusion of knowledge.[331] Finally, these agreements result in product market competition.[332]

324. The chronology of events is described in the European Commission Memo entitled 'Antitrust: Commission consults on proposal for revised competition regime for technology transfer agreements – frequently asked questions Memo/13/120 (Brussels, 20 February 2013), 2.
325. This consultation resulted in 38 replies.
326. Communication from the Commission – Guidelines on the application of Article 101 of the Treaty on the Functioning of the European Union to technology transfer agreements. (2014/C 89/03).
327. TTBER 2014, recital para. 4.
328. TTBER 2014, recital para. 4.
329. TTBER 2014, recital para. 4.
330. TTBER 2014, recital para. 4.
331. TTBER 2014, recital para. 4.
332. TTBER 2014, recital para. 4.

[B] The Format of the TTBER 2014

The TTBER 2014 contains 19 recitals and 11 articles which contrasts with the previous regulations governing technology transfer agreements. The 1996 Technology Transfer Agreements Regulation contained 27 recitals and 13 articles and the TTBER 2004 consisted of 20 recitals and 11 articles.

The Recitals and Articles in the TTBER 2014 are summarised below.

[1] The Recitals

Recital 1

The Commission's power to apply Article 101(3) TFEU by regulation to various categories of TT agreements and corresponding concerted practices.

Recital 2

The legislative basis on which TTBER 2004 and TTBER 2014 were adopted and the reasons for the adoption of TTBER 2014.

Recitals 3 and 4

The aims of TTBER 2014 and the importance of technology transfer agreements.

Recital 5

The centrality of the market power of the contracting undertakings.

Recital 6

The application of TTBER 2014 to agreements involving licensee and licensor even if the agreement contains conditions that govern more than one level of trade.

Recital 7

The application of TTBER 2014 to the exploitation of licensed technology rights for the purpose of producing goods or services.

The non-applicability of TTBER 2014 to licencing in the context of R&D agreements (Regulation 1217/201), licencing in the context of specialisation agreements (Regulation 1218/2010), agreements governing the reproduction and distribution of software copyright protected products and agreements involving the establishment of technology pools.

Recitals 8 and 9

The manner in which technology transfer agreements are to be dealt with.

Recitals 10–13

The impact of market share thresholds.

Recitals 14 and 15

The impact of hardcore restrictions (Recital 14) and excluded restrictions (Recital 15).

Recital 16

The rationale behind market share thresholds, the non-exemption of technology transfer agreements containing hardcore restrictions and the treatment of excluded restrictions.

Recitals 17 and 18

Revocation of the benefit of the Regulation by the Commission and national competition authorities (Recital 17 & 18 respectively).

Recital 19

The power of the Commission to exclude from the scope of the Regulation, by regulation, technology transfer incorporating restrictive measures affecting the market concerned, in a bid to improve the monitoring of parallel networks of technology transfer agreements which have similar restrictive effects and which cover more than half of a given market.

[2] The Articles

Article 1

This Article sets out the definitions of key terms and expressions used through the TTBER 2014 ('agreement', 'technology rights', 'technology transfer agreement', 'reciprocal agreement', 'non-reciprocal agreement', 'product', 'contract product', 'intellectual property rights', 'know-how', 'relevant product market', 'relevant technology market', 'relevant geographic market', 'relevant market', 'competing undertakings', 'selective distribution system', 'exclusive licence', 'exclusive territory', 'exclusive customer group' and 'connected undertaking').

Article 2

This Article sets out the core exemption. Noting that in line with Article 101(3) TFEU and subject to the provisions of TTBER 2014, Article 101(1) TFEU will not apply to technology transfer agreements. (Article 2(1))

This Article defines the parameters of this exemption. (Article 2(2) and Article 2(3)) Stating that the exemption set out in Article 2(1) will be applicable to technology transfer agreements with anti-competitive restrictions that fall within the scope of Article 101(1) TFEU. (Article 2(2)) Adding that the exemption will be applicable until such a time as the licenced technology rights have expired, lapsed or been declared invalid or in the case of know-how for as long as the same remains secret. (Article 2(2))

Asserting that the exemption set out in Article 2(1) will apply to provisions addressing the purchase of products by the licensee or addressing the licencing or assignment of other intellectual property right or know-how to the licensee so long as these provisions are 'directly related to the production or sale of the contract products'. (Article 2(3))

Article 3

This Article sets out the market share thresholds that the undertakings that are party to the agreement must not surpass. A distinction is drawn here between competing undertakings (Article 3(1)) and non-competing undertakings (Article 3(2)). In effect between horizontal agreements and vertical agreements (respectively).[333]

Article 4

This Article sets out the hardcore restrictions that will have the effect of excluding the exemption in Article 2 from applying to the agreement(s) within which they are contained.

A distinction is drawn in this Article between hardcore restrictions applicable to agreements made between competing undertakings (Article 4(1)) and those applicable to agreements made between non-competing undertakings (Article 4(2)).

Certain hardcore restrictions are subject to permitted qualifications, which effectively means that where the agreement contains a hardcore restriction and the latter falls within the permitted qualification, it will not have the effect of taking the agreement outside the scope of the exemption in Article 2.[334]

For agreements concluded between competing undertakings (Article 4(1)), the hardcore restrictions are:

- restrictions on the ability of a party to set prices when selling goods to third parties (Article 4(1)a)
- restrictions on output except limitations on outputs imposed on the licensee in a non-reciprocal agreement or imposed on only one licensee in a reciprocal agreement (output limitation) (Article 4(1)b)
- market and client allocation (Article 4(1)c)
- curbing the capacity of the licensee to exploit its own technology rights (Article 4(1)d)
- curtailing the capacity of any party to the agreement to undertake R&D (Article 4(1)d)

For agreements concluded between non-competing undertakings (Article 4(2)), the hardcore restrictions are:

- restrictions on the ability of a party to set prices when selling products to third parties except for the possibility of imposing a maximum sale price or recommending a sale price on the proviso that it does not amount to either a fixed sale price or a minimum sale price due to pressure or incentives from any of the parties (Article 4(2)a)

333. Anderson 2010: 666.
334. Anderson 2010: 666.

- restrictions on the territory into which the licensee may passively sell contract goods except for restrictions on passive sales into an exclusive territory reserved for the licensor (Article 4(2)b)
- restrictions on the clients to whom the licensee may passively sell contract goods except for restrictions on passive sales to an exclusive client group reserved for the licensor (Article 4(2)b)
- restriction on sales by a licensee to end-users, which are passive or active, when the licensee is a member of a selective distribution system operating at the retail level (Article 4(2)c)

Article 5

This article sets out the excluded restrictions to which the exemption in Article 2 will not apply. Where an agreement contains a provision containing one of the excluded restrictions, the offending provision rather than the agreement itself will be taken outside the scope of the exemption in Article 2.[335] The excluded restrictions are:

- an obligation on the licensee to grant an exclusive licence or to assign rights to the licensor or another party appointed by the licensor in relation to the licensee's improvements to the licensed technology or new applications of the licensed technology. (Article 5(1)a);
- an obligation imposed on a contracting party not to challenge the validity of the intellectual property rights held by the other party in the EU. (Article 5(1)b);
- where the agreement is made between non-competing undertakings, an obligation limiting the capacity of the licensee to exploit its own technology rights. (Article 5(1)c);
- where the agreement is made between non-competing undertakings, an obligation limiting the capacity of either party to the agreement to undertake R&D. (Article 5(1)c).

Article 6

This Article allows the Commission and the national competition authorities (NCA) to withdraw the benefit of the Regulation – in accordance with Article 29 of Regulation (EC) No 1/2003 – where the agreement that benefits from the exemption has effects that are incompatible with Article 101(3) TFEU. (Article 6(1) and Article 6(2) respectively)

Article 7

This Article allows the Commission by regulation to declare that where parallel networks of similar technology transfer agreements cover more than half the relevant market, the Regulation is inapplicable to technology transfer agreements containing

335. Anderson 2010: 666.

specific restrictions relevant to that market. (Article 7(1)) Once adopted, the regulation will not be applicable for a period of 6 months post-adoption. (Article 7(2))

Article 8

This Article sets out the methods used to calculate the market share thresholds denoted in Article 3.

Article 9

This Article addresses the relationship between TTBER 2014 and other block exemption regulations. Stating that the TTBER 2014 will not apply to licencing arrangements in the context of R&D agreements (these fall under Regulation 1217/201) and licencing arrangements in the context of specialisation agreements (these fall under Regulation 1218/2010).

Article 10

This Article addresses the transitional period. During the period 1 May 2014 until 30 April 2015, the prohibition in Article 101(1) TFEU did not apply to agreements already in force on 30 April 2014 that did not satisfy the conditions for the exemption contained in TTBER 2014 but which on 30 April 2014 satisfied the conditions for the exemption contained in TTBER 2004.

Article 11

This Article denotes the period of validity of TTBER 2014 namely from 1 May 2014 until 30 April 2026.

[C] The Scope of the TTBER 2014

The TTBER 2014, which was made in Brussels on 21 March 2014 and was issued on 28 March 2014, will expire on 30 April 2026.[336]

Where the agreement concerned respects all the criteria set out in the block exemption governing technology transfer agreements (TTBER) and defined by the Commission, then in line with Article 101(3) TFEU the pertinent agreement is exempted from the prohibition contained in Article 101 TFEU.[337]

To the extent that technology transfer agreements fall within the scope of Article 101(1) TFEU, the block exemption in the TTBER operates on the assumption that those agreements that qualify for the block exemption satisfy the four stipulations articulated in Article 101(3) TFEU.[338] In other words, it is presumed therefore that such agreements contribute to the improvement of production or distribution of goods or to the

336. TTBER 2014, Art. 11.
337. European Commission Memo entitled 'Antitrust: Commission consults on proposal for revised competition regime for technology transfer agreements – frequently asked questions Memo/13/120 (Brussels, 20 February 2013), 1.
338. Article 101(3) TFEU reads 'The provisions of paragraph 1 may, however, be declared inapplicable in the case of any agreement or category of agreements between undertakings ...

promotion of technical or economic progress, whilst affording consumers a fair share of the resulting benefit, and these agreements do not contain restrictions that are not indispensable to the attainment of such efficiencies and do not afford these undertakings the possibility of eliminating competition in relation to a major part of the products concerned.[339]

The provisions in the Block Exemption, notably the articles governing market share thresholds, hardcore restrictions and excluded restrictions, aim to ensure that 'only restrictive agreements that can reasonably be presumed to fulfil the four conditions of Article 101(3) are block exempted'.[340]

Agreements that are exempted by the TTBER are both 'legally valid and enforceable'.[341] Such agreements can only be prohibited if the block exemption is revoked by the Commission or by an NCA. An agreement exempted by the TTBER cannot be forbidden by a judgement of a national court in private litigation.[342]

The TTBER will only cover those provisions in the technology transfer agreements that relate to the purchase of products by the licensee, if, and only to the degree that, these provisions are directly connected with the production or the sale of the contract products.[343] As such the TTBER will not cover those provisions in the technology transfer agreement that relate to materials or data employed for purposes other than the production of the contract products.[344]

The TTBER will only cover provisions in the technology transfer agreement that relate to the licensing of other forms of intellectual property (beside software copyright) if, and to the degree that, they are directly connected with the production or sale of the contract products. Thereby ensuring that these other forms of intellectual

---

which contributes to improving the production or distribution of goods or to promoting technical or economic progress, while allowing consumers a fair share of the resulting benefit, and which does not:

(a) impose on the undertakings concerned restrictions which are not indispensable to the attainment of these objectives;
(b) afford such undertakings the possibility of eliminating competition in respect of a substantial part of the products in question.'

339. Communication from the Commission - Guidelines on the application of Article 101 of the Treaty on the Functioning of the European Union to technology transfer agreements. (2014/C 89/03), C89/12, para. 41.
340. Communication from the Commission - Guidelines on the application of Article 101 of the Treaty on the Functioning of the European Union to technology transfer agreements. (2014/C 89/03), C89/12, para. 41.
341. Communication from the Commission - Guidelines on the application of Article 101 of the Treaty on the Functioning of the European Union to technology transfer agreements. (2014/C 89/03), C89/12, para. 40.
342. Communication from the Commission - Guidelines on the application of Article 101 of the Treaty on the Functioning of the European Union to technology transfer agreements. (2014/C 89/03), C89/12, para. 40.
343. Communication from the Commission - Guidelines on the application of Article 101 of the Treaty on the Functioning of the European Union to technology transfer agreements. (2014/C 89/03), C89/13, para. 46.
344. Communication from the Commission - Guidelines on the application of Article 101 of the Treaty on the Functioning of the European Union to technology transfer agreements. (2014/C 89/03), C89/13, para. 46.

property are only exempted when they are used by the licensee to make better use of the licensed technology rights.[345]

Where the licensee is granted the right to make use of the licensor's trademark on products manufactured using the licensor's technology, the licensed trademark will be exempted alongside the technology licensed if the licensed trademark allows the licensee to make better use of the licensed technology rights, by for example allowing buyers of the products manufactured to make an immediate connection between the product manufactured and the features inputted to the product by the licensed technology rights.[346]

This exemption provided for by the TTBER will apply to the extent that the technology transfer agreement contains measures that restrict competition and fall within the scope of the prohibition contained in Article 101(1) TFEU.[347]

This exemption will apply for as long as the technology rights licensed have not expired, lapsed or been declared invalid or for as long as the know-how remains secret.[348] In circumstances where the know-how is made public due to an action taken by the licensee, the exemption will apply for the term of the agreement.[349]

In the TTBER 2014[350] the expression 'technology transfer agreement' is treated as encompassing not only licensing agreements, but also assignments of technology rights.[351]

A licensing agreement, in the context of this Regulation, is an agreement pursuant to which the licensor (or an undertaking connected to the licensor) permits one or more parties to use its technology rights in the production of contract products by the licensee or a connected undertaking and/or its sub-contractor(s).[352,353]

An assignment of technology rights, in this context, is defined as an agreement between two undertakings for the purpose of producing contract products 'where part of the risk associated with the exploitation of the technology remains with the assignor'.[354]

345. Communication from the Commission – Guidelines on the application of Article 101 of the Treaty on the Functioning of the European Union to technology transfer agreements. (2014/C 89/03), C89/13, para. 47.
346. Communication from the Commission – Guidelines on the application of Article 101 of the Treaty on the Functioning of the European Union to technology transfer agreements. (2014/C 89/03), C89/13, para. 47.
347. TTBER 2014, Art. 2(2).
348. TTBER 2014, Art. 2(2).
349. TTBER 2014, Art. 2(2).
350. Pursuant to the Technology Transfer Block Exemption Regulation (TTBER) as supplemented by the Guidance Accompanying the TTBER.
351. TTBER 2014, Art. 1(c).
352. European Commission Memo entitled 'Antitrust: Commission consults on proposal for revised competition regime for technology transfer agreements – frequently asked questions Memo/13/120 (Brussels, 20 February 2013), 1.
353. TTBER 2014, Art. 1(c) read alongside Art. 1(f) and Art. 1(g).
354. TTBER 2014, Art. 1(c) read alongside Art. 1(f) and Art. 1(g).

Excluded from this Regulation are licensing arrangements in research and development agreements (these fall within the scope of Regulation (EU) No 1217/2010) and licensing arrangements in specialisation agreements (these fall within the scope of Regulation (EU) No 1218/2010).[355]

[D] Concepts That Typify the TTBER

Certain concepts characterise the TTBER 2004 and 2014. First the emphasis on the distinction between competing and non-competing undertakings. Second the prominence given to the market share of the undertakings.

Though these concepts were present in the forerunner to the TTBER 2004 Technology (Technology Transfer Regulation 1996), these concepts did not take centre stage.

[1] Competing Undertakings and Non-competing Undertakings[356]

Due to the higher level of risk to competition posed by agreements concluded between competing undertakings, a distinction is made in different provisions of the Regulation between agreements involving competing undertakings and those involving non-competing undertakings. This distinction can be found in the context of the market share thresholds (in Article 3, TTBER 2014), the hardcore restrictions (in Article 4, TTBER 2014) and the excluded restrictions (Article 5, TTBER 2014).

To ascertain the nature of the competitive relationship existing between the undertakings, it is essential to clarify if the contracting parties 'would have been actual or potential competitors in the absence of the agreement'.[357]

'Competing undertakings' are entities that are in competition with one another on the 'relevant market' in which either the technology rights are licensed or in the alternative in which the contract products are sold.[358] In the context of the latter, these undertakings may be either actual competitors on the 'relevant market' or indeed potential competitors on the 'relevant market'.[359]

In the context of technology rights, 'competing undertakings' are engaged in competition with one another on the 'relevant market' in which the 'technology rights' are licensed. As such they are 'actual competitors on the relevant market'.[360] Such

355. TTBER 2014, Art. 9.
356. Communication from the Commission – Guidelines on the application of Article 101 of the Treaty on the Functioning of the European Union to technology transfer agreements. (2014/C 89/03), C89/10, para. 27.
357. Communication from the Commission – Guidelines on the application of Article 101 of the Treaty on the Functioning of the European Union to technology transfer agreements. (2014/C 89/03), C89/10, para. 28.
358. TTBER 2014, Art. 1(1)n(i) and Art. 1(1)n(ii).
359. TTBER 2014, Art. 1(1)n(ii).
360. TTBER 2014, Art. 1(1)n(ii).

competition manifests itself in the fact that these undertakings are engaged in licensing out competing technology rights.[361]

In the context of contract products, 'competing undertakings' are entities that but for the technology transfer agreement would be in actual competition with one another on the 'relevant market' on which the 'contract products' are on sale or would be potential competitors on the said market.[362] These undertakings would both be actual competitors if, in the absence of the technology transfer agreement, they were both 'active on the relevant market(s) on which the contract products are sold'.[363]

If the undertakings are not both active on the relevant market(s) on which the contract products are sold, they would both be potential competitors on the relevant market if, in the absence of the technology transfer agreement, by virtue of the fact that they would 'on realistic grounds and not just as a mere theoretical possibility, in response to a small and permanent increase in relative prices, be likely to undertake, within a short period of time, the necessary additional investments or other necessary switching costs to enter the relevant market(s)'.[364] A licensee will be viewed, for example, as a potential competitor on the product market if, in the absence of the agreement, it would incur the expenditure and time of entering the relevant market in response to a nominal but ongoing increase in the prices of the product.[365] The likely entry must be assessed realistically based on the circumstances of the case at hand by looking for example at whether the licensee has assets that would make an entry into the relevant market more easier and considering whether the licensee has developed concrete plans to address such an eventuality.[366]

If the undertakings were already active on the same relevant product market before the conclusion of the agreement between them, then they will be actual competitors.[367]

Two further issues that relate to competing undertakings are the presence of intra-technology competition and the existence of a one-way or two-way blocking position.[368]

361. TTBER 2014, Art. 1(1)n(ii).
362. TTBER 2014, Art. 1(1)n(ii).
363. TTBER 2014, Art. 1(1)n(ii).
364. TTBER 2014, Art. 1(1)n(ii).
365. Communication from the Commission – Guidelines on the application of Article 101 of the Treaty on the Functioning of the European Union to technology transfer agreements. (2014/C 89/03), C89/10, para. 31.
366. Communication from the Commission – Guidelines on the application of Article 101 of the Treaty on the Functioning of the European Union to technology transfer agreements. (2014/C 89/03), C89/10, para. 31.
367. Communication from the Commission – Guidelines on the application of Article 101 of the Treaty on the Functioning of the European Union to technology transfer agreements. (2014/C 89/03), C89/10, para. 30.
368. Communication from the Commission – Guidelines on the application of Article 101 of the Treaty on the Functioning of the European Union to technology transfer agreements. (2014/C 89/03), C89/10, para. 27 and 29 (respectively).

Intra-technology competition exists where there is competition between undertakings that employ identical technology.[369] Where intra-technology competition exists this is capable of reducing the prices of the products that make use of the technology in question, which may be beneficial to consumers of these products and may promote additional competition between the undertakings that use competing technologies.[370]

Where the contracting parties are in a one-way blocking position or two-way blocking position they are not regarded as competitors.

A one-way blocking position will exist when 'a technology right cannot be exploited without infringing upon another valid technology right, or where one party cannot be active in a commercially viable way on the relevant market without infringing the other party's valid technology right. This is, for instance, the case where one technology right covers an improvement of another technology right and the improvement cannot be legally used without a licence of the basic technology right'.[371]

A two-way blocking position will exist when 'neither technology right can be exploited without infringing upon the other valid technology right or where neither party can be active in a commercially viable way on the relevant market without infringing the other party's valid technology right and where the parties thus need to obtain a licence or a waiver from each other'.[372]

[2] Market Share Thresholds of the Safe Harbour[373]

According to the TTBER 2014, the likelihood that the positive effect of technology transfer agreements (in terms of efficiency enhancement and the furtherance of competition) will exceed the negative effects of such agreements, on account of the constraints contained in these agreements, is largely contingent on the market power of the undertakings concerned and in turn on the degree to which these undertakings are confronted with competition from other undertakings owning substitute technologies or producing substitute goods.[374]

369. Communication from the Commission – Guidelines on the application of Article 101 of the Treaty on the Functioning of the European Union to technology transfer agreements. (2014/C 89/03), C89/10, para. 27.
370. Communication from the Commission – Guidelines on the application of Article 101 of the Treaty on the Functioning of the European Union to technology transfer agreements. (2014/C 89/03), C89/10, para. 27.
371. Communication from the Commission – Guidelines on the application of Article 101 of the Treaty on the Functioning of the European Union to technology transfer agreements. (2014/C 89/03), C89/10, para. 29.
372. Communication from the Commission – Guidelines on the application of Article 101 of the Treaty on the Functioning of the European Union to technology transfer agreements. (2014/C 89/03), C89/10, para. 29.
373. The concept of market share will be reviewed in detail further on in this chapter.
374. TTBER 2014, recital para. 5.

In order to better gauge the effect(s) of a licensing agreement on competition,[375] it is imperative to determine the relevant markets – the relevant product market(s)[376] as well as the relevant technology market(s)[377] – and then to ascertain market share.

In order to analyse the impact of such an agreement on competition, the Commission will ordinarily limit its examination to the impact of the agreement on competition within the existing product and technology markets.[378]

[3] Other Concepts Present in the TTBERs and Regulation 240/96

Concepts that run through the instruments governing transfer of technology (namely Regulation 240/96, TTBER 2004 and TTBER 2014) are the distinction made between bilateral and multilateral agreements, the notion of a transfer, certain key terminology (such as contract products, relevant markets, technology rights and connected undertakings) and the prospect of revocation.

[a] Bilateral Agreements Versus Multilateral Agreements

The TTBER 2004 and 2014 as well as Regulation 240/96 only apply to bilateral agreements.

Multilateral agreements (referred as 'multiparty agreements') that entail more than two undertakings are not cover by these instruments.[379] Agreements involving the formation and running of technology pools (structures used by two or more parties to pool their respective technologies before licensing these out) are typically multilateral agreements and are as such outside the scope of the TTBER 2014.[380]

375. Communication from the Commission – Guidelines on the application of Article 101 of the Treaty on the Functioning of the European Union to technology transfer agreements. (2014/C 89/03), C89/9, para. 20.
376. Made up of the contract products and all other products that the buyer deems to be interchangeable with or substitutable for the contract products, by virtue of the product's features, the prices and the intended purpose. (Communication from the Commission – Guidelines on the application of Article 101 of the Treaty on the Functioning of the European Union to technology transfer agreements. (2014/C 89/03), C89/9, para. 21) More later on in this chapter.
377. Made up of the licensed technology rights and all other technologies that are viewed by licensees as interchangeable with the licensed technologies or substitutable for them, bearing in mind the features of the technologies, the royalties and their intended purpose. (Communication from the Commission – Guidelines on the application of Article 101 of the Treaty on the Functioning of the European Union to technology transfer agreements. (2014/C 89/03), C89/9, para. 22) More later on in this chapter.
378. Communication from the Commission – Guidelines on the application of Article 101 of the Treaty on the Functioning of the European Union to technology transfer agreements. (2014/C 89/03), C89/9, para. 26.
379. In the context of TTBER 2014, *see* Communication from the Commission – Guidelines on the application of Article 101 of the Treaty on the Functioning of the European Union to technology transfer agreements. (2014/C 89/03), C89/14, para. 54.
380. Communication from the Commission – Guidelines on the application of Article 101 of the Treaty on the Functioning of the European Union to technology transfer agreements. (2014/C 89/03), C89/14, para. 56.

A bilateral agreement is capable of being exempted by the TTBER even when the agreement addresses more than one level of trade.[381] This could arise for example where the licensing agreement addresses the stages of production and distribution.[382]

[b] *The Notion of a Transfer*

In the context of technology transfer agreements, there must be a transfer. As such, the technology must flow from one undertaking to another.[383]

The concept of transfer is present in the context of a licensing agreement, as there is a grant of the right to make use of the licensor's technology, by the licensor to the licensee, in exchange for the payment of royalties by the licensee to the licensor.[384]

Equally there is a transfer where an assignment of technology rights takes place.[385] The assignor will retain part of the risk associated with the exploitation of the technology rights and will receive payment in consideration of the assignment.[386] This payment will often depend on the turnover generated by the assignee in relation to the products produced using the assigned technology, the volume of products or the number of operations executed using the assigned technology.[387]

[c] *Key Terminology*

[i] 'Contract Products'

If the aim of the licensing agreement is not the production of contract products, as the licensing agreement is merely used to limit or to block the ability of one of the parties

381. Communication from the Commission – Guidelines on the application of Article 101 of the Treaty on the Functioning of the European Union to technology transfer agreements. (2014/C 89/03), C89/14, para. 55.
382. Communication from the Commission – Guidelines on the application of Article 101 of the Treaty on the Functioning of the European Union to technology transfer agreements. (2014/C 89/03), C89/14, para. 55.
383. Communication from the Commission – Guidelines on the application of Article 101 of the Treaty on the Functioning of the European Union to technology transfer agreements. (2014/C 89/03), C89/13, para. 51.
384. Communication from the Commission – Guidelines on the application of Article 101 of the Treaty on the Functioning of the European Union to technology transfer agreements. (2014/C 89/03), C89/13, para. 51.
385. Communication from the Commission – Guidelines on the application of Article 101 of the Treaty on the Functioning of the European Union to technology transfer agreements. (2014/C 89/03), C89/13, para. 51.
386. Communication from the Commission – Guidelines on the application of Article 101 of the Treaty on the Functioning of the European Union to technology transfer agreements. (2014/C 89/03), C89/13, para. 51.
387. Communication from the Commission – Guidelines on the application of Article 101 of the Treaty on the Functioning of the European Union to technology transfer agreements. (2014/C 89/03), C89/13, para. 51.

to develop competing technology,[388] then the licensing agreement will not be covered by the TTBER.[389] In other words, in order for a technology transfer agreement to benefit from the TTBER, it is imperative that the agreement is made for the purpose of producing the contract products.[390,391]

Under the Regulation, a contract product is a product that is produced directly or indirectly using the technology rights licensed.[392] Reference to a product in the context of the Regulation is taken to mean not only a good but also a service and encompasses intermediary goods and services as well as final goods and services.[393]

[ii] 'Technology Rights'

In the context of the Regulation, the phrase 'technology rights' encompasses know-how[394] alongside the following right/s:

- patents;
- utility models;
- design rights;
- topographies of semiconductor products;
- supplementary protection certificates for medicinal products or other products for which such supplementary protection certificates may be obtained;
- plant breeder's certificates; and
- software copyrights.[395]

Such rights may be awarded alone or together.[396]

388. Communication from the Commission - Guidelines on the application of Article 101 of the Treaty on the Functioning of the European Union to technology transfer agreements. (2014/C 89/03), C89/14, para. 59.
389. Communication from the Commission - Guidelines on the application of Article 101 of the Treaty on the Functioning of the European Union to technology transfer agreements. (2014/C 89/03), C89/14, para. 59.
390. Communication from the Commission - Guidelines on the application of Article 101 of the Treaty on the Functioning of the European Union to technology transfer agreements. (2014/C 89/03), C89/14, para. 59.
391. TTBER 2014, Art. 1(1)c. 'Technology transfer agreement' means: '(i) a technology rights licensing agreement entered into between two undertakings for the purpose of the production of contract products by the licensee and/or its sub-contractor(s), (ii) an assignment of technology rights between two under takings for the purpose of the production of contract products where part of the risk associated with the exploitation of the technology remains with the assignor.'
392. TTBER 2014, Art. 1(1)g.
393. TTBER 2014, Art. 1(1)f.
394. Know-how is 'a package of practical information, resulting from experience and testing, which is secret, substantial and identified'. (Art. 1(1)i TTBER 2014).
395. TTBER 2014, Art. 1(1)b.
396. Communication from the Commission - Guidelines on the application of Article 101 of the Treaty on the Functioning of the European Union to technology transfer agreements. (2014/C 89/03), C89/12, para. 44.

The technology rights licensed should be sufficient 'to allow the licensee, with or without other input, to produce the contract products'.[397]

[iii] 'Relevant Market'

The expression relevant market, which is employed in Article 3 of the TTBER 2014, is defined by Article 1(1) as 'the combination of the relevant product *or* technology market *with* the relevant geographic market'.[398]

When assessing the 'relevant market' reference should be made to:

- the *relevant product market* and the *relevant geographic market*; or
- the *relevant technology market* and the *relevant geographic market*

The relevant product market is defined as the 'market for the *contract products* and *their substitutes*, that is to say all those products which are regarded as interchangeable or substitutable by the buyer, by reason of the products' characteristics, their prices and their intended use'.[399] Contract products may be either part of a finished product market or an intermediary product market.[400]

The relevant technology market is described as the 'market for the *licensed technology rights* and *their substitutes*, that is to say all those technology rights which are regarded as interchangeable or substitutable by the licensee, by reason of the technology rights' characteristics, the royalties payable in respect of those rights and their intended use'.[401]

Two methods may be employed in order to determine the relevant technology market in this context.[402]

According to the first method, the point of departure is the technology promoted by the licensor, thereafter it is essential to isolate other technologies to which licensees 'could switch in response to a small but permanent increase in relative prices, that is to say, to the royalties'.[403]

In the alternative, reference may be made to 'the market for products incorporating the licensed technology rights'.[404]

397. Communication from the Commission – Guidelines on the application of Article 101 of the Treaty on the Functioning of the European Union to technology transfer agreements. (2014/C 89/03), C89/12, para. 44.
398. TTBER 2014, Art. 1(1)m. Emphasis added by writer.
399. TTBER 2014, Art. 1(1)j. Emphasis added by writer.
400. Communication from the Commission – Guidelines on the application of Article 101 of the Treaty on the Functioning of the European Union to technology transfer agreements. (2014/C 89/03), C89/9, para. 21.
401. TTBER 2014, Art. 1(1)k. Emphasis added by writer.
402. Communication from the Commission – Guidelines on the application of Article 101 of the Treaty on the Functioning of the European Union to technology transfer agreements. (2014/C 89/03), C89/9, para. 22.
403. Communication from the Commission – Guidelines on the application of Article 101 of the Treaty on the Functioning of the European Union to technology transfer agreements. (2014/C 89/03), C89/9, para. 22.
404. Communication from the Commission – Guidelines on the application of Article 101 of the Treaty on the Functioning of the European Union to technology transfer agreements. (2014/C 89/03), C89/9, para. 22.

The relevant geographic market is determined by reference to 'the area in which the undertakings concerned are involved in the supply of and demand for products or the licensing of technology rights, in which the conditions of competition are sufficiently homogeneous and which can be distinguished from neighbouring areas because the conditions of competition are appreciably different in those areas'.[405] The geographic market of the relevant technology market(s) may be distinct from that of the relevant product market(s).[406]

- Analysis of the terms 'relevant product market' and 'relevant technology market'

Two of the terms on which the definition of the 'relevant market' depends, namely 'relevant product market' and 'relevant technology market' – are defined by reference to contract products[407] (in the context of the 'relevant product market'), technology rights[408] (in the context of the 'relevant technology market') as well as their substitutes (for both the 'relevant product market' and the 'relevant technology market').

The notion of substitutes, in the context of the Regulation, is taken to encompass products or technology rights viewed by the buyer and the licensee (respectively) as 'interchangeable or substitutable'.

The reasoning from the perspective of the buyer of the contract products in the context of the 'relevant product market' will depend first upon the features of the (intermediary or final) goods or services,[409] second their cost and finally their intended purpose.[410]

The reasoning from the viewpoint of the licensee in the context of the 'relevant technology market' will depend first on the features of the technology rights, second on the royalties that are payable for these rights and finally upon their intended purpose.[411]

[iv] 'Connected Undertakings'

Reference in the Regulation to an undertaking, licensor or licensee is taken to include their respective connected undertakings.[412] A connected undertaking is defined by the Regulation as an undertaking:

405. TTBER 2014, Art. 1(1)l.
406. Communication from the Commission – Guidelines on the application of Article 101 of the Treaty on the Functioning of the European Union to technology transfer agreements. (2014/C 89/03), C89/9, para. 24.
407. Reviewed above.
408. Reviewed above.
409. TTBER 2014, Art. 1(1)f and Art. 1(1)g read together. Reviewed above in more detail.
410. TTBER 2014, Art. 1(1)j.
411. TTBER 2014, Art. 1(1)k.
412. TTBER 2014, Art. 1(2).
A connected undertaking is:An undertaking that is controlled by a party to the technology transfer agreement (TTBER 2014, Art. 1(2)a).
An undertaking that controls a party to the technology transfer agreement (TTBER 2014, Art. 1(2)b).

- *that is controlled* by a party to the technology transfer agreement (TTBER 2014, Article 1(2)a);
- *that controls* a party to the technology transfer agreement (TTBER 2014, Article 1(2)b);
- in which an undertaking that controls a party to the technology transfer agreement has directly or indirectly the powers denoted in point (a) (TTBER 2014, Article 1(2)c);
- in which a party to the technology transfer agreement together with at least one of the undertakings listed in points (a)-(c) jointly have the powers listed in point (a) (TTBER 2014, Article 1(2)d);
- in which two or more of the undertakings listed in points (a)-(c) jointly have the powers listed in point (a) (TTBER 2014, Article 1(2)d);
- in which the powers listed in point (a) are jointly held by the parties to the technology transfer agreement or their connected undertakings or jointly held by at least one of the parties to the technology transfer agreement (TTBER 2014, Article 1(2)e).

[E] Revocation (TTBER 2014, Article 6)

The benefit of the block exemption may be withdrawn in individual cases by either the Commission or an NCA.

The Commission on its own initiative or in response to a complaint[413] may withdraw the benefit of this block exemption if it finds that in any particular case the

---

An undertaking in which an undertaking that controls a party to the TT agreement has directly or indirectly the powers denoted in point (a) (TTBER 2014, Art. 1(2)c).

An undertaking in which a party to the TT agreement together with at least one of the undertakings listed in points (a)-(c) jointly have the powers listed in point (a) (TTBER 2014, Art. 1(2)d).An undertaking in which two or more of the undertakings listed in points (a)-(c) jointly have the powers listed in point (a) (TTBER 2014, Art. 1(2)d).

An undertaking in which the powers listed in point (a) are jointly held by the parties to the TT agreement or their connected undertakings or jointly held by at least one of the parties to the TT agreement (TTBER 2014, Art. 1(2)e).An undertaking controlled by a party to the technology transfer agreement (point a) (TTBER 2014, Art. 1(2)a).

An undertaking controlled by a party to the technology transfer agreement is one in which a party to the technology transfer agreement, directly or indirectly, has the power to:

Exercise a majority of the voting rights;Appoint a majority of the members on the supervisory or management board or any other body that legally represents the undertaking; or

Direct the business of the undertaking.An undertaking that controls a party to the technology transfer agreement (TTBER 2014, Art. 1(2)b).

An undertaking that controls a party to the technology transfer agreement is one that enjoys one or more of the powers listed in point (a) (majority of voting rights, power to appoint members onto the body that governs or represents the undertaking and the power to direct the business of the undertaking).

413. Council Regulation (EC) No 1/2003 of 16 December 2002 on the implementation of the rules on competition laid down in Articles 81 and 82 of the Treaty (OJ L 1, 4.1.2003, p. 1), Article 29(1). This Articles reads 'Where the Commission, empowered by a Council Regulation, such as Regulations 19/65/EEC, (EEC) No 2821/71, (EEC) No 3976/87, (EEC) No 1534/91 or (EEC) No 479/92, to apply Article 81(3) of the Treaty by regulation, has declared Article 81(1) of the

agreement to which the exemption applies has certain effects that are incompatible with Article 101(3) TFEU.[414] Such a situation may arise for example when 'the incentives to innovate are reduced or where access to markets is hindered'.[415]

Incentives to innovate may be curbed in circumstances where the access to the market of third parties' technologies is curtailed by for example 'the cumulative effect of parallel networks of similar restrictive agreements prohibiting licensees from using third parties' technologies'.[416]

Access to markets may be hindered when the access of potential licensees to the market is curtailed by for example 'the cumulative effect of parallel networks of similar restrictive agreements prohibiting licensors from licensing to other licensees or because the only technology owner licensing out relevant technology rights concludes an exclusive licence with a licensee who is already active on the product market on the basis of substitutable technology rights'.[417]

An NCA is permitted to withdraw the benefit of this block exemption[418] in respect of the entire territory of the Member State or part of the said territory, in circumstances where the agreement to which the exemption applies has effects that are incompatible with Article 101(3) TFEU in the entire territory of the Member States or in part of the said territory and where the territory concerned possesses 'all the characteristics of a distinct geographic market'.[419] It may do so in the same situations as the Commission.[420]

[F] Market Share Thresholds of the Safe Harbour

Central to the review of the market share thresholds of the safe harbour are the relevant markets. Once these relevant markets have been ascertained, it is possible to designate

Treaty inapplicable to certain categories of agreements, decisions by associations of undertakings or concerted practices, it may, acting on its own initiative or on a complaint, withdraw the benefit of such an exemption Regulation when it finds that in any particular case an agreement, decision or concerted practice to which the exemption Regulation applies has certain effects which are incompatible with Article 81(3) of the Treaty.'

414. TTBER 2014, recital para. 17 citing Council Regulation (EC) No 1/2003 of 16 December 2002 on the implementation of the rules on competition laid down in Articles 81 and 82 of the Treaty (OJ L 1, 4.1.2003, p. 1), Article 29(1).
415. TTBER 2014, recital para. 17.
416. TTBER 2014, Art. 6(1)a.
417. TTBER 2014, Art. 6(1)b.
418. TTBER 2014, recital para. 18 citing Council Regulation (EC) No 1/2003 of 16 December 2002 on the implementation of the rules on competition laid down in Articles 81 and 82 of the Treaty (OJ L 1, 4.1.2003, p. 1), Article 29(2). Article 29(2) reads 'Where, in any particular case, agreements, decisions by associations of undertakings or concerted practices to which a Commission Regulation referred to in paragraph 1 applies have effects which are incompatible with Article 81(3) of the Treaty in the territory of a Member State, or in a part thereof, which has all the characteristics of a distinct geographic market, the competition authority of that Member State may withdraw the benefit of the Regulation in question in respect of that territory.'
419. TTBER 2014, recital para. 18.
420. TTBER 2014, Art. 6(2).

market shares to the different sources of competition in the market and to then employ these market shares to determine the relative strength of the different market actors.[421]

Two mechanisms are available that may be employed in order to ascertain market shares in the context of technology markets.

The first method involves the computation of market shares 'on the basis of each technology's share of total licensing income from royalties, representing a technology's share of the market where competing technologies are licensed'.[422]

The second of the two methods is the one outlined in Article 8(d) TTBER 2014. This method ascertains 'market shares on the technology market on the basis of sales of products incorporating the licensed technology on downstream product markets'.[423]

The first of the two methods used to calculate the market shares on the technology market is oftentimes more theoretical than practical due to the fact that no coherent data is available on royalties.[424] Both methods may be useful when assessing individual cases that fall outside the safe harbour offered by the TTBER. These methods may be used to determine the market strength of the licensor with more accuracy.[425]

[1] Key Terms in the Assessment of Market Share Thresholds

Central to the review of market share thresholds are certain staple concepts namely 'relevant market', 'relevant product market', 'relevant technology market', 'relevant geographic market' and 'competing undertakings'. These terms are defined in Article 1(1) of the TTBER 2014.

[2] Market Share Thresholds of the Safe Harbour: Competing Undertakings

In the case of technology transfer agreements concluded between competing undertakings, where the combined market share of the contracting parties 'does not exceed 20% on the relevant market(s)'[426] and the agreements in question do not contain certain anti-competitive restraints, it is presumed by the TTBER 2014 that these

421. Communication from the Commission - Guidelines on the application of Article 101 of the Treaty on the Functioning of the European Union to technology transfer agreements. (2014/C 89/03), C89/9, para. 25.
422. Communication from the Commission - Guidelines on the application of Article 101 of the Treaty on the Functioning of the European Union to technology transfer agreements. (2014/C 89/03), C89/9, para. 25.
423. Communication from the Commission - Guidelines on the application of Article 101 of the Treaty on the Functioning of the European Union to technology transfer agreements. (2014/C 89/03), C89/9, para. 25.
424. Communication from the Commission - Guidelines on the application of Article 101 of the Treaty on the Functioning of the European Union to technology transfer agreements. (2014/C 89/03), C89/9, para. 25.
425. Communication from the Commission - Guidelines on the application of Article 101 of the Treaty on the Functioning of the European Union to technology transfer agreements. (2014/C 89/03), C89/9, para. 25.
426. TTBER 2014, Art. 3(1).

agreements will generally 'lead to an improvement in production or distribution and allow consumers a fair share of the resulting benefits'.[427]

[3] *Market Share Thresholds of the Safe Harbour: Non-competing Undertakings*

In the case of technology transfer agreements concluded between non-competing undertakings, where the individual market share of each of the contracting parties 'does not exceed 30% on the relevant market(s)'[428] and the agreements in question do not contain certain anti-competitive restraints, it is presumed by the TTBER 2014 that these agreements 'generally lead to an improvement in production or distribution and allow consumers a fair share of the resulting benefits'.[429]

Conversely the block exemption will not extend to agreements in circumstances where 'the applicable market-share threshold is exceeded on one or more product or technology markets' for the relevant markets concerned.[430]

[4] *Application of the Market Share Thresholds*

In order to apply the market share thresholds (reviewed in Article 3 of the TTBER 2014), reference should be made to the guidance on the calculation of the market share of the undertakings concerned contained in Article 8.

Based on this Article, market share is calculated using:[431]

- the market sales value data for the preceding calendar year (where this data is available); or
- estimations deriving from other reliable market data relating to the preceding calendar year *inter alia* market sales volumes (where market sales value data is not available).

[G] Substantive Contractual Terms

Beyond the relevance of the market share (individual or aggregated) of the parties contracting, due consideration is given by the block exemptions governing technology

427. TTBER 2014, recital para. 10 which reads 'For technology transfer agreements between competitors it can be presumed that, where the combined share of the relevant markets accounted for by the parties does not exceed 20 % and the agreements do not contain certain severely anti-competitive restrictions, they generally lead to an improvement in production or distribution and allow consumers a fair share of the resulting benefits.'
428. TTBER 2014, Art. 3(2).
429. TTBER 2014, recital para. 11 which reads 'For technology transfer agreements between non-competitors it can be presumed that, where the individual share of the relevant markets accounted for by each of the parties does not exceed 30% and the agreements do not contain certain severely anti-competitive restrictions, they generally lead to an improvement in production or distribution and allow consumers a fair share of the resulting benefits.'
430. TTBER 2014, recital para. 12.
431. TTBER 2014, Art. 8(a) and Art. 8(b) read together.

transfer agreements (the former and current TTBER) to the substantive contractual terms and their impact on effective competition.

Pertinent contractual terms that impact on effective competition are divided into two categories. In the first category are the restrictions that are referred to as hardcore restrictions and in the second category are the restrictions that are referred to as excluded restrictions.

These restrictions are distinguished by reference to the consequences that they generate. Where an agreement contains one or more hardcore restrictions, the agreement itself will not be exempted by the Regulation. In contrast, where agreements contain excluded restrictions, the restrictions themselves will be excluded from the benefit of the block exemption.

[1] Hardcore Restrictions under TTBER 2014 (Article 4)

The Regulation does not exempt technology transfer agreements that contain within them restrictive provisions 'which are not indispensible to the improvement of production or distribution'.[432] More specifically, the Regulation will not exempt agreements that contain 'certain severely anti-competitive restrictions, such as the fixing of prices charged to third parties…' In such circumstances, such agreements are excluded from the benefit of the block exemption without regard to market share.[433]

The hardcore restrictions in the Regulation are classified by reference to whether the contracting parties are competing undertakings (TTBER 2014, Article 4(1)) or non-competing undertakings (TTBER 2014, Article 4(2)).

A further classification found within the hardcore restrictions is the one made between reciprocal and non-reciprocal agreements.

A reciprocal agreement is defined as 'a technology transfer agreement where two undertakings grant each other, in the same or separate contracts, a technology rights licence, and where those licences concern *competing technologies or can be used for the production of competing products*'.[434] In other words, this is a cross licensing agreement where the licensed technologies are competing technologies or can be used in the production of competing goods.[435]

A non-reciprocal agreement is defined as 'a technology transfer agreement where one undertaking grants another undertaking a technology rights licence, or where two undertakings grant each other such a licence but where those licences *do not concern competing technologies and cannot be used for the production of competing products*'.[436] In other words, this agreement is one where only one party licenses its technology rights to the other or if there is a cross licensing agreement, the licensed technologies

432. TTBER 2014, recital para. 14.
433. TTBER 2014, recital para. 14.
434. TTBER 2014, Art. 1(1)d; emphasis added by writers.
435. TTBER 2014 Guidelines, para. 98.
436. TTBER 2014, Art. 1(1)e; emphasis added by writers.

are *not* competing technologies and the rights being licensed *cannot* be used in the manufacturing of competing goods.[437]

An agreement will not be a reciprocal agreement for the purposes of the TTBER 2014 simply because it contains a grant-back obligation or because the licensee licenses back its own improvements of the licensed technology.[438]

The hardcore list is far more stringent for reciprocal agreements, than it is for non-reciprocal agreements between competing undertakings.[439]

[a] Hardcore Restrictions Applicable to Competing Undertakings under the TTBER 2014 (Article 4 (1))

The block exemption contained in Article 2 of the TTBER 2014 will not apply to agreements concluded between competing undertakings that either directly or indirectly, alone or together with other factors under the control of the contracting parties aim to:[440]

- limit the ability of a party to set prices when selling products to third parties including products incorporating the licensed technology[441]
  - Here it is immaterial whether the agreement concerns fixed, minimum, maximum or indeed recommended prices, though an obligation on a licensee to pay a certain minimum royalty will not in itself amount to price fixing[442]
- limit output by restricting the quantities that a party may produce and sell[443] except for output limitations on the licensee in a non-reciprocal agreement or output limitations imposed on one of the licensees in a reciprocal agreement so long as the output limitation only concerns products produced using the licensed technology[444]
  - This hardcore restriction found in Article 4(1)b effectively targets competitors who agree to impose reciprocal output limitations in turn reducing output on the market as well as output restrictions imposed on the licensor in relation to its own technology, thereby targeting agreements that reduce the incentive of the parties to expand output[445]
- allocate markets or customers save for select scenarios where allocation is permitted[446]

437. TTBER 2014 Guidelines, para. 98.
438. TTBER 2014 Guidelines, para. 98.
439. TTBER 2014 Guidelines, para. 98.
440. TTBER 2014, Art. 4(1).
441. TTBER 2014, Art. 4(1)a as supplemented by TTBER 2014 Guidelines, para. 99.
442. TTBER 2014 Guidelines, para. 99.
443. TTBER 2014 Guidelines, para. 103.
444. TTBER 2014, Art. 4(1)b as supplemented by TTBER 2014 Guidelines, para. 103.
445. TTBER 2014 Guidelines, para. 103.
446. TTBER 2014, Art. 4(1)c.

  - Agreements between competitors that share markets and customers have as their object the restriction of competition.[447] An agreement between competitors (in a reciprocal agreement) not to produce in certain markets or not to sell actively and/or passively into certain markets or to certain clients reserved for the other party is considered a hardcore restriction.[448] As such a reciprocal exclusive licensing agreement concluded between competing undertakings is considered market sharing.[449]
- limit the parties' ability to carry out research and development[450] 'irrespective of whether the restriction applies to a field covered by the licence or to other fields'.[451] The parties should accordingly remain free to perform independent R&D.[452]
  - An agreement between the parties to furnish each other with future improvements made to their respective technologies will not amount to a hardcore restriction.[453]
  - Restrictions imposed on a party's ability to carry out R&D with third parties where such a restriction is necessary to protect the know-how of the licensor against disclosure will not fall within Article 4(1)d.[454] In order to qualify under this exception, any restrictions must be both necessary and proportionate to ensure such protection.[455]
- limit the ability of the licensee to make use of its own technology rights thereby reducing the competitiveness of the licensee's technology[456]
  - The licensee should accordingly enjoy unfettered freedom in the use of its own competing technology rights so that the licensee is not limited in terms of 'where it produces or sells, the technical fields of use or product markets within which it produces, how much it produces or sells and the price at which it sells'.[457] Moreover the licensee should not be restricted in licensing its' own technology rights to third parties.[458]
  - On the proviso that in doing so, the licensee does not make use of the technology rights licensed from the licensor.[459]

447. TTBER 2014 Guidelines, para. 105.
448. TTBER 2014 Guidelines, para. 105.
449. TTBER 2014 Guidelines, para. 105.
450. TTBER 2014, Art. 4(1)d, as supplemented by the TTBER 2014 Guidelines, para. 115.
451. TTBER 2014 Guidelines, para. 115.
452. TTBER 2014 Guidelines, para. 115.
453. TTBER 2014 Guidelines, para. 115.
454. TTBER 2014 Guidelines, para. 115.
455. TTBER 2014 Guidelines, para. 115.
456. TTBER 2014 Guidelines, para. 116.
457. TTBER 2014 Guidelines, para. 116.
458. TTBER 2014 Guidelines, para. 116.
459. TTBER 2014 Guidelines, para. 116.

[b] Hardcore Restrictions Applicable to Non-competing Undertakings under the TTBER 2014 (Article 4(2))

The exemption contained in Article 2 of the TTBER 2014 will not apply to agreements, concluded by non-competing undertakings, which either directly or indirectly, alone or together with other factors under the control of the parties to the contract, aim to:[460]

- limit the capacity of a party to set 'its prices when selling products' to other parties
  - Though this is 'without prejudice to the possibility of imposing a maximum sale price or a recommending a sale price', so long as this does not equate to either 'a fixed or minimum sale price as a result of pressure from, or incentives offered by, any of the parties'.[461]
- limit the territory into which the licensee is permitted to 'passively sell the contract products'[462] or restrict the customers to whom the licensee is permitted to 'passively sell the contract products'[463] except for a restriction on passive sales into an exclusive territory reserved for the licensor or to an exclusive group of customers reserved for the licensor[464];
- curtail the 'active or passive sales to end-users by a licensee operating at the retail level which is a member of a selective distribution system[465]
  - Though this is without prejudice to the prospect of precluding 'a member of the system from operating out of an unauthorised place of establishment'.[466]

[c] Transformation from a Non-competing Undertaking to a Competing Undertaking

If at the time of conclusion of the agreement, the parties to the agreement are non-competing undertakings but at a later date they become competing undertakings then Article 4(2) will be applicable to the agreement for the full duration of the agreement (i.e., the hardcore restrictions applicable to non-competing undertakings under the TTBER 2014). This is so on the proviso that the agreement is not subsequently amended in any material respect.[467] In the event that the agreement is

460. TTBER 2014, Art. 4(2).
461. TTBER 2014, Art. 4(2)a.
462. TTBER 2014, Art. 4(2)b.
463. TTBER 2014, Art. 4(2)b.
464. TTBER 2014, Art. 4(2)b.
465. A 'selective distribution system' is defined as 'a distribution system where the licensor undertakes to license the production of the contract products, either directly or indirectly, only to licensees selected on the basis of specified criteria and where those licensees undertake not to sell the contract products to unauthorised distributors within the territory reserved by the licensor to operate that system'. (TTBER 2014, Art. 1(1)o).
466. TTBER 2014, Art. 4(2)c.
467. TTBER 2014, Art. 4(3).

amended in a material respect (e.g., a new agreement is concluded between the parties concerning competing technology rights) then this waiver will no longer apply.[468]

[2] Excluded Restrictions under the TTBER 2014 (Article 5)

In an effort to stimulate innovation by safeguarding the impetus to innovate, the block exemptions (both the TTBER 2014 and its predecessor) exclude certain restrictive measures from the benefit of the block exemption.[469] Where such restrictive measures appear in a licence, only the restriction itself is excluded from the benefit of the block exemption.[470]

Three categories of restrictions are excluded from the benefit of the block exemption, namely grant-back obligations, non-challenge clauses[471] and non-exploitation clauses.

The grant-back obligations that are excluded from the benefit of the block exemption are those measures that directly or indirectly oblige the licensee to grant an exclusive licence or to assign rights to the licensor or to a third party designated by the licensor in respect of improvements made by the licensee to the licensed technology or new applications made by the licensee of the licensed technology.[472]

The non-challenge clauses that are excluded from the benefit of the block exemption are those measures that directly or indirectly oblige a party 'not to challenge the validity of intellectual property rights held by the other party in the Union'.[473] Where a measure in an exclusive licence provides for the termination of the technology transfer agreement in the event that the licensee challenges the validity of any of the licensed technology rights, such a measure will not be excluded from the benefit of the block exemption.[474]

The non-exploitation clauses that are excluded from the benefit of the block exemption are those measures, used in agreements concluded between non-competing undertakings, that either directly or indirectly curtail the ability of the licensee 'to exploit its own technology rights'.[475]

Other measures that are excluded from the benefit of the block exclusion are those measures, used in agreements concluded between non-competing undertakings restricting 'the ability of any of the parties to the agreement to carry out research and development'.[476]

---

468. TTBER 2014, Art. 4(3).
469. TTBER 2014, recital para. 15.
470. TTBER 2014, recital para. 15. Reiterated by TTBER 2014, Art. 5(1) which states 'The exemption provided for in Article 2 shall not apply to any of the following obligations contained in technology transfer agreements ... .'
471. TTBER 2014, recital para. 15.
472. TTBER 2014, Art. 5(1)a.
473. TTBER 2014, Art. 5(1)b.
474. TTBER 2014, Art. 5(1)b.
475. TTBER 2014, Art. 5(2).
476. TTBER 2014, Art. 5(2).

§6.11 THE MATERIAL TERMS OF A TECHNOLOGY LICENSING AGREEMENT[477,478]

The following section of the chapter reviews the key terms typically contained in technology licensing agreements.

Whilst the terms that should be contained in such licensing agreements depend largely on the nature of the technology being licensed, certain common matters frequently arise in such deals.

The provisions that are reviewed are representative of the types of provisions that the parties should consider incorporating into their licensing agreement. The goal of this review is to provide an introductory overview of the key provisions and the matters that are frequently encountered in the context of these terms. This review is by no means intended to be exhaustive.

Due to the legal regulation governing such clauses in certain jurisdictions it is sensible for the parties to seek legal advice before incorporating these clauses into their licensing agreement.

[A] Checklist of Provisions

In the preface to this section, a checklist of the key provisions reviewed is included. This checklist aims to help the reader plan their agreement before the drafting and negotiation of the said accord.

477. Anderson 2010, Chapter 2; Exchanging value – Negotiating technology licensing agreements (WIPO), 44-82; Fisher & Fisher, Export Best Practice – Commercial and Legal Aspects, 228-233; Cannady, Technology Licensing and Development Agreements (2013, OUP) (on Google books; not available yet for sale).

478. Anderson, Chapter 2; Exchanging value – Negotiating technology licensing agreements (WIPO), 44-82; Fisher & Fisher, Export Best Practice – Commercial and Legal Aspects, 228-233; Cannady, Technology Licensing and Development Agreements (2013, OUP) (on Google books); UNICO guides key issues, 42-59; Successful Technology Licensing (WIPO 2004), 15-37. *See also* Chapter 5 of the Draft International Code of Conduct on the Transfer of Technology (1985 version) – this chapter lists a number of contractual obligations that the contracting parties should consider including in their technology transfer agreement. These provisions address *inter alia* the resolution of disputes and governing law, confidentiality, training and support. Chapter 4 adopts a regulatory model by addressing the use of competition-related provisions. This chapter was the one of the hardest parts of the Draft Code to negotiate. (UNCTAD 2001, 70) The 'failure to agree on its terms was a major reason for the eventual non-adoption of the Code'. (UNCTAD 2001, 70-5) In spite of the fact that the countries generally agree on the practices that should be regulated (a list of these provisions can be found at UNCTAD 2001, 75), they disagree about the test that should be used to judge these provisions. Whilst the major developed countries support a reasonableness-based approach, the developing countries support an outright ban on the use of such provisions in a contract. This latter approach completely bans the use of such provisions since they reflect 'the superior bargaining power of the technology owner and could act against the best interests of the technology recipient'. (UNCTAD 2001, 75, citing Davidow 2001; Miller and Davidow 2001; Roffe 1998; Sell 2001; and Verma 2001) Pursuant to the reasonableness-based approach, such provisions should only be banned when their positive (pro-competitive) ramifications are outweighed by their negative (anti-competitive) implications. (UNCTAD 2001, 75).

The following checklist lists some of the key provisions that should be borne in mind by the parties contracting or the party drafting the agreement.

This agreement is intended for use in cross-jurisdictional transactions between commercial parties. Not all of the provisions noted in the checklist are mandatory. However, when planning, negotiating and agreeing on the format of the terms of the contract it is sensible for each party contracting to consider each of these provisions in turn before deciding whether or not to use it.

Box 11.1 Checklist of provisions

Preface to the contract

✓ Cover sheet

✓ Table of contents (optional in longer contracts)

✓ Index of defined terms

Front of the contract

✓ Title

✓ Introductory clause (type of agreement, date of agreement, parties to agreement)

✓ Recitals

Body of the contract

✓ Definitions clause

✓ Grant

✓ Term of the agreement

✓ Relationship of the parties[479]

✓ Confidentiality[480]

✓ Work obligations

✓ Obligations of the licensee

✓ Obligations of the licensor

✓ Termination (grounds and consequences)

Boilerplate clauses

✓ Assignment clause

✓ Change of control and ownership clause

479. *See* the corresponding section in Chapter 1 of this book.
480. *See* the corresponding section in Chapter 1 of this book.

✓ Merger clause

✓ Modifications clause

✓ Severance clause

✓ Notice clause

✓ Representation clause

✓ Dispute resolution (informal discussions, renegotiation, adaption, ADR, choice of jurisdiction, choice of law)

✓ Language clause

Back of the contract

✓ Concluding clause

✓ Signature blocks

✓ Attachment (exhibits and schedules)

[B] Preface of the Contract

The preface of the contract is addressed in Chapter 1 of this book.

[C] Front of the Contract

The front of the contract is addressed in Chapter 1 of this book.

[D] Body of the Contract

[1] Definitions Clause

The definitions clause denotes the key terms used throughout the agreement and determines the scope of these terms. Due to the importance of these definitions to the ensuing relationship between the parties, it is sensible to verify the precision of these terms.

In agreements that address the licensing of technology typically the definitions clause will encompass terms such as Licenced Property, Licenced Patent, Licenced Technology, Licenced Trademarks, Licenced Products, Net Sales, Improvements, New Products and Licenced Territory.

The writing of technical terminology may necessitate a joint effort involving a lawyer or party drafting the commercial agreement and a scientist, to guarantee the accuracy of these terms.[481]

[a] Licensed Technology

It is sensible for the parties contracting to take the time needed to define the subject matter of the licence. Whilst the licensor may be concerned about limiting the scope of the licence by narrowing down the subject matter of the licence, the licensee for its part will probably be fairly keen on defining the subject matter of the agreement as broadly as possible.[482]

The parties should ask themselves in this context *inter alia*[483] whether the intended licence should encompass one patent or a series of patents? Whether the licence is intended to cover all the intellectual property and technology needed in order to meet a specific standard or a series of standards? Whether the licence will need to cover the schematics? Whether a source code/object code will be required under the licence? If software is required, which version of the software will be provided? In the event that training and assistance are needed in addition to the licensed intellectual property (especially important where the licensed technology is complex) whether the licence will encompass such training and assistance? In the event that the licensor plans to continue developing the technology, will such future developments also fall within the scope of the licence?

Occasionally the parties will consciously define the scope of the licence ambivalently for strategic reasons. This may arise where the parties are uncertain about the state of the technology and the intended use to which the technology will be put.[484] In this context, it is sensible to acquire a more precise understanding of the state of the technology and the intended purposes for which the technology will be used by speaking to colleagues and clients before the commencement of negotiations and during the course of these negotiations.[485]

In order to verify that the technology licensed is defined with precision, the licence should be accompanied by a clear written specification or document describing the technology that is the subject matter of the licensing agreement and attention should be given to ensuring that the description of the technology licensed corresponds exactly with the needs of the client.[486]

The description contained within the licensing agreement should be comprehensive and precise and the level of detail given should be enough for a third party who has no knowledge of the technology to know what the subject matter of the licence is.[487]

481. Anderson 2010: 56.
482. Successful Technology Licensing (WIPO 2004), 16.
483. Successful Technology Licensing (WIPO 2004), 16.
484. Successful Technology Licensing (WIPO 2004), 16.
485. Successful Technology Licensing (WIPO 2004), 16.
486. Successful Technology Licensing (WIPO 2004), 16.
487. Successful Technology Licensing (WIPO 2004), 16.

This is crucial in the event that a dispute ensues between the parties in relation to the licence.[488]

[b] Unfinished Technology

The state of the technology is an important consideration when defining the subject matter of the licensing agreement. In circumstances where further work is required, the parties should consider whether the technology is usable *as is* and whether the agreement permits the development of the unfinished technology.[489]

In the event the agreement requires a finished product, the licensor should consider whether the deal is conditional upon the completion of its work, whether the anticipated completion date is a feasible objective and whether testing (acceptance testing and functionality testing for example) is prerequisite for the deal proceeding.[490]

The ideal position from the point of view of the licensor, in this context, will be that the licensed technology need not meet any particular standard of performance or function.[491] For the licensee, this would not be an ideal position unless suitable concessions were made by the licensor in terms of the licence.[492] Such concessions may be reflected in the royalties due,[493] the availability of rights in the technology developed by the licensee and so forth.

In circumstances where further work is required it is advisable for the parties to draw up a distinct agreement setting out deadlines and deliverables, as well as delegation of tasks (if at all) and performance.[494] The ideal position for the licensee in such circumstances is that the licensed technology meets defined specifications.[495]

[c] Licensed Territory[496]

Due consideration should be given by the parties to the definition of territory. In this context, the licensee should consider where it intends to use the technology? Where it plans to sell, market or distribute the goods developed using the technology?

The parties may agree that the rights granted under the licence are worldwide in scope. Alternately they may decide that the granted rights are limited to a specific territory (region, country, continent and so forth). A further concern here is whether distribution over the internet is granted to the licensee under the terms of the agreement.[497]

488. Successful Technology Licensing (WIPO 2004), 17.
489. Successful Technology Licensing (WIPO 2004), 17.
490. Successful Technology Licensing (WIPO 2004), 17.
491. Successful Technology Licensing (WIPO 2004), 18.
492. Successful Technology Licensing (WIPO 2004), 18.
493. Successful Technology Licensing (WIPO 2004), 18.
494. Successful Technology Licensing (WIPO 2004), 18.
495. Successful Technology Licensing (WIPO 2004), 18.
496. Successful Technology Licensing (WIPO 2004), 23.
497. Successful Technology Licensing (WIPO 2004), 23.

[2] Grant[498,499]

The grant provision furnishes the licensee with a licence in relation to the intellectual property owned by the licensor. This provision is central to the parties for a number of reasons.[500]

Once the parties have established the subject matter of their licence namely the component(s) that they wish to licence in or licence out, the licensee should give due consideration to that which it wishes to achieve using the licensed intellectual property and technology.[501]

By identifying its business objectives, the licensee should be able to isolate the categories of rights that it will require under the licence.[502] The rights granted under a licence will be governed not only by the needs of the contracting parties but also by the intellectual property law applicable to the agreement.[503]

Typically grants under a technology licence will encompass one or more of the following rights:[504]

(1) the right to reproduce the technology;
(2) the right to display the technology;
(3) the right to change the technology, so that for instance the licensed technology is adapted to the operational needs of the licensee;
(4) the right to produce derivative products that are either inspired by or based on the licensed technology thus allowing the licensee to develop improvements and new products or processes using the technology licensed to it;
(5) the right to produce the technology or have the technology produced by another on behalf of the licensee;
(6) the right to distribute the technology (distribution licence);
(7) the right to trade in the technology;
(8) the right to utilise the technology; and
(9) the right to sublicence the technology to others in its current state or in an enhanced form.

When a licensee is granted the right to produce derivative products the licensee should bear in mind whether it will also require the right to produce or have produced these products.[505]

498. The grant clause is reviewed in Chapter 1 of this book. A template clause can be found in this chapter.
499. The grant clause is linked to the provision governing the fields of use discussed below. For this reason it is worthwhile considering the two together.
500. These reasons are reviewed in detail in Chapter 1 of this book.
501. Successful Technology Licensing (WIPO 2004), 21.
502. Successful Technology Licensing (WIPO 2004), 21.
503. Successful Technology Licensing (WIPO 2004), 21.
504. Successful Technology Licensing (WIPO 2004), 21.
505. Successful Technology Licensing (WIPO 2004), 21.

[a] Territorial Exclusivity[506,507]

[i] Exclusive Arrangements[508]

Under an exclusive licence the ability of the licensor to award further licences in the assigned territory to other parties aside from the licensee is typically curtailed. Such an arrangement will be beneficial to the licensee as it will be the sole actor on the designated market with the right to use the licensed technology reducing or eliminating its exposure to intra-technology competition in its assigned territory.

A licensee is likely to insist on exclusivity in the context of technology licences for a variety of reasons.[509] There may be an expectation under the licensing agreement that the licensee invest resources in the development of the technology licensed to it.

In situations where the licensor has not got the resources needed in order to develop the technology (a public entity for instance) it may be relying on the licensee for the investment needed in order to take the technology to the next stage. In such scenarios it will be the licensee that will assess whether the technology can be commercialised. In the event that the technology has commercial applications, the licensee may be the party responsible for developing products (goods and services) using the technology of the licensor.

By insisting on exclusivity, the licensee is able to ward against the risk of free-riding which occurs where a party other than the licensee (another licensee, a distributor, the licensor and so forth) is able to benefit from the work of the licensee on the given market. Where the licensee is responsible for commercialising the licensed technology, it is probably going to insist on exclusivity so that free-riding is not possible. This is especially important in circumstances where the technology is novel and its commercial value unknown.

[3] Term of the Agreement

This topic is reviewed in detail in Chapter 1 of this book.[510]

[4] Work Obligations

Where work is undertaken under a technology transfer agreement, a list of the tasks to be executed by the party or parties charged with these tasks should be comprehensively and accurately drafted either within the body of the agreement itself or in a schedule or attachment to the said agreement.[511]

506. This topic is reviewed in detail in Chapter 1 of this book.
507. For further details *see* the discussion in Meiselles 2013: 255.
508. For further details *see* the discussion in Meiselles 2013: 256.
509. These reasons are reviewed in detail in Chapter 1 of this book.
510. For further details *see* the discussion in Meiselles 2013: 256-257.
511. Anderson 2010: 57.

[5] Improvements and New Products

During the course of this agreement:

(1) Each Party shall inform the other promptly [or by written notice within (___) days] of any Improvements and/or New Goods of which it becomes aware.

(2) (Optional) The Licensor shall have sole ownership of the Improvements and/or New Goods developed by the Licensee.

(3) Each Party shall have the sole right to file a patent pertaining to such Improvements and/or New Goods made by it or acquired by it.

(4) In order to discuss potential innovative developments or joint projects, the Parties shall meet [or convene meetings by written notice of (___) days] [(___) times a year or on a monthly basis or as and when required] at a time that is convenient for the Parties.

[a] Option to Buy (Optional Provision)

1. For the period of (___) following receipt of written notice of the availability of Improvements and/or New Goods, the Party that is notified shall have the right to reach an agreement with the other Party on a price that is agreeable to the Parties in relation to the Improvements and/or New Goods and any technology and know-how connected to the Improvements and/or New Goods.

2. The Parties shall keep the existence of any such discussions and the content of any such discussions confidential.

3. Such discussions shall be exclusive to the Parties.

[b] Licence to Improvements and/or New Goods Developed by the Licensee (Optional Provision)

Option A

The Licensee shall grant the Licensor the right to use or make use of any Improvements and/or New Goods, in connection with which the Licensee shall have the right to grant such licences, on the same terms as are contained within this agreement.

Option B

1. In response to a request by the Licensor, the Licensee shall grant to the Licensor for the duration of this agreement a royalty-free licence in relation to Improvements and/or New Goods in connection with which the Licensee shall have the right to grant such licences (for all the world save the Licenced Territory or for a specific territory or for specific territories) (on an exclusive/non-exclusive basis).

2. (Optional) Upon the expiration of this agreement and in response to a request by the Licensor, the Licensee shall grant to the Licensor a non-exclusive worldwide royalty-free licence in relation to Improvements and/or New Goods.

[c] Licence to Improvements and/or New Goods Developed by the Licensor (Optional Provision)

Option A

The Licensor shall grant to the Licensee the right to use or make use of any Improvements and/or New Goods in connection with which the Licensor shall have the right to grant such licences on the same terms as are contained within this agreement.

Option B

In response to a request by the Licensee, the Licensor shall grant to the Licensee for the duration of this agreement a licence in relation to Improvements and/or New Goods in connection with which the Licensor shall have the right to grant such licences in the Licenced Territory (on an exclusive/non-exclusive basis).

[d] Improvements and/or New Goods Developed by the Contracting Parties

[i] Licensor's Improvements and/or New Goods

A licensee for its part will be interested in acquiring the rights to use the technology developed by the licensor after the date the agreement was executed. In this context, if a new product is developed by the licensor post-agreement using the licensed technology, the licensee may look to the licensor for the right to make use of the same.

As such the parties should give due consideration to whether this further technology and new products will be come under the terms of the licence they plan to conclude or whether it will be the subject matter of a separate licence.

[ii] Licensee's Improvements and/or New Goods

A material issue that will arise in circumstances where the licensee is granted the right to produce derivative products is the question of ownership of such products. More precisely who will enjoy ownership of the improvements made by the licensee and any new products developed by the licensee.[512] Consideration should be duly accorded by the parties in the pre-negotiation and the negotiation phases to whether they will seek sole ownership or will be prepared to accord joint ownership in relation to such improvements and new products.

In circumstances where the parties agree that the licensee enjoys sole ownership of improvements and new products developed by the licensee, the parties should determine whether the licensor be extended an option to buy or a licence in relation to the same.

From the vantage point of the licensor, motivation on the part of the licensee will be of prime importance. In order to create incentives for innovation on the part of the licensee, a sustainable solution should be sought by the contracting parties. Such innovation on the part of the licensee is not only beneficial to the licensee, it may also be beneficial to the licensor when the improvements and new products allow it to enhance its own operational efficiency whilst increasing its profitability and standing on the marketplace.

If the contracting parties decide that rights will be granted to the licensee in relation to improvements and new products that the licensee has developed (using the licenced property), then due consideration should be given by them to an array of different issues.

First, the parties should decide whether they wish to make a distinction between the rights the licensor and the licensee will acquire in relation to improvements and the rights that each party will acquire in relation to new products.

Should the parties decide to make such a distinction, they should exercise care and attention when defining each of the two terms (improvements versus new products) so that each is distinct from the other. In order to do so, they should give due consideration to the inclusion of a precise description of the parameters that will be used in order to differentiate between improvements on the one hand and new products on the other. The provision of illustrations may be useful in such a situation to alleviate potential misunderstandings at a later stage.

Second, one further concern from the point of view of the licensor is the importance of ensuring the distinctiveness of the improvements and/or new products on the one hand from the Licensed Goods on the other.

With this concern in mind, the contracting parties generally and the licensor specifically should give due consideration to whether or not a new product will be defined as one that is *entirely produced using the intellectual property of the licensee* and whether or not a new product should be distinct from *products produced using the joint background intellectual property of the parties*.

512. Successful Technology Licensing (WIPO 2004), 21.

For example, will a new product be one that contains an internal mechanism that is distinct from the one used in the Licensed Goods? What percentage of new parts (in other words parts that were not previously used in any Licensed Goods) should make up a new product? Will a new product for example need to comprise of fifty or seventy-five or one hundred percent new parts?

Third, the parties contracting should give thought to the types of rights that will be acquired by the licensor in relation to improvements the licensee makes and/or the new products the licensee develops. An exclusive licence, a non-exclusive licence and an option to buy are illustrations of the rights that could be acquired by the licensor in relation to the improvements the licensee makes and/or the new products the licensee develops.

Fourth, consideration should be given to the temporal and the geographic scope of any rights awarded to the licensor in relation to improvements and/or new goods developed by the licensee.

In terms of temporal scope, several alternatives are available. The licensee may grant the licensor a licence:

- allowing the licensor to use the improvements and/or new goods for the duration of the underlying agreement (in other words such a licence granted to the licensor will expire at the same time as the underlying licence);
- that comes into effect upon the expiry of the underlying agreement; or
- that runs indefinitely (in other words, a licence that runs for the duration of the underlying agreement as well as thereafter).

In terms of geographic scope, a number of options are available to the contracting parties. The licence granted by the licensee to the licensor may be for the whole world excluding the Licensed Territory. Another option would be for the licensee to grant a licence to the licensor that is limited to one or more territories thereby allowing the licensee to optimise profitability and to partition its risk.

Fifth, the parties should give thought to the nature of the consideration that should be provided by the licensor in exchange for the grant of rights to the improvements and/or new products developed by the licensee.

The parties should decide for example whether a licence granted to the licensor will be royalty-free and if so whether the grant will remain indefinitely royalty-free.

From the point of view of the licensee, beyond the *right to use* the improvements and/or new products it has developed using the technology of the licensor, it will probably attempt to reserve itself one of the following rights:

(1) the right to sell improvements and/or new goods developed by it in circumstances where the licensor is not prepared to pay a mutually acceptable price for these; or
(2) the right to extend a non-exclusive licence to the licensor in relation to the improvements and/or new goods so that it is able to licence the same to other parties besides the licensor.

Finally, a common concern that will confront a licensor in circumstances where the licensee is tasked with the development of the licensed technology will be a failure on the part of the licensee to develop the licensed technology.[513] This may arise in a variety of circumstances. When the licensed technology is under review by the licensee, where the licensed technology is no longer the most pressing concern for the licensee and the development of the licensed technology is drawn out and when the licensee is working on rival technology and is adamant about retention of the licence in order to prevent the technology licensed being used by a rival of entity.[514]

[6] Obligations of the Licensee

This topic is reviewed in detail in Chapter 1 of this book.[515]

[7] Payment Terms (Structure and Time; Currency; Consequence of Non-payment)[516,517]

The question of payment should be clearly and comprehensively addressed in the technology transfer agreement.[518] The matters that should be addressed in the context of payment are the structure of payment, the currency and the timing of payments and the consequences of failing to pay or paying late.

[8] Non-compete Provisions

This topic is reviewed in detail in Chapter 1 of this book. A template clause can be found in this chapter.

[9] Sublicensing

This topic is reviewed in detail in Chapter 1 of this book. A template clause can be found in this chapter.

[10] Intellectual Property Concerns

Intellectual property granted under the terms of technology licences typically consist of existing intellectual property (background intellectual property) and intellectual

513. Anderson 2010, 85.
514. Anderson 2010, 85.
515. For further details *see* the discussion in Meiselles 2013: 257-266.
516. This topic is reviewed in detail in Chapter 1 of this book. A template clause can be found in this chapter.
517. For further details *see* the discussion in Meiselles 2013: 257-266.
518. Anderson 2010: 57.

property generated during the term of the agreement (foreground intellectual property).[519]

Such agreements will address in relation to each category the following issues:[520]

- ownership of intellectual property
- control of intellectual property
- use of intellectual property
- maintenance of intellectual property protection
- handling of intellectual property infringements by third parties.

National law will primarily govern the protection of intellectual property as such the licensor should look to secure protection of the intellectual property licensed under the national law in the target market. In this context, the licensor will have two options open to it. First, it could opt to delegate the protection of the intellectual property licensed to the licensee. Second, the licensor may decide to assume this responsibility itself. The latter option is beneficial from the point of view of the licensor in circumstances where it is keen on ensuring certainty and where it is looking to ensure the efficacy of protection.

[11] Retention of Title

1. Except as provided for under this agreement, the Licensee shall acquire no rights in relation to the Licenced Property, Licenced Technology, Licenced Know-how and any information and property licenced to it by the Licensor.

2. The Licensee confirms that, except as expressly provided for in this agreement, it shall acquire no rights in relation to the Licenced Property, Licenced Technology, Licenced Know-how and any information and property licenced to it by the Licensor.

3. The Licensee confirms that all such rights and goodwill in relation to the Licenced Property, Licenced Technology, Licenced Know-how and any information and property licenced to it by the Licensor are, and shall remain, vested in the Licensor.

[12] Quality Control

This topic is reviewed in detail in Chapter 1 of this book. A template clause can be found in this chapter.

519. Anderson 2010: 58.
520. Anderson 2010: 58.

[13] Maintenance of Licensed Property

This topic is reviewed in detail in Chapter 1 of this book. A template clause can be found in this chapter.

[14] Restrictions on the Fields of Use

This topic is reviewed in detail in Chapter 1 of this book. A template clause can be found in this chapter.

[15] Obligations of the Licensor

This topic is reviewed in detail in Chapter 1 of this book. A template clause can be found in this chapter.

[16] Assistance and Training to the Licensee Provided by the Licensor

This topic is reviewed in detail in chapter one of this book. A template clause can be found in this chapter.

[17] Warranties, Liabilities and Indemnities

[a] Representations and Warranties

This topic is reviewed in detail in Chapter 1 of this book. A template clause can be found in this chapter.

[b] Indemnities

This topic is reviewed in detail in Chapter 1 of this book. A template clause can be found in this chapter.

[18] Termination

General clauses, boilerplate clauses and the back of the contract are addressed in Chapter 1 of this book.

[19] General Clauses, Boilerplate Clauses and the Back of the Contract

General clauses, boilerplate clauses and the back of the contract are addressed in Chapter 1 of this book.

§6.12 CASE STUDY[521]

Technology licensing is one of several types of technology transfer agreements concluded by the national laboratories operated and owned by the DOE in the US.

These federal laboratories perform collaborative research with educational research institutions, which are either privately or publicly funded, and include universities, state or local government, non-profit organisations as well as privately funded laboratories.[522]

This programme of collaborative research is governed by federal law. Since the early 1980s, the US Congress has introduced several bodies of legislation governing the transfer of technology programme.

One of the foundational pieces of legislation governing this programme is the Stevenson-Wydler Technology Innovation Act of 1980.[523] This Act highlights the primacy of technology transfer noting this objective as a federal priority.[524] In turn it calls for the establishment of an office of research and technology applications by the federal laboratories and the allocation of funding and resources to the promotion of technological collaboration and to the transfer of technologies.[525]

A further relevant item of legislation from 1980 is the Bayh-Dole Act.[526] This Act which promotes the utilisation of federal technologies and the generation of profits from the same places an obligation on federal agencies to ensure 'the right to elect title to new inventions made under their federal funding agreements' to outside concerns notably SMEs, educational institutions and not-for-profit organisations.[527]

Once technology is developed by one of the national laboratory of the DOE and the office of research and technology applications at the relevant laboratory (referred to as the technology transfer office) deems the technology in question to be of a commercial value, the technology transfer office assumes responsibility for applying for patents and different forms of legal protection pertaining to the technology generated,[528] for promoting this technology to prospective licensees[529] and for ultimately licensing the technology in question to the external entity or entities (if the agreement is not exclusive).

The licensee(s) will take charge of commercialising the licensed technology by assuming responsibility for the production, marketing, distribution and sale of products developed using the licensed technology.[530]

521. This case study is based on one set out in GAO Report 2009, 4-7.
522. GAO Report 2009, 2.
523. GAO Report 2009, 4.
524. GAO Report 2009, 4.
525. GAO Report 2009, 4.
526. GAO Report 2009, 4.
527. GAO Report 2009, 5. Other relevant items of federal legislation governing technology transfer rules as they pertain to the DOE include the Atomic Energy Act of 1954 and the Federal Nonnuclear Energy Research and Development Act of 1974.
528. GAO Report 2009, 6.
529. GAO Report 2009, 6.
530. GAO Report 2009, 6.

In exchange for this grant of rights in the intellectual property, a licensing fee and royalties are payable to the laboratory.[531] On occasion the licensee will assume responsibility for further research and development in a bid to ensure that the product produced using the licensed technology is marketable.[532]

531. GAO Report 2009, 6.
532. GAO Report 2009, 7.

CHAPTER 7

International Dispute Resolution*

§7.01 INTRODUCTION

International trade and cross-border investment have increased considerably since the end of World War II, bringing about an increase in the volume of multijurisdictional commercial disputes.[1] As such due consideration should be given by contracting parties to the inclusion of provisions addressing dispute resolution in turn articulating the procedure that will be used to resolve disputes between them, and the substantive elements of their dispute resolution infrastructure.

When looking to resolve a dispute, the parties may first consider attempting an out-of-court settlement with or without the assistance of their respective lawyers. At first, the parties are likely to try to resolve matters between them by means of negotiation which is especially important when a long-term relationship is at stake which the parties are keen to salvage. The process of negotiation is advantageous since it permits the parties to control both the format of the negotiation and the solution found.

If such negotiations prove futile, the parties may decide to resort to one or more alternative mechanisms to resolve their differences. In situations where the contracting parties decide to opt for an extrajudicial structure to resolve their dispute, they should take time to define with clarity in their contract the role of the extrajudicial entity or person. In other words, they should decide whether this third party will be endowed with the power to impose a decision on them, and determine issues in a definitive manner (*definitive determination*) or whether the third party will be allocated the role

* The authors owe a debt of gratitude to Professor Dr. Peter Mankowski of Universitat Hamburg who took the time to review this draft chapter, providing us with insightful and comprehensive recommendations as well as extensive feedback on the content and layout of the draft chapter. Any omissions are the sole responsibility of the authors.

1. Born, Gary, International Arbitration and Forum Selection Agreements: Drafting and Enforcing (3rd ed. Wolters Kluwer 2010), 1.

of helping the contracting parties reach a resolution of their dispute (*agreement-based resolution*).

As a last resort one of the parties may decide to take the matter to a court of law for adjudication on the dispute.

This chapter looks at the key issues that contracting parties must address when negotiating the clauses addressing resolution of international disputes.

§7.02 ALTERNATIVE DISPUTE RESOLUTION

[A] What Does This Term Mean?

Alternative Dispute Resolution (ADR) is a term with a variety of meanings. In Europe and most of the world this term is taken to encompass all dispute resolution mechanisms save for litigation and arbitration.[2] In the US, in contrast, this term is wider in scope encompassing all mechanisms of dispute resolution except litigation.[3]

On occasion ADR may not just be optional but rather an obligation under the contract or by virtue of the operation of the law. Extrajudicial mechanisms are not only used in the commercial context but also in the context of consumer disputes,[4] community disputes,[5] divorce,[6] parent-child disputes,[7] intra-institutional disputes, and the claims by citizens against public institutions.[8]

Extrajudicial mechanisms may be either independent of the court structure or affiliated with this structure. Court-annexed mechanisms were developed in response to the growing popularity of ADR.[9]

ADR has four often overlapping goals.[10] First, the need to relieve congestion in the courts as well as the associated costs and delays that such congestion generates.[11] Second, the need to increase community involvement in the resolution of disputes.[12]

2. Margaret L. Moses, *The Principles and Practice of International Commercial Arbitration* (2nd edn, Cambridge University Press) (Kindle edition): 14 (hereafter Moses 2012).
3. Moses 2012: 14.
4. Frank Sander, 'Alternative Methods of Dispute Resolution: An Overview', (1985) 37 University of Florida Law Review 1, 5 (hereafter Sander 1985).
5. Disputants looking to resolve present disputes, and to prevent future conflicts often opt for mediation over adjudication so that they are better able to settle their problems jointly. Free standing or court affiliated neighbourhood justice centres developed in the 1970s and 1980s to handle disputes. These centres handle two categories of disputes. Those disputes referred to it by the courts, the police, the prosecutor or community agencies. Those disputes involving disputants that come into the centres on a walk in basis (Sanders 1985:1).
6. In 1981, California became the first state in the United States to introduce a system requiring mandatory mediation in cases involving disputes over child custody (Sander 1985: 7).
7. Sander 1985: 7.
8. Sander 1985: 7.
9. Sander 1985: 8.
10. Sander 1985: 3.
11. Sander 1985: 3.
12. Sander 1985: 3.

Third, the need to improve access to justice generally.[13] Finally the need to offer disputing parties more effective dispute resolution mechanisms.[14]

[B] Definitive Determination Mechanisms[15]

The first category of mechanisms consists of those that impose decisions and determine issues in a definitive manner.[16] These mechanisms allow a third party to impose a decision on the parties; so once the parties agree on such a mechanism they are not permitted to unilaterally withdraw from this process.[17]

Definitive determination mechanisms include expert determination, adjudication, rent-a-judge (also known as private judging), baseball arbitration (also known as final arbitration, last offer arbitration, or pendulum arbitration).

[1] Expert Determination

This mechanism allows for the referral of a dispute to an independent third party whose role it is to resolve the dispute or aspects of the dispute using their expertise. Such a method is useful where the issues involved require the application of certain specific expertise which may occur when the dispute involves IP, accounting, and technical matters.

This set-up may be faster, and cheaper than arbitration as the expert may be able to carry out their own investigations without relying on or having to wait for information from the parties.[18]

[2] Adjudication

This mechanism provides for a binding, though not necessarily final, resolution of disputes.[19] The decision made on adjudication may not necessarily represent the final resolution of the dispute as the parties may have reserved themselves the right to have the matter re-heard in its entirety.[20] Where the matter is reheard the arbiter will not be bound by the decision of the adjudicator.[21]

Adjudication provides for the resolution of disputes in an expedited fashion.[22] Though intended as an interim mechanism of dispute resolution, oftentimes decisions

13. Sander 1985: 3.
14. Sander 1985: 3.
15. Julian D. M. Lew, Loukas A. Misterlis, and Stefan Michael Kröll, *Comparative International Arbitration* (Kluwer Law International 2003), 9-10 (hereafter Lew 2003).
16. Lew 2003: 9-10.
17. Lew 2003: 9-10.
18. Lew 2003:10.
19. Lew 2003:12.
20. Lew 2003: 12.
21. Lew 2003:12.
22. Lew 2003: 12.

made under the auspices of adjudication result in the disposal of disputes without further proceedings.[23]

[3] Rent a Judge (Private Judging)

This court-annexed or private dispute resolution method involves a referral of cases to neutral third parties for formal trials.[24] The parties to which these matters are referred are typically retired members of the judiciary.[25] The procedures used in this context will be similar to those used in a common court trial.[26] Once made the decision will be referred to the competent court and will be viewed as the decision of this court.[27] The right of appeal will be identical to that applicable to a common court judgment.[28]

[4] Baseball Arbitration (Final or Last Offer or Pendulum Arbitration)

The arbitrators involved in this procedure are be bound by the parties' perceptions and assessments.[29] Once the matter is submitted to the arbitral panel each party will provide the panel with its best offer leaving the panel to select the offer that is nearest to its assessment.[30]

The panel is obliged to choose between the proposals[31] and will not replace this offer with its own evaluation, this procedure in turn forces the disputing parties to assess the strength of their respective claims in a realistic manner.[32]

[C] Agreement-Based Resolution Mechanisms[33]

The second category of mechanisms includes those that provide the parties with the infrastructure needed to allow them to reach an agreed solution or settlement. Negotiation, mini-trial, mediation, conciliation, early neutral evaluation and expert evaluation are all illustrations of this second category.

[1] Negotiation

Negotiation between the parties with or without their advisors, or between the parties' advisors represents the easiest, cheapest and most flexible method of resolving

23. Lew 2003: 12.
24. Lew 2003: 12.
25. Lew 2003: 12.
26. Lew 2003: 12-3.
27. Lew 2003: 13.
28. Lew 2003: 13.
29. Lew 2003: 13.
30. Lew 2003: 13.
31. Moses 2012: 16.
32. Lew 2003: 13.
33. Lew 2003: 9-10.

differences.[34] The process is informal and party-directed reflecting the concerns of the parties themselves.[35] The parties will control location, timing, agenda, participants and so forth.[36] Personal differences, entrenched positions, insufficient communication, the fear of losing face are all reasons why a negotiation may fail.[37]

[2] Mini-trial[38]

In a mini-trial a panel is assembled comprising a neutral decision-maker, and one executive from each entity involved in the dispute, where these executives will have the authority to make decisions on behalf of the respective entities they represent.[39]

To ensure neutrality these executives should not be personally involved in the circumstances that led to the dispute.[40]

In the course of the mini-trial, each party will present its case and supporting evidence before the panel retires in a bid to reach a settlement.[41] The proceedings, which typically last for one to two days, are confidential and non-binding and their goal is to provide the high-level executives with the opportunity to resolve the dispute.[42]

Pioneered in the US by Telecredit and TRW in order to resolve a long-standing dispute between the two entities.[43] After three years of unsuccessful litigation, the parties agreed to a non-binding arbitration involving executives from both corporations, and a former judge (Judge James Davis).[44] Thirty minutes into the proceedings the matter had been settled.[45]

[3] Mediation[46]

Mediation is a process that is commonly used in the context of disputes, and occasionally in the context of negotiations[47] whereby a third person or persons are approached by the parties to assist in the settlement of their dispute or to facilitate the negotiation of their contract.

34. Lew 2003: 13.
35. Lew 2003: 13.
36. Lew 2003: 13.
37. Lew 2003: 13.
38. Sander 1985: 11.
39. Moses 2012: 16.
40. Moses 2012: 16.
41. Moses 2012: 16.
42. Moses 2012: 16.
43. Green, Recent Developments in Alternative Forms of Dispute Resolutions, 100 F.R.D 512, 514–516 (1983).
44. Green, Recent Developments in Alternative Forms of Dispute Resolutions, 100 F.R.D 512, 514–516 (1983).
45. Green, Recent Developments in Alternative Forms of Dispute Resolutions, 100 F.R.D 512, 514–516 (1983).
46. The distinction between mediation and conciliation on the one hand, and arbitration on the other is discussed in detail in Fouchard, Gaillard, and Goldman on International Commercial Arbitration, Gaillard, Emmanuel, and Savage, John (eds) (Kluwer Law International, 1999), 15-6.
47. Moses 2012: 14.

The role of the mediator is to help the parties reach common ground in order to resolve the dispute or conclude the contract, by helping each party understand the viewpoint of the other.[48] In this context the mediator will meet in private with each of the parties in order to explore their concerns, interests, priorities, and objectives.[49]

The process itself is typically confidential so that any matters discussed during the course of the mediation cannot be referred to at a later stage.[50] If the rules selected do not provide for this, a provision should be included in writing in the agreement drawn up by the parties.[51]

Mediation and conciliation procedures are occasionally referred to as formalised negotiations;[52] whilst these procedures involve negotiations between the parties facilitated by a neutral third party, any settlements reached by the parties must be reached voluntarily as the neutral third party does not have the authority to impose a decision on the parties.[53]

Where a settlement is reached under the auspices of mediation, it must generally be put into writing to be binding.[54] Until such a time as the agreement is enforceable, either party may change its mind, with anything discussed or disclosed during the course of the mediation remaining confidential.[55]

[4] Conciliation

Conciliation is defined by the UNCITRAL as 'a process, whether referred to by the expression conciliation, mediation or an expression of similar import, whereby parties request a third person or persons ("the conciliator") to assist them in their attempt to reach an amicable settlement of their dispute arising out of or relating to a contractual or other legal relationship. The conciliator does not have the authority to impose upon the parties a solution to the dispute'.[56,57]

In multiparty disputes involving interests and issues that are complex, conciliation may be a suitable way of resolving certain issues if not the dispute itself.[58]

A good example of a situation where conciliation has been used as a way of avoiding complex and drawn-out litigation is the insolvency scenario where the competing needs and the conflicting interests of the different classes of creditors and the different creditors themselves as well as the debtors make it hard to find a suitable

48. Moses 2012: 14.
49. Moses 2012: 14.
50. Moses 2012: 14.
51. Moses 2012: 14.
52. Jeffrey Dasteel, *International Commercial Arbitration for Law Students* (2014, published by author) (Kindle edition), 2.10 (hereafter Dasteel 2014).
53. Dasteel 2014: 2.10.
54. Dasteel 2014: 2.10.
55. Martin Mendelsohn, *The Guide to Franchising* (7th edn, Thomson Learning 2004), 198 (hereafter Mendelsohn 2004).
56. Article 1(3), UNCITRAL Model Law on International Commercial Conciliation (2002).
57. Article 1(3) and para 5, Guide to Enactment and Use of the UNCITRAL Model Law on International Commercial Conciliation (2002).
58. Article 1(3) and para 5, Guide to Enactment and Use of the UNCITRAL Model Law on International Commercial Conciliation (2002).

solution for all the parties.[59] These varying and competing interests and needs will draw out an attempt to resolve the matters by negotiation between the parties themselves with or without the help of the insolvency practitioner or lawyers, or adjudication.[60]

Conciliation is distinct from the process of negotiation between the parties, as instead of attempting to handle the dispute alone, the parties approach the conciliator, as an independent third party, to assist them in resolution of their dispute.[61]

In contrast with the process of arbitration, where the parties entrust resolution of the dispute and the outcome of the dispute to an arbitral tribunal that imposes a binding decision on the parties, the conciliator, in response to an approach by the parties, provides independent, and impartial assistance to the parties, in a bid to help the parties *themselves* resolve their dispute.[62]

Another reason, this process differs from arbitration, is the fact that conciliation is a non-adjudicatory process in which the parties retain control over the process, and its outcome.[63] Unlike the arbitration process, the conciliator lacks the authority to impose a solution upon the parties themselves.[64] The role of the conciliator in the conciliation process is to help the parties negotiate a settlement that will meet their needs and interests.[65]

Any information disclosed during the course of the conciliation is confidential, unless disclosure is mandated by law or is required for the purposes of implementation or enforcement of a settlement agreement.[66]

Though the parties to a conciliation retain the right to resort to arbitral or judicial proceedings, where the parties agree in relation to an existing dispute or a future one to conciliate, and have expressly agreed not to initiate such proceedings during a set period of time or until a specific event arises, their undertaking is upheld by the arbitral tribunal or the court until such a time as the terms of the undertaking have been complied with.[67]

A settlement agreement reached by the parties to a conciliation may be binding, and enforceable subject to the rules in the jurisdiction of enforcement.[68]

---

59. Article 1(3) and para 5, Guide to Enactment and Use of the UNCITRAL Model Law on International Commercial Conciliation (2002).
60. Article 1(3) and para 5, Guide to Enactment and Use of the UNCITRAL Model Law on International Commercial Conciliation (2002).
61. Article 1(3) and para 5, Guide to Enactment and Use of the UNCITRAL Model Law on International Commercial Conciliation (2002).
62. Article 1(3) and para 5, Guide to Enactment and Use of the UNCITRAL Model Law on International Commercial Conciliation (2002).
63. UNCITRAL Model Law on International Commercial Conciliation (2002), Part 2 Guide to Enactment and Use of the UNCITRAL Model Law on International Commercial Conciliation (2002), para 6.
64. Article 1(3), UNCITRAL Model Law on International Commercial Conciliation (2002).
65. UNCITRAL Model Law on International Commercial Conciliation (2002), Part 2 Guide to Enactment and Use of the UNCITRAL Model Law on International Commercial Conciliation (2002), para 6.
66. Article 9, UNCITRAL Model Law on International Commercial Conciliation (2002).
67. Article 13, UNCITRAL Model Law on International Commercial Conciliation (2002).
68. Article 14, UNCITRAL Model Law on International Commercial Conciliation (2002).

[5] Neutral Evaluation

This mechanism entails the appointment of a neutral party by the parties themselves or the institution selected by the parties to listen to each party and provide a non-binding determination in relation to an issue of fact or law or a technical matter.[69] Typically the neutral party will help the parties themselves evaluate their claims enabling them to adopt a more realistic about their claims.[70]

[6] Expert Determination

Expert determination is known in Germany as *schiedsgutachten* (expert arbitration), in France as *expertise amiable*, in Belgium as *tiere decision-amiable*, and in Italy as *perizia contrattual*.[71]

In technical cases, the parties may agree that an expert be appointed to determine certain technical aspects of their case.[72] The determination of the expert is generally binding, though the parties may agree to use an expert under rules that permit a non-binding opinion.[73] The expert's report may be admissible in any judicial or arbitral proceedings, unless the parties agree otherwise.[74]

In Germany, this mechanism is wide in scope encompassing the establishment of a fact, the determination of a disputed aspect of the legal relationship (e.g., damages or the liability of a party), as well as the definition of the components of an incomplete legal relationship.[75]

§7.03 CONTRACTUAL CONSIDERATIONS ASSOCIATED WITH ADR[76]

Where ADR is an obligation under the contract and one party issues without exhausting the procedure set out in the contract, the non-defaulting party may apply to court to halt the litigation pending resolution of the dispute by means of ADR.[77]

Occasionally the parties contracting will agree on alternative dispute resolution provisions that provide for more than two levels or tiers of ADR. Such provisions are alternately known as multi-tiered dispute resolution clauses or escalation clauses. Where the contracting parties opt to use such clauses they are required to reach a

69. Moses 2012: 15.
70. Moses 2012: 15.
71. Jean-François Poudret and Sébastien Besson, *Comparative Law of International Arbitration* (Sweet & Maxwell Ltd 2007), 14.
72. Moses 2012: 15.
73. Moses 2012: 15, citing ICC Rules of Expertise, Article 12(3). This Article states that the findings of the expert, unless otherwise agreed upon by the parties, are not binding on the parties.
74. ICC Rules of Expertise, Article 12(4).
75. Jean-François Poudret and Sébastien Besson, *Comparative Law of International Arbitration* (Sweet & Maxwell Ltd 2007), 14.
76. Klaus Peter Berger, *Private Dispute Resolution in International Business – Negotiation, Mediation, Arbitration* (Kluwer Law International), 48.
77. UNCITRAL 1958 Convention on the Recognition and Enforcement of Arbitral Awards, aka NY Convention.

settlement of their disputes by going through the different consecutive steps that they agreed upon.[78] Such provisions aim to 'filter' out all or specific aspects of the disagreement narrowing down the scope of disagreement using a multi-tiered dispute resolution mechanism. Commonly this process commences with negotiations proceeding through mediation or other types of ADR structures terminating with arbitration or litigation before national courts. The question of whether each of the tiers 'is a condition precedent to proceeding to the next tier' is a matter of construction.[79]

Certain contracts may specify that the parties continue in the performance of their contract even if a dispute should arise.

§7.04 ARBITRATION

[A] Arbitration Defined[80]

Arbitration ranks first as dispute resolution mechanism in commercial cases.[81] Amongst the other dispute resolution mechanisms used, commercial litigation is in second place and mediation in third.[82] The popularity of arbitration varies from sector to sector with a higher take-up rate in the energy and construction sectors.[83]

Various definitions are available for the term 'arbitration'.[84] These different definitions attempt to define arbitration in a manner that reflects 'the evolving general understanding and essential legal forms of arbitration'.[85] One such definition is the one provided by Professor René David who defines arbitration as 'a device whereby the settlement of a question, which is of interest for two or more persons, is entrusted to one or more other persons – the arbitrator or arbitrators – who derive their powers from

78. Jean-François Poudret and Sébastien Besson, *Comparative Law of International Arbitration* (Sweet & Maxwell Ltd 2007), Preface.
79. Susan Blake, Julie Browne and Stuart Sime, *A Practical Approach to Alternative Dispute Resolution* (3rd edn, Oxford University Press 2014) 426.
80. The definition of the term 'arbitration' is discussed in detail in Chapter 1, Fouchard 1999.
81. 52% of the respondents to the survey carried out note arbitration as their preferred dispute resolution mechanism, according to the PWC International Arbitration Study entitled Corporate Choices in International Arbitration – Industry Perspectives (2013), page 6 accessible at at http://www.pwc.com/gx/en/arbitration-dispute-resolution/assets/pwc-international-arbitration-study.pdf (last accessed February 2015) (PWC 2013 Report).
82. 28% of the respondents to the survey note that litigation is their preferred dispute resolution mechanism, and 18% note mediation. (PWC 2013 Report, 6).
83. Arbitration is the most popular dispute resolution mechanism amongst respondents in the Energy (56% of respondents opt for this mechanism versus 22% who opt for litigation; whilst adjudication and mediation are favoured by 17% and 5% of respondents respectively) and the Construction sectors (68% of respondents opt for arbitration versus mediation and litigation favoured by 22% and 11% of respondents respectively). (PWC 2013 Report, 7).
84. Definitions of the term 'arbitration' are provided in Shorter Oxford English Dictionary (3rd edition, 1969); Saunders (ed), Words and Phrases Legally Defined (3rd ed, Butterworths 1988), 105; Domke, Arbitration, 1; Halsbury' Laws of England (4th ed, Butterworths 1991), para 601, 332; Rene David, *Arbitration in International Trade* (Springer Netherlands 1985), 5.
85. Lew et al, 2.

a private agreement, not from the authorities of a State, and who are to proceed and decide the case on the basis of such an agreement'.[86]

[1] Rules Governing Arbitration

The public sources of rules governing arbitrations can be found in national and international law.[87] In addition to these public sources, certain opt-in rules have also been formulated. These rules are optional in so far as they are 'simply recommended to, rather than imposed upon, potential users'.[88] These optional rules do however play an important role, alongside the traditional bilateral treaties and multilateral treaties governing arbitration.[89]

These opt-in rules include the rules of the institutions offering arbitration services, as well as the UNCITRAL (United Nations' Commission on International Trade Law) Arbitration Rules (last revised in 2010).[90] Opt-in arbitration rules have been drawn up by the likes of the International Chamber of Commerce (ICC),[91] LCIA (London Court of International Arbitration),[92] AAA (American Arbitration Association)[93] and ICDR (International Centre for Dispute Resolution).[94]

To assist nations in the formulation of domestic substantive law governing arbitrations, the UNCITRAL has also issued draft rules - in its Model Law on International Commercial Arbitration 1985 (as amended in 2006)[95] (Model Law 2006) - that can be incorporated into substantive domestic law. The provisions of the Model

86. Rene David, *Arbitration in International Trade* (Springer Netherlands 1985), 5.
87. For a discussion of these rules, *see* Chapter 2, Fouchard 1999.
88. Fouchard 1999: 103-104.
89. Fouchard 1999: 104.
90. UNCITRAL Arbitration Rules (as revised in 2010). These can be accessed at https://www.uncitral.org/pdf/english/texts/arbitration/arb-rules-revised/arb-rules-revised-2010-e.pdf (last accessed 26/5/18).
91. At the time of writing, the latest version of the ICC's Arbitration Rules came into effect on 1 March 2017. A copy of these Rules is available at https://cdn.iccwbo.org/content/uploads/sites/3/2017/01/ICC-2017-Arbitration-and-2014-Mediation-Rules-english-version.pdf.pdf (last accessed 26/5/18).
92. At the time of writing, the latest version of the LCIA's Arbitration Rules came into effect on 1 October 2014. A copy of these Rules is available at http://www.lcia.org//Dispute_Resolution_Services/lcia-arbitration-rules-2014.aspx (last accessed 26/5/18).
93. At the time of writing, the latest version of the AAA's Commercial Arbitration Rules and Mediation Procedures came into effect on 1 October 2013 (the amended Fee Schedule became effective 1 July 2016). A copy of these Rules is available at https://www.adr.org/sites/default/files/Commercial%20Rules.pdf (last accessed 26/5/18).
94. The latest version of the ICDR's rules, at the time of writing, is entitled International Dispute Resolution Procedures (including Mediation and Arbitration Rules) which came into effect on 1 June 2014. A copy of these Rules can be found at https://www.icdr.org/sites/default/files/document_repository/ICDR_Rules.pdf (last accessed 25/5/18).
95. UNCITRAL Model Law on International Commercial Arbitration 1985 (with amendments as adopted in 2006) (UNCITRAL Model Law 2006) accessible at https://www.uncitral.org/pdf/english/texts/arbitration/ml-arb/07-86998_Ebook.pdf (last accessed 26/5/18).

Law 2006 are intended for use by nations formulating arbitration rules, or revising existing rules governing arbitration.

Originally issued on 21 June 1985 and revised on 7 June 2006,[96] the Model Law 2006 covers all stages of the arbitration process from the agreement to arbitrate to the recognition and enforcement of arbitral awards.[97] Reflecting 'a worldwide consensus on the principles and important issues of international arbitration practice',[98] this body of rules is intended to act as a 'vehicle for harmonisation and modernisation',[99] addressing the considerable disparties in the national laws governing arbitrations and the need for improvement to existing laws to ensure that these are tailored to international cases.[100] The UNCITRAL suggests that use of these rules in national law will help enhance 'the confidence of foreign parties, as the primary users of international arbitration, in the reliability of arbitration law in the enacting State'.[101]

[B] Arbitration: Its Features

The arbitration process is typified by four key features.[102] First, it is private mechanism for the resolution of disputes.[103] Second, this forum serves as an alternative to the national court system.[104] Third, this structure is one that is chosen by the contracting parties and administered by them.[105] Finally, it typically offers a procedure which is final and binding upon the contracting parties determining their rights, and obligations.[106]

96. Paragraph 1, Explanatory Note by the UNCITRAL secretariat on the 1985 Model Law on International Commercial Arbitration as amended in 2006 accessible at https://www.uncitral.org/pdf/english/texts/arbitration/ml-arb/07-86998_Ebook.pdf (last accessed 26/5/18).
97. Paragraph 2, Explanatory Note by the UNCITRAL secretariat on the 1985 Model Law on International Commercial Arbitration as amended in 2006 accessible at https://www.uncitral.org/pdf/english/texts/arbitration/ml-arb/07-86998_Ebook.pdf (last accessed 26/5/18).
98. Paragraph 2, Explanatory Note by the UNCITRAL secretariat on the 1985 Model Law on International Commercial Arbitration as amended in 2006 accessible at https://www.uncitral.org/pdf/english/texts/arbitration/ml-arb/07-86998_Ebook.pdf (last accessed 26/5/18).
99. Paragraph 3, Explanatory Note by the UNCITRAL secretariat on the 1985 Model Law on International Commercial Arbitration as amended in 2006 accessible at https://www.uncitral.org/pdf/english/texts/arbitration/ml-arb/07-86998_Ebook.pdf (last accessed 26/5/18).
100. Paragraph 5, Explanatory Note by the UNCITRAL secretariat on the 1985 Model Law on International Commercial Arbitration as amended in 2006 accessible at https://www.uncitral.org/pdf/english/texts/arbitration/ml-arb/07-86998_Ebook.pdf (last accessed 26/5/18).
101. Paragraph 3, Explanatory Note by the UNCITRAL secretariat on the 1985 Model Law on International Commercial Arbitration as amended in 2006 accessible at https://www.uncitral.org/pdf/english/texts/arbitration/ml-arb/07-86998_Ebook.pdf (last accessed 26/5/18).
102. Lew 2003: 4.
103. Lew 2003: 4.
104. Lew 2003: 4.
105. Lew 2003: 4.
106. Lew 2003: 4.

[1] Feature One: An Alternative to the National Court System

Whilst the court system is perhaps the traditional forum used to resolve mainstream disputes, arbitration as a structure offers parties to a dispute an alternative, extrajudicial forum for the resolution of their differences.[107]

Courts are established, controlled and administered by the state for a variety of ends including the resolution of disputes between private parties.[108] The state in this context is responsible for ensuring that the court system exists and is properly administered.[109] In contrast with the court system, arbitrators are non-governmental decision-makers, as such they do not act as representatives of the state.[110]

In international transactions, differences in language, culture and legal traditions pose as concerns to the contracting parties, coupled with the potential exposure of national courts to political, media, and popular pressures.[111]

International arbitration 'is intended to be neutral, in that it usually seeks to provide a dispute resolution mechanism that takes place outside either party's home jurisdiction and judicial system, and that adopts no nation's litigation procedures'.[112] As arbitration is not affiliated with the national court system, when the parties agree to arbitrate they are effectively removing their relationship and disputes associated with this relationship from the national courts.[113]

[2] Feature Two: A Private Dispute Resolution Mechanism

Arbitration is generally a private forum, whereas the courts are public structures.[114]

When a dispute arises between the parties and they opt for arbitration as the forum for the resolution of their dispute, the dispute itself will be resolved to a large extent in private, subject to certain safeguards.[115]

[3] Feature Three: Selected and Administered by the Parties Themselves

The agreement to arbitrate 'is ordinarily consensual as the parties themselves agree to arbitrate their differences'.[116] The power of an arbitrator 'to resolve a dispute is founded upon the common intention of the parties to that dispute'.[117]

107. Lew 2003: 4.
108. Lew 2003: 4.
109. Lew 2003: 4.
110. Born 2010: 2.
111. Born 2010: 2.
112. Born 2010: 2.
113. Lew 2003: 4.
114. Lew 2003: 4.
115. Lew 2003: 4.
116. Born 2010: 2.
117. Fouchard 1999: 29.

Beyond the choice to arbitrate, the parties themselves enjoy significant procedural flexibility,[118] determining not only the general format of the arbitration (ad hoc or institutional), but also *inter alia* the rules governing the arbitration process itself and the law used by the arbitrator/s.[119]

This flexibility enables the parties to select or tailor the process to their specific needs, transaction and industry.[120]

In most jurisdictions, national law will only seek to give effect to, supplement and support the parties' agreement, acting as a facilitator rather than looking to intervene with the parties' choice.[121] In certain circumstances, for example, where the parties are silent on certain issues, national law may provide default provisions.[122]

These procedures are commonly adjudicative allowing each contracting party to present evidence and be heard in accordance with quasi-judicial procedures.[123]

[4] Feature Four: Final and Binding

When the parties agree to arbitrate as a result of their contractual commitment and the impact of national law, they will effectively be agreeing to be bound by the arbitral award and the procedural rules of the arbitration body they select, as well as forfeiting their right to appeal to a national court.[124] The arbitration will produce a definitive and binding award rather than merely a precatory recommendation.[125] One of the key features of international commercial arbitration is 'the absence of appellate review of arbitral awards'.[126] Review of arbitral awards in most developed nations is typically limited to questions of procedural fairness, concerns about jurisdiction and public policy considerations.[127] Dispensing with appellate review helps reduce litigation costs whilst preventing delays.[128] This feature, on the other hand, also means that 'wildly eccentric or simply wrong' awards are not open to challenge.[129] Though the risk of this occurring may be mitigated by mandating for a three-person arbitral tribunal to resolve disputes.[130]

118. Born 2010: 2.
119. Lew 2003: 4.
120. Born 2010: 2.
121. Lew 2003: 4.
122. Lew 2003: 4.
123. Born 2010: 2.
124. Lew 2003: 4.
125. Born 2010: 2.
126. Born 2010: 6.
127. Born 2010: 6.
128. Born 2010: 6.
129. Born 2010: 6.
130. Born 2010: 6.

[C] Why Arbitrate?

Arbitration clauses are popular in many international commercial agreements. According to PWC International Arbitration Study 2006,[131] the advantages associated with arbitration include (in order of importance) the enforceability of the award (29% of respondents), privacy (21%), being able take part in the constitution of the arbitral panel (20%) and the flexibility of the procedure (13%).[132] Other advantages identified by the respondents (17% of the respondents) include cost, speed, possibility of avoiding specific legal systems, and the neutrality of the process.[133]

Many view international arbitration as the most effective method of ensuring industrial and business processes, trade secrets, IP, and the existence of the proceedings are kept confidential.[134]

Many benefits are associated with arbitration including[135] its suitability to international transactions, its perceived neutrality, its apparent flexibility, its finality, the enforceability of arbitral awards, the autonomy enjoyed by the contracting parties, the speed, privacy and informality of the procedure.

[1] Reason One: Suitability to International Transactions

National courts may have little experience adjudicating over international commercial disputes.[136] Moreover such courts may lack the correct infrastructure to handle matters of a cross-border nature, as they inevitably apply local procedural rules to such disputes which may be unsuitable when parties come from different legal traditions.[137] Language may also result in misunderstandings when evidence and legal authorities need to be translated into the language of the forum.[138]

Even the most perfect of translations may be insufficient to ward against misunderstandings. Some matters may be lost in translation, especially when the judges adjudicating the matter are unfamiliar with the legal nuances associated with the substantive law governing the contractual relationship, the different backgrounds of the parties and witnesses and the language of the contract.

Arbitration bodies do not belong to any national system and are accordingly attractive to parties drawn from different jurisdictions.[139] One party to a dispute may not wish to submit to the national courts of the other party due to a fear of bias, as such the neutrality and the independence of the arbitration process are its key attractions.[140]

---

131. PWC International Arbitration Study (2006) accessible at http://www.pwc.be/en_BE/be/publications/ia-study-pwc-06.pdf (last accessed February 2015) (PWC 2006 Report).
132. PWC 2006 Report, 6.
133. PWC 2006 Report, 6.
134. PWC 2006 Report, 6.
135. Lew 2003: 6.
136. Born 2010: 8.
137. Born 2010: 8.
138. Born 2010: 8.
139. Lew 2003: 5.
140. Lew 2003: 6.

Beyond the fact that judges are drawn from that specific nationality and do not necessarily possess the requisite expertise needed to handle cross-border disputes, the procedures used by national courts are generally considered to be fairly rigid when compared to the procedures used in arbitration tribunals.[141] Arbitrations in contrast offer international character. With arbitrators drawn from different backgrounds and possessing technical and business expertise, as well as a familiarity with cross-border disputes.[142] In addition, arbitrations are conducted under distinct legal systems, using different arbitration rules.[143]

[2] Reason Two: Flexibility

Arbitrations offer flexibility due to the private nature of the arbitration.[144] As such the parties are free to fix the procedures and select their arbitrators taking into account their specific requirements.

Major international arbitration rules allow the parties and the arbitrators to determine the procedure that they consider appropriate.[145]

Parties also have the freedom to balance the tribunal by selecting a panel made up of arbitrators with pertinent expertise and complementary knowledge.[146] Arbitrators will be selected based on whether they possess the expertise necessary to consider and resolve the dispute,[147] which is crucial when the dispute involves specialised commodities (chemicals compounds, pharmaceutical products for example) or services (construction etc). In addition, the selection of arbitrators will be motivated by their understanding of the issues at hand,[148] their background, language skills and experience.[149]

[3] Reason Three: Finality of Decisions

The finality of decisions made by arbitration bodies is a crucial benefit associated with arbitrations. In limited circumstances the parties may look to set aside or vary an award in the courts based on a procedural irregularity.[150]

141. Lew 2003: 5.
142. Lew 2003: 5-6.
143. Lew 2003: 5-6.
144. Lew 2003: 5-6.
145. Article 14(2), LCIA Arbitration Rules (2014); Article 37(a), WIPO Arbitration Rules (effective from 1 June 2014).
146. Lew 2003: 5-6.
147. Lew 2003: 5-6.
148. Lew 2003: 5-6.
149. Lew 2003: 5-6.
150. Walker 2012: 1-02.

[4] Reason Four: Enforceability of Awards

Recognition and enforcement of arbitral awards are provided for in the New York Convention[151] and in turn in the countries that have ratified the Convention.[152] This Convention is virtually worldwide in its adoption.[153] Roughly 80% of awards are voluntarily complied with.[154]

[5] Reason Five: Speed and Cost

Relative to national court proceedings arbitration proceedings are generally faster. Arbitrators are obliged to ensure that there are no unnecessary delays in the conduct of arbitration, pursuant to §33(1)b Arbitration Act 1996,[155] and Articles 24(1) and 30(1) ICC Rules.[156,157]

A final arbitral award will typically be made in an international commercial arbitration within an 18-36 month period.[158] Challenges to arbitrators, litigation over jurisdiction and difficulties timetabling arbitrators and counsel can all hold up the arbitration process,[159] though it is possible to expedite the arbitration process by inclusion of a 'fast track' arbitration clause.[160]

Arguably this speed should render the process cheaper when compared to litigation in national court.[161] In practice, however, this is not always the case as international arbitration cases may be fairly complex and involve several arbitrators which increase costs.[162] International commercial arbitration notably in substantial cases is rarely cheap when one factors in the cost of legal representation, arbitration fees (including the fees of the arbitrator/s and where applicable the institution administering the arbitration) and costs associated with logistics (hiring the room, travel and so forth).[163]

Nevertheless such costs may pale in comparison with the costs of legal representation in cases involving 'parallel or multiplicitous proceedings in national courts' which may arise when the parties are unable to agree on an exclusive forum selection

151. 1958 UNCITRAL Convention on the Recognition and Enforcement of Arbitral Awards (New York Convention).
152. The New York Convention is reviewed in detail later on in this chapter.
153. Walker 2012: 1-04.
154. Walker 2012: 1-02.
155. §33(1)b Arbitration Act 1996 Chapter 23 reads '(1) The tribunal shall ... (b) adopt procedures suitable to the circumstances of the particular case, avoiding unnecessary delay or expense, so as to provide a fair means for the resolution of the matters falling to be determined.'
156. Accessible at http://www.iccwbo.org/products-and-services/arbitration-and-adr/arbitration/icc-rules-of-arbitration/ (last accessed 25th July 2016).
157. Lew 2003: 9.
158. Born 2010: 7.
159. Born 2010: 7.
160. Born 2010: 7.
161. Lew 2003: 9.
162. Lew 2003: 9.
163. Born 2010: 7.

clause, or this clause is held to be unenforceable.[164] Costs are especially high when a matter is relitigated.[165] What is more, arbitrations do not typically involve costly discovery or many of the procedural steps involved in certain common law jurisdictions.[166]

[6] Reason Six: Privacy

Importantly the process is private, so that the fact that the matter is being arbitrated upon is confidential as is any final settlement or arbitral order made. This in turn helps protect the parties' reputation, their goodwill and brand image. Also privacy may help stem an influx of similar claims.

In contrast with national court proceedings with 'open public dockets and court proceedings', international commercial arbitrations are typically private affairs; hearings are virtually always closed to the public and press, and in practice submissions and awards are usually kept confidential.[167]

National laws do not always impose a clear duty of confidentiality on the parties to arbitrations, as such due consideration should be given to the incorporation of confidentiality provisions in the arbitration clause/agreement, and the use of non-disclosure agreements signed by the parties, their legal representatives, witnesses, and the arbitrators themselves, in the event of proceedings.[168]

[7] Reason Seven: Comparative Informality

The rules governing admissibility of evidence are generally more flexible, and proceedings are less adversarial than court proceedings.

[D] The Disadvantages of Arbitration

According to PWC International Arbitration Study 2006, the disadvantages associated with arbitration (in order of importance) are expense, the lapse of time between the date of filing (of the application), and the rendering of the award.[169]

[1] Disadvantage One: Expense

According to a survey conducted by a leading arbitrator Klaus Sachs in 2006 roughly 85% of the costs associated with the arbitration process relate to legal fees with the remaining 15% relating to institutional costs consisting of the costs of the arbitrators,

164. Born 2010: 7.
165. Born 2010: 7.
166. Born 2010: 7.
167. Born 2010: 12.
168. Born 2010: 12.
169. PWC International Arbitration Study (2006).

and the administrative expenses of the institution.[170] The hourly rate of a leading QC or a lawyer with a magic circle firm (in England) is roughly £1,000 per hour, and the hourly rate of an arbitrator is between £150 and £450 per hour.[171] With high value arbitrations typically requiring three arbitrators.[172]

The expense of arbitration consists of the costs of arbitration lawyers, arbitrators, and the arbitration institution.[173] Such costs associated with arbitrations may be placed into two distinct categories namely arbitration costs and counsel's fees.[174]

Arbitration costs consist of the fees of the arbitrator or arbitrators, the institution (where an institution is used), the expenses associated with the hearings (the cost of renting a venue, the fees of the translators, and so forth), and the costs of the experts appointed by the tribunal (their profit costs, and expenses).[175]

This is cited as a one of the three top concerns amongst 70 out of 80 respondents with 50% of respondents ranking it as their primary concern.[176]

Fifty-two per cent of the respondents indicated that the costs incurred in cross-border arbitration cases range from $100,000 to $500,000 with 12% of respondents suggesting that the costs incurred were over $5 million.[177] According to respondents in 64% of cases, the fees of counsel make up more than half the overall costs associated with an arbitration.[178]

Corporations in most common law jurisdictions and several civil law jurisdictions including Sweden, France and Italy view such costs as acceptable in view of the expertise of the arbitrators, and the overall level of service provided by the institution, and the arbitrators.[179]

[2] Disadvantage Two: Time Lapse

The time lapse from filing to award is a concern to many commercial parties.[180] According to data provided by the ICC, and the AAA/ICDR in the majority of cases the period between the filing of the claim, and the making of the award is 18 months.[181] In certain cases this time lapse (of 18 months) is far shorter than the period associated with cross-border litigation of commercial disputes.[182]

170. Walker 2012:1-06.
171. Walker 2012: 1-06.
172. Walker 2012: 1-06.
173. PWC International Arbitration Study 2006: 6.
174. PWC International Arbitration Study 2006: 19.
175. PWC International Arbitration Study 2006: 19.
176. PWC International Arbitration Study 2006: 6.
177. PWC International Arbitration Study 2006: 19.
178. PWC International Arbitration Study 2006: 19.
179. PWC International Arbitration Study 2006: 20.
180. PWC International Arbitration Study 2006: 7.
181. PWC International Arbitration Study 2006: 7.
182. PWC International Arbitration Study 2006: 7.

[3] Disadvantage Three: Likelihood of National Court Intervention

Certain jurisdictions allow international arbitrations to be conducted with no or minimal intervention by the national courts.[183] Where domestic law permits intervention, there is little that the arbitral tribunal can do to prevent this from happening.[184] For this reason the choice of seat is extremely important in arbitration agreements.[185]

[4] Disadvantage Four: Lack of an Appeal Structure

There is no international forum that has jurisdiction to handle appeals in relation to arbitral awards, though certain institutions will have internal review procedures. This is noted as a disadvantage by some of the respondents that took part in the survey conducted by PWC.[186] The writers of this survey suggest that this finding demonstrates that parties using arbitration would probably prefer an appeal infrastructure within the arbitration framework rather than using the court system to appeal a decision of the arbitrators or that such parties are increasingly willing to challenge arbitral awards.[187]

No appeals are possible on points of law or fact unless the contracting parties have reserved this right in their arbitration agreement.

[5] Disadvantage Five: Lack of a Third-Party Procedure

Another widely recognised concern highlighted by the respondents to the PWC survey is the difficulty of bring third parties into the international arbitration procedure when such entities were not party to the arbitration agreement.[188]

Whilst the arbitral tribunal has jurisdiction over the parties to the arbitration agreement, it has no power over parties linked to the transaction who are not subscribed to the arbitration agreement.

Arbitration agreements governing multi-party and multi-contract transactions are often difficult to formulate.[189] In some cases, parties to related transactions may refuse to agree to a multi-party arbitration, and in other cases, international arbitration rules may be ill-suited to deal with complex disputes.[190]

Sub-licencees, subcontractors, researchers, developers and assignees are examples of parties that could potentially be linked to a licence. For this reason, the licensor and licensee should give due consideration to the conclusion of a separate arbitration agreement reflecting the terms of the master arbitration agreement with each party connected to the licence.

183. PWC International Arbitration Study 2006: 7.
184. PWC International Arbitration Study 2006: 7.
185. PWC International Arbitration Study 2006: 7.
186. PWC International Arbitration Study 2006: 7.
187. PWC International Arbitration Study 2006: 7.
188. PWC International Arbitration Study 2006: 7.
189. Born 2010: 12.
190. Born 2010: 12.

[6] Disadvantage Six: Lack of Enforcement Mechanisms

Arbitral tribunals lack the jurisdiction to enforce awards; in order to enforce an award granted by an arbitral tribunal the winning party will need to apply to court.[191]

[7] Disadvantage Seven: Arbitral Tribunals Are Unable to Issue Subpoenas

Arbitral tribunals cannot force attendance of *inter alia* the parties, the witnesses of fact and the expert witnesses using subpoenas or similar orders compelling a person to attend a court under penalty. In order to address this the parties to an arbitration agreement should give consideration to the inclusion of a provision in their arbitration agreement allowing for an application to the court in this context.

[8] Disadvantage Eight: Lack of Default Judgment Mechanism

Generally where the respondent fails to appear, the arbitral tribunal will not grant the equivalent of default judgment. In order to address potential abuse, the parties should consider including a default mechanism in their arbitration agreement allowing the tribunal to penalise the party who fails to attend without good reason.

§7.05 DRAFTING ARBITRATION AGREEMENTS

When concluding an arbitration agreement, the parties should give due consideration to the format of their arbitration by opting for either an ad hoc arbitration or an institutional one.

An ad hoc arbitration is one without the benefit of an arbitration institution, in turn permitting the parties to devise a framework specifically suited to their unique needs and to organise and conduct the arbitration process in line with these needs.[192] The parties will accordingly agree on the procedural and substantive framework addressing *inter alia* the criteria to be used for the selection, and reappointment of arbitrators, the procedural rules that the arbitral tribunal will use, and the substantive law that will be used by the tribunal in addressing the contract, and the dispute before it.[193] An institutional arbitration is one administered by an institution set up specifically to provide an arbitration service.[194] For a fee the institution will administer the process in accordance with the rules established by the institution.[195]

191. A more detailed review can be found later on in this chapter in the context of recognition and enforcement.
192. Walker 2012: 1-05.
193. Walker 2012: 1-05.
194. Walker 2012: 1-05.
195. Walker 2012: 1-05.

Once the parties have determined the format of their arbitration, they should give due consideration to a number of general and specific issues. Amongst the general considerations that the parties should consider when negotiating, and drafting an arbitration agreement are:

- the clarity, and comprehensiveness of the agreement;
- the need for compliance with formalities in order to ensure the validity of this agreement under national or international law;[196]
- making use of template arbitration agreements;
- the need to exercise caution when adapting the institutional rules selected as such a step could result in a refusal to administer the arbitration;[197] and
- making use of the UNCITRAL Arbitration Rules[198] when opting for an ad hoc arbitration.

Parties to an ad hoc arbitration should give due consideration to the need for court intervention to resolve disagreements between them. The UNCITRAL Arbitration Rules also permit an application to be made by any one of the parties to the Secretary General of the Permanent Court of Arbitration to allocate an appointing authority, if the parties cannot agree on the appointment of an arbitrator or appointing authority.[199]

Certain specific matters should also be addressed by the parties when negotiating and drafting their arbitration agreement. Amongst the specific concerns that the parties should consider are the:

- identity of the institution chosen
- procedure for the selection of arbitrators
- seat of arbitration (locus of arbitration), and the procedural rules for the arbitration
- language of the arbitration
- substantive law
- evidential rules
- availability of interim relief
- technical expertise
- multiparty dispute resolution clause
- legal expenses
- confidentiality.

196. A more detailed review of formalities can be found later on in this chapter.
197. Yves Derains and Eric Schwartz (2005) A Guide to the ICC Rules of Arbitration, 8.
198. UNCITRAL Arbitration Rules (as revised in 2010). These can be accessed at https://www.uncitral.org/pdf/english/texts/arbitration/arb-rules-revised/arb-rules-revised-2010-e.pdf (last accessed 26/5/18).
199. Art 6(2), UNCITRAL Arbitration Rules which reads 'If all parties have not agreed on the choice of an appointing authority within 30 days after a proposal made in accordance with paragraph 1 has been received by all other parties, any party may request the Secretary-General of the PCA to designate the appointing authority.'

[A] Procedure for the Selection of Arbitrators[200]

When choosing between one or three arbitrators, certain factors should be borne in mind by the parties. The number of arbitrators selected should reflect the[201] complexity of the transaction, the value of any potential dispute that could arise between the parties, and the general likelihood of a potential dispute arising.

In disputes involving contractual interpretation where the disputed sum is likely to be lower than $1 million, one arbitrator should suffice.[202] Whereas in complex issues where the sums involved exceed $1 million, generally there is a preference for three arbitrators.[203]

The expense and delay associated with having three arbitrators are arguably offset by the belief that 'three minds are generally better than one at absorbing all the necessary information, and arriving at a reasonable resolution'.[204]

There is a correlation between the number of arbitrators on the one hand, and the length and expense of the arbitration procedure on the other hand.[205] With one arbitrator, it is generally easier to schedule hearings, costs are lower, the proceedings progress at a faster pace and the award is issued more rapidly.[206] Where the parties opt for a three-arbitrator panel, this could lead to delays in scheduling, more discussion and the potential for a lack of accord when deliberating.[207]

In cross-border disputes, a party should consider a number of factors when selecting its arbitrator.[208] The arbitrator's understanding of the party's culture, and legal system, the arbitrator's expertise, and experience in the field concerned, and the language skills of the arbitrator, which are crucial when the hearings are in one language, and the evidence is in another language.[209]

When the parties agree on the appointment of three arbitrators, each appoints an arbitrator, and either the two appoint a third or the third is appointed by the parties or by the institution.[210] The third arbitrator may be designated as the chair of the arbitral tribunal.[211] As institutional rules address the appointment procedure, such rules may be used when the parties disagree on the appointment process.[212] Usually when only one arbitrator is agreed upon, the appointment will be made by the institution.[213]

Care should be taken when appointing specific arbitrators in the arbitration agreement or clause as it is usually unclear at that precise point in time what the nature

200. Moses 2012: 46-7.
201. Moses 2012: 46.
202. Moses 2012: 46.
203. Moses 2012: 46.
204. Moses 2012: 46.
205. Moses 2012: 46.
206. Moses 2012: 46.
207. Moses 2012: 46.
208. Moses 2012: 47.
209. Moses 2012: 47.
210. Walker 2012: 2-17.
211. Moses 2012: 47.
212. Moses 2012: 47.
213. Walker 2012: 2-17.

of the dispute will be, and whether the arbitrator in question will be available if and when a dispute arises.[214]

[B] Seat of Arbitration (Locus of Arbitration) and the Procedural Rules for the Arbitration

The arbitration law of the seat of the arbitration will be the law governing the arbitration proceedings (*lex arbitri*) alongside any institutional rules referred to or ad hoc rules formulated by the parties.[215] Failure to select procedural rules for the arbitration will result in the selection being made by the arbitrators and will be determined by reference to the arbitration law of the primary jurisdiction.[216]

The strategic value of the seat of arbitration cannot be overstated.[217] The choice of seat is important for a number of reasons, prime amongst these is the prospect of domestic court intervention. On the one hand such intervention could lead to a lack of procedural finality, delays, and expense as the court may be asked to intervene in the arbitral proceedings when one party believes it is unfairly treated or in circumstances where a party is dissatisfied with the award granted by the tribunal.[218] On the other hand, domestic court intervention is a way of securing the support and guidance of the courts. Seat will determine the degree of support that may be requested from the local courts during the course of the arbitral proceedings, as for example the correct choice of seat may allow a party to challenge an award in circumstances where the basic procedural standards of fairness are not adhered to.[219] Local courts may also be petitioned to provide guidance if the choice of arbitral procedure by the parties is not sufficiently comprehensive.[220]

Seat is also important since it defines the procedural rules that will govern the arbitral proceedings in concert with the institutional or ad hoc rules selected by the parties governing *inter alia* burden of proof and admissibility of evidence.[221]

[C] Language of the Arbitration

Whilst it is often assumed that the language of the contract will also be the language of the arbitration proceedings this is not the case unless the parties expressly stipulate so in their agreement.[222] The tribunal may decide differently in the absence of such an indication.[223] In circumstances where the parties come from different countries even when they habitually use the same working language when transacting, it is sensible to

214. Walker 2012: 2-18.
215. PWC International Arbitration Study 2006, 13.
216. Dasteel, 16-2-1.
217. PWC International Arbitration Study 2006, 3.
218. PWC International Arbitration Study 2006, 7.
219. PWC International Arbitration Study 2006: 13.
220. PWC International Arbitration Study 2006: 13.
221. PWC International Arbitration Study 2006: 13.
222. Moses 2012: 48.
223. Moses 2012: 48.

ensure the inclusion of a language provision to avoid doubt, and disagreement.[224] It is typically best to ensure that the language selected is the same as the one used in the principal contractual documentation to avoid the cost, and delays associated with translation, and the commissioning of interpreters.[225]

[D] Substantive Law

Whilst the law governing the contract is likely to be used in the event that the parties fail to make a selection in their arbitration clause, it is best to include this information in the arbitration clause as well to prevent doubt, and disagreement.[226]

According to the UNCITRAL Model Law 2006, the arbitral tribunal will decide a dispute in line with the rules of law selected by the parties as applicable to the substance of their dispute.[227] In such a context, any 'designation of the law or legal system in a given state shall be construed, unless expressed, as directly referring to the substantive law of that State and not to its conflict of laws rules'.[228] In the event that the parties fail to designate such rules of law, the arbitral tribunal will apply the law 'determined by the conflict of laws rules which it considers applicable'.[229]

The reference to 'rules of law' rather than 'law' in the UNCITRAL Model Law 2006 is intended to widen the range of options open to the parties when designating the law applicable to the substance of the disputes, permitting them to agree on rules of law formulated by an international forum which may have not been incorporated into any national legal system.[230]

[E] Evidential Rules

As many arbitration institutions do not necessarily address in any detail the issues of evidence, the parties should consider incorporating evidential rules into their arbitration agreement. Dedicated rules have been developed by the International Bar Association (IBA) for use in international arbitrations.[231] When the parties require additional discovery they should make provision for this in terms of their agreement.[232]

224. Walker 2012: 2-16.
225. Walker 2012: 2-16.
226. Moses 2012: 48.
227. A28(1), UNCITRAL Model Law on International Commercial Arbitration 1985 (with amendments as adopted in 2006) (UNCITRAL Model Law 2006) accessible at https://www.uncitral.org/pdf/english/texts/arbitration/ml-arb/07-86998_Ebook.pdf (last accessed 26/5/18).
228. Article 28(1), UNCITRAL Model Law 2006.
229. Article 28(2), UNCITRAL Model Law 2006.
230. Paragraph 39, Explanatory Note by the UNCITRAL secretariat on the 1985 Model Law on International Commercial Arbitration as amended in 2006 accessible at https://www.uncitral.org/pdf/english/texts/arbitration/ml-arb/07-86998_Ebook.pdf (last accessed 26/5/18).
231. Moses 2012: 49 referring to the IBA's Rules on the Taking of Evidence in International Arbitrations. The Rules adopted by the IBA in May 2010 can be accessed in PDF at http://www.ibanet.org/Publications/publications_IBA_guides_and_free_materials.aspx#Practice%20Rules%20and%20Guidelines (last accessed 19th July 2016).
232. Moses 2012: 49.

[F] Availability of Interim Relief

The availability of interim relief from the arbitral tribunal will be determined by the applicable institutional rules (if at all), and the ability to enforce such relief will vary, it is accordingly worthwhile including a provision in the arbitration agreement permitting the parties to apply to a court of applicable jurisdiction for interim relief.[233] In the absence of such a provision, the ability to apply to a court for interim relief will be determined by applicable law.[234]

The parties should consider the inclusion of a provision addressing the availability of interim relief so that either one of them may petition for such relief prior to the formation of the arbitral tribunal.[235]

[G] Technical Expertise

Disputes relating to technical matters may require the expertise of a suitably qualified person as such the contracting parties should consider including such a provision in their arbitration agreement.[236] Such a provision may stipulate that the expert's decision is either binding or non-binding. Where the decision of the expert is non-binding, the parties may add that in the event of disagreement the matter proceed to a binding arbitration.[237]

[H] Multistep Dispute Resolution Clause

Where such a clause is used, the parties should give due consideration to the inclusion of a stipulation that highly ranked executives with the requisite decision-making authority be present at such meetings held at the initial stages.[238]

[I] Legal Expenses

The parties may elect to determine the question of costs preemptively in their arbitration agreement.[239] They may decide for example that the arbitral tribunal will determine the question of costs. Alternately they may decide that the losing party will be responsible for costs, or that each party bears its own costs.

233. Chapter 11 (written by Thierry Calame and Martin Aebi), Arbitration of International Intellectual Property Disputes (edited by Thomas D. Halket) (JurisNet 2012), 548.
234. Chapter 11 (written by Thierry Calame and Martin Aebi), Arbitration of International Intellectual Property Disputes (edited by Thomas D. Halket) (JurisNet 2012), 548.
235. Moses 2012: 50.
236. Moses 2012: 50.
237. Moses 2012: 50.
238. Moses 2012: 52.
239. Moses 2012: 53.

[J] Confidentiality

Certain institutional rules impose a duty of confidentiality on institutional administrators, and arbitrators.[240] As such it is imperative that the parties address the question of confidentiality more generally by addressing the responsibilities of the contracting parties, the experts and the witnesses.[241] With this in mind, due consideration should be given to the inclusion of a provision in the arbitration agreement stipulating that all witnesses, and experts sign confidentiality agreements. Moreover a provision should be included in the arbitration agreement expressly stipulating that the parties themselves comply with such an obligation.[242]

§7.06 INTERNATIONAL INSTRUMENTS GOVERNING ARBITRATION

Alongside the international treaties governing arbitration agreements and arbitral awards such as the New York Convention,[243] and the Panama Convention,[244] model laws, and contractual texts governing arbitration are also available.

International instruments governing arbitration include instruments drawn up by the likes of the United Nations Commission on International Trade Law (UNCITRAL[245]), and the Hague Conference on Private International Law (HCCH[246]). Both organisations have been instrumental in preparing legislative, and non-legislative texts aimed at facilitating international commerce and improving the legal framework for international trade.

[A] 1958 UNCITRAL Convention on the Recognition and Enforcement of Arbitral Awards (New York Convention)

Adopted in June 1958 by the United Nations Conference on International Commercial Arbitration, and ratified by over 145 countries,[247] the New York Convention requires Contracting States to uphold arbitration clauses, and to recognise, and enforce arbitral awards made in a territory of a Contracting State other than the Contracting State in which recognition, and enforcement of the award is sought.[248]

240. Moses 2012: 53.
241. Moses 2012: 53.
242. Moses 2012: 53.
243. 1958 UNCITRAL Convention on the Recognition and Enforcement of Arbitral Awards (New York Convention).
244. Inter-American Convention on International Commercial Arbitration (1976 Panama Convention).
245. Further information can be found at www.uncitral.org.
246. Further information can be found at http://www.hcch.net/index_en.php?act=text.display&tid=26.
247. *See* www.uncitral.org for an updated list of State Parties.
248. Article 1, UNCITRAL 1958 Convention on the Recognition and Enforcement of Arbitral Awards.

[1] Article 2: Recognition of Arbitration Agreements

Each Contracting State to the Convention is obligated, pursuant to Article 2 of the Convention, to recognise agreements concluded in writing according to which the parties agree to submit to an arbitration process all or certain differences that have arisen between them or may arise between them in relation to a defined legal relationship, contractual or otherwise.

An agreement in writing may include an arbitration clause contained within a contract or an arbitration agreement 'signed by the parties or contained in an exchange of letters or telegrams'.[249]

The parties may have agreed to refer all disputes or only certain disputes to arbitration.[250] Moreover the agreement to arbitrate may have been made before or after the dispute arose.[251]

[2] Article 3: Recognition, and Enforcement of Arbitral Awards

Subject to certain qualifications set out in Article 5 of the New York Convention, each Contracting State to the Convention is first bound to recognise arbitral awards as binding, and second to enforce such awards in line with the procedural rules in place in the territory where the award is relied upon subject to the conditions set out in the Convention.[252]

§7.07 LITIGATION VERSUS PRIVATE DISPUTE RESOLUTION MECHANISMS

Litigation has certain key advantages when compared to private dispute resolution mechanisms.

First, the courts generally possess the power to deal with third parties who are not parties to the contract.

Second, the courts in certain jurisdictions have the power to produce a decision that may influence the determination of similar disputes in future.

Third, the courts are able to grant remedies which private fora cannot. Courts may have the power to grant orders, and injunctions either in response to a request by one of the parties to the litigation or on its own initiative.

A court may issue an order demanding that a party do something. A court could for example issue an order demanding that one of the parties produce evidence in its possession to the other party, and to the court. In the alternative the court may issue an

249. Article 2(2), UNCITRAL 1958 Convention on the Recognition and Enforcement of Arbitral Awards.
250. Article 2, UNCITRAL 1958 Convention on the Recognition and Enforcement of Arbitral Awards.
251. Article 2, UNCITRAL 1958 Convention on the Recognition and Enforcement of Arbitral Awards.
252. Article 3, UNCITRAL 1958 Convention on the Recognition and Enforcement of Arbitral Awards. Article 4 of the Convention describes the procedural steps that an applicant seeking recognition and enforcement must follow.

injunction demanding that a party refrain from doing something. For example, it may grant an injunction restraining a breach of one or more of the contractual terms[253] or stopping the publication of certain information.

Fourth, the courts may summon parties by issuing orders that oblige the parties summoned to appear before court.

Finally, and quite importantly, judgments issued by the courts will have legal force and will be capable of execution using a variety of remedies available in law.

§7.08 JURISDICTION IN THE EUROPEAN UNION[254,255]

Intellectual property law is international in its scope of application, since immaterial objects (such as ideas, innovations and authored works) cross borders with ease, and travel through Cyberspace at the touch of a button.[256] Jurisdiction and applicable law concerns accordingly arise on a regular basis when the enforcement of Intellectual Property Rights is involved, against an infringer, or in the context of a licensing agreement or assignment:[257]

> In an era in which IPRs are still for the most part national rights – and a proprietor mostly owns a bundle of national IPRs instead of one supranational IPR – having to deal with an infringement in multiple jurisdictions still means, as a starting position, that one may have to litigate in a great number of countries to enforce one's IPR. Needless to say that the financial and economic costs of such an exercise are horrendous and that the outcome usually resembles a 'patchwork quilt' with different results for different countries.[258]

Private International Law (PIL) rules are the rules found in domestic law which are used to determine which cases it will accept and deal with.[259] The goal of such rules is to determine 'the appropriate or most suited court to deal with cases with a cross-border element'.[260] The rule that is standard to most jurisdictions looks at the

253. Mendelsohn 2004: 197.
254. European Convention on Jurisdiction and Enforcement of Judgements in Civil and Commercial Matters, done at Brussels, 27 September 1968, 41 OJ Eur Comm C27/1, 26 January 1998 (consolidated and updated version of the 1968 Convention and the Protocol of 1971, following the 1996 accession of the Republic of Austria, the Republic of Finland and the Kingdom of Sweden) (**Brussels Convention**). Council Regulation No 44/2001 of 22 December 2000 on Jurisdiction and the Recognition and Enforcement of Judgements in Civil and Commercial Matters OJ L12, 16 January 2001, pages 1-23 (**Brussels Regulation 2000**). Regulation (EU) No 1215/2012 Of the European Parliament and of the Council of 12 December 2012 on jurisdiction and the recognition and enforcement of judgments in civil and commercial matters (**Brussels Regulation 2012**).
255. For further reading regarding Rome I Regulation, please *see* Mankowski, Peter, Contracts relating to Intellectual or Industrial Property Rights under the Rome I Regulation, in Leible and Ohly (eds), Intellectual Property and Private International Law, Tubingen 2009, 31.
256. Van Engelen, Th. C. J. A., Jurisdiction and Applicable Law in Matters of Intellectual Property (2010), Electronic Journal of Comparative Law, 14(3), 1 (hereinafter Van Engelen 2010).
257. Van Engelen 2010: 1.
258. Van Engelen 2010: 3.
259. Paul, Torremans, Jurisdiction for Cross-border Intellectual Property Infringement Cases in Europe (2016) CMLR 53(6), 1625-1645, 1626.
260. Torremans 2016: 1626.

domicile or habitual residence of the defendant as the 'connecting factor between the case and the court',[261] to help redress any imbalance between the parties to the litigation; with the plaintiff choosing the course of action, this rule affords the defendant the possibility of 'playing at home' when choosing to defend.[262]

In cases involving an infringement or tort, it is the place of the tort that is used as an alternative connecting factor, since the underlying facts and ensuing consequences lie at the heart of the case.[263] When a case involves a matter of public interest, national interest dictates that national courts enjoy exclusive jurisdiction.[264]

Once a court has jurisdiction, it will then proceed to determine the law applicable using its national Private International Choice-of-Law rules.[265]

Rules governing jurisdiction determine whether the arbiter possesses the power to deal with a case.

Brussels Regulation 2012 – concluded on 12 December 2012, and applicable from January 2015[266] – repeals the Brussels Regulation 2000,[267] and applies to proceedings commenced, to court settlements approved or concluded on or after 10 January 2015 on the proviso that these fall within the scope of the Brussels Regulation 2012.

Brussels Regulation 2000 applies to judgments awarded in cases instituted, to court settlements approved or concluded before 10 January 2015 on the proviso that these fall within the scope of the Brussels Regulation 2000.[268]

[A] Scope of the Brussels Regulation 2012[269]

The Brussels Regulation seeks to 'unify the rules of conflict of jurisdiction in civil and commercial matters by way of rules of jurisdiction which are highly predictable'.[270] The current Regulation (Brussels Regulation 2012) like its predecessor (Brussels Regulation 2000) pursues 'an objective of legal certainty which consists in strengthening the legal protection of persons established in the European Community, by enabling the applicant to identify easily the court in which he may sue and the defendant reasonably to foresee before which court he may be sued'.[271]

261. Torremans 2016: 1626-1627.
262. Torremans 2016: 1627.
263. Torremans 2016: 1627.
264. Torremans 2016: 1627.
265. Torremans 2016: 1627.
266. Pippa Rogerson, *Collier's Conflict of Laws* (2013, Cambridge University Press) (Kindle book) (hereafter Rogerson 2013).
267. Article 80, Brussels Regulation 2012.
268. Article 66, Brussels Regulation 2012.
269. Merrett, Commercial conflict of laws, in Commercial Law Edited by Michael Furmstone and Jason Chuah (Pearson 2013), 591 (hereafter Merrett 2013).
270. Case C-533/07 *Falco Privatstiftung and Thomas Rabitsch v Gisela Weller-Lindhorst*, 23 April 2009, para. 21 of ECJ judgement.
271. Paragraph 22, ECJ decision in Falco.

Article 1, Brussels Regulation 2012

1. This Regulation shall apply in civil and commercial matters whatever the nature of the court or tribunal. It shall not extend, in particular, to revenue, customs or administrative matters or to the liability of the State for acts and omissions in the exercise of State authority (*acta iure imperii*).

2. This Regulation shall not apply to:

(a) the status or legal capacity of natural persons, rights in property arising out of a matrimonial relationship or out of a relationship deemed by the law applicable to such relationship to have comparable effects to marriage;

(b) bankruptcy, proceedings relating to the winding-up of insolvent companies or other legal persons, judicial arrangements, compositions and analogous proceedings;

(c) social security;

(d) arbitration;

(e) maintenance obligations arising from a family relationship, parentage, marriage or affinity;

(f) wills and succession, including maintenance obligations arising by reason of death.

Article 4(1), Brussels Regulation 2012

Subject to this Regulation, persons domiciled in a Member State shall, whatever their nationality, be sued in the courts of that Member State.

The first question that a court or tribunal in a Member State disposed of a matter should ask is whether the dispute is one that falls within the material scope of the Brussels Regulation.[272]

The Brussels Regulation 2012 applies in *civil and commercial matters* whatever the nature of the *court or tribunal* by virtue of Article 1(1), Brussels Regulation 2012.

To ensure that the Regulation is not confined to any particular understanding of any legal system, the phrase 'civil and commercial matters' is left undefined.

Certain matters are excluded from the scope of the Brussels Regulation 2012. Prime amongst these is arbitration (Article 1(2), Brussels Regulation 2012).[273]

272. Merrett 2013: 591.
273. Case C190/89 *Marc Rich & Co AG v Societa Italiana Impianti PA* ECR 1991 I-03855.

[B] Arbitration Exclusion

Originally contained in the 1968 Brussels Convention (the drafters of the 1968 Convention had believed that a Community instrument would be introduced to unify the law governing arbitrations, but in fact this has never happened[274]), this exclusion meant that the Brussels Convention did not apply to recognition, and enforcement of arbitral awards, jurisdiction of the courts in relation to litigation involving arbitration, and the judgments resulting from such litigation.[275] In 1989 the CJEU extended the scope of this exclusion so that it included all ancillary proceedings related to the arbitration proceedings, including proceedings intended to assess the validity of an arbitration agreement.[276]

The Brussels Regulation 2012 enhances the arbitration exclusion. The exclusion is elaborated upon in Recital 12, Brussels Regulation 2012 which confirms that the Brussels Regulation 2012 does not apply 'to any action or ancillary proceedings relating to, in particular, the establishment of an arbitral tribunal, the powers of arbitrators, the conduct of an arbitration procedure or any other aspects of such a procedure, nor to any action or judgment concerning the annulment, review, appeal, recognition or enforcement of an arbitral award'.[277]

Recital 12 adds that a ruling issued by a court of a Member State relating to 'whether or not the arbitration agreement is null and void, inoperative or incapable of being performed should not be subject to the rules of recognition and enforcement set out in the Regulation, regardless of whether the court decided on this as a principal issue or as an incidental question'. As such there is less of an incentive for parties to issue proceedings in a Member State 'simply with a view to obtaining an order that their arbitration agreement is invalid, because such an order will not be capable of recognition in other member states'.[278]

Whilst Recital 12 confirms that the Regulation should not apply to arbitration it does not prevent the courts of the Member States from referring parties to arbitration, from staying or dismissing proceedings in favour of arbitration, or from examining whether an arbitration agreement is null and void, inoperative or incapable of being performed.[279]

In the event that a court of a Member State exercising its jurisdiction under the Regulation or under national law, determines that an arbitration agreement is null and void, inoperative or incapable of being performed, Recital 12 states that, 'this should not preclude that court's judgment on the substance of the matter from being recognised or, as the case may be, enforced in accordance with this Regulation. This

274. Rogerson 2013: 4460.
275. Rogerson 2013: 4460 citing Jenard Report [1979] OJ C59/1, p.13.
276. Rogerson 2013: 4472 citing Case C190/89 *Marc Rich & Co AG v Societa Italiana Impianti PA* ECR 1991 I-03855.
277. Recital 12, Brussels Regulation 2012.
278. Sarah Garvey, 'Brussels Regulation (Recast): Are you ready?' 18 March 2015, p.6. Accessible at http://www.allenovery.com/publications/en-gb/Pages/BRUSSELS-REGULATION-(RECAST)-ARE-YOU-READY.aspx (last accessed 18 July 2016).
279. Recital 12, Brussels Regulation 2012.

should be without prejudice to the competence of the courts of the Member States to decide on the recognition and enforcement of arbitral awards in accordance with the Convention on the Recognition and Enforcement of Foreign Arbitral Awards, done at New York on 10 June 1958 ('the 1958 New York Convention'), which takes precedence over this Regulation'.[280]

[C] Article 4: General Rule on Jurisdiction[281]

Article 4, Brussels Regulation 2012

1. Subject to this Regulation, persons domiciled in a Member State shall, whatever their nationality, be sued in the courts of that Member State.

2. Persons who are not nationals of the Member State in which they are domiciled shall be governed by the rules of jurisdiction applicable to nationals of that Member State.

The rules of jurisdiction in the Brussels Regulation 2012, and its predecessor (Brussels Regulation 2001) are 'founded on the principle that jurisdiction is generally based on the defendant's domicile'.[282] Accordingly, the starting point for the exercise of jurisdiction is the notion that jurisdiction should be exercised by the courts of the Member State in which the defendant is domiciled regardless of the defendant's nationality. This general rule applies unless the jurisdiction of the courts of the defendant's domicile is ousted, which is the case when a valid jurisdiction agreement is concluded, or another court has exclusive jurisdiction.[283]

Article 4, Brussels Regulation 2012 allows for 'the separate prosecution of every defendant in the country where he or she resides'.[284]

This approach is likely to be less convenient for a potential party looking to pursue a claim, if the defendant resides in a Member State that is not proximate to the Member State where the affected IP holder is based, or if several defendants are involved – Article 4 does not permit the whole matter, in the latter scenario, to be brought before the same court, effectively splitting-up the case into 'as many cases are there are Member States in which a defendant is based'.[285]

280. Recital 12, Brussels Regulation 2012.
281. Article 4, Brussels Regulation 2012 ex Article 2, Brussels Regulation 2000.
282. Paragraph 23, ECJ decision in Falco.
283. Merrett 2013: 595.
284. Torremans 2016: 1627-8.
285. Torremans 2016: 1628.

[D] Articles 62 and 63: Domicile

Article 62, Brussels Regulation 2012

1. In order to determine whether a party is domiciled in the Member State whose courts are seised of a matter, the court shall apply its internal law.

2. If a party is not domiciled in the Member State whose courts are seised of the matter, then, in order to determine whether the party is domiciled in another Member State, the court shall apply the law of that Member State.

Article 63, Brussels Regulation 2012

For a company and other legal person, as well as an association of natural or legal persons, domicile is the place where it has its

(a) statutory seat;

(b) central administration; or

(c) principal place of business

When for the purposes of Ireland, Cyprus and the UK, statutory seat is defined as the registered office or, where there is no such office anywhere, the place of incorporation or, where there is no such place anywhere, the place under the law of which the formation took place.

The Brussels Regulation 2012 defines domicile from the point of view of a natural person as well as a legal person.

Whilst this Regulation does not provide for an autonomous definition of domicile from the point of view of a natural person,[286] it does provide for an autonomous definition of domicile from the point of view of a legal person.[287]

A legal person, and an association of persons is capable of having several domiciles in the context of Article 63, Brussels Regulation 2012 pursuant to subsections (a), (b), and (c).[288]

'Principal place of business' it has been said means 'most important' rather than 'main', and refers *inter alia* to the importance of the offices to the activities of the business.[289] In contrast 'central administration' is likely to be the locus of the operational functions rather than the locus of executive functions.[290]

286. Article 62, Brussels Regulation 2012.
287. Article 63, Brussels Regulation 2012.
288. Merrett 2013: 594.
289. Merrett 2013: 594 citing The Rewia [1991] 2 Lloyds's Rep 325.
290. Merrett 2013: 594 citing *Ministry of Defence and Support of the Armed Forces for the Islamic Republic of Iran v FAZ Aviation Ltd* [2007] EWHC 1042 (Comm); [2007] 1 LPr 42.

[E] Article 7: Special Rules on Jurisdiction[291]

Article 7(1), Brussels Regulation 2012

A person domiciled in a Member State may be sued in another Member State:

(1) (a) in matters relating to a contract, in the courts for the place of performance of the obligation in question;

(b) for the purpose of this provision and unless otherwise agreed, the place of performance of the obligation in question shall be:

— in the case of the sale of goods, the place in a Member State where, under the contract, the goods were delivered or should have been delivered,

— in the case of the provision of services, the place in a Member State where, under the contract, the services were provided or should have been provided;

(c) if point (b) does not apply then point (a) applies;

(2) in matters relating to tort, delict or quasi-delict, in the courts for the place where the harmful event occurred or may occur ... .

The general rule on jurisdiction, namely that jurisdiction is based upon the domicile of the defendant, is supplemented by the rules of special jurisdiction.[292]

These special rules on jurisdiction confer jurisdiction on courts other than the courts of the Member State where the defendant is domiciled, thus according to the party issuing proceedings the choice of where to sue the defendant.

Rather than ousting the jurisdiction of the courts of the defendant's domicile, these special heads of jurisdiction – laid out in Article 7 – allocate further jurisdiction to the courts of this other Member State.[293] As a result, the party issuing proceedings is free to make the final selection themselves; opting to sue in the courts of the defendant's domicile, or alternately in the courts endowed with jurisdiction pursuant to Article 7.[294]

[1] In Cases Relating to a Tort

In cases relating to a tort, the rule that jurisdiction is generally based on the domicile of the defendant is complemented by a rule of special jurisdiction, which states that in matters relating to tort, a person domiciled in a Member State may be sued in the courts

291. Article 7, Brussels Regulation 2012 ex Article 5, Brussels Regulation 2000.
292. Paragraph 23, ECJ decision in Falco.
293. Merrett 2013: 595.
294. Merrett 2013: 595.

of the Member State 'for the place where the harmful event occurred or may occur'.[295,296]

[2] In Cases Relating to a Contract

In matters involving a contract, the rule that jurisdiction is generally based on the domicile of the defendant is complemented by a rule of special jurisdiction.[297] Pursuant to which, a person domiciled in a Member State may be sued in the courts of the Member State 'for the place of performance of the obligation in question'.[298] The rationale for this rule of special jurisdiction in matters relating to a contract is 'the desire for proximity'[299] through 'the existence of a close link between the contract and the court called upon to hear and to determine the case'.[300]

Article 7(1)b Brussels Regulation 2012 defines the 'place of performance of the obligation in question' in the absence of an agreement to the contrary. For contracts involving sales of goods, this place of performance is deemed to be 'the place in a Member State where, under the contract, the goods were delivered or should have been delivered'.[301] For contracts involving the supply of services, this place of performance is deemed to be 'the place in a Member State where, under the contract, the services were provided or should have been provided'.[302]

In the event that Article 7(1)b does not apply then Article 7(1)a applies,[303] effectively allocating jurisdiction to the courts for the place of performance of the obligation concerned, when the matter relates to a contract.

The CJEU (at the time the ECJ) stated, in its decision in the Falco case, that 'a contract under which the owner of an intellectual property right grants its contractual partner the right to use that right in return for remuneration is not a contract for the provision of services',[304] within the meaning of Article 7(1)b, Brussels Regulation 2012[305] (at the time Article 5(1)b, Brussels Regulation 2001).[306] The only obligation that 'the owner of the right granted undertakes with regard to its contractual partner is not to challenge the use of that right by the latter'.[307] The owner of the right concerned

295. Article 7(2), Brussels Regulation 2012.
296. Van Engelen 2010: 6.
297. Paragraph 24, ECJ decision in Falco.
298. Article 7(1)a, Brussels Regulation 2012.
299. Paragraph 24, ECJ decision in Falco.
300. Paragraph 24, ECJ decision in Falco.
301. Article 7(1)b, Brussels Regulation 2012.
302. Article 7(1)b, Brussels Regulation 2012.
303. Article 7(1)c, Brussels Regulation 2012.
304. Paragraph 44, ECJ decision in Falco.
305. The germane part of Article 7(1)b, Brussels Regulation 2012 reads '(b) for the purpose of this provision and unless otherwise agreed, the place of performance of the obligation in question shall be: .... in the case of the provision of services, the place in a Member State where, under the contract, the services were provided or should have been provided'.
306. Paragraph 44, ECJ decision in Falco.
307. Paragraph 31, ECJ decision in Falco.

'does not perform any service in granting a right to use that property' rather the owner of this right merely undertakes 'to permit the licensee to exploit that right freely'.[308]

The fact that the licensing agreement is not a contract for the provision of services under Article 7(1)b, Brussels Regulation 2012,[309] added the CJEU, does not preclude that contract from being subject to the Regulation, and its other rules governing jurisdiction;[310] if a contract for the sale of goods is not involved, then jurisdiction is not determined only on the basis of the rules applicable to contracts for the provision of services, since – by virtue of Article 7(1)c, Brussels Regulation 2012,[311] – Article 7(1)a, Brussels Regulation 2012[312] applies to contracts which are neither contracts for the sale of goods, nor contracts for the provision of services.[313]

This decision of the CJEU in Falco case has been criticised for failing to address how courts should deal with cases involving mixed contracts containing a licence alongside the provision of services or goods.[314] A distribution agreement is an illustration of such a contract.[315] Under such an arrangement, the manufacturer often sells goods to the distributor, whilst granting the latter the right to exploit its trademark in the sale and marketing of the goods. In such a scenario, 'would the court of the distributor's domicile be required to take jurisdiction over a dispute involving the supply of goods ... but no over the brand licence?'[316]

The term 'contract' in this context is given an autonomous definition that is not defined with reference to the law of the forum or the law applicable to the contract,[317] and is assumed to be 'an undertaking freely assumed by one party towards another'.[318]

The rule in Article 7(1)b Brussels Regulation (formerly Article 5(1)b Brussels 2000) determining place of performance can 'be "displaced" by an explicit agreement on the place of performance'.[319]

[F] Article 7(5): Operations of a Branch, Agency or Other Establishment

Article 7(5) Brussels Regulation 2012

A person domiciled in a Member State may be sued in another Member State:

...

308. Paragraph 31, ECJ decision in Falco.
309. At the time Article 5(1)b, Brussels Regulation 2001.
310. Paragraph 36, ECJ decision in Falco.
311. At the time Article 5(1)c, Brussels Regulation 2001.
312. At the time Article 5(1)a, Brussels Regulation 2001.
313. Paragraph 40, ECJ decision in Falco.
314. Joseph, P., ECJ rules on jurisdiction for IP licence disputes, Journal of Intellectual Property Law and Practice (2009), 4(9), 616-617, 617.
315. Joseph 2009: 617.
316. Joseph 2009: 617.
317. Merrett 2013: 596 citing Case C-34/82 *Martin Peters v Zuid* [1983] ECR I-987.
318. Merrett 2013: 596 citing Case C-26/91 *Handte v TMCS* [1982] ECR I-3967.
319. Merrett 2013: 597 citing Proposal for a Council regulation on jurisdiction and the recognition and enforcement of judgments in civil and commercial matters 99/0154 (CNS), p.14.

> (5) as regards a dispute arising out of the operations of a branch, agency or other establishment, in the courts for the place where the branch, agency or other establishment is situated; ...

A defendant domiciled in a Member State (MS A) may be sued in another Member State (MS B) in which its branch, agency or other establishment is situated but only 'as regards a dispute arising out of the operations of (the) branch, agency or other establishment'.[320]

Article 7(5) Brussels Regulation 2012 sets out two requirements that must be met. First the defendant must have a branch, agency or other establishment. Second the dispute must arise out of the operations of a branch, agency or other establishment.

To satisfy the first requirement the place of business of the entity in the second Member State (MS B) must possess 'an appearance of permanence with a local management which is materially equipped to negotiate business with third parties'.[321] And this operation must be subject to 'the direction and control of the parent body'.[322]

To meet the second requirement the negotiations or the execution of the contract must take place in the second Member State (MS B).[323]

[G] Article 24: Exclusive Jurisdiction[324]

> **Article 24, Brussels Regulation 2012**
>
> The following courts of a Member State shall have exclusive jurisdiction, regardless of the domicile of the parties: ...
>
> (4) in proceedings concerned with the registration or validity of patents, trademarks, designs, or other similar rights required to be deposited or registered, irrespective of whether the issue is raised by way of an action or as a defence, the courts of the Member State in which the deposit or registration has been applied for, has taken place or is under the terms of an instrument of the Union or an international convention deemed to have taken place.
>
> Without prejudice to the jurisdiction of the European Patent Office under the Convention on the Grant of European Patents, signed at Munich on 5 October

320. Article 7(5) Brussels Regulation 2012.
321. Merrett 2013: 599 citing Case C-33/78 *Somafer v Saar-Ferngas* [1978] ECR I-2182, at [12].
322. Merrett 2013: 600 citing Case C-14/76 *De Bloss v Bouyer* [1976] ECR I-1479, at [21].
323. Merrett 2013: 600 citing *Anton Durbeck GmbH v Den Norske Bank ASA* [2003] 2 WLR 1296. *See also* Case-439/93 *Lloyd's Register v Campenon Bernard* [1995] ECR I-961 c.f. Case C-33/78 *Somafer v Saar-Ferngas* [1978] ECR I-2182.
324. Article 24, Brussels Regulation 2012 ex Article 22, Brussels Regulation 2000.

> 1973, the courts of each Member State shall have exclusive jurisdiction in proceedings concerned with the registration or validity of any European patent granted for that Member State; ....

Pursuant to Article 24 Brussels Regulation 2012 regardless of the domicile of the parties exclusive jurisdiction will be endowed upon the courts of a specific Member State in a limited number of situations.[325]

In the context of intellectual property, Article 24(4) is relevant. This provision states that in proceedings involving the registration or validity of patents, trademarks, designs or other similar rights required to be deposited or registered, exclusive jurisdiction will be endowed upon the courts of the Member State in which the deposit or registration has been applied for, has taken place or, is under the terms of an instrument of the Union or an international convention, deemed to have taken place.[326] This will be the case whether the issue is raised by way of an action or as a defence.[327] The courts of each Member State will have exclusive jurisdiction 'in proceedings concerned with the registration or validity of any European patent granted for that Member State'.[328]

[H] Article 25: Jurisdiction Agreements[329]

> **Article 25, Brussels Regulation 2012**
>
> 1. If the parties, regardless of their domicile, have agreed that a court or the courts of a Member State are to have jurisdiction to settle any disputes which have arisen or which may arise in connection with a particular legal relationship, that court or those courts shall have jurisdiction, unless the agreement is null and void as to its substantive validity under the law of that Member State. Such jurisdiction shall be exclusive unless the parties have agreed otherwise. The agreement conferring jurisdiction shall be either:
>
> (a) in writing or evidenced in writing;
>
> (b) in a form which accords with practices which the parties have established between themselves; or
>
> (c) in international trade or commerce, in a form which accords with a usage of which the parties are or ought to have been aware and which in such trade or commerce is widely known to, and regularly observed by, parties to contracts of the type involved in the particular trade or commerce concerned.

325. Preamble to Article 24, Brussels Regulation 2012.
326. Article 24(4), Brussels Regulation 2012.
327. Article 24(4), Brussels Regulation 2012.
328. Article 24(4), Brussels Regulation 2012.
329. Article 25, Brussels Regulation 2012 ex Article 23, Brussels Regulation 2000.

2. Any communication by electronic means which provides a durable record of the agreement shall be equivalent to 'writing'.

In almost every cross-border dispute, one of the first questions asked is 'where, and by whom, will this dispute be decided?'[330] The answer to this critical question will often determine the eventual outcome of the ensuing dispute since the procedure, and substantive law differ from nation to nation, as does the character, ability and integrity of the tribunals.[331]

Private parties engaged in a contract linked to more than one country will usually agree between them to include within the contract a provision fixing jurisdiction (jurisdiction agreement). Such an agreement between the parties either obliges or allows the parties to pursue their claims against each other in a designated forum.[332]

Also known as forum clause/agreement, or choice-of-court clause/agreement, a jurisdiction agreement[333] looks to eliminate forum-shopping by indicating in advance which forum will have jurisdiction over any future disputes between the parties. If such an agreement does not eliminate the risk of forum-shopping at the very least it reduces the likelihood of one of the parties engaging in forum-shopping.

Jurisdiction agreements are either exclusive or non-exclusive in nature.

Exclusive agreements require all litigation between the parties to be pursued only in the forum selected by them.[334] In exclusive agreements, the parties select a named entity – person (e.g., arbitrator, and mediator), institution (in the context of arbitration, mediation and so forth), court or courts of a named country – to handle any disputes that arise between them.

Less frequently, jurisdiction agreements take the non-exclusive form; pursuant to which the parties contracting agree that the dispute may be referred to an entity – body or court – without precluding any other possible forum. Non-exclusive jurisdiction agreements allow litigation between the parties to take place in the forum selected in the contract, but also permit claims to be brought in other fora possessing jurisdiction.[335]

Non-exclusive jurisdiction agreements may be used for a variety of reasons. Occasionally as part of a concession to ensure conclusion of the agreement. Also as a strategic tool in order to address uncertainty regarding the nature of any ensuing dispute thus affording the parties operational flexibility if, and when, a dispute arises.

The Brussels Regulation 2012 has removed the domicile requirement for parties to an Article 25 jurisdiction agreement, so that a jurisdiction agreement will fall within

330. Born 2010: 1.
331. Born 2010: 1.
332. Born 2010: 2.
333. Born 2010: 1.
334. Born 2010: 2.
335. Born 2010: 2.

the scope of Article 25 Brussels Regulation 2012 'even if none of the parties are domiciled in a Member State'.[336]

An agreement compliant with the predicate conditions in this Regulation will give the court or tribunal selected jurisdiction under the Regulation, and unless there is a contrary agreement, such jurisdiction will be exclusive.[337]

To be valid under the Brussels Regulation 2012, the agreement must fulfil the following conditions. The jurisdiction agreement must be between parties.[338] The parties must be in agreement on the jurisdiction of the court or courts, as such lack of mutual consent will render the jurisdiction agreement invalid.[339] The jurisdiction agreement must be connected with a particular legal relationship by virtue of Article 25(1) which states that the parties have to agree 'that a court or the courts of a Member State are to have jurisdiction to settle any disputes which have arisen or which may arise in connection with a particular legal relationship ... .'[340] To be valid the agreement must comply with certain requirements as to form. In this context such an agreement may take one of four forms – indicated in Article 25(1)(a)-(c), Brussels Regulation 2012 – it may be in writing, evidenced in writing, be in a form that conforms with a practice established by the parties contracting, or be in a form that conforms with a usage of which the parties are aware or ought to have been aware, and which in such a trade is widely known to parties to contracts of the kind involved in the particular trade, and regularly observed by such parties.[341]

§7.09 JURISDICTION AGREEMENTS IN INTERNATIONAL LAW

[A] Hague Convention on Choice of Court Agreements 2005 (Hague Convention 2005)[342]

This Convention entered into force in October 2015. It has been acceded to by Mexico (in 2007), the EU (in 2015), and Singapore (in 2016),[343] and signed by the US (in 2009), and Ukraine (in 2016).

This Convention, which 'provides a litigation counterpart to the 1958 United Nations Convention on the Recognition and Enforcement of Foreign Arbitral Awards

336. Sarah Garvey, 'Brussels Regulation (Recast): Are you ready?' 18 March 2015, p.2. Accessible at http://www.allenovery.com/publications/en-gb/Pages/BRUSSELS-REGULATION-(RECAST)-ARE-YOU-READY.aspx (last accessed 18 July 2016).
337. Article 25(1), Brussels Regulation 2012.
338. Article 25(1), Brussels Regulation 2012 ex Article 23(1), Brussels Regulation 2000.
339. C-387/98 *Coreck Maritime GmbH v Handelsveem BV*.
340. Article 25(1) Brussels Regulation 2012.
341. Case C-106/95 *Mainschiffahrts-Genossenschaft eG v Les Gravieres Rhenanes SARL*, para 19.
342. For a detailed review of the Hague Convention *see* Rogerson 2013: Chapter 6.2.
343. The European Community became a member of the Hague Conference on Private International Law on 3 April 2007 by depositing its instrument of acceptance of the Statute of the Hague Convention. This was made possible due to the amendment of the Hague Conference Statute to allow for the admission of Regional Economic Integration Organisations, and the adoption by the EC Council of Decision 2006/719 on the accession of the Community to the Hague Conference on Private International Law [2006] OJ L297/1 (Peter Stone, *EU Private International Law* (2nd edn, Edward Elgar Publishing Limited 2012), 13).

(New York Convention)',[344] establishes a set of rules that 'allow parties to obtain both the *enforcement* of exclusive choice of court agreements and the *recognition and enforcement of the resulting judgments* rendered by courts of Contracting States'.[345,346]

Subject to a number of narrow exceptions set out in Article 2, Hague Convention 2005, this Convention is intended to apply to civil and commercial matters in international cases when the parties have used an exclusive choice of court agreement or incorporated an exclusive choice of court clause into their contract.[347]

An array of matters and transactions are excluded from the scope of the Hague Convention 2005 by virtue of Article 2.

The Convention will *not* apply to an exclusive choice of court agreement where one or more of the contracting parties are natural persons acting primarily for personal, family or household purposes.[348]

Arbitrations and related proceedings fall outside the scope of the Convention,[349] alongside intellectual property cases involving either the *validity of IPR* (excluding copyright)[350] or the *infringement of IPR*, except where such an *infringement arises out of a breach of contract relating to such rights*.[351]

Arguably in contractual cases involving claims of breach of IPRs, the Hague Convention 2005 would apply.[352]

Where a licence for example is concluded in the context of a distribution or franchise agreement then any breach of the IPRs by one of the contracting parties should arguably be caught by the Hague Convention 2005. If a distributor breaches one or more of its obligations in relation to the IPRs of the manufacturer, the matter would arguably be caught by the Hague Convention 2005. Similarly if the franchisee is in

344. Ronald A Brand, U.S. Implementation Vel Non of the 2005 Hague Convention on Choice of Court Agreements, in Yearbook of Private International Law, Vol. XII 2010 eds Andrea Bonomi and Gian Paolo Romano (Sellier European Law Publishers), pp 107-108 (available on Google Books).
345. Ronald A Brand, U.S. Implementation Vel Non of the 2005 Hague Convention on Choice of Court Agreements, in Yearbook of Private International Law, Vol. XII 2010 eds Andrea Bonomi and Gian Paolo Romano (Sellier European Law Publishers), p 108 (available on Google Books).
346. Italics added by authors.
347. Article 1, Hague Convention 2005 which reads '(1) This Convention shall apply in international cases to exclusive choice of court agreements concluded in civil or commercial matters. (2) For the purposes of Chapter II, a case is international unless the parties are resident in the same Contracting State and the relationship of the parties and all other elements relevant to the dispute, regardless of the location of the chosen court, are connected only with that State. (3) For the purposes of Chapter III, a case is international where recognition or enforcement of a foreign judgment is sought.'
348. Article 2(1), Hague Convention 2005.
349. Article 2(4), Hague Convention 2005.
350. Article 2(2)n, Hague Convention 2005 reads 'This Convention shall not apply to the following matters – ... the validity of intellectual property rights other than copyright and related rights.'
351. Article 2(2)o, Hague Convention 2005 reads 'This Convention shall not apply to the following matters -... infringement of intellectual property rights other than copyright and related rights, except where infringement proceedings are brought for breach of a contract between the parties relating to such rights, or could have been brought for breach of that contract'.
352. By virtue of Article 2(2)o, Hague Convention 2005.

breach of the IPRs set out in the franchise agreement, this claim would also arguably be caught by the Hague Convention 2005.

Article 2(2) – listing the exclusions above – should be read subject to Article 2(3) which states that proceedings are not excluded from the scope of the Convention where the matter excluded under Article 2(2) 'arises merely as a *preliminary question* and not as an object of the proceedings. In particular, the mere fact that a matter excluded under paragraph 2 arises by way of defence does not exclude proceedings from the Convention, if that matter is not an object of the proceedings'.[353]

[B] Article 3: Exclusive Choice of Court Agreements

Article 3, Hague Convention 2005

For the purposes of this Convention –

a) 'exclusive choice of court agreement' means an agreement concluded by two or more parties that meets the requirements of paragraph c) and designates, for the purpose of deciding disputes which have arisen or may arise in connection with a particular legal relationship, the courts of one Contracting State or one or more specific courts of one Contracting State to the exclusion of the jurisdiction of any other courts;

b) a choice of court agreement which designates the courts of one Contracting State or one or more specific courts of one Contracting State shall be deemed to be exclusive unless the parties have expressly provided otherwise;

c) an exclusive choice of court agreement must be concluded or documented –

i) in writing; or

ii) by any other means of communication which renders information accessible so as to be usable for subsequent reference;

d) an exclusive choice of court agreement that forms part of a contract shall be treated as an agreement independent of the other terms of the contract. The validity of the exclusive choice of court agreement cannot be contested solely on the ground that the contract is not valid.

At the international level, an agreement between the parties designating a court or courts with jurisdiction can only be deemed valid if it fulfils certain formalities defined within the provisions of the Hague Convention 2005.

First, the agreement must be what the Hague Convention 2005 terms an *exclusive choice of court agreement*.

353. Article 2(3), Hague Convention 2005. Italics added by authors.

Article 3 of this Convention sets out five distinct prerequisites for an exclusive choice of court agreement. There must be an agreement between two or more persons. The agreement must meet the requirements as to form as such it must be concluded or documented in writing or using any other means of communication rendering the information accessible so that it may be used for subsequent reference.[354] The agreement must designate the courts of one state or one or more specific courts of one state to the exclusion of all other courts. The court or courts so designated must be located in a Contracting State. The agreement must designate the court or courts to determine disputes connected to a particular legal relationship.[355]

Such an agreement may effectively arise in one of two situations. It may arise explicitly. In the alternative it may arise implicitly.

An explicit exclusive choice of court agreement is an agreement concluded by the parties which select the courts of one Contracting State or one or more specific courts of one Contracting State to the exclusion of the jurisdiction of any other courts.[356]

An implicit exclusive choice of court agreement is an agreement concluded by the parties that designates the courts of one Contracting State or one or more specific courts of one Contracting State in circumstances where the parties do not expressly provide otherwise.[357]

Second, the matter must be of an international character.[358]

A case will be regarded as being of an international character unless the following cumulative criteria are met. First, the parties are resident in the same Contracting State, and second, the relationship between the parties, and all the other elements relevant to the dispute are connected with that Contracting State.[359]

A legal person is considered to be resident in the Contracting State where it has its statutory seat, under whose law it was incorporated or formed, where it has its central administration or where it has its principal place of business.[360]

[C] Article 5: Obligations of the Designated Court

Article 5, Hague Convention 2005

1. The court or courts of a Contracting State designated in an exclusive choice of court agreement shall have jurisdiction to decide a dispute to which the agreement applies, unless the agreement is null and void under the law of that State.

354. Article 3(c), Hague Convention 2005.
355. Faye Fangfei Wang, *Internet Jurisdiction and Choice of Law: Legal Practices in the EU, US and China* (Cambridge University Press 2010), 22, citing from Hartley and Dogauchi (2007) Explanatory Report on the 2005 Hague Choice of Court Agreements Convention, HCCH Publications, p 38-39.
356. Article 3(a), Hague Convention 2005.
357. Article 3(a), Hague Convention 2005.
358. Article 1(2), Hague Convention 2005.
359. Article 1(2), Hague Convention 2005.
360. Article 4(2), Hague Convention 2005.

2. A court that has jurisdiction under paragraph 1 shall not decline to exercise jurisdiction on the ground that the dispute should be decided in a court of another State.

3. The preceding paragraphs shall not affect rules –

a) on jurisdiction related to subject matter or to the value of the claim;

b) on the internal allocation of jurisdiction among the courts of a Contracting State. However, where the chosen court has discretion as to whether to transfer a case, due consideration should be given to the choice of the parties.

The 'positive effect of exclusive choice of court agreements in the State chosen'[361] is addressed in Article 5 of the Hague Convention that states that the chosen court *must* hear the dispute.[362]

The court designated by the parties cannot accordingly decline to exercise jurisdiction on the ground that the dispute should be decided in a court of another State.[363] The chosen court may however refuse to hear the case where the exclusive choice of court agreement is null and void under the law of that State.[364]

[D] Article 6: Obligations of the Non-designated Court

Article 6, Hague Convention 2005

A court of a Contracting State other than that of the chosen court shall suspend or dismiss proceedings to which an exclusive choice of court agreement applies unless –

a) the agreement is null and void under the law of the State of the chosen court;

b) a party lacked the capacity to conclude the agreement under the law of the State of the court seised;

c) giving effect to the agreement would lead to a manifest injustice or would be manifestly contrary to the public policy of the State of the court seised;

d) for exceptional reasons beyond the control of the parties, the agreement cannot reasonably be performed; or

e) the chosen court has decided not to hear the case.

361. Peter Stone, *EU Private International Law* (2nd edn, Edward Elgar Publishing Limited 2012), 185.
362. Article 5, Hague Convention 2005.
363. Article 5, Hague Convention 2005.
364. Article 5, Hague Convention 2005.

The 'negative effect of an exclusive choice of court agreements in other Contracting States'[365] is addressed in Article 6 of the Hague Convention that states that a court of a Contracting State other than the court chosen by the parties is *obliged to suspend or dismiss proceedings* to which the exclusive choice of court agreement applies.[366]

[1] Hague Convention 2005 and the Brussels Regulation 2012

One of the concerns remaining unanswered by the Brussels Regulation 2012 is the question of the effect of a choice of court agreement designating the courts of a country *other than a Member State.*[367]

Article 25, Brussels Regulation 2012 addresses only choice of court agreements designating the courts of a Member State.[368,369] The Lugano Convention[370] extends this provision to agreements selecting the courts of Iceland, Norway or Switzerland.

Professor Hartley gives the example of an exclusive choice of court agreement concluded between two parties domiciled in the EU – one in England,[371] and the other in Spain – designating the courts of Hong Kong, and asks what would happen if the Spanish party sues the English party in England? Would the English court be permitted to decline jurisdiction in favour of the courts of Hong Kong?[372]

Professor Hartley suggests that since the English courts have jurisdiction – pursuant to Article 4(1), Brussels 2012 – and since Article 25, Brussels 2012 does not apply when the designated court is not in a Member State, then the English court would be obliged to hear the matter.[373]

---

365. Stone 2012: 185-186.
366. Article 6, Hague Convention 2005.
367. Hartley, Trevor C., International Commercial Litigation – Text, Cases and Materials on Private International Law (2nd Edition, Cambridge University Press, 2015), 195.
368. Hartley 2015: 195.
369. The active part of Article 25(1), Brussels Regulation 2012 states 'If the parties, regardless of their domicile, have agreed that *a court or the courts of a Member State* are to have jurisdiction to settle any disputes which have arisen or which may arise in connection with a particular legal relationship, that court or those courts shall have jurisdiction ...' (italics added by authors).
370. The Lugano Convention was originally adopted on 16 September 1988 (Hartley 2015: 195). The new version of the Lugano Convention came into effect on 30 October 2007 (Hartley 2015: 195). The recent Lugano Convention – Convention on jurisdiction and the recognition and enforcement of judgments in civil and commercial matters OJ 2009 L147/5 – can be accessed at https://eur-lex.europa.eu/legal-content/EN/TXT/?uri=uriserv:OJ.L_.2009.147.01.0005.01.ENG&toc=OJ:L:2009:147:TOC (last accessed 26/5/18). The original Lugano Convention – Convention on jurisdiction and the enforcement of judgements in civil and commercial matters OJ 1988 L319/9 – can be accessed at http://eur-lex.europa.eu/legal-content/EN/TXT/PDF/?uri=CELEX:41988A0592&from=en (last accessed 26/5/18).
371. At the time of writing this book, the UK is in the process of discussing the parameters of a withdrawal agreement, with the EU.
372. Hartley 2015: 195.
373. Hartley 2015: 195.

§7.10 CHOICE OF LAW (COL) RULES GOVERNING CONTRACTUAL CASES UNDER EU LAW

Internationalisation of IP related contracts raises a number of concerns amongst them the identification of applicable law in situations where a licence involves a conflict of laws.[374] This situation is made even more complex if one bears in mind the fact that a number of right holders may look to exploit IPRs at the same time in an array of jurisdictions using multistate licences.[375] Such fragmentation can potentially 'lead to the application of different national laws to the IP rights which are the subject matter of a multistate licence'.[376]

Public interest concerns may also impact on IP-related contracts justifying the application of overriding mandatory provisions, irrespective of the law selected in the contract.[377]

The rules governing jurisdiction determine *which arbiter can hear a claim*, whereas the rules governing choice of law determine the *substantive law which this arbiter will use* to determine the case before it.[378]

In the European Union, contracts generally are governed by the provisions of Rome I,[379] or those of the Rome Convention,[380] depending on the date on which the contract was concluded. Rome I governs all contracts concluded after 17 December 2009, whereas the Rome Convention governs contracts concluded before or on 17 December 2009. Rome I, and the Rome Convention, both apply to contractual obligations in situations where there is a choice between the laws of different countries.[381] Both instruments contain rules which effectively define the law applicable to a contract. The rules contained in both are mandatory in application.

Whilst the rules governing the law applicable to contracts involving IPRs, their transfer, and licensing are set out in Rome I,[382] the latter does not contain regimes that are specific to cases involving IP.[383] A dedicated provision on IP-related contracts was

374. De Miguel Asensio, Pedro Alberto, The Law Governing International Intellectual Property Licensing Agreements, Research Handbook on Intellectual Property Licensing (a conflict of laws analysis) (edited by J de Werra) (Cheltenham, Edward Elgar Publishing 2013), 312-336, 312.
375. De Miguel Asensio 2013: 312.
376. De Miguel Asensio 2013: 312.
377. De Miguel Asensio 2013: 312.
378. Merrett 2013: 632.
379. The full title of Rome I is Regulation (EC) No 593/2008 of the European Parliament and the Council of 17 June 2008 on the Law Applicable to Contractual Obligations. It is available at http://eurlex.europa.eu/LexUriServ/LexUriServ.do?uri=OJ:L:2008:177:0006:0006:en:PDF (last accessed 21 January 2013).
380. Convention on the Law Applicable to Contractual Obligations Opened for Signature in Rome on 19 June 1980, available at http://eurlex.europa.eu/LexUriServ/LexUriServ.do?uri=CELEX:41980A0934:EN:HTML (last accessed 21 January 2013).
381. Where states have several territorial units each of which has its own rules of law in relation to contractual obligations then each territorial unit will be treated as a country for the purposes of identifying the law applicable under Rome I (Article 22.1, Rome I).
382. Yuko, Nishitani, Contracts concerning Intellectual Property Rights, in Franco Ferrari and Stefan Leible (eds), Rome I Regulation - The Law Applicable to Contractual Obligations in Europe (Sellier 2009), 51, 52.
383. Van Engelen 2010: 18.

incorporated into draft Article 4(1)f of the Commission's Proposal for the Rome I Regulation,[384] but this provision was later abandoned.[385]

[A] Scope of Rome I

Rome I applies 'in situations involving a conflict of laws, to contractual obligations in civil and commercial matters'.[386] The phrase 'contractual obligations' is defined autonomously without reference to national law, and is widely considered to include situations which would not be classed as enforceable contractual obligations under national law.[387]

The applicable law - determined by virtue of Articles 3 and 4, Rome I - can be displaced or supplemented by mandatory rules and/or rules of public policy.[388]

[B] Article 3: Freedom of Choice[389]

Article 3(1), Rome I

A contract shall be governed by the law chosen by the parties. The choice shall be made expressly or clearly demonstrated by the terms of the contract or the circumstances of the case. By their choice the parties can select the law applicable to the whole or to part only of the contract.

Article 3(2), Rome I

The parties may at any time agree to subject the contract to a law other than that which previously governed it, whether as a result of an earlier choice made under this Article or of other provisions of this Regulation...

The notion that the parties contracting are free to select the law applicable to their relationship is one that is rooted in European private international law, and traceable back to Roman law.[390]

Article 3, Rome I permits the contracting parties to elect the law governing their contract. The parties are free to choose the law applicable to the whole of their contract,

384. Proposal for a Regulation of the European Parliament and the Council on the law applicable to contractual obligations (Rome I) COM (2005) 650 Final.
385. Yuko: 53-54.
386. Article 1(1), Rome I.
387. Merrett 2013: 633, citing Re Bonacina [1912] 2 Ch 394.
388. *See* Merrett 2013: 641-4.
389. H. Heiss, Party Autonomy, Franco Ferrari and Stefan Leible (eds), *Rome I Regulation – The Law Applicable to Contractual Obligations in Europe* (Sellier 2009).
390. Jan-Jaap Kuipers, *EU law and Private International Law: The interrelationship in contractual obligations (*Martinus Nijhoff Publishers 2012), 44, citing from Ranouil, V., L'autonomie de la volonté.

or in the alternative the bodies of law that will govern different sections of their contract.[391]

Parties entering into an IP related agreement enjoy the autonomy extended to other categories of contracts, allowing them to designate the law governing their IP-related contract,[392] guaranteeing substantive freedom, clarity, predictability, and transactional security.[393]

In such situations the parties enjoy wide flexibility, as they are free to select any law they wish including 'neutral law' with no 'territorial connection to the contract'.[394] They are also free to opt for a hybrid clause by selecting several laws for the different parts of their contract (*dépeçage*).[395]

Such freedom is curtailed in limited circumstances by the special provisions on mandatory regimes (Articles 3(3), 3(4), 6(2), and 8(1), Rome I), the overriding mandatory rules (Article 9, Rome I), and public policy (Article 21, Rome I).

In order for a selection to stand, the parties contracting are obliged to make their selection expressly or, at the very least, clearly.[396] If the choice of the parties is not expressly made, their selection must be ascertainable by reference to the terms of the contract or the circumstances of the case.[397]

The parties are free if they so wish to make a *ex post* change to their selection of applicable law pursuant to Article 3(2) Rome I, though Professor Heiss suggests that the notion that the parties are free to select the law governing their contractual relationship is subject to the proviso that any *ex post* selection does not undermine the rights acquired by a third party.[398]

When IPRs are licensed in the context of a technology transfer or joint venture arrangement, the IP-related agreement does not constitute the subject-matter of the agreement but is instead ancillary to it.[399] In such a situation, it is generally understood that the intent of the parties is for the entire agreement to be subject to a single body of governing law, unless the parties designate a different body of law to specifically govern the licensing agreement.[400]

The parties are entitled to alter the governing law at a later stage, even during the course of court proceedings.[401]

391. Article 3(1), Rome I.
392. Yuko: 53.
393. Yuko: 54.
394. Yuko: 54.
395. Yuko: 54.
396. Article 3(1), Rome I.
397. Article 3(1), Rome I.
398. H. Heiss, Party Autonomy, Franco Ferrari and Stefan Leible (eds), *Rome I Regulation – The Law Applicable to Contractual Obligations in Europe* (Sellier 2009), 2 citing Article 3 paragraph 2 Rome I, and Article 3 paragraph 2 Rome Convention.
399. Yuko: 54.
400. Yuko: 55.
401. Yuko: 55, citing A3(2), Rome I.

[C] Implied Choice of Law[402]

The Giuliano-Lagarde Report[403] accompanying the Rome Convention provides for three types of situations in which a choice of law may be implied.[404] These are standard form contracts, jurisdiction clauses (including arbitration clauses), and previous course of dealings between the parties.

[D] Standard Form Contracts

Choice of law will be implied when a contract is in a standard form known to be governed by a specific system of law.[405] Lloyd's policy of marine insurance is an example of such a contract.[406]

[E] Jurisdiction Clauses

Whilst choice of jurisdiction is not the same as choice of law, the parties' choice of jurisdiction, and the locus of any intended arbitration may be taken to demonstrate that the parties intended for the contract to be governed by the law of their selected jurisdiction.[407] Any such assessment should however be made bearing in mind the other terms of the contract, and the facts of the case.[408]

[F] Previous Course of Dealings

Where a previous course of dealings between the same parties entails a specific choice of law clause this will leave a court in no doubt if the parties then omit this clause in a later deal, unless there is evidence of a deliberate change in policy.[409]

402. A detailed review of implied choice of law clauses is provided in Merrett 2013: 634-6.
403. Giuliano-Lagarde Report OJ 1980 C/282/1 (hereafter Giuliano-Lagarde Report).
404. Whilst this Report accompanies the Rome Convention its recommendations are arguably of relevance when approaching Rome I.
405. Merrett 2013: 634.
406. Merrett 2013: 634, citing Giuliano-Lagarde Report.
407. Merrett 2013: 635. *See also* Recital 2, Rome I which states that 'an agreement between the parties to confer on one or more courts or tribunals of a Member State exclusive jurisdiction to determine disputes under the contract should be one of the factors to be taken into account in determining whether a choice of law has been clearly demonstrated'.
408. Merrett 2013: 635, citing Giuliano-Lagarde Report.
409. Merrett 2013: 635, citing *Marubeni Hong Kong and South China Ltd v Mongolia* [2002] 2 All ER (Comm) 873.

[G] Article 4: In the Absence of a Choice by the Parties

Article 4(1), Rome I

1. To the extent that the law applicable to the contract has not been chosen in accordance with Article 3 and without prejudice to Articles 5 to 8, the law governing the contract shall be determined as follows:

(a) a contract for the sale of goods shall be governed by the law of the country where the seller has his habitual residence;

(b) a contract for the provision of services shall be governed by the law of the country where the service provider has his habitual residence;

(e) a franchise contract shall be governed by the law of the country where the franchisee has his habitual residence;

(f) a distribution contract shall be governed by the law of the country where the distributor has his habitual residence; ...

In the absence of an explicit or implicit choice, the law governing the contract is determined by reference to Article 4, Rome I, on the proviso that the contract does not fall within the remit of the special provisions in Articles 5-8, Rome I.[410]

In the law-finding process, Article 4 starts with a provision which sets out the law applicable to a number of types of agreements, 'by means of fixed and direct rules which may be disregarded only in exceptional circumstances'.[411] Article 4(1) sets out specific choice of law rules for particular categories of cases including contracts for the sale of goods, supply of services as well as franchise and distribution agreements.[412]

Pursuant to Article 4(1):

- a contract for the sale of goods shall be governed by the law of the country where the seller has his habitual residence;
- a contract for the provision of services shall be governed by the law of the country where the service provider has his habitual residence;
- a franchise contract shall be governed by the law of the country where the franchisee has his habitual residence; and
- a distribution contract shall be governed by the law of the country where the distributor has his habitual residence.

410. Yuko: 55.
411. De Miguel Asensio 2013: 322.
412. Merrett 2013: 637.

The presumptions set out in Article 4(1) aim to identify the law with which the contract is most closely connected.[413] These presumptions are rebuttable, and as such can be set aside in favour of another closely connected law (Article 4(3), Rome I).[414]

Once the court has determined the law applicable to the contract, this body of law will govern most of the substantive matters that will arise in the contract.[415]

In those situations where the contract is not categorised as one of those contracts listed in Article 4(1), Article 4(2) requires only identification of characteristic performance to determine the law governing the contract.[416]

[1] Licensing and Choice-of-Law under Rome I

The Commission's Proposal for the Rome I Regulation,[417] presented in 2005, included – in draft Article 4(1)f – a rule stating that contracts relating to IP or industrial property rights should be governed by the law of the country where the party transferring or assigning the property rights has his habitual residence.[418]

Intended to introduce a fixed criterion governing all contracts having as their main object the transfer or licensing of IPR, this provision was suppressed during the legislative process due in the main 'to the impossibility of finding a fixed rule capable of providing an adequate response to the diverse typology of IP contracts that have been developed in business practice'.[419]

[a] Franchsie Agreements

The law applicable to franchise agreements – according to Article 4(1)e – is the law of the country in which the franchisee has his habitual residence.[420] Recital 17[421] clearly states that, in the absence of choice of applicable law, the default rule applicable to franchise agreements is 'driven by the perspective that franchise contracts ... are regarded to be *contracts for services*'.[422]

Certain contracts having IP rights as their subject matter are capable of falling within one of the categories listed in Article 4(1) suggests De Miguel Asensio.[423] Other

413. Merrett 2013: 637.
414. Merrett 2013: 637.
415. Merrett 2013: 639. A review of the scope of applicable law can be found in Merrett 2013: 639-41.
416. De Miguel Asensio 2013: 322.
417. Proposal for a Regulation of the European Parliament and the Council on the law applicable to contractual obligations (Rome I) COM (2005) 650 Final.
418. De Miguel Asensio 2013: 323.
419. De Miguel Asensio 2013: 323.
420. De Miguel Asensio 2013: 323.
421. Recital 17, Rome I reads 'As far as the applicable law in the absence of choice is concerned, the concept of "provision of services" and "sale of goods" should be interpreted in the same way as when applying Article 5 of Regulation (EC) No 44/2001 in so far as sale of goods and provision of services are covered by that Regulation. Although franchise and distribution contracts are contracts for services, they are the subject of specific rules.'
422. Van Engelen 2010: 18.
423. De Miguel Asensio 2013: 323.

contracts listed in Article 4(1) which may include provisions involving IPR are distribution agreements, which may include trademark licences.[424] 'Inasmuch as an agreement falls within the category of a distribution contract in terms of Article 4.1(f) Rome I Regulation, the criterion that the contract shall be governed by the law of the country where the distributor has his habitual residence applies irrespective of the presence of IP rights in its subject matter.'[425]

Notwithstanding the decision of the CJEU in the Falco case, De Miguel Asensio suggests that certain IP-related service agreements are capable of being classed as service agreements under Article 4(1).[426]

In its decision in the Falco case, the CJEU states that 'a contract under which the owner of an intellectual property right grants its contractual partner the right to use that right in return for remuneration is not a contract for the provision of services within the meaning (of the second indent of Article 5(1)b, Brussels Regulation 2001).[427,428]

The diversity of IP-related contracts could, suggests De Miguel Asensio, mean that certain contracts may be classified as contracts for the provision of services within the scope of Article 7(1)b, Brussels Regulation 2012, and Article 4(1)b, Rome I Regulation.[429]

This may occur when 'the permission for use granted to the licensee by the owner of the IP right is functionally subordinated to the main obligation of one of the parties to provide certain services to the other party.'[430] This may occur when the contract includes a patent licence with an obligation on the licensor of the patent to furnish technical assistance and support to the licensee along with training to the licensee's workforce.[431] In such a scenario, the obligations related to the patent licence are likely to be ancillary to the promise to furnish services since the patent-related obligations 'are economically and functionally less significant than the promise to provide services to the other party.'[432]

Another category of service provision contracts to which Article 4(1)b may apply are agreements with an R&D component; in certain categories of R&D agreements under which the researcher/developer is granted a right to exploit technology owned by the other contracting party, the obligations related to research/development are viewed as the critical object of the contractual relationship.[433]

Certain agreements which may straddle more than one of the categories listed in Article 4(1) include production and supply agreements covering patented products.[434] Characterised as supply contracts with production licences and no marketing and sales

424. De Miguel Asensio 2013: 323.
425. De Miguel Asensio 2013: 323.
426. De Miguel Asensio 2013: 324.
427. Now Article 7(1)b, Brussels Regulation 2012.
428. Paragraph 44, ECJ decision in Falco.
429. De Miguel Asensio 2013: 324.
430. De Miguel Asensio 2013: 324.
431. De Miguel Asensio 2013: 324.
432. De Miguel Asensio 2013: 324.
433. De Miguel Asensio 2013: 324.
434. De Miguel Asensio 2013: 324.

licence,[435] under such agreements the licensee produces goods on behalf of the licensor exploiting the licensor's technology, and then supplies these goods to the licensor who is contractually bound to buy the entire stock of goods produced by the licensee.[436] The licensee in such an arrangement is not visible in the marketplace as an independent supplier of these goods.[437] Though such agreements include a licence within the framework of Article 4(1), they could be classified on the one hand as contracts for the sale of goods, and on the other hand as contracts for the supply of services (namely the production on behalf of the licensor).[438] By virtue of Articles 4(1)a and 4(1)b, the law applicable is that of the country of the same party respectively the producer of the goods/supplier of services, who also happens to be the licensee.[439] In both scenarios, Article 4(1) makes identification of the party who is to effect characteristic performance possible.[440]

Bearing in mind the difficulties deciphering with certainty the law governing IP-related contracts under Article 4, Rome I, Yuko recommends that parties choose their applicable law.[441]

[H] Default Position (Article 4(2), Rome I)

Article 4(2) Rome I

Where the contract is not covered by paragraph 1 or where the elements of the contract would be covered by more than one of points (a) to (h) of paragraph 1, the contract shall be governed by the law of the country where the party required to effect the characteristic performance of the contract has his habitual residence.

Article 4(3) Rome I

Where it is clear from all the circumstances of the case that the contract is manifestly more closely connected with a country other than that indicated in paragraphs 1 or 2, the law of that other country shall apply.

Article 4(4) Rome I

Where the law applicable cannot be determined pursuant to paragraphs 1 or 2, the contract shall be governed by the law of the country with which it is most closely connected.

435. De Miguel Asensio 2013: 324-325.
436. De Miguel Asensio 2013: 325.
437. De Miguel Asensio 2013: 325.
438. De Miguel Asensio 2013: 325.
439. De Miguel Asensio 2013: 325.
440. De Miguel Asensio 2013: 325.
441. Yuko: 53.

Article 4(3), Rome I which provides for the application of the law of the country of closest connection, will be important in those situations where a number of related deals are concluded. In such situations, it is commercially important that a single body of law be applied to the whole transaction rather than different laws being applied to each of the separate deals.

[I] Habitual Residence

Habitual residence is defined for companies, and other bodies, corporate or unincorporated, as the place of central administration, and for natural persons acting in the course of their business activities, as their principal place of business.[442]

In the event of a contract being concluded in the course of the operations of a branch, agency or other establishment, or where performance under the contract is the responsibility of such a branch, agency or other establishment, then the location of the branch, agency or any other establishment is treated as the place of habitual residence for the purposes of Rome I.[443]

The temporal point at which habitual residence is determined is the point in time when the contract was concluded.[444]

§7.11 RECOGNITION AND ENFORCEMENT OF FOREIGN JUDGMENTS UNDER EUROPEAN UNION LAW

Pursuant to the Brussels Regulation 2012, a judgment given in a Member State must be recognised in other Member States without any special procedure being required.[445] Brussels Regulation 2012 introduced a simplified procedure for the recognition and enforcement of judgments by removing the need for a declaration of enforceability in the courts of the Member State of enforcement.[446] Now a party wishing to invoke in a Member State a judgment given in another Member State is required to produce a copy of the judgment, and a standard form certificate.[447] Where the judgment contains a measure or an order not known in the law of the Member State of enforcement that measure or order will be adapted 'to the extent possible' to a measure or an order known in the law of the Member State of enforcement.[448]

Recognition of a judgment will be refused on an application of any interested party in certain limited circumstances[449] *inter alia* if recognition of the judgment is manifestly contrary to public policy in the Member State addressed; if the judgment

442. Article 19(1), Rome I.
443. Article 19(2), Rome I.
444. Article 19(3), Rome I.
445. Article 36(1), Brussels Regulation 2012.
446. Sarah Garvey, 'Brussels Regulation (Recast): Are you ready?' 18 March 2015, p.6. Accessible at http://www.allenovery.com/publications/en-gb/Pages/BRUSSELS-REGULATION-(RECAST)-ARE-YOU-READY.aspx (last accessed 18 July 2016).
447. Article 37(1), Brussels Regulation 2012.
448. Article 54(1), Brussels Regulation 2012.
449. Article 45(1), Brussels Regulation 2012.

was given in default of appearance, if the defendant was not served with the document which instituted the proceedings in sufficient time, and in such a way to enable the defendant to arrange a defence, unless the defendant failed to commence proceedings to challenge the judgment when it was possible for the defendant to do so; if the judgment is irreconcilable with a judgment given between the same parties in the Member State addressed; or if the judgment is irreconcilable with an earlier judgment given in another Member State or in a third State involving the same cause of action, and between the same parties.[450]

§7.12 RECOGNITION AND ENFORCEMENT OF FOREIGN JUDGMENTS UNDER INTERNATIONAL LAW

A judgment given by a court of a Contracting State selected by the parties in an exclusive choice of court agreement (the designated court) must be recognised, and enforced by all courts in other Contracting States.[451] There will be no review of the merits of the judgment given by the court of origin, and the court addressed is bound by the findings of fact on which the court of origin based its jurisdiction.[452] In limited circumstances the court of a Contracting State may postpone recognition or enforcement or refuse to recognise or give force to a judgment of the designated court.[453]

The term *judgment* in this context is widely defined to include any decision on merits made by a court whatever its title including a decree and order.[454] An interim measure of protection is however excluded from this definition.[455] The term *judgment* encompasses determinations relating to the question of costs or expenses issued by the court including an officer of the court so long as the determination relates to a decision on merits, and is capable of being recognised or enforced under the Convention.[456]

The States may agree by declaration to recognise and enforce judgments rendered pursuant to a non-exclusive choice of court agreement.[457]

§7.13 CONCLUSION

Licensing agreements are increasingly international in so far as they are linked to more than one system of law. When negotiating, and drafting international licensing agreements the contracting parties should consider the way in which they wish to resolve disputes that arise between them.

First as a preemptive measure, and in a bid to prevent disputes from arising the contracting parties should determine whether they will hold informal meetings to address interpretative differences on a regular or ad hoc basis, and whether revisions

450. Article 45(1), Brussels Regulation 2012.
451. Article 8(1), Hague Convention 2005.
452. Article 8(2), Hague Convention 2005.
453. Article 8(4), and Article 9, Hague Convention 2005.
454. Article 4(1), Hague Convention 2005.
455. Articles 4(1) and 7, Hague Convention 2005.
456. Stone 2012: 183.
457. Article 22, Hague Convention 2005.

agreed by them to the terms of the agreement will be incorporated into the body of the agreement at regular intervals.

Second they should decide whether they will use ADR to resolve their differences, and if so whether they will use one or more ADR mechanism. When negotiating an ADR clause the parties should consider whether they wish to resort to definitive determination mechanisms or agreement based resolution mechanisms. When opting for definitive determination mechanisms, the contracting parties should assess whether they wish to reserve themselves a right to appeal. When agreeing a right of appeal, the parties should give due consideration to the scope of this right, in other words will the right be general in scope (providing a general right of appeal) or specific (limiting the circumstances in which an appeal may be made).

Third in the event that the contracting parties opt for arbitration as the sole mechanism for the resolution of their disputes or as one step in a multi-tiered dispute resolution infrastructure, the parties should determine the format of the arbitration (ad hoc versus institutional) before considering the general and specific concerns associated with arbitrations.[458] Arbitration offers certain advantages from the point of view of parties to a licence.

This mechanism offers a private dispute resolution structure administered by the parties with arbitrators selected for their experience, and expertise. From the perspective of parties to a licence arbitration may be problematic, though most of the problems associated with arbitration may be addressed to a certain degree in the agreement.[459] The risk of national court intervention may be addressed to a certain degree by selecting the seat of the arbitration with care.

To address the lack of third-party procedures, parties to a licensing agreement should consider entering into distinct arbitration agreements with connected parties to which the licensor and licensee are also party thereby ensuring the arbitral tribunal has jurisdiction over all the parties. The question of reserving the right of appeal is a key concern the parties to a licensing agreement should bear in mind. Whilst finality offers certainty the right to challenge the decision of the arbitral tribunal is an issue that should be assessed.

Finally if there is a risk of the matter proceeding to court the parties should address jurisdiction, and substantive law in the terms of the licensing agreement.

When negotiating a jurisdiction clause each of the contracting parties should imagine itself as the party initiating the claim, and each party should ask itself what a chosen jurisdiction has to offer. Choice of jurisdiction is usually motivated by a variety of factors including the experience and expertise of the arbiters, the cost of pursuing a claim in that jurisdiction, ease of access, the language used, the speed with which matters are dealt with, the remedies available, the location of evidence and witnesses, and the scope of discovery. When litigation is involved consideration should also be given *inter alia* to the availability of public funding, the array of interim measures of protection available, the possibility of class actions, and the availability of punitive damages.

458. A full discussion can be found earlier in this chapter.
459. A full discussion can be found earlier in this chapter.

Table of Cases

Case C-234/89 *Stergios Delimitis v. Henninger Bräu* [1991] ECR I-935 (hereinafter *Delimitis* case), para. 13, **120, 122**
Case C-8/08 *T-Mobile* [2009] ECR I-4529, [2009] 5 CMLR 1701, para. 43, **120, 121**
Case C-73/95 *Viho Europe BV v. Commission P* [1996] ECR I-5457 [1997] 4 CMLR 419, para. 16, **114, 115**
Case C-5/69 *Völk v. Vervaecke* [1969] ECR 295, [1969] CMLR 273, **125, 131**
Case C-36/74 *Walrave and Kock* [1974] ECR 1405, para. 4, **108**
Case C-309/99 *Wouters, Savelbergh and Price Waterhouse Belastingadviseurs BV v. Algemene Raad van de Nederlandsche Orde van Advocaten* [2002] ECR I-I 1577, [2002] 4 CMLR 913 (hereinafter *Price Waterhouse* case), para. 46, **105–108, 113, 124**
Case C-27/87 *Erauw-Jacquery Sprl v. La Hesbignonne Société Coopérative* [1988] ECR 1919, [1988] 4 CMLR 576, **123**
Case C-22/78 *Hugin Kassaregister AB and Hugin Cash Registers Ltd v. Commission of the European Communities* [1979] ECR 1869, 1899, [1979] 3 CMLR 345, **117**
Case C-48/69 *ICI v Commission* [1972] ECR 619, para s 133 and 134, 115, 116
Case C-48/69 *Imperial Chemical Industries Ltd v. Commission of the European Communities* [1972] ECR 619 (hereinafter *Dyestuffs* case), para. 64, **101, 115**
Case C-319/82 *Kerpen & Kerpen* [1983] ECR 4 173, paras. 11 and 12, **133**
Case C-258/78 *LC Nungesser KG v. Commission* [1982] ECR 2015, [1983] 1 CMLR 278, **123**
Case C-439/93 *Lloyd's Register v Campenon Bernard* [1995] ECR I-961 c.f., **473**
Case C-49/07 *Motosykletistiki Omospondia Ellados NPID* (hereinafter *MOTOE* case) *v. Elliniko Dimosio* [2008] ECR I-4863, [2008] 5 CMLR 790, para. 25, **108**
Case C-161/84 *Pronuptia de Paris v. Schilligalis* [1986] ECR 353, [1986] 1 CMLR 414, **123, 135**
Cases C-29/83 and 30/83, paras.25-6, **121**
Cases C-43/82 and 63/82 *VBVB and VVVB v. Commission* [1984] ECR 19, para. 61, **135**
Cases C-159/91 & C-160/91 *Poucet & Pistre,* paras. 18 & 19, **112**
Cases C-501/06 P etc *GlaxoSmithKline v. Commission* [2009] ECR I-9291, [2010] 4 CMLR 50, paras. 59-60, **120, 121**
Cases C-180/98 to C-184/98, para. 107**, 107, 111, 112**
Case C-56/65 *Société Technique Minière (L.T.M.) v. Maschinenbau Ulm GmbH (M.B.U.)* [1966] ECR 235, 337, 249, [1966] CMLR 357, 375, **97, 118, 120, 123, 133**
Cases T-374, 375, 384 and 388/94 *European Night Services v. Commission* [1998] ECR II-3141, para. 136, **120**
Cases T-68, 77 and 78/89 *Societa Vetro v. Commission* [1992] ECR II-1403, para. 358, **105**
Cases T-25/95 etc *Cimenteries CBR SA v. Commission* [2000] ECR II-491, [2000] 5 CMLR 204, para. 1320, **101**
Cases T-374/94 etc. *European Night Services v. Commission* [1988] ECR II-3141, [1998] 5 CMLR 718, paras. 136, 139-147, **122, 123**
Case T-128/98 *Aéroports de paris v. Commission* [2000] ECR II-3929, para 108, **106**
Case T-112/05 *Akzo Nobel NV v. Commission* [2007] ECR II-5049, [2008] 4 CMLR 321, paras. 57 & 58, **114, 115**

Table of Legislation

Index

B

U

V

W

www.ingramcontent.com/pod-product-compliance
Lightning Source LLC
LaVergne TN
LVHW020003031026
849161LV00023B/854
* 9 7 8 9 4 0 3 5 0 3 3 2 5 *